Comparative Research on Earnings Management, Corporate Governance, and Economic Value

Elisabete S. Vieira
University of Aveiro, Portugal

Mara Madaleno
University of Aveiro, Portugal

Graça Azevedo
University of Aveiro, Portugal

IGI Global
PUBLISHER of TIMELY KNOWLEDGE

A volume in the Advances in Finance, Accounting, and Economics (AFAE) Book Series

Published in the United States of America by
IGI Global
Business Science Reference (an imprint of IGI Global)
701 E. Chocolate Avenue
Hershey PA, USA 17033
Tel: 717-533-8845
Fax: 717-533-8661
E-mail: cust@igi-global.com
Web site: http://www.igi-global.com

Library of Congress Cataloging-in-Publication Data

Names: Vieira, Elisabete S., editor. | Madaleno, Mara, 1981- editor. | Azevedo, Graça Maria do Carmo, editor.
Title: Comparative research on earnings management, corporate governance, and economic value / Elisabete S. Vieira, Mara Madaleno, and Graça Azevedo, editors.
Description: Hershey, PA : Business Science Reference, [2021] | Includes bibliographical references and index. | Summary: "This book discusses the accounting policies firms use in different opportunistic circumstances in order to manage earnings, and to understand the corporate governance practices in different countries, and its relationship to firms' performance, and other dimensions of companies"-- Provided by publisher.
Identifiers: LCCN 2020049325 (print) | LCCN 2020049326 (ebook) | ISBN 9781799875963 (hardcover) | ISBN 9781799875970 (paperback) | ISBN 9781799875987 (ebook)
Subjects: LCSH: Earnings management. | Corporate governance. | Accounting.
Classification: LCC HG4028.E27 C66 2021 (print) | LCC HG4028.E27 (ebook) | DDC 658.15/54--dc23
LC record available at https://lccn.loc.gov/2020049325
LC ebook record available at https://lccn.loc.gov/2020049326

This book is published in the IGI Global book series Advances in Finance, Accounting, and Economics (AFAE) (ISSN: 2327-5677; eISSN: 2327-5685)

British Cataloguing in Publication Data
A Cataloguing in Publication record for this book is available from the British Library.

All work contributed to this book is new, previously-unpublished material. The views expressed in this book are those of the authors, but not necessarily of the publisher.

For electronic access to this publication, please contact: eresources@igi-global.com.

Advances in Finance, Accounting, and Economics (AFAE) Book Series

Ahmed Driouchi
Al Akhawayn University, Morocco

ISSN:2327-5677
EISSN:2327-5685

Mission

In our changing economic and business environment, it is important to consider the financial changes occurring internationally as well as within individual organizations and business environments. Understanding these changes as well as the factors that influence them is crucial in preparing for our financial future and ensuring economic sustainability and growth.

The **Advances in Finance, Accounting, and Economics (AFAE)** book series aims to publish comprehensive and informative titles in all areas of economics and economic theory, finance, and accounting to assist in advancing the available knowledge and providing for further research development in these dynamic fields.

Coverage

- Auditing
- Ethics in Accounting and Finance
- Macroeconomics
- Finance and Accounting in SMEs
- Accounting Standards
- Risk Analysis and Management
- Economics of Risks, Uncertainty, Ambiguity, and Insurance
- Bankruptcy
- Environmental and Social Accounting
- Development Economics

IGI Global is currently accepting manuscripts for publication within this series. To submit a proposal for a volume in this series, please contact our Acquisition Editors at Acquisitions@igi-global.com or visit: http://www.igi-global.com/publish/.

The Advances in Finance, Accounting, and Economics (AFAE) Book Series (ISSN 2327-5677) is published by IGI Global, 701 E. Chocolate Avenue, Hershey, PA 17033-1240, USA, www.igi-global.com. This series is composed of titles available for purchase individually; each title is edited to be contextually exclusive from any other title within the series. For pricing and ordering information please visit http://www.igi-global.com/book-series/advances-finance-accounting-economics/73685. Postmaster: Send all address changes to above address.

Titles in this Series

For a list of additional titles in this series, please visit: http://www.igi-global.com/book-series/advances-finance-accounting-economics/73685

Influence of FinTech on Management Transformation
Amira Sghari (Faculty of Economics and Management, University of Sfax, Tunisia) and Karim Mezghani (Al Imam Mohammad Ibn Saud Islamic University, Saudi Arabia & University of Sfax, Tunisia)
Business Science Reference • © 2021 • 273pp • H/C (ISBN: 9781799871101) • US $215.00

Handbook of Research on Institutional, Economic, and Social Impacts of Globalization and Liberalization
Yilmaz Bayar (Bandirma Onyedi Eylul University, Turkey)
Information Science Reference • © 2021 • 699pp • H/C (ISBN: 9781799844594) • US $445.00

Bridging Microeconomics and Macroeconomics and the Effects on Economic Development and Growth
Pantelis C. Kostis (National and Kapodistrian University of Athens, Greece)
Business Science Reference • © 2021 • 340pp • H/C (ISBN: 9781799849339) • US $195.00

Machine Learning Applications for Accounting Disclosure and Fraud Detection
Stylianos Papadakis (Hellenic Mediterranean University, Greece) Alexandros Garefalakis (Hellenic Mediterranean University, Greece) Christos Lemonakis (Hellenic Mediterranean University, Greece) Christiana Chimonaki (University of Portsmouth, UK) and Constantin Zopounidis (School of Production Engineering and Management, Technical University of Crete, Greece & Audencia Business School, France)
Business Science Reference • © 2021 • 270pp • H/C (ISBN: 9781799848059) • US $225.00

Corporate Governance and Its Implications on Accounting and Finance
Ahmad Alqatan (University of Portsmouth, UK) Khaled Hussainey (University of Portsmouth, UK) and Hichem Khlif (University of Sfax, Tunisia)
Business Science Reference • © 2021 • 425pp • H/C (ISBN: 9781799848523) • US $195.00

Recent Applications of Financial Risk Modelling and Portfolio Management
Tihana Škrinjarić (University of Zagreb, Croatia) Mirjana Čižmešija (University of Zagreb, Croatia) and Bryan Christiansen (Global Training Group, Ltd, UK)
Business Science Reference • © 2021 • 432pp • H/C (ISBN: 9781799850830) • US $195.00

Fostering Innovation and Competitiveness With FinTech, RegTech, and SupTech
Iustina Alina Boitan (Bucharest University of Economic Studies, Romania) and Kamilla Marchewka-Bartkowiak (Poznan University of Economics and Business, Poland)
Business Science Reference • © 2021 • 313pp • H/C (ISBN: 9781799843900) • US $215.00

IGI Global
PUBLISHER of TIMELY KNOWLEDGE

701 East Chocolate Avenue, Hershey, PA 17033, USA
Tel: 717-533-8845 x100 • Fax: 717-533-8661
E-Mail: cust@igi-global.com • www.igi-global.com

Editorial Advisory Board

List of Reviewers

Table of Contents

Detailed Table of Contents

This chapter intends to contribute to the analysis and comparison of the earnings management (EM) practices through a bibliometric review of the existent literature, in order to understand the current state of EM research, as well as to identify the main determinants for these kind of practices in firms. Although there are extensive research on EM, no recent study tries to update the current state of the research over this topic. To do so, a bibliometric analysis is conducted. The study describes the evolutional research studies published in the digital library Scopus, between 2010 and 2019, and compares the results obtained in evolutionary terms. It ends up concentrating the bibliometric analysis in the Scopus database, leading to a total database of 2,377 documents. Regarding the most recent articles published, the years of 2019 and 2020 were studied, ending with a final sample of 389 articles. Research avenues are provided based on these results and more recent published articles regarding EM.

In contexts characterized by high ownership concentration, institutional investors may lose their monitoring role and might not be effective in constraining earnings management. So, this study investigates whether directors appointed by institutional shareholders are more effective in inhibiting earnings management for companies with a high ownership concentration, rather than the mere presence of institutional investors. Based on a sample of Italian listed companies, findings suggest a negative relationship between minority directors appointed by institutional shareholders and abnormal accruals, while no relationship is found

The assessment of the implementation of the corporate governance practices is important because it contributes to the efficient use of resources and, thus, increases corporate performance. However, the practice of CG in Portugal is below European standards due to several issues related to weak legal protection, concentrated ownership structures, and limited information transparency. Using a panel data of 17 firms listed on PSI20, this chapter investigates the impact of the internal CG mechanisms on corporate performance, in 2014-2018. Results show that the size of the audit committee impacts positively on firm performance. However, the number of independent members of audit committee decreases corporate performance in firms operating in services, and ownership of related parties increases corporate performance. Also, fewer leveraged firms are likely to exhibit better performances. This research provides understanding of the relationships between internal mechanisms of CG and corporate performance by comparing results across groups of sectors.

This chapter aimed at assessing the contribution of a bank's listing to its governance and performance. Using a single case study, it collected data on bank governance, performance, and stability over the period 2009-18. Findings show that listing improved I&M Bank's internal governance in particular soon after it listed on the Rwanda Stock Exchange in 2008. Its board's independence, size, and ownership showed significant changes soon after it listed and listing improved its performance as well as stability through governance. A change in both the board's size and independence significantly reduced the bank's non-performing loans and increased the bank's resilience (Z-score) and lending.

Current practice shows that firms throughout the world are in favor of high cash holdings; yet, they are still performing well. This situation contradicts the agency and free cash flow theories, which suggest that excessive cash may increase agency costs and lower firm performance. The purpose of this study is to examine the relationship between corporate governance, cash holdings, and firm performance. Five thousand four hundred twenty observations were conducted, and a balanced panel data analysis was performed. The results indicate that corporate governance has a significant impact on cash holdings, corporate governance has a significant impact on firm performance, and cash holding has a significant impact on a firm's performance. The findings of this study do not show any evidence to support the agency and free cash flow theories among non-financial Malaysian firms listed on Bursa Malaysia. Thus, this study contributes to the finance and accounting literature by gaining a better understanding of firm performance indicators in Malaysia, specifically.

In this chapter, the impacts of corporate governance mechanisms on accounting conservatism are examined by using a sample that includes 85 non-financial firms quoted in Borsa Istanbul during the years of 2013 to 2018. The results of empirical analysis indicate that board size, board independency, institutional ownership, and firm size are positively related with accounting conservatism. However, leverage is negatively related with accounting conservatism, while there is no statistically significant association between CEO duality and accounting conservatism. This chapter contributes to limited literature on the association between accounting conservatism practices and corporate governance in the emerging market.

The regulations related to corporate governance mechanisms such as the sensitivity of pay and performance of chief executive officers, board characteristics, and watches outside of those that are well connected in related party transactions (RPTs)in Malaysia are struggling from the monitoring and enforcement of good corporate governance. The primary aims of this study are to investigate the gap that exists in Malaysian company failures due to appropriate related party transactions and to evaluate the impact of good corporate governance on shareholders' confidence in related party transaction (RPTs) disclosures from the Malaysian Accounting Standards Board (MASB) of regulations. In the year 2000, a study was done by Claessens that examined the data of 236 Malaysian public organizations. The study found the dominancy of a large block of shareholders in organizations in addition to weak institutional structures. This chapter focuses on the usage of related party transactions undertaken to benefit Malaysian companies which have led to financial reporting disclosure information.

Preface

ABOUT THE SUBJECT

The topics of earnings management, corporate governance and economic value have gained a huge international relevance.

Earnings management deals with maximization, minimization, and smoothing earnings in order to achieve benefits associated with opportunistic actions that allow managers to obtain the desire level of earnings. Consequently, research on earnings management allows us to predict future manager behavior, helping identifying managers' behavioral patterns and understanding how they use accounting policies in distinct opportunistic circumstances.

Earnings management may be difficult for individual investors to detect due to the complexity of accounting rules, the characteristics of corporate governance structures, the kind of linguistics used by managers, and the inability of auditing some sets of disclosures. However, corporate governance can reduce or even eliminate the extent of earnings management. An institutional environment providing better legal protection can control managers' self-interest to a certain extent. Takeover force can exert market pressure on managers to do the best for shareholders. Board independence can enhance certain monitoring behaviors in managers, including the misappropriation of assets. Female directors can develop trust leadership, which requires managers to share information, and are more likely to be risk-averse to frauds and opportunistic earnings management. An audit committee can oversee the internal control for financial reporting and the quality of financial information. Directors with financial expertise can provide incremental control effects on earnings management, especially in firms with weak corporate governance.

Earnings management and corporate governance characteristics have impact on firms' performance, leverage and cash holdings, among other financial topics. Inevitably, it has consequences on economic value.

It is fruitful to investigate and disseminate the results of theoretical and empirical studies that reveal different aspects of earnings management phenomenon, different corporate governance dimensions and impact on firms and consequences on economic value, in order to obtain insightful knowledge on how to promote effectively the financial decision making-process.

This book folds several coherent chapters which allow, on a scientific basis, to discuss at an international level the new directions in earnings management, corporate governance and economic value, mainly associated with ownership concentration, family businesses, liquidity, cash flows, leverage, accounting, social responsibility and companies performance.

EXPECTATIONS

The editors intend this book to be useful for regulatory authorities and researchers in the field of corporate governance, capital markets finance, investments, corporate finance, economics, and accounting.

Through dissemination of the research findings on the rigor of finance, this publication could also be valuable to develop and inspire further studies by researchers and students in postgraduate courses, whose research interests are related to earnings management, corporate governance and economic value.

The book intends to provide a clear comparison of major trends regarding the earnings management and corporate governance, showing similarities and striking differences in the practices of different countries and economies. The idea of this book is to be a compilation of ideas in new trends that are currently shaping the modern corporate governance.

This book aims to achieve the following main objectives:

- Document the state of the art related to earnings management;
- Disseminate the methodologies that would ensure the quality of financial information;
- Document the relationship between earnings management and free cash flows, liquidity and leverage;
- Review processes/governance models that promote better earnings quality;
- Document the state of the art related to corporate governance;
- Analyze the corporate governance effects on earnings management;
- Analyze the corporate governance effects on social responsibility;
- Document the corporate governance effects on firms performance;
- Analyze the relationship between accounting conservatism and corporate governance;
- Analyze the gender effect on firm economic value.

ORGANIZATION OF THE BOOK

This book is organized by 17 chapters. The first chapter is focused on the literature review of earnings management phenomenon. Thus:

- Chapter 1 – *Research on Earnings Management: Bibliometric Analysis* – offers a literature review on earnings quality based on the bibliometric analysis methodology.

The next five chapters provide studies analyzing the issue of earnings management associated with specific characteristics of companies, such as institutional investors, owner managers, family firms, liquidity, as well as environmental characteristics. In this way:

- Chapter 2 – *Institutional Investors' Representativeness and Earnings Management: Evidence From a High Ownership Concentration Context* – investigates whether directors appointed by institutional shareholders, rather than the mere presence of institutional investor, are more effective in inhibiting earnings management for companies with a high ownership concentration.
- Chapter 3 – *Owner Managers, Family Business, and Earnings Management Preceding Management Buyouts* – hypothesizes that concentrated ownership in private non-family firms provides suffi-

cient wealth incentives and power to owner/managers to manage earnings upwards before the acquisition, while family owners use management buyouts as a succession tool in the absence of a suitable family successor out of concern for the future of family business.

- Chapter 4 – *Earnings Management and Stock Liquidity: Evidence From Turkey* – tests whether the earnings management practices in Turkey are considered informative or opportunistic by outside investors by examining its effect on stock liquidity.
- Chapter 5 – *Free Cash Flow and Earnings Management: The Moderating Role of Leverage* – draws on Jensen's (1986) free cash flow hypothesis to evaluate the relationship between free cash flow and earnings management. It also examines whether the level of leverage moderate the relationship between free cash flow and earnings management.
- Chapter 6 – *Bi-Level Programming for Earning Management in Imprecise and Random Environment* – to deal with the dualism the authors consider a fuzzy stochastic bi-level programming problem in mathematical model. The fuzziness and randomness concept has been taken care by fuzzy random variable as the parameter of the bi-level programming problem.

The Chapters 7 and 8 present a literature review on corporate governance. Thus:

- Chapter 7 – *Research on Corporate Governance: Bibliometric Analysis* – offers a literature review on corporate governance based on the bibliometric analysis methodology.
- Chapter 8 – *Corporate Governance in Portugal: A Literature Review* – provides a literature review of the research on the corporate governance mechanisms of Portuguese firms.

The following eight chapters cover the impact of corporate governance on corporate issues, such as social responsibility, companies' performance, accounting conservatism, and investment decision-making. Thus:

- Chapter 9 – *The Social Responsibility of the Firm: A Corporate Governance Perspective* – intends to show that from a welfare economics perspective there is room for improvement if governments are willing to revisit the legal framework and redesign the institutional boundaries of the firm.
- Chapter 10 – *How Different Corporate Governance and Corporate Social Responsibility Impact Earnings Management: Eastern and Western European Countries* – addresses the question of the role of corporate governance and corporate social responsibility in earnings management. The objective of the study is to test whether the effectiveness of both in constraining earnings management is the same or vary within the Eastern and Western Europe.
- Chapter 11 – *Corporate Governance and Company Performance: A Comparative Analysis Across Sectors in Portugal* – investigates the impact of the internal corporate governance mechanisms on corporate performance in Portugal.
- Chapter 12 – *Corporate Governance Mechanisms and Firm Performance in a Young Stock Exchange: The Case of I&M Bank-Rwanda* – contributes to the debate on corporate governance by exploring how listing either constrains or improves the corporate governance mechanisms, as well as their effects on a firm's performance.
- Chapter 13 – *Investigating the Relationship of Corporate Cash Holdings, Corporate Governance, and Firm Performance in Malaysia* – examine the relationship between corporate governance, cash holdings, and firm performance.

- Chapter 14 – *Accounting Conservatism and Corporate Governance Firm-Level Evidence From Turkey* – the impacts of corporate governance mechanisms on accounting conservatism are examined by using a sample that includes 85 non-financial firms quoted in Borsa Istanbul during the years of 2013 to 2018.
- Chapter 15 – *Why Malaysian Companies are Involved in Related Party Transactions (RPT) in the Context of Corporate Governance (CG)* – investigate the gap that exists in Malaysian company failures due to appropriate related party transactions. Also, to evaluate the impact of good corporate governance on shareholders' confidence in related party transaction (RPTs) disclosures from the Malaysian Accounting Standards Board (MASB) of regulations.
- Chapter 16 – *Analysis of Investment Decision Making in Private Hospitals: Qualitative Study of the Process of Investment* – exploratory study seeking to develop a model for outlining the role of the managers of private hospitals in Brazil and Canada, through qualitative analysis of interviews to identify the specific factors influencing decision-making on investment.

Finally, the last chapter addresses the issue of gender effect on firm economic value. Thus:

- Chapter 17 – *Executive Women and Firm Economic Value* – analyses the relationship between gender diversity on the board of directors' executive roles and the firm economic value. Based on a sample of Portuguese non-financial listed firms, between 2010 and 2018.

Elisabete Vieira
University of Aveiro, Portugal

Mara Madaleno
University of Aveiro, Portugal

Graça Azevedo
University of Aveiro, Portugal

Acknowledgment

The editors would like to thank all the people involved in this project for all the help provided, especially to the authors and reviewers. We sincerely appreciate the contributions provided by all of you. It was an excellent and relevant input to the publication process. Without your support, this project would not be possible to achieve.

The editors would like to thank each of the authors of the chapters who contributed deeply dispending their time and expertise to this book, making it so special.

It is never too much to thank and recognize the valuable work of the members of the IGI Editorial Advisory Board in improving the quality, consistency and presentation of the content of the chapters, which has ensured the highest accuracy in the double-blind review process. We would like to thank the Editorial Advisory Board for its precise collaboration, as well as to some of the authors who have taken on a double task, serving as well as referees for their pairs.

To all, our most sincere thank you.

Elisabete S. Vieira
University of Aveiro, Portugal

Mara Madaleno
University of Aveiro, Portugal

Graça Azevedo
University of Aveiro, Portugal

Chapter 1
Research on Earnings Management:
Bbibliometric Analysis

Elisabete S. Vieira
https://orcid.org/0000-0003-3593-368X
GOVCOPP, University of Aveiro, Portugal

Mara Madaleno
https://orcid.org/0000-0002-4905-2771
GOVCOPP, University of Aveiro, Portugal

Graça Azevedo
https://orcid.org/0000-0002-6346-4035
Research Centre on Accounting and Taxation (CICF), University of Aveiro, Portugal

ABSTRACT

This chapter intends to contribute to the analysis and comparison of the earnings management (EM) practices through a bibliometric review of the existent literature, in order to understand the current state of EM research, as well as to identify the main determinants for these kind of practices in firms. Although there are extensive research on EM, no recent study tries to update the current state of the research over this topic. To do so, a bibliometric analysis is conducted. The study describes the evolutional research studies published in the digital library Scopus, between 2010 and 2019, and compares the results obtained in evolutionary terms. It ends up concentrating the bibliometric analysis in the Scopus database, leading to a total database of 2,377 documents. Regarding the most recent articles published, the years of 2019 and 2020 were studied, ending with a final sample of 389 articles. Research avenues are provided based on these results and more recent published articles regarding EM.

DOI: 10.4018/978-1-7998-7596-3.ch001

INTRODUCTION

No bibliometric research should start without previously defining what the main subject under analysis is. The study concentrate on earnings management articles published in the recent years of 2010-2019. As well, what is earnings management? Earnings management is the use of accounting techniques to produce financial statements that present an overly positive view of a company's business activities and financial position. Many accounting rules and principles require that a company's management make judgments in following these principles. Earnings management takes advantage of how accounting rules are applied and creates financial statements that inflate or "smooth" earnings. These earnings smoothness has as a main consequence the loss of credibility over the firm by stakeholders if mistakes are to be found, or even if these earnings manipulations come out to the public (Flayyih et al., 2020).

This chapter intends to analyze the firms' motivation to implement earnings management (EM) practices and their consequences on firms, by trying to understand how the literature has researched the topic in recent years. By doing this through a bibliometric analysis, the authors are able to find the main reported determinants for this behavior in comparative terms among the different fields of analysis.

The authors are faced with the EM problem when management deliberately exerts their influence to change the truth and fairness of a financial statement. The goal is to conceal the real economic condition or to obtain private gains of contractual outcomes, which are accounting-based (Healy and Wahlen, 1999). There are various methods of EM calculation, being one of the main research gaps in this field of study (Agustia et al., 2020), as it was also possible to infer from our bibliometric analysis. A deeper understanding of these different measurements and the respective literature review the study leave for ongoing work. Moreover, other research gaps have been identified concerning EM and debt financing, earnings control, gender and EM, board characteristics and EM (including behavioral biases), as well as, business strategy and bankruptcy risks relationship with EM. The authors do not intend to present a literature review, but yes a bibliometric analysis stating clearly what are the relevant topics being analyzed in more recent years (2010-2019) and the current state of research, since there is a lack of studies in this respect, as it was possible to identify and is clearly stated at the conclusions section. Additionally, and respecting the book title, the authors have an additional section relating to corporate governance and EM's present state of research.

As will be evidenced in the next section, these results report different findings that could lead us to other research fields. As such, it is intended to present the state of the current literature regarding research on earnings management. The first document researching under the keyword earnings management was published in 1974 according to our bibliometric research. The rest of this chapter develops as follows. Section two presents a brief literature review on the EM topic and its relationship with corporate governance. Section three presents the general status of earnings management research from 2010 to 2019. Section four presents the redefinition of our research and focuses it on the most recent published articles in the years 2019 and 2020, while section five provides some insights for possible future research regarding the recent scientific research and the literature that relates corporate governance and earnings management (2018-2020). Section six concludes this chapter.

BRIEF LITERATURE REVIEW ON EARNINGS MANAGEMENT

Some reasons motivate firms to practice actions of EM, namely to smooth earnings, avoiding positive or negative picks (Abeyratna & Power, 2002), or to reach a target in earnings level (Buckmaster, 2001; Leuz, Nanda, & Wysocki, 2003). However, studies are finding no evidence of significant EM practices, such as Ball and Shivakumar (2005). The authors believe that different country's specificities can cause different evidence among them, such as the development of the regulatory framework, the capital markets development, the investor protection in the different countries, the concentration of property, and the type of property (family versus non-family firms).

According to Jaggi, Leung, and Gul (2009), the level of ownership concentration and the system of civil law or common law of countries can lead to differences among countries. González and García-Meca (2014) argue that results may differ according to the level of investors' protection by the legal system, the level of transparency, and the dispersion of equity ownership. According to Maijoor and Vanstraelen (2006), the magnitude of EM is not uniform across the European countries. Indeed, Leuz et al. (2003) find higher EM in countries with lower investor protection and with undeveloped capital markets, and Ball, Robin, and Wu (2003) conclude that institutional factors have a significant influence on the managerial incentives for financial reporting. Persakis and Iatridis (2016) find that EM is lower (higher) in countries with strong (weak) investor protection.

Dechow, Sloan, and Sweeney (1996) study a sample of UK firms, concluding that the higher the firms' EM, the more the board is dominated by insiders and Beasley (1996) conclude that firms with a higher proportion of outside directors on boards are less likely to practice financial statement fraud. Using a sample of USA and UK firms, Xie, Davidson, and DaDalt (2003) find a negative relationship between corporate board independence and discretionary accruals. Dimitrasa, Kyriakoua, and Iatridis (2015) investigate the EM practices during recession years, considering a sample of firms from five European countries: Greece, Ireland, Italy, Portugal, and Spain. Greece, Italy, Portugal, and Spain are civil-law countries, characterized by low financial transparency. Thus, the authors were expecting that these countries displayed higher EM manipulation. However, despite the financial crisis, these countries behaved as common-law countries and the managers of these countries' firms seemed to reduce EM manipulation during the recession. The quality of financial statements most affected by the financial crisis were the ones of Ireland. As a common-law country with high financial transparency, the authors expect Ireland to display a lower possibility for EM. Surprisingly, the impact of the financial crisis stimulated the Irish managers to manipulate earnings to avoid bankruptcy.

Kousenidis, Ladas, and Negatis (2013) examined whether the crisis in the European Union (EU) had some impact on the quality of the reported earnings of firms in countries with weak fiscal sustainability (Greece, Ireland, Italy Portugal, and Spain), as well as on EM. Overall, the results show that during the crisis, the change in most determinants of earnings quality favors' higher earnings quality. The evidence indicated that, on average, earnings quality has improved during the crisis period. Arthur, Tang, and Lin (2015) examined earnings quality during the 2008-2010 financial crisis, considering a sample of 14 European countries. The results showed that the sample of firms presented higher-quality financial reports during the financial crisis than before it, concluding that reduced investor confidence and market liquidity engendered by the financial crisis motivates management to strategically enhanced earnings quality in an attempt to increase investor confidence and reduce the negative impact of the economic recession. Papadaki and Tzovas (2017) investigated whether firms engage more intensively in earnings management in a period of the financial crisis, using a sample of firms from 19 EU countries. The results suggest that in periods of financial crisis firms are less likely to use accruals for EM purposes, while real EM is not affected by the financial crisis. Ball and Shivakumar (2005) find no significant EM practices in UK firms.

Beuselinck et al. (2019) examined the determinants of EM within multinational corporations. Their results suggest that to meet the consolidated reporting objectives, multinational corporations practice EM through an orchestrated reporting strategy across subsidiaries over which they exert considerable influence. Another phenomenon that can influence the EM is the family involvement in firms' management, which is a complex issue (Ferramosca & Allegrini, 2018).

EM tends to be lower in family firms than in non-family firms, namely because family firms tend to monitor managerial decision-making processes, which reduces the opportunities to participate in EM actions (Vieira & Madaleno, 2019). Besides, family-firms have a long-term orientation (Anderson, Mansi, & Reeb, 2003; Jiraporn & DaDalt, 2009; Cascino et al., 2010) as well as a motivation to protect firms wealth for future generations (Achleitner et al., 2014), which decreases the incentive for EM practices. However, European empirical results are mixed. On one hand, studies are showing that family firms are less likely to practice EM than their counterparts, such as Prencipe, Bar-Yosef, and Dekker (2008), in Italy, Achleitner et al. (2014), in Germany, and Vieira and Madaleno (2019), in Portugal. On the other hand, some studies provide evidence that family firms do not differ from non-family firms in what concerns EM, such as Vieira (2016), in Portugal. Besides, Ferramosca and Allegrini (2018), considering a sample of Italian firms, find an inverted U-shaped relation between discretionary accruals and family involvement in a firm's management and control.

In what concerns the presence of women in firms' management, female directors tend to be more ethical than male directors (Betz, O'Connell, & Shepard, 1989). Indeed, Vieira and Madaleno (2019) find evidence that women contribute to a limitation on EM in Portuguese firms. Some other studies relate EM practices to the audit environment and audit firms' quality (Maijoor & Vanstraelen, 2006; Reicher & Ngo, 2020). Maijoor and Vanstraelen (2006) examine EM in a European context, namely considering the effect of audit environment and audit firm quality, expecting that the restrictions imposed by national audit environments on EM vary.

Analyzing three EU countries with clearly distinct audit environments (France, Germany, and the UK), the authors find evidence that a stricter audit environment reduces the magnitude of EM. Considering the different countries, the authors concluded that, in France and the UK, the magnitude of abnormal accruals to increase income is not significantly different from the dimension of abnormal accruals to decrease income. However, in Germany, the results show that the magnitude of abnormal accruals to increase income is significantly greater than the magnitude of abnormal accruals to decrease income. The authors conclude that Germany has a less rigorous audit quality regime than France and the UK. Reicher and Ngo (2020) used a sample of firms listed in the STOXX Europe 600, which comprises 600 small, medium, and large companies in the EU financial market. The authors conclude that firms in the STOXX Europe 600 Index should shorten the audit tenure by rotating their audit engagement more often to decline the degree of EM because longer audit tenure leads to more EM in the firms that belong to the analyzed index.

GENERAL BIBLIOMETRIC ANALYSIS ON EARNINGS MANAGEMENT: 2010-2019

Bibliometric analysis is a method that turns easier the research of the relationship between research criteria and variables related to the research and environment of that research. During this research, it was applied the exploratory, descriptive, and bibliographic research methodology, performing a content analysis through the keyword earnings management. The search was performed at the beginning of July 2020 and as such the authors excluded from it articles published after 2019. Provided the authors wanted a recent analysis period, they concentrate the chapter research during the period 2010-2019. Even so, just by searching for the keyword earnings management in the Scopus database, it was find 3473 documents (from all types) published from 1974 until 2021.

Another classification performed in our study is the kind of quantitative and qualitative research that takes on its basis a content analysis. The acquired data has on its basis several sources which are found in Scopus (https://www.scopus.com/search/), a database with a huge quantity of articles. The process of data collection in this platform is divided into several parameters: the choice of the database, the definition of keywords, the identification of the article, the journal identification, and the classification of the articles. The study performed and presented next will follow over some of these parameters.

Figure 1 presents the evolution of the documents collected during 2010 and 2019, after applying the parameters defined in the Scopus database, leading us to a total database of 2377 documents. It is visible a jump in the number of publications after 2002, being at the date the year of 2019 that with the highest number of documents published.

Figure 1. Number of documents published during 2010-2019, by year
Source: Scopus

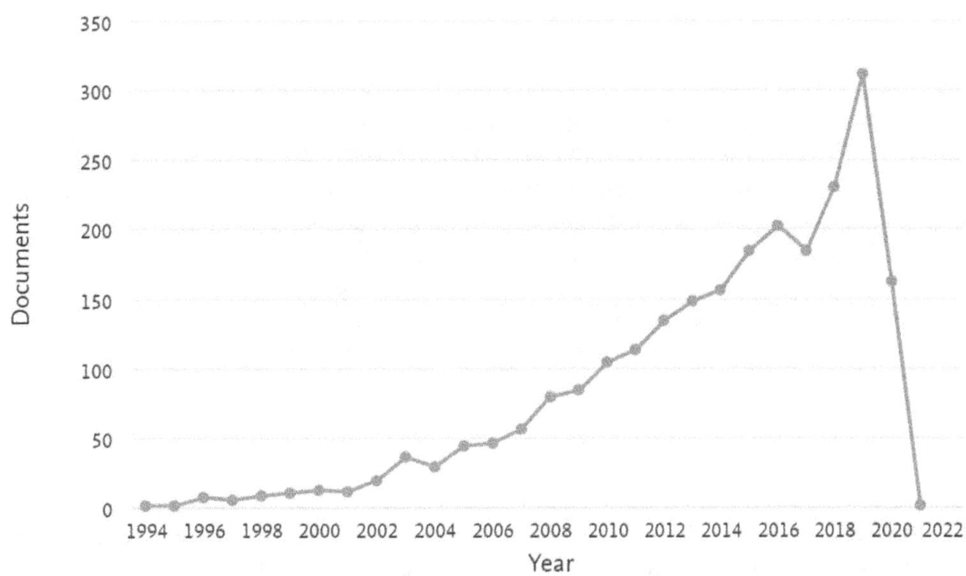

It is even denoted a short break in the year 2017, which may be due to the lack of a deeper exploration of the subject by researchers. Just by curiosity, up to the present date, 227 documents have already been published using as keyword earnings management, which leads us to argue that this continues to be a hot topic on the subject areas of Business, Management, and Accounting; Economics, Econometrics and Finance; and in Social Sciences.

Figure 2. Documents published in 2010-2019 by Source Title
Source: Scopus

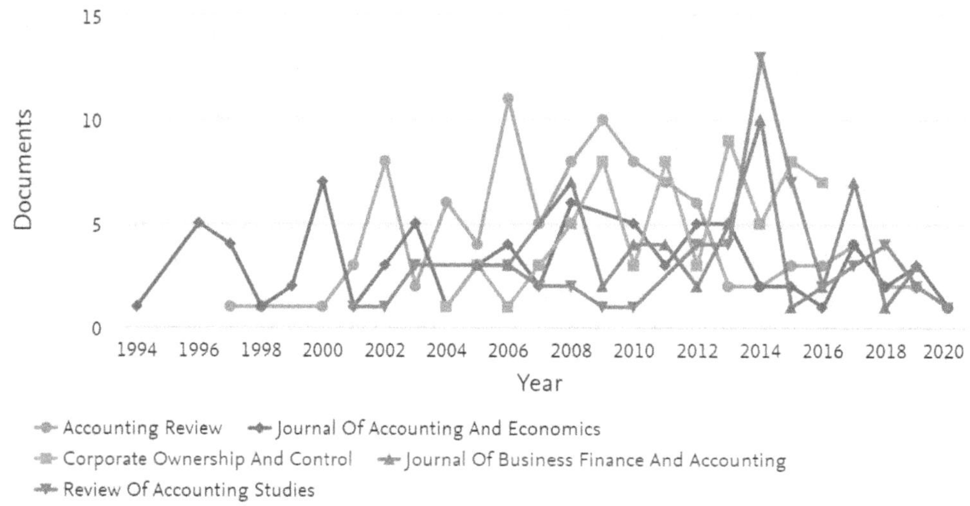

Figure 3. Documents published during 2010-2019 by author
Source: Scopus

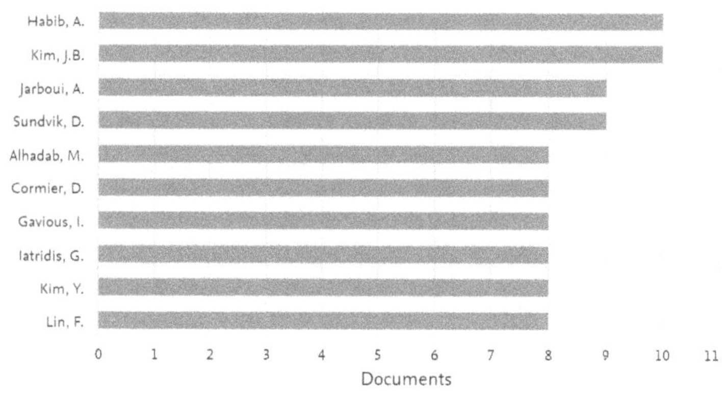

From the 2377 documents collected, Figure 2 shows the journals to which correspond the major sources of publishing journals, namely the Accounting Review, Journal of Accounting and Economics, Corporate Ownership and Control, Journal of Business Finance and Accounting, and the Review of Accounting Studies. It is clear a peak of published documents during 2006 and 2009 in the Accounting

Review, whereas both the Journal of Business Finance and Accounting and the Review of Accounting Studies published more documents whose keywords included earnings management in the year 2014.

Figure 4. Documents published by affiliation during 2010-2019 under the keyword earnings management
Source: Scopus

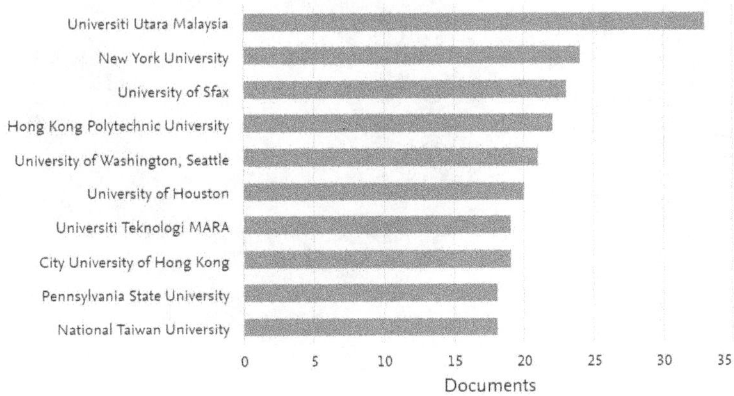

Figure 3 highlights the authors which most published in the field of earnings management during 2010 and 2019. With 10 documents each during this period, there are the authors Habib, A., and Kim, J.B., followed with 9 documents each Jarboui and Sunddvik. With 8 documents there are 6 more authors. The authors want to highlight that up to this phase they are considering all kinds of published documents under the earnings management keyword for the period of analysis, being full articles or not as it will be described in Figure 6.

Figure 5. Documents by country or territory during 2010-2019
Source: Scopus

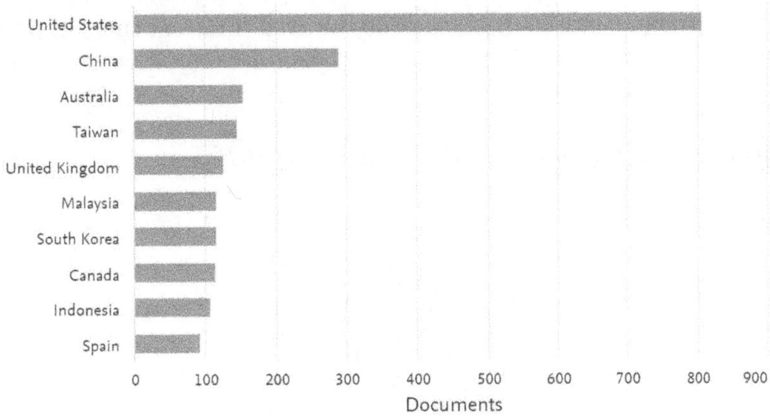

Figure 6. Documents published during 2010-2019 by type
Source: Scopus

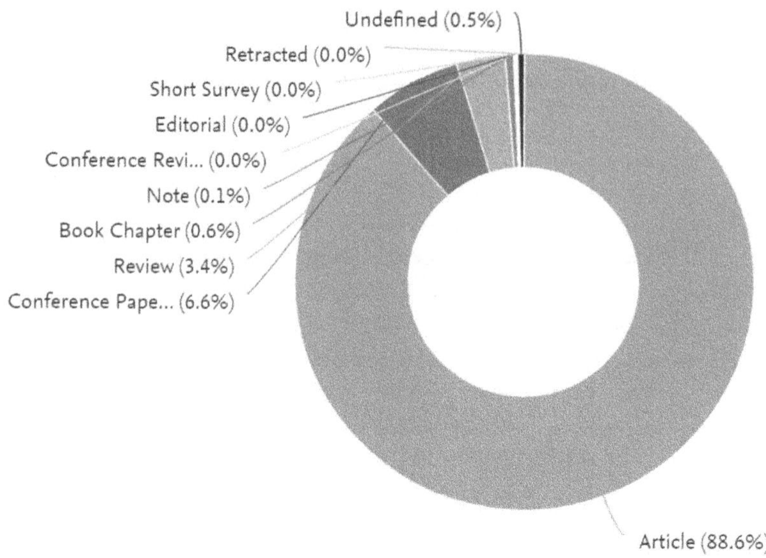

Regarding the affiliation of these authors, Figure 4 exposes that the University of Utara Malaysia is the one with the highest number of affiliated authors and co-authors publishing during 2010 and 2019. This is followed by the New York University, being the Pennsylvania State University and the National Taiwan University in the lowest top ten of affiliations.

Regarding the number of documents published by country or territory, it can be seen that research on earnings management is being focused on the United States, countries in Asia lead the top ten with only two European countries inside this top ten of research, namely the United Kingdom and Spain. This would mean that a lot more research is needed on countries within Europe, where there is still a scarcity of research under the earnings management subject and that the lack of research in other specific countries maybe be due to the scarcity of data to be explored. Moreover, a comparative analysis of earnings management is necessary within regions and among regions to observe if mixed results found by the literature are due to the country's heterogeneity or even different rules imposed related to earnings management.

Figure 7. Documents by Subject Area published during 2010-2019
Source: Scopus

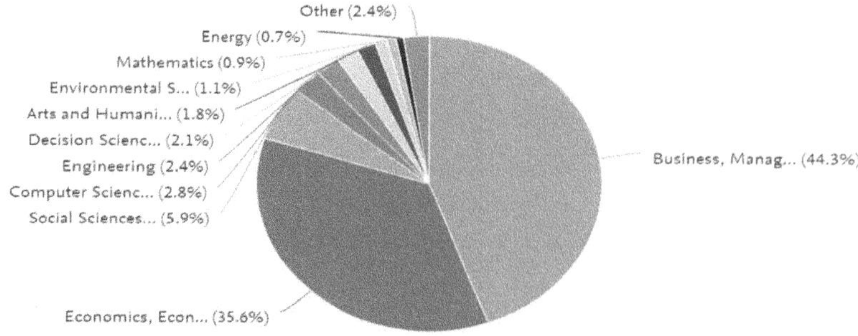

Figure 5 displays the documents by country or territory during 2010-2019.

Clearly (Figure 6), the most published documents during this period were made in the form of scientific articles (88.6%). Conference papers within our initial sample represented solely 6.6%, while Review and Book Chapters represent 3.4% and 0.6%, respectively.

Regarding the main subject areas of publication, Figure 7 shows that mostly (44.3%) are within the Business, Management and Accounting area, followed by the area of Economics, Econometrics and Finance (35.6%) and Social Sciences with 5.9%. However, it is visible that earnings management is being explored in other knowledge areas such as Computer Science, Engineering, Decision Sciences, Environmental Science, Energy, Mathematics, and Agricultural and Biological Sciences.

Regarding the funding sponsor of these documents (Figure 8),it can be observed from the figure that the National Natural Science Foundation of China, the Social Sciences and Humanities Research Council of Canada, the Ministério de Ciência e Inovação, the National Science Council, and the Fundamental Research Funds for the Central Universities are those which mostly sponsored all these documents under analysis.

Figure 8. Documents published during 2010-2019 by funding sponsor
Source: Scopus

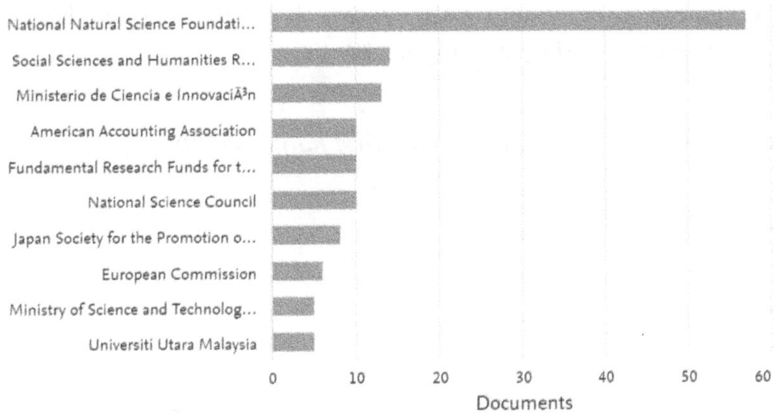

Bibliometric Analysis of Earnings Management Research During 2019 and Up to July 2020

In this section,the study has proceeded in four steps. First, the database from Scopus was used to gather documents that have been published during the years 2019 and 2020 (the search was made at the beginning of July 2020) under the subject keyword earnings management as previously. Second, the keyword earnings management was the one used, eliminating all the documents which do not have it as keyword defined. Third, it was identified all documents and journals which used earnings management as a keyword. Fourth, and finally, the study was limited the bibliographic database to solely scientific peer-reviewed articles in scientific journals during 2019 and the first six months of 2020, which were classified in the categories Business, Management and Accounting and that of Economics, Econometrics, and Finance. As such only final articles and published already were considered to perform the bibliometric analysis in this section, totaling 389 articles.

While exporting this data to the VOSviewer, the authors were able to verify that there were four distinct clusters (or groups) of authors that work together. One of these clusters has 7 authors, another 5 authors, and two other clusters had 3 main authors, as evidenced in Figure 9.

Figure 9. Authors and coauthors analysis for earnings management articles published during 2019 and the first half of 2020.
Source: VosViewer

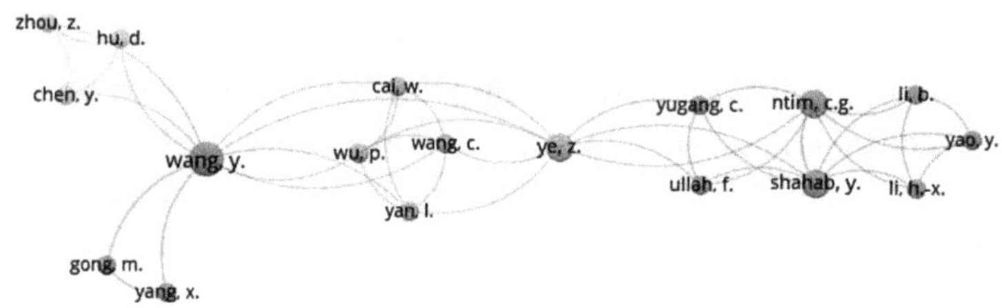

From the 389 articles considered, the research was redefined by the h-index resulting in a total of 7 articles that were cited at least 7 times. As such, our bibliometric analysis in the following exposition will be concentrated on these seven scientific articles which were more cited during 2019 and the first six months of 2020. The results are shown in Figure 10.

Figure 10. Documents h-index during 2019 and the first half of 2020.
Source: Scopus

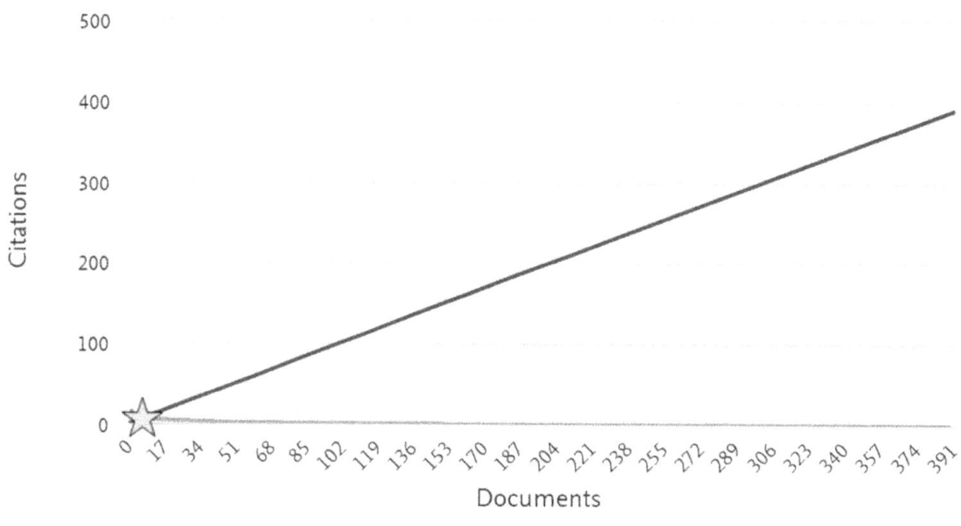

The most cited articles are those described in Table 1. The article gathering more citations was published in 2019 in the Journal of Business Ethics with 15 citations at the moment of this chapter writing. The author analyzed earnings management from the perspective of financial reports and social capital. Obviously, given our search criteria, only 2019 articles are presented in the list of the most cited ones, or with more than or equal to 7 citations.

Table 1. Top 7 cited articles during 2019 and the first half of 2020

	Document Title	Authors	Year	Source	Cited by
1	Financial Reports and Social Capital	Jha, A.	2019	Journal of Business Ethics 155(2), pp. 567-596	15
2	The influence of CEO and CFO power on accruals and real earnings management	Baker, T.A., Lopez, T.J., Reitenga, A.L., Ruch, G.W.	2019	Review of Quantitative Finance and Accounting 52(1), pp. 325-345	8
3	Activity strategies, information asymmetry, and bank opacity	Tran, D.V., Hassan, M.K., Houston, R.	2019	Economic Modelling 83, pp. 160-172	7
4	Pre-merger management in developing markets: The role of earnings glamor	Huang, W., Goodell, J.W., Zhang, H.	2019	International Review of Financial Analysis 65,101375	7
5	Strangers on the board: The impact of board internationalization on earnings management of Nordic firms	Hooghiemstra, R., Hermes, N., Oxelheim, L., Randøy, T.	2019	International Business Review 28(1), pp. 119-134	7
6	A study of interaction effects of political influences and earnings management on organisational performance	Sadiq, M., Othman, Z., Keong, O.C.	2019	Asian Economic and Financial Review 9(5), pp. 642-653	7
7	Individualistic cultures and crash risk	Dang, T.L., Faff, R., Luong, H., Nguyen, L.	2019	European Financial Management 25(3), pp. 622-654	7

Source: Own Development

Table 2. Total citations made by other articles to the most cited articles in 2019

	Documents	Citations	2018	2019	2020	Total
	Total		1	18	39	58
1	Financial Reports and Social Capital	2019	1	3	11	15
2	The influence of CEO and CFO power on accruals and real earnings management	2019		2	6	8
3	Activity strategies, information asymmetry, and bank opacity	2019		1	6	7
4	Pre-merger management in developing markets: The role of earnings glamor	2019			7	7
5	Strangers on the board: The impact of board internationalization on earnings management of Nordic firms	2019		5	2	7
6	A study of interaction effects of political influences and earnings management on organisational performance	2019		3	4	7
7	Individualistic cultures and crash risk	2019		4	3	7

Source: Own Development

The thematic under research includes earnings management, financial reports, social capital, board characteristics, information asymmetry, mergers and acquisitions, political influences, and culture. Jha (2019) examines social capital's impact on financial reports for the USA finding that firms located in regions with high social capital have lower levels of discretionary accruals, lower probability of committing fraud by misrepresenting financial information, and more readable annual reports. Considering board characteristics, Baker et al.'s (2019) results suggest that the power of the CEO relative to the CFO is an important factor in the type and magnitude of EM. For Nordic firms, Hooghiemstra et al. (2019) found that the presence of non-Nordic foreign directors is associated with EM, that foreign board members' accounting knowledge negatively affects board monitoring, and also that different language structures affect perception and detection of EM.

A positive relationship between EM and bank diversification was found by Tran et al. (2019), where diversification was associated with manager discretionary power in small banks. The authors end by stating that the financial crisis has mitigated the value of diversification on EM. In a different vein and market, Huang et al. (2019) examined a sample of mergers by Chinese listed firms to conclude that EM increases the probability of deal payment in stock and that acquirer firms take advantage of informational voids by signaling. Sadiq et al. (2019), using a sample of Pakistani firms, results point that politically influenced firms to manipulate earnings through accruals to report poor organizational performance and lower taxable income. Analyzing national culture impact on stock price risk, Dang et al. (2019) conclude that firms influence is higher for firms in more individualistic cultural settings. They argue that EM, excessive managerial risk-taking, investors' difference of opinion, and overconfidence all contribute to the positive impact of individualism on crash risk. Having these specific 7 articles summarized, it can be argued that these are the hot topics in EM at the present moment provided the number of citations thus far.

Table 3. Total citations made by other articles to the most cited articles in 2019 (excluding self-citations from all authors)

	Documents	Citations	2018	2019	2020	Total
	Total		1	15	30	46
1	Financial Reports and Social Capital	2019	1	3	11	15
2	The influence of CEO and CFO power on accruals and real earnings management	2019		1	6	7
3	Activity strategies, information asymmetry, and bank opacity	2019		0	0	0
4	Pre-merger management in developing markets: The role of earnings glamor	2019		0	7	7
5	Strangers on the board: The impact of board internationalization on earnings management of Nordic firms	2019		5	2	7
6	A study of interaction effects of political influences and earnings management on organisational performance	2019		2	1	3
7	Individualistic cultures and crash risk	2019		4	3	7

Source: Own Development

In terms of citations made by other authors of these same 7 articles, it can be seen in Table 2 the total number and by year of citation, by article. It is possible to observe that even in 2018 there is 1 article citing the paper written by Jha (2019), but most of the citations have already been made during the first 6 months of 2020 (11). Table 3 presents the total number of citations made by other articles during the same periods but at this time excluding all self-citations of all authors. The numbers are especially different considering totals but curiously not in the more identified cited article of Jha (2019). Self-citations are particularly relevant in article 3. It can be seen that from Table 2 to Table 3, there is no citations in the years of 2018-2020. This means that being on the top 7 of citations for Tran et al. (2019) depends on the self-citations of one or more of these same authors.

Table 4. Articles collaboration for the top 7 cited articles during 2018-2020: number of authors

	Documents	Number of Authors
1	Financial Reports and Social Capital	1
2	The influence of CEO and CFO power on accruals and real earnings management	4
3	Activity strategies, information asymmetry, and bank opacity	3
4	Pre-merger management in developing markets: The role of earnings glamor	3
5	Strangers on the board: The impact of board internationalization on earnings management of Nordic firms	4
6	A study of interaction effects of political influences and earnings management on organisational performance	3
7	Individualistic cultures and crash risk	3

Source: Own Development

Table 5. Research activity and facts for the authors of the most cited articles in 2019

	Author	Documents by Author	Total Citation	h-Index	Co-authors
1	Jha, Anand	12	175	4	16
2	Baker, Terry A.	5	114	4	5
	Lopez, Thomas J.	20	398	11	24
	Reitenga, Austin L.	17	376	11	19
	Ruch, George W.	4	48	2	7
3	Tran, Dung Viet	12	22	3	9
	Kabir Hassan, M.	246	3217	29	247
	Houston, Reza	9	40	4	7
4	Huang, Wei	20	104	6	17
	Goodell, John W.	48	498	12	44
	Zhang, Hong	1	7	1	2
5	Hooghiemstra, Reggy B.H.	22	811	11	21
	Hermes, Niels	52	2049	23	43
	Oxelheim, Lars	65	658	13	37
	Randoy, Trond	35	1099	17	35
6	Sadiq, Muhammad	4	11	2	6
	Othman, Zaleha	15	15	2	19
	Keong, Ooi Chee	10	7	1	16
7	Dang, Tung Lam	13	65	3	26
	Luong, Hoang	3	46	2	7
	Nguyen, Lily H.G.	10	81	5	20

Source: Own Development

Table 6. Facts related to the Journals of the most cited articles in EM during 2019

	Author	CiteScore 2019	SJR 2019	SNIP 2019	Citations 2016-2019	Documents 2016-2019
1	Journal of Business Ethics	7.0	1.972	2.700	10.574	1.518
2	Review of Quantitative Finance and Accounting	2.4	0.669	1.399	771	320
3	Economic Modelling	4.2	0.972	1.603	4.645	1.114
4	International Review of Financial Analysis	3.8	0.874	1.666	1.805	474
5	International Business Review	7.6	1.453	2.213	2.898	383
6	Asian Economic and Financial Review	1.6	0.233	1.951	321	201
7	European Financial Management	2.6	0.995	1.533	357	138

Source: Own Development

By doing a more detailed analysis of the articles' collaboration it is easily perceived that most of these articles are composed by a team of authors composed of three authors (Table 4). Those with the highest number of collaborators are the articles "The influence of CEO and CFO power on accruals and real earnings management" and "Strangers on the board: The impact of board internationalization on earnings management of Nordic firms" as it can be seen in Table 4, while the only article written by a sole author is the most cited one and with no self-citations, namely the article "Financial Reports and Social Capital", by Anad Jha (2019).

Within this context of the number of articles collaborators, Table 5 shows the number of documents created by each, the total citations considering each author, the h-index of each author, and the number of co-authors that each author has added in the documents explored and identified. The author with the highest number of published documents, number of citations, h-index, and co-authors as well is Kabir Hassan, M., one of the co-authors identified in Table 3 where only self-citations were identified in a total of 7.

It should be as well noticed that the author with the lowest numbers in these components is Hong Zhang, maybe because it is a junior researcher, which will be reflected in these lowest numbers identified at the date.

To conclude this section, the authors present in Table 6 some stylized facts at the date of the journals were the most cited articles during 2019 have been published. The article that published more articles was the Journal of Business Ethics, the one which also received the highest number of citations.

Regarding the CiteScore index the highest one was attributed to the International Business Review, whereas following both SJR and SNIP, the highest score is attributed to the Journal of Business Ethics.

Table 7. Summary of articles exploring simultaneously corporate governance and earnings management from 2018 - 2020

Publication Year	Document Title	Authors	Citations	2018	2019	2020	Total
			Journal Title	17	48	101	166
2020	Are insiders equal? Evidence from earnings management in closely held East Asian firms	Attig N., Chen R., El Ghoul S., Guedhami O., Kwok C., Pittman J.	Research in International Business and Finance	0	0	0	0
2020	The impact of corporate governance and agency effect on earnings management – A test of the dual banking system	Alam N., Ramachandran J., Nahomy A.H.	Research in International Business and Finance	0	0	0	0
2020	Economic bonding, corporate governance and earnings management: Evidence from UK publicly traded family firms	Al-Okaily J., BenYoussef N., Chahine S.	International Journal of Auditing	0	0	0	0
2020	Corporate governance and earnings management practices in indonesian banking sector	Puryandani S., Kusumawati H.A., Robiyanto R.	Quality - Access to Success	0	0	0	0
2020	Financial flexibility and managerial short-termism	Gu Y., Zhou Q., Ho K.-C.	Annals of Economics and Finance	0	0	0	0
2020	Are loyalty shares an effective antidote against short-termism? Empirical evidence from Italy	Mio C., Soerger Zaro E., Fasan M.	Business Strategy and the Environment	0	0	0	0
2020	Earnings management under different ownership and corporate governance structure: A natural experiment with master limited partnerships	Chen H., Jory S., Ngo T.	Quarterly Review of Economics and Finance	0	0	0	0
2020	Insider trading restrictions and earnings management	Garcia Osma B., Scarlat E., Shields K.	Accounting and Business Research	0	0	0	0
2020	Corporate governance and earnings management: Evidence from listed firms at Palestine exchange	Abdelkarim N., Zuriqi K.	Asian Economic and Financial Review	0	0	0	0
2020	A triple of corporate governance, social responsibility and earnings management	Huynh Q.L.	Journal of Asian Finance, Economics and Business	0	0	1	1
2020	Audit certification, earnings management and risk governance: a moderated-mediation analysis	Fakhfakh I., Jarboui A.	Journal of Financial Reporting and Accounting	0	0	0	0
2020	How do the ownership structure and board of directors' features impact earnings management? The Spanish case	Saona P., Muro L., Alvarado M.	Journal of International Financial Management and Accounting	0	0	1	1
2020	CEO discretion, political connection and real earnings management in Nigeria	Sani A.A., Abdul Latif R., Al-Dhamari R.A.	Management Research Review	0	0	0	0
2020	Impact of corporate governance on firm performance and earnings management a study on vietnamese non-financial companies	Dao B.T.T., Ngo H.A.	Asian Economic and Financial Review	0	0	0	0
2020	Corporate governance factors as predictors of earnings management	Wasan P., Mulchandani K.	Journal of General Management	0	0	0	0
2020	Real earnings management and corporate governance: a study of Latin America	Mellado C., Saona P.	Economic Research-Ekonomska Istrazivanja	0	0	0	0
2020	Corporate governance and earnings management in concentrated markets	El Diri M., Lambrinoudakis C., Alhadab M.	Journal of Business Research	0	0	1	1
2020	Corporate social responsibility and earnings management: The moderating effect of corporate governance mechanisms	Buertey S., Sun E.-J., Lee J.S., Hwang J.	Corporate Social Responsibility and Environmental Management	0	0	4	4
2019	Relationship between earnings management, CEO compensation, and stock return on Tehran Stock Exchange	Moardi M., Salehi M., Poursasan S., Molavi H.	International Journal of Organization Theory and Behavior	0	0	0	0
2019	Effect of audit committee independence, board ethnicity and family ownership on earnings management in Malaysia	Wan Mohammad W.M., Wasiuzzaman S.	Journal of Accounting in Emerging Economies	0	0	1	1
2019	Board gender diversity, corporate governance, and earnings management: Evidence from an emerging market	Orazalin N.	Gender in Management	0	0	2	2
2019	The impact of corporate governance mechanisms on real and accrual earnings management practices: evidence from Jordan	Al-Haddad L., Whittington M.	Corporate Governance (Bingley)	0	0	5	5
2019	Female directors, earnings management, and CEO incentive compensation: UK evidence	Harakeh M., El-Gammal W., Matar G.	Research in International Business and Finance	0	1	2	3
2019	Shareholder litigation risk and real earnings management: a causal inference	Liao Q., Ouyang B.	Review of Accounting and Finance	0	0	0	0
2019	Corporate governance, foreign direct investment, and bank income smoothing in African countries	Pinto I., Gaio C., Goncalves T.	International Journal of Emerging Markets	0	0	1	1
2019	Busy boards and earnings management – an Australian perspective	Tham Y.H., Sultana N., Singh H., Taplin R.	Asian Review of Accounting	0	1	0	1
2019	Audit committee chairman characteristics and earnings management: The influence of family chairman	Al-Absy M.S.M., Ku Ismail K.N.I., Chandren S.	Asia-Pacific Journal of Business Administration	0	0	0	0
2019	Corporate governance mechanisms, whistle-blowing policy and real earnings management	Al-Absy M.S.M., Ismail K.N.I.K., Chandren S.	International Journal of Financial Research	0	0	0	0
2019	The effect of outside blockholders on earnings management around seasoned equity offerings in French listed companies on the SBF120	Jerbi Maatougui A., Halioui K.	Journal of Financial Reporting and Accounting	0	0	1	1
2019	Do female and independent directors explain the two-way relationship between corporate social responsibility and earnings management of Chinese listed firms?	Sial M.S., Chunmei Z., Khuong N.V.	International Journal of Accounting and Information Management	0	0	5	5

continued on following page

Table 7. Continued

Publication Year	Document Title	Authors	Citations	2018	2019	2020	Total
			Journal Title	17	48	101	166
2019	Duration of equity overvaluation and managers' choice to use aggressive underlying earnings disclosure and accrual-based earnings management: Australian evidence	Yang Y., Abeysekera I.	Journal of Contemporary Accounting and Economics	0	0	1	1
2019	The role of foreign institutional investors in restraining earnings management activities across countries	Lel U.	Journal of International Business Studies	0	1	4	5
2019	Discretionary accruals: signalling or earnings management in Australia?	Pham H.Y., Chung R.Y.-M., Roca E., Bao B.-H.	Accounting and Finance	0	2	2	4
2019	Voting with hands, earnings management and corporate governance	Li T., Zhao X., Zhao A.	Review of Accounting and Finance	0	0	0	0
2019	Managing the Conflicting Interests of Workers and Shareholders: Evidence from Pension-Assumption Manipulations	Cobb J.A.	ILR Review	0	0	0	0
2019	Corporate governance quality and premature revenue recognition: evidence from the UK	Okaily J.A., Dixon R., Salama A.	International Journal of Managerial Finance	0	1	1	2
2019	[Women on the board: Do they manage earnings? empirical evidence from european listed firms, Mulheres no Board: Elas gerem resultados? Evidência empírica das empresas europeias cotadas]	Goncalves T., Gaio C., Santos T.	Revista Brasileira de Gestao de Negocios	0	0	2	2
2019	The effect of corporate board diversity: Real earnings management among Malaysian listed firms	Ghazali A.W., Nurullah M., Ibrahim S., Sanusi Z.M., Mohame N.	International Journal of Business and Management Science	0	0	0	0
2019	Impact of corporate governance on earnings management: Large sample evidence from India	Sehrawat N.K., Kumar A., Lohia N., Bansal S., Agarwal T.	Asian Economic and Financial Review	0	0	0	0
2019	Earnings management: Esop and Corporate Governance	Susanto Y.K., Pradipta A., Cecilia E.	Academy of Accounting and Financial Studies Journal	0	0	0	0
2019	Firm attributes, earnings management, and anti-corruption activities in Thai-listed firms	Benyasrisawat P.	Afro-Asian Journal of Finance and Accounting	0	0	0	0
2019	Unmasking the fraud at toshiba	Caplan D.H., Dutta S.K., Marcinko D.J.	Issues in Accounting Education	0	0	2	2
2019	The associations between earnings management, corporate environmental disclosure, corporate financial performance and corporate governance mechanisms	Utomo S.D., Machmuddah Z., Oktafiyani M.	WSEAS Transactions on Business and Economics	0	0	1	1
2019	Board of director's gender diversity and its impact on earnings management: An empirical analysis for select european firms	Saona P., Muro L., San Martin P., Baier-Fuentes H.	Technological and Economic Development of Economy	0	0	1	1
2019	Female directorship and real earnings management in Bangladesh: Towards an analytical assessment	Debnath N.C., Patnaik B.C.M., Satpathy I.	Management Science Letters	0	0	1	1
2019	The impact of corporate fraud on director-interlocked firms: Evidence from bank loans	Lai T.-K., Lei A.C.H., Song F.M.	Journal of Business Finance and Accounting	0	1	0	1
2018	Related party transactions, corporate governance and earnings management	Marchini P.L., Mazza T., Medioli A.	Corporate Governance (Bingley)	0	1	2	3
2018	Good corporate governance mechanism and earnings management: Study on manufacturing companies in Indonesia stock exchange	Mukhtaruddin M., Zuryati E., Robiani B., Saftiana Y.	Journal of Applied Economic Sciences	0	0	0	0
2018	The relationship between managerial entrenchment, earnings management and firm innovation	Salehi M., Mahmoudabadi M., Adibian M.S.	International Journal of Productivity and Performance Management	0	1	2	3
2018	The effect of ownership composition on earnings management: evidence for the Mexican stock exchange	San Martin Reyna J.M.	Journal of Economics, Finance and Administrative Science	0	0	2	2
2018	The relationship between external financing activities and earnings management: Evidence from enterprise risk management	Wang T.-S., Lin Y.-M., Werner E.M., Chang H.	International Review of Economics and Finance	0	4	5	9
2018	Firm- and Country-Level Attributes as Determinants of Earnings Management: An Analysis for Latin American Firms	Saona P., Muro L.	Emerging Markets Finance and Trade	0	2	6	8
2018	National corporate governance, GMI ratings and earnings management: A country level study	El-Helaly M., Shehata N.F., El-Sherif R.	Asian Review of Accounting	0	0	0	0
2018	Ex ante and ex post overvalued equities: The roles of corporate governance and product market competition	Kao L., Chen A., Lu C.-S.	Asia Pacific Management Review	0	0	0	0
2018	Gender diverse board and earnings management: evidence from French listed companies	Triki Damak S.	Sustainability Accounting, Management and Policy Journal	1	2	3	6
2018	Do dimensions of corporate social responsibility affect earnings management?: Evidence from France	Ben Amar A., Chakroun S.	Journal of Financial Reporting and Accounting	1	2	3	6
2018	[The right person at the right time: Audit committee members and the quality of financial information ¹, La persona adecuada en el momento adecuado: Los miembros del comité de auditoría y la calidad de la información financiera]	Herranz C.Z., Iturriaga F.J.L., Reguera-Alvarado N.	UCJC Business and Society Review	0	0	0	0
2018	Effect of corporate governance mechanism, independence and management of earnings integrity of financial statements (In manufacturing companies listed on the stock exchange)	Khaddafi M., Wahyuddin, Heikal M., Falahuddin, Maulida R.	Quality - Access to Success	0	1	0	1
2018	When institutions passively curb earnings management: Evidence from the Korean market	Chung C.Y., Hwang J.H., Kim D., Liu C.	Finance Research Letters	0	0	0	0

continued on following page

Table 7. Continued

Publication Year	Document Title	Authors	Citations	2018	2019	2020	Total
			Journal Title	**17**	**48**	**101**	**166**
2018	Audit quality, debt financing, and earnings management: Evidence from Jordan	Alzoubi E.S.S.	Journal of International Accounting, Auditing and Taxation	0	4	6	10
2018	The consequences of managerial indiscretions: Sex, lies, and firm value	Cline B.N., Walkling R.A., Yore A.S.	Journal of Financial Economics	1	4	3	8
2018	Earnings management in developing countries. The case of Brazilian real estate industry	Matteo P., Francesco P.	Academy of Accounting and Financial Studies Journal	0	0	1	1
2018	Does hometown advantage matter? the case of institutional blockholder monitoring on earnings management in Korea	Liu C., Chung C.Y., Sul H.K., Wang K.	Journal of International Business Studies	4	9	15	28
2018	Effects of borrowing costs, firm size, and characteristics of board of directors on earnings management types: a study at Borsa Istanbul[*]	Turegun N.	Asia-Pacific Journal of Accounting and Economics	0	1	0	1
2018	The effect of corporate governance attributes on earnings management: A study of listed companies in Nigeria	Tolulope I., Uwuigbe U., Uwuigbe O.R., Emmanuel O., Oriabie S., Asiriuwa O.	Academy of Strategic Management Journal	0	1	1	2
2018	An exploratory analysis of earnings management practices in Australia and New Zealand	Sun L., Al Farooque O.	International Journal of Accounting and Information Management	0	1	2	3
2018	The analysis of effects of good corporate governance on earnings management in Indonesia with panel data approach	Muda I., Maulana W., Siregar H.S., Indra N.	Iranian Economic Review	10	4	9	23
2018	Corporate governance compliance and accrual earnings management in eastern Africa: Evidence from Kenya and Tanzania	Waweru N.M., Prot N.P.	Managerial Auditing Journal	0	4	2	6
Total			**Excluding self-citations**	15	35	77	127

Source: Own Development

BIBLIOMETRIC ANALYSIS OF ARTICLES CONSIDERING CORPORATE GOVERNANCE AND EARNINGS MANAGEMENT

As for the design of research in this section, the authors concentrate on the keywords "Corporate Governance" and "Earnings Management" in the Scopus database. In total, 340 documents were identified. After limiting our search to the years 2018, 2019, and 2020 (first six months), to only already published articles in Journals and to the subject areas Business, Management, and Accounting and Economics, Econometrics and Finance, the study ends up with a total of 68 documents. Considering the subject area of these 68 documents, it can be seen that 50.4% correspond to the area of Business, Management and Accounting (59) and 37.6% classified as Economics, Econometrics, and Finance (in a total of 44 documents). The h-index of these articles considering their citations is 6, whereof the 68 documents considered for the h-index, 6 have been cited at least 6 times. This data is summarized in Table 7.

The highly cited articles were published in 2018. Self-citations in 2018 have been 2, in 2019 the number increased to 13 and in 2020, own citations that can be count (see Table 7) 24. In total for these three years, there are 39 self-citations. 2019 was the year with the highest number of articles published by scientific journals. There has been a total of 147 document results that cited the selected 68 articles. The year 2020 already counts with 18 articles published, 28 were published in 2019, whereas in 2018 it has 22 articles published in refereed journals. The authors which most published during this period were Muro, followed by Al-Absy, Chandren, Cheng and Gaio, each with 2 articles.

There are three journals each with 3 articles published analyzing the relationship between corporate governance and earnings management. These were the Asian Economic and Financial Review, the Journal of Financial Reporting and Accounting, and the Research in International Business and Finance. Both with two articles from the 68 published, there are the Academy of Accounting and Financial Studies Journal, the Asian Review of Accounting, the Review of Accounting and Finance, and four other Journals. All the others identified in Table 7 had only one article published, from the 68, during this period.

CONCLUSION

In accounting, earnings management is a method of manipulating financial records to improve the appearance of the company's financial position. EM has been explored in this bibliometric review accounting first for all the documents published between 2010 and 2019. Afterward, and provided that companies use earnings management to present the appearance of consistent profits and to smooth earnings' fluctuations, our bibliometric research was redefined to contemplate solely articles published in journals during 2019 and the first half of 2020 where the most cited ones (in a total of 7) were presented. Hot research topics include mergers and acquisitions, financial reports manipulation, cultural differences, political instability, and corporate governance. One of the most popular ways to manipulate financial records is to use an accounting policy that generates higher short-term earnings. Therefore, the authors moved to perform a bibliometric analysis of the articles published in referred journals studying the relationship between corporate governance and earnings management.

Mixed evidence has been reported in the literature leaving space for new developments in research terms. European markets exploration is still in deeper need of analysis. Corporate governance can be used as a tool for earnings management control. Board characteristics like gender, education, commitment, experience, image, age, and independence are still being explored and new findings emerge bringing with these new research developments. Different methodologies are being applied to explore these relationships and these sometimes drive to different reported results. A deeper understanding of institutional and market pressures, legal environments, macroeconomic conditions, and many others are still in need of research or deserve more understanding. Relating these two themes with the economic value of the firm is still in its infancy even though much research has emerged in recent years.

REFERENCES

Abdelkarim, N., & Zuriqi, K. (2020). Corporate governance and earnings management: Evidence from listed firms at palestine Palestine exchange. *Asian Economic and Financial Review, 10*(2), 200–217. doi:10.18488/journal.aefr.2020.102.200.217

Abeyratna, G., & Power, D. (2002). The post-announcement performance of dividend-changing companies: The dividend-signalling hypothesis revisited. *Accounting and Finance, 42*(2), 131–151. doi:10.1111/1467-629X.00071

Achleitner, A., Günther, N., Kaserer, C., & Siciliano, G. (2014). Real earnings management and accrual based earnings management in family firms. *European Accounting Review, 23*(3), 431–461. doi:10.1080/09638180.2014.895620

Agustia, D., Muhammad, N. P. A., & Permatasari, Y. (2020). Earnings management, business strategy, and bankruptcy risk: Evidence from Indonesia. *Heliyon, 6*(2), e03317. doi:10.1016/j.heliyon.2020.e03317 PMID:32055735

Al-Absy, M. S. M., Ismail, K. N. I. K., & Chandren, S. (2019). Corporate governance mechanisms, whistle-blowing policy and real earnings management. *International Journal of Financial Research, 10*(6), 265–282. doi:10.5430/ijfr.v10n6p265

Al-Absy, M. S. M., Ku Ismail, K. N. I., & Chandren, S. (2019). Audit committee chairman characteristics and earnings management: The influence of family chairman. *Asia-Pacific Journal of Business Administration, 11*(4), 339–370. doi:10.1108/APJBA-10-2018-0188

Al-Haddad, L., & Whittington, M. (2019). The impact of corporate governance mechanisms on real and accrual earnings management practices: Evidence from jordan. *Corporate Governance, 19*(6), 1167–1186. doi:10.1108/CG-05-2018-0183

Al-Okaily, J., BenYoussef, N., & Chahine, S. (2020). Economic bonding, corporate governance and earnings management: Evidence from UK publicly traded family firms. *International Journal of Auditing, 24*(2), 185–204. doi:10.1111/ijau.12186

Alam, N., Ramachandran, J., & Nahomy, A. H. (2020). The impact of corporate governance and agency effect on earnings management – A test of the dual banking system. *Research in International Business and Finance, 54*, 101242. Advance online publication. doi:10.1016/j.ribaf.2020.101242

Alzoubi, E. S. S. (2018). Audit quality, debt financing, and earnings management: Evidence from jordan. *Journal of International Accounting, Auditing & Taxation, 30*, 69–84. doi:10.1016/j.intaccaudtax.2017.12.001

Anderson, R. C., Mansi, S. A., & Reeb, D. M. (2003). Founding family ownership and the agency cost of debt. *Journal of Financial Economics, 68*(2), 263–285. doi:10.1016/S0304-405X(03)00067-9

Arthur, N., Tang, Q., & Lin, Z. (2015). Corporate accruals quality during the 2008–2010 Global Financial Crisis. *Journal of International Accounting, Auditing & Taxation, 25*, 1–15. doi:10.1016/j.intaccaudtax.2015.10.004

Attig, N., Chen, R., El Ghoul, S., Guedhami, O., Kwok, C., & Pittman, J. (2020). Are insiders equal? evidence from earnings management in closely held east asian firms. *Research in International Business and Finance, 54*, 101243. Advance online publication. doi:10.1016/j.ribaf.2020.101243

Baker, T. A., Lopez, T. J., Reitenga, A. L., & Ruch, G. W. (2019). The influence of CEO and CFO power on accruals and real earnings management. *Review of Quantitative Finance and Accounting, 52*(1), 325–345. doi:10.100711156-018-0711-z

Ball, R., Robin, A., & Wu, J. (2003). Incentives versus standards: Properties of accounting income in four East Asian countries. *Journal of Accounting and Economics, 36*(1-3), 235–270. doi:10.1016/j.jacceco.2003.10.003

Ball, R., & Shivakumar, L. (2005). Earnings quality in UK private firms: Comparative loss recognition timeless. *Journal of Accounting and Economics, 39*(1), 83–128. doi:10.1016/j.jacceco.2004.04.001

Beasley, M. (1996). An empirical analysis of the relation between the board of director composition and financial statement fraud. *The Accounting Review, 71*(4), 443–464.

Ben Amar, A., & Chakroun, S. (2018). Do dimensions of corporate social responsibility affect earnings management?: Evidence from france. *Journal of Financial Reporting and Accounting, 16*(2), 348–370. doi:10.1108/JFRA-05-2017-0033

Benyasrisawat, P. (2019). Firm attributes, earnings management, and anti-corruption activities in thai-listed firms. *Afro-Asian Journal of Finance and Accounting*, *9*(4), 439–458. doi:10.1504/AAJFA.2019.102982

Betz, M., O'Connell, L., & Shepard, J. M. (1989). Gender differences in proclivity for unethical behavior. *Journal of Business Ethics*, *8*(5), 321–324. doi:10.1007/BF00381722

Beuselinck, C., Cascino, S., Deloof, M., & Vanstraelen, A. (2019). Earnings Management within Multinational Corporations. *The Accounting Review*, *94*(4), 45–76. doi:10.2308/accr-52274

Buckmaster, D. (2001). *Development of the Income Smoothing Literature 1893–1998: A Focus on the United States*. Elsevier Science Ltd.

Buertey, S., Sun, E., Lee, J. S., & Hwang, J. (2020). Corporate social responsibility and earnings management: The moderating effect of corporate governance mechanisms. *Corporate Social Responsibility and Environmental Management*, *27*(1), 256–271. doi:10.1002/csr.1803

Caplan, D. H., Dutta, S. K., & Marcinko, D. J. (2019). Unmasking the fraud at toshiba. *Issues in Accounting Education*, *34*(3), 41–57. doi:10.2308/iace-52429

Cascino, S., Pugliese, A., Mussolino, D., & Sansone, C. (2010). The influence of family ownership on the quality of accounting information. *Family Business Review*, *23*(3), 246–265. doi:10.1177/0894486510374302

Chen, H., Jory, S., & Ngo, T. (2020). Earnings management under different ownership and corporate governance structure: A natural experiment with master limited partnerships. *The Quarterly Review of Economics and Finance*, *76*, 139–156. doi:10.1016/j.qref.2019.05.005

Chung, C. Y., Hwang, J. H., Kim, D., & Liu, C. (2018). When institutions passively curb earnings management: Evidence from the korean market. *Finance Research Letters*, *25*, 274–279. doi:10.1016/j.frl.2018.02.033

Cline, B. N., Walkling, R. A., & Yore, A. S. (2018). The consequences of managerial indiscretions: Sex, lies, and firm value. *Journal of Financial Economics*, *127*(2), 389–415. doi:10.1016/j.jfineco.2017.11.008

Cobb, J. A. (2019). Managing the conflicting interests of workers and shareholders: Evidence from pension-assumption manipulations. *Industrial & Labor Relations Review*, *72*(3), 523–551. doi:10.1177/0019793918789155

Dang, T. L., Faff, R., Luong, H., & Nguyen, L. (2019). Individualistic cultures and crash risk. *European Financial Management*, *25*(3), 622–654. doi:10.1111/eufm.12180

Dao, B. T. T., & Ngo, H. A. (2020). Impact of corporate governance on firm performance and earnings management a study on vietnamese non-financial companies. *Asian Economic and Financial Review*, *10*(5), 480–501. doi:10.18488/journal.aefr.2020.105.480.501

Debnath, N. C., Patnaik, B. C. M., & Satpathy, I. (2019). Female directorship and real earnings management in bangladesh: Towards an analytical assessment. *Management Science Letters*, *9*(11), 1723–1740. doi:10.5267/j.msl.2019.6.018

Dechow, P., Sloan, R., & Sweeney, A. (1996). Causes and consequences of earnings manipulation: An analysis of firms subject to enforcement actions by the SEC. *Contemporary Accounting Research, 13*(1), 1–36. doi:10.1111/j.1911-3846.1996.tb00489.x

Dimitrasa, A. I., Kyriakoua, M. I., & Iatridis, G. (2015). Financial crisis, GDP variation and earnings management in Europe. *Research in International Business and Finance, 34*, 338–354. doi:10.1016/j.ribaf.2015.02.017

El Diri, M., Lambrinoudakis, C., & Alhadab, M. (2020). Corporate governance and earnings management in concentrated markets. *Journal of Business Research, 108*, 291–306. doi:10.1016/j.jbusres.2019.11.013

El-Helaly, M., Shehata, N. F., & El-Sherif, R. (2018). National corporate governance, GMI ratings and earnings management: A country level study. *Asian Review of Accounting, 26*(3), 373–390. doi:10.1108/ARA-07-2017-0124

Fakhfakh, I., & Jarboui, A. (2020). Audit certification, earnings management and risk governance: A moderated-mediation analysis. *Journal of Financial Reporting and Accounting, 18*(2), 277–299. doi:10.1108/JFRA-01-2019-0015

Ferramosca, S., & Allegrini, M. (2018). The complex role of family involvement in earnings management. *Journal of Family Business Strategy, 9*(2), 128–141. doi:10.1016/j.jfbs.2018.01.001

Flayyih, H.H., Salih, J.I., Rahma, N.G.A., & Mohammed, Y.N. (2020). Earnings Management between the fact of manipulation and credibility of management procedures: a literature review. *SSHJ, 4*(5), 1898-1908.

Garcia Osma, B., Scarlat, E., & Shields, K. (2020). Insider trading restrictions and earnings management. *Accounting and Business Research, 50*(3), 205–237. doi:10.1080/00014788.2020.1712650

Ghazali, A. W., Nurullah, M., Ibrahim, S., Sanusi, Z. M., & Mohame, N. (2019). The effect of corporate board diversity: Real earnings management among malaysian listed firms. *International Journal of Business and Management Science, 9*(2), 257–276. www.scopus.com

Gonçalves, T., Gaio, C., & Santos, T. (2019). Women on the board: Do they manage earnings? empirical evidence from european listed firms [Mulheres no Board: Elas gerem resultados? Evidência empírica das empresas europeias cotadas]. *Revista Brasileira de Gestão de Negócios, 21*(3), 582–597. doi:10.7819/rbgn.v21i3.4010

González, J. S., & García-Meca, E. (2014). Does corporate governance influence earnings management in Latin American markets? *Journal of Business Ethics, 121*(3), 419–440. doi:10.100710551-013-1700-8

Gu, Y., Zhou, Q., & Ho, K. (2020). Financial flexibility and managerial short-termism. *Annals of Economics and Finance, 21*(1), 189–208. www.scopus.com

Harakeh, M., El-Gammal, W., & Matar, G. (2019). Female directors, earnings management, and CEO incentive compensation: UK evidence. *Research in International Business and Finance, 50*, 153–170. doi:10.1016/j.ribaf.2019.05.001

Healy, P. M., & Wahlen, J. M. (1999). A review of the earnings management literature and its implications for standard setting. *Accounting Horizons, 13*(4), 365–383. doi:10.2308/acch.1999.13.4.365

Herranz, C. Z., Iturriaga, F. J. L., & Reguera-Alvarado, N. (2018). The right person at the right time: Audit committee members and the quality of financial information 1. [La persona adecuada en el momento adecuado: Los miembros del comité de auditoría y la calidad de la información financiera] UCJC. *Business and Society Review*, *15*(2), 18–35. doi:10.3232/UBR.2018.V15.N2.01

Hooghiemstra, R., Hermes, N., Oxelheim, L., & Randøy, T. (2019). Strangers on the board: The impact of board internationalization on earnings management of Nordic firms. *International Business Review*, *28*(1), 119–134. doi:10.1016/j.ibusrev.2018.08.007

Huang, W., Goodell, J. W., & Zhang, H. (2019). Pre-merger management in developing markets: The role of earnings glamor. *International Review of Financial Analysis*, *65*(C), 101375. Advance online publication. doi:10.1016/j.irfa.2019.101375

Huynh, Q. L. (2020). A triple of corporate governance, social responsibility and earnings management. *Journal of Asian Finance. Economics and Business*, *7*(3), 29–40. doi:10.13106/jafeb.2020.vol7.no3.29

Jaggi, B., Leung, S., & Gul, F. (2009). Family control, board independence and earnings management: Evidence based on Hong Kong firms. *Journal of Accounting and Public Policy*, *28*(4), 281–300. doi:10.1016/j.jaccpubpol.2009.06.002

Jerbi Maatougui, A., & Halioui, K. (2019). The effect of outside blockholders on earnings management around seasoned equity offerings in french listed companies on the SBF120. *Journal of Financial Reporting and Accounting*, *17*(3), 449–467. doi:10.1108/JFRA-02-2018-0012

Jha, A. (2019). Financial Reports and Social Capital. *Journal of Business Ethics*, *155*(2), 567–596. doi:10.100710551-017-3495-5

Jiraporn, P., & DaDalt, P. (2009). Does founding family control affect earnings management? *Applied Economics Letters*, *16*(2), 113–119. doi:10.1080/17446540701720592

Kao, L., Chen, A., & Lu, C. (2018). Ex ante and ex post overvalued equities: The roles of corporate governance and product market competition. *Asia Pacific Management Review*, *23*(3), 209–221. doi:10.1016/j.apmrv.2017.07.002

Khaddafi, M., Wahyuddin, Heikal, M., Falahuddin, & Maulida, R. (2018). Effect of corporate governance mechanism, independence and management of earnings integrity of financial statements (in manufacturing companies listed on the stock exchange). *Quality - Access to Success*, *19*(164), 94–97.

Kousenidis, D. V., Ladas, A. C., & Negakis, C. I. (2013). The effects of the European debt crisis on earnings quality. *International Review of Financial Analysis*, *30*, 351–362. doi:10.1016/j.irfa.2013.03.004

Lai, T., Lei, A. C. H., & Song, F. M. (2019). The impact of corporate fraud on director-interlocked firms: Evidence from bank loans. *Journal of Business Finance & Accounting*, *46*(1-2), 32–67. doi:10.1111/jbfa.12362

Lel, U. (2019). The role of foreign institutional investors in restraining earnings management activities across countries. *Journal of International Business Studies*, *50*(6), 895–922. doi:10.105741267-018-0195-z

Leuz, C., Nanda, D., & Wysocki, D. (2003). Earnings management and investor protection: An international comparison. *Journal of Financial Economics*, *69*(3), 505–527. doi:10.1016/S0304-405X(03)00121-1

Li, T., Zhao, X., & Zhao, A. (2019). Voting with hands, earnings management and corporate governance. *Review of Accounting and Finance*, *18*(2), 178–197. doi:10.1108/RAF-02-2016-0016

Liao, Q., & Ouyang, B. (2019). Shareholder litigation risk and real earnings management: A causal inference. *Review of Accounting and Finance*, *18*(4), 557–588. doi:10.1108/RAF-06-2018-0122

Liu, C., Chung, C. Y., Sul, H. K., & Wang, K. (2018). Does hometown advantage matter? the case of institutional blockholder monitoring on earnings management in korea. *Journal of International Business Studies*, *49*(2), 196–221. doi:10.105741267-017-0093-9

Maijoor, S. J., & Vanstraelen, A. (2006). Earnings management within Europe: The effects of member state audit environment, audit firm quality and international capital markets. *Accounting and Business Research*, *36*(1), 33–52. doi:10.1080/00014788.2006.9730005

Marchini, P. L., Mazza, T., & Medioli, A. (2018). Related party transactions, corporate governance and earnings management. *Corporate Governance*, *18*(6), 1124–1146. doi:10.1108/CG-11-2017-0271

Matteo, P., & Francesco, P. (2018). Earnings management in developing countries. the case of brazilian real estate industry. Academy of Accounting and Financial Studies Journal, 22(1).

Mellado, C., & Saona, P. (2020). Real earnings management and corporate governance: A study of latin america. *Economic Research-Ekonomska Istrazivanja*, *33*(1), 2229–2268. doi:10.1080/1331677X.2019.1691930

Mio, C., Soerger Zaro, E., & Fasan, M. (2020). Are loyalty shares an effective antidote against short-termism? empirical evidence from italy. *Business Strategy and the Environment*, *29*(4), 1785–1796. doi:10.1002/bse.2473

Moardi, M., Salehi, M., Poursasan, S., & Molavi, H. (2019). Relationship between earnings management, CEO compensation, and stock return on tehran stock exchange. *International Journal of Organization Theory and Behavior*, *23*(1), 1–22. doi:10.1108/IJOTB-12-2018-0133

Muda, I., Maulana, W., Siregar, H. S., & Indra, N. (2018). The analysis of effects of good corporate governance on earnings management in indonesia with panel data approach. *Indian Economic Review*, *22*(2), 599–625.

Mukhtaruddin, M., Zuryati, E., Robiani, B., & Saftiana, Y. (2018). Good corporate governance mechanism and earnings management: Study on manufacturing companies in indonesia stock exchange. *Journal of Applied Economic Sciences*, *13*(8), 2298–2308. www.scopus.com

Okaily, J. A., Dixon, R., & Salama, A. (2019). Corporate governance quality and premature revenue recognition: Evidence from the UK. *International Journal of Managerial Finance*, *15*(1), 79–99. doi:10.1108/IJMF-02-2018-0047

Orazalin, N. (2019). Board gender diversity, corporate governance, and earnings management: Evidence from an emerging market. *Gender in Management*, *35*(1), 37–60. doi:10.1108/GM-03-2018-0027

Papadaki, A., & Tzovas, C. (2017). Financial crisis and accrual and real earnings management in Europe. *Corporate Ownership & Control*, *14*(3), 8–19. doi:10.22495/cocv14i3art1

Persakis, A., & Iatridis, G. E. (2016). Audit quality, investor protection and earnings management during the financial crisis of 2008: An international perspective. *Journal of International Financial Markets, Institutions and Money*, *41*, 70–101. doi:10.1016/j.intfin.2015.12.006

Pham, H. Y., Chung, R. Y., Roca, E., & Bao, B. (2019). Discretionary accruals: Signalling or earnings management in australia? *Accounting and Finance*, *59*(2), 1383–1413. doi:10.1111/acfi.12275

Pinto, I., Gaio, C., & Gonçalves, T. (2019). Corporate governance, foreign direct investment, and bank income smoothing in african countries. *International Journal of Emerging Markets*, *15*(4), 670–690. doi:10.1108/IJOEM-04-2019-0297

Prencipe, A., Bar-Yosef, S., & Dekker, H. (2014). Accounting research in family firms: Theoretical and empirical challenges. *European Accounting Review*, *23*(3), 361–385. doi:10.1080/09638180.2014.895621

Puryandani, S., Kusumawati, H. A., & Robiyanto, R. (2020). Corporate governance and earnings management practices in indonesian banking sector. *Quality - Access to Success*, *21*(176), 102–108.

Reicher, R., & Ngo, T. N. (2020). The propensity for mandatory audit rotation and its impact on earnings management in Europe. *International Journal of Engineering and Management Sciences*, *5*(1), 1–10. doi:10.21791/IJEMS.2020.1.19

Sadiq, M., Othman, Z., & Keong, O. C. (2019). A study of interaction effects of political influences and earnings management on organisational performance. *Asian Economic and Financial Review*, *9*(5), 642–653. doi:10.18488/journal.aefr.2019.95.642.653

Salehi, M., Mahmoudabadi, M., & Adibian, M. S. (2018). The relationship between managerial entrenchment, earnings management and firm innovation. *International Journal of Productivity and Performance Management*, *67*(9), 2089–2107. doi:10.1108/IJPPM-03-2018-0097

San Martin Reyna, J. M. (2018). The effect of ownership composition on earnings management: Evidence for the mexican stock exchange. *Journal of Economics, Finance and Administrative Science*, *23*(46), 289–305. doi:10.1108/JEFAS-01-2017-0011

Sani, A. A., Abdul Latif, R., & Al-Dhamari, R. A. (2020). CEO discretion, political connection and real earnings management in nigeria. *Management Research Review*, *43*(8), 909–929. doi:10.1108/MRR-12-2018-0460

Saona, P., & Muro, L. (2018). Firm- and country-level attributes as determinants of earnings management: An analysis for latin american firms. *Emerging Markets Finance & Trade*, *54*(12), 2736–2764. doi:10.1080/1540496X.2017.1410127

Saona, P., Muro, L., & Alvarado, M. (2020). How do the ownership structure and board of directors' features impact earnings management? the spanish case. *Journal of International Financial Management & Accounting*, *31*(1), 98–133. doi:10.1111/jifm.12114

Saona, P., Muro, L., San Martín, P., & Baier-Fuentes, H. (2019). Board of director's gender diversity and its impact on earnings management: An empirical analysis for select european firms. *Technological and Economic Development of Economy*, *25*(4), 634–663. doi:10.3846/tede.2019.9381

Sehrawat, N. K., Kumar, A., Lohia, N., Bansal, S., & Agarwal, T. (2019). Impact of corporate governance on earnings management: Large sample evidence from india. *Asian Economic and Financial Review, 9*(12), 1335–1345. doi:10.18488/journal.aefr.2019.912.1335.1345

Sial, M. S., Chunmei, Z., & Khuong, N. V. (2019). Do female and independent directors explain the two-way relationship between corporate social responsibility and earnings management of chinese listed firms? *International Journal of Accounting and Information Management, 27*(3), 442–460. doi:10.1108/IJAIM-03-2018-0027

Sun, L., & Al Farooque, O. (2018). An exploratory analysis of earnings management practices in australia and new zealand. *International Journal of Accounting and Information Management, 26*(1), 81–114. doi:10.1108/IJAIM-09-2016-0087

Susanto, Y. K., Pradipta, A., & Cecilia, E. (2019). Earnings management: Esop and corporate governance. *Academy of Accounting and Financial Studies Journal, 23*(1).

Tham, Y. H., Sultana, N., Singh, H., & Taplin, R. (2019). Busy boards and earnings management – an australian perspective. *Asian Review of Accounting, 27*(3), 464–486. doi:10.1108/ARA-08-2018-0149

Tolulope, I., Uwuigbe, U., Uwuigbe, O. R., Emmanuel, O., Oriabie, S., & Asiriuwa, O. (2018). The effect of corporate governance attributes on earnings management: A study of listed companies in nigeria. Academy of Strategic Management Journal, 17(6).

Tran, D. V., Hassan, M. K., & Houston, R. (2019). Activity strategies, information asymmetry, and bank opacity. *Economic Modelling, 83*, 160–172. doi:10.1016/j.econmod.2019.02.008

Triki Damak, S. (2018). Gender diverse board and earnings management: Evidence from french listed companies. Sustainability Accounting. *Management and Policy Journal, 9*(3), 289–312. doi:10.1108/SAMPJ-08-2017-0088

Türegün, N. (2018). Effects of borrowing costs, firm size, and characteristics of board of directors on earnings management types: A study at borsa istanbul*. *Asia-Pacific Journal of Accounting & Economics, 25*(1-2), 42–56. doi:10.1080/16081625.2016.1246192

Utomo, S. D., Machmuddah, Z., & Oktafiyani, M. (2019). The associations between earnings management, corporate environmental disclosure, corporate financial performance and corporate governance mechanisms. *WSEAS Transactions on Business and Economics, 16*, 345–354.

Vieira, E., & Madaleno, M. (2019). Earnings Management and Corporate Governance in Family Firms: Evidence from a small market. In Handbook International Financial Reporting Standards and New Directions in Earnings Management. IGI Global. doi:10.4018/978-1-5225-7817-8

Vieira, E. S. (2016). Earnings management in public family firms under economic adversity. *Australian Accounting Review, 26*(2), 190–207. doi:10.1111/auar.12096

Wan Mohammad, W. M., & Wasiuzzaman, S. (2019). Effect of audit committee independence, board ethnicity and family ownership on earnings management in malaysia. *Journal of Accounting in Emerging Economies, 10*(1), 74–99. doi:10.1108/JAEE-01-2019-0001

Wang, T., Lin, Y., Werner, E. M., & Chang, H. (2018). The relationship between external financing activities and earnings management: Evidence from enterprise risk management. *International Review of Economics & Finance*, *58*, 312–329. doi:10.1016/j.iref.2018.04.003

Wasan, P., & Mulchandani, K. (2020). Corporate governance factors as predictors of earnings management. *Journal of General Management*, *45*(2), 71–92. doi:10.1177/0306307019872304

Waweru, N. M., & Prot, N. P. (2018). Corporate governance compliance and accrual earnings management in eastern africa: Evidence from kenya and tanzania. *Managerial Auditing Journal*, *33*(2), 171–191. doi:10.1108/MAJ-09-2016-1438

Xie, B., Davidson, W. N. III, & DaDalt, P. J. (2003). Earnings management and corporate governance: The roles of the board and the audit committee. *Journal of Corporate Finance*, *9*(3), 295–316. doi:10.1016/S0929-1199(02)00006-8

Yang, Y., & Abeysekera, I. (2019). Duration of equity overvaluation and managers' choice to use aggressive underlying earnings disclosure and accrual-based earnings management: Australian evidence. *Journal of Contemporary Accounting and Economics*, *15*(2), 167–185. doi:10.1016/j.jcae.2019.04.004

KEY TERMS AND DEFINITION

Bibliometric Analysis: Is the attempt to quantitatively assess the academic quality of journals or authors by statistical methods such as citation rates.

Content Analysis: Is the study of documents and communication artifacts, which might be texts of various formats, pictures, audio or video. Social scientists use content analysis to examine patterns in communication in a replicable and systematic manner.

Corporate Governance: Is the system of rules, practices, and processes by which a firm is directed and controlled. Corporate governance essentially involves balancing the interests of a company's many stakeholders, such as shareholders, senior management executives, customers, suppliers, financiers, the government, and the community. Since corporate governance also provides the framework for attaining a company's objectives, it encompasses practically every sphere of management, from action plans and internal controls to performance measurement and corporate disclosure.

Earnings Management: Is the use of accounting techniques to produce financial statements that present an overly positive view of a company's business activities and financial position. Many accounting rules and principles require that a company's management make judgments in following these principles. Earnings management takes advantage of how accounting rules are applied and creates financial statements that inflate or "smooth" earnings.

Measurement: Is the numerical quantitation of the attributes of an object or event, which can be used to compare with other objects or events. The scope and application of measurement are dependent on the context and discipline.

Chapter 2
Institutional Investors' Representativeness and Earnings Management:
Evidence From a High Ownership Concentration Context

Pietro Fera
https://orcid.org/0000-0002-4770-9741
University of Campania "Luigi Vanvitelli", Italy

Nicola Moscariello
University of Campania "Luigi Vanvitelli", Italy

Michele Pizzo
University of Campania "Luigi Vanvitelli", Italy

Giorgio Ricciardi
University of Campania "Luigi Vanvitelli", Italy

ABSTRACT

In contexts characterized by high ownership concentration, institutional investors may lose their monitoring role and might not be effective in constraining earnings management. So, this study investigates whether directors appointed by institutional shareholders are more effective in inhibiting earnings management for companies with a high ownership concentration, rather than the mere presence of institutional investors. Based on a sample of Italian listed companies, findings suggest a negative relationship between minority directors appointed by institutional shareholders and abnormal accruals, while no relationship is found between the latter and the mere presence of institutional investors. Moreover, results also highlight that the difference between strategic and no strategic institutional investors does not count in a context characterized by high ownership concentration. Overall, this study suggests that institutional investors, regardless of their characteristics, are more effective in constraining earnings management when they can count on an agent on the board of directors.

DOI: 10.4018/978-1-7998-7596-3.ch002

INTRODUCTION

Accounting earnings are considered as key performance indicators and represent one of the main sources of information for a firm's stakeholders (Graham et al., 2005). However, scholars and practitioners have recognized that preparers often use their private information and discretion in terms of accounting rules to manage the reported earnings in a wide variety of contexts and for many purposes. Therefore, the topic of earnings management has been deeply examined by academic researchers, financial market regulators, operators, and investors.

Although it has been recognized that earnings management is a complex phenomenon with a non-univocal interpretation (Arya et al., 2003; Ronen and Yaari, 2008), a substantial body of literature has stressed the negative impact of earnings management on the quality of earnings and on financial market efficiency (e.g., Dechow et al., 2010; Lang et al., 2012; Bhattacharya et al., 2012), while there is little evidence of the beneficial effects of earnings management activities (e.g., Subramanyam, 1996; Linck et al., 2013; Moscariello et al., 2020).

Based on the negative effects of earnings management mainly supported by the previous literature, a substantial research strand has focused on a variety of external and internal factors that can constrain earnings management activities.

As for the former, several authors argue that country-level institutional factors matter when it comes to financial reporting quality. For instance, Leuz et al. (2003), analyzing earnings management activities across 31 countries, suggest that earnings management is positively associated with ownership concentration and is negatively associated with the quality of minority shareholder rights.

As for the internal factors, many studies highlight that internal corporate governance mechanisms have an impact on corporate accounting behaviour, including earnings management (Dechow et al., 1996). Among other aspects, the impact of institutional ownership on the quality of earnings has been widely discussed in the previous literature, since it is well known that the presence of institutional shareholders can provide an important monitoring mechanism (Rajgopal and Venkatachalam, 1997; Bushee, 1998; Koh, 2003). Specifically, institutional shareholders are considered as sophisticated investors and, therefore, are assumed to be skilled in interpreting financial reports, and easily able to detect the presence of earnings management (Peasnell et al., 2005). In particular, Bushee (1998) found that managers are less likely to cut R&D to reverse earnings decline when institutional ownership is high, implying that institutional shareholders are sophisticated investors who typically serve a monitoring role in reducing pressures resulting from myopic behaviour. Chung et al. (2002) document that the presence of large institutional shareholdings inhibits managers from increasing or decreasing reported profits in terms of their desired level or range. Moreover, Koh (2003) observes a negative association between higher institutional ownership levels and earnings management consistent with the view that long-term oriented institutional investors' monitoring limits managerial accruals discretion.

In addition, the previous literature considers the situation in-depth and suggests that institutional investors can be clustered in the form of short-term oriented or transient institutional investors and long-term oriented or strategic institutional investors (Bushee, 1998; Koh, 2003). On the one hand, the former, usually holding a limited number of shares, tend to have a short-term investment horizon creating incentives for managers to manage earnings upward (Graves and Waddock, 1990; Porter, 1992). On the other hand, the latter, usually holding higher share quotas, are considered as strategic investors due to their long-term investment horizon and are assumed to be able to better act as a complementary effective corporate governance mechanism in mitigating myopic aggressive earnings management activities (Bushee, 1998; Collins et al., 2003).

However, it is worth noting that the above-mentioned studies are focused on contexts – such as the U.S.A. and Australia – characterized by a low ownership concentration, thus mitigating the global generalizability of their results. Indeed, it has also been observed that the relationship between the presence of institutional investors and earnings management activities is not always negative (Porter, 1992; Sundaramurthy et al., 2005), since peculiar context characteristics, such as high ownership concentration, seem to limit the positive effects that the institutional shareholders may have on earnings management. Specifically, contexts characterized by both a high ownership concentration and a weak protection of minority shareholders' rights may represent a barrier to the effective monitoring role of institutional investors. In this regard, Alves (2012), analysing a sample of firms listed in Portugal, denies the hypothesis that there is a negative relationship between firms having institutional ownership and earnings management activities.

In these contexts, the previous literature suggests that the minority shareholders' representativeness might be an important mechanism for promoting greater director accountability, and for easing tensions between corporate controllers and outside investors (Enriques, 2009; Belcredi and Enriques, 2014). Several authors have documented that directors appointed by minority shareholders (minority directors) play a key role in fostering corporate transparency and disclosure quality (Bianchi et al., 2011; Lefort and Urzúa, 2008; Cornett et al., 2008; Marchetti et al., 2017). Thus, it is reasonable to assume that, in contexts with high ownership concentration, the institutional investors' inefficacy in constraining earnings management activities may be overcome through the appointment of an agent on the board.

Relying on these aspects, the aim of this study is to investigate if the institutional investor representativeness on the board rather than the mere presence of institutional shareholders, is more effective in constraining earnings management activities and enhancing the quality of financial reporting in contexts characterized by high ownership concentration and weak investor protection. Thus, this study contributes to the literature adding new evidence to the debate relating to the effectiveness of internal corporate governance mechanisms, by analyzing a still partially unexplored topic.

BACKGROUND AND HYPOTHESES DEVELOPMENT

Since engaging in earnings management is not a risk-free operation, the previous literature has identified a set of main incentives that can be clustered in terms of external and internal factors. External factors point to a manager's manipulation of earnings to meet the expectations of financial analysts and markets (Kasznick, 1999). Internal factors, on the other hand, refer to personal incentives such as bonus plans (Healy, 1985) and budget targets (Merchant, 1990). More recently, Leuz et al. (2003) argued that incentives to misrepresent a firm's performance through earnings management also arise, at least in part, from a conflict of interest between the firm's insiders and outsiders, since the former, such as controlling owners or managers, can exercise their control to the detriment of other stakeholders.

The previous literature also identifies several other factors affecting earnings management activities. First, there is a wide strand of literature concerning the impact of corporate governance characteristics on the earnings management (Dechow et al., 1996; Klein, 2002; Peasnell et al., 2005). In addition, based on previous research that identified investor protection as a key institutional factor affecting corporate policy choices (Shleifer and Vishny, 1997; La Porta et al., 2000), several scholars focused on investor protection as a significant determinant of earnings management activity (Leuz et al., 2003; Francis and Wang, 2008; Ben-Nasr et al., 2015). Specifically, Francis and Wang (2008) document higher earnings quality as investor protection regimes become stricter throughout the mediating role of the Big 4 auditors. Moreover, Leuz et al. (2003) document a negative association between earnings management and the degree of investor protection at the country level, suggesting that earnings management is positively associated with ownership concentration, and is negatively associated with the quality of minority shareholder rights. For instance, Italy has been found exhibiting a higher level of earnings management activities compared to countries having different characteristics in terms of investor protection and ownership structure (e.g., the U.K., Ireland, U.S.). Similarly, Reverte (2008) provides evidence that earnings management practices are higher in those EU countries (e.g., Italy) with higher ownership concentration and lower degree of investor protection.

However, the previous literature also suggests that a better protection of minority shareholder rights is not always enough, especially in high ownership concentration contexts, since minority shareholders could exercise their voting rights for purposes that differ from the firm's value maximization as colluding with the controlling shareholders and expropriating wealth from other minority shareholders (Bainbridge, 2006; Kahn and Rock, 2007; Listokin, 2010).

The Role Played by Institutional Investors

The agency theory suggests that the presence of institutional shareholders can represent an important monitoring mechanism. Specifically, several scholars have collected evidence concerning the impact exercised by institutional investors on earnings management activities. Chung et al. (2002) hypothesize that there will be less opportunistic earnings management in firms with more institutional investor ownership because the institutions will either put pressure on the firms to adopt better accounting policies, or they will be able to unravel the earnings management ruse so that it will not benefit the managers. As expected, they find that when institutional investors own a large percentage of a firm's outstanding shares, there is less opportunistic earnings management. Moreover, several studies have examined the relationship between a firm's aggregate institutional ownership and its R&D investment to see if institutional ownership affects managerial behaviour. In relation thereto, Bushee (1998) suggests that institutions in aggregate reduce the pressure that induces management to behave myopically, implying that managers are less likely to cut R&D to reverse an earnings decline. Furthermore, Bange and De Bondt (1998) found that there is less earnings management (R&D) when institutional investors own a larger share of the firm. More recently, Koh (2003) has documented a non-linear association between institutional ownership and income increasing discretionary accruals, consistent with the view that long-term oriented institutional investors' monitoring limits managerial accruals discretion. Moreover, Chung et al. (2002) document that the presence of large institutional shareholdings inhibits managers from increasing or decreasing reported profits in line with the managers' desired level or range of profits. Yet, Benkraiem (2008) shows that institutional investors can move corporate managers away from using discretionary accruals to adjust reported earnings.

However, it is noteworthy that the above-mentioned studies assert that the inverse relationship between the presence of institutional shareholders and earnings management activities occurs when the former hold a consistent proportion of shares. Thus, contexts characterized by high ownership concentration, which imply limited share quotas owned by institutional investors, represent a barrier to the monitoring role of such shareholders. Indeed, as mentioned before, in these contexts, minority shareholders face the risk of being deprived of their interests due to expropriation by the controlling shareholders, who usually gain effective control of the firm's management (La Porta et al., 1999). In this respect, it has been found that institutional shareholders lose their influence on management decision in concentrated ownership contexts. For instance, Hamdani and Yafeh (2013) state that dominant shareholders may limit institutional shareholder's voting power aiming to discipline corporate insider. Moreover, Fich and Slezak (2008) assert that in contexts characterized by high ownership concentration, institutional shareholders are less proactive in governance since they have short-term objectives. Thus, less influence over the management and less activism in governance suggests less control on firms' accounting behaviour. To this regard, Prencipe et al. (2011), analysing the Italian context, find that there is no significant relation between institutional ownership and income smoothing. In addition, an empirical study focused on Portugal, which is a country characterized by high ownership concentration, shows that there is no negative relationship between firms having institutional ownership and earnings management activities (Alves, 2012).

Therefore, relying on the above-mentioned literature, this study tests the first hypothesis:

Hypothesis One: the presence of institutional investors has no effect on earnings management activities in contexts characterized by high ownership concentration.

Institutional Investors Characteristics

The previous literature focused on the role of institutional ownership in preserving the integrity of financial reporting activities went in-depth and found that its impact on earnings management depends on the institutional shareholders' characteristics. Indeed, the previous literature makes a sharp distinction between short-term oriented or transient institutional investors and long-term oriented or strategic institutional investors (Bushee, 1998; Koh, 2003). In particular, institutional shareholders usually holding a limited number of shares tend to have a short investment horizon which implies an excessive focus on current earnings. Such a characteristic creates incentives for a firm's managers to manage earnings upwards (Graves and Waddock, 1990; Porter, 1992). On the other hand, institutional shareholders investing in firms with the aim of holding their ownership stake over a long-time run are more likely to be identified as strategic investors, having strong incentives to monitor activities. Indeed, Bushee (1998) argues that when the investment size grows, institutional investors could act to reduce managerial incentives to manage earnings aggressively. Additionally, more recent studies also show that the association between earnings quality and institutional investors varies with institutional investor categories. Collins et al. (2003) indicate that stock prices reflect the persistence of accruals more accurately in firms with a high level of institutional ownership, while it has also been found that only short-term oriented institutional investors are associated with more discretionary accruals management (Burns et al., 2010). Overall, there is supporting evidence for the notion that long-term oriented institutional investors are associated with a higher quality of earnings.

However, with regard to the previous strand of literature, the above-mentioned empirical evidence refers to contexts characterized by dispersed ownership, such as is found in the U.S.A and Australia. Indeed, in contexts characterized by high ownership concentration, the monitoring role of strategic institutional shareholders may be hindered by the controlling shareholders, who usually gain effective control of the firm's management (La Porta et al., 1999).

Thus, relying on these aspects, this study aims to test the second hypothesis:

Hypothesis Two: the presence of strategic institutional investors has no effect on earnings management activities in contexts characterized by high ownership concentration.

Institutional Investors as Minority Directors

Several scholars assert that there are also different corporate governance mechanisms able to constrain earnings management activities in firms having a highly concentrated ownership. Gutiérrez and Sáez (2013) assert that companies operating in institutional settings characterized by high ownership concentration would benefit from the introduction of the so-called minority directors. Indeed, allowing minority shareholders to have representatives on the board can represent an important mechanism for promoting greater director accountability, and for easing tensions between corporate controllers and outside investors (Enriques, 2009; Belcredi and Enriques, 2014). In fact, several studies assert the positive impact exercised by minority directors on both corporate governance and financial performance (Lefort and Urzua, 2008; Bianchi et al., 2011; Melis et al., 2012; Moscariello et al., 2019).

Relying on the previous literature, this study aims to test the third hypothesis:

Hypothesis Three: the institutional investors representativeness in the board of directors (as proxied by the minority directors appointed from the institutional investors' slate) can constrain earnings management activities.

INSTITUTIONAL SETTING AND SAMPLE COMPOSITION

To test the above-mentioned hypotheses, this study focuses on the Italian institutional setting, which represents the most suitable context for analysis since Italian listed companies have a highly concentrated ownership composition, with a dominant shareholder capable of effectively monitoring and influencing the companies' senior managers (Melis, 2000; Volpin, 2002). Moreover, these characteristics are traditionally coupled with both a weak legal protection of minority shareholders and the prevalent use of control-enhancing mechanisms that encourage the corporate controller to extract diversionary private benefits of control to the detriment of outside investors and increase the agency costs in a principal-principal relationship (La Porta et al., 1998; Gilson, 2006; Bianchi and Bianco, 2006). In addition, since June 2007, a 'slate-vote-system' based on quotas has been established by law, with the aim of boosting minority shareholders' voting power, protecting them against possible abuse (Bianchi et al., 2011; Belcredi et al., 2013). Specifically, the slate voting system is a peculiar characteristic of the current Italian corporate governance regulations that gives minority shareholders the right to appoint at least one member of the board of directors (De Poli and De Gioia Carabellese, 2017).

Thus, the sample consists of non-financial companies listed on the Italian Stock Exchange during the reference period, from 2012 to 2016. We exclude all firms that refer to the GICS 40 (financials) and to GICS 60 (real estate) because of their peculiar financial reporting rules. In addition, firms with a lack of financial market, accounting, and corporate governance data, and firms involved in business combinations are dropped from the sample.

As shown in Table 1, the basic sample is composed of 125 firms from which a final sample of 625 firm-year observations is obtained.

Table 1. Sample Selection Process

Population of non-financial listed firms	228
Financial and accounting data not available	-48
Corporate governance data not available	-53
Companies involved in extraordinary operations	-2
Basic sample	125

Data were collected from different sources: financial market and accounting data were collected from Thomson Reuters Eikon and DataStream, while corporate governance data were hand-picked from Co.N.So.B. (the Italian supervisory authority for financial markets) online databases, and from companies' annual reports on corporate governance and ownership structure.

RESEARCH DESIGN

To test the first hypothesis the following heteroskedastic-robust standard errors panel data regression model with random effects is set up to evaluate if the presence of institutional investors per se among the company shareholders has an impact on the level of earnings management:

$$\begin{aligned} AA_{it} &= \beta_0 + \beta_1 InstInvestors_{it} + \beta_2 BoD\_Size_{it} + \beta_3 BoD\_Indep_{it} + \beta_4 Duality_{it} + \beta_5 \%Own_{it} \\ &+ \beta_6 Big4_{it} + \beta_7 Size_{it} + \beta_8 OCF\_Vol_{it} + \beta_9 Neg\_Earn_{it} + \beta_{10} ROA_{it} + \beta_{11} Lev_{it} + \beta_{12} STAR_{it} \\ &+ \sum\left(Years\_Effects\right)_{it} + \sum\left(Industry\_Effects\right)_{it} + \varepsilon_{it} \end{aligned} \quad (1)$$

where i is the specific firm, t indicates the reference year, and ε_{it} stands for the regression error.

The dependent variable (AA) is the proxy for the magnitude of abnormal accruals that are one of the most commonly-used proxies to detect earnings management. Specifically, AA is defined using the Dechow and Dichev (2002) model as modified by McNichols (2002).

The main dependent variable ($InstInvestors$) is a dummy variable which takes the value of 1 if, among the shareholders, there is at least one institutional investor, defined as banks, insurance companies, investment found, and other certified financial brokers.

Moreover, to better test the hypothesis, several control variables that might affect the accrual-based earnings management, and that are widely used in the accounting and corporate governance literature, are included in the model (Dechow et al., 1996; Klein, 2002; Bedard and Johnstone, 2004; Peasnell et al., 2005; Prencipe et al., 2008).

Specifically, as to the corporate governance attributes, the model controls for the number of constituents of the board of directors (BoD_Size), since prior studies assert that board size can affect earnings quality, although the sign of the relationship is not clear (Dechow et al., 1996; Beasley and Salterio, 2001; Peasnell et al., 2005). Then the model controls for the proportion of independent directors within the board (BoD_Indep), because empirical evidence generally supports the expectation that board independence reduces earnings management (Dechow et al., 1996; Klein, 2002). The CEO duality ($Duality$) and the ownership concentration ($\%Own$) are also included in the model, with a positive sign being expected for both variables. It also considers the presence of an external auditor belonging to the Big 4 group (*Big4*), since audit companies belonging to this group are expected to positively affect the reliability of the accounting information and thus are assumed to reduce earnings management (Bedard and Johnstone, 2004).

Relative to the firm-accounting attributes, several variables have been included (Francis et al., 2005; Klein, 2002): the annual sales' natural logarithm as a proxy for the firm size ($Size$), the volatility of operating cash flows (OCF_Vol) computed as the year-over-year relative change, and the frequency of negative earnings (Neg_Earn) as a dummy variable that takes the value of 1 for each firm-year observation with a reported loss. It has also been included a measure for the firm's profitability (as proxied by ROA) which may affect the magnitude of abnormal accruals (McNichols, 2000) and the annual leverage (Lev) computed as the ratio between total assets and equity.

Finally, the model controls for firms belonging to the STAR segment of the Italian Stock Exchange.

To test if the presence of strategic institutional investors has an incremental impact on the level of earnings management in contexts with high ownership concentration (Hp_2), the same regression model has been set up, but with the addition of a new main independent variable ($Strategic\_InstInv$). This is a dummy variable that takes the value of 1 if an institutional investor has more than 5% of the share capital (Zhong et al., 2017).

$$\begin{aligned} AA_{it} &= \beta_0 + \beta_1 InstInvestors_{it} + \beta_2 Strategic\_InstInv_{it} + \beta_3 BoD\_Size_{it} + \beta_4 BoD\_Indep_{it} \\ &+ \beta_5 Duality_{it} + \beta_6 \%Own_{it} + \beta_7 Big4_{it} + \beta_8 Size_{it} + \beta_9 OCF\_Vol_{it} + \beta_{10} Neg\_Earn_{it} + \beta_{11} ROA_{it} \\ &+ \beta_{12} Lev_{it} + \beta_{13} STAR_{it} + \Sigma\left(Years\_Effects\right)_{it} + \Sigma\left(Industry\_Effects\right)_{it} + \varepsilon_{it} \end{aligned} \quad (2)$$

where i is the specific firm, t indicates the reference year, and ε_{it} stands for the regression error.

Finally, to determine whether or not institutional investor representativeness on the board, rather than the mere presence of institutional shareholders, can constrain earnings management activities (Hp_3), this study provides a two-fold analysis. First, it employs the same heteroskedastic-robust standard errors panel data regression from Model 1, adding a new main independent variable ($Min\_InstInv$). This is a dummy variable that takes the value of 1 for each firm-year observation with at least one minority director appointed by the institutional shareholders' minority slate.

$$\begin{aligned} AA_{it} &= \beta_0 + \beta_1 InstInvestors_{it} + \beta_3 Min\_InstInv_{it} + \beta_3 BoD\_Size_{it} + \beta_4 BoD\_Indep_{it} \\ &+ \beta_5 \%Own_{it} + \beta_6 Duality_{it} + \beta_7 Big4_{it} + \beta_8 Size_{it} + \beta_9 OCF\_Vol_{it} + \beta_{10} Neg\_Earn_{it} + \beta_{11} ROA_{it} \\ &+ \beta_{12} Lev_{it} + \beta_{13} STAR_{it} + \Sigma\left(Years\_Effects\right)_{it} + \Sigma\left(Industry\_Effects\right)_{it} + \varepsilon_{it} \end{aligned} \quad (3a)$$

where i is the specific firm, t indicates the reference year, and ε_{it} stands for the regression error.

Second, to test if the strategic institutional investors' representativeness on the board of directors has a different impact on earnings management, this study adds an additional main regressor ($Min\_Strategic\_InstInv$) to Model 3a. This is a dummy variable that takes the value of 1 if the minority director has been appointed by a strategic institutional investor, along with the variable $Strategic\_InstInv$ as defined in the description of Model 2.

$$\begin{aligned}AA_{it} &= \beta_0 + \beta_1 InstInvestors_{it} + \beta_2 Strategic\_InstInv_{it} + \beta_3 Min\_InstInv_{it} \\ &+\beta_4 Min\_Strategic\_InstInv_{it} + \beta_5 BoD\_Size_{it} + \beta_6 BoD\_Indep_{it} + \beta_7 \%Own_{it} \\ &+\beta_8 Duality_{it} + \beta_9 Big4_{it} + \beta_{10} Size_{it} + \beta_{11} OCF\_Vol_{it} + \beta_{12} Neg\_Earn_{it} + \beta_{13} ROA_{it} \\ &+\beta_{14} Lev_{it} + \beta_{15} STAR_{it} + \Sigma\left(Years\_Effects\right)_{it} + \Sigma\left(Industry\_Effects\right)_{it} + \varepsilon_{it}\end{aligned} \tag{3b}$$

where i is the specific firm, t indicates the reference year, and ε_{it} stands for the regression error.

In particular, the double version of Model 3 is performed in order to seek if, in contexts characterized by high ownership concentration, the relationship between institutional ownership and earnings management activities depends on the institutional investor type (Model 3b) or is just driven by the representativeness of the whole set of institutional investors (Model 3a).

MAIN RESULTS

This section presents the descriptive statistics of the variables defined above, followed by the univariate correlation matrix, and a discussion of the results from the multivariate analysis.

Table 2 shows that the average value of the magnitude of abnormal accruals (AA) is about 4.5% of total assets (with a median value of about 3%) and that in 340 out of 625 firm-year observations, there is at least one institutional investor (54,4%). Moreover, among the firms revealing at least an institutional shareholder among the owners, in 196 out of 340 (57,6%) firm-year observations the institutional investor can be defined as a strategic one. In addition, among the firms having one or more institutional shareholders, in less than 50% of the cases (153 firm-year observations) at least one minority director has been elected from the institutional investors' slate and, among them, in 40 firm-year observations, the minority director has been appointed by a strategic institutional investor.

As for the other variables, results from Table 2 highlights some characteristics of the sample. In particular, the boards of directors on average are composed of 9 or10 members (mean value and median are respectively 9.52 and 9) and usually the 43% of them are independents (mean value of 43.18%). Table 2 also reflects a high ownership concentration among the sample (median value of 66.72%) reinforcing the previous discussion about the Italian institutional context.

Table 3 provides the Pairwise correlations matrix for all the variables. In particular, the table shows that the proxy for earnings management activities (AA) is negatively correlated with the presence of minority directors elected from the institutional shareholders' slate ($Min\_InstInv$). Conversely, there is no significant relationship between the magnitude of abnormal accruals (AA) and the mere presence of an institutional investor among the shareholders ($InstInvestors$). The same result is observed with regard to the strategic institutional investors ($Strategic\_InstInv$). As for the control variables, a negative correlation with the dependent variable (AA), which implies a positive impact on the level of earning management, is also detected for $Big4$, $Size$ and ROA. On the other hand, a negative impact on the quality of accounting numbers, as proxied by AA, can be noticed for the ownership concentration ($\%Own$), the frequency of negative earnings (Neg_Earn), and the total amount of leverage (Lev). In addition, Table 3 highlights that none of the variables included in the regression model suffers from collinearity matters, as all coefficients are much lower than 0.8 (Wulferth, 2013).

Table 2. Descriptive Statistics

	Obs	Min	Max	Mean	Median	StdDev
AA	625	0.001	0.223	0.044	0.030	0.045
InstInvestors	340	-	-	-	-	-
Strategic_InstInv	196	-	-	-	-	-
Min_InstInv	153	-	-	-	-	-
Min_Strategic_InstInv	40	-	-	-	-	-
BoD_Size	625	4	17	9.517	9	2.701
BoD_Indep	625	0.111	0.818	0.431	0.408	0.155
Duality	180	-	-	-	-	-
%Own	625	21.781	99.483	64.997	66.726	14.927
Big4	560	-	-	-	-	-
Size	625	15.582	25.014	19.867	19.662	1.869
OCF_Vol	625	-6.600	55.817	1.203	0.096	6.478
Neg_Earn	170	-	-	-	-	-
ROA	625	-0.296	0.262	0.040	0.043	0.079
Lev	625	1.206	17.092	3.738	2.977	2.800
STAR	250	-	-	-	-	-

Although the total number of observations equals to 625 for each variable, as for the dummies ($InstInvestors, Strategic\_InstInv$, $Min\_InstInv$, $Min\_Strategic\_InstInv$, $Duality$, $Big4$, Neg_Earn, $STAR$) the fist column refers to the number of observations that meet the condition for which each dummy was included).

After controlling for a set of variables that affect the quality of accounting numbers, Model 1 allows to test our first hypothesis.

Table 4 shows that there is no significant relationship between $InstInvestors$ and AA (|t| = 0.05 / pv = 0.964), highlighting that, as expected, in contexts characterized by high ownership concentration, the mere presence of institutional investors is not sufficient to constrain earnings management activities. Therefore, this evidence leads us to accept the first hypothesis.

As expected, Table 4 also shows that, all else being equal, the magnitude of abnormal accruals is lowered by the presence of a Big 4 auditor and tends to decrease when firms are bigger. On the other hand, a higher frequency of negative earnings, and the overall firm's leverage, reveal a positive and significant relationship with the magnitude of abnormal accruals.

In order to deepen the analysis, Model 2 allows us to test the second hypothesis. Table 5 shows that there is no significant relationship between $Strategic\_InstInv$ and AA (|t| = 0.13/ pv = 0.898), highlighting that, as expected, in contexts characterized by high ownership concentration, even if institutional investors are long-term oriented, they are not able to constrain earnings management activities. Therefore, this evidence leads to an acceptance of the second hypothesis.

As for the control variables, Model 2 highlights the same relationship obtained from Model 1.

Thus, since the first and second models confirm that, in a context characterized by high ownership concentration and weak legal protection of minority shareholders, institutional investors also lose their monitoring role when they are long-term oriented, Model 3 allows us to test the third hypothesis, that aims

Table 3. Univariate Correlations Matrix

		(1)	(2)	(3)	(4)	(5)	(6)	(7)	(8)	(9)	(10)	(11)	(12)	(13)	(14)	(15)
(1)	AA	1.000*														
(2)	InstInvestors	-0.056*	1.000*			*	*	*								
(3)	Strategic_ InstInv	-0.009*	0.618*	1.000*												
(4)	Min_InstInv	-0.142*	0.277*	0.244*	1.000*											
(5)	BoD_Size	-0.067*	0.187*	0.131*	0.127*	1.000*										
(6)	BoD_Indep	-0.057*	0.192*	0.156*	0.347*	0.651*	1.000*									
(7)	Duality	-0.006*	0.035*	0.049*	-0.116*	-0.196*	-0.312*	1.000*								
(8)	%Own	0.085*	-0.058*	-0.087*	-0.148*	-0.099*	-0.222*	0.078*	1.000*							
(9)	Big4	-0.146*	0.104*	0.126*	0.077*	0.064*	0.154*	-0.087*	-0.051*	1.000*						
(10)	Size	-0.160*	0.339*	0.228*	0.307*	0.464*	0.537*	-0.258*	-0.150*	0.305*	1.000*					
(11)	OCF_Vol	0.058*	-0.010*	-0.071*	-0.043*	-0.017*	-0.056*	0.030*	0.055*	-0.069*	0.011*	1.000*				
(12)	Neg_Earn	0.195*	-0.101*	-0.027*	-0.040*	-0.113*	-0.088*	-0.017*	-0.100*	-0.120*	-0.266*	-0.053*	1.000*			
(13)	ROA	-0.138*	0.099*	-0.019*	-0.024*	0.090*	0.044*	-0.037*	0.152*	0.180*	0.238*	-0.001*	-0.674*	1.000*		
(14)	Lev	0.161*	0.021*	0.117*	0.003*	-0.018*	0.156*	-0.056*	0.006*	0.020*	0.077*	0.013*	0.113*	-0.240*	1.000*	
(15)	STAR	-0.052*	-0.040*	-0.186*	-0.143*	-0.112*	-0.250*	0.208*	-0.062*	-0.090*	-0.244*	0.080*	-0.127*	0.121*	-0.227*	1.000*

to address if, in such settings, institutional investor representativeness on the board rather than just the presence of institutional shareholders, is more effective in constraining earnings management activities.

As mentioned before, Model 3 has been split in two sub-models in order to highlight if the institutional investors' representativeness affects the level of earnings management *per se,* or when coupled with specific institutional investor characteristics.

In particular, results from both Model 3a and Model 3b highlight once more a non-significant relationship between $InstInvestors$ and AA (pv = 0.540; pv = 0.729, respectively), confirming that, in contexts characterized by high ownership concentration, institutional investors may not be effective in constraining earnings management activities.

However, Model 3a shows that there is a negative and significant relationship between $Min\_InstInv$ and AA (|t| = - 2.55 / pv = 0.012), underlining that minority directors appointed by an institutional shareholder can constrain earnings management activities and enhance the quality of financial reporting. Moreover, Model 3b shows that there is no significant relationship between AA and both $Strategic\_InstInv$ and $Min\_Strategic\_InstInv$ with a p-value of 0.368 and 0.110 respectively.

As far as it concerns the control variables, similarly to the previous model, the presence of a Big 4 lowers the magnitude of abnormal accruals as well as the firms' size. In contrast, a higher frequency of negative earnings and the overall firm's leverage have a positive and significant relationship with the magnitude of abnormal accruals.

Overall, the empirical evidence from this study leads to the acceptance of the third hypothesis according to which the institutional investor representativeness, rather than the presence *per se* of an institutional investor, can constrain earnings management activities in contexts characterized by high ownership concentration and weak legal protection of minority shareholders. In addition, these results confirm that, in such contexts, the positive impact that institutional investors have on earnings management activities does not depend on the institutional investors' nature (short-term or long-term oriented) but rather on their activism.

Table 4. Multivariate Analysis from Model 1

Dependent Variable: AA	McNichols (2002)		
	Coefficient	***t*-Stat**	**P > |t|**
Intercept	0.099	2.80	0.006
InstInvestors	**-0.002**	**0.05**	**0.964**
BoD_Size	0.001	0.45	0.655
BoD_Indep	0.006	0.34	0.735
Duality	-0.004	-0.81	0.419
%Own	0.001	1.36	0.177
Big4	-0.015	-1.77	0.079
Size	-0.003	-2.39	0.019
OCF_Vol	0.001	1.09	0.280
Neg_Earn	0.018	2.49	0.014
ROA	0.033	0.86	0.390
Lev	0.003	2.29	0.024
STAR	-0.003	-0.64	0.524
Year effects	Included		
Industry effects	Included		
R^2	0.1231		
F-value	3.01		
Prob. >*F*	0.0000		
Root MSE	0.0431		
No. of Observations	625		
No. of Groups	125		

CONCLUSION

Previous studies provide evidence that institutional ownership represents an effective monitoring mechanism for detecting and constraining earnings management activities, especially when institutional investors are long-term oriented (Bushee, 1998; Bange and De Bondt, 1998; Chung et al., 2002; Koh, 2003; Benkraiem, 2008). On the other hand, in contexts characterized by high ownership concentration, institutional investors seem to lose their monitoring role. Indeed, it has been shown that in these contexts, where minority shareholders may be deprived of their interests (La Porta et al., 1999), there is no negative relationship between firms having institutional ownership and earnings management activities (Alves, 2012).

Therefore, this study aims to examine if institutional investor representativeness on the board of directors, rather than the mere presence of institutional shareholders, is more effective in constraining earnings management activities in such contexts.

Table 5. Multivariate Analysis from Model 2

Dependent Variable: AA	McNichols (2002)		
	Coefficient	*t*-Stat	P > |t|
Intercept	0.099	2.77	0.006
InstInvestors	**-0.001**	**-0.04**	**0.970**
Strategic_InstInv	**0.001**	**0.13**	**0.898**
BoD_Size	0.001	0.43	0.655
BoD_Indep	0.005	0.34	0.735
Duality	-0.004	-0.81	0.420
%Own	0.001	1.36	0.177
Big4	-0.015	-1.76	0.081
Size	-0.003	-2.39	0.021
OCF_Vol	0.001	1.08	0.281
Neg_Earn	0.018	2.50	0.014
ROA	0.033	0.87	0.386
Lev	0.003	2.31	0.023
STAR	-0.003	-0.62	0.534
Year effects	Included		
Industry effects	Included		
R^2	0.1232		
F-value	2.90		
Prob. >*F*	0.0001		
Root MSE	0.0431		
No. of Observations	625		
No. of Groups	125		

Focusing on the Italian institutional context, that features high ownership concentration and weak legal protection of minority shareholders, the empirical findings suggest that the presence of institutional investors *per se* among the company' shareholders has no impact on the level of earnings management, regardless of the institutional investors' characteristics. However, this study also highlights a significant and negative relationship between the presence of minority directors appointed by an institutional shareholder and the magnitude of abnormal accruals. Thus, this study suggests that, in contexts characterized by high ownership concentration and weak protection of minority shareholders' rights, institutional investors are more effective in constraining earnings management activities and enhancing the quality of financial reporting when they can count on an agent on the board of directors. In addition, since no significant relationship has been found between the level of earnings management and the presence of minority directors appointed by strategic institutional investors, this study concludes that the positive impact that institutional investors have on earnings management activities does not depend on the institutional investors' nature (short-term or long-term oriented), but rather on their activism.

Table 6. Multivariate Analysis from Model 3

Dependent Variable: AA	Model 3a			Model 3b		
	Coeff.	*t*-Stat	P > |t|	Coeff.	*t*-Stat	P > |t|
Intercept	0.093	2.70	0.008	0.099	2.99	0.003
InstInvestors	**-0.003**	**0.61**	**0.540**	**-0.001**	**0.35**	**0.729**
Strategic_InstInv				**0.004**	**0.90**	**0.368**
Min_InstInv	**-0.014**	**-2.55**	**0.012**	**-0.008**	**-2.01**	**0.047**
Min_Strategic_InstInv				**-0.018**	**-1.66**	**0.110**
BoD_Size	0.001	0.51	0.611	0.001	0.34	0.733
BoD_Indep	0.016	0.81	0.417	0.015	0.84	0.405
Duality	-0.005	-0.88	0.380	-0.005	-0.96	0.337
%Own	0.001	1.39	0.167	0.001	1.71	0.089
Big4	-0.015	-1.86	0.066	-0.015	-1.99	0.049
Size	-0.003	-2.34	0.021	-0.003	-2.68	0.008
OCF_Vol	0.001	1.04	0.300	0.001	1.01	0.312
Neg_Earn	0.017	2.36	0.020	0.017	2.53	0.013
ROA	0.025	0.64	0.525	0.027	0.70	0.486
Lev	0.002	2.28	0.024	0.002	2.48	0.014
STAR	-0.003	-0.57	0.569	-0.002	-0.42	0.673
Year effects	Included			Included		
Industry effects	Included			Included		
R^2	0.1363			0.1421		
F-value	3.62			3.60		
Prob. >*F*	0.0000			0.0000		
Root MSE	0.0428			0.0427		
No. of Observations	625			625		
No. of Groups	125			125		

The contribution of this study is twofold. First, it adds new evidence to the debate relating to the effectiveness of internal corporate governance mechanisms, by analyzing a still partially unexplored topic. Indeed, there is still little effort being made with regard to analyzing contexts characterized by high ownership concentration and weak legal protection of investors, although they are very common in Europe and throughout the world. Second and most important, evidence from this study provides useful insight for practitioners and regulators, as it reveals the effectiveness of a specific corporate governance mechanism, established by the law although not mandatory, in overcoming the institutional settings limitations.

However, this study also comes with some potential caveats. Indeed, it focuses on one country and, therefore, implies a relatively small sample size. Thus, future researchers should consider these aspects and enrich the empirical evidence in different contexts, by assessing the peculiarity of the Italian corporate governance institutional regulations relative to other comparable institutional settings. Moreover, another possible avenue of future research could be the analysis of some country level variables as a mediator of the relationship examined in this study.

REFERENCES

Alves, S. (2012). Ownership structure and earnings management: Evidence from Portugal. *Australasian Accounting. Business and Finance Journal*, *6*(1), 57–74.

Arya, A., Glover, J. C., & Sunder, S. (2003). Are unmanaged earnings always better for shareholders? *Accounting Horizons*, *17*(s-1), 111–116. doi:10.2308/acch.2003.17.s-1.111

Bainbridge, S. (2006). Director Primacy and Shareholder Disempowerment. *Harvard Law Review*, *119*(6), 1735–1758.

Bange, M. M., & De Bondt, W. F. (1998). R&D budgets and corporate earnings targets. *Journal of Corporate Finance*, *4*(2), 153–184. doi:10.1016/S0929-1199(98)00006-6

Beasley, M. S., & Salterio, S. E. (2001). The relationship between board characteristics and voluntary improvements in audit committee composition and experience. *Contemporary Accounting Research*, *18*(4), 539–570. doi:10.1506/RM1J-A0YM-3VMV-TAMV

Bedard, J. C., & Johnstone, K. M. (2004). Earnings manipulation risk, corporate governance risk, and auditors' planning and pricing decisions. *The Accounting Review*, *79*(2), 277–304. doi:10.2308/accr.2004.79.2.277

Belcredi, M., Bozzi, S., & Di Noia, C. (2013). Board elections and shareholders activism: The Italian experiment. In M. Belcredi & G. Ferrarini (Eds.), *Boards and shareholders in European listed companies*. Cambridge University Press. doi:10.1017/CBO9781139629126.008

Belcredi, M., & Enriques, L. (2014). *Institutional investor activism in a context of concentrated ownership and high private benefits of control: The case of Italy.* ECGI, law working paper, No. 225.

Ben-Nasr, H., Boubaker, S., & Rouatbi, W. (2015). Ownership structure, control contestability, and corporate debt maturity. *Journal of Corporate Finance*, *35*, 265–285. doi:10.1016/j.jcorpfin.2015.10.001

Benkraiem, R. (2008). The influence of institutional investors on opportunistic earnings management. *International Journal of Accounting. Auditing and Performance Evaluation*, *5*(1), 89–106. doi:10.1504/IJAAPE.2008.020195

Bhattacharya, N., Ecker, F., Olsson, P. M., & Schipper, K. (2012). Direct and mediated associations among earnings quality, information asymmetry, and the cost of equity. *The Accounting Review*, *87*(2), 449–482. doi:10.2308/accr-10200

Bianchi, M., & Bianco, M. (2006). *Italian corporate governance in the last 15 years: From pyramids to coalitions?* ECGI, finance working paper, No. 144.

Bianchi, M., Ciavarella, A., Novembre, V., & Signoretti, R. (2011). Comply or explain: Investor protection through the italian corporate governance code. *Journal of Applied Corporate Finance*, *23*(1), 107–121. doi:10.1111/j.1745-6622.2011.00319.x

Burns, N., Kedia, S., & Lipson, M. (2010). Institutional ownership and monitoring: Evidence from financial misreporting. *Journal of Corporate Finance*, *16*(4), 443–455. doi:10.1016/j.jcorpfin.2010.06.001

Bushee, B. J. (1998). The influence of institutional investors on myopic R&D investment behavior. *The Accounting Review*, *73*(3), 305–333.

Chung, R., Firth, M., & Kim, J. B. (2002). Institutional monitoring and opportunistic earnings management. *Journal of Corporate Finance*, *8*(1), 29–48. doi:10.1016/S0929-1199(01)00039-6

Collins, D. W., Gong, G., & Hribar, P. (2003). Investor sophistication and the mispricing of accruals. *Review of Accounting Studies*, *8*(2-3), 251–276. doi:10.1023/A:1024417513085

Cornett, M., Marcus, A., & Tehranian, H. (2008). Corporate governance and pay-for-performance: The impact of earnings management. *Journal of Financial Economics*, *87*(2), 357–373. doi:10.1016/j.jfineco.2007.03.003

De Poli, M., & De Gioia Carabellese, P. (2017). The minority directors in the corporate governance of EU listed institutions: A chimaera or a possibility? *Maastricht Journal of European and Comparative Law*, *24*(1), 43–62. doi:10.1177/1023263X17693187

Dechow, P., Ge, W., & Schrand, C. (2010). Understanding earnings quality: A review of the proxies, their determinants and their consequences. *Journal of Accounting and Economics*, *50*(2-3), 344–401. doi:10.1016/j.jacceco.2010.09.001

Dechow, P. M., & Dichev, I. D. (2002). The quality of accruals and earnings: The role of accruals estimation error. *The Accounting Review*, *77*(1), 35–39. doi:10.2308/accr.2002.77.s-1.35

Dechow, P. M., Sloan, R. G., & Sweeney, A. P. (1996). Causes and consequences of earnings manipulation: An analysis of firms subject to enforcement actions by the SEC. *Contemporary Accounting Research*, *13*(1), 1–36. doi:10.1111/j.1911-3846.1996.tb00489.x

Enriques, L. (2009). *Modernizing Italy's corporate governance institutions: mission accomplished?* ECGI Law Working Paper, n. 123.

Fich, E. M., & Slezak, S. L. (2008). Can corporate governance save distressed firms from bankruptcy? An empirical analysis. *Review of Quantitative Finance and Accounting*, *30*(2), 225–251. doi:10.100711156-007-0048-5

Francis, J., Schipper, K., & Vincent, L. (2005). Earnings and dividend informativeness when cash flow rights are separated from voting rights. *Journal of Accounting and Economics*, *39*(2), 329–360. doi:10.1016/j.jacceco.2005.01.001

Francis, J. R., & Wang, D. (2008). The joint effect of investor protection and Big 4 audits on earnings quality around the world. *Contemporary Accounting Research*, *25*(1), 157–191. doi:10.1506/car.25.1.6

Gilson, R. J. (2006). Controlling shareholders and corporate governance: Complicating the comparative taxonomy. *Harvard Law Review, 119*(6), 1642–1679.

Graham, J. R., Harvey, C. R., & Rajgopal, S. (2005). The economic implications of corporate financial reporting. *Journal of Accounting and Economics, 40*(1), 3–73. doi:10.1016/j.jacceco.2005.01.002

Graves, S. B., & Waddock, S. A. (1990). Institutional ownership and control: Implications for long-term corporate strategy. *The Academy of Management Perspectives, 4*(1), 75–83. doi:10.5465/ame.1990.4274714

Gutiérrez, M., & Sáez, M. (2013). Deconstructing Independent Directors. *Journal of Corporate Law Studies, 13*(1), 63–94. doi:10.5235/14735970.13.1.63

Hamdani, A., & Yafeh, Y. (2013). Institutional investors as minority shareholders. *Review of Finance, 17*(2), 691–725. doi:10.1093/rof/rfr039

Healy, P. (1985). The impact of bonus schemes on the selection of accounting principles. *Journal of Accounting and Economics, 7*(1-3), 85–107. doi:10.1016/0165-4101(85)90029-1

Kahn, M., & Rock, E. (2007). Hedge funds in corporate governance and corporate control. *University of Pennsylvania Law Review, 155*(5), 1021–1093.

Kasznick, R. (1999). On the Association between Voluntary Disclosure and Earnings Management. *Journal of Accounting Research, 37*(1), 57–82. doi:10.2307/2491396

Klein, A. (2002). Audit committee, board of director characteristics, and earnings management. *Journal of Accounting and Economics, 33*(3), 375–400. doi:10.1016/S0165-4101(02)00059-9

Koh, P. S. (2003). On the association between institutional ownership and aggressive corporate earnings management in Australia. *The British Accounting Review, 35*(2), 105–128. doi:10.1016/S0890-8389(03)00014-3

La Porta, R., Lopez-de-Silanes, F., & Shleifer, A. (1999). Corporate ownership around the world. *The Journal of Finance, 54*(2), 471–517. doi:10.1111/0022-1082.00115

La Porta, R., Lopez-de-Silanes, F., Shleifer, A., & Vishny, R. (2000). Investor protection and corporate governance. *Journal of Financial Economics, 58*(1-2), 3–27. doi:10.1016/S0304-405X(00)00065-9

La Porta, R., Lopez-de-Silanes, F., Shleifer, A., & Vishny, R. W. (1998). Law and Finance. *Journal of Political Economy, 106*(6), 1113–1155. doi:10.1086/250042

Lang, M., Lins, K. V., & Maffett, M. (2012). Transparency, liquidity, and valuation: International evidence on when transparency matters most. *Journal of Accounting Research, 50*(3), 729–774. doi:10.1111/j.1475-679X.2012.00442.x

Lefort, F., & Urzua, F. (2008). Board independence, firm performance and ownership concentration: Evidence from Chile. *Journal of Business Research, 61*(6), 615–622. doi:10.1016/j.jbusres.2007.06.036

Leuz, C., Nanda, D., & Wysocki, P. D. (2003). Earnings management and investor protection: An international comparison. *Journal of Financial Economics, 69*(3), 505–527. doi:10.1016/S0304-405X(03)00121-1

Linck, J. S., Netter, J., & Shu, T. (2013). Can managers use discretionary accruals to ease financial constraints? Evidence from discretionary accruals prior to investment. *The Accounting Review*, *88*(6), 2117–2143. doi:10.2308/accr-50537

Listokin, Y. (2010). If you give shareholders power, do they use it? An empirical analysis. *Journal of Institutional and Theoretical Economics*, *166*(1), 38–53. doi:10.1628/093245610790711438

Marchetti, P., Siciliano, G., & Ventoruzzo, M. (2017). Dissenting directors. *European Business Organization Law Review*, *18*(4), 659–700. doi:10.100740804-017-0093-z

McNichols, M. F. (2000). Research design issues in earnings management studies. *Journal of Accounting and Public Policy*, *19*(4-5), 313–345. doi:10.1016/S0278-4254(00)00018-1

McNichols, M. F. (2002). Discussion of the quality of accruals and earnings: The role of accrual estimation errors. *The Accounting Review*, *77*(s-1), 61–69. doi:10.2308/accr.2002.77.s-1.61

Melis, A. (2000). Corporate governance in Italy. *Corporate Governance*, *8*(4), 347–355. doi:10.1111/1467-8683.00213

Melis, A., Carta, S., & Gaia, S. (2012). Executive remuneration in blockholder-dominated firms. How do Italian firms use stock options? *The Journal of Management and Governance*, *16*(3), 511–541. doi:10.100710997-010-9163-0

Merchant, K. A. (1990). The effects of financial controls on data manipulation and management myopia. *Accounting, Organizations and Society*, *15*(4), 297–313. doi:10.1016/0361-3682(90)90021-L

Moscariello, N., Fera, P., & Cinque, E. (2020). The information content of discretionary accruals during systemic crises. *Journal of Applied Accounting Research*, *21*(3), 455–476. doi:10.1108/JAAR-04-2018-0054

Moscariello, N., Pizzo, M., Govorun, D., & Kostyuk, A. (2019). Independent minority directors and firm value in a principal–principal agency setting: Evidence from Italy. *The Journal of Management and Governance*, *23*(1), 165–194. doi:10.100710997-018-9421-0

Peasnell, K. V., Pope, P. F., & Young, S. (2005). Board Monitoring and Earnings Management: Do Outside Directors Influence Abnormal Accruals? *Journal of Business Finance & Accounting*, *32*(7-8), 1311–1346. doi:10.1111/j.0306-686X.2005.00630.x

Porter, M. E. (1992). Capital choices: Changing the way America invests in industry. *Journal of Applied Corporate Finance*, *5*(2), 4–16. doi:10.1111/j.1745-6622.1992.tb00485.x

Prencipe, A., Bar-Yosef, S., Mazzola, P., & Pozza, L. (2011). Income smoothing in family-controlled companies: Evidence from Italy. *Corporate Governance*, *19*(6), 529–546. doi:10.1111/j.1467-8683.2011.00856.x

Prencipe, A., Markarian, G., & Pozza, L. (2008). Earnings management in family firms: Evidence from R&D cost capitalization in Italy. *Family Business Review*, *21*(1), 71–88. doi:10.1111/j.1741-6248.2007.00112.x

Rajgopal, S., & Venkatachalam, M. (1997). *The role of institutional investors in corporate governance: An empirical investigation*. Graduate School of Business, Stanford University.

Reverte, C. (2008). Institutional differences in EU countries and their relationship with earnings management differences. *Journal of Accounting & Organizational Change*, *4*(2), 182–200. doi:10.1108/18325910810878964

Ronen, J., & Yaari, V. (2008). *Earnings management* (Vol. 372). Springer US.

Shleifer, A., & Vishny, R. W. (1997). A survey of corporate governance. *The Journal of Finance*, *52*(2), 737–783. doi:10.1111/j.1540-6261.1997.tb04820.x

Subramanyam, K. R. (1996). The pricing of discretionary accruals. *Journal of Accounting and Economics*, *22*(1-3), 249–281. doi:10.1016/S0165-4101(96)00434-X

Sundaramurthy, C., Rhoades, D. L., & Rechner, P. L. (2005). A meta-analysis of the effects of executive and institutional ownership on firm performance. *Journal of Managerial Issues*, *17*(4), 494–510.

Volpin, P. (2002). Governance with poor investor protection: Evidence from top executive turnover in Italy. *Journal of Financial Economics*, *64*(1), 61–90. doi:10.1016/S0304-405X(02)00071-5

Wulferth, H. (2013). *Managerial Discretion and Performance in China*. Springer-Verlag Berlin and Heidelbe. doi:10.1007/978-3-642-35837-1

Zhong, L., Chourou, L., & Ni, Y. (2017). On the association between strategic institutional ownership and earnings quality: Does investor protection strength matter? *Journal of Accounting and Public Policy*, *36*(6), 429–450. doi:10.1016/j.jaccpubpol.2017.09.002

KEY TERMS AND DEFINITIONS

Anormal Accruals: The amount of accrued assets and liabilities that does not maps into cash flows because of distortions caused by the wrong application of accounting rules or earnings management.

Institutional Investor: A market operator that makes systematic and substantial investments and can be identified as banks, credit unions, insurance companies, pension funds, hedge funds, REITs, investment advisors, endowments, and mutual funds.

Minority Director: A member of the Board of Director that is elected from a slate presented by at least one minority shareholder.

Ownership Concentration: The amount of share capital that are not actively traded in the open market and, therefore, it represents a significant internal governance mechanism in which the block-owners can control and influence the management of the firm to protect their interests.

Strategic Institutional Investor: An institutional investor investing in firms with the aim of holding their ownership stake over a long-time run and, therefore, having strong incentives to monitor activities.

Chapter 3
Owner Managers, Family Business, and Earnings Management Preceding Management Buyouts

Lokman Tutuncu
https://orcid.org/0000-0002-8653-9546
Bulent Ecevit University, Turkey

ABSTRACT

This study investigates earnings management prior to management buyouts in a sample of 269 UK private family and non-family firms. It hypothesizes that concentrated ownership in private non-family firms provides sufficient wealth incentives and power to owner/managers to manage earnings upwards before the acquisition, while family owners use management buyouts as a succession tool in the absence of a suitable family successor out of concern for the future of family business. The results are consistent with this prediction. Owner/managers in non-family firms tend to overstate earnings preceding the buyout while family ownership is negatively associated with discretionary accruals one year before the buyout transaction.

INTRODUCTION

Prior research investigates earnings management (EM) in listed family firms (Wang, 2006; Prencipe, Markarian, & Pozza, 2008; Tong, 2007; Achleitner, Gunther, Kaserer, & Siciliano, 2014), private family businesses (Stockmans, Lybaert, & Voordeckers, 2010), and going private buyouts (Perry & Williams, 1994; Mao & Renneboog, 2015). This study examines EM preceding management buyouts (MBO) of private firms. Private firms constitute majority of MBO acquisitions worldwide (Strömberg, 2008) and family firms are an important source for these deals (Howorth, Westhead, & Wright, 2004; Scholes, Westhead, & Burrows, 2008). The research on the non-listed family and non-family firms is scarce due to difficulty in obtaining private firm data (Prencipe, Bar-Yosef, & Dekker, 2014; Paiva, Lourenco, &

DOI: 10.4018/978-1-7998-7596-3.ch003

Branco, 2016). This study pays special attention to private family and non-family owned firms, whose managers, in the MBO context, have varying motivations to engage in or refrain from earnings management. Analysis of EM behaviour in family and non-family private firm acquisitions provides an ideal setting to observe managerial deviations from fiduciary duties and moral hazard problems pointed in the prior research.

Existing family studies examine financial reporting in a conventional setting that lack the unique managerial incentives and agency conflicts induced by the initiation of the acquisition process. The underlying moral hazard in MBOs involves incumbent managers of listed firms expropriating shareholders by exploiting their decision-making powers and dispersed ownership structure of the firm (Perry & Williams, 1994). The manager-owner relation is; however, more complicated as far as private firms are concerned, which characteristically have concentrated ownership and as a consequence, blurred owner/manager responsibilities. More importantly, the selling owner/managers or family members often possess control powers to manipulate earnings upwards to the detriment of the acquiring team. This contrasts with public firms, where managers tend to possess opportunistic incentives to understate earnings for the benefit of the acquiring investors of which they are part. An examination of private MBO acquisitions, therefore, provides an opportunity to shed light on an important but unanswered question: whether/why private firms in general, and private family firms in particular, engage in earnings management prior to a major event associated with their wealth. For many private firms, financial statements are the only source of public information. A better understanding of the quality of this information is important for investors, creditors, and regulators.

The entrepreneurship literature highlights the need for more studies on agency conflicts during private family firm successions (Howorth et al., 2004; Scholes et al., 2008), especially those that compare EM practice in family and non-family firms (Salvato & Moores, 2010). Past studies do not make any distinction between private family and non-family owned businesses (Burgstahler, Hail, & Leuz, 2006), and future contributions would come in the form of comparative studies in this field (Paiva et al., 2016). Although private family firms represent the majority of firms worldwide (IFERA, 2003), little is known about the family firms' accounting practices (Hutton, 2007; Salvato & Moores, 2010; Prencipe et al., 2014). This study attempts to fill a gap by comparatively investigating private family and non-family firms.

The study hypothesizes that owner/managers will have enhanced motives to inflate income before MBO due to their selling position in the deal, their large ownership stakes and the corresponding wealth considerations associated with the transaction. Family firms are, in contrast, predicted to be more concerned about their family identity and culture than their wealth to prevent EM prior to succession of the family business to managers. These two different private firm positions are tested by discretionary accruals models in a sample of 269 UK buyouts. As expected, private family owned firms show no evidence of EM and non-family firms report significant income-increasing EM one year before the acquisition. Regressions of family dummy and ownership on the discretionary accruals support the results. The results underline positive impact of family succession on wealth motivated moral hazard, while cautioning against extrapolating the results from exclusively listed firms to the overall population of MBOs.

This chapter makes two contributions to the existing literature. First, it contributes to the family business literature by presenting the first analysis of EM related to a major corporate event which coincides with or leads to family succession and where event-specific incentives to engage in EM are present (i.e., acquisition via buyout). Second, it adds to the literature by providing the first comparative analysis of EM in non-listed firms and showing that owner/managers inflate earnings in the absence of family culture. Overall, the chapter presents comparative empirical research on non-listed family and non-family firms, which is rare due to extensive archival data concerns (Prencipe et al., 2014; Paiva et al., 2016).

BACKGROUND AND HYPOTHESES

Managers in public companies manage earnings in order to influence information available to investors and/or financial intermediaries, to avoid violation of contractual terms and to influence the information set of third parties (Walker, 2013). The existing evidence shows that managers have incentives to manage earnings upward to achieve their targets (Gore, Pope, & Singh, 2007). They might also be motivated to engage in EM for personal benefits related to bonus schemes (Healy & Wahlen, 1999), and to obtain higher valuation for firms going public (IPO) (Teoh, Welch, & Wong, 1998). Private businesses are often thought to have less severe agency conflicts, monitoring and regulatory pressures compared to public corporations (Fama & Jensen, 1983), yet Burgstahler et al. (2006) show that they tend to exhibit more severe EM than their public counterparts. They argue that private firms have fewer incentives to report informative earnings because the information may be conveyed through private channels, which could obfuscate financial statements and lead to more aggressive EM.

This study relies on agency theory and socioemotional wealth theory to make predictions about managerial behaviour. The agency theory emphasizes the conflict of interest between owners and managers in a public company setting where ownership is relatively dispersed and delegated managers may exploit their superior knowledge and ability to run daily operations to the detriment of shareholders and their benefit (Jensen & Meckling, 1976). This hazard is manifested in several ways and empirically examined in settings such as managerial entrenchment, capital structure, earnings management, and pay-out policy decisions (Berger, Ofek, & Yermack, 1997; Hu & Kumar, 2004; Meo, Lara, & Surroca, 2017). The moral hazard is reduced when owners also participate in the management affairs (Jensen & Meckling, 1976); however, private ownership and concentration of power in the hands of owner manager may lead to or exacerbate a self-control problem that reduces the effectiveness of control mechanisms (Jensen, 1994; Schulze, Lubatkin, Dino, & Buchholtz, 2001). The family business is a particular case, where agency costs are reduced further by means of special relationships between principals and agents and without separation of management and control decisions (Fama & Jensen, 1983). Aside from these universal observations in public, private and family firms, agency costs play an important role in acquisitions and going private decisions (Jensen, 1986; Weir, Laing, & Wright, 2005; Fung, Jo, & Tsai, 2009). In the unique case of going private buyouts, managers act on their superior information about company value and attempt to take over when it is undervalued. The managers then have an interest in understating earnings to acquire it at a lower price (Perry & Williams, 1994; Francis, Hasan, & Li; 2016), which clashes with their fiduciary duties that require them to guard the interests of shareholders. When the takeover is in the form of a change in private ownership; however, the agency proposition is reversed, and the owner/managers' interest lies in overstating earnings to sell at a higher price. The evidence from going private MBOs conclusively shows earnings understatement (Perry & Williams, 1994; Wu, 1997; Fischer & Louis, 2008; Mao & Renneboog, 2015) and downwards real earnings management (Francis et al., 2016). In private firms; however, earnings could be inflated by outgoing owner/managers before the acquisition since their engagement with the firm is often terminated ex-post and they do not suffer from the cost of accrual reversals (Mao & Renneboog, 2015; Tutuncu, 2019). The incentive to overstate earnings would be associated with the size of the ownership sold by the outgoing owner/managers. The evidence points out that managers, who are not part of the incoming management team, divest large parts of their shares (Kaplan, 1989). In the private firm setting, these owner/managers are likely to have even larger shareholdings and consequently enhanced wealth incentives and powers to inflate earnings. A key difference between MBOs of public and private companies is that it is the outgoing incumbents in private companies who are likely to be motivated to manage earnings whereas in public companies it is the incoming owner/managers who tend to manage earnings. Shareholders of public firms often do not have the controlling powers to influence accounting decisions, thus they are exposed to expropriation by opportunistic managerial behaviour. On the contrary, owner/managers in private firms can actively influence vital decisions and accounting practices. These selling owner/managers would be sufficiently powerful and motivated to overstate earnings at the expense of buying managers in the MBO team, since the resulting deal price will directly influence their wealth. Thus, author conjectures that owner/managers in private firms engage in systematic earnings overstatement prior to acquisition. This discussion suggests following hypotheses:

Hypothesis One: Owner/managers in private firms manipulate earnings upwards prior to MBO transaction.
Hypothesis Two: Pre-MBO managerial ownership is positively associated with discretionary accruals in private non-family firms acquired by their management.

Private Family Management Buyouts

Prior research shows that family firms may overstate earnings to mask the poorer performance (Stockmans et al., 2010; Demsetz & Villalonga, 2001) resulting from conflicts between family members that arise due to pursuit of non-economic business goals (Chrisman, Chua, & Litz, 2004; Stockmans et al., 2010), and agency conflicts which are hard to resolve because of the reluctance to impose strict monitoring over family members (Eisenhardt, 1989; Schulze, Lubatkin, & Dino, 2003). While large shareholders may attempt to expropriate minority shareholders in private firms (Chrisman et al., 2004; Salvato & Moores, 2010), private family firms are less likely to do so because the family wealth is itself dependent on the overall value of the business (Schulze et al., 2003). Socioemotional wealth theory (Gomez-Mejia, Haynes, Nunes-Nickel et al., 2007) provides an excellent framework to the MBO setting for advocating family reputation and long-term non-economic utility than short-term gains. Investigating German family firms going public, Leitterstorf and Rau (2014) find that family businesses prioritize preservation of socioemotional wealth and underprice more by offering larger discounts. They conduct the offering despite the fact that partial transfer of family ownership reduces their influence in the company. However, faced with a dilemma to raise required capital and relinquishing partial control versus remaining private, they choose the former because conducting the initial public offering (IPO) might be the only way to preserve the long-term socioemotional wealth. The IPO concept is similar to our setting, where family owners partially or fully relinquish control to a management team in the absence of a family successor (Westhead, 1997; Howorth et al., 2004; Scholes et al., 2008). The MBO is an extraordinary corporate event, which is devoid of the survival instinct of the family and replaces it with a suitable successor. Nearly 20% of all buyouts in Europe are takeovers of family firms. Unlike public firms where family is often the minority shareholder, private firms are strictly-held businesses (Ansari, Goergen, & Mira, 2014), and the minority shareholding in family-owned businesses may not be large enough to deserve expropriation. In this scenario, the family would be better off finding a successor to take over the business and protect its identity and reputation, instead of risking a pointless conflict with minority shareholders for small gains. The succession of business to known managers also allows preservation of long-term relationships with suppliers and lenders (Burkart, Panunzi, & Shleifer, 2003; Anderson, Mansi, & Reeb, 2003). Since the successor manager or the steward should ideally identify with the established values and culture of the family business (Davis, Schoorman, & Donaldson, 1997; Gomez-Mejia et al., 2007; Chrisman et al., 2004; Corbetta & Salvato, 2004), the family would be less concerned about short-term economic gains and incentives to inflate earnings would be minimal in these succession MBOs. This discussion produces the following hypothesis:

Hypothesis Three: Pre-MBO family ownership is negatively associated with discretionary accruals in private family firms acquired by their management.

RESEARCH DESIGN

Sample Selection and Data

This study comprises MBO deals between 2004 and 2015 in the UK. The market choice is based on the fact that UK is the largest buyout market after the US and regulations allow access to private firm financial statements. Thomson One Banker (TOB) is used to collect the list and source of deals. To be included in the sample; the acquisition target must be a private company, transaction must be led by an incumbent manager, and at least 2-year historical accounting data must be available to estimate discretionary accruals preceding the transaction. Secondary management buyouts (SMBO), former subsidiaries, and public-to-private buyouts are excluded from the sample. SMBOs are complex deals and very different from primary buyout transactions. Divestments are dropped as their managers are less likely to have discretion in the ex-ante accounting practices. Following Perry and Williams (1994), buyouts originating from liquidations are excluded since they are likely to have zero managerial discretion and considerably limited ability for EM prior to acquisition. Finally, MBOs involving financial firms are dropped following the tradition in corporate finance because their financial statements do not follow the mainstream practice and cannot be used to estimate discretionary accruals. These restrictions allow testing an independent sample of private firms for EM practices. The annual reports and return filings obtained from Fame database are used to gather accounting data, and to document family relationships; to obtain surname and residence of owners and managers in order to identify family members and blood relations. Table 1 presents sample construction steps. The initial sample has 1886 deals, which is substantially reduced by the lack of accounting data because the sample contains a large number of small and medium sized firms which are exempt from reporting full accounts. In particular, UK regulations stipulate that medium companies may withhold sales data while small companies may avoid reporting income statement altogether. The EM cannot be tested if income statement items such as sales and depreciation are unavailable. Cross-sectional models require at least two years of historical data to detect discretionary accruals, therefore the accounting data must be available for at least two successive years preceding the transaction. Final sample includes 269 MBOs after eliminating missing observations, of which 113 are family and 156 are non-family firms.

Table 1. Sample selection

Procedure	MBOs
MBO observations during 2004-2015	1886
Financial firms	-151
Public-to-private buyouts, secondary and divisional buyouts	-165
Firms missing accounting data, sales etc.	-1280
Firms missing ownership information and original filings	-21
Remaining sample	269
Family MBO firms (FMBO)	113
Non-family MBO firms (NFMBO)	156

Definition of Family Business

Defining family firms is one of the most challenging aspects of the empirical family business research (Prencipe et al., 2014), and the literature employs various definitions of family business depending on the research question. This study focuses on the common factors to construct its criteria. A family firm is often defined as business owned and managed by multiple family members (Chua, Chrisman, & Sharma, 1999; Miller, Le Breton-Miller, Lester, & Cannella, 2007). However, different requirements with regard to ownership, management and control are employed in private and public firms to qualify. The qualification criteria appear more relaxed in public firms due to their dispersed ownership. In these firms, a minority family ownership is often combined with the family CEO, one or multiple family managers, or board members to identify as family firm (Anderson & Reeb, 2003; Gomez-Mejia, Larraza-Kintana, & Makri, 2003; Ali, Chen, & Radhakrishnan, 2007; Achleitner et al., 2014), where family control is wielded through strategic positions or majority voting rights (Barontini & Caprio, 2006) rather than majority ownership, while in private businesses majority ownership is a pre-requisite to qualify, even absent family managers (Westhead & Howorth, 2006; Scholes et al., 2008; Stockmans et al., 2010). Nonetheless, one can deduce that family owners also often occupy managerial positions due to blurred lines between owner and manager responsibilities in private firms. To capture the essence of family business, a strict family definition is adopted requiring the firms to have either majority family ownership or voting rights, as well as having a family member on the board to qualify. Two or more shareholders or managers must be connected with blood or marriage to be part of the same family. Residence addresses and surnames of individuals are used to identify these connections. This definition is similar to Wilson, Wright, and Scholes (2013; however, different from Prencipe et al. (2008) and Stockmans et al. (2010), who absolve managerial position requirement. Firms that do not meet these criteria are classified as non-family firms, including firms owned and controlled by a single entrepreneur and firms jointly owned and controlled by two unrelated entrepreneurs.

Table 2. Distribution of management buyouts

Year	MBO Observations	Family MBOs (FMBO)		Non-family MBOs (NFMBO)		FM_OWN	
		N	%	N	%	FMBO	NFMBO
2004	15	6	40%	9	60%	85.43%	64.17%
2005	39	14	35.89%	25	64.10%	86.42%	79.82%
2006	46	17	36.95%	29	63.04%	90.60%	83.68%
2007	37	17	45.94%	20	54.05%	89.41%	79.87%
2008	22	12	54.54%	10	45.45%	90.63%	65.70%
2009	5	4	80%	1	20%	87.18%	0%
2010	15	6	40%	9	60%	85.12%	68.50%
2011	9	3	33.33%	6	66.67%	100%	83.16%
2012	19	8	42.10%	11	57.90%	93.62%	63.87%
2013	22	8	36.36%	14	63.64%	86.25%	85.36%
2014	31	15	48.38%	16	51.61%	78.53%	93.88%
2015	9	3	33.33%	6	66.67%	85.67%	83.67%
Total	269	113	42%	156	58%	87.64%	79.08%

Table 2 shows distribution of MBOs across years and ownership status. Average family and non-family ownership (FM_OWN) statistics are also displayed in the last column. The average family ownership for 113 firms is 87%, which shows that these firms are closely held and non-family shareholders are a small minority. Non-family firms are also tightly controlled by owner/managers, average non-family firm managers holding 79% of the equity. These statistics support the early propositions that non-family shareholding is not large enough to deserve expropriation, and owner/managers may have enhanced incentives to inflate earnings parallel with their large equity. Note that 50% family ownership threshold is imposed for firms to qualify as family business whereas for non-family firms no threshold exists, yet the average entrepreneurial ownership is still a large 79%. Untabulated statistics show that there are 76 leading family owners (LFO) and 85 leading non-family owners (LNFO), where lead owner is defined as a family member or manager holding at least 50% of the ordinary shares or voting rights. Total number of lead owners is 161, amounting to 60% of the sample. 36 firms (13.4% of the sample) are lone founder firms, defined as an entrepreneur holding 100% of the ordinary voting shares, of which 14 are family firms and 22 are non-family firms. The heavy concentration of managerial ownership is not due to the selection criteria, but a natural representation of the private firm characteristics.

RESULTS

Table 3 reports summary statistics on governance and other firm-specific characteristics for 113 family and 156 non-family firms. Tests show differences in the mean and medians of family and non-family owned firms. Average sample firm has 83.7% of its ownership controlled by family or owner/managers (FM_OWN) and median firm has 97% of its ownership under family or owner/manager control. Average family has a larger ownership (87.6%) than average owner/manager (79.1%) while median family ownership (95%) and owner/manager ownership (100%) are about the same level. The percentages are considerably higher than previous studies. For instance, Achleitner et al. (2014) report 35.8% average and 37.6% median family ownership for family firms, and Anderson and Reeb (2003) report 17.88% average family ownership. Average sample firm has 57% of board seats controlled by family members or owner/managers (BOARDCONTROL). Family firms allocate over 40% of the managerial positions to family members while owner/managers occupy over 60% of the board seats. Non-family firm boards tend to be more tightly controlled by their owners. On average, 67.2% of family firms and 53.8% of non-family firms are have a single controlling shareholder (LEADOWNER) defined as an entrepreneur holding at least 50% of the shares. Relative to average non-family firm, family firms have a higher ownership concentration (HERF), average statistic is 0.547 for family and 0.493 for non-family firms. With regards to firm characteristics, family and non-family firms are comparable to each other in terms of size, auditing by BIG4 auditors (AUDIT), private equity sponsorship (PE), implementation of IFRS and reporting loss before management buyout. Compared to family firms, non-family firms have higher profitability (PERF), better industry-adjusted performance (MPERF), higher sales growth, and more institutional shareholders (INST). Close to half of family (48.6%) and non-family firms (49.3%) have secured private equity backing for the MBO. Average sample firm is 23.78 years old (AGE), and family firms (mean age 30.89 and median age 23 years) are significantly older than non-family firms (mean age 19.93 and median age 14 years).

The study employs total accruals calculated as non-cash working capital minus depreciation expense following Perry and Williams (1994), Dechow, Sloan, and Sweeney (1995), and Burgstahler et al. (2006). The cross-sectional variant of the Jones (1991) model is employed to estimate parameters of the base model and compute discretionary total and current accruals. Discretionary current accruals are estimated since several studies suggest their relevance at the time of major corporate events (Jones, 1991; Teoh et al., 1998). Jones (1991) time-series model requires extensive historical data and therefore it is better suited for public companies. Ultimately, the choice of accrual-based earnings management metric is imposed by the available data and information disclosure of UK private firms, not only for the MBOs but for the control sample which we rely on to obtain the parameter estimates. Although it is mandatory for UK private firms to disclose financial statements as per EU 4th Directive Article 47(1) and 51(1), cash flow statement is an exception and voluntarily published (Tutuncu, 2019). Therefore, to use cash-flow based earnings management proxies, the researcher faces a choice between working with a small number of companies engaging in voluntary disclosure or limiting the measurement to accruals-based metrics. As voluntary disclosure is likely to be associated with positive bias and will considerably reduce the sample size, the latter is the preferred way of measurement. The metrics in this study could be used for public and private companies alike since the regulations impose the same disclosure and auditing requirements on them. For example, Burgstahler et al. (2006) utilize accruals-based metrics to compare earnings management in European public and private companies. The population of the UK private firms with available data are used to estimate non-discretionary accruals parameters. Overall, 160000 control firms are matched on 2-digit industry code and event year with buyouts to construct parameter estimation portfolios.

Table 4 presents estimated discretionary accruals for family and non-family firms in the two years preceding MBO transaction. The second year is included to examine differences in earnings management behaviour with and without the prospect of MBO. With the exception of mean current accruals, sample mean and median discretionary accruals are significantly positive in Year -1. Breakdown of the sample into family and non-family components reveals significant differences between subsamples. Family firm mean and median discretionary accruals have low percentages, and they are insignificantly different from zero. Non-family firms have large positive and significantly higher percentage of discretionary accruals estimates than family firms. In Year -2, both family and non-family firms tend to report significantly negative accruals and the differences between the two are not significant.

The results suggest that non-family firms overstate earnings and family firms avoid earnings management practice prior to MBO transaction. Differences in means and medians between family and non-family firms are significant in all models, indicating that earnings management in the preceding year is limited to non-family firms only. Hypothesis One is, therefore, supported. The findings are consistent with a scenario where family firms are unaffected by managerial moral hazard induced by MBO transaction since buyout is initiated to ensure smooth transition of family ownership to a trusted management team. In this scenario, family culture and socioemotional wealth concerns (i.e., long term value of the firm) dominate MBO process and manipulative incentives are suppressed or stay minimal, while non-family firms are more exposed to moral hazard and opportunistic practice, since leaving owner/managers possess large wealth incentives proportional to their high ownership levels to extract maximum value from the deal absent such pervasive family culture. The behavioural reversal from Year -2 to Year -1 also presents an interesting concept. Although private firms are known to manage earnings (Burgstahler et al., 2006), family firm behaviour is generally expected to be different than non-family firm behaviour. On the contrary, findings show that both family and non-family firms manage earnings downwards in the absence of MBO. Discretionary accruals are more negative for non-family firms, contrary to prior evidence that family firms display more negative accruals than non-family firms (Ali et al., 2007; Achleitner et al., 2014), although the differences between them are not significant. The results are consistent with an explanation that family firms have higher earnings quality and are less likely to manage earnings (Cascino, Pugliese, Mussolino, & Sansone, 2010; Jiraporn & Dadalt, 2009).

Overall, the results are consistent with family succession (Howorth et al., 2004; Scholes et al., 2008), stewardship theory (Davis et al., 1997), and socioemotional wealth (Stockmans et al., 2010) explanations in the sense that incentives of family and succeeding managers are aligned when dealing parties identify with and/or committed to the family business.

Additional Tests

Additional tests are carried out in family and non-family firms controlled by lead owners, defined as a person holding at least 50% of shares or voting rights, and in firms with and without lead owners. The separate treatment of lead family owners (LFO) and non-family owners (LNFO) is important (Miller et al., 2007; Stockmans et al., 2010) because LFOs may have stronger incentives to preserve special family features of their business which may result in different EM practices. In these closely held firms, intra-family conflicts are expected to be minimal and family culture most pervasive. Moreover, MBOs in these type of family firms are often initiated to replace the LFO, who has more interest in leaving his business in safe hands than making personal gains. On the contrary, leading owners in non-family firms would have stronger incentives to manipulate earnings since wealth gains from MBO deal are proportionate to their majority shareholding. Separate examination of earnings management in family firms with and without LFOs also contributes to the family firm heterogeneity debate (Corbetta & Salvato, 2004; Stockmans et al., 2010). In the spirit of Stockmans et al. (2010), who differentiate between lone founder firms and true family firms, a different family definition is adopted by including lone founder firms in the family firm sample to examine its effect on the overall family sample. Lastly, the family vs. non-family concept is ignored to set up lead owner vs. non-lead owner samples to investigate minority shareholder expropriation. If controlling shareholders expropriate minority shareholders prior to buyout, upwards earnings management should be stronger in lead owner firms.

Table 3. Descriptive statistics for family and non-family management buyouts

Variables	All MBOs		FMBO		NFMBO		Standard Deviation		Differences		Observations		
	Mean	Median	Mean	Median	Mean	Median	FMBO	NFMBO	Mean	Median	FMBO	NFMBO	Total
Governance Characteristics													
FM_OWN	0.827	0.97	0.876	0.95	0.791	1	0.154	0.298	***	n.s.	113	150	263
BOARDCONTROL	0.573	0.5	0.451	0.4	0.665	0.714	0.241	0.321	***	***	113	151	264
LEADOWNER	0.594	1	0.672	1	0.538	1	0.471	0.5	**	-	113	156	269
HERF	0.516	0.5	0.547	0.5	0.493	0.471	0.299	0.286	n.s.	n.s.	113	150	263
Firm Characteristics													
PERF	0.084	0.086	0.064	0.079	0.099	0.095	0.199	0.134	*	*	113	156	269
MPERF	0.019	0.019	0.002	0.014	0.034	0.027	0.204	0.134	***	**	113	156	269
SIZE	9.114	9.035	9.096	9.025	9.127	9.064	1.089	0.896	n.s.	n.s.	113	156	269
GROWTH	0.282	0.105	0.124	0.096	0.397	0.118	0.229	2.159	**	**	113	156	269
AGE	23.78	17	30.89	23	19.93	14	24.23	22.58	***	***	113	156	269
AUDIT	0.223	0	0.195	0	0.243	0	0.398	0.431	n.s.	-	113	156	269
PE	0.491	0	0.486	0	0.493	0	0.502	0.502	n.s.	-	113	156	269
INST	0.119	0	0.026	0	0.185	0	0.161	0.39	***	-	113	156	269
LOSS	0.115	0	0.133	0	0.102	0	0.341	0.304	n.s.	-	113	156	269
IFRS	0.007	0	0.008	0	0.006	0	0.094	0.08	n.s.	-	113	156	269

Table 4. Discretionary accruals

	All MBOs		FMBO		NFMBO		Difference	
	Mean	Median	Mean	Median	Mean	Median	Mean	Median
Year -1								
DTA	0.329***	0.030***	0.145	0.018	0.463***	0.035***	***	***
DCA	0.027	0.018**	-0.012	0.006	0.055**	0.028***	**	**
N	269	269	113	113	156	156		
Year -2								
DTA	-0.101**	-0.071***	-0.098***	-0.044***	-0.115***	-0.075***	n.s.	n.s.
DCA	-0.124**	-0.007	-0.046	-0.005	-0.14*	-0.009	n.s.	n.s.
N	193	193	81	81	112	112		

This table shows discretionary total (DTA) and current accruals (DCA) in the two years before MBO deal. Significance in means is assessed by two-tailed t-test and significance in medians is assessed by Wilcoxon/Mann-Whitney sign tests. ***, ** represent significance at 1% and 5% levels. n.s. = not significant.

Table 5 presents the results of tests. Untabulated statistics for 22 lone founder firms show that mean and median total discretionary accruals are 0.784 and 0.112, of which median is significant at 5% despite the low count. Mean and median statistics for current accruals are 0.003 and 0.02. Inclusion of lone founder firms in the family sample significantly skews the mean discretionary total accruals, increasing the magnitude from the original 0.145 to 0.249. Median discretionary total accruals also increase from 0.018 to 0.034 and weakly significant. Discretionary current accruals are not affected. Remaining non-family firms continue to show upwards management of both total and current accruals. The differences between family and non-family samples, however, become mostly insignificant after the inclusion of lone founder firms to family sample. Lone founder firms appear to manage long term accruals, they have larger discretionary total accruals than family firms and behave identical to a non-family owner/manager with substantial wealth motives. In Panel B, LFO firms display slightly smaller discretionary accruals compared to overall family firms and LNFO firms show larger discretionary accruals than other non-family firms, supporting the argument that LFO's have a larger concern for the family than their wealth while LNFO's have larger wealth concern. The Panel C shows stratified sample along lead and non-lead owners, each representing concentrated and a relatively dispersed ownership structure. Both of these subsamples include family and non-family firms. The mean and median accruals statistics are in the middle of family and non-family statistics, and differences between subsamples are not significant. This goes to show that classification along the family and non-family lines is more correct when it comes to agency conflicts and having a lead owner does not result in minority shareholder expropriation in private firms when these lines are ignored. Family effect aside, this is an expected result of small minority shareholding in private firms unworthy of expropriation. Instead, they can opt for inflating earnings to increase sale proceeds from MBO.

Table 5. Additional tests

	Mean	**Median**	**Mean**	**Median**	**Differences**		
Panel A: Adopting a Different Family Definition							
	Family (N=135)		Non-family (N=134)		Mean	Median	N
DTA	0.249**	0.034*	0.411***	0.025**	n.s.	n.s.	269
DCA	-0.01	0.006	0.064**	0.027**	**	n.s.	269
Panel B: Lead Family Owner (LFO) vs Lead Non-family Owner (LNFO)							
	LFO (N=76)		LNFO (N=85)				
DTA	0.123	0.017	0.477***	0.057***	n.s.	n.s.	161
DCA	-0.017	0.005	0.074*	0.029**	*	n.s.	161
Panel C: Lead Owner vs Non-lead Owners (Concentrated vs Dispersed Ownership)							
	Lead Owner (N=161)		Non-Lead Owners (N=108)				
DTA	0.31***	0.041**	0.359***	0.02*	n.s.	n.s.	269
DCA	0.031	0.018	0.013	0.011	n.s.	n.s.	269

Regression of Discretionary Accruals

To test the relationship between discretionary accruals, firm status and ownership, a model similar to Wang (2006) and Achleitner et al. (2014) is employed. Ownership variables FOWN and NFMOWN are added to test the Hypothesis Two and Three that earnings management is negatively (positively) related to family (owner/manager) ownership levels. Full list and definition of variables can be found in Appendix. The full models with controls are as follows:

$$DTA = \alpha + \beta_1 FDUMMY + \beta_2 SIZE + \beta_3 GROWTH + \beta_4 PERF + \beta_5 AUDIT + \beta_6 LOSS + \varepsilon$$
$$DTA = \alpha + \beta_1 FOWN + \beta_2 SIZE + \beta_3 GROWTH + \beta_4 PERF + \beta_5 AUDIT + \beta_6 LOSS + \varepsilon$$
$$DTA = \alpha + \beta_1 NFMOWN + \beta_2 SIZE + \beta_3 GROWTH + \beta_4 PERF + \beta_5 AUDIT + \beta_6 LOSS + \varepsilon$$

The models are tested by cross-sectional OLS with year fixed effects and robust standard errors, and the tests are repeated using discretionary current accruals (DCA) as dependent variable. Leverage cannot be included in the model since short and long term debt items are mostly missing in the annual reports around MBO deals. This variable is excluded instead of setting missing values to zero. Panel A of Table 7 presents the results for simple regressions for the main variables of interest and Panel B presents full model results with controls. Model R^2 ranges from a 17.89% in the second DTA model to 6.74% in the second DCA model. The results in Panel A show negative and significant relationship between family firms and discretionary accruals (DTA, DCA). Likewise, family ownership is negatively associated with DTA and DCA. Non-family ownership is positively related to discretionary accruals in both models. Overall, results suggest that family firms are less likely to manage earnings, family owners tend to avoid earnings management and non-family owners engage in upwards management before MBO transaction, supporting Hypothesis Two and Three. The findings are also consistent with the previous evidence that discretionary accruals are more negative for family firms (Ali et al., 2007; Achleitner et al., 2014).

CONCLUSION

Based on a unique sample of 269 non-listed UK family and non-family firms, this study examines earnings management preceding MBO transactions, which are peculiar transactions since they facilitate change and/or succession in ownership whilst firms remain private. By examining this type of buyouts, the study attempts to shed light on an important question as whether/why private firms in general, and private family firms in particular, engage in earnings management, and contribute to the private firms' heterogeneity debate by comparing earnings management practices in family and non-family owned private firms.

The study hypothesizes that private non-family firms overstate earnings due to wealth concerns associated with outgoing owner/managers and to secure deal financing, and family firms do not manage earnings due to pervasive family culture and transition of family ownership. In line with the hypotheses, the study finds no evidence of earnings management in private family owned firms. In subsample of non-family firm; however, significant upward earnings management is reported preceding MBOs. The earnings management practice is significantly associated with the percentage ownership of family and non-family owners. The above findings remain consistent across total and current accruals models. For many private firms, financial statements are the only source of public information. The results of this study contribute to a better understanding of the quality of this information and are therefore important for investors in private equity, creditors, and regulators. The limitations of this study are largely pertinent to the information disclosure and data accessibility issues common with private firms such as reporting exemptions, unavailability of cash flow statements and market data. An interesting area for further research would be earnings management in private family and non-family firms in the absence of an acquisition (i.e., management buyout). The results for Year -2, in which both types of firms report negative discretionary accruals absent buyout acquisition, deserve more investigation.

Table 6. Pairwise Pearson correlations

	DTA	DCA	FOWN	NFMOWN	SIZE	GROWTH	AGE	PERF	MPERF	AUDIT	LOSS
DTA											
DCA	0.108*										
FOWN	-0.128**	-0.102*									
NFMOWN	0.134**	0.127**	-0.845***								
SIZE	-0.076	-0.088	-0.016	-0.019							
GROWTH	-0.036	-0.111*	-0.112*	0.064	0.085						
AGE	-0.115*	-0.02	0.265***	-0.184**	-0.011	-0.326***					
PERF	0.018	0.112*	-0.137**	0.112*	-0.094	0.052	0.069				
MPERF	-0.144**	0.111*	-0.118*	0.113*	-0.142**	0.051	0.032	0.943***			
AUDIT	-0.085	0.032	-0.071	-0.014	0.199***	-0.054	-0.037	0.002	0.009		
LOSS	-0.077	-0.031	0.061	-0.084	-0.121	-0.012	-0.113*	-0.584***	-0.547***	-0.053	
HERF	0.000	-0.007	0.162***	0.075	-0.038	-0.055	0.052	-0.088	-0.067	-0.087	0.115**

Variables are defined in Appendix. ***, ** and * are two-tailed significance at 1, 5, and 10% levels respectively.

Table 7. OLS regressions with discretionary accruals

	Dependent Variable: DTA			Dependent Variable: DCA		
	Model 1	**Model 2**	**Model 3**	**Model 1**	**Model 2**	**Model 3**
Panel A: Basic Model						
Intercept	1.011***	1.069***	0.781***	0.039	0.031	-0.033
	[3.45]	[3.47]	[2.95]	[1.27]	[0.94]	[-0.93]
FDUMMY	-0.303**			-0.071**		
	[-2.39]			[-2.07]		
FOWN		-0.345**			-0.072**	
		[-2.36]			[-1.98]	
NFMOWN			0.367**			0.085**
			[2.32]			[1.99]
R^2	0.1122	0.1181	0.1205	0.0332	0.0315	0.0361
N	269	263	263	269	263	263
Panel B: Full Model With Controls						
Intercept	2.536***	2.516***	2.124**	0.267	0.269	0.191
	[2.69]	[2.68]	[2.33]	1.14	[1.13]	[0.84]
FDUMMY	-0.366***			-0.072**		
	[-2.79]			[-2.31]		
FOWN		-0.416***			-0.075**	
		[-2.77]			[-2.13]	
NFMOWN			0.381**			0.084**
			[2.45]			[2.16]
SIZE	-0.142*	-0.135*	-0.131	-0.023	-0.024	-0.022
	[-1.76]	[-1.69]	[-1.61]	[-0.93]	[-0.94]	[-0.90]
GROWTH	-0.185	-0.186	-0.143	-0.134	-0.144	-0.138
	[0.473]	[-0.67]	[-0.51]	[-1.29]	[-1.32]	[-1.26]
PERF	-2.605***	-2.572***	-2.503***	0.345*	0.357*	0.365*
	[-2.94]	[-2.87]	[-2.83]	[1.78]	[1.77]	[1.84]
AUDIT	-0.285**	-0.295**	-0.254**	0.02	0.015	0.023
	[-2.39]	[-2.37]	[-2.12]	[0.57]	[0.42]	[0.63]
LOSS	-0.803***	-0.812***	-0.788***	0.025	0.018	0.023
	[-3.28]	[-3.27]	[-3.17]	[0.38]	[0.27]	[0.34]
R^2	0.1762	0.1789	0.1753	0.0682	0.0674	0.0708
N	269	263	263	269	263	263

This table shows results of OLS regressions with year-fixed effects and robust standard errors for the relation between discretionary accruals, family firms, family and non-family managerial ownership in Year -1. Variables are defined in Appendix. t-values are in brackets. ***, ** and * are two-tailed significance at 1, 5 and 10% levels respectively.

ACKNOWLEDGMENT

This research received no specific grant from any funding agency in the public, commercial, or not-for-profit sectors.

REFERENCES

Achleitner, A. K., Gunther, N., Kaserer, C., & Siciliano, G. (2014). Real earnings management and accrual based earnings management in family firms. *European Accounting Review*, *23*(3), 431–461. doi:10.1080/09638180.2014.895620

Ali, A., Chen, T. Y., & Radhakrishnan, S. (2007). Corporate disclosures by family firms. *Journal of Accounting and Economics*, *44*(1-2), 238–286. doi:10.1016/j.jacceco.2007.01.006

Anderson, R. C., Mansi, S. A., & Reeb, D. M. (2003). Founding family ownership and the agency cost of debt. *Journal of Financial Economics*, *68*(2), 263–285. doi:10.1016/S0304-405X(03)00067-9

Anderson, R. C., & Reeb, D. M. (2003). Founding-family ownership and firm performance: Evidence from the S&P 500. *The Journal of Finance*, *58*(3), 1301–1327. doi:10.1111/1540-6261.00567

Ansari, I. F., Goergen, M., & Mira, S. (2014). The determinants of the CEO successor choice in family firms. *Journal of Corporate Finance*, *28*, 6–25. doi:10.1016/j.jcorpfin.2013.12.006

Barontini, R., & Caprio, L. (2006). The effect of family control on firm value and performance: Evidence from Continental Europe. *European Financial Management*, *12*(5), 689–723. doi:10.1111/j.1468-036X.2006.00273.x

Berger, P. G., Ofek, E., & Yermack, D. L. (1997). Managerial entrenchment and capital structure decisions. *The Journal of Finance*, *52*(4), 1411–1438. doi:10.1111/j.1540-6261.1997.tb01115.x

Burgstahler, D. C., Hail, L., & Leuz, C. (2006). The importance of reporting incentives: Earnings management in European private and public firms. *The Accounting Review*, *81*(5), 983–1016. doi:10.2308/accr.2006.81.5.983

Burkart, M., Panunzi, F., & Shleifer, A. (2003). Family firms. *The Journal of Finance*, *58*(5), 2167–2201. doi:10.1111/1540-6261.00601

Cascino, S., Pugliese, A., Mussolino, D., & Sansone, C. (2010). The influence of family ownership on the quality of accounting information. *Family Business Review*, *23*(3), 246–265. doi:10.1177/0894486510374302

Chrisman, J. J., Chua, J. H., & Litz, R. A. (2004). Comparing the agency costs of family and non-family firms: Conceptual issues and exploratory evidence. *Entrepreneurship Theory and Practice*, *28*(4), 335–354. doi:10.1111/j.1540-6520.2004.00049.x

Chua, J. H., Chrisman, J. J., & Sharma, P. (1999). Defining the family business by behaviour. *Entrepreneurship Theory and Practice*, *23*(4), 19–39. doi:10.1177/104225879902300402

Corbetta, G., & Salvato, C. (2004). Self-serving or selfactualizing? Models of man and agency costs in different types of family firms. *Entrepreneurship Theory and Practice*, *28*(4), 355–362. doi:10.1111/j.1540-6520.2004.00050.x

Davis, J. H., Schoorman, F. D., & Donaldson, L. (1997). Toward a stewardship theory of management. *Academy of Management Review*, *22*(1), 20–47. doi:10.5465/amr.1997.9707180258

Dechow, M. P., Sloan, R. G., & Sweeney, A. P. (1995). Detecting earnings management. *The Accounting Review*, *70*(2), 193–225.

Demsetz, H., & Villalonga, B. (2001). Ownership structure and corporate performance. *Journal of Corporate Finance*, *7*(1), 209–233. doi:10.1016/S0929-1199(01)00020-7

Eisenhardt, K. M. (1989). Agency theory: An assessment and review. *Academy of Management Review*, *14*(1), 57–74. doi:10.5465/amr.1989.4279003

Fama, E., & Jensen, M. (1983). Separation of ownership and control. *The Journal of Law & Economics*, *26*(2), 321–325. doi:10.1086/467037

Fischer, P. E., & Louis, H. (2008). Financial reporting and conflicting managerial incentives: The case of management buyouts. *Management Science*, *54*(10), 1700–1714. doi:10.1287/mnsc.1080.0895

Francis, B., Hasan, I., & Li, L. (2016). Evidence for the existence of downwards real-activity earnings management. *Journal of Accounting, Auditing & Finance*, *31*(2), 212–248. doi:10.1177/0148558X15582086

Fung, S., Jo, H., & Tsai, S. (2009). Agency problems in stock market driven acquisitions. *Review of Accounting and Finance*, *8*(4), 388–430. doi:10.1108/14757700911006958

Gomez-Mejia, L. R., Haynes, K., Nunez-Nickel, M., Jacobson, K., & Moyano-Fuentes, F. (2007). Socioemotional wealth and business risks in family controlled firms. *Administrative Science Quarterly*, *52*(1), 106–137. doi:10.2189/asqu.52.1.106

Gomez-Mejia, L. R., Larraza-Kintana, M., & Makri, M. (2003). The determinants of executive compensation in family controlled public corporations. *Academy of Management Journal*, *46*(2), 226–237.

Gore, P., Pope, P. F., & Singh, A. K. (2007). Earnings management and the distribution of earnings relative to targets: UK evidence. *Accounting and Business Research*, *37*(2), 123–150. doi:10.1080/00014788.2007.9730065

Healy, P. M., & Wahlen, J. M. (1999). A review of the earnings management literature and its implications for standard setting. *Accounting Horizons*, *13*(4), 365–383. doi:10.2308/acch.1999.13.4.365

Howorth, C., Westhead, P., & Wright, M. (2004). Buyouts, information asymmetry and family management dyad. *Journal of Business Venturing*, *19*(4), 509–534. doi:10.1016/j.jbusvent.2003.04.002

Hu, A., & Kumar, P. (2004). Managerial entrenchment and payout policy. *Journal of Financial and Quantitative Analysis*, *39*(4), 759–790. doi:10.1017/S0022109000003203

Hutton, A. P. (2007). A discussion of "Corporate disclosure by family firms". *Journal of Accounting and Economics*, *44*(1-2), 287–297. doi:10.1016/j.jacceco.2007.01.004

International Family Enterprise Research Academy (IFERA). (2003). Family businesses dominate. *Family Business Review*, *16*(4), 235–240. doi:10.1177/08944865030160040201

Jensen, M. C. (1986). Agency costs of free cash flow, corporate finance, and takeovers. *The American Economic Review*, *76*(2), 323–329.

Jensen, M. C. (1994). Self-interest, altruism, incentives, and agency theory. *Journal of Applied Corporate Finance*, *7*(2), 40–45. doi:10.1111/j.1745-6622.1994.tb00404.x

Jensen, M. C., & Meckling, W. H. (1976). Theory of the firm: Managerial behavior, agency costs and ownership structure. *Journal of Financial Economics*, *3*(4), 305–360. doi:10.1016/0304-405X(76)90026-X

Jiraporn, P., & Dadalt, P. J. (2009). Does founding family control affect earnings management? *Applied Economics Letters*, *16*(2), 113–119. doi:10.1080/17446540701720592

Jones, J. J. (1991). Earnings management during relief investigations. *Journal of Accounting Research*, *29*(2), 193–228. doi:10.2307/2491047

Kaplan, S. (1989). Management buyouts: Evidence on taxes as a source of value. *The Journal of Finance*, *44*(3), 611–632. doi:10.1111/j.1540-6261.1989.tb04381.x

Leitterstorf, M. P., & Rau, S. B. (2014). Socioemotional wealth and IPO underpricing of family firms. *Strategic Management Journal*, *35*(5), 751–760. doi:10.1002mj.2236

Mao, Y., & Renneboog, L. (2015). Do managers manipulate earnings prior to management buyouts? *Journal of Corporate Finance*, *35*, 43–61. doi:10.1016/j.jcorpfin.2015.08.005

Meo, F. D., Lara, J. M. G., & Surroca, J. M. (2017). Managerial entrenchment and earnings management. *Journal of Accounting and Public Policy*, *36*(5), 399–414. doi:10.1016/j.jaccpubpol.2017.07.003

Miller, D., Le Breton-Miller, I., Lester, R. H., & Cannella, A. A. Jr. (2007). Are family firms really superior performers? *Journal of Corporate Finance*, *13*(5), 829–858. doi:10.1016/j.jcorpfin.2007.03.004

Paiva, I. S., Lourenco, I. C., & Branco, M. C. (2016). Earnings management in family firms: Current state of knowledge and opportunities for future research. *Review of Accounting and Finance*, *15*(1), 85–100. doi:10.1108/RAF-06-2014-0065

Perry, S., & Williams, T. (1994). Earnings management preceding management buyout offers. *Journal of Accounting and Economics*, *18*(2), 157–179. doi:10.1016/0165-4101(94)00362-9

Prencipe, A., Bar-Yosef, S., & Dekker, H. C. (2014). Accounting research in family firms: Theoretical and empirical challenges. *European Accounting Review*, *23*(3), 361–385. doi:10.1080/09638180.2014.895621

Prencipe, A., Markarian, G., & Pozza, L. (2008). Earnings management in family firms: Evidence from R&D cost capitalization in Italy. *Family Business Review*, *21*(1), 71–88. doi:10.1111/j.1741-6248.2007.00112.x

Salvato, C., & Moores, K. (2010). Research on accounting in family firms: Past accomplishments and future challenges. *Family Business Review*, *23*(3), 193–215. doi:10.1177/0894486510375069

Scholes, L., Westhead, P., & Burrows, A. (2008). Family firm succession: The management buy-out and buy-in routes. *Journal of Small Business and Enterprise Development*, *15*(1), 8–30. doi:10.1108/14626000810850829

Schulze, W. S., Lubatkin, M., & Dino, R. N. (2003). Exploring the agency consequences of ownership dispersion among the directors of private family firms. *Academy of Management Journal*, *45*(2), 179–194.

Schulze, W. S., Lubatkin, M., Dino, R. N., & Buchholtz, A. K. (2001). Agency relationships in family firms: Theory and evidence. *Organization Science*, *12*(2), 99–116. doi:10.1287/orsc.12.2.99.10114

Stockmans, A., Lybaert, N., & Voordeckers, W. (2010). Socioemotional wealth and earnings management in private family firms. *Family Business Review*, *23*(3), 280–294. doi:10.1177/0894486510374457

Strömberg, P. (2008). The new demography of private equity. *The Global Impact of Private Equity Report*, *2008*, 3–26.

Teoh, S. H., Welch, I., & Wong, T. J. (1998). Earnings management and the long run performance of initial public offerings. *The Journal of Finance*, *53*(6), 1935–1974. doi:10.1111/0022-1082.00079

Tong, Y. H. (2007). Financial reporting practices of family firms. *Advances in Accounting*, *23*, 231–261. doi:10.1016/S0882-6110(07)23009-3

Tutuncu, L. (2019). Earnings management and performance of management buyouts. *Managerial Finance*, *45*(10-11), 1363–1381. doi:10.1108/MF-01-2018-0007

Walker, M. (2013). How far can we trust earnings numbers? What research tells us about earnings management? *Accounting and Business Research*, *43*(4), 445–481. doi:10.1080/00014788.2013.785823

Wang, D. (2006). Founding family ownership and earnings quality. *Journal of Accounting Research*, *44*(3), 619–656. doi:10.1111/j.1475-679X.2006.00213.x

Weir, C., Laing, D., & Wright, M. (2005). Undervaluation, private information, agency costs and the decision to go private. *Applied Financial Economics*, *15*(13), 947–961. doi:10.1080/09603100500278221

Westhead, P. (1997). Ambitions, external environment and strategic factor differences between family and non-family companies. *Entrepreneurship and Regional Development*, *9*(2), 127–157. doi:10.1080/08985629700000007

Westhead, P., & Howorth, C. (2006). Ownership and management issues associated with family firm performance and company objectives. *Family Business Review*, *19*(4), 301–316. doi:10.1111/j.1741-6248.2006.00077.x

Wilson, N., Wright, M., & Scholes, L. (2013). Family business survival and the role of boards. *Entrepreneurship Theory and Practice*, *37*(6), 1369–1389. doi:10.1111/etap.12071

Wright, M., Thompson, S., & Robbie, K. (1992). Venture capital and management-led, leveraged buy-outs: A European perspective. *Journal of Business Venturing*, *7*(1), 47–71. doi:10.1016/0883-9026(92)90034-O

Wu, W. Y. (1997). Management buyouts and earnings management. *Journal of Accounting, Auditing & Finance*, *12*(4), 373–389. doi:10.1177/0148558X9701200402

KEY TERMS AND DEFINITIONS

Discretionary Accruals: Deviation of accruals from the estimated normal accruals, computed as total accruals minus non-discretionary (normal) accruals.

Family Firm: A firm majority owned, controlled, and managed by multiple family members connected by blood or marriage.

Lead Family Owner (LFO): A member of family owning at least 50% of firm equity.

Lead Non-Family Owner (LNFO): A non-family or standalone entrepreneur owning at least than 50% of firm equity.

Management Buyout: Takeover of a firm by its incumbent manager(s) often with the assistance of private equity sponsors and high leverage.

Non-Discretionary Accruals: Accruals arising from normal activities, estimated via modified Jones models and private control firms.

Owner Manager: A non-family entrepreneur in non-listed firms holding substantial equity and managerial positions, often as a lone founder and shareholder.

APPENDIX

Table 8. List of variables and definitions

Variables	Definition	Source
FM_OWN FDUMMY	Cumulative percentage of common shares owned by family members (for family firms) or owner/managers (for non-family firms) at time t-1 (year preceding the MBO). Dummy variable, equal to 1 if family firm at time t-1, 0 otherwise.	Annual report and return filings. Own construction.
FOWN	Cumulative percentage of common shares owned by family members in a family firm at time t-1.	Annual report and return filings.
NFMOWN	Cumulative percentage of common shares owned by owner/managers in a non-family firm at time t-1.	Annual report and return filings.
BOARDCONTROL	Proportion of family members (for family firms) or owner/managers (for non-family firms) on board one year prior to MBO transaction.	Annual reports.
LEADOWNER	Dummy variable, equal to one if one member of family or owner/manager holds at least 50% of common shares or voting rights, zero otherwise.	Annual report and return filings.
HERF	Herfindahl Index is calculated as sum of squared percentage ownership of all blockholders at time t-1 and takes values between 0 and 1. Higher values indicate higher ownership concentration.	Annual report and return filings.
DTA	Discretionary total accruals at time t-1, estimated using corresponding industry-year regressions.	Fame, own estimation.
DCA	Discretionary current accruals at time t-1, estimated using corresponding industry-year regressions.	Fame, own estimation.
PERF	Net income at time t-1, divided by total assets at time t-1.	Fame.
MPERF	Industry adjusted net income divided by total assets one year prior to MBO transaction, matched on year and 2-digit SIC code.	Fame, own estimation.
SIZE	Natural logarithm of total assets at time t-1.	Fame.
GROWTH	Change in sales from t-2 to t-1. Year t-1 is one year prior to MBO.	Fame.
AGE	Firm age is calculated as MBO deal year minus incorporation year.	Fame.
AUDIT	Dummy variable, equal to one if the firm is audited by a BIG4 auditor (Deloitte, PWC, KPMG, EY) at time t-1, zero otherwise.	Fame, annual reports.
PE	Dummy variable, equal to one, if the firm is subsequently backed by a private equity investor in MBO, zero otherwise.	Thomson One Banker.
INST	Dummy variable, equal to one if the firm has institutional shareholder at time t-1, zero otherwise.	Annual return filings.
LOSS	Dummy variable, equal to one if net income at time t-1 is less than zero, zero otherwise.	Fame.
IFRS	Dummy variable, equal to one if the firm applies IFRS, zero if applies UK GAAP.	Annual reports.

Chapter 4
Earnings Management and Stock Liquidity:
Evidence From Turkey

Hakan Özkaya
https://orcid.org/0000-0001-7810-5943
Dokuz Eylul University, Turkey

ABSTRACT

This chapter tests whether the earnings management practices in Turkey are considered informative or opportunistic by outside investors by examining its effect on stock liquidity. Earnings management is measured by discretionary accruals calculated by two different competing methods. Stock liquidity is also proxied by two different measures: the illiquidity measure of Amihud and the turnover ratio. Amihud's illiquidity measure indicates firms' daily price responses associated with the trading volume and the turnover ratio indicates how many times a stock changes its owner in a year. Relevant control variables are also included in the models. A positive association between earnings management and stock liquidity implies informative earnings management and vice versa. Earnings management is found to be positively associated with stock market liquidity. Results favor the informative earnings management view for Turkish firms and are robust to alternative specifications of earnings management and stock liquidity measures.

1. INTRODUCTION

Earnings management can be defined as the managers' purposeful interventions to mislead some stakeholders about the firm's true performance (Schipper, 1989; Healy and Wahlen, 1999). The fact that this "true performance" does not always necessarily mean "a bad performance" is the central intuition behind this study.

Earnings management is a heavily researched phenomenon, and a lot is known about the adverse effects of earnings management. The characteristic feature of definitions of earnings management is that they draw attention to its adverse effects. The vast majority of the previous literature has indeed

DOI: 10.4018/978-1-7998-7596-3.ch004

provided abundant evidence on these adverse effects. The concise bottom-line of the literature is that earnings management is not favored due to its misleading nature. However, in this chapter, whether there might be some favorable outcomes of earnings management or not is inquired. In a sense, the stream of research, including this one and its antecedents, attempts to reveal some favorable outcomes of earnings management.

It is known both intuitively and from agency costs literature that managers are better informed about firms' prospects, and they have different motivations for engaging in earning management practices. Another known fact from the literature is that using discretionary accruals is the most common way of managing earnings. Managers might manage their earnings not only to conceal their bad performance but also to reveal their good performance based on their motivation.

This chapter draws investors and scholars' attention to one of the very few favorable outcomes of earnings management. Earnings management is not solely "opportunistic", but it is sometimes "informative". That is, it can be beneficial to shareholders even by concealing information. This study is the first to examine the relationship between earnings management and stock liquidity for Turkey where there is a relatively weaker equity culture, a dominant of long-term debt finance and less legal protection. Results contribute to the scarce literature by providing additional evidence for a debated issue of the "informative" versus "opportunistic" earnings management from an emerging market.

Disentangling earnings management into opportunistic and informative parts enables scholars and practitioners to better understand the effectiveness of the mechanisms employed to prevent or at least minimize the overall earnings management. From an academic point of view this may be one of the possible explanations of the conflicting results in earning management literature. When some of the mechanisms that serve to both aspects of earnings management at various degrees, they would be inappropriately labeled as having no effect on overall earnings management. From the practitioners' point of view, the financial consequences of their reporting actions would be more predictable as they comprehend informative earnings management. On the other hand, as investors become more aware of informative earnings management, they would prioritize their investments on companies with informative earnings management as opposed to opportunistic earnings management.

The objective of this chapter is to examine the effect of earnings management on stock liquidity in an emerging country market. Since the liquidity of stocks proxies the degree of informativeness about the stock, the association between earnings management and stock liquidity enables us to test whether the earnings management practices in Turkey are considered as informative or opportunistic by the outside investors.

2. EARNINGS MANAGEMENT IN TURKEY

There is a bunch of literature on Turkey that modeled earnings management as the dependent variable and investigated the effects of particular characteristics on earnings management.

The relationship between corporate governance and earnings management was heavily investigated for Turkey. Their findings on the effect of various aspects of corporate governance on earnings management are mixed. Önder (2012) reports that while; block ownership, managerial ownership, audit committee size and management board size increase earnings management, the independence of the audit committee and the independence of management board decrease earnings management practices. Memiş and Çetenak (2012) investigated the association between corporate governance characteristics and earnings management. They report that while board size and audit by big 4 four audit firms reduce earnings management practices, there is no significant association between ISE corporate governance index, ownership concentration, CEO duality and earnings management. However, Yaşar (2013) argues that there is no difference between the earnings management practices of firms audited by Big Four audit companies and those audited by non-Big Four companies. Adıgüzel (2013) investigated the effectiveness of corporate governance practices like independent boards, audit committees, and internal audits in family-owned firms. Her results suggest that total accruals management is lower in family-owned firms when compared to that in non-family-owned firms. Aygun et al. (2014) investigated the impact of corporate ownership (managerial ownership and institutional ownership) and board size on earnings management. They report that while institutional ownership and the board size have a significant negative effect on earnings management, managerial ownership has a statistically significant positive impact on earnings management. Cengiz, Gör and Terzi (2016) also investigated the relationship between earnings management and corporate governance (institutional management, the board size, board independence, board members' ownership ratio, institutional investor's percentage, independence of inspection committee, the size of inspection committee). The authors did not report any significant relationship between corporate governance and earnings management. Yavuzaslan and Kalmış (2016) report that; non-executive members of the board of directors and the audit committee and audit committee size were found to reduce earnings management. They also report that firm size, measured by total assets, was found to increase earnings management practices.

Using quarterly data between 2006 and 2009, Karaibrahimoğlu (2010) found that Turkish firms are engaged in income decreasing discretionary accruals, but the discretionary accruals tend to decrease following the adoption of IFRS in 2005. Karaibrahimoğlu (2010) reports that firms that are audited by one of the Big 4 Audit Companies and industry specialized audit companies have less income decreasing earnings management practices. Audit firm tenure also constrains earnings management practices. These results are also backed by Özcan (2019) who analyzes the effect of audit quality in terms of auditor independence, audit industry specialization and auditor tenure on earnings management in the period 2013 to 2018. Karaibrahimoğlu (2010) further reports that the independence of the board of directors does not limit earnings management but increase such practices. Board size was also find less effective in constraining earnings management. Moreover, CEO duality has a positive association with income increasing earnings management. The presence of the institutional owner, ownership concentration and blockholdership, which are internal corporate governance characteristics that are thought to constrain earnings management, was found to have no association with earnings management. Karaibrahimoğlu (2010) argued that the subsistence, magnitude and direction of the relation between corporate governance and earnings management change over time, thus it is not a straightforward task to capture the relationship between corporate governance and earnings management.

Gündüz (2016) aims at determining the characteristics of earnings management practices in Turkey. She reports that the average of discretionary accruals for Turkish firms between 2013 and 2015 shows a normal distribution, revealing that there is no significant effect of economic development on total accruals. She also reports that Turkish firms were involved in revenue increasing practices in 2014 and revenue decreasing practices in 2013 and 2015. The impact of global financial crisis of 2008 on earnings management is investigated by Türegün (2020) for the period of 2007–2012. Her results indicated increase in earnings management practices in the postcrisis period in Turkey. Cengiz, Dilsiz and Aslanoğlu (2016) tested the relationship between dividend policy and earnings management, but their results revealed no significant relationship. Kaya and Yazan (2017) report that corporate social responsibility decreases earnings management and hence enhances the accounting information quality for Turkish firms. Besides financial performance, the difficulty of audit and debt financing also increase earnings management. Arioglu (2020a) tests whether presence of female directors and their attributes affect earnings quality, but he reports no such association.

One of the recent works conducted on the different perspectives of earnings management in Turkey is Arioglu (2020b). Focusing on the conservatism levels of provinces of birth of company chairmen, he investigates whether the intentions behind earnings management in Turkey is opportunistic or informative by using a sample of non-financial companies quoted at the Borsa Istanbul. He concludes that the managers of Turkish companies are engages in earnings management with an informative intent.

This study differs from this stream of literature by investigating the earnings management as one of the independent variables determining stock liquidity. Above all, so far, there is no research done on the relationship between the earnings management and stock liquidity of Turkish firms.

3. THEORETICAL BACKGROUND

Buckmaster (1997), who reviewed the antecedents of modern earnings management research, states that Hepworth (1953) was the first publication on income smoothing which makes it one of the most prominent antecedents of earnings management literature. Income smoothing is defined as "a form of earnings management designed to remove peaks and valleys from a normal earnings series" (Mulford and Comiskey, 2002:3)

Hepworth (1953) argued that the significance of periodic net income had increased as opposed to balance sheet information and he surveyed some accounting techniques that apply to smoothing or leveling the magnitude of periodic net income fluctuations. He considered the motivators for income smoothing like the existence of tax levies, better management relations with investors and workers, reducing the effect of waves of optimism and pessimism. He listed accounting techniques to the smoothing of periodic income as; manipulation of gross revenue, deferred charge and intangible asset accounting, valuation of inventory, property accounting (acquisition of plant assets, depreciation rates and methods), reserve accounting and treatment of non-recurring charges or credit. (Hepworth, 1953). Schipper (1989) equates earnings management with "disclosure management" and defines earnings management as "the purposeful intervention of managers in the external financial reporting processes with the intent of gaining some private gain" (Schipper, 1989: 92). Mulford and Comiskey (2002:3) define earnings management as "the active manipulation of earnings toward a predetermined target."

Healy (1985) argued and documented that managers can choose accounting procedures and use discretion on accruals to maximize their bonus awards. They show that managers choose either income-decreasing accruals or income-increasing accruals dependent upon their bonus plans. Although Healy (1985) did not use the term "earnings management" explicitly, this paper is also one of the earliest works that postulate the selection of accounting practices by managers to increase their bonuses. Healy and Wahlen (1999) define earnings management as altering financial reports by managers to mislead some stakeholders about the company's performance or to influence contractual outcomes dependent on the financial reports. The misled stakeholders can sometimes be the government, sometimes the creditors, sometimes the current shareholders or sometimes outside investors, etc. Managers alter financial reports by exercising judgments in preparing financial statements. They are required to use judgments in estimating some future economic events (i.e., expected lives, salvage values, obligations for future benefits, deferred taxes, losses from bad debts, etc.), in choosing an accounting method (i.e., valuation methods, depreciation methods, etc.). Managers are also required to use their judgments in managing working capital (i.e., policies regarding inventory and receivables, etc.) and structuring of corporate transactions (i.e., keeping of lease obligations on or off-balance sheet, etc.) (Healy and Wahlen, 1999).

There is an information asymmetry on the financial outcomes between managers and outside investors. This asymmetry lessens as disclosure gets more qualified and is exacerbated as accurate financial information is masked intentionally. Earnings management is one of the very influential practices that increases information asymmetry between insiders and other stakeholders (Park and Shin, 2004; Bar-Yosef and Prencipe, 2013).

Gul et al. (2003) categorize earnings management as "informative" and "opportunistic" based on the private information held by the managers. They categorize the earnings management as "informative" if the private information of the managers is high value relevant. Otherwise, they categorize earnings management as "opportunistic." They provide an example to clarify the decomposition of any given discretionary accruals into informative earnings management and opportunistic earnings management. Let us assume that a manager estimates her company's earnings as $2 per share by using her expertise and private information but due to the reporting standards resulting earnings are $1.95 per share without any managing of earnings. If the manager uses discretionary accruals to increase the earnings to $2 per share, then it would be informative earnings management. If she uses income increasing discretionary accruals to manage the earnings to more than $2 per share (say $2.10 per share), then the remaining part would be opportunistic earnings management. It is not possible to judge whether the earnings management is informative or opportunistic ex-ante, which constitutes the effective limitation in the execution of scientific research on the subject. One can only observe the perception of stakeholders by their responses to reported earnings.

Putra and Mela (2019) examine the effect of ownership types (i.e., managerial ownership, institutional ownership, foreign ownership) on informative earnings management on a sample of Indonesian manufacturing companies. Informative earnings management is captured by a dummy variable that compared discretionary accruals and earnings growth. Their results show that while managerial ownership has no effect on informative earnings management, institutional and foreign ownership enhance informative earnings management. In their recent work, Shoaib and Siddiqui (2020) identify the impact of earning management, earning quality, accrual quality on the earning information content for countries of Asia Pacific Trade Agreement (APTA) (China, India, Bangladesh, Sri Lanka, and Pakistan). They investigated whether the managers' intentions of the earning management are opportunistic or efficient. They detected opportunistic behavior of earning management for all countries in their sample except for Bangladesh. Not only accrual-based earnings management but also real earnings management is investigated in terms of its effect on informativeness about the company. Li (2019) investigates the effect of real earnings management on earnings' informativeness about future cash flows and concludes that real earnings management deteriorates earnings quality in terms of persistence and informativeness.

Earnings management is defined as the act of managers' using judgment in preparing financial statements to mislead some stakeholders about the true performance of the company (Healy and Wahlen, 1999). Chung et al. (2009) define earnings management as the intentional use of discretion in the financial statements to manage the company's financial results. These definitions (as many others do) highlight and reveal the opportunistic facet of earnings management. If managers distort or conceal information to mask their poor performance, this type of earnings management is called opportunistic. Managers who engage in opportunistic earnings management decrease transparency, accuracy, and disclosure quality (Al-Jaifi, 2017). The liquidity of stock markets is highly influenced by the information asymmetries created by weak investor protection (Brockman and Chung, 2003). Because one of the effects of opportunistic earnings management is higher adverse selection costs (Chung et al.,2009) and earnings management worsens the information asymmetry (Bar-Yosef and Prencipe 2013), higher earnings management is expected to lead to lower stock liquidity.

Verrecchia (1986) proposes an analytical model, which suggests that managers chose the "post outcome costly action" when faced with private information. They argue that this costly action yields more accurate financial reports and the condition that the principal (i.e., investors) allow agents (i.e., managers) is dependent on the improvement in profit. Demski (1998) provides a two-period model showing manipulation of financial information (i.e., performance measure) might be socially efficient and may be motivated contingent upon the content of the information. These models suggest that managers' engaging in earnings management is not solely opportunistic but sometimes informative. Arya et al. (2003) also argue that earnings management can be beneficial to shareholders even by concealing information. Jiraporn et al. (2008) provide evidence supporting an alternative view of earnings management's effect. Although the detrimental effects of earnings management on information quality are mostly posited, it can be informative as well. They provide empirical evidence that firms engage in more earnings management suffer fewer agency costs, and hence, they document a positive association between earnings management and firm value.

The relationship between several corporate governance and control characteristics and stock liquidity was investigated in the literature. Some papers examine the relationship between institutional ownership and stock liquidity and report that as institutional ownership increase, stock liquidity increase (Dang et al. (2018); Ali and Hashmi (2018); Hunjra et al. (2020); Rubin (2007); Yaghoobnezhad et al. (2011)). Evidence on the effect of ownership concentration on stock liquidity is mixed. While some papers report a negative association between ownership concentration and stock market liquidity (Jacoby and Zheng (2010); Leano and Pedraza (2018); Rubin (2007); Al-Sharif et al. (2015), Yosra and Sioud (2011); Yaghoobnezhad et al. (2011), Staglianò et al. (2017)), a recent paper by Hunjra et al. (2020) report a positive association.

There is a bunch of literature that examines the relationship between stock liquidity and earnings management as earnings management is the dependent variable and the stock liquidity is the independent variable. Chen et al. (2015) employ earnings management as the proxy for managerial short-termism. Accrual based earnings management is measured by the discretionary accruals while real earnings management is measured by; abnormal production costs, abnormal discretionary expenses and abnormal operating cash. Along with some control variables, the independent variable stock liquidity is measured as the relative effective spread. Their results show that; stock liquidity is associated with less earnings management in both accrual-based and real terms. On the other hand, Huang et al. (2017) argue that there is a positive association between stock liquidity and accrual-based earnings management. They support their argument by commonly used regression models and their difference-in-differences estimation accounting for exogenous shocks.

Parallel to analytical studies, evidence stems from empirical studies regarding the relationship between earnings management and stock liquidity is mixed. Results of Chung et al. (2009) show that firms engaged in higher earnings management signal higher adverse selection costs and suffer lower equity liquidity. Ascioglu et al. (2012) argue that earnings management increases information asymmetry, and their results show that greater earnings management is associated with lower market liquidity. Ajina and Habib (2017) report wider bid-ask spreads for firms that engage in earnings management and provide evidence that information quality improves stock market liquidity for a sample of French firms from 2008 to 2011. Using a sample of companies from Pakistan, India, Australia and Singapore, Hunjra et al. (2020) report that earnings management has a negative effect on stock market liquidity. They argue that the reliability of companies' financial statements, which engage in earnings management practices, are lower. On the other hand, Riahi et al. (2013) report a positive and significant relationship between earnings management and market liquidity in the Tunisian market. Al-Jaifi (2017) provides supporting evidence for the favorable informative earnings management view. Their analyses show that the liquidity of firms with high earnings management is improved.

Based on the competing views and evidence in the literature, the chapter's central hypothesis can be formulated as follows:

H_0: There is a negative relationship between earnings management and stock market liquidity.

4. RESEARCH METHODOLOGY

4.1. Model

Following regression model is estimated to test the relationship between earnings management and stock market liquidity:

$$\begin{aligned} ILLIQ_{i,t} &= \beta_0 + \beta_1 ERNMAN_{i,t} + \beta_2 SIZE_{i,t} + \beta_3 LEV_{i,t} \\ &+ \beta_4 ROA_{i,t} + \beta_5 TANG_{i,t} + \beta_6 VOLT_{i,t} + \beta_7 1 / PRICE_{i,t} + \varepsilon_{i,t} \end{aligned} \tag{1}$$

In this equation, ILLIQ is the illiquidity measure, which is the daily price response to one unit of the trading volume. ERNMAN is the earnings management variable measured as the absolute discretionary accruals, SIZE variable is the logarithm of total assets, LEV is the leverage ratio which is the total debt divided by total assets, ROA is the variable for profitability and measured as the net income divided by total assets, TANG is the tangibility variable and measured as net property, plant, and equipment divided by total assets, VOLT is the volatility variable and is calculated as the standard deviation of daily returns, 1/PRICE is the inverse of year-end prices, and ε is the error term.

Both Pearson's and Spearman's rank-order correlation coefficients between variables are calculated to check for multicollinearity. The differences between two sets of values are taken into consideration by Pearson, while changes in rank order are calculated by Spearman. The correlation matrix is presented in Table 1. Pearson's correlation coefficients r are displayed in the lower-half while Spearman's rank-order correlation coefficients ρ are shown in the upper half of the matrix. All correlation coefficients are below the critical values, which indicate that there is no multicollinearity problem for independent variables.

Table 1. Correlation Matrix for Independent Variables

	ERNMAN	LEV	ROA	TANG	SIZE	VOLT	PRICEINV
ERNMAN		0.019	-0.004	-0.106**	-0.033	0.019	0.065*
LEV	0.033		-0.450	-0.035	0.101**	0.164**	0.023
ROA	-0.005	-0.010**		-0.162**	0.280**	-0.327**	-0.393**
TANG	-0.106**	-0.017	-0.087**		0.064*	-0.016	-0.014
SIZE	-0.043	0.039	0.041	-0.006		-0.433**	-0.295**
VOLT	0.045	0.148**	-0.093**	-0.005	-0.120**		0.243**
PRICEINV	0.010	0.119**	-0.160**	-0.011	-0.149**	0.192**	

Pearson's correlation r (lower-half), Spearman's rank-order correlation ρ (upper-half), ERNMAN (earnings management) is absolute discretionary accruals, SIZE is the logarithm of total assets, LEV (leverage) is the total debt divided by total assets, ROA (Return on Assets) is the net income divided by total assets, TANG (Tangibility) is the net property, plant, and equipment divided by total assets, VOLT (Volatility) is the standard deviation of daily returns, 1/PRICE is the inverse of year-end prices.

* Correlation is significant at the 0.05 level (2-tailed).

** Correlation is significant at the 0.01 level (2-tailed).

4.2. Sample

The sample of this study is comprised of 119 Turkish manufacturing firms, which are listed in Borsa İstanbul throughout 2006 and 2017. For the sake of uniformity and comparability in financial reports, the starting year of the analysis period is chosen as 2005 when all listed firms in Turkey adopted the International Financial Reporting Standards. Using of lagged variables in estimating discretionary accruals hindered using variables in 2005 in the overall analyses. Due to some missing data during the analysis period, the final data set consists of 1,185 firm-year observations. The stock market variables are taken from DataStream, and other firm characteristics are taken from WorldScope databases. The descriptive statistics for the sample are presented in Table 2.

4.3. Data and Variable Description

4.3.1. Liquidity Measure

Stock market liquidity is measured by using Amihud's (2002) illiquidity formula. This very widely used measure has both a robust theoretical appeal and ease of computation. It enables the researchers to capture, month by month, variations in the illiquidity. It is also documented to be the best among proxies employed to capture Kyle's lambda (Marcelo and Quirós, 2006). It measures how much one unit of trading volume result in absolute price change by showing the daily price responses to one-dollar unit of trading volume (Prommin et al., 2014).

The illiquidity measure of stock i in year y is calculated as:

$$ILLIQ_{i,y} = \frac{1}{D_{i,y}} \sum_{t=0}^{D_{i,y}} \frac{|R_{i,y,d}|}{VOL_{i,y,d}} \quad (2)$$

where; $|R_{i,y,d}|$ is the absolute return on stock i on day d of year y; $VOL_{i,y,d}$ is the daily volume of stock i on day d of year y in Turkish Liras; $D_{i,y}$ is the number of the trading days for stock i in year y. Illiquidity ratio shows the average daily absolute change associated with one Turkish Lira of the trading volume. The higher the values of the ratio, the lower the stock liquidity.

Table 2. Descriptive Statistics of Variables

	Mean	Median	Max.	Min.	Std. Dev.	Number of Observations
ILLIQ	2.77E-07	2.46E-08	7.84E-05	9.40E-11	2.87E-06	1,185
ERNMAN1	-0.0010	-0.007	0.441	-0.256	0.091	1,185
LEV	0.502	0.451	8.674	0.027	0.470	1,185
ROA	0.040	0.039	6.805	-2.885	0.240	1,185
TANG	0.365	0.363	0.911	0.005	0.167	1,185
SIZE	1.22E+09	3.07E+08	3.82E+10	7.54E+06	3.09E+09	1,185
VOLT	0.027	0.025	0.221	0.010	0.013	1,185
PRICEINV	0.537	0.318	7.946	0.003	0.680	1,185

ILLIQ is the Amihud (2002)'s illiquidity measure calculated as the daily price response to one unit of trading volume, ERNMAN (earnings management) is absolute discretionary accruals, SIZE is the logarithm of total assets, LEV (leverage) is the total debt divided by total assets, ROA (Return on Assets) is the net income divided by total assets, TANG (Tangibility) is the net property, plant, and equipment divided by total assets, VOLT (Volatility) is the standard deviation of daily returns, 1/PRICE is the inverse of year-end prices

4.3.2. Earnings Management Measure

Financial manipulation is mostly conducted by using the accruals basis of accounting (Findik and Öztürk, 2016). Thus, following prior research, discretionary accruals are used as the measure of earnings management. Being one of the most widely used proxies of earnings management, discretionary accruals, cannot be observed. The most common way of measuring discretionary accruals is to calculate the total accruals using accounting relations and to estimate non-discretionary accruals by using regressors. The discretionary accruals are what remains when non-discretionary accruals are subtracted from total accruals. Total accruals are calculated by using the cash flow approach. Total accruals (by using cash flow approach) are calculated as follows:

$$TAcc_{i,t} = NetInc_{i,t} - CFO_{i,t}$$

where;

$TAcc_{i,t}$ = Total accruals of firm i in year t;

$NetInc_{i,t}$ = Net income of firm i in year t;

$CFO_{i,t}$ = Cash flows from operations of firm i in year t.

In this study, a performance matched discretionary measure model by Kothari et al. (2005) was used. Kothari et al. (2005) adjust the modified Jones model by adding performance measure, which is the ROA. So the non-discretionary accruals are estimated by using the equation below:

$$TAcc_{i,t} / A_{i,t-1} = \beta_0 + \beta_1 \left(1 / A_{i,t-1}\right) + \beta_2 \left(\Delta Rev_{i,t} - \Delta AR_{i,t}\right) / A_{i,t-1}\big) \\ +\beta_3 \left(PPE_{i,t} / A_{i,t-1}\right) + \beta_3 ROA_{i,t} + \varepsilon_{i,t} \quad (3)$$

where;

$TAcc_{i,t}$ = Total accruals of firm *i* in year *t*,

$A_{i,t-1}$ = Total assets of firm *i* in year *t-1*,

$\Delta Rev_{i,t}$ = Change in revenues of firm i from year *t-1* to *t*,

$\Delta AR_{i,t}$ = Change in net account receivables of firm *i* from year *t-1* to *t*,

$PPE_{i,t}$ = Gross property, plant, and equipment of firm *i* in year *t*,

$ROA_{i,t}$ = Return on assets of firm *i* in year *t*,

$\varepsilon_{i,t}$ = Error term of firm *i* in year *t*.

Equation 3 is estimated by using the Ordinary-Least Squares (OLS) cross-sectional regression for each separate year to determine the coefficients of β_0, β_1, β_2 and β_3. The fitted values calculated by using these coefficients give the non-discretionary accruals. The difference between the observed values and the fitted values (i.e., the residuals) proxies the discretionary accruals.

4.3.3. Control Variables

Although the main research question to be answered is how earnings management affects stock market liquidity, several control variables, which are found to be associated with liquidity in the literature, are employed in empirical analyses.

The first control variable is the firm size, measured by the book value of total assets. Firm size is used as a proxy for the degree of public information available for the investors (Harris, 1994). Bigger companies are assumed to be with a higher level of public information. Thus, a positive association is expected between firm size and liquidity. Tangibility variable, measured as net property, plant, and equipment divided by total assets, is included. Since payoffs of tangible assets are easier to observe, firms with relatively more tangible assets in their asset structure are less prone to asymmetric information problems (Chung et al., 2010). Firms with more liquidity stocks are assumed to have a lower cost of equity, which encourages these firms to be financed by equity over debt. Hence leverage, which is measured as the total debt divided by total assets, is expected to have an inverse association with liquidity measure (Udomsirikul et al., 2011). Following previous literature (Ascioglu et al., 2012; Al-Jaifi, 2017) profitability, volatility, and stock price measures are also used as control variables. Profitability is measured as the net income divided by total assets; the volatility is calculated as the standard deviation of daily returns and effect of price on liquidity is controlled by using the inverse of year-end prices in the regression estimations.

4.4. Robustness Check

To add robustness to the study results, alternative measures of the variables of interest are used. Discretionary accruals, which is used as the earnings management variable, is also calculated by using total accruals calculated by using the balance sheet approach. Total accruals calculated by the balance sheet approach (also known as the indirect approach) will serve as a robustness check as this method is documented to be more erroneous in the literature (Hribar and Collins, 2002).

Total accruals (by using the balance sheet approach) are calculated as follows:

$$TAcc_{i,t} = \left(\Delta CA_{i,t} - \Delta Cash_{i,t}\right) - \left(\Delta CL_{i,t} - \Delta LTD_{i,t}\right) - DepExp_{i,t} \quad (4)$$

where;

$TAcc_{i,t}$ = Total accruals of firm *i* in year *t*,
$\Delta CA_{i,t}$ = Change in total current assets of firm i from year *t-1* to *t*,
$\Delta Cash_{i,t}$ = Change in cash and cash equivalents of firm i from year *t-1* to *t*,
$\Delta CL_{i,t}$ = Change in total current liabilities of firm i from year *t-1* to *t*,
$\Delta LTD_{i,t}$ = Change in long term debt of firm i from year *t-1* to *t*,
$DepExp_{i,t}$ = Depreciation and amortization expense of firm *i* in year *t*.

The dependent variable, stock liquidity, is also calculated using an alternative approach to add more robustness to the results. Turnover ratio is the total trading volume (in terms of the number of shares) in a particular year divided by the total number of shares outstanding in that year. The turnover ratio, which is presented below, indicates how many times a stock changes its owner in a year. Thus, the higher the turnover ratio, the more the liquidity (Al-Jaifi, 2017).

$$TURN_{i,y} = \sum_{t=0}^{D_{i,y}} \frac{Vol_{i,y}}{N_{i,y}} \quad (5)$$

where $Vol_{i,y}$ is the total number of shares traded, while $N_{i,y}$ is the total number of shares outstanding.

5. RESULTS

To test the effect of earnings management on stock liquidity, Equation (1) is estimated using two different measures of earnings management and liquidity. The results of the estimations for four models are presented in Table 3. T-values are presented in parentheses below the regression coefficients. Model 1 employs the main dependent and independent variables of the study where the illiquidity measure of Amihud (2002) is the dependent variable (see Equation (2)) and the discretionary accruals estimated by using cash flow approach for total accruals (see Equation (3)). Model 2, Model 3, and Model 4 employ variations of alternative measures of illiquidity and discretionary accruals. These models serve as a robustness check to the main model of the study. To control for autocorrelation, time and cross-section pooled data is clustered at the firm level. To control autocorrelation and heteroskedasticity, the equations are estimated using Generalized Least Square (GLS) with cross-section weights. Moreover, White (1980) robust standard errors are estimated.

Table 3. Regression Results

	Model 1	Model 2	Model 3	Model 4
Dependent Variable	**LOG(ILLIQ)**	**LOG(ILLIQ)**	**LOG(TURN)**	**LOG(TURN)**
Independent Variables				
Intercept	-5.305	-4.827	6.357	5.985
	(-12.489)***	(-11.468)***	(18.097)***	(16.692)***
ERNMAN1	-0.958		0.748	
	(-1.846)*		(1.816)*	
ERNMAN2		-0.707		0.362
		(-5.054)***		(3.636)***
LEV	0.050	0.136	0.290	0.243
	(0.563)	(1.424)	(3.311)***	(2.816)***
ROA	0.140	-0.010	-0.720	-0.685
	(0.770)	(-0.049)	(-3.872)***	(-3.749)***
TANG	1.242	1.168	-0.460	-0.426
	(7.009)***	(6.929)***	(-3.054)***	(-2.855)***
SIZE	-0.669	-0.690	-0.340	-0.319
	(-33.460)***	(-34.545)***	(-20.760)***	(-19.126)***
VOLT	4.515	4.929	32.210	30.933
	(1.821)*	(2.082)**	(11.410)***	(11.114)***
PRICEINV	0.564	0.491	-0.069	-0.062
	(13.319)***	(14.244)***	(-1.500)	(-1.400)
Adjusted R-square	0.632	0.705	0.429	0.422
F-statistic	291.182	411.813	128.071	126.249
Number of Clusters	119	119	119	119
Number of Observations	1,185	1,203	1,184	1,201

ILLIQ is the Amihud's (2002) illiquidity measure calculated as the daily price response to one unit of the trading volume. TURN is the turnover ratio indicating how many times a stock changes its owner in a year. ERNMAN1 (earnings management) is absolute discretionary accruals where total accruals are calculated using the cash flow approach. ERNMAN2 (earnings management) is absolute discretionary accruals where total accruals are calculated by using the balance sheet approach. LEV (leverage) is the total debt divided by total assets. ROA (Return on Assets) is the net income divided by total assets. TANG (Tangibility) is the net property, plant, and equipment divided by total assets. SIZE is the logarithm of total assets. VOLT (Volatility) is the standard deviation of daily returns, 1/PRICE is the inverse of year-end prices.

*Significant at the 0.1 level.

**Significant at the 0.05 level.

***Significant at the 0.01 level.

Table 3 shows that the coefficient of the EARNMAN1, which is the independent variable of this study, is -0.958 (t=-1.846) in Model 1. It is significantly negative at the 0.1 level. The negative relationship with the illiquidity proxy indicates a positive relationship with stock liquidity, implying that, on average, the liquidity of stocks increases with an increase in the earnings management level of companies. The positive effect of EARNMAN1 variable, which is the absolute discretionary accruals calculated by the cash flow approach, is robust. Its coefficient is also statistically significant and positive (0.748 with a t value of 1.816) in Model 3. Since the dependent variable of Model 3, the TURN variable, is a measure of stock liquidity, the positive coefficient positive of EARNMAN1 shows that stock liquidity is greater for higher levels of earnings management practices. This implication is robust to an alternative measure of earnings management as well. Table 3 shows that the coefficient of the EARNMAN2, which is the absolute discretionary accruals where total accruals are calculated using the balance sheet approach, is -0.707 (t=-5.054) and 0.748 (t=1.816) for the Model 2 and Model 3 respectively. These findings indicate that the positive association between earnings management practices and stock liquidity is even more significant with this alternative measure.

Table 3 shows that while the effect of leverage on Amihud's stock illiquidity measure is insignificant, it has a statistically positive effect on the turnover variable with coefficients of 0.290 (t=3.311) and 0.243 (t=2.816). It is the case for the profitability variable ROA as well. The profitability has no significant effect on the stock illiquidity measure (Models 1 and 2). Still, it has a significantly negative effect on the turnover variable with coefficients of -0.720 (t=-3.872) and -0.685 (t=-3.749) for Models 3 and 4, respectively. The tangibility variable, TANG, has a statistically significant negative effect on the stock liquidity, evidenced by all four models. While the PRICEINV variable's negative effect on illiquidity measure is statistically significant, its effect on the turnover ratio is also negative though not significant.

6. FUTURE RESEARCH DIRECTIONS

Future research can be directed towards measuring informative earnings management and test its specific effect on stock liquidity. Further theoretical models and their empirical tests that address the nature of the relationship between earnings management and stock liquidity will be valuable contributions. Last but not least consideration of real earnings management besides accrual earnings management in future research will add valuable insights to informative perspective of earnings management.

7. CONCLUSION

The relationship between the level of earnings management and stock liquidity was examined in this chapter. It is known from the literature that providing the market with more information yields higher stock liquidity, and people abstain from trading stocks with less information. Hence the basic argument of the chapter was that controlling for the known determinants; if stock liquidity increases with a higher level of earnings management, this indicates that there is a room of informativeness of earnings management. This chapter does not measure how much portion of the earnings management is informative and how much portion is opportunistic but merely observes the results.

The results of the study show that as the earnings management practices measured by the discretionary accruals increase, the stock liquidity also increases. This relationship implies that managing earnings by the managers is another way of attracting traders for their companies' stocks in the market. These results support the findings of Al-Jaifi (2017) and Riahi et al. (2013) but contrast with those of Ascioglu et al. (2012) and Chung et al. (2009). Al-Jaifi (2017) explains this peculiar effect with the relatively limited number of information sources about firm performance. That is, managers of companies in countries where there are limited ways of providing information about their companies' true performance are more motivated to convey their private information through informative earnings management. This explanation can be valid for Turkey's case as well. The fact that better corporate governance leads to less earnings management is highly evidenced in the literature. However, the results of Lin et al. (2016) that corporate governance has a positive impact on the informative earnings management modify this widely documented relationship and provide the basis for the results of this study. Stock liquidity is also a function of information asymmetry. Intuitively one can say that the higher the information asymmetry, the lower the stock liquidity. Thus, evidence that documents less information asymmetry for the underinvesting firms whose managers manage earnings also supports the results of this study (Rahman et al., 2013). Since underinvestment is one of the problems that exist relatively more often for firms in emerging markets, managers of these firms can be motivated to convey informational earnings management as implied by Rahman et al. (2013).

Some of the common features of emerging markets can be listed as; lacking legal regulations, deficiencies in applications of existent sanctions, lacking standardizations in accounting and auditing practices, few numbers of controlling groups dominating the significant portion of shares in the market, and limited capital movements in the stock market. Adiguzel (2013) characterizes the Turkish financial environment as weak equity culture, the dominance of long-term debt finance, and inadequate legal protection. Because the capital stock in Turkey is quite limited, both foreign and domestic investments in the Turkish stock market are crucial for Turkey to achieve sustainable growth and competitiveness and deal with the unemployment problem. Liquidity is one of the most desired features of well-functioning stock markets. Stock liquidity, one of the preconditions of health and depth of the stock market, becomes more important for emerging markets like Turkey.

Like every work this chapter is bounded with several limitations. First limitation is that the chapter does not employ proxies for opportunistic and informative earnings management separately. Measuring informative earnings management was beyond the scope of this chapter. Secondly, the positive relationship between earnings management and stock market liquidity is implicitly considered as a sign of informative perspective of earnings management outweighing its opportunistic perspective. However, this relationship may also be explained by other mechanisms besides informative earnings management that could not be controlled in the research design of this chapter. Thirdly, due to data availability earnings management measures are based on two traditional models in the chapter where there are other competing measures (some are arguably more powerful) in the literature.

REFERENCES

Adiguzel, H. (2013). Corporate governance, family ownership and earnings management: Emerging market evidence. *Accounting and Finance Research*, *2*(4), 17–33. doi:10.5430/afr.v2n4p17

Ajina, A., & Habib, A. (2017). Examining the relationship between earning management and market liquidity. *Research in International Business and Finance*, *42*, 1164–1172. doi:10.1016/j.ribaf.2017.07.054

Al-Jaifi, H. A. (2017). Ownership Concentration, Earnings Management and Stock Market Liquidity: Evidence from Malaysia. *Corporate Governance: The International Journal of Business in Society*, *17*(3), 490–510. doi:10.1108/CG-06-2016-0139

Ali, M. S., & Hashmi, S. H. (2018). Impact of institutional ownership on stock liquidity: Evidence from Karachi Stock Exchange, Pakistan. *Global Business Review*, *19*(4), 939–951. doi:10.1177/0972150918772927

Amihud, Y. (2002). Illiquidity and stock returns: Cross-section and time-series effects. *Journal of Financial Markets*, *5*(1), 31–56. doi:10.1016/S1386-4181(01)00024-6

Arioglu, E. (2020a). The affiliations and characteristics of female directors and earnings management: Evidence from Turkey. *Managerial Auditing Journal*, *35*(7), 927–953. doi:10.1108/MAJ-07-2019-2364

Arioglu, E. (2020b). *Upper Echelons Theory, Conservative Chairmen and Informative Earnings Management*. Available at: https://www.researchgate.net/profile/Emrah_Arioglu/publication/343657293_Upper_Echelons_Theory_Conservative_Chairmen_and_Informative_Earnings_Management/links/5f39367192851cd302faa29f/Upper-Echelons-Theory-Conservative-Chairmen-and-Informative-Earnings-Management.pdf

Arya, A., Glover, J. C., & Sunder, S. (2003). Are Unmanaged Earnings Always Better for Shareholders? *Accounting Horizons*, *17*(1), 111–116. doi:10.2308/acch.2003.17.s-1.111

Ascioglu, A., Hegde, S. P., Krishnan, G. V., & McDermott, J. B. (2012). Earnings management and market liquidity. *Review of Quantitative Finance and Accounting*, *38*(2), 257–274. doi:10.100711156-010-0225-9

Aygun, M., Ic, S., & Sayim, M. (2014). The Effects of corporate ownership structure and board size on earnings management: Evidence from Turkey. *International Journal of Business and Management*, *9*(12), 123–132. doi:10.5539/ijbm.v9n12p123

Bar-Yosef, S., & Prencipe, A. (2013). The Impact of Corporate Governance and Earnings Management on Stock Market Liquidity in a Highly Concentrated Ownership Capital Market. *Journal of Accounting, Auditing & Finance*, *28*(3), 292–316. doi:10.1177/0148558X13492591

Brockman, P., & Chung, D. Y. (2003). Investor Protection and Firm Liquidity. *The Journal of Finance*, *58*(2), 921–937. doi:10.1111/1540-6261.00551

Buckmaster, D. (1997). Antecedents of Modern Earnings Management Research: Income smoothing in literature, 1954–1965. *The Accounting Historians Journal*, *24*(1), 75–91. doi:10.2308/0148-4184.24.1.75

Cengiz, S., Dilsiz, M. Ş., & Aslanoğlu, S. (2016). Kar Dağıtım Politikasının Kazanç Yönetimi Uygulamaları Üzerindeki Etkisi. *Muhasebe ve Finansman Dergisi*, (70), 39–54. doi:10.25095/mufad.396677

Cengiz, S., Gör, Y., & Terzi, S. (2016). Kurumsal Yönetim ve Kazanç Yönetimi Arasındaki İlişki: Borsa İstanbul'da İşlem Gören Şirketler Üzerine Uygulama. *Uluslararası Yönetim İktisat ve İşletme Dergisi*, *30*, 756–770.

Chung, H., Elder, J., & Kim, J. C. (2010). Corporate governance and liquidity. *Journal of Financial and Quantitative Analysis*, *45*(2), 265–291. doi:10.1017/S0022109010000104

Chung, H., Sheu, H. J., & Wang, J. L. (2009). Do firms' earnings management practices affect their equity liquidity? *Finance Research Letters*, *6*(3), 152–158. doi:10.1016/j.frl.2009.03.003

Dang, T. L., Nguyen, T. H., Tran, N. T. A., & Vo, T. T. A. (2018). Institutional ownership and stock liquidity: International evidence. *Asia-Pacific Journal of Financial Studies*, *47*(1), 21–53. doi:10.1111/ajfs.12202

Demski, J. S. (1998). Performance measure manipulation. *Contemporary Accounting Research*, *15*(3), 261–285. doi:10.1111/j.1911-3846.1998.tb00560.x

Findik, H. & Öztürk, E. (2016). Finansal Bilgi Manipülasyonunun Beneish Modeli Yardımıyla Ölçülmesi: BIST İmalat Sanayi Üzerine Bir Araştırma. *İşletme Araştırmaları Dergisi*, *8*(1), 483-499.

Gul, F. A., Leung, S., & Srinidhi, B. (2003). *Informative and opportunistic earnings management and the value relevance of earnings: Some evidence on the role of IOS*. Available from https://papers.ssrn.com/sol3/papers.cfm?abstract_id=429800

Gündüz, M. (2016). Determination of earnings management: An application in BIST Kazanç yönetiminin tespiti: BIST'de bir uygulama. *Journal of Human Sciences*, *13*(3), 6080–6091. doi:10.14687/jhs.v13i3.4367

Harris, L. (1994). Minimum Price Variations, Discrete Bid-Ask Spreads, and Quotation Sizes. *Review of Financial Studies*, *7*(1), 149–178. doi:10.1093/rfs/7.1.149

Healy, P. M. (1985). The effect of bonus schemes on accounting decisions. *Journal of Accounting and Economics*, *7*(1-3), 85–107. doi:10.1016/0165-4101(85)90029-1

Healy, P. M., & Wahlen, J. M. (1999). A Review of the Earnings Management Literature and Its Implications for Standard Setting. *Accounting Horizons*, *13*(4), 365–383. doi:10.2308/acch.1999.13.4.365

Hepworth, S. R. (1953). Smoothing periodic income. *The Accounting Review*, *28*(1), 32–39.

Hribar, P., & Collins, D. W. (2002). Errors in estimating accruals: Implications for empirical research. *Journal of Accounting Research*, *40*(1), 105–134. doi:10.1111/1475-679X.00041

Huang, K., Lao, B., & McPhee, G. (2017). Does stock liquidity affect accrual-based earnings management? *Journal of Business Finance & Accounting*, *44*(3-4), 417–447. doi:10.1111/jbfa.12236

Hunjra, A. I., Perveen, U., Li, L., Chani, M. I., & Mehmood, R. (2020). Impact of ownership concentration, institutional ownership and earnings management on stock market liquidity. *Corporate Ownership & Control*, *17*(2), 77–87. doi:10.22495/cocv17i2art7

Jacoby, G., & Zheng, S. X. (2010). Ownership dispersion and market liquidity. *International Review of Financial Analysis*, *19*(2), 81–88. doi:10.1016/j.irfa.2010.01.008

Jiraporn, P., Miller, G. A., Yoon, S. S., & Kim, Y. S. (2008). Is earnings management opportunistic or beneficial? An agency theory perspective. *International Review of Financial Analysis*, *17*(3), 622–634. doi:10.1016/j.irfa.2006.10.005

Karaibrahimoğlu, Y. (2010). *The role of corporate governance on earnings management: Quarterly evidence from Turkey* (Unpublished Doctoral Dissertation). Izmir University of Economics, Turkey.

Kaya, U., & Yazan, Ö. (2017). Kurumsal Sosyal Sorumluluk-Kazanç Yönetimi ve Finansal Performans İlişkisi. *Muhasebe ve Denetime Bakis*, *17*(51), 15–40.

Kothari, S. P., Leone, A. J., & Wasley, C. E. (2005). Performance matched discretionary accrual measures. *Journal of Accounting and Economics*, *39*(1), 163–197. doi:10.1016/j.jacceco.2004.11.002

Li, V. (2019). The effect of real earnings management on the persistence and informativeness of earnings. *The British Accounting Review*, *51*(4), 402–423.

Lin, Z., Liu, M., & Noronha, C. (2016). The impact of corporate governance on informative earnings management in the Chinese market. *Abacus*, *52*(3), 568–609.

Marcelo, J. L. M., & Quirós, M. D. M. M. (2006). The role of an illiquidity risk factor in asset pricing: Empirical evidence from the Spanish stock market. *The Quarterly Review of Economics and Finance*, *46*(2), 254–267.

Memiş, M. Ü. & Çetenak, E. H. (2012). Kurumsal Yönetimin Kazanç Yönetimi Uygulamaları Üzerine Etkisi: İmkb'de İşlem Gören Şirketler Üzerine Uygulama. *Çukurova Üniversitesi Sosyal Bilimler Enstitüsü Dergisi*, *21*(3), 205-224.

Mulford, C. W., & Comiskey, E. E. (2002). *The financial numbers game: detecting creative accounting practices*. John Wiley & Sons.

Önder, Ş. (2012). *İşletmelerin Kar Yönetimi Uygulamalarında Kurumsal Yönetim Yapılarının Etkisi İMKB üzerine Bir Uygulama*. Basılmamış Doktara Tezi, Kütahya Üniversitesi.

Özcan, A. (2019). Audit Quality and Earnings Management: Evidence From Turkey. *International Journal of Economic & Administrative Studies*, *23*, 67–78.

Park, Y. W., & Shin, H. H. (2004). Board composition and earnings management in Canada. *Journal of Corporate Finance*, *10*(3), 431–457.

Pedraza, A. (2018). Ownership concentration and market liquidity: Evidence from a natural experiment. *Economics Letters*, *167*, 56–59.

Prommin, P., Jumreornvong, S., & Jiraporn, P. (2014). The effect of corporate governance on stock liquidity: The case of Thailand. *International Review of Economics & Finance*, *32*, 132–142.

Putra, A. A., & Mela, N. F. (2019). Effect of Ownership Types on Informative Earnings Management. *International Journal of Academic Research in Accounting. Finance and Management Sciences*, *9*(2), 74–82.

Rahman, A. F., Hassan, M. S., Saleh, N. M., & Shukor, Z. A. (2013). The effect of underinvestment on the relationship between earnings management and information asymmetry. *Asian Academy of Management Journal of Accounting and Finance*, *9*(2), 1–28.

Riahi, Y., Lamiri, I., & Ben Arab, M. (2013). The Impact of Earnings Management on Liquidity: Case of the Tunisian Stock Market. *International Journal of Business and Commerce*, *2*(10), 38–57.

Rubin, A. (2007). Ownership level, ownership concentration and liquidity. *Journal of Financial Markets*, *10*(3), 219–248.

Schipper, K. (1989). Earnings management. *Accounting Horizons*, *3*(4), 91–102.

Sharif, F. A., Bino, A., & Tayeh, M. (2015). The impact of ownership structure on stock liquidity: Evidence from Amman Stock Exchange. *Jordan Journal of Business Administration*, *11*(1), 239–251.

Shoaib, A., & Siddiqui, M. A. (2020). Earning information content changes based on accrual measures and quality measures: Evidence from member countries of Asia Pacific trade agreement. *International Journal of Finance & Economics*.

Staglianò, R., La Rocca, M., & Gerace, D. (2018). The impact of ownership concentration and analyst coverage on market liquidity: Comparative evidence from an auction and a specialist market. *Economic Modelling*, *70*, 203–214.

Türegün, N. (2020). Does financial crisis impact earnings management? Evidence from Turkey. *Journal of Corporate Accounting & Finance*, *31*(1), 64–71.

Udomsirikul, P., Jumreornvong, S., & Jiraporn, P. (2011). Liquidity and capital structure: The case of Thailand. *Journal of Multinational Financial Management*, *21*(2), 106–117.

Verrecchia, R. E. (1986). Managerial discretion in the choice among financial reporting alternatives. *Journal of Accounting and Economics*, *8*(3), 175–195.

White, H. (1980). A heteroskedasticity-consistent covariance matrix estimator and a direct test for heteroskedasticity. *Econometrica*, *48*(4), 817–838.

Yaghoobnezhad, A., Roodposhti, R. F., & Zabihi, A. (2011). The study of relationship between institutional ownership and stock liquidity in Tehran stock exchange. *Journal of Basic and Applied Scientific Research*, *12*(1), 2736–2742.

Yaşar, A. (2013). Big Four Auditors' Audit Quality and Earnings Management: Evidence from Turkish Stock Market. *International Journal of Business and Social Science*, *4*(17), 153–163.

Yavuzaslan, S. & Kalmis, H. (2016). İşletmelerin Kurumsal Yönetim Uygulamalarinin Kâr Yönetimi Üzerindeki Etkisi ve Borsa Istanbul AS Sirketleri Üzerinde Bir Uygulama. *Çanakkale Onsekiz Mart Üniversitesi Yönetim Bilimleri Dergisi*, *14*(27), 353-384.

Yosra, G., & Sioud, O. B. O. (2011). Ultimate ownership structure and stock liquidity: Empirical evidence from Tunisia. *Studies in Economics and Finance*, *28*(4), 282–300.

KEY TERMS AND DEFINITIONS

Corporate Governance: Set of rule and mechanisms tailored to align the interests of various stakeholders of companies.

Discretionary Accruals: The unobserved part of total accruals left when the estimated non-discretionary accruals are deducted from total accruals.

Earnings Management: Intentionally alterations of financial figures of companies by managers.

Information Asymmetry: Possession of superior information by some parties about the subject of an economic transaction.

Informative Earnings Management: Earnings management conducted by motivations of conveying information of managers about firms' prospects.

Opportunistic Earnings Management: Earnings management conducted by motivations of concealing unfavorable performance of firms.

Stock Liquidity: The ease of selling of a particular stock in the market.

Chapter 5
Free Cash Flow and Earnings Management: The Moderating Role of Leverage

Sandra Alves
University of Aveiro, Portugal

ABSTRACT

This study draws on Jensen's free cash flow hypothesis to evaluate the relationship between free cash flow and earnings management. This study also examines whether the level of leverage moderate the relationship between free cash flow and earnings management. This study uses a fixed effects regression model to examine the effect of free cash flow on earnings management and to test whether leverage levels moderate that relationship for an unbalanced panel of 13,850 firms' year observations from 2011 to 2018 across five European countries. Consistent with the free cash flow hypothesis of Jensen, this study suggests that firms with high free cash flow are more likely to manage earnings. Further, the results also suggest that the positive impact of free cash flow on earnings management is attenuated in firms with high leverage levels. This study contributes to the literature by examining how free cash flow affects the extent of earnings management and by shedding light on the mediating effect of leverage on the relationship between free cash flow and earnings management.

INTRODUCTION

Free cash flow (FCF) is important because it shows how much actual cash a company has at its disposal. This FCF allows company to search for opportunities going up shareholder's value. Ideally, managers of firms with free cash flow are expected to invest excessive cash in profitable investment in order to generate high returns to shareholders. However, firms with a large amount of free cash flow are normally affected with major agency problems. Jensen (1986) suggests that the existence of free cash flow increases the potential conflicts of interests between managers and shareholders as managers have discretion over the use of free cash flow. There is an increased risk that managers may spend this money on unprofitable projects rather than returning the money to shareholders, for example, in the form of dividends.

DOI: 10.4018/978-1-7998-7596-3.ch005

Managers do not have any obligation to disclose to their investors the rationale behind investment decisions or the investment's feasibility. Therefore, investors may not be able to know the prospect and the advantages or disadvantages of the project for their wealth (Chung, Firth, & Kim, 2005). Likewise, managers may not provide adequate discloses to investors on investment's cash flow projections and underlying assumptions, which increases the opportunity for managers to divert corporate resources to gain personal advantage. Wang (2010) finds that free cash flow increases agency costs due to managerial perquisite consumption.

Excessive free cash flow in the hands of managers leads to overinvestment due to investment in projects with negative net present value (Jensen, 1986, Jensen & Meckling, 1976). Cai (2013) and Chen et al. (2016) find that firms with higher free cash flow show more pronounced overinvestment.

Non-value-maximising investments eventually reduce earnings and will result in lower stock prices. This could lead shareholders to remove directors and senior executives (Habib, 2011). However, to camouflage the effects of the non-wealth-maximizing investments, managers may use accounting techniques that increase (decrease) reported income. Earnings management allows managers to finance sub-optimal investments that maximize their own utilities at the expense of some informationally disadvantaged stakeholders (An, Li, & Yu, 2016). In this vein, Chung et al. (2005) and Astami et al. (2017) find that management use accounting discretion to obscure the earnings impact of investments in negative net present value projects and other self-serving activities.

According to Jensen (1986), leverage is helpful for reducing free cash flow in the hands of company managers as well as reducing agency cost. The interest and principal payments reduce the cash available to management for non-optimal spending. When a firm employs debt financing, it undergoes the scrutiny of lenders and is often subject to lender-induced spending restriction (Jensen, 1986). Hence, leverage reduces the agency costs of free cash flow by reducing the cash flow available for spending at the discretion of managers. Park & Jang (2013) find that the reduction of free cash flow in managers' control reduce agency cost and raise company worth. This suggests that higher level of debt reduces the free cash flows available to managers and therefore limits their discretionary behaviour, and thus reduce earnings management. However, some studies also show that leverage intensifies earnings management (Defond & Jiambalvo, 1994, Iatridis & Kadorinis, 2009, Chamberlain, Butt, & Sarkar, 2014).

Using a sample of non-financial listed European firms-year from 2011 to 2018, this study aims to test whether earnings management is higher for firms with more free cash flow. Additionally, this study examines how leverage influence the impact of free cash flow on earnings management.

The study makes some contributions to the existing literature. First, although many studies have examined the incentives for earnings management, the relationship between free cash flow and earnings management in the Europe region has received little attention. Second, to our knowledge, this study is the first to investigate the role of leverage on the association between free cash flow and earnings management in the European context. Third, the findings of this study can provide useful information mainly for shareholders and auditors whether free cash flow affect earnings management, and especially whether leverage moderate the relationship between free cash flow and earnings management. Finally, findings based on European data also help build a more expansive international understanding of the relation between free cash flow, leverage and earnings management debate.

LITERATURE REVIEW AND TESTABLE HYPOTHESES

Earnings Management and Free Cash Flow

According to Healy & Wahlen (1999, p. 6) earnings management "occurs when managers use judgment in financial reporting and in structuring transactions to alter financial reports to either mislead some stakeholders about the underlying economic performance of the company, or to influence contractual outcomes that depend on reported accounting numbers". Therefore, managers may have incentives to use their control to extract private benefits at the expense of other stakeholders.

Previous studies suggest that the opportunity for earnings management is higher among companies with high free cash flow (Cheung & Jiang, 2016; Chung et al., 2005). Firms with a large amount of free cash flow are normally affected with major agency problems (Lanhane & Mahakud, 2016; Wang, 2010). Jensen (1986) suggests that the existence of free cash flow increases the potential conflicts of interests between managers and shareholders as managers have discretion over the use of free cash flow. There is an increased risk that managers may spend this money on unprofitable projects rather than returning the money to shareholders, for example, in the form of dividends. Managers of firms with high FCF act opportunistically for personal gain, and tend to get involved in unprofitable projects, overinvestments and misuse the funds (Jensen, 1986). In fact, firms with high FCF tend to overinvest (Richardson, 2006), to exhibit higher stock return synchronicity and to reduce disclosure quality (Cheung & Jiang, 2016), to exhibit poor future profitability (Chung et al., 2005) and act sub-optimally in acquisition (Lang, ReneM Stulz, & Walkling, 1991).

Investments that do not maximize shareholder wealth can reduce earnings and consequently lower stock price. This may trigger efforts by shareholders to remove managers (Chung et al., 2005). Therefore, to camouflage the impact of investments with negative or marginal net present value on earnings, managers may use accounting procedures to increase earnings. In this vein, Astami et al. (2017), Friska et al. (2019), Jones and Sharma (2001), Raeisi and Vaez (2016), Rusmin et al. (2014), Toumeh et al. (2020) and Yendrawati and Asy'ari (2017) find that firms with high free cash flow are more likely to engage in earnings management.

Hence, under Jensen's (1986) free cash flow hypothesis it is expected that firms with high free cash flow are more likely to manage earnings:

Hypothesis 1: The level of free cash flow will be positively associated with earnings management.

The Role of Leverage in the Relationship Between Earnings Management and Free Cash Flow

Leverage is a disciplining mechanism that limits management's engagement in self-dealing activities (Ghorbani & Salehi, 2020; Jensen 1986; Stulz 1990; Harvey, Lins, & Roper, 2004). According to Jensen (1986), leverage is helpful for reducing free cash flow in the hands of company managers as well as reducing agency cost. The interest and principal payments reduce the cash available to management for non-optimal spending. When a firm employs debt financing, it undergoes the scrutiny of lenders and is often subject to lender-induced spending restriction (Jensen, 1986). Hence, leverage reduces the agency costs of free cash flow by reducing the cash flow available for spending at the discretion of managers. Park & Jang (2013) find that the reduction of free cash flow in managers' control reduce agency cost and raise company worth. The literature has supported the role of leverage as a mechanism which reduces this overinvestment problem by decreasing the free cash flow under managerial discretionary control (Ahn, Denis, & Denis, 2006; D'Mello & Miranda, 2010; Fernandez, 2011; Firth, Lin, & Wong, 2008; Harvey et al., 2004).

Since debt mitigates the amount of free cash flow, it reduces the amount of liquid resources under managers' control, increases the monitoring activity by financial markets and commits future cash flows to debt-related payments. So, leverage may mitigate the impact of free cash flow problem on earnings management.

The above discussion leads to the following hypothesis:

Hypothesis 2: High leverage will mitigate the positive effect of free cash flow on earnings management.

SAMPLE AND RESEARCH DESIGN

Sample Selection

Our sample includes all the non-financial listed firms of the five European countries for the period 2011-2018. The choice for studying more than one European country is motivated by the fact that it offers the opportunity to examine to what extent free cash flow affects earnings management, if any, is uniform across countries. The data used in this study come from the November 2019 version of the Amadeus database managed by Bureau Van Dijk and Informa D&B, S.A.. The five countries used in this study are Spain, France, Germany Italy and United Kingdom. The choice for studying these countries is by the fact that the Madrid Stock Exchange (Bolsa de Madrid), Euronext Paris, Frankfurt Stock Exchange (Börse Frankfurt), Italian Stock Exchange (Borsa Italiana) and London Stock Exchange are considered as important Stock Exchanges in Europe.

Table 1 details how the selection criteria resulted in a final total unbalanced panel of 13.850 firm-year observations over the 2011 to 2018 period.

Table 1. Sample selection criteria during the years 2011-2018

Sample Selection	Number of Firm Years					
	Spain	**France**	**Germany**	**Italy**	**United Kingdom**	**Total**
Non-financial firms listed	896	6.021	3.864	2.488	8.840	22.109
(-) Firms with missing data	(345)	(1.629)	(897)	(616)	(4.772)	(8.259)
Number of firm-year observations in the final sample	551	4.492	2.967	1.872	4.068	13.850

RESEARCH DESIGN

Measuring Earnings Management

Following standard accounting literature, we use discretionary accruals as a proxy for earnings management. Discretionary accruals are estimated using the cross-sectional variation of the modified Jones model proposed by Dechow et al. (1995), that is commonly used by most of earnings management research (Alzoubi, 2016; Ayedh, Fatima, & Mohammad, 2019; Matteo & Francesco, 2018; Ongsakul, Jiraporn, & Kim, 2020; Peasnell, Pope, & Young, 2005; Warfield, Wild, & Wild, 1995).

The modified Jones' model consists of regressing total accruals (*TACC*) on three variables: the change in revenues (*ΔRev*), the change in receivables (*ΔRec*) and the level of gross property, plant and equipment (*PPE*). All variables and the intercept are divided by lagged total assets in order to avoid problems of heteroskedasticity. Non-discretionary accruals (NDACC) are the predictions from the ordinary least squares (OLS) estimation of model (1), while discretionary accruals (DACC) are the residuals.

The modified Jones model is as follows:

$$\frac{TACC_{it}}{TA_{it-1}} = \alpha_1\left(\frac{1}{TA_{it-1}}\right) + \alpha_2\left(\frac{\Delta Rev_{it} - \Delta Rec_{it}}{TA_{it-1}}\right) + \alpha_3\left(\frac{PPE_{it}}{TA_{it-1}}\right) + \varepsilon_{it} \quad (1)$$

Where,

TACC = total accruals in year t, calculated as the difference between net income and operating cash flows.
TA = total assets at the beginning of year t.
Δ *Rev* = change in revenues.
Δ *Rec* = change in accounts receivable.
PPE = gross property, plant and equipment.
i,t = firm and year index.

Measuring Free Cash Flow

As in Astami et al. (2017), Bhundia (2012), Cheung and Jiang (2016) and Toumeh et al. (2020) this study uses the model of Lehn and Poulsen (1989) to measure the amount of free cash flow (*Free_Cash*). Thus, *Free_Cash* is measured by operating income before depreciation minus expenses such as tax expense, interest expense and dividend (Lehn & Poulsen, 1989).

Control Variables

Given that the *Free cashflow* is not the only factor affecting earnings management, several control variables are introduced to isolate other factors that may influence the earnings management. This study includes the value of total accruals (*T_Accruals*) to control for a firm's "accrual-generating potential" (Becker, DeFond, Jiambalvo, & Subramanyam, 1998). According to Krishnan (2003) firms with higher values of total accruals are likely to have greater discretionary accruals. *T_Accruals* is the value of total accruals divided by total assets for firm i for year t-1. This study also includes growth opportunities (*Growth*) as a number of previous studies suggest that high-growth firms are by nature more difficult to monitor due to the existence of discretionary investments and measurement problems associated with future assets (Myers, 1977). Managers in high-growth firms are more likely to have opportunistic behaviour (Skinner, 1993; Watts & Zimmerman, 1986). High-growth firms are more likely to engage in earnings management, which will further aggravate the situation of lower observability in growth firms (Chen, Elder, & Hung, 2010; Zalata, Tauringana, & Tingbani, 2018). *Growth* is the market to book of firm *i* for period *t*. According to Kapoor and Goel (2017), firm profitability is an important variable in the context of earnings management. Managers of firms with lower profitability are more likely to engage in earnings management (Chen, Cheng, & Wang, 2015; Kapoor & Goel, 2017). Profitability (*ROA*) is the return on assets of firm *i* for period *t*. Firm size (*Size*) is also included because positive accounting theory suggests that managers of large firms are more likely to exploit latitude in accounting to reduce political costs (Watts & Zimmerman, 1978). Therefore, large firms are more likely to choose income-decreasing earnings management in order to reduce the probability of adverse impact from political exposure (the size hypothesis) (Peasnell, Pope, & Young, 2000; Jiang, Lee, & Anandarajan, 2008; Banderlipe, 2009). *Size* is measured as the natural logarithm of total assets of firm *i* for period *t*.

Regression Model

To test the hypothesis 1, the impact of free cash flow on earnings management, it is estimated the following regression:

$$Earnings\ Management_{it} = \lambda_0 + \lambda_1 (Free\_Cash_{it}) + \lambda_2 (T\_Accruals_{it-1})$$

$$+ \lambda_3 (Growth_{it}) + \lambda_4 (ROA_{it}) + \lambda_5 (Size_{it}) + \varepsilon_{it} \quad (2)$$

Where:

Earnings Management$_{it}$ = is the discretionary accruals measured by the modified Jones (1991) model for firm *i* for period *t*;
Free_Cash$_{it}$ = is measured by operating income before depreciation minus expenses such as tax expense, interest expense and dividend divided by market value of equity of firm *i* for period *t*;
T_Accruals$_{it}$ = is the value of total accruals divided by total assets for firm *i* for period *t*;
Growth$_{it}$ = is the market to book of firm *i* for period *t*;
ROA$_{it}$ = is the net income deflated by total assets of firm *i* for period *t*;
Size$_{it}$ = logarithm of total assets of firm *i* for period *t*.

To test hypothesis 2, the effect of the level of leverage on the relationship between free cash flow and earnings management, it is expanded equation (2) by including the leverage level and an interaction term between *Free_Cash* and *Leverage* level:

$$Earnings\ Management_{it} = \lambda_0 + \lambda_1 (Free\_Cash_{it}) + \lambda_2 (T\_Accruals_{it-1}) + \lambda_3 (Growth_{it})$$

$$+ \lambda_4 (ROA_{it}) + \lambda_5 (Size_{it}) + \lambda_6 (Leverage_{it}) + \lambda_7 (Free\_Cash{*}Leverage_{it}) + \varepsilon_{it} \quad (3)$$

Where:

$Leverage_{it}$ = ratio between the book value of long-term debt and the total assets;
$Free\_Cash_{it}*Leverage_{it}$ = Interaction variable of free cash flow and leverage.

RESULTS AND DISCUSSION

Descriptive Statistics and Correlations

Table 2 presents the sample descriptive statistics for the variables used in this research. Spearman correlations between the explanatory variables are documented in Table 3.

Earnings management is the discretionary accruals measured by the modified Jones (1991) model; *Free_Cash* is the free cash flow deflated by the market value of equity; *T_Accruals* is the value of total accruals divided by total assets; *Growth* is the market to book of firm; *ROA* is the net income deflated by total assets; *Size* represents the firm's size; *Leverage* represents the ratio between the book value of long-term debt and the total assets.

Table 2, panel F, shows that, while *Earnings Management*, ranges between about -0.349 and 0.878, the mean and median are about 0.037 and 0.031. At country level, the mean for *Earnings Management* range from a low of -0.003 in Italy to 0.087 for Germany. Panel F of table 2, shows that, while *Free_Cash*, ranges between about -16.846 and 21.538, the mean and median are about 0.063 and 0.071. At country level, the mean for *Free_Cash* range from a low of -0.019 in United Kingdom to 0.164 for Spain. The mean (median) *T_Accruals* is -0.088 (-0.036), with a minimum of -29.800 and a maximum of 1.018. At country level, the mean for *T_Accruals* range from a low of -0.131 in France to -0.019 for Spain. Table 2, panel F, also shows that the mean (median) *Growth* is 3.325 (1.529), with a minimum of -429.980 and a maximum of 823.000. At country level, the mean for *Growth* range from a low of 1.268 in France to 6.205 for Germany. The mean (median) ROA is 0.560 (3.103), with a minimum of -99.590 and a maximum of 90.260. At country level, the mean for ROA range from a low of -1.584 in France to 2.875 for Spain. The mean of firm size (*Size*) is about EUR 4.329.227 thousand with a minimum of EUR 46 thousand and a maximum of EUR 458.156.000 thousand. At country level, the mean for *Size* range from a low of 3.254.470 thousand in Italy to 8.599.900 thousand for Spain. *Leverage* variable represents on average 0.200 of the total assets of the company (with a median of 0.116). At country level, the mean for *Leverage* range from a low of 0.154 in France to 0.220 for Spain.

Table 2. Summary of Descriptive Statistics

	Mean	Median	Min.	Max.
Panel A – Spain: Number of Observations: 551				
Earnings Management	0.025	-0.058	-0.248	0.318
Free_Cash	0.164	0.086	-7.254	4.122
T_Accruals	-0.019	-0.030	-4.009	-3.486
Growth	3.055	1.245	-9.467	102.30
ROA	2.875	2.956	-51.367	55.022
Size (th EUR)	8.599.900	777.454	1.036	129.773.000
Leverage	0.220	0.203	0.000	0.701
Panel B – France: Number of Observations: 4.492				
Earnings Management	0.004	-0.015	-0.349	0.418
Free_Cash	0.099	0.092	-16.846	7.212
T_Accruals	-0.131	-0.027	-7.019	0.558
Growth	1.268	1.367	-292.851	283.234
ROA	-1.584	2.302	-99.590	90.260
Size (th EUR)	4.445.719	109.013	83	283.169.000
Leverage	0.156	0.106	0.000	6.532
Panel C – Germany: Number of Observations: 2.967				
Earnings Management	0.087	0.070	0.000	0.796
Free_Cash	0.109	0.094	-16.760	7.599
T_Accruals	-0.081	-0.038	-7.634	-3.361
Growth	6.205	1.557	-429.980	628.200
ROA	1.185	3.742	-98.420	79.610
Size (th EUR)	5.122.472	192.327	152	458.156.000
Leverage	0.206	0.122	0.000	54.375
Panel D – Italy: Number of Observations: 1.872				
Earnings Management	-0.003	0.011	-0.232	0.398
Free_Cash	0.077	0.095	-8.048	21.538
T_Accruals	-0.083	-0.043	-0.228	-9.048
Growth	1.986	1.174	-106.061	204.045
ROA	0.414	1.712	-92.000	57.960
Size (th EUR)	3.254.470	175.982	46	202.670.000
Leverage	0.154	0.120	0.000	0.962
Panel E – United Kingdom: Number of Observations: 4.068				
Earnings Management	0.058	0.044	0.000	0.878
Free_Cash	-0.019	0.044	-16.720	14.630
T_Accruals	-0.064	-0.039	-29.80	1.018
Growth	3.843	1.910	-64.610	823.000
ROA	1.949	4.396	-94.750	59.340
Size (th EUR)	3.566.088	224.877	57	248.521.264
Leverage	0.157	0.099	0.000	14.640
Panel F – Total Sample: Number of Observations: 13.850				
Earnings Management	0.037	0.031	-0.349	0.878
Free_Cash	0.063	0.071	-16.846	21.538
T_Accruals	-0.088	-0.036	-29.800	1.018
Growth	3.325	1.529	-429.980	823.000
ROA	0.560	3.103	-99.590	90.260
Size (th EUR)	4.329.227	185.238	46	458.156.000
Leverage	0.200	0.116	0.000	54.375

Table 3. Pearson Correlation Coefficients Matrix

	Earnings Management	Free_cash	T_Accruals	Growth	ROA	Size	Leverage
Earnings Management	1						
Free_cash	0.354**	1					
T_Accruals	0.567**	0.098*	1				
Growth	-0.052	0.034	-0.054	1			
ROA	0.128*	0.234*	0.165*	0.231*	1		
Size	-0.098*	0.145*	-0.088	0.077	0.293**	1	
Leverage	-0.274*	-0.139*	0.078	0.053	-0.127**	0.136*	1

Earnings management is the discretionary accruals measured by the modified Jones (1991) model; *Free_Cash* is the free cash flow deflated by the market value of equity; *T_Accruals* is the value of total accruals divided by total assets; *Growth* is the market to book of firm; *ROA* is the net income deflated by total assets; *Size* represents the firm's size; *Leverage* represents the ratio between the book value of long-term debt and the total assets.

** Correlation is significant at the 0.01 level (2-tailed); * Correlation is significant at the 0.05 level (2-tailed).

Spearman correlations between the explanatory variables are documented in Table 3. The analysis of Table 3 shows that there are some significant correlations between the variables. *Free_cash, T_Accruals* and *ROA* are positively associated with Earnings Management, suggesting that firms with high levels of *Free_cash, T_Accruals* and *ROA* are more likely to engage earnings management. In contrast *Size and Leverage* are negatively associated with *Earnings Management.* This may suggest that large firms and with high leverage have a lower tendency to manage earnings. *Free_cash* is positively associated with *T_Accruals, ROA* and *Size*, suggesting that firms with high *T_Accruals, ROA* and *Size* present more *Free_cash. Free_cash* is negatively associated with *Leverage*, suggesting that firms with higher *Free_cash* have lower leverage levels. *ROA* is positively associated with *T_Accruals* and *Growth*, suggesting that firms with high *ROA* present higher levels of *T_Accruals* and *Growth. Size* is positively associated with *ROA*, suggesting that greater the size of the firm, the higher the *ROA* of the firm. *ROA* is negatively associated with *Leverage*, suggesting that firms with high *ROA* have lower leverage levels. *Size* is positively associated with *Leverage*, suggesting that larger firms have higher levels of leverage. Correlation coefficients are, in general, low (below the 0.9 threshold) (Tabachnick & Fidell, 2001), suggesting the absence of serious statistical problems related with multicollinearity.

Regression Results

The author began with a pooled Ordinary Least Squares (OLS) model, a random effects model and a fixed effects model and ran different tests to check the suitability of each model. On one hand, it is compared the results of the pooled OLS model to those of the random effects model by means of the Breusch-Pagan test for random effects. This test revealed that using the random effects model was preferable to the pooled regression model. On the other hand, it is estimated a fixed effects model, and the F test for significance of fixed effects revealed that using fixed effects was also preferable to the pooled regression. Finally, it is used the Hausman specification test to compare random and fixed effects models and, based on the test results, the fixed effects model is appropriate.

Table 4. Fixed Effects Regression Results Period: 2011-2018

	Spain		France		Germany		Italy		United Kingdom		Total sample	
Dependent Variable	**Earnings Management**		**Earnings Management**		**Earnings Management**		**Earnings Management**		**Earnings Management**		**Earnings Management**	
Independent Variables	**Coefficient**	**t-Values**	**Coefficient**	**t-Values**	**Coefficient**	**t-Values**	**Coefficient**	**t-Values**	**Coefficient**	**t-Values**	**Coefficient**	**t-Values**
Constant	-0.024	-3.900***	0.360	1.167	0.126	2.067**	-0.007	-0.279	0.025	3.574***	0.226	2.828***
Free_Cash	0.002	1.720*	0.135	3.883***	0.024	0.154	-0.013	-4.535***	0.003	1.951*	0.026	2.178**
T_Accruals	0.040	4.744***	0.274	2.987***	0.130	2.145**	0.005	1.905*	0.099	7.806***	0.069	2.721***
Growth	-0.001	-1.408	0.014	0.651	-0.001	-1.972**	0.001	0.697	0.000	0.249	-0.001	-2.706***
ROA	0.012	2.061**	0.001	0.321	-1.085	-0.008	0.002	8.362***	-0.002	-2.652***	0.002	0.916
Size	0.063	6.679***	-1.141	-3.748***	-0.009	-1.920*	0.001	0.3862	-0.016	-5.965***	-0.013	-2.055**
Observations	551		4.492		2.967		1.872		4.068		13.850	
R-squared	69.37%		39.145		52.54%		35.53%		74.76%		77.30%	
F-statistic	25.778***		7.365***		12.507***		7.007***		27.965***		28.235***	

Earnings management is the discretionary accruals measured by the modified Jones (1991) model; *Free_Cash* is the free cash flow deflated by the market value of equity; *T_Accruals* is the value of total accruals divided by total assets; *Growth* is the market to book of firm; *ROA* is the net income deflated by total assets; *Size* represents the firm's size.

*** Significant at the 1-percent level; ** Significant at the 5-percent level; * Significant at the 10-percent level.

Table 5. Fixed Effects Regression Results Period: 2011-2018

	Spain		France		Germany		Italy		United Kingdom		Total sample	
Dependent Variable	**Earnings Management**		**Earnings Management**		**Earnings Management**		**Earnings Management**		**Earnings Management**		**Earnings Management**	
Independent Variables	**Coefficient**	**t-Values**	**Coefficient**	**t-Values**	**Coefficient**	**t-Values**	**Coefficient**	**t-Values**	**Coefficient**	**t-Values**	**Coefficient**	**t-Values**
Constant	-0.002	-0.895	0.004	0.144	0.115	1.854*	-0.019	-0.725	0.025	3.576***	0.296	2.931***
Free_Cash	0.004	2.094**	0.092	2.803***	0.007	0.164	-0.012	-3.887***	0.004	2.593***	0.029	2.208**
T_Accruals	0.081	7.485***	0.374	3.275***	0.168	2.720***	0.005	1.916*	0.099	7.778***	0.097	3.106***
Growth	0.001	1.471	0.007	0.278	-0.001	-2.019**	0.001	0.8293	0.000	0.037	-0.001	-2.711***
ROA	0.041	5.636***	0.001	0.228	-0.001	-2.026**	0.003	8.137***	-0.037	-4.727***	0.002	0.932
Size	0.002	4.400***	-0.080	-1.959*	-0.013	-2.695***	0.002	1.133	-0.172	-2.910***	-0.013	-2.062**
Leverage	-0.041	5.363***	-1.467	-4.609***	0.091	1.939*	-0.052	-2.467**	-0.002	-1.321	-0.009	-0.521
Free_Cash*Leverage	-0.004	-0.515	-1.908	-1.915*	0.026	1.098	-0.014	-0.843	-0.022	-3.014***	-0.033	-2.428**
Observations	551		4.492		2.967		1.872		4.068		13.850	
R-squared	61.14%		39.30%		62.91%		42.11%		74.86%		81.35%	
F-statistic	27.071***		7.891***		14.862***		8.117***		28.319***		29.054***	

Earnings management is the discretionary accruals measured by the modified Jones (1991) model; *Free_Cash* is the free cash flow deflated by the market value of equity; *T_Accruals* is the value of total accruals divided by total assets; *Growth* is the market to book of firm; *ROA* is the net income deflated by total assets; *Size* represents the firm's size; *Leverage* represents the ratio between the book value of long-term debt and the total assets; *Free_Cash* Leverage* is the interaction variable of free cash flow and leverage.

*** Significant at the 1-percent level; ** Significant at the 5-percent level; * Significant at the 10-percent level.

Table 4 presents the results from fixed effects regression for the equation 2 (hypothesis 1) and Table 5 presents the results from fixed effects regression for the equation 3 (hypothesis 2).

Tables 4 and 5 present the results from fixed effects regression for the equations 2 and 3.

To Spain, France, United Kingdom and total sample the results show that free cash flow is positively related to earnings management. The Hypothesis 1 predicts a positive relationship between free cash flow and earnings management. The findings support this hypothesis, which suggests that firms with more free cash flow could be more likely to engage earnings management practices. Therefore, the results of this study support the Jensen's (1986) free cash flow hypothesis. This result suggests that earnings of firms with high free cash flow are of low quality. However, to Italy the results in Tables 4 and 5 show that free cash flow is negatively related to earnings management.

To Spain, France and Italy, the coefficient for *Leverage* is negative and significant, suggesting that high leverage may restrict managers' ability to manipulate earnings. In contrast, to Germany the results suggest that highly leveraged firms are more likely to engage in earning management activities.

To France, United Kingdom and total sample, the coefficient on *Free_Cash*Leverage* is negative and statistically significant, suggesting that leverage affects the relationship between free cash flow and earnings management. Thus, the level of earnings quality reduction associated with the presence of free cash flow is attenuated when leverage is higher.

Regarding the control variables, growth, is negatively and significantly associated with earnings management to Germany and to total sample. To Spain and Italy, the results indicate that ROA influence managers' opportunistic behaviour. Differently, to United Kingdom, profitable firms seem to have better quality of reporting. To Spain, large firms are more likely to engage earnings management. Contrarily, to France, Germany and United Kingdom, firm size is negatively associated with discretionary accruals, suggesting that large firms have better earnings quality.

DISCUSSION

This study examines the relationship between earnings management and free cash flow using the free cash flow theory of Jensen (1986). Furthermore, this study examines how leverage influence the impact of free cash flow on earnings management. Agency theory suggests that the existence of free cash flow increases the potential conflicts of interests between managers and shareholders as managers have discretion over the use of free cash flow (Jensen, 1986). Leverage is helpful for reducing free cash flow in the hands of company managers as well as reducing agency cost. Therefore, leverage may reduce the agency costs of free cash flow by reducing the cash flow available for spending at the discretion of managers.

The findings of this research show evidence that free cash flow affects earnings management. In line with agency theory, free cash flow is positively related to earnings management. Accordingly, earnings management is higher among companies with high free cash flow. However, to Italy the results suggest that firms with high free cash flow engage less earnings management. One possible explanation for this result is that in Italy more free cash flow in the hands of managers may lead to higher performance, and consequently, less need to engage in earnings management. That is, firms that have sufficient free cash flow may have greater confidence in their financial performance, and hence are less likely to engage in earnings management. Another alternative explanation for this result is that Italian listed companies have effective corporate governance structure to control the managerial opportunistic behavior over the use of free cash flow.

Leverage is a disciplining device that limits management's engagement in self-dealing activities (Jensen, 1986; Stulz, 1990; Harvey et al., 2004). To France, United Kingdom and total sample, in line with agency theory, the results suggest that leverage is effective in alleviating free cash flow problem. As a result, leverage seems to reduce earnings management problems arising from free cash flow.

Overall, this study suggests that (1) free cash flow intensifies the agency problem (lower earnings quality); and (2) leverage can act as a monitoring mechanism to alleviate the agency cost of free cash flow.

SENSITIVITY ANALYSES

To ensure the robustness of results, the author performs several sensitivity checks. The first sensitivity analysis tests the impact of using alternative definition for the earnings management and firm size variables on regression results. Discretionary accruals are determined using the Kothari et al. (2005) model instead of the modified Jones model. The results (not reported here) of the regression, using alternative variable to measure earnings management has implications on *Free_Cash* variable on regression results in both tables 4 and 5, for Italy, which lost significance level (from $p<0.01$ to $p<0.10$). The other results remain unchanged (at coefficient signal and significant level). The results are also robust to using either the reported market value of equity or reported sales as alternative proxies of firm size.

The second sensitivity analysis examines the effect of influential observations on results. Where outliers are found (namely in the variables *Growth*, *ROA* and *Leverage*), a winserization method is used to test the robustness of the results. Extreme values (defined as values that are more than three standard deviations away from the mean) are replaced by values that are exactly three standard deviations away from the mean. The results (not reported here) do not differ from results presented previously. Thus, the influential observations do not seem affect the results.

Overall, the several sensitivity analyses conducted largely corroborate the results presented previously.

CONCLUSION

This research draws on Jensen's (1986) free cash flow hypothesis to evaluate the relationship between free cash flow and earnings management, proxied by discretionary accruals. Additionally, this study examines whether the level of leverage moderate the relationship between free cash flow and earnings management. To the author's knowledge, this study is the first to examine this mediating effect of leverage levels on the relationship between free cash flow and earnings management in the European context. The study aims to contribute to the literature by examining how free cash flow affects the extent of earnings management and by shedding light on the mediating effect of leverage on the relationship between free cash flow and earnings management. These effects have important implications for top managers, shareholders, corporate boards and policy makers.

Consistent with the free cash flow hypothesis of Jensen (1986), this study suggests that firms with high free cash flow are more likely to manage earnings, supporting the notion that high free cash flow intensifies the agency problem (lower earnings quality). Specifically, the results suggest that high free cash flow affects negatively earnings quality. This study also shows that the level of leverage has a moderating negative effect on earnings management in the presence of free cash flow. Therefore, this study suggests that leverage is able to reduce the agency cost of free cash flow (lower earnings quality).

The results of this study make the following contributions. First, this study contributes to the literature by examining how free cash flow affects the extent of earnings management in the European context. The results show lower earnings quality (greater earnings management) for firms with high free cash flow, which is consistent with the free cash flow hypothesis of Jensen (1986). Second, this study shows that leverage promote earnings quality and mitigates the positive effect of free cash flow on earnings management. Therefore, leverage may serve as an external control mechanism to alleviate the agency cost of free cash flow. Finally, the findings based on this study provide useful information to investors, corporate boards and policy makers in evaluating the impact of free cash flow on earnings quality and the mediating effect of leverage on the relationship between free cash flow and earnings management. Results suggest that the practice of earnings management may exist when a company has high free cash flow. In addition, results also suggest that leverage can act as a control mechanism to reduce the agency cost of free cash flow. Therefore, investors are recommended to pay attention to free cash flow and leverage and regard them as factors influencing companies' earnings management in their decision-making models when taking decisions on investment. Shareholders and boards of directors are also recommended to pay further attention in the presence of large free cash flow in order to promote earnings quality and, in consequence, to reduce earnings management.

REFERENCES

Ahn, S., Denis, D. J., & Denis, D. K. (2006). Leverage and investment in diversified firms. *Journal of Financial Economics*, *79*(2), 317–337. doi:10.1016/j.jfineco.2005.03.002

Alzoubi, E. S. S. (2016). Audit quality and earnings management: Evidence from Jordan. *Journal of Applied Accounting Research*, *17*(2), 170–189. doi:10.1108/JAAR-09-2014-0089

An, Z., Li, D., & Yu, J. (2016). Earnings management, capital structure, and the role of institutional environments. *Journal of Banking & Finance*, *68*, 131–152. doi:10.1016/j.jbankfin.2016.02.007

Astami, E. W., Rusmin, R., Hartadi, B., & Evans, J. (2017). The role of audit quality and culture influence on earnings management in companies with excessive free cash flow – Evidence from the Asia-Pacific region. *International Journal of Accounting and Information Management*, *25*(1), 21–42. doi:10.1108/IJAIM-05-2016-0059

Ayedh, A. M., Fatima, A. H., & Mohammad, M. H. S. (2019). Earnings Management in Malaysian Companies during the Global Financial Crisis and the Coincidental Effect of IFRS Adoption. *Australasian Accounting, Business, and Finance Journal, 13*(1), 4-26. doi:10.14453/aabfj.v13i1.2

Banderlipe, M. R. S. (2009). The impact of selected corporate governance variables in mitigating earnings management in the Philippines. *DLSU Business & Economics Review*, *19*(1), 17–27. doi:10.3860/ber.v19i1.1110

Becker, C. L., DeFond, M. L., Jiambalvo, J., & Subramanyam, K. R. (1998). The Effect of Audit Quality on Earnings Management. *Contemporary Accounting Research*, *15*(1), 1–24. doi:10.1111/j.1911-3846.1998.tb00547.x

Bhundia, A. (2012). A comparative study between free cash flows and earnings management. *Business Intelligence Journal*, *5*(1), 123–129.

Cai, J. (2013). Does corporate governance reduce the overinvestment of free cash flow? Empirical evidence from China. *Journal of Finance and Investment Analysis*, *2*(3), 97–126.

Chamberlain, T. W., Butt, U. R., & Sarkar, S. (2014). Accruals and Real Earnings Management Around Debt Covenant Violations. *International Advances in Economic Research*, *20*(1), 119–120. doi:10.100711294-013-9422-3

Chen, K. Y., Elder, R. J., & Hung, S. (2010). The investment opportunity set and earnings management: Evidence from the role of controlling shareholders. *Corporate Governance*, *18*(3), 193–211. doi:10.1111/j.1467-8683.2010.00793.x

Chen, X., Cheng, Q., & Wang, X. (2015). Does increased board independence reduce earnings management? Evidence from recent regulatory reforms. *Review of Accounting Studies*, *20*(2), 899–933. doi:10.100711142-015-9316-0

Chen, X., Sun, Y., & Xu, X. (2016). Free cash flow, over-investment and corporate governance in China. *Pacific-Basin Finance Journal*, *37*, 81–103. doi:10.1016/j.pacfin.2015.06.003

Cheung, W. M., & Jiang, L. (2016). Does free cash flow problem contribute to excess stock return synchronicity? *Review of Quantitative Finance and Accounting*, *46*(1), 123–140. doi:10.100711156-014-0464-2

Chung, R., Firth, M., & Kim, J.-B. (2005). Earnings management, surplus free cash flow, and external monitoring. *Journal of Business Research*, *58*(6), 766–776. doi:10.1016/j.jbusres.2003.12.002

D'Mello, R., & Miranda, M. (2010). Long-term debt and overinvestment agency problem. *Journal of Banking & Finance*, *34*(2), 324–335. doi:10.1016/j.jbankfin.2009.07.021

Dechow, P. M., Sloan, R. G., & Sweeney, A. P. (1995). Detecting Earnings Management. *The Accounting Review*, *70*(2), 193–225. https://www.jstor.org/stable/248303

DeFond, M. L., & Jiambalvo, J. (1994). Debt covenant violation and manipulation of accruals. *Journal of Accounting and Economics*, *17*(1-2), 145–176. doi:10.1016/0165-4101(94)90008-6

Fernandez, R. (2011). *Explaining the decline of the Amsterdam financial centre: Globalizing finance and the rise of a hierarchical inter-city network* (PhD Thesis). University of Amsterdam, The Netherlands.

Fernandez, R. (2011). *Explaining the decline of the Amsterdam financial centre: Globalizing finance and the rise of a hierarchical inter-city network* (PhD Thesis). University of Amsterdam, The Netherlands.

Fernandez, V. (2011). The Driving Factors of Firm Investment: Latin American Evidence. *Emerging Markets Finance & Trade*, *47*(5), 4–26. doi:10.2753/REE1540-496X470501

Firth, M., Lin, C., & Wong, S. M. L. (2008). Leverage and investment under a state-owned bank lending environment: Evidence from China. *Journal of Corporate Finance*, *14*(5), 642–653. doi:10.1016/j.jcorpfin.2008.08.002

Friska, F., & Kashan, P. (2019). Company Characteristics, Corporate Governance, Audit Quality Impact on Earnings Management. *Accounting & Finance Review*, *4*(2), 43–49. doi:10.35609/afr.2019.4.2(2)

Ghorbani, A., & Salehi, N. (2020). Earnings management and the informational and disciplining role of debt: Evidence from Iran. *Journal of Asia Business Studies*. Advance online publication. doi:10.1108/JABS-11-2019-0336

Habib, A. (2011). Growth opportunities, earnings permanence and the valuation of free cash flow. *Australasian Accounting, Finance, and Business Journal*, *5*(4), 101–122.

Harvey, C. R., Lins, K. V., & Roper, A. H. (2004). The effect of capital structure when expected agency costs are extreme. *Journal of Financial Economics*, *74*(1), 3–30. doi:10.1016/j.jfineco.2003.07.003

Healy, P. M., & Wahlen, J. M. (1999). A Review of the Earnings Management Literature and its Implications for Standard Setting. *Accounting Horizons*, *13*(4), 365–383. doi:10.2308/acch.1999.13.4.365

Iatridis, G., & Kadorinis, G. (2009). Earnings management and firm financial motives: A financial investigation of UK listed firms. *International Review of Financial Analysis*, *18*(4), 164–173. doi:10.1016/j.irfa.2009.06.001

Jensen, M. C. (1986). Agency costs of free cash flow, corporate finance, and takeovers. *The American Economic Review*, *76*(2), 323–329. https://www.jstor.org/stable/1818789

Jensen, M. C., & Meckling, W. H. (1976). Theory of the Firm: Managerial Behavior, Agency and Ownership Structure. *Journal of Financial Economics*, *3*(4), 305–360. doi:10.1016/0304-405X(76)90026-X

Jiang, W., Lee, P., & Anandarajan, A. (2008). The association between corporate governance and earnings quality: Further evidence using the GOV-score. *Advances in Accounting incorporating. Advances in International Accounting*, *24*(2), 191–201. doi:10.1016/j.adiac.2008.08.011

Jones, S., & Sharma, R. (2001). The impact of free cash flow, financial leverage and accounting regulation on earnings management in Australia's "old" and "new" economies. *Managerial Finance*, *27*(12), 18–39. doi:10.1108/03074350110767420

Kapoor, N., & Goel, S. (2017). Board Characteristics, Firm Profitability and Earnings Management: Evidence from India. *Australian Accounting Review*, *81*(27), 180–194. doi:10.1111/auar.12144

Kothari, S. P., Leone, A. J., & Wasley, C. E. (2005). Performance matched discretionary accrual measures. *Journal of Accounting and Economics*, *39*(1), 163–197. doi:10.1016/j.jacceco.2004.11.002

Krishnan, G. V. (2003). Audit Quality and the Pricing of Discretionary Accruals. *Auditing*, *22*(1), 109–126. doi:10.2308/aud.2003.22.1.109

Labhane, N. B., & Mahakud, J. (2016). Determinants of dividend policy of Indian companies: A panel data analysis. *Paradigm*, *20*(1), 36–55. doi:10.1177/0971890716637698

Lang, H. P., René, M., Stulz, L., & Walkling, R. A. (1991). A test of the free cash flow hypothesis: The case of Bidder returns. *Journal of Financial Economics*, *29*(2), 315–335. doi:10.1016/0304-405X(91)90005-5

Lehn, K., & Poulsen, A. (1989). Free Cash Flow and Stockholder Gains in Going Private Transactions. *The Journal of Finance*, *44*(3), 771–787. doi:10.1111/j.1540-6261.1989.tb04390.x

Matteo, P., & Francesco, P. (2018). Earnings Management in Developing Countries. The Case of Brazilian Real Estate Industry. *Academy of Accounting and Financial Studies Journal*, *22*(1), 1–12.

Myers, S. (1977). Determinants of corporate borrowing. *Journal of Financial Economics*, *5*(2), 147–175. doi:10.1016/0304-405X(77)90015-0

Ongsakul, V., Jiraporn, P., & Kim, Y. S. (2020). The effect of earnings management on shareholder value and the role of board gender diversity: Evidence from terrorism. *Pacific Accounting Review*, *32*(3), 323–334. Advance online publication. doi:10.1108/PAR-09-2019-0110

Park, K., & Jang, S. (2013). Capital structure, free cash flow, diversification and firm performance: A holistic analysis. *International Journal of Hospitality Management*, *33*, 51–63. doi:10.1016/j.ijhm.2013.01.007

Peasnell, K. V., Pope, P. F., & Young, S. (2000). Accrual Management to meet earnings targets: UK evidence pre- and post-Cadbury. *The British Accounting Review*, *32*(4), 415–445. doi:10.1006/bare.2000.0134

Peasnell, K. V., Pope, P. F., & Young, S. (2005). Board Monitoring and Earnings Management: Do Outside Directors Influence Abnormal Accruals? *Journal of Business Finance & Accounting*, *32*(7-8), 1311–1346. doi:10.1111/j.0306-686X.2005.00630.x

Raeisi, A., & Vaez, S. A. (2016). An evaluation of the relationships between the corporate governance mechanisms, the free cash flow, and earnings management in Tehran stock exchange listed companies. *International Journal of Humanities and Cultural Studies*, 122-140.

Richardson, S. (2006). Over-investment of free cash flow. *Review of Accounting Studies*, *11*(2-3), 159–189. doi:10.100711142-006-9012-1

Rusmin, R. W., Astami, E., & Hartadi, B. (2014). The impact of surplus free cash flow and audit quality on earnings management: The case of growth triangle countries. *Asian Review of Accounting*, *22*(3), 217–232. doi:10.1108/ARA-10-2013-0062

Skinner, D. (1993). The investment opportunity set and accounting procedure choice. *Journal of Accounting and Economics*, *16*(4), 407–445. doi:10.1016/0165-4101(93)90034-D

Stulz, R. (1990). Managerial discretion and optimal financing policies. *Journal of Financial Economics*, *26*(1), 3–27. doi:10.1016/0304-405X(90)90011-N

Tabachnick, B. G., & Fidell, L. S. (2001). *Using Multivariate Statistics*. Allyn and Bacon.

Toumeh, A. A., Yahya, S., & Amran, A. (2020). Surplus Free Cash Flow, Stock Market Segmentations and Earnings Management: The Moderating Role of Independent Audit Committee. *Global Business Review*, 1–30. doi:10.1177/0972150920934069

Wang, G. Y. (2010). The impacts of free cash flows and agency costs on firm performance. *Journal of Service Science and Management*, *3*(04), 408–418. doi:10.4236/jssm.2010.34047

Warfield, T., Wild, J., & Wild, K. (1995). Managerial Ownership, Accounting Choices and Informativeness of Earnings. *Journal of Accounting and Economics*, *20*(1), 61–91. doi:10.1016/0165-4101(94)00393-J

Watts, R. L., & Zimmerman, J. L. (1978). Towards a positive theory of the determination of accounting standards. *The Accounting Review*, *53*(1), 112–134. https://www.jstor.org/stable/245729

Watts, R. L., & Zimmerman, J. L. (1986). *Positive Accounting Theory*. Prentice Hall.

Yendrawati, R., & Asy'ari, E. F. (2017). The Role of Corporate Governance as a Leverage Moderating and Free Cash Flow on Earnings Management. *Jurnal Keuangan dan Perbankan, 21*(3), 412-424. doi:10.26905/jkdp.v21i3.704

Zalata, A. M., Tauringana, V., & Tingbani, I. (2018). Audit committee financial expertise, gender, and earnings management: Does gender of the financial expert matter? *International Review of Financial Analysis*, *55*, 170–183. doi:10.1016/j.irfa.2017.11.002

ADDITIONAL READING

Ahmed AL-Dhamari, R., & Nor Izah Ku Ismail, K. (2014). An investigation into the effect of surplus free cash flow, corporate governance and firm size on earnings predictability. *International Journal of Accounting and Information Management*, *22*(2), 118–133. doi:10.1108/IJAIM-05-2013-0037

Bukit, R. B., & Nasution, F. N. (2015). Employee Diff, Free Cash Flow, Corporate Governance and Earnings Management. *Procedia: Social and Behavioral Sciences*, *211*, 585–594. doi:10.1016/j.sbspro.2015.11.077

Cardoso, F. T., Martinez, A. L., & Teixeira, A. J. C. (2014). Free Cash Flow and Earnings Management in Brazil: The Negative Side of Financial Slack. *Global Journal of Management and Business Research: Accounting and Auditing*, *14*(1), 84–96.

Griffin, P. A., Lont, D. H., & Sun, Y. (2010). Agency problems and audit fees: Further tests of the free cash flow hypothesis. *Accounting and Finance*, *50*(2), 321–350. doi:10.1111/j.1467-629X.2009.00327.x

Kadioglu, E., & Yilmaz, E. A. (2017). Is the free cash flow hypothesis valid in Turkey? *Borsa Istanbul Review*, *17*(2), 111–116. doi:10.1016/j.bir.2016.12.001

Lin, D., & Lin, L. (2016). How does Corporate Governance Affect Free Cash Flow? *Journal of Applied Finance & Banking*, *6*(3), 145–156.

Rahman, A. F., & Mohd-Saleh, N. (2008). The Effect of Free Cash Flow Agency Problem on the Value Relevance of Earnings and Book Value. *Journal of Financial Reporting and Accounting*, *6*(1), 75–90. doi:10.1108/19852510880000636

Smith, D. D., & Pennathur, A. K. (2019). Signaling Versus Free Cash Flow Theory: What Does Earnings Management Reveal About Dividend Initiation? *Journal of Accounting, Auditing & Finance*, *34*(2), 284–308. doi:10.1177/0148558X17724051

Staglianò, R., La Rocca, M., & La Rocca, T. (2014). Agency costs of free cash flow, internal capital markets and unrelated diversification. *Review of Managerial Science*, *8*(2), 145–174. doi:10.100711846-013-0098-0

Zamri, N., Rahman, R. A., & Isa, N. S. M. (2013). The Impact of Leverage on Real Earnings Management. *Procedia Economics and Finance*, *7*, 86–95. doi:10.1016/S2212-5671(13)00222-0

KEY TERMS AND DEFINITIONS

Earning Management: Occurs when managers exercise their discretion over the accounting numbers to achieve specific objective.

Free Cash Flow: Represents the cash a firm generates after accounting for cash outflows to support operations and maintain its capital assets.

Leverage: Is the amount of debt that a firm uses to finance assets.

Manager: An individual who exercises executive managerial functions.

Chapter 6
Bi-Level Programming for Earning Management in Imprecise and Random Environments

Vishnu Pratap Singh
https://orcid.org/0000-0002-6846-6187
Visvesvaraya National Institute of Technology, Nagpur, India

ABSTRACT

Organizations striving in today's environment of active technological and business transformations are confronted with the difficulties of "twofoldness," that is, performing efficiently in the present while innovating effectively for the future. Administrators inside these organizations not only have to concentrate on the business benefit and profitability of each of their authorized commodities and services but must also guarantee their ability to introduce into next-generation contributions that output properties that will maintain and even enhance their renewed global competitiveness. The surprisingly fast breakdown of so many probably great companies over the last decade gives an extensive declaration to the consequence of accomplishing this dualism. In this chapter, to deal with this dualism, the authors consider a fuzzy stochastic bi-level programming problem in the mathematical models. The fuzziness and randomness concept has been taken care of by the fuzzy random variable as the parameter of the bi-level programming problem. A two-stage approach has been defined to solve the problem.

1. INTRODUCTION

In a hierarchical organizational structure, decision-makers frequently trade with conflicting goals. At one level of the hierarchy, a DM may hold his individual goal and decision area and due to another level of the hierarchy, it may be affected by the distinct levels. The hierarchical organization trades with decentralized programming problems with various decision-makers which can be referred to as multi-level programming (MLP). The bi-level programming problem (BLPP) is a specific instance of MLP. There are

DOI: 10.4018/978-1-7998-7596-3.ch006

two separate hierarchical levels including a couple of decision-makers in BLPP. Both the DM examines their variables individually. The upper-level decision-maker is called the leader who can influence the objective function of the lower level (Decision-maker of the lower level is called the follower). Both the DM wants to optimize its objective function and is influenced by the judgments of one another. The nested structure of the overall problem requires that a solution to the upper-level problem may be feasible only if it is an optimal solution to the lower level problem. Bi-level programming is complicated to deal with due to its inherent non-convexity. The principal component of analysis on the bi-level programming problem is yet concerned in the deterministic case. In the literature, Bi-level programming problem has been first formulated by Candler and Townsley (1982) and *Fortuny & McCarl (1981)*.

The BLPP models defined by *Candler and Townsley (1982)*, *Bialas and Karwan (1984)*, and *Bard (1991)*can be formulated as:

$$\max_{X} G_1\left(X, Y\right) = AX + BY$$

where Y solves

$$\max_{Y} G_2\left(X, Y\right) = CX + DY$$

s.t. $EX + FY \leq R,$

Here $A, C \in \mathbb{R}^{n_1}$, $B, D \in \mathbb{R}^{n_2}$, $R \in \mathbb{R}^{m}$, E is an $m \times n_1$ matrix, F is an $m \times n_2$ matrix. $\left(X, Y\right) \in \mathbb{R}^{n}$ is a vector of decision variables which can be controlled by the decision makers. $X \in \mathbb{R}^{n_1}$ is a vector control by leader and $Y \in \mathbb{R}^{n_2}$ by follower, where $n_1 + n_2 = n$. G_1 & G_2 are the objectives functions of leader and follower respectively. In the past several approaches have been studied by *Bard (1984)*, *Bard(1991)*, *Wen and Hsu (1991)*, *Wen and Hsu (1991)*, *Bialas and Karwan (1984)* and others to solve the bi-level programming problem.

Bi-level programming problems are usually encountered in the field of economics, transportation, environmental economics, decision science, engineering, business, etc. Yet, in real-world circumstances, chance and impreciseness are included in describing the parameters. It is challenging to establish parameters in the objective functions and constraints in this case. Both the DMs have to take a decisiveness even if they do not comprehend the parameter of the problem with complete conviction hence bi-level programming problem with fuzzy parameter and Stochastic bi-level programming problem (bi-level programming with random variable coefficients) has been developed separately. *Sakawa et. al. (2000)* described the bi-level programming problem with fuzzy parameter and introduced a fuzzy programming method to solve it. *Zhang and Lu (2005)* designed a fuzzy number based Kuhn-Tucker condition to solve bi-level programming problem with the fuzzy parameter. Some multi-objective bi-level programming also has been studied with fuzzy parameter *Gao et. al. (2009)* and *Zhang and Lu (2010)*. For the randomness, *Nishizaki et. al. (2003)* solved the bi-level programming problem with random variable coefficients. They considered the variance of the objective function of the leader and means of the objective function of the follower to find the deterministic programming problem. Stochastic bi-level programming problem has been solved by Kosuch et. al. with probabilistic knapsack constraints, which can be used to jointly optimize network resources and service pricing. *Li et. al. (2018)* introduced a bi-level optimization model consisting of power market clearing and DSR aggregator internal scheduling. *Gholami et. al. (2020)* extended the single-period decentralized channel optimization problem with stochastic demand into a multi-period, non-autonomous one and propose an efficient general solution algorithm for it. A supply channel composed of two price-setting agents in a bi-level (Stackelberg) framework has to address an uncertain dynamic demand for a perishable good at different times. An evolutionary optimization model for maximizing the profits of the transportation agency that considers conflicts between executive decision making and passenger flow was developed by *Chou et. al. (2020)*. To resolve these conflicts, the bi-level planning approach was applied to consider both upper-level and lower-level planning and reflect passenger behavior and transportation profit management. *Liu et. al. (2020)* proposed a bi-level programming model for the coordinated DG and EVCSs planning problem. The maximisation of annual overall profit for the power supply company is taken as the objective function for the upper planning level. Then, each scenario is optimised at the lower level by using active management strategies. The management of fast-growing plantations involves two-layer decision makers, such as forestry management departments and direct operators. Direct operators are interested in the economic benefits of plantation management, while forestry management departments aim to preserve reasonable age structures and sustainable development within plantations. A bi-level programming model has been introduced by *Zhai et. al. (2014)* for optimizing the management of fast-growing plantations. *Rashidizadeh et. al. (2019)* investigated a stochastic bi-level scheduling model for decision-making of a load-serving entity (LSE) in competitive day-ahead (DA) and regulating markets with uncertainties. To model the actions of Disco, a bi-level optimization method is developed by *Bahramara (2018)* where Disco problem is modeled at the upper-level problem, whereas the MGs problem together with the day-ahead market clearing procedure are modeled as the lower-level problems.

But in real-world decision-making conditions, the simultaneous occurrence of randomness and fuzziness is a basic demand. An interactive fuzzy programming method by using fuzzy goals with fractile criterion optimization has been developed by *Sakawa et. al. (2011)* to deal with the fuzzy random bi-level programming problem. *Sakawa and Katagiri (2012)* used level sets and fractile criterion optimization to solve a fuzzy random bi-level programming problem. *Sakawa et. al. (2014)* used level set and probability maximization to solve a fuzzy random bi-level programming problem. Recently, *Sakawa and Matsui (2013)* developed an interactive fuzzy programming approach to solve fuzzy random bi-level linear programming problems through probability maximization with possibility. *Ren and Wang (2014)* and *Ren and Wang (2015)* considered a kind of bi-level linear programming problem where the coefficients of objective functions are fuzzy random variables. The approach first transforms the fuzzy random bi-level programming problem into an α-stochastic interval bi-level linear programming problem. The α-stochastic interval bi-level linear programming problem can be converted into a deterministic multi-objective bi-level linear programming problem. Considering the collective response of the decision-makers, two-level linear programming problems involving random variables in constraints are considered by *Sakawa et. al. (2014)*. Using the theory of simple recourse, the formulated stochastic two-level simple recourse problems are transformed into deterministic two-level programming ones.

In the literature, fuzzy random variable has been considered only in the objective functions of the fuzzy random bi-level linear programming problem. Inspired by *Chakraborty D. (2015), Singh V. P. (2020), Singh et. al. (2020), Singh & Sharma (2020)* and *Singh and Chakraborty (2019),* paper on solving different types of programming problem in the mixed environment, In this chapter, fuzzy stochastic bi-level programming has been considered to deal with fuzziness and randomness simultaneously. Here the coefficients of both the objective functions as well as constraints are fuzzy random variable. *Kwakernaak H. (1978), Kwakernaak H. (1979)* and *Puri et. al. (1993)* presented the concept of fuzzy random variable, fuzzy expectation and its fuzzy variance.

The chapter is arranged as follows. In section 2, fuzzy Stochastic bi-level programming problem has been introduced first which is followed by the methodology of solving this type problem. Section 3 deals with a numerical example and the conclusion has been made in section 4.

2. DEFINITIONS AND PRELIMINARIES

2.1 Fuzzy numbers [*Zimmermann (2011)*]**:** A convex normalized fuzzy set is said to be the fuzzy number if the universe of discourse is given by $X = \mathbb{R}$ (the set of all real number) and the membership function $\mu_{\tilde{A}}(x)$ is a piecewise continuous function.

(Reference Function) A function, usually denoted by “ L ” or “ R ”, is a reference function if and only if

1. $L(x) = L(-x)$,
2. $L(0) = 1$,
3. $L(.)$ is non-increasing on $[0, \infty)$.

2.2 Triangular Fuzzy Number [*Zimmermann (2011)*]: It is a normalized fuzzy number represented with three points as $\tilde{A} = (a_1, a_2, a_3)$, where a_1, a_2, a_3 are real numbers. The membership function $\mu_{\tilde{A}}(x)$ of a triangular fuzzy number is a function from $\mathbb{R}$ to $[0,1]$ and given by

$$\mu_{\tilde{A}}(x) = \begin{cases} 0, & x < a_1 \\ \dfrac{x - a_1}{a_2 - a_1}, & a_1 \le x \le a_2 \\ \dfrac{a_3 - x}{a_3 - a_2}, & a_2 \le x \le a_3 \\ 0, & x > a_3 \end{cases}$$

2.3 L-R type Fuzzy Number [*Zimmermann (2011)*]: A fuzzy number $\tilde{M}$ is of L-R type if there exist reference functions L (for left), R (for right), and scalars $\alpha > 0, \beta > 0$ with

$$\mu_{\tilde{M}}(x) = \begin{cases} L\left(\dfrac{m - x}{\alpha}\right), & for\, x \le m \\ R\left(\dfrac{x - m}{\beta}\right), & for\, x \ge m \end{cases} \tag{2}$$

m , called the mean value of $\tilde{M}$, is a real number and α and β are called the left and right spreads, respectively. Symbolically $\tilde{M}$ is denoted by $(m,\alpha,\beta)_{LR}$.

For reference function L , different functions can be chosen, for instance, $L(x) = \max(0,1-x)^p$, $L(x) = \max(0,1-x^p)$, with $p>0$, $L(x) = e^{-x}$ or $L(x) = e^{-x^2}$. If m is not a real number but an interval $[\underline{m},\overline{m}]$ then the fuzzy set $\tilde{M}$ is not a fuzzy number but a fuzzy interval.

For *L*-*R* type fuzzy number the computations necessary for the arithmetic operations are considerably simplified. Let $\tilde{A} = (a,\alpha,\beta)_{LR}, \tilde{B} = (b,\gamma,\delta)_{LR}$ be two fuzzy number of *L*-*R* type. Then,

1. $(a,\alpha,\beta)_{LR} \oplus (b,\gamma,\delta)_{LR} = (a+b,\alpha+\gamma,\beta+\delta)_{LR}$
2. $-(a,\alpha,\beta)_{LR} = (-a,\beta,\alpha)_{LR}$
3. $(a,\alpha,\beta)_{LR} \ominus (b,\gamma,\delta)_{LR} = (a-b,\alpha+\delta,\beta+\gamma)_{LR}$

2.4 Fuzzy random variable: A fuzzy random variable may be thought of as random variables whose values are fuzzy number. *H. Kwakernaak (1978, 1979)* and *M.L. Puri and D.A. Ralescu* (1993) introduced the notion of a fuzzy random variable.

Let (Ω, A, P) be probability space where Ω is the sample space, A is σ-*algebra* on Ω and P is the probability measure. Let $F(\mathbb{R})$ be the set of all fuzzy numbers on $\mathbb{R}$. A function $\tilde{\xi} : \Omega \to \mathbb{R}$ is said to be fuzzy random variable if $\underline{\xi}_\alpha$ and $\overline{\xi}_\alpha$ are two real valued random variables for all $\alpha \in [o,1]$ which are defined as follows:

$$\underline{\xi}_\alpha(x) = \inf\left(x \in \mathbb{R} : \mu_{\tilde{\xi}}(x) \geq \alpha\right) \text{and}$$

$$\overline{\xi}_\alpha(x) = \sup\left(x \in \mathbb{R} : \mu_{\tilde{\xi}}(x) \geq \alpha\right)$$

where $A \subset 2^{\copyright}$ is said to be $\sigma - algebra$ if it satisfies the following three properties:

- $\Omega \in A$ i.e. A contains the sample space Ω.
- If a set $S \in A$ then $S^c \in A$ i.e. A is closed under complements.
- If $S_i \in A$ then $\left(\bigcup_{i=1}^{\infty} S_i\right) \in A$ i.e. A is closed under countable union.

So if $\tilde{\xi}$ is a fuzzy random variable, then $\left[\tilde{\xi}\right]_\alpha = \left[\underline{\xi}_\alpha, \overline{\xi}_\alpha\right]$, $\alpha \in [0,1]$ is a random closed interval set.

Bur according to *M.L. Puri and D.A. Ralescu* (1993), the fuzzy random variable is directly generated as a fuzzy valued variable. For the probability space (Ω, A, P), a function $\tilde{\xi} : \Omega \to F(\mathbb{R}^n)$ is said to be fuzzy random variable if for all $\alpha \in [0,1]$ the set value mappings $\xi_\alpha : \Omega \to C(\mathbb{R}^n)$ are random sets where $C(\mathbb{R}^n)$ denotes the set of all compact subset of $\mathbb{R}^n$.

H. Kwakernaak defined fuzzy random variable such that for each $\alpha \in [0,1]$ $\tilde{\xi}_\alpha$ are real valued random variables. On the other hand by definition given by Puri and Ralescu α-*cuts* are set value mappings. Though their approaches are different, [?] proved that both the definitions are equivalent.

2.4.1 Discrete Fuzzy Random Variable:

Suppose (Ω, A, P) be probability space and $\tilde{\xi}$ be is a fuzzy random variable, $\tilde{\xi}$ is said to be discrete fuzzy random variable if Ω is a countable set.

Expectation and Variance

Expectation of fuzzy random variable $\tilde{\xi}$ is denoted by $E(\tilde{\xi})$ and defined by

$$E(\tilde{\xi}) = \int \tilde{\xi} dP = \left\{\left(\int \underline{\xi}_\alpha dP, \int \overline{\xi}_\alpha dP\right) : 0 \le \alpha \le 1\right\}$$

If $\tilde{\xi}$ is a discrete fuzzy random variable such that $P\left(\tilde{\xi} = \tilde{\xi}(s)\right) = \tilde{p}_s$, $s = 1,2\ldots S$, then its expectation and variance are defined by

$$E[\tilde{\xi}] = \sum_{s=1}^{S} \tilde{p}_s \odot \tilde{\xi}(s),$$

$$Var[\tilde{\xi}] = E[(\tilde{\xi} - E[\tilde{\xi}])^2]$$

3. FUZZY STOCHASTIC BI-LEVEL PROGRAMMING PROBLEM

We consider the bi-level programming problem where the coefficients of both the objective functions as well as constraints are fuzzy random variable and it is defined as:

$$\widetilde{\max_X} \tilde{G}_1(X,Y) \doteqdot \sum_{i=1}^{n} \tilde{a}_i x_i + \sum_{j=1}^{m} \tilde{b}_j y_j$$

where Y solves

$$\widetilde{\max_{Y}}\tilde{G}_2\left(X,Y\right) \doteq \sum_{i=1}^{n} \tilde{c}_i x_i + \sum_{j=1}^{m} \tilde{d}_j y_j$$

$$\tilde{H}_k\left(X,Y\right) \doteq \sum_{i=1}^{n} \tilde{m}_{ik} x_i + \sum_{j=1}^{m} \tilde{n}_{jk} y_j \lesssim \tilde{r}_k,$$

$$x_1, x_2 \ldots x_n \geq 0, y_1, y_2 \ldots y_m \geq 0.$$

$$i = 1,2,\ldots n, j = 1,2,\ldots m, k = 1,2\ldots p. \tag{1}$$

Here $X \in \mathbb{R}^n$ and $\tilde{G}_1$, $Y \in \mathbb{R}^m$ and $\tilde{G}_2$ are the decision variables and objective functions for leader and follower respectively. $\tilde{H}_k, k = 1,2\ldots p.$ represents the number of constraints for fuzzy Stochastic bi-level programming problem. $\tilde{a}_i$, $\tilde{c}_i$, $\tilde{m}_{ik}$ for $i = 1,2\ldots n, k = 1,2\ldots p$, $\tilde{b}_j$, $\tilde{d}_j$, $\tilde{n}_{jk}$,for $j = 1,2\ldots m, k = 1,2\ldots p$ are positive fuzzy random variable with finite support. For the sake of simplicity all the fuzzy random variable and $\tilde{r}_k, k = 1,2\ldots p$ can be considered as triangular type fuzzy number. We have considered that all the fuzzy random variables have finite support, i.e all the fuzzy random variables have finite number of realization or scenarios with respective fuzzy probabilities. If $\tilde{a}_i$ is a fuzzy random variable, has finite number of realizations and scenarios $\tilde{a}_{is}$ (say) with respective fuzzy probabilities say $\tilde{p}_{as}$ where $s \in \left\{1,2\ldots S\right\}$ such that $\sum_{s=1}^{S} \tilde{p}_{as} = \tilde{1}$ (*Chakraborty D. (1995)*) then we can define the notation of scenarios and fuzzy probabilities for all fuzzy random variables in the same way. Such type of problem can be considered as fuzzy stochastic bi-level programming problem.

Further assumptions may be considered to define the above model as a fuzzy two-stage stochastic bi-level programming problem. At first Stage, we convert the above model in fuzzy programming problem. Later on the second stage, the fuzzy programming problem is converted into deterministic programming problem using *Bellman and Zadeh (1970)* minimum operator and the upper bound of the $\alpha - cut$ of the follower's objective function. We use the fuzzy goal programming approach (*Aouni et. al. (2009)*) to solve deterministic programming problem at the second stage.

3.1 The Optimization Procedure

To take on the above problem, first we need to define $\widetilde{\max}\tilde{G}_1\left(X,Y\right)$ and $\widetilde{\max}\tilde{G}_2\left(X,Y\right)$. It is possible to model the above fuzzy stochastic bi-level programming problem into fuzzy equivalent form i.e. Fuzzy BLPP. A fuzzy equivalent objective functions for leader and follower may be built as:

$$\widetilde{\max_{X}} k_1.E\left(\tilde{G}_1\left(X,Y\right)\right) - k_2.Var\left(\tilde{G}_1\left(X,Y\right)\right) \tag{2}$$

$$\widetilde{\max_{Y}} k_1.E\left(\tilde{G}_2\left(X,Y\right)\right) - k_2.Var\left(\tilde{G}_2\left(X,Y\right)\right) \tag{3}$$

where the numerical values of $k_1 \geq 0$ and $k_2 \geq 0$ indicate the relative importance of expected value and variance of fuzzy random objective functions. Mean and variance of objective functions are fuzzy numbers $E\left(\tilde{G}_1\left(X,Y\right)\right)$ and $E\left(\tilde{G}_2\left(X,Y\right)\right)$ can be defined as:

$$E\left(\tilde{G}_1\left(X,Y\right)\right) = \sum_{s=1}^{S} \tilde{p}_s \odot \tilde{G}_1\left(X,Y,\tilde{a}_{is},\tilde{b}_{js}\right)$$

$$E\left(\tilde{G}_2\left(X,Y\right)\right) = \sum_{s=1}^{S} \tilde{p}_s \odot \tilde{G}_2\left(X,Y,\tilde{c}_{is},\tilde{d}_{js}\right)$$

After calculating expectations of each objective functions, Variance can be calculated as

$$Var\left(\tilde{G}_1\left(X,Y\right)\right) = E[\tilde{G}_1\left(X,Y\right) - E\left(\tilde{G}_1\left(X,Y\right)\right)]^2$$

$$Var\left(\tilde{G}_2\left(X,Y\right)\right) = E[\tilde{G}_2\left(X,Y\right) - E\left(\tilde{G}_2\left(X,Y\right)\right)]^2$$

The constraints set may also be newly defined as

$$k_1.E\left(\tilde{H}_k\left(X,Y\right)\right) + k_2.Var\left(\tilde{H}_k\left(X,Y\right)\right) \lesssim \tilde{r}_k$$

for all $k = 1,2\ldots p.$ (4)

Thus the final form of fuzzy equivalent fuzzy stochastic BLPP in fuzzy BLPP is given as follows:

$$\widetilde{\max_{X}} k_1.E\left(\tilde{G}_1\left(X,Y\right)\right) - k_2.Var\left(\tilde{G}_1\left(X,Y\right)\right)$$

where Y solves

$$\widetilde{\max_{Y}} k_1.E\left(\tilde{G}_2\left(X,Y\right)\right) - k_2.Var\left(\tilde{G}_2\left(X,Y\right)\right)$$

s.t. $k_1.E\left(\tilde{H}_k\left(X,Y\right)\right) + k_2.Var\left(\tilde{H}_k\left(X,Y\right)\right) \lesssim \tilde{r}_k,$

$$k = 1,2\ldots p. \tag{5}$$

Now we have a fuzzy BLPP, to handling with the fuzzy constraints *Rommelfanger H. (1996)* method and for finding the aspiration level of leader or follower *Chakraborty D. (1995)* method can be used.

3.2 Fuzzy Inequality Constraint to Crisp Inequality Constraints

Rommelfanger H. (1996) has suggested that how a fuzzy inequality can be replaced by a combination of crisp inequality and an objective function. If $\tilde{C}(x) \tilde{\leq} \tilde{D}$ be a fuzzy inequality where $\tilde{C}(x) = (c(x), \alpha(x), \beta(x))_{LR}$ and $\tilde{D} = (d, \eta, \nu)_{LR}$ then the corresponding crisp inequality can be given as,

$$\tilde{C}(x) \tilde{\leq} \tilde{D} \Rightarrow \begin{cases} c(x) + \beta(x) R^{-1}(\varepsilon) \leq d + \nu R^{-1}(\varepsilon) \\ \mu_{\tilde{D}(x)} \to maximize \end{cases} \tag{6}$$

Where, $\varepsilon \in [0,1]$ is chosen by decision maker and $\mu_{\tilde{D}(x)}$ is defined as

$$\mu_{\tilde{D}}(x) = \begin{cases} 1 & c(x) \leq d \\ \dfrac{d + \nu R^{-1}(\varepsilon) - c(x)}{\nu R^{-1}(\varepsilon)} & d \leq c(x) \leq d + \nu R^{-1}(\varepsilon) \\ 0 & c(x) \geq d + \nu R^{-1}(\varepsilon) \end{cases} \tag{7}$$

In our model, we have fuzzy constraints in equation (5). Let us consider the form

$$\tilde{H}_k(X,Y) = (H_k(X,Y), \alpha_k^G(X,Y), \beta_k^G(X,Y))_{LR}$$

$$= \tilde{k}_1.E(\tilde{H}_k(X,Y)) + k_2.Var(\tilde{H}_k(X,Y)) \tilde{\leq} \tilde{r}_k \tag{8}$$

$$\tilde{r}_k = (r_k, 0, \delta_k)_{LR} \tag{9}$$

For $\varepsilon = 0$, $R^{-1}(\varepsilon) = 1$ So the fuzzy constraints can be written as

$$H_k(X,Y) + \beta_k^G(X,Y) \leq r_k + \delta_k \\ k = 1,2 \ldots p. \tag{10}$$

$$\mu_{\tilde{D}}(X,Y) \to maximize \tag{11}$$

where

$$\mu_{\tilde{D}}(X,Y)=\begin{cases}1 & H_k(X,Y)\leq r_k\\ \dfrac{r_k+\delta_{ks}-H_k(X,Y)}{\delta_k} & r_k\leq H_k(X,Y)\leq r_k+\delta_k\\ 0 & H_k(X,Y)\geq r_k+\delta_k\end{cases}$$

So if there are p number of fuzzy constraints in equations (10). These fuzzy constraints are converted to $2.p$ number of crisp inequalities.

3.3 Maximization of Objective Functions

From the equation 3 let us consider

$$(G_2(X,Y),\alpha_2(X,Y),\beta_2(X,Y))_{LR}\equiv \widetilde{\max_X k_1}.E(\tilde{G}_2(X,Y))-k_2.Var(\tilde{G}_2(X,Y)) \tag{12}$$

Which is a fuzzy objective function. To convert this objective function into crisp, since our goal is to maximize the objective one can select the upper bound of $\alpha-cut$ of this $LR-type$ fuzzy number. Which can be written as:

$$[G_2(X,Y)]_\alpha^U=k_1.[E(\tilde{G}_2(X,Y))]_\alpha^U-k_2.[Var(\tilde{G}_2(X,Y))]_\alpha^U \tag{13}$$

While in case of leader's objective function, from the equation 2, let us consider

$$(G_1(X,Y),\alpha_1(X,Y),\beta_1(X,Y))_{LR}\equiv \widetilde{\max_X k_1}.E(\tilde{G}_1(X,Y))-k_2.Var(\tilde{G}_1(X,Y)) \tag{14}$$

is the objective function. Suppose leader wants to find an aspiration level (*Chakraborty D. (1995)*) $\tilde{N}=(n,0,\delta)_{LR}$ such that $(G_1(X,Y),\alpha_1(X,Y),\beta_1(X,Y))_{LR}\tilde{\leq}\tilde{N}$ Since this is a fuzzy inequality, the crisp equivalent form of this can be written as

$$\begin{cases}G_1(X,Y)+\beta_1(X,Y)\leq n+\delta\\ \mu_{\tilde{D}_1(X,Y)}\rightarrow maximize\end{cases}$$

where

$$\mu_{\tilde{D}_1}(X,Y)=\begin{cases}1 & G_1(X,Y)\le n\\ \dfrac{n+\delta-G_1(X,Y)}{\delta} & n\le G_1(X,Y)\le n+\delta\\ 0 & G_1(X,Y)\ge n+\delta\end{cases}$$

for n solve

$\max G_1(X,Y)$ subject to 10

$x_1,x_2\ldots x_n\ge 0, y_1,y_2\ldots y_m\ge 0.$

$$i=1,2,\ldots n, j=1,2,\ldots m, k=1,2\ldots p. \tag{15}$$

For $n+\delta$

$\max G_1(X,Y)+\beta_1(X,Y)$ subject to 10

$x_1,x_2\ldots x_n\ge 0, y_1,y_2\ldots y_m\ge 0.$

$$i=1,2,\ldots n, j=1,2,\ldots m, k=1,2\ldots p. \tag{16}$$

3.4 Equivalent Deterministic Model

The final form of the equivalent crisp model can be written as, using 13 and (*Bellman and Zadeh (1970)*) min operator.

$\max\ \lambda$

$$\max_Y k_1.\left[E\left(\tilde{G}_2(X,Y)\right)\right]_\alpha^U - k_2.\left[Var\left(\tilde{G}_2(X,Y)\right)\right]_\alpha^U$$

subject to

$G_1(X,Y)+\lambda.\delta\le n+\delta$

$G_1(X,Y)+\beta_1(X,Y)\le n+\delta$

$$H_k(X,Y)+\lambda.\delta_k \le r_k+\delta_k$$

$$H_k(X,Y)+\beta_k(X,Y).r_k \le r_k+\delta_k.r_k$$

$$i=1,2,\dots n, j=1,2,\dots m, k=1,2\dots p. \tag{17}$$

Now this is a BLPP which can be solved using fuzzy goal programming approach. Let X^* and Y^* be the optimal solution of this model, then

$$k_1.E\left(\tilde{G}_1\left(X^*,Y^*\right)\right)-k_2.Var\left(\tilde{G}_1\left(X^*,Y^*\right)\right)$$

and

$$k_1.E\left(\tilde{G}_2\left(X^*,Y^*\right)\right)-k_2.Var\left(\tilde{G}_2\left(X^*,Y^*\right)\right)$$

is the equivalent optimal objective value of leader and follower respectively.

4. NUMERICAL EXAMPLE

Let us consider the following fuzzy stochastic bi-level programming problem:

$$\widetilde{\max_X}\tilde{G}_1(X,Y) \doteqdot \tilde{c}_1x_1+\tilde{c}_2x_2+\tilde{c}_3y_1$$

where Y solves

$$\widetilde{\max_Y}\tilde{G}_2(X,Y) \doteqdot \tilde{c}_4x_2+\tilde{c}_1y_1-\tilde{c}_2y_2$$

s.t. $\tilde{H}_1(X,Y) \doteqdot \tilde{c}_2x_1+\tilde{c}_2x_2+\tilde{c}_4y_1+\tilde{c}_3y_2 \lesssim \tilde{8},$

$$\tilde{H}_2(X,Y) \doteqdot \tilde{1}x_1+\tilde{1}x_2+\tilde{1}y_1+ \lesssim \tilde{2},$$

$$\tilde{H}_3(X,Y) \doteqdot \tilde{1}x_2+\tilde{1}y_1+\tilde{1}y_2+ \lesssim \tilde{3},$$

$$H_4(X,Y)=x_1 \le 4,$$

$H_5(X,Y) = x_2 \leq 4,$

$H_6(X,Y) = y_1 \leq 2,$

$H_7(X,Y) = y_2 \leq 2,$

$$x_1, x_2 \geq 0, y_1, y_2 \geq 0. \quad (18)$$

Table 1. Fuzzy random variables and its probability distribution for FSBLPP

	$\tilde{c}_1$	$\tilde{c}_2$	$\tilde{c}_3$	$\tilde{c}_4$	**Probability**
ω_1	$(5,2,3)_{LR}$	$(2,1,1)_{LR}$	$(4,2,2)_{LR}$	$(3,1,2)_{LR}$	$(.4,.05,0)_{LR}$
ω_2	$(10,5,5)_{LR}$	$(8,2,2)_{LR}$	$(12,3,3)_{LR}$	$(10,2,1.5)_{LR}$	$(.6,0,.02)_{LR}$

where $\tilde{c}_1$, $\tilde{c}_2$, $\tilde{c}_3$, $\tilde{c}_4$ are positive discrete random variable and $\tilde{1} = (1,0,0.2)_{LR}$. Now let us assume there are two points in the sample space © $= \{\omega_1, \omega_2\}$ where ω_1, ω_2 are sample points and $\tilde{c}_1$, $\tilde{c}_2$, $\tilde{c}_3$, $\tilde{c}_4$ are independently distributed with fuzzy probability distribution given in the table. We use the optimization procedure given in the section 2.1 to convert the leader's and follower's objective function in fuzzy equivalent form. Considering $k_1 = 1$ and $k_2 = 0$, the leader's objective function can be calculated in fuzzy equivalent form as follows:

$$\widetilde{\max_X} E\left[\tilde{G}_1(X,Y)\right] = \sum_{s=1}^{2} \tilde{p}_s \odot \tilde{G}_{1s}(X,Y)$$

$$= \left(G_1(X,Y), \alpha_1(X,Y), \beta_1(X,Y)\right)_{LR}$$

where

$\tilde{G}_1(X,Y) = 8x_1 + 5.6x_2 + 8.8y_1$

$\tilde{\alpha}_1(X,Y) = 3.9x_1 + 1.7x_2 + 2.8y_1$

$\tilde{\beta}_1(X,Y) = 4.2x_1 + 1.76x_2 + 2.84y_1$

Similarly, the follower's objective function and constraints can also be calculated in fuzzy equivalent form and the final model in fuzzy form can be written as:

$$\widetilde{\max_X}(8x_1 + 5.6x_2 + 8.8y_1, 3.9x_1 + 1.7x_2 + 2.8y_1, 4.2x_1 + 1.76x_2 + 2.84y_1)_{LR}$$

where Y solves

$$\widetilde{\max_Y}(1.8x_2 + 8y_1 - 5.6y_2, 1.75x_2 + 3.95y_1 + 1.5y_2, 1.9x_2 + 4.4y_1 + 1.44y_2)_{LR}$$

subject to

$$(5.6x_1 + 5.6x_2 + 7.2y_1 + 8.8y_2, 1.7x_1 + 1.7x_2 + 1.75y_1$$
$$+2.8y_2, 1.7x_1 + 1.7x_2 + 1.9y_1 + 2.8y_2)_{LR} \le \tilde{8}$$

$$2x_1 + 2x_2 + 1.5y_1 + 3y_2)_{LR} \le (8, 0, 0.2)_{LR}$$

$$(x_1 + x_2 + y_1, 0, 0.2(x_1 + x_2 + y_1))_{LR} \le (2, 0, 0.2)_{LR}$$

$$(x_2 + y_1 + y_2, 0, 0.2(x_2 + y_1 + y_2))_{LR} \le (3, 0, 0.2)_{LR}$$

$$x_1 \le 4$$

$$x_2 \le 4$$

$$y_1 \le 2$$

$$y_2 \le 2$$

$$x_1, x_2 \ge 0, y_1, y_2 \ge 0. \quad (19)$$

Now the procedure given in 2.2 has been used to convert the fuzzy inequalities to crisp inequalities. The condition

$$\tilde{H}_1(X, Y) = (5.6x_1 + 5.6x_2 + 7.2y_1 + 8.8y_2, 1.7x_1 + 1.7x_2 + 1.75y_1$$
$$+2.8y_2, 1.7x_1 + 1.7x_2 + 1.9y_1 + 2.8y_2)_{LR} \le (8, 0, 0.2)_{LR}$$

is equivalent to

$$\tilde{H}_1(X,Y)=\begin{cases}7.3x_1+7.3x_2+9.1y_1+11.64y_2\leq 8.2\\ \mu_{\tilde{G}_1}\rightarrow maximize\end{cases}$$

where

$$\mu_{\tilde{H}_1}==\begin{cases}1, & H_1\leq 8\\ \dfrac{8.2-H_1}{0.2}, & 8\leq H_1\leq 8.2\,.\\ 0, & H_1>8.2\end{cases}$$

Here,

$$H_1(X,Y)=5.6x_1+5.6x_2+7.2y_1+8.8y_2$$

$$\tilde{H}_2(X,Y)=\begin{cases}1.2(x_1+x_2+y_1)\leq 2.2\\ \mu_{\tilde{H}_2}\rightarrow maximize\end{cases}$$

where

$$\mu_{\tilde{H}_2}=\begin{cases}1, & H_2\leq 2\\ \dfrac{2.2-H_2}{0.2}, & 2\leq H_2\leq 2.2\\ 0, & H_2>2.2\end{cases}$$

Here,

$$H_2(X,Y)=x_1+x_2+y_1$$

$$\tilde{H}_3(X,Y)=\begin{cases}1.2(x_2+y_1+y_2)\leq 3.2\\ \mu_{\tilde{H}_3}\rightarrow maximize\end{cases}$$

where

$$\mu_{\tilde{H}_3} = \begin{cases} 1, & H_3 \leq 3 \\ \dfrac{3.2 - H_3}{0.2}, & 3 \leq H_3 \leq 3.2 \\ 0, & H_3 > 3.2 \end{cases}$$

Here,

$$H_2\left(X,Y\right) = x_2 + y_1 + y_2$$

Using 2.3 and 2.4, we convert the above fuzzy model into the deterministic model and given as:

$\max \lambda$

where Y solves

$$\max_{Y} 2.75x_2 + 10.2y_1 - 4.88y_2$$

subject to

$$8x_1 + 5.6x_2 + 8.8y_1 + 1.9\lambda \leq 11.71$$

$$12.2x_1 + 7.36x_2 + 11.6y_1 \leq 13.70$$

$$7.3x_1 + 7.3y_2 + 9.1y_1 + 11.64y_2 \leq 8.2$$

$$5.6x_1 + 5.6x_2 + 7.2y_1 + 8.8y_2 + 0.2\lambda \leq 8.2$$

$$x_1 + x_2 + y_1 + .2\lambda \leq 2.2$$

$$x_2 + y_1 + y_2 + .2\lambda \leq 2.2$$

$$x_1 + x_2 + y_1 \leq 1.8$$

$$x_2 + y_1 + y_2 \leq 2.7$$

$$x_1 \leq 4$$

$x_2 \leq 4$

$y_1 \leq 2$

$y_2 \leq 2$

$$x_1, x_2 \geq 0, y_1, y_2 \geq 0. \tag{20}$$

Using Goal programming approach

$$\min \frac{1}{6.16} d_1^+ + \frac{1}{0.62} d_2^- + \frac{1}{9.19} d_3^+ + \frac{1}{0.4} d_4^-$$

subject to

$$\frac{\lambda}{6.16} + d_1^- - d_1^+ = 1$$

$$\frac{x_1 - 0.5}{0.62} + d_2^- - d_2^+ = 1$$

$$\frac{2.75x_2 + 10.2y_1 - 4.88y_2}{8.28} + d_3^- - d_3^+ = 1$$

$$\frac{y1 - 0.5}{0.4} + d_4^- - d_4^+ = 1$$

S

where S represents the constraints of equations (20) and d_i^-, d_i^+ are the deviational variables for $i = 1, 2 \ldots 4$.

On solving we get $x_1 = 0.0013$, $x_2 = 0$, $y_1 = 0.9$, $y_2 = 0$ with leader's objective value $(7.93, 2.525, 2.555)_{LR}$ and follower's objective value $(7.2, 3.5, 3.96)_{LR}$.

5. CONCLUSION

It would be moderately honest if everyone operating in a company could accept on the approaches and means by which this twofoldness could be accomplished, but such agreement is exceptional. Among the distinct requirements of everyday work specifications and compensations, administrators interpreting various market units and departmental fields normally bother on the comparable benefits of earmarking already limited sources and expertise amongst the variety of ventures that might serve "today's" versus "tomorrow's" commodities and services. Furthermore, utmost managerial methods and schemes cannot submit mere, ready-made clarifications that are adjusting to what are actually genetically contradictory requirements and difficulties. To deal with these difficulties we have developed a mathematical model with bi-level programming problem involving fuzzy random variable coefficients and named it as the fuzzy stochastic bi-level programming problem. The fuzzy programming problem has been formulated by handling the expectation and variance of the objective functions of the leader as well as follower's. Once we get the fuzzy programming model, using the aspiration level and $\alpha\text{-}cut$ for deterministic formulation of objective functions, the fuzzy programming problem is converted to the deterministic bi-level programming problem. The proposed methodology provides an optimal solution of fuzzy stochastic bi-level programming problem.

The presented method to find the optimal solution of the fuzzy stochastic bi-level programming problem is based on finding the equivalent crisp bi-level programming problem which can be solved by a goal programming approach. In other classical methods used for solving fuzzy bi-level programming problems, issues like the random nature of the coefficients because of various conditions on the given data have not been discussed. In this work, fuzziness and randomness have been dealt with by using fuzzy random variables. The expectation of a fuzzy random variable has been used to convert the given imprecise and random model into the corresponding fuzzy model, where coefficients are given by fuzzy numbers.

Table 2. Comparison of various methods

Method	Leader's Objective Value	Follower's Objective Value
Sakawa et. al. (2000)	$(6.802, 2.203, 1.001)_{LR}$	$(6.9, 2.05, 2.56)_{LR}$
Ren and wang (2015)	$(6.932, 3.06., 2.221)_{LR}$	$(7.10, 2.35, 1.24)_{LR}$
Zang and Lu (2014)	$(7.213, 2.81., 1.785)_{LR}$	$(6.992, 2.96., 2.89)_{LR}$
Zang and Lu (2005)	$(7.332, 3.06., 1.991)_{LR}$	$(7.001, 3.11., 2.98)_{LR}$
Proposed method	$(7.93, 2.525, 2.555)_{LR}$	$(7.2, 3.5, 3.96)_{LR}$

The method presented earlier can solve the fuzzy bi-level programming problem whereas the proposed method has been given with consideration of impreciseness and randomness of BLPP, which has not been discussed earlier. Comparison of the method with other works can only be done once a fuzzy bi-level programming problem has been obtained from the corresponding fuzzy stochastic bi-level programming problem. The table 2 comprises the comparison of the method presented in this paper with other method of solving fuzzy bi-level programming problem. Clearly, the proposed method gives the best result.

REFERENCES

Aouni, B., Martel, J. M., & Hassaine, A. (2009). Fuzzy goal programming model: An overview of the current state-of-the art. *Journal of Multi-Criteria Decision Analysis*, *16*(5-6), 149–161. doi:10.1002/mcda.448

Bahramara, S., Sheikhahmadi, P., Damavandi, M. Y., Shafie-Khah, M., Osório, G. J., & Catalão, J. P. (2018, June). Strategic Behavior of a Distribution Company in the Wholesale Energy Market: A Risk-Based Stochastic Bi-Level Model. In *2018 IEEE International Conference on Environment and Electrical Engineering and 2018 IEEE Industrial and Commercial Power Systems Europe (EEEIC/I&CPS Europe)* (pp. 1-6). IEEE. 10.1109/EEEIC.2018.8493872

Bard, J. F. (1984). Optimality conditions for the bilevel programming problem. *Naval Research Logistics Quarterly*, *31*(1), 13–26. doi:10.1002/nav.3800310104

Bard, J. F. (1991). Some properties of the bilevel programming problem. *Journal of Optimization Theory and Applications*, *68*(2), 371–378. doi:10.1007/BF00941574

Bellman, R. E., & Zadeh, L. A. (1970). Decision-making in a fuzzy environment. *Management Science*, *17*(4), B-141–B-164. doi:10.1287/mnsc.17.4.B141

Bialas, W. F., & Karwan, M. H. (1984). Two-level linear programming. *Management Science*, *30*(8), 1004–1020. doi:10.1287/mnsc.30.8.1004

Candler, W., & Townsley, R. (1982). A linear two-level programming problem. *Computers & Operations Research*, *9*(1), 59–76. doi:10.1016/0305-0548(82)90006-5

Chakraborty, D. (1995). *Optimization in imprecise and uncertain environment* (Doctoral dissertation, Ph. D. Thesis). Department of Mathematics, IIT Kharagpur.

Chakraborty, D. (2002). Redefining chance-constrained programming in fuzzy environment. *Fuzzy Sets and Systems*, *125*(3), 327–333. doi:10.1016/S0165-0114(00)00133-0

Chakraborty, D. (2015). Solving geometric programming problems with fuzzy random variable coefficients. *Journal of Intelligent & Fuzzy Systems*, *28*(6), 2493–2499. doi:10.3233/IFS-141528

Chou, J. S., Ongkowijoyo, C. S., Ngo, N. T., & Chen, S. Y. (2020). Evolutionary bi-level model for optimizing ticket fares and operations profit of Taiwan high-speed rail. *Research in Transportation Business & Management*, *37*, 100548. doi:10.1016/j.rtbm.2020.100548

Fortuny-Amat, J., & McCarl, B. (1981). A representation and economic interpretation of a two-level programming problem. *The Journal of the Operational Research Society*, *32*(9), 783–792. doi:10.1057/jors.1981.156

Gao, Y., Zhang, G., Ma, J., & Lu, J. (2009). A ${\bm\lambda} $-Cut and Goal-Programming-Based Algorithm for Fuzzy-Linear Multiple-Objective Bilevel Optimization. *IEEE Transactions on Fuzzy Systems*, *18*(1), 1–13. doi:10.1109/TFUZZ.2009.2030329

Gholami, R. A., Sandal, L. K., & Ubøe, J. (2020). A solution algorithm for multi-period bi-level channel optimization with dynamic price-dependent stochastic demand. *Omega*. doi:10.1016/j.omega.2020.102297

Kosuch, S., Le Bodic, P., Leung, J., & Lisser, A. (2012). On a stochastic bilevel programming problem. *Networks*, *59*(1), 107–116. doi:10.1002/net.20482

Kwakernaak, H. (1978). Fuzzy random variables—I. Definitions and theorems. *Information Sciences*, *15*(1), 1–29. doi:10.1016/0020-0255(78)90019-1

Kwakernaak, H. (1979). Fuzzy random variables—II. Algorithms and examples for the discrete case. *Information Sciences*, *17*(3), 253–278. doi:10.1016/0020-0255(79)90020-3

Li, B., Jiang, C., Zhang, G., & He, Y. (2018). Management and performance evaluation of DSR aggregator based on a bi-level optimization model. *IEEJ Transactions on Electrical and Electronic Engineering*, *13*(3), 432–441. doi:10.1002/tee.22584

Liu, L., Zhang, Y., Da, C., Huang, Z., & Wang, M. (2020). Optimal allocation of distributed generation and electric vehicle charging stations based on intelligent algorithm and bi-level programming. *International Transactions on Electrical Energy Systems*, *30*(6), e12366. doi:10.1002/2050-7038.12366

Nishizaki, I., Sakawa, M., & Katagiri, H. (2003). Stackelberg solutions to multiobjective two-level linear programming problems with random variable coefficients. *Central European Journal of Operations Research*, *11*(3).

Puri, M. L., Ralescu, D. A., & Zadeh, L. (1993). Fuzzy random variables. In *Readings in fuzzy sets for intelligent systems* (pp. 265–271). Morgan Kaufmann. doi:10.1016/B978-1-4832-1450-4.50029-8

Rashidizadeh-Kermani, H., Vahedipour-Dahraie, M., Anvari-Moghaddam, A., & Guerrero, J. M. (2019). A stochastic bi-level decision-making framework for a load-serving entity in day-ahead and balancing markets. *International Transactions on Electrical Energy Systems*, *29*(11), e12109. doi:10.1002/2050-7038.12109

Ren, A., & Wang, Y. (2014). Optimistic Stackelberg solutions to bilevel linear programming with fuzzy random variable coefficients. *Knowledge-Based Systems*, *67*, 206–217. doi:10.1016/j.knosys.2014.05.010

Ren, A., & Wang, Y. (2015). An interval approach based on expectation optimization for fuzzy random bilevel linear programming problems. *The Journal of the Operational Research Society*, *66*(12), 2075–2085. doi:10.1057/jors.2015.13

Rommelfanger, H. (1996). Fuzzy linear programming and applications. *European Journal of Operational Research*, *92*(3), 512–527. doi:10.1016/0377-2217(95)00008-9

Sakawa, M., & Katagiri, H. (2012). Stackelberg solutions for fuzzy random two-level linear programming through level sets and fractile criterion optimization. *Central European Journal of Operations Research*, *20*(1), 101–117. doi:10.100710100-010-0156-5

Sakawa, M., Katagiri, H., & Matsui, T. (2011). Interactive fuzzy random two-level linear programming through fractile criterion optimization. *Mathematical and Computer Modelling*, *54*(11-12), 3153–3163. doi:10.1016/j.mcm.2011.08.006

Sakawa, M., Katagiri, H., & Matsui, T. (2012). Stackelberg solutions for fuzzy random bilevel linear programming through level sets and probability maximization. *Operations Research*, *12*(3), 271–286. doi:10.100712351-010-0090-2

Sakawa, M., Katagiri, H., & Matsui, T. (2014). Interactive fuzzy stochastic two-level linear programming with simple recourse. *Information Sciences, 278*, 67–75. doi:10.1016/j.ins.2014.03.020

Sakawa, M., & Matsui, T. (2013). Interactive fuzzy programming for fuzzy random two-level linear programming problems through probability maximization with possibility. *Expert Systems with Applications, 40*(7), 2487–2492. doi:10.1016/j.eswa.2012.10.052

Sakawa, M., Nishizaki, I., & Uemura, Y. (2000). Interactive fuzzy programming for multi-level linear programming problems with fuzzy parameters. *Fuzzy Sets and Systems, 109*(1), 3–19. doi:10.1016/S0165-0114(98)00130-4

Singh, V. P. (2020). An Approach to Solve Fuzzy Knapsack Problem in Investment and Business Model. In *Networked Business Models in the Circular Economy* (pp. 154–173). IGI Global. doi:10.4018/978-1-5225-7850-5.ch007

Singh, V. P., & Chakraborty, D. (2019). Solving Knapsack Problem with Fuzzy Random Variable Coefficients. In *International Conference on Innovation in Modern Science and Technology* (pp. 1037-1048). Springer.

Singh, V. P., & Sharma, K. (2020). Capacitated Vehicle Routing Problem with Interval Type-2 Fuzzy Demands. In *Advances in Mechanical Engineering* (pp. 83–89). Springer.

Singh, V. P., Sharma, K., & Chakraborty, D. (2020). Solving the shortest path problem in an imprecise and random environment. *Sadhana, 45*(1), 1–10. doi:10.100712046-020-01403-4

Wen, U. P., & Hsu, S. T. (1991). Linear bi-level programming problems—A review. *The Journal of the Operational Research Society, 42*(2), 125–133.

Wen, U. P., & Hsu, S. T. (1992). Efficient solutions for the linear bilevel programming problem. *European Journal of Operational Research, 62*(3), 354–362. doi:10.1016/0377-2217(92)90124-R

Zhai, W., Zhao, Y., Lian, X., Yang, M., & Lu, F. (2014). Management planning of fast-growing plantations based on a bi-level programming model. *Forest Policy and Economics, 38*, 173–177. doi:10.1016/j.forpol.2013.08.009

Zhang, G., & Lu, J. (2005). The Definition of Optimal Solution and Extended Kuhn-Tucker Approach for Fuzzy Linear Bilevel Programming. *The IEEE Intelligent Informatics Bulletin.*

Zhang, G., & Lu, J. (2010). Fuzzy bilevel programming with multiple objectives and cooperative multiple followers. *Journal of Global Optimization, 47*(3), 403–419. doi:10.100710898-008-9365-z

Zimmermann, H. J. (2011). *Fuzzy set theory—and its applications*. Springer Science & Business Media.

Chapter 7
Research on Corporate Governance:
Bibliometric Analysis

Elisabete S. Vieira
https://orcid.org/0000-0003-3593-368X
GOVCOPP, University of Aveiro, Portugal

Mara Madaleno
https://orcid.org/0000-0002-4905-2771
GOVCOPP, University of Aveiro, Portugal

Graça Azevedo
https://orcid.org/0000-0002-6346-4035
Research Centre on Accounting and Taxation (CICF), University of Aveiro, Portugal

ABSTRACT

This chapter intends to contribute to the analysis of corporate governance (CG) practices through a bibliometric review of the existent literature in order to understand the current state of CG, providing an overview of the main trends in this field of research. Although there is extensive research on CG, no recent studies try to update the current state of the art on this topic. It is conducted a bibliometric analysis. The study describes the evolutional research studies published in the digital library Scopus between 2010 and 2019 and compares the results obtained in evolutionary terms. The bibliometric analysis is based in the Scopus database, leading to a total database of 4,430 documents. Regarding the most recent articles published, the study focuses on the period between 2018 and July 2020, ending with a final sample of 887 articles. Finally, a bibliometric analysis on the 16 scientific articles that were more cited in the more recent period is made. Research avenues are provided based on these results and on more recent published articles regarding the CG subject.

DOI: 10.4018/978-1-7998-7596-3.ch007

INTRODUCTION

The debate on best practices in Corporate Governance (CG) to protect investors, remains one of the most fascinating research topics, especially after several international firms' financial scandals related to CG, the audit committee, and the role of the board on firms' performance (Soltani & Maupetit, 2015).

The CG system consists of a set of principles and rules that firms must follow in their activity to ensure that the board of directors' decisions go to the meeting of the different stakeholder's interests. Indeed, the Organization for Economic Co-operation and Development (OECD) considers the CG as a system through which organizations are controlled.

Although the variety of CG definitions, all of them are concerned with the alignment of interests between managers and shareholders.

For example, Shleifer and Vishny (1997) define CG as a framework to safeguard the interests of corporate claim holders, managerial share ownership, and block ownership, which can be considered as instruments of CG. Vaz (2013) considers that CG is a system to manage and supervise firms from a legal perspective, intending to mediate the interests of ownership and management of firms. Although the existence of many other definitions, CG proposes a set of practices to reduce the conflicts between managers and shareholders (Vieira & Neiva, 2019).

Crowther and Sefi (2011) argue that CG consists of a model that enforces the board of director's mission to protect the interests of shareholders, inducing an environment of ethics, confidence, and morality and, simultaneously, maximizing the firm's value. Indeed, Happ and Schiereck (2017) analyze a sample of firms from 12 European countries, concluding that a structure of concentrated ownership may be beneficial due to managerial incentive alignment and active monitoring by block holders, which may align managerial incentives and, consequently, maximize shareholder value.

The board of directors has a key position in CG since they are responsible for the strategy and development of firms. The simplest and most concise definition of CG was provided by the Cadbury Report in 1992. Here it is written that "Corporate governance is the system by which companies are directed and controlled", and all the responsibility is placed over their leaders. For most companies, those leaders are the directors, responsible for the decision of the long-term strategy of the company, to serve the best interests of the owners and, more broadly, all the stakeholders.

In what concerns the CG systems in Europe, the Western Continental European firms are known for higher levels of ownership concentration and the dominance of family owners (Aganin & Volpin, 2002; Högfeldt, 2003), while the Central European countries are presently in the stage of economic development, consolidating their CG systems and trying to improve investor protection and transparency (Svejnar, 2002). Eastern Europe reveals far different CG characteristics with strong ownership concentration and poor investor protection. According to the study results of Aluchna (2016), Continental European firms are often controlled by families as well as by institutional investors, and the United Kingdom (UK) characteristics relating to ownership concentration and shareholder identity remains closer to the American characteristics, providing strong investor protection, public information, and supervision over the capital market. More specifically, the UK is categorized by dispersed ownership, strong capital market, transparency, and high investors' protection (Aluchna, 2016). Finally, France, Germany, and Italy made extensive efforts to improve the stock market efficiency, investor protection, as well as best practice codes (Aluchna, 2016).

Several studies analyze the impact of the crisis on CG practices, and some of them report significant changes in CG practices because of the global financial crisis. Some of them find evidence that firms with good CG practices are less affected in the periods of crisis (Watkins, Spronk, & Dick, 2009; Suvankulov & Ogucu, 2012; Ezzine & Olivero; 2013). However, studies are finding that CG influences negatively the firms' performance during the financial crisis (Erkens, Hung, & Matos, 2012; Peni & Sami, 2012; Orazalin et al., 2016). Al-Gamrh et al. (2018) find that in normal periods, CG mitigates the negative influence of leverage and risk on the accounting and economic firm performance. However, during crisis periods, this synergy effect varies across performance indicators. Using a sample of non-financial firms from 10 countries throughout the financial crisis, Andries et al. (2020) find that CG has a nonlinear (inverted U-shape) impact on the firms' investment risk, since the investment risk increases up to a level of CG score, while at higher levels of CG, the investment risk decreases. Besides, other authors report that poor CG is one of the main causes of the crisis (Mahenthiran, Rahman, & Hamid, 2006; Yeoh, 2010). Aldamen et al. (2020) investigate the impact of CG on Australian family firms' performance during the financial crisis, finding that better CG is associated with better performance during the crisis period, regardless of whether it is a family or non-family firm.

A vast number of studies explore the impact of CG on earnings management. There is large evidence that CG helps reducing strategies of earnings management (Klein, 2002; Liu & Lu, 2007; Shen & Chih, 2007; Marchini, Mazza, & Medioli, 2018; Al-Haddad & Whittington, 2019). However, some studies find no significant relationship between these variables, such as Park and Shin (2004) and Agrawal and Chadha (2005). On the other side, Sehrawat et al. (2019), considering the Indian market, find that managerial ownership is positively related to earnings management.

Damak (2018) analyses the influence of board gender diversity on earnings management practices, considering a sample of French firms. The results show a significant negative effect of board women's presence on earnings management level, suggesting that women on boards are effective in their monitoring role. His evidence is in agreement with the majority of earlier studies, such as the ones of Lakhal et al. (2015), also in the French market, Kyaw, Olugbode and Petracci (2015) in European countries, and Adams and Ferreira (2009), Gul, Srinidhi, & Tsui (2011) and Srinidhi, Gul, & Tsui et al. (2011), in the USA market. Orazalin (2020) scrutinizes whether board gender diversity, as well as other board characteristics, affect earnings management practices of top public companies in Kazakhstan, finding that firms with greater board gender diversity and with larger boards are more effective in constraining earnings management practices. However, the results provide weak evidence of a significant relationship between board independence and earnings quality.

Al-Okaily, Youssef, & Chahine (2019) investigate whether CG moderates the earnings management, in the context of UK family firms. Although the authors find that earnings management is lower in family firms, such impact may be moderated by good governance mechanisms.

More recently, Alam, Ramachandran, & Nahomy (2020) examine the impact of the board characteristics of Islamic banks on earnings management, finding that board size has a significant negative influence on earnings management. El Diri, Lambrinoudakis, & Alhadab (2020) investigate the role of CG in mitigating earnings management activities between high and low concentrated markets, finding that CG is more effective in mitigating earnings management in non-concentrated markets than in their counterparts. However, the authors find evidence that CG in concentrated markets drives managers to substitute accrual with real earnings management because the latter is harder to detect and its negative consequences on firm value in a long-term perspective are likely to be mitigated by the higher competitive power of firms.

This chapter intends to present a bibliometric analysis of CG providing some additional insights into the current state of CG research and an overview of the main trends in this field of research. The information will be collected from the Scopus database, which includes studies recognized by their high level of standards. Besides, it analysis the h-index (Hirsch, 2005), which combines productivity (number of papers) and the influence of a research subject (number of citations).

The remainder of the chapter is organized as follows: Section two presents the general status of CG research during the period between 2010 and 2019. Section three presents the redefinition of our research and focus on the most recent published works in the last three years (2018-2020). Finally, section four concludes the chapter.

BIBLIOMETRIC ANALYSIS ON CORPORATE GOVERNANCE: 2010-2019

The bibliometric analysis, which studies and quantitatively classifies bibliographic material, has become more popular in the last decades (Merigó & Yang, 2017).

The concept of bibliometric analysis and the underlying methods have undergone some evolution over time. According to Sengupta (1992), Campbell (1896) made the first bibliometric study, using statistical methods to analyze scattered publications on a specific topic. Some years later, Machlup and Mansfield (1983) note that bibliometric studies are associated with the development and the dissemination of the literature. After these studies, bibliometric analysis studies grew significantly in a wide range of subjects, being considered that this kind of study provides a lot of information regarding a research discipline (Wagstaff & Culyer, 2012).

Several authors have used bibliometric indicators to assess the general state of the art in what concerns finance research (Olheten, Theoharakis, & Travlos, 2005; Borokhovich, Bricker, & Simkins, 2000; Currie & Pandher 2011), but few studies have focused specifically on CG subjects, such as Huang and Ho (2011) and Tunger and Eulerich (2018). However, the former study covers the period between 1992 and 2008, which is an old period to analyze the current trends and the latter study only analyses the German-speaking countries.

For the bibliometric analysis, the authors use the Scopus database (https://www.scopus.com/search/), which, according to Elsevier, is the largest database of abstracts and citations of peer-reviewed scientific literature, with tools available to make several analyzes of the research carried out.

Just by searching for the keyword "Corporate Governance", at the beginning of July, the authors find 7,527 documents (from all types) published from 1978 to 2020.

Limiting the search to:

- **Subject area:** Business, Management, and Accounting and Economics, Econometrics and Finance;
- **Document type:** article;
- **Words:** TITLE ("Corporate Governance") AND (LIMIT-TO (DOCTYPE, "ar")) AND (LIMIT-TO (SUBJAREA, "BUSI") OR LIMIT-TO (SUBJAREA, "ECON")), the authors obtain 4,430 document results, distributed from the period between 1978 and 2020.

Figure 1 shows the evolution of the documents by year, after applying the definition of the parameter in the Scopus database.

Figure 1. Documents published by year
Source: Scopus

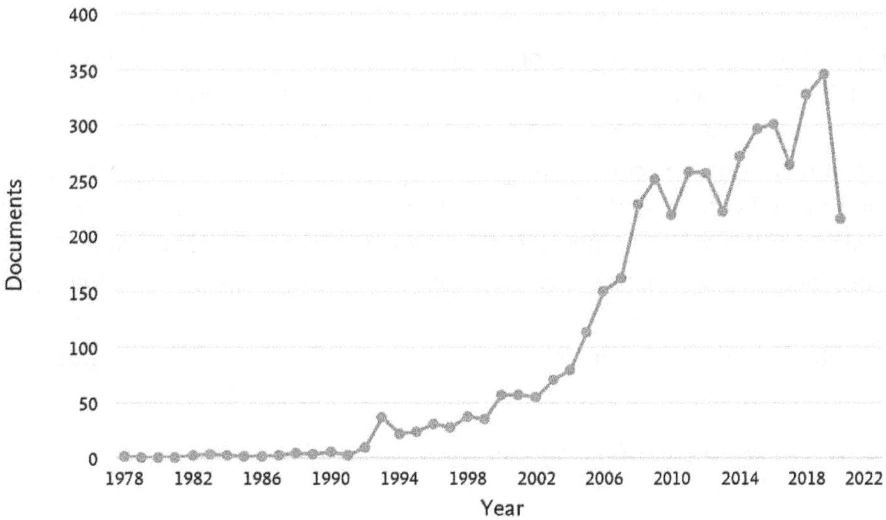

It is clear the high growth of the number of publications after 2002, reflecting the growing and progressive research interest in the CG subject. The graphic shows some instability in the number of publications between 2009 and 2020. However, the publications vary between 215 and 345, suggesting that CG is a hot topic in the subject areas of Business, Management and Accounting, Economics, Econometrics, and Finance. The year 2019 presents the highest number of documents published (345). It is important to note that the decline in 2020 (215) is justified by the fact that the researchers are analyzing only seven months (from January to July).

Figure 2 highlights the documents published by source title.

Figure 2. Documents published by source title
Source: Scopus

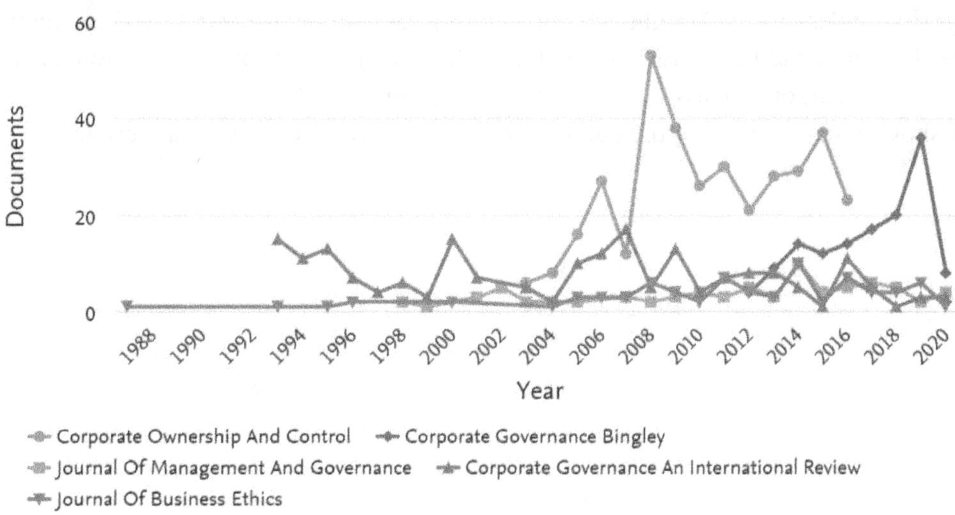

It can be observed that, from the 4,430 documents collected, the journals that correspond to the major sources of publishing journals are the Corporate Ownership and Control, Corporate Governance: An International Review, and the Corporate Governance Bingley. Between 2008 and 2016, Corporate Ownership and Control registered the biggest number of publications. However, this journal was discontinued in Scopus as of 2016. The publication Corporate Governance: An International Review registered a high number of publications in the CG subjects. Nevertheless, Corporate Governance Bingley exceeded the number of publications from the previous magazine in 2013. Consistent with the previous Figure, we can see a decrease in publications in the 2020 year, because of the records concern about seven months.

During the period 1992-2008, the journals that published more articles in this research field were Corporate Governance: An International Review and the Journal of Financial Economics (Huang & Ho, 2011).

Figure 3 presents the authors which most published in the field of CG during 2010 and 2019.

Figure 3. Documents published during the period 2010-2019 by author
Source: Scopus

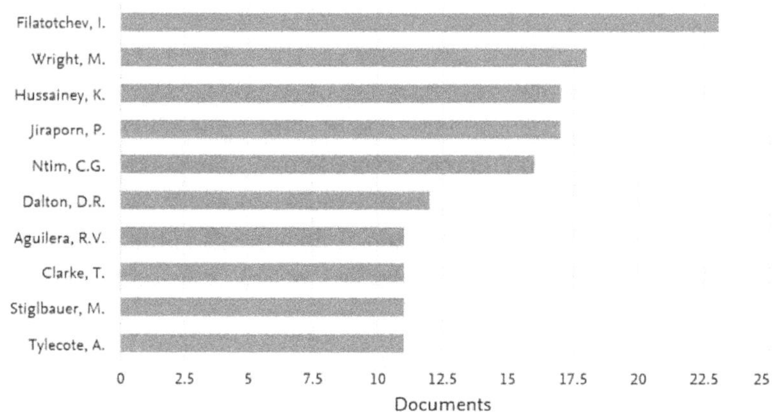

As it can be seen, the author Filatochev, I. stands out from the others, with 23 published documents during the period under review. Wright, M. register 18 publications, followed by Hussainey, K. and Jiraporn, P., both with 17 publications. Ntim, C.G. published 16 documents, and Dalton, D.R. published 12 documents. Four authors are associated with 11 documents.

Figure 4 shows the affiliation of the authors under the keyword corporate governance.

Figure 4. Documents published during the period 2010-2019 by affiliation
Source: Scopus

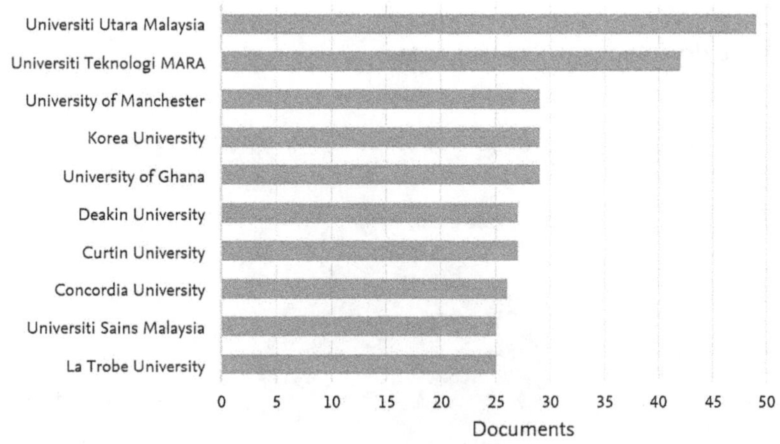

The University Utara Malaysia is the one with the highest number of affiliated authors and co-authors publishing during 2010 and 2019, with 49 publications, followed by the University Teknologi MARA, with 42 publications. All the other top ten affiliations have less than 30 publications. Three universities register 29 publications, two of them present 27 works, and one register 26 publications. The University Sains Malaysia and La Trobe University are in the lowest top ten of affiliations, with 25 publications.

Figure 5 displays the documents by country or territory during 2010-2019.

Figure 5. Documents published during the period 2010-2019 by country or territory
Source: Scopus

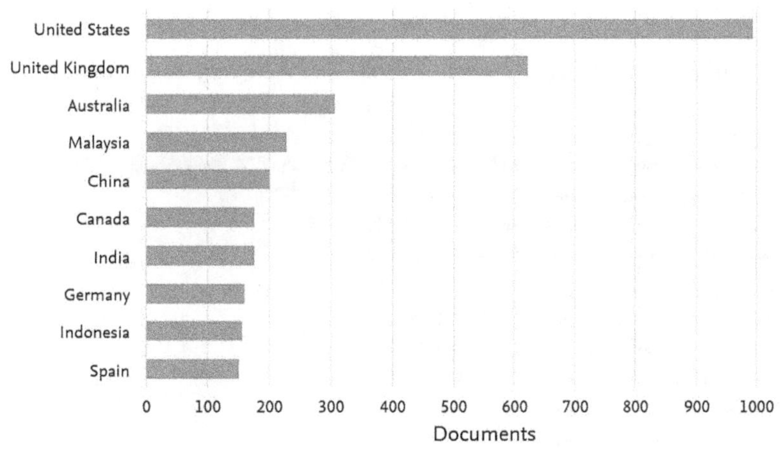

In what concerns the documents published by country or territory, it is clear that research on CG is concentrated on the Anglo-Saxon countries. The country with more publications is the United States (993), followed by the UK (621) and Australia, with less than half of the UK publications. Malaysia, China, Canada, and India appears after the first three countries. In the lowest top ten countries, there are Germany, Indonesia, and Spain, with 160, 156, and 150 publications, respectively. This evidence suggests that is it needed more research on countries within Europe, where there is still a scarcity of research under the CG subject.

Figure 6 presents the documents by subject area.

Figure 6. Documents published during the period 2010-2019 by subject area
Source: Scopus

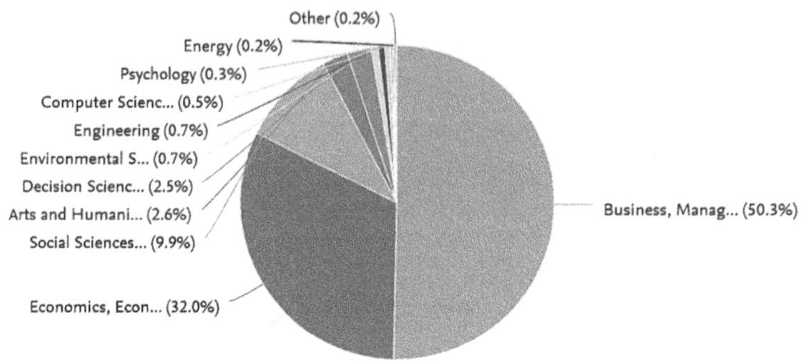

In what concerns the main subject areas of publication, most of the publications (50.3%) are from Business, Management and Accounting area, followed by the area of Economics, Econometrics, and Finance (32%) and Social Sciences (9.9%). With about 2.5% of the publications, there are the Art and Humanities and the Decision Sciences areas. All the other areas register less than 1% of the publications.

Huang and Ho (2011) conclude that, during the period 1992-2008, the main area of publication was from Economics and Business.

Finally, Figure 7 shows the documents by the funding sponsor.

Figure 7. Documents published during the period 2010-2019 by funding sponsor
Source: Scopus

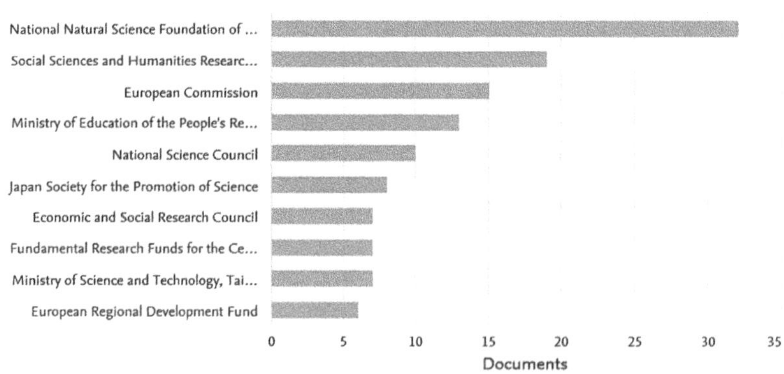

Regarding the funding sponsor of these documents, the National Natural Science Foundation of China, the Social Sciences and Humanities Research Council of Canada, the European Commission, the Ministry of Education of the People's Republic of China, and the National Science Council are the institutions that mostly sponsored all the documents under analysis.

Figure 8. Keywords analysis for CG articles published during the period 2018-July 2020
Source: VosViewer

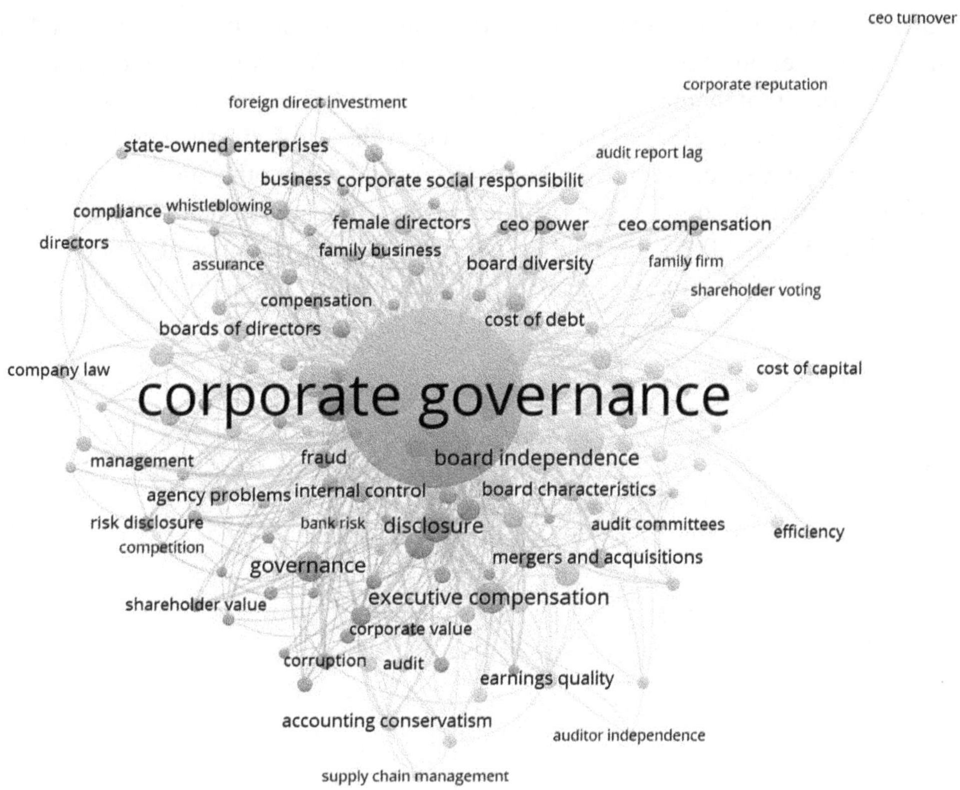

Bibliometric Analysis of Corporate Governance Research During the period Between 2018 and July 2020

In this section, the authors limit their bibliographic analysis to solely scientific peer-reviewed articles in scientific journals considering the period from 2018 to the middle of 2020 (July), which were classified in the categories Business, Management and Accounting, Economics, Econometrics, and Finance, under the subject keyword corporate governance, as previously.

Limiting the search to:

- **Subject area:** Business, Management, and Accounting and Economics, Econometrics and Finance;
- **Words:** TITLE ("Corporate Governance") AND (LIMIT-TO (PUBYEAR, 2020) OR LIMIT-TO (PUBYEAR, 2019) OR LIMIT-TO (PUBYEAR, 2018)) AND (LIMIT-TO (SUBJAREA, "BUSI")

OR LIMIT-TO (SUBJAREA, "ECON")) AND (LIMIT-TO (DOCTYPE, "ar")) obtaining 887 articles between 2018 and July 2020.

Exporting the data to the VOSviewer, it can be observed the clusters of keywords most used in articles containing the CG subject. Figure 8 shows the keywords used when researching CG at Scopus analysis, for articles published during 2018 and the first seven months of 2020.

The regularity and relevance of each keyword are related to the size of each circle and the distance between them allows assessing the level of association between keywords. The keywords used in the articles are related to different themes within the great theme of CG, represented by different colors. As it can be seen, the CG issue is researched jointly with many other subjects, such as disclosure, the board of directors, board independence, executive compensation, and many others.

Then, the search was narrowed, sorting the articles by those that are most cited. To do so, the researchers reach the h-index (Hirsch, 2005), an analysis that conjugates the number of papers and the number of citations, in the option "view citation overview". The results are shown in Figure 9.

Figure 9. h-index during the period 2018-July 2020
Source: Scopus

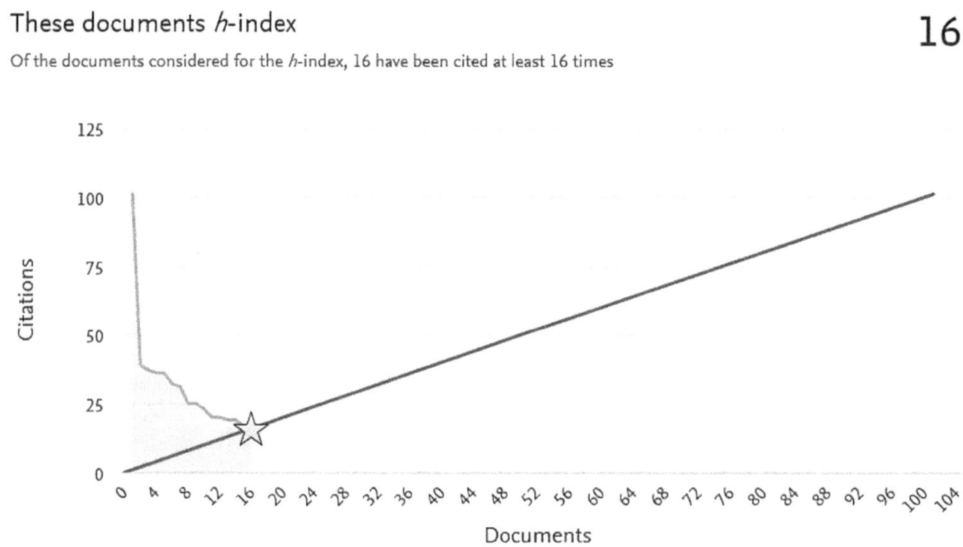

It was reached an h-index of 16, which means that of the 887 articles analyzed, 16 have at least 16 citations.

Consequently, our bibliometric analysis is now concentrated on the 16 scientific articles which were more cited between 2018 and the first seven months of 2020.

Table 1 describes the articles ranked by citations.

Table 1. Top 16 articles during the period 2018-July 2020, ranked by citations

	Document Title	Authors	Year	Source	Cited by
1	Corporate Governance and Sustainability Performance: Analysis of Triple Bottom Line Performance	Hussain, N., Rigoni, U., Orij, R.P.	2018	Journal of Business Ethics 149(2), pp. 411-432	101
2	The role of corporate governance in creating a capable supply chain: A case of Indonesian Tin industry	Chatchawanchanchanakij, P., Arpornpisal, C., Jermsittiparsert, K.	2019	International Journal of Supply Chain Management 8(3), pp. 855-864	39
3	Corporate Boards and Ownership Structure as Antecedents of Corporate Governance Disclosure in Saudi Arabian Publicly Listed Corporations	Al-Bassam, W.M., Ntim, C.G., Opong, K.K., Downs, Y.	2018	Business and Society 57(2), pp. 335-377	37
4	Corporate governance deviance	Aguilera, R.V., Judge, W.Q., Terjesen, S.A.	2018	Academy of Management Review 43(1), pp. 87-109	36
5	Corporate Governance and Tobin's Q as a Measure of Organizational Performance	Singh, S., Tabassum, N., Darwish, T.K., Batsakis, G.	2018	British Journal of Management 29(1), pp. 171-190	36
6	Corporate governance and financial performance: The role of ownership and board structure	Paniagua, J., Rivelles, R., Sapena, J.	2018	Journal of Business Research 89, pp. 229-234	32
7	Corporate governance and firm performance in emerging markets: Evidence from Turkey	Ciftci, I., Tatoglu, E., Wood, G., Demirbag, M., Zaim, S.	2019	International Business Review 28(1), pp. 90-103	31
8	System approach to achieving new quality of corporate governance in the context of innovation development	Veselovsky, M.Y., Izmailova, M.A., Bogoviz, A.V., Lobova, S.V., Ragulina, Y.V.	2018	Quality - Access to Success 19(163), pp. 30-36	25
9	On the relationship between corporate governance and firm performance: Evidence from GCC countries	Pillai, R., Al-Malkawi, H.A.N.	2018	Research in International Business and Finance 44, pp. 394-410	25
10	The analysis of effects of good corporate governance on earnings management in Indonesia with panel data approach	Muda, I., Maulana, W., Siregar, H.S., Indra, N.	2018	Iranian Economic Review 22(2), pp. 599-625	23
11	Corporate Governance in China: A Meta-Analysis	Mutlu, C.C., Van Essen, M., Peng, M.W., Saleh, S.F., Duran, P.	2018	Journal of Management Studies 55(6), pp. 943-979	20
12	Risk in Islamic banking and corporate governance	Safiullah, M., Shamsuddin, A.	2018	Pacific Basin Finance Journal 47, pp. 129-149	20
13	Complementary or Substitutive Effects? Corporate Governance Mechanisms and Corporate Social Responsibility	Oh, W.Y., Chang, Y.K., Kim, T.Y.	2018	Journal of Management 44(7), pp. 2716-2739	19
14	What drives green banking disclosure? An institutional and corporate governance perspective	Bose, S., Khan, H.Z., Rashid, A., Islam, S.	2018	Asia Pacific Journal of Management 35(2), pp. 501-527	19
15	Innovative solutions for improving the quality of corporate governance in Russian companies	Veselovsky, M.Y., Izmailova, M.A., Bogoviz, A.V., Lobova, S.V., Alekseev, A.N.	2018	Quality - Access to Success 19(162), pp. 60-66	17
16	Corporate governance and board of directors: The effect of a board composition on firm sustainability performance	Naciti, V.	2019	Journal of Cleaner Production, 237, 117727	16

Source: Scopus

The article gathering, by far, more citations were published in 2018 in the Journal of Business Ethics, with 101 citations at the date of the data bibliometric analysis (Hussain, Rigoni, & Orij, 2018). The authors analyze the relationship between CG and sustainability performance. The citations of the rest of the papers vary between 16 and 39. The thematic under research includes besides CG, disclosure, performance, innovation, earnings management, risk, and social responsibility. Most of these articles associate CG and the firm's performance. Thirteen of the sixteen (about 81%) publications are from 2018.

In what concerns the relationship between CG mechanisms and a firm's performance, the results are mixed. Overall, Paniagua, Rivelles, and Sapena (2018), Mutlu et al. (2018), Ciftci et al. (2019), and Naciti (2019) find that CG mechanisms, such as larger boards, diversity, and independence have positive effects on firm's performance. However, Ciftci et al. (2019) argue that an increase in cross-ownership does not influence market performance, but is negatively associated with accounting performance and Naciti (2019) reveals that a higher number of independent directors leads to lower sustainability performance. Besides, Pillai and Al-Malkawi (2018) find evidence that family shareholding affects positively the firm's performance in the Gulf Cooperation Council, but in what concerns other variables, such as the governmental shareholding, the results are mixed between countries. Singh et al. (2018) analyze a sample of Pakistani firms, finding that board size, the number of board committees, and ownership concentration are positively related to performance, while board independence and CEO duality display a negative relationship between the two variables.

Al-Bassam et al. (2018) and Bose et al. (2018) find that CG mechanisms, such as board size and institutional ownership affect positively the level of organization disclosure. Aguilera, Judge, and Terjesen (2018) argue that as the firm's governance discretion increases, more likely they are to adopt over or underconforming governance practices that deviate from established norms and practices. Oh, Chang, & Kim (2018) study a sample of American firms, finding that multiple governance mechanisms mainly act as substitutes to promote corporate social responsibility.

Muda et al. (2018) study a sample of Indonesian listed firms, concluding that the independent CG variable which consists of the composition of commissioners and audit committee, affects the manufacturing firms' earning management. However, the board of commissioners and the audit committee have no effects on earnings management practices.

Safiullah and Shamsuddin (2018) examine the differences in risk between Islamic and conventional banks. Considering the role of Shariah supervisory board composition, the authors find that Islamic banks have higher liquidity risk, lower credit risk, and lower insolvency risk, but meet similar operational risk when comparing with conventional banks.

Veselovsky et al. (2018a) conclude that the role of the board of directors in Russian firms increases its relevance in the nearest period, being important to achieving higher levels of quality on corporate management. Veselovsky et al. (2018b) focus its study on the implementation of the basic recommendations of the Russian CG Code of 2014, concluding that it is necessary to use an innovative approach to improve the quality of CG in the Russian economy.

The prime objective of Chatchawanchanchanakij, Arpornpisal, and Jermsittiparsert (2019) is to examine the role of CG in determining supply chain capability. The results show that along with the customer focus approach, the firms follow also the production focus approach.

The agency theory (Jensen and Meckling, 1976) was the one most cited by the top 16 articles analyzed to base their studies, which is in agreement with the evidence of Huang and Ho (2011).

Having the 16 articles summarized, it can be argued that these are the hot topics in CG nowadays, provided the citations shown.

Table 2 provides the number of citations, by articles of 2018 and 2019, during the period 2018-2020 (7 first months of the year).

Table 2. Total citations made by other articles to the most cited studies of 2018 and 2019, during the period 2018-July 2020

	Documents	Citations	2018	2019	2020	Total
	Total		71	228	181	480
1	Corporate Governance and Sustainability Performance: Analysis of Triple Bottom Line Performance	2018	19	41	41	101
2	The role of corporate governance in creating a capable supply chain: A case of Indonesian Tin industry	2019		39		39
3	Corporate Boards and Ownership Structure as Antecedents of Corporate Governance Disclosure in Saudi Arabian Publicly Listed Corporations	2018	12	13	12	37
4	Corporate governance deviance	2018	9	16	11	36
5	Corporate Governance and Tobin's Q as a Measure of Organizational Performance	2018	1	19	16	36
6	Corporate governance and financial performance: The role of ownership and board structure	2018	1	18	13	32
7	Corporate governance and firm performance in emerging markets: Evidence from Turkey	2019		11	20	31
8	System approach to achieving new quality of corporate governance in the context of innovation development	2018	11	11	3	25
9	On the relationship between corporate governance and firm performance: Evidence from GCC countries	2018	6	9	10	25
10	The analysis of effects of good corporate governance on earnings management in Indonesia with panel data approach	2018	10	4	9	23
11	Corporate Governance in China: A Meta-Analysis	2018		10	10	20
12	Risk in Islamic banking and corporate governance	2018	1	9	10	20
13	Complementary or Substitutive Effects? Corporate Governance Mechanisms and Corporate Social Responsibility	2018	1	12	6	19
14	What drives green banking disclosure? An institutional and corporate governance perspective	2018	2	10	7	19
15	Innovative solutions for improving the quality of corporate governance in Russian companies	2018	11	5	1	17
16	Corporate governance and board of directors: The effect of a board composition on firm sustainability performance	2019		1	15	16

Source: Scopus

It is not possible to compare directly the citations for all three years for two reasons. First, some articles were published in 2018 and others in 2019. Second, in what respects to 2020, the study only considers seven months of the year, expecting more citations for this year. In terms of citations made by other authors to the top 16 articles in analysis, it is possible to see that the year 2019 is the one with the higher number of citations (228), followed by the year 2020 (181). The most cited work (Hussain et al., 2019) presents the same number of citations in 2019 (41) and the first 7 months of 2020 (41). Curiously, the study of Chatchawanchanchanakij et al. (2019) presents all the citations in 2019 (39).

To do a more detailed analysis, it were considered the articles collaboration for the top 16 cited articles during the period from 2018 to 2020, July, as can be seen in Table 3.

Table 3. Number of authors for the top 16 cited articles, during the period 2018-July 2020

	Documents	**Number of Authors**
1	Corporate Governance and Sustainability Performance: Analysis of Triple Bottom Line Performance	3
2	The role of corporate governance in creating a capable supply chain: A case of Indonesian Tin industry	3
3	Corporate Boards and Ownership Structure as Antecedents of Corporate Governance Disclosure in Saudi Arabian Publicly Listed Corporations	4
4	Corporate governance deviance	3
5	Corporate Governance and Tobin's Q as a Measure of Organizational Performance	4
6	Corporate governance and financial performance: The role of ownership and board structure	3
7	Corporate governance and firm performance in emerging markets: Evidence from Turkey	5
8	System approach to achieving new quality of corporate governance in the context of innovation development	5
9	On the relationship between corporate governance and firm performance: Evidence from GCC countries	2
10	The analysis of effects of good corporate governance on earnings management in Indonesia with panel data approach	4
11	Corporate Governance in China: A Meta-Analysis	5
12	Risk in Islamic banking and corporate governance	2
13	Complementary or Substitutive Effects? Corporate Governance Mechanisms and Corporate Social Responsibility	3
14	What drives green banking disclosure? An institutional and corporate governance perspective	4
15	Innovative solutions for improving the quality of corporate governance in Russian companies	5
16	Corporate governance and board of directors: The effect of a board composition on firm sustainability performance	1

Source: Scopus

It is easily perceived that a team of authors between three and five composes most of these articles. A group of three authors wrote the work with more citations (Hussain et al., 2019). Only one study is developed individually, which is in the one on the bottom of the top 16 articles.

Table 4 presents the journals where the most cited articles were published in 2019.

Table 4. Facts related to the journals of the most cited articles on CG in 2019

	Journals	CiteScore 2019	SJR 2019	SNIP 2019	Citations 2016-2019	Documents 2016-2019
1	Journal of Business Ethics	7.0	1.972	2.700	10.574	1.518
2	International Journal of Supply Chain Management	1,0	0.190	1.176	1.292	1.329
3	Business and Society	9.4	1.796	2.419	1.518	161
4	Academy of Management Review	13.0	7.482	5.026	2.137	164
5	British Journal of Management	5.6	1.522	1.993	1.062	188
6	Journal of Business Research	8.9	1.871	2.760	18.010	2.031
7	International Business Review	7.6	1.453	2.213	2.898	383
8	Quality - Access to Success	1.2	0.280	0.918	1.410	1.161
9	Research in International Business and Finance	3.7	0.638	1.323	2.475	671
10	Iranian Economic Review	0.6	0.193	0.402	104	162
11	Journal of Management Studies	9.4	4.608	3.413	1.781	189
12	Pacific Basin Finance Journal	2.8	0.671	1.473	1.113	401
13	Journal of Management	17.6	6.982	6.280	6.565	374
14	Asia Pacific Journal of Management	4.8	1.302	1.867	755	157
15	Quality - Access to Success	1.2	0.280	0.918	1.410	1.161
16	Corporate Governance: An International Review	6.0	1.471	1.887	648	108

Source: Scopus

The journal that publishes more articles, and that receives the highest number of citations, is the Journal of Business Research, followed by the Journal of Business Ethics.

Regarding the CiteScore index and the SNIP, the highest one was attributed to the Journal of Management, followed by the Academy of Management Review. Finally, in what concerns the SJR, the highest score is attributed to the Academy of Management Review and the second one respects the Journal of Management.

The authors conclude this section by presenting in Table 5 the number of documents created by the author, the total citations considering each author, the h-index, and the number of co-authors that an author has added in the documents explored and identified.

Table 5. Research activity and facts for the authors of the most cited articles in 2019

	Author	Documents by Author	Total Citation	h-Index	Co-authors
1	Hussain, Nazim	8	166	5	12
	Rigoni, Ugo	7	130	3	9
	Orij, René P.	3	207	2	4
2	Chatchawanchanchanakij, Petcharaporn	1	39	1	2
	Arpornpisal, Chanapong	1	39	1	2
	Jermsittiparsert, Kittisak	346	3716	36	377
3	Al-Bassam, Waleed M.	1	37	1	3
	Ntim, Collins G.	64	1199	20	74
	Opong, Kwaku Kyekyeku	26	495	11	28
	Downs, Yvonne	13	102	5	11
4	Aguilera, Ruth V.	83	6628	33	92
	Judge, William Q.	86	3813	28	72
	Terjesen, Siri	89	3489	33	335
5	Singh, Satwinder	32	417	12	36
	Tabassum, Naeem	1	36	1	3
	Darwish, Tamer Khalil	23	279	10	203
	Batsakis, Georgios K.	17	144	6	14
6	Paniagua, Jordi	27	249	8	19
	Rivelles, Rafael	2	33	1	2
	Sapena, Juan	20	218	7	16
7	Ciftci, Ilhan	1	31	1	4
	Tatoglu, Ekrem	94	3147	31	82
	Wood, Geoffrey T.	214	2581	26	177
	Demirbag, Mehmet	89	2683	28	80
	Zaim, Selim	57	2277	27	65
8	Veselovsky, Mikhail Yakovlevich	32	252	10	195
	Izmailova, Marina Alekseevna	18	85	5	49
	Bogoviz, Aleksei Valentinovich	141	1009	17	144
	Lobova, Svetlana V.	78	412	12	80
	Ragulina, Julia V.	74	711	16	73
9	Pillai, Rekha	5	84	4	4
	Al-Malkawi, Husam Aldin Nizar	10	111	6	12
10	Muda, Iskandar	34	64	4	79
	Maulana, Weldi	1	23	1	3
	Siregar, H. S.	7	264	7	16
	Indra, Naleni	1	23	1	3
11	Mutlu, Canan C.	8	92	4	14
	Van Essen, Marc V.	50	1554	17	48
	Peng, Michael W.	158	19656	61	142
	Saleh, Sabrina F.	2	20	1	8
	Duran, Patricio	15	356	7	32
12	Safiullah, Md	7	27	2	3
	Shamsuddin, Abul F.M.	46	605	12	27
13	Oh, Won-yong	29	700	10	31
	Chang, Young Kyun	23	483	11	30
	Kim, Taeyeol	52	1847	21	110
14	Bose, Sudipta	6	43	3	10
	Khan, Habib Zaman	13	293	5	19
	Rashid, Afzalur	20	199	9	13
	Islam, Shajul	2	33	2	4
15	Veselovsky, Mikhail Yakovlevich	32	252	10	60
	Izmailova, Marina Alekseevna	18	85	5	49
	Bogoviz, Aleksei Valentinovich	141	1009	17	144
	Lobova, Svetlana V.	78	412	12	80
	Alekseev, Alexander Nikolaevich	50	328	11	60
16	Naciti, Valeria	1	16	1	0

Source: Scopus

The author with the highest number of published documents as well as coauthors in his studies is Kittisak Jermsittiparsert. However, the one with the highest number of citations (19656) and h-index (61) is Michael W. Peng. The author with the lowest numbers in these components is Valeria Naciti, which is justified because she is a junior researcher.

CONCLUSION

Research trends about Corporate Governance have been explored in this bibliometric review, considering first all the documents published between 2010 and 2019. Besides, the authors consider the most recent articles published, analyzing the period between 2018 and the middle of 2020 (July). Afterward, our bibliometric research was redefined to consider only articles published in journals during 2018, 2019, and the first seven months of 2020, presenting the results for the 16 most cited articles.

The mainstream of CG research is in disclosure, performance, innovation, earnings management, risk, and social responsibility. Most of these articles associates CG and a firm's performance, and the most adopted theory to CG research is the agency theory. During the analyzed period, the Journal of Business Research published the most CG related articles, followed by the Journal of Business Ethics.

Since one of the explored topics in the top 16 articles is the relationship between CG and earnings management, which are the main subjects of this book, the researchers made a brief literature review on the relationship between CG and earnings management.

Mixed evidence and the countries analyzed leave space for new developments in research on the CG topic. It is clear from the study that European countries require research, so, authors can focus future research on these markets. Corporate governance characteristics like gender, education, commitment, experience, image, age, and independence are still being explored and new findings can emerge with new research developments. Different methodologies can also be applied to explore CG research. The authors suppose that another possible avenue of future research is a comparative analysis of CG among regions to analyze whether observe mixed results found by the literature are due to the country's heterogeneity or associated with different CG rules and practices. A deeper understanding of institutional pressures, legal environments, and macroeconomic conditions can also be explored, contributing to a better understanding of CG practices and consequences differences in firms performance, risk, and earnings management, among other relations.

Even though much research has emerged in recent years on CG, there is still a long way to go.

REFERENCES

Adams, R. B., & Ferreira, D. (2009). Women in the boardroom and their impact on governance and performance. *Journal of Financial Economics*, *94*(2), 291–309. doi:10.1016/j.jfineco.2008.10.007

Aganin, A., & Volpin, P. (2002). The history of corporate ownership in Italy. In R. A. Morck (Ed.), *A history of corporate governance around the World* (pp. 325–365). The University of Chicago Press.

Agrawal, A., & Chadha, S. (2005). Corporate governance and accounting scandals. *The Journal of Law & Economics*, *48*(2), 371–406. doi:10.1086/430808

Aguilera, R. V., Judge, W. Q., & Terjesen, S. A. (2018). Corporate governance deviance. *Academy of Management Review*, *43*(1), 87–109. doi:10.5465/amr.2014.0394

Al-Bassam, W. M., Ntim, C. G., Opong, K. K., & Downs, Y. (2018). Corporate boards and ownership structure as antecedents of corporate governance disclosure in Saudi Arabian publicly listed corporations. *Business & Society*, *57*(2), 335–377. doi:10.1177/0007650315610611

Al-Gamrh, B., Izah, K. N., Ismail, K., & Al-Dhamari, R. (2018). The role of corporate governance strength in crisis and non-crisis times. *Applied Economics*, *50*(58), 6263–6284. doi:10.1080/00036846.2018.1489513

Al-Haddad, L., & Whittington, M. (2019). The impact of corporate governance mechanisms on real and accrual earnings management practices: Evidence from Jordan. *Corporate Governance*, *19*(6), 1167–1186. doi:10.1108/CG-05-2018-0183

Al-Okaily, J., Youssef, N. B., & Chahine, S. (2019). Economic bonding, corporate governance and earnings management: Evidence from UK publicly traded family firms. *International Journal of Auditing*, *24*(2), 185–204. doi:10.1111/ijau.12186

Alam, N., Ramachandran, J., & Nahomy, A. H. (2020). The impact of corporate governance and agency effect on earnings management - A test of the dual banking system. *Research in International Business and Finance*, *54*, 1–16. doi:10.1016/j.ribaf.2020.101242

Aldamen, H., Duncan, K., Kelly, S., & McNamara, R. (2020). Corporate governance and family firm performance during the global financial crisis. *Accounting and Finance*, *60*(2), 1673–1701. doi:10.1111/acfi.12508

Aluchna, M. (2016). Applying corporate governance in Europe. In G. Aras (Ed.), *Global Perspectives on Corporate Governance and CSR* (pp. 47–71). Routledge.

Andries, A. M., Balutel, D., Ihnatov, I., & Ursu, S. G. (2020). The nexus between corporate governance, risk taking, and growth. *PLoS One*, *15*(2), 1–24. doi:10.1371/journal.pone.0228371 PMID:32017781

Borokhovich, K. A., Bricker, R. J., & Simkins, B. J. (2000). An analysis of finance journal impact factors. *The Journal of Finance*, *55*(3), 1457–1469. doi:10.1111/0022-1082.00254

Bose, S., Khan, H. Z., Rashid, A., & Islam, S. (2018). What drives green banking disclosure? An institutional and corporate governance perspective. *Asia Pacific Journal of Management*, *35*(2), 501–527. doi:10.100710490-017-9528-x

Campbell, F. B. F. (1896). *The theory of the national and international bibliography: with special reference to the introduction of system in the record of modern literature*. Library Bureau.

Chatchawanchanchanakij, P., Arpornpisal, C., & Jermsittiparsert, K. (2019). The role of corporate governance in creating a capable supply chain: A case of Indonesian Tin industry. *International Journal of Supply Chain Management*, *8*(3), 855–864.

Ciftci, I., Tatoglu, E., Wood, G., Demirbag, M., & Zaim, S. (2019). Corporate governance and firm performance in emerging markets: Evidence from Turkey. *International Business Review*, *28*(1), 90–103. doi:10.1016/j.ibusrev.2018.08.004

Crowther, D., & Seifi, S. (2011). Corporate governance and risk management. *Ventus Publishing*, *58*, 2–16.

Currie, R. R., & Pandher, G. S. (2011). Finance journal rankings and tiers: An active scholar assessment methodology. *Journal of Banking & Finance*, *35*(1), 7–20. doi:10.1016/j.jbankfin.2010.07.034

Damak, S. T. (2018). Gender diverse board and earnings management: Evidence from French listed companies. *Sustainability Accounting. Management and Policy Journal*, *9*(3), 289–312.

El Diri, M., Lambrinoudakis, C., & Alhadab, M. (2020). Corporate governance and earnings management in concentrated markets. *Journal of Business Research*, *108*, 291–306. doi:10.1016/j.jbusres.2019.11.013

Erkens, D. H., Hung, M., & Matos, P. (2012). Corporate governance in the 2007-2008 financial crisis: Evidence from financial institutions worldwide. *Journal of Corporate Finance*, *18*(2), 389–411. doi:10.1016/j.jcorpfin.2012.01.005

Ezzine, H., & Olivero, B. (2013). Evolution of corporate governance during the recent financial crises. *The International Journal of Business and Finance Research*, *7*(1), 85–100.

Gul, F. A., Srinidhi, B., & Tsui, J. (2011). Female directors and earnings quality. *Journal of Contemporary Accounting Research*, *28*(5), 1610–1643. doi:10.1111/j.1911-3846.2011.01071.x

Happ, C., & Schiereck, D. (2017). Seasoned equity offerings and corporate governance in Europe. *Journal of European Real Estate Research*, *10*(2), 170–194. doi:10.1108/JERER-05-2016-0019

Hirsch, J. E. (2005). An index to quantify an individual's scientific research output. *Proceedings of the National Academy of Sciences of the United States of America*, *102*(46), 16569–16572. doi:10.1073/pnas.0507655102 PMID:16275915

Högfeldt, P. (2003). The history and politics of corporate ownership in Sweden. In R. A. Morck (Ed.), *History of corporate governance around the world* (pp. 517–579). The University of Chicago Press.

Huang, C. Y., & Ho, Y. S. (2011). Historical research on corporate governance: A bibliometric analysis. *African Journal of Business Management*, *5*(2), 276–284.

Hussain, N., Rigoni, U., & Orij, R. P. (2018). Corporate governance and sustainability performance: Analysis of triple bottom line performance. *Journal of Business Ethics*, *149*(2), 411–432. doi:10.100710551-016-3099-5

Jensen, M. C., & Meckling, W. H. (1976). Theory of the firm: Managerial behavior, agency costs and ownership structure. *Journal of Financial Economics*, *3*(4), 305–360. doi:10.1016/0304-405X(76)90026-X

Klein, A. (2002). Audit committee, board of director characteristics, and earnings management. *Journal of Accounting and Economics*, *33*(3), 375–400. doi:10.1016/S0165-4101(02)00059-9

Kyaw, K., Olugbode, M., & Petracci, B. (2015). Does gender diverse board mean less earnings management? *Finance Research Letters*, *14*, 135–141. doi:10.1016/j.frl.2015.05.006

Lakhal, F., Aguir, A., Lakhal, N., & Malek, A. (2015). Do women on boards and in top management reduce earnings management? Evidence in France. *Journal of Applied Business Research*, *31*(3), 1107–1118. doi:10.19030/jabr.v31i3.9236

Liu, Q., & Lu, Z. J. (2007). Corporate governance and earnings management in the Chinese listed companies: A tunneling perspective. *Journal of Corporate Finance, 13*(5), 881–906. doi:10.1016/j.jcorpfin.2007.07.003

Machlup, F., & Mansfield, U. (1983). *The study of information, interdisciplinary messages*. John Wiley & Sons.

Mahenthiran, H. M., Rahman, R. A., & Hamid, N. A. (2006). Agency costs as a factor in the suspension of companies from the Kuala Lumpur stock exchange. *Journal of Contemporary Accounting & Economics, 2*(1), 99–121. doi:10.1016/S1815-5669(10)70018-7

Marchini, P. L., Mazza, T., & Medioli, A. (2018). Related party transactions, corporate governance and earnings management. *Corporate Governance, 18*(6), 1124–1146. doi:10.1108/CG-11-2017-0271

Merigó, J. M., & Yang, J. B. (2017). Accounting research: A bibliometric analysis. *Australian Accounting Review, 80*(27), 71–100. doi:10.1111/auar.12109

Muda, I., Maulana, W., Siregar, H. S., & Indra, N. (2018). The analysis of effects of good corporate governance on earnings management in Indonesia with panel data approach. *Indian Economic Review, 22*(2), 599–625.

Mutlu, C. C., Van Essen, M., Peng, M. W., Saleh, S. F., & Duran, P. (2018). Corporate governance in China: A meta-analysis. *Journal of Management Studies, 55*(6), 943–979. doi:10.1111/joms.12331

Naciti, V. (2019). Corporate governance and board of directors: The effect of a board composition on firm sustainability performance. *Journal of Cleaner Production, 237*, 117727. doi:10.1016/j.jclepro.2019.117727

Oh, W. Y., Chang, Y. K., & Kim, T. Y. (2018). Complementary or substitutive effects? Corporate governance mechanisms and corporate social responsibility. *Journal of Management, 44*(7), 2716–2739. doi:10.1177/0149206316653804

Olheten, E., Theoharakis, V., & Travlos, N. G. (2005). Faculty perceptions and readership patterns of finance journals: A global view. *Journal of Financial and Quantitative Analysis, 40*(1), 223–239. doi:10.1017/S0022109000001800

Orazalin, N. (2020). Board gender diversity, corporate governance, and earnings management: Evidence from an emerging market. *Gender in Management, 35*(1), 37–60. doi:10.1108/GM-03-2018-0027

Orazalin, N., Orazalin, N., Mahmood, M., Mahmood, M., & Lee, K. J. (2016). Corporate governance, financial crises and bank performance: Lessons from top Russian banks. *Corporate Governance: The International Journal of Business in Society, 16*(5), 798-814.

Paniagua, J., Rivelles, R., & Sapena, J. (2018). Corporate governance and financial performance: The role of ownership and board structure. *Journal of Business Research, 89*, 229–234. doi:10.1016/j.jbusres.2018.01.060

Park, Y. W., & Shin, H. H. (2004). Board composition and earnings management in Canada. *Journal of Corporate Finance, 10*(3), 431–457. doi:10.1016/S0929-1199(03)00025-7

Peni, E., & Sami, V. (2012). Did good corporate governance improve bank performance during the financial crisis. *Journal of Financial Services Research*, *41*(1-2), 19–35. doi:10.100710693-011-0108-9

Pillai, R., & Al-Malkawi, H. A. N. (2018). On the relationship between corporate governance and firm performance: Evidence from GCC countries. *Research in International Business and Finance*, *44*, 394–410. doi:10.1016/j.ribaf.2017.07.110

Safiullah, M., & Shamsuddin, A. (2018). Risk in Islamic banking and corporate governance. *Pacific-Basin Finance Journal*, *47*, 129–149. doi:10.1016/j.pacfin.2017.12.008

Sehrawat, N. K., Kumar, A., Lohia, N., Bansal, S., & Agarwal, T. (2019). Impact of corporate governance on earnings management: Large sample evidence from India. *Asian Economic and Financial Review*, *9*(12), 1335–1345. doi:10.18488/journal.aefr.2019.912.1335.1345

Sengupta, I. N. (1992). Bibliometrics, informetrics, scientometrics and librametrics: An overview. *Libri*, *42*(2), 75–98. doi:10.1515/libr.1992.42.2.75

Shen, C. H., & Chih, H. L. (2007). Earnings management and corporate governance in Asia's emerging markets. *Corporate Governance*, *15*(5), 999–1021. doi:10.1111/j.1467-8683.2007.00624.x

Shleifer, A., & Vishny, R. W. (1997). A survey of corporate governance. *The Journal of Finance*, *52*(2), 737–783. doi:10.1111/j.1540-6261.1997.tb04820.x

Singh, S., Tabassum, N., Darwish, T. K., & Batsakis, G. (2018). Corporate governance and Tobin's Q as a measure of organizational performance. *British Journal of Management*, *29*(1), 171–190. doi:10.1111/1467-8551.12237

Soltani, B., & Maupetit, C. (2015). Importance of core values of ethics, integrity and accountability in the European corporate governance codes. *The Journal of Management and Governance*, *19*(2), 259–284. doi:10.100710997-013-9259-4

Srinidhi, B. I. N., Gul, F. A., & Tsui, J. (2011). Female directors and earnings quality. *Contemporary Accounting Research*, *28*(5), 1610–1644. doi:10.1111/j.1911-3846.2011.01071.x

Suvankulov, F., & Ogucu, F. (2012). Have firms with better corporate governance fared better during the recent financial crisis in Russia. *Applied Economics Letters*, *19*(8), 769–773. doi:10.1080/13504851.2011.603685

Svejnar, J. (2002). Transition economies: Performance and challenges. *The Journal of Economic Perspectives*, *16*(1), 3–28. doi:10.1257/0895330027058

Tunger, D., & Eulerich, M. (2018). Bibliometric analysis of corporate governance research in German-speaking countries: Applying bibliometrics to business research using a custom-made database. *Scientometrics*, *117*(3), 2041–2059. doi:10.100711192-018-2919-z

Vaz, J. C. (2013). A OPA e o controlo societário: A Regra de não frustração [Lexical characteristics of Portuguese language]. Edições Almedina, S.A.

Veselovsky, M. Y., Izmailova, M. A., Bogoviz, A. V., Lobova, S. V., & Alekseev, A. N. (2018b). Innovative solutions for improving the quality of corporate governance in Russian companies. *Quality - Access to Success*, *19*(162), 60–66.

Veselovsky, M. Y., Izmailova, M. A., Bogoviz, A. V., Lobova, S. V., & Ragulina, Y. V. (2018a). System approach to achieving new quality of corporate governance in the context of innovation development. *Quality - Access to Success*, *19*(163), 30–36.

Vieira, E., & Neiva, J. (2019). Corporate governance board of directors and firm performance in Portugal. In Handbook of Board of Directors and Company Performance: An International Outlook (pp. 121-150). Virtus Interpress.

Wagstaff, A., & Culyer, A. J. (2012). Four decades of health economics through a bibliometric lens. *Journal of Health Economics*, *31*(2), 406–439. doi:10.1016/j.jhealeco.2012.03.002 PMID:22481096

Watkins, K., Spronk, J., & Dick, V. D. (2009). Corporate governance and performance during normal and crisis periods: Evidence from an emerging market perspective. *International Journal of Corporate Governance*, *1*(4), 382–399. doi:10.1504/IJCG.2009.032726

Yeoh, P. (2010). Causes of the global financial crisis: Learning from the competing insights. *International Journal of Disclosure and Governance*, *7*(1), 42–69. doi:10.1057/jdg.2009.18

KEY TERMS AND DEFINITION

Bibliometric Analysis: Is the attempt to quantitatively assess the academic quality of journals or authors by statistical methods such as citation rates.

Corporate Governance: Is the system of rules, practices, and processes by which a firm is directed and controlled. Corporate governance essentially involves balancing the interests of a company's many stakeholders, such as shareholders, senior management executives, customers, suppliers, financiers, the government, and the community. Since corporate governance also provides the framework for attaining a company's objectives, it encompasses practically every sphere of management, from action plans and internal controls to performance measurement and corporate disclosure.

Disclosure: In the financial world, disclosure refers to the timely release of all information about a company that may influence an investor's decision. It reveals both positive and negative news, data, and operational details that impact its business.

Earnings Management: Is the use of accounting techniques to produce financial statements that present an overly positive view of a company's business activities and financial position. Many accounting rules and principles require that a company's management make judgments in following these principles. Earnings management takes advantage of how accounting rules are applied and creates financial statements that inflate or "smooth" earnings.

Financial Statements: Financial statements are written records that convey the business activities and the financial performance of a company. Financial statements are often audited by government agencies, accountants, firms, etc. to ensure accuracy and for tax, financing, or investing purposes.

Chapter 8
Corporate Governance in Portugal:
A Literature Review

João Teodósio
https://orcid.org/0000-0002-7877-1564
Polytechnic Institute of Santarém, Portugal & GOVCOPP, University of Aveiro, Portugal

ABSTRACT

This study provides a literature review of the research on the corporate governance mechanisms of Portuguese firms. Based on a sample of 47 articles published, between 2004 and 2019, it is documented that research is predominantly focused on corporate governance mechanisms as determinants of the performance on non-financial listed firms. Literature reports, in its majority, that board size decreases firm performance while CEO (Chief Executive Officer) non-duality promotes it; board size, board independence, and CEO non-duality improve the level of firms' information disclosure; CEO age is positively associated with an increase of CEO pay but CEO duality has an opposite effect; board independence increases firm risk-taking. These results should be of interest to national authorities in the development of future regulation related to firms' corporate governance and to national and international investors that intend to invest in Portuguese companies.

INTRODUCTION

What do we know on the corporate governance mechanisms effects on the outcomes of Portuguese firms and non-profit organizations (NPOs)? The aim of this research is to provide answers to this fundamental question.

The governance structure of the organizations is crucial since they execute the strategic plan approved by shareholders and manage the daily operations. Shareholders also define the governance model of their organizations in order to better protect their own interests. Despite the shareholders' power in the organizations, there is a constant conflict of interests between the managers they hire to run the organization and their own interests. The agency theory addresses this tension and suggests ways to mitigate

DOI: 10.4018/978-1-7998-7596-3.ch008

this problem (Jensen & Mecklin, 1976). Following the findings and recommendations of researchers, countries started to develop regulations (e.g. Cadbury Report,1992, for the United Kingdom) related to how organizations should draw their governance structures, in terms of executive management and internal (e.g. independent directors and audit committees) and external (e.g. auditing firms) control mechanisms. Concomitantly, these regulations also framed the scope of information that management should publicize in order to protect shareholders' interests, namely the interests of minority shareholders.

The first Portuguese Corporate Governance Code (PCGC) is dated from 1999, and was developed by the *Comissão de Mercado de Valores Mobiliários* (CMVM, 1999). This document contains 17 recommendations organized in five chapters: the dissemination of information; voting and representation of shareholders; institutional investors; the corporate rules; and the structure and functioning of the board. Since then, the Portuguese Corporate Governance Code has been updated and it was created, in 2003, the *Instituto Português de Corporate Governance* (IPGC). The current PCGC is dated from 2018, and the responsibility to evaluate the code, the level of firms' compliance and to update it is presently in the hands of the *Comissão de Acompanhamento e Monitorização* (CAM), created by IPGC.

Vieira and Neiva (2019) and Lisboa, Guilherme and Teixeira (2020) provide a compelling vision of the corporate governance practices conducted by Portuguese firms. According to Vieira and Neiva (2019), the prevailing governance model of the Portuguese firms is the Latin model, where the governance structure is composed by a board of directors (BoD) or a sole director and an audit committee or a statutory auditor. In addition, the authors conclude for an increase of the fraction of independent directors and the fraction of women directors on the BoD, over the past years. Lisboa et al. (2020) provide additional information and report that almost half of the Portuguese listed firms are family firms, that the firms' remuneration plans of the board members have increase its fixed component to around 75%, and a small percentage of firms uses stock options in their remuneration systems. The authors also document a consistent increase of merger and acquisitions (M&A) operations and a growing presence of international institutional investors in the shareholders' structures.

Literature on the corporate governance mechanisms impact in Portuguese firms had its beginning with the investigation conducted by Alves and Mendes (2004). In this research, the authors conclude for a positive association between the level of compliance of some of the recommendations of the Portuguese Corporate Governance Code and firms' performance. Nevertheless, the authors conclude for a non-systematic effect between the level of compliance and performance. Research on this topic has been growing and covers a wide range of governance mechanisms, firm outputs and firm types.

Using a sample of 47 articles, published between 2004 and 2019[1], it is possible to organize the research on five major topics: firm performance; earnings management; information disclosure; executive compensation and risk. The most of the variables used by research presents contingent effects, however it is possible to highlight some of the most consistent findings. Firstly, there is a tendency to report that board size is detrimental do firm performance, while CEO non-duality is a governance mechanism that improves it. Secondly, board size and board independence are positively associated with corporate governance disclosure, CSR disclosure and risk-related disclosure while CEO duality is detrimental to corporate governance disclosure and CSR disclosure. Thirdly, Latin model of governance, board gender diversity and a higher number of board meetings promote lower levels of earnings management. In opposition, executive compensation based on stock options, older CEOs, CEOs with business or finance background, and CEOs that accumulate the Chairperson position are more prone to manage earnings. Fourthly, CEO age is positively associated with an increase of CEO pay while CEO duality has an opposite effect. Fifthly, board independence increases firms risk-taking.

The contributions of this investigation are twofold: First, and to the best of the author knowledge, this is the first attempt to systematize the corporate governance research focus on Portuguese organizations; Second, this research encapsulates literature on corporate governance covering all topics studied until now, which contributes to extend the study of Vieira and Neiva (2019), that focus only on the determinants of firm performance.

The remaining of the chapter is organized as follows: Section 2, describes the evolution of the Portuguese Corporate Governance Code; Section 3, presents the methodology of the study; Section 4 describes and discusses the results and; Section 5, concludes.

BACKGROUND

The Evolution of the Portuguese Corporate Governance Code

The Portuguese Corporate Governance Code had its first version in 1999. The first recommendation of the Portuguese Securities Market Commission *(Comissão de Mercado de Valores Mobiliários - CMVM)* contemplates 17 recommendations organized in five chapters: the dissemination of information; voting and representation of shareholders; institutional investors; the corporate rules; and the structure and functioning of the board. In the fifth chapter, the CMVM recommends, in section 15, that the board should include one or more independent directors, to protect other interests than the larger shareholders. In addition, in section 17, it is suggested to companies to create internal control commissions in matters of potential conflict of interests between managers and shareholders, such as the appointment of directors and managers, the analysis of remuneration policy, and the assessment of corporate structure and governance.

In 2001, it was published the first regulation *(Regulamento da CMVM nº7/2001)* about corporate governance obligations of listed firms. This regulation presents, for the first time, a formal structure of the Corporate Governance Report that listed firms should produce and publicize to the stock markets. This legislation was exclusively related to rules of corporate information disclosure and introduced in the Portuguese legislation the principle of *"comply or explain"*. This principle, presented in the article nº 1 a), demands that listed companies publicize the level of the adoption of the regulation and, in case of non-adoption, the necessity to explain why they are not following the recommendations.

In 2005, the CMVM published a new regulation *(Regulamento da CMVM nº 10/2005)* to update the previous regulation published in 2001 *(Regulamento da CMVM nº7/2001)* and 2004 *(Regulamento da CMVM nº 4/2004)*. The new regulation aimed to transport for Portuguese legislation: (1) the EU Commission Recommendation (2005/162/EC), of 15 February 2005, on the role of non-executive or supervisory directors of listed companies and the committees of the (supervisory) board; (2) the EU Commission Recommendation (2004/913/CE), of 14 December 2004, fostering an appropriate regime for the remuneration of directors of listed companies. These two European recommendations focus, among others: (a) on the definition of a more strict concept of directors' independence; (b) on a clear distinction between executive and non-executive directors and, among the last, the distinction between independent and non-independent directors; (c) on the publication of the list of specific commissions created by corporate boards, with indication of their composition and the number of independent members belonging to each commission; (d) on the description of the remuneration policies; (e) on the publication of semiannual information (based on the adoption of the IAS 34) and; (f) on the changes on the Annexes related to the structure of the Corporate Governance Report. In sum, the focus of this legislation was in the internal control systems of the listed firms.

In September of 2007, the CMVM published the first Portuguese Corporate Governance Code - *"Código do Governo das Sociedades da CMVM"*. This Recommendation reorganizes the previous Recommendations in a new systematic way and accommodates the new rules of the Commercial Code provided by the Decree-Law nº 76-A/2006, of March 29th. In this Decree-Law, it is presented an extensive list of new rules framing the conditions of Corporate Governance committees' composition, the list of requirements to consider a director as "independent", it is reinforced the independence of the audit committees and it is added a new Corporate Governance Model. While the previous legislation contemplated only two Corporate Governance Models (Board and Fiscal Council; and Board, General Council and External Auditor), the new one, expand the firms' possibilities to implement a model composed by one Executive Board, a General and Supervisory Council and an External Auditor. In this Recommendation, it is suggested, for the first time, a proportion of independent directors on board. According to section II.1.2.2, the number of independent directors shouldn't be lower than 25% of the total number of board members. Also, the document postulate a number of recommendations related to the independence of internal control governance mechanisms: First, according to the Governance Model adopted by firms, the President of the Fiscal Council, or the audit commission or the commission for financial matters must be independent (section II.1.3.10.); Second, the members of the remuneration committee must be independent (section II.5.2.).

In November of 2007, the CMVM published another regulation *(Regulamento da CMVM nº 1/2007)*, to conciliate, until that date, regulations and recommendations related to firms' information disclosure from different sources, namely: from itself (CMVM); from the European Commission; and the Organization for Economic Co-operation and Development (OECD). In addition, this regulation also comprises the new obligations postulated by the Decree-Law nº 76-A/2006, of March 29th. In *"Regulamento da CMVM nº 1/2007"* it is proposed a new structure for the Corporate Governance Reports, much more demanding in terms of information disclosure.

In 2010, the CMVM publishes the Regulation *"Regulamento da CMVM nº 1/2010"* to substitute *"Regulamento da CMVM nº 1/2007"* with two main purposes: (a) to allow listed firms to choose the Corporate Governance Code they want to follow, respecting the law requirements and; (b) to communicate to markets the remuneration of all members of the committees that have control duties.

In the same year, the CMVM produces two additional documents: *"Consolidação de fontes normativas e do código de governo das sociedades (2010)"* and *"Recomendações da CMVM sobre o governo das sociedades cotadas (2010)"*. While in the first document, there is a consolidation of the national recommendations and regulations related to the Corporate Governance of listed firms, the second document does not present any substantial change in terms of firms' corporate governance structure.

In 2013, the CMVM authorizes, without previous consent, that listed firms adopt the Corporate Governance Code that is more suitable to their reality, as long as they respect the Portuguese Law and CMVM requirements *(Regulamento da CMVM nº 4/2013)*. In the same legislation, the structure of the Corporate Governance Reports is updated. In the same year, it was published the last Recommendation related to the Portuguese Corporate Code by CMVM, whose major innovation related to firms' Corporate Governance structure, is the elimination of a minimal numerical proportion of independent directors' presence on board (section II.1.7.).

In 2014, the Portuguese Institute of Corporate Governance *(Instituto Português de Corporate Governance - IPCG)* published an updated version of its first Corporate Governance Code, dated from 2012.

This improved version started to be adopted by some firms, and created some noise and confusion along with firms and markets, due to the existence of two alternative Corporate Governance Codes produced by two different institutions: CMVM and IPCG. To solve this disruption, both institutions initiated a dialogue to produce a unified Corporate Governance Code and create a new mechanism to evaluate the firms' level of compliance. As a result of their discussion, in 2016, both institutions announced that CMVM transferred the responsibility for the development of a new and unified Corporate Code to IPGC. The IPGC also became responsible to develop the necessary conditions to evaluate the code, the level of firms' compliance and to update the code. After a relatively long period of public discussion with all interested parts, the IPCG published the new Portuguese Corporate Governance Code, in 2018.

The Portuguese Corporate Governance Code of 2018 presents some innovations in the structure of the Corporate Governance mechanisms to be adopted by firms, when compared with the last version of the Code produced by CMVM, namely: (a) it recommends that the number of non-executive directors must be higher than the number of executive directors (section III.3.); (b) it recovers the idea of the establishment of a minimum proportion of independent directors on boards but in a more demanding way. While in the previous Codes the recommended fraction of independent directors was 25%, the new code recommends a fraction of 33% (section III.4.); (c) it recommends, for the first time, that the majority of the members of the nomination committee should be independent directors (section V.4.3.). Until now, the Portuguese Corporate Governance Code of 2018, is still in use, without any update. The responsibility to evaluate the code, the level of firms' compliance and to update the code is presently in the hands of the *CAM - Comissão de Acompanhamento e Monitorização*, created by IPGC.

METHODOLOGY

According to Xie, Reddy and Liang, (2017: 134) a "literature review is a process of searching, reviewing, consolidating, and integrating the most prevalent issues examined in the discipline, thus to present research trends, research synthesis and research direction [...]". Our study follows the systematic approach as review technique, in order to establish a compelling perspective of the relevant literature. To build our database with quality research we define a set of procedures. Firstly, it were only considered publications in journals indexed to Web of Science[2] (subject areas: Business; Business Finance; Economics; and Management) and Scopus (subject areas: Business, Management and Accounting; and Economics, Econometrics and Finance) databases. Secondly, articles were searched with the following keywords: *"(Portugal OR Portuguese OR Euronext Lisbon) AND (director OR board OR executive OR chief OR CEO OR CFO)"*. The search provided a list of 46 articles published at the Web of Science database and 169 published at the Scopus database. Thirdly, both lists were merged in order to eliminate duplications, which resulted in a list of 186 articles. Finally, all articles were analyzed in order to check if they used corporate governance mechanisms as determinants of firm outcomes in their econometric models. This procedure generated a final sample of 47 articles.

This study encapsulates a combination of quantitative and qualitative methods. While the quantitative approach was used to produce descriptive data, the documental analysis was the primary qualitative technic.

RESULTS AND DISCUSSION

On Table 1, it is presented the list of the final articles that results from the adopted research criteria. The information is organized by alphabetic order of the authorships. For each article it is mentioned the research topic and the sample characteristics.

The first article published in Scopus or Web of Science databases, related to Corporate Governance in the Portuguese context, is dated from 2004. In this pioneering work, Alves and Mendes (2004) analyze the relationship between the level of compliance of the Portuguese Corporate Governance Code and the financial performance of listed firms. The authors conclude for a significant association between the compliance of some recommendations and the level of firms' excess returns. The study reveals, in the first step of econometric analysis, a negative association between the group of recommendations related to information disclosure and excess returns, but a positive association between the group of recommendations related to improvements in the board composition and internal control committees. In additional tests, the authors analyze some specific recommendations and conclude for a beneficial effect of an appropriate dimension of the executive committee on financial performance, and a detrimental effect of information disclosure related to dividend policies and meeting attendance.

Since the innovative article of Alves and Mendes (2004), the literature on Corporate Governance in Portugal has been slowly growing. Figure 1 presents the evolution of the publications related to Corporate Governance in Portugal.

As Figure 1 shows, the literature on Portuguese Corporate Governance has been facing a positive trend, being 2016 and 2018 the most productive years. However, it is our understanding that this phenomenon is still clearly understudied in Portugal.

Figure 2 illustrates the topics that have been the focus of research related to corporate governance.

Figure 2 demonstrates that Portuguese research can be grouped in five major topics: The first topic is devoted to financial performance and represents 40% of the research, meaning that it is the preferred topic of researchers; the second, is related to information disclosure, with a weight of around 23%; the third, is about earnings management policies, with a share of 19%; the remaining two topics (executive compensation and corporate risk) are the less investigated topics, with weights of 10% and 8%, respectively.

Figures 3 and 4 highlight the type of sample used by researchers.

According to Figures 3 and 4, 79% of the studies focus on firms listed at the Euronext Lisbon Stock Market, while non-financial firms are the most used type of firms used by researchers, representing 45% of the total sample. In addition, 36 out of 47 of the studies are single country based and the remaining contemplates a multi-country sample.

The following subsections are organized by the relevance of the aforementioned research topics.

Table 1. List of articles

Authors	Research Topic	Sample		
		Country Level	Firm Type	Period of Analysis
Alves (2011)	Financial performance	Single country	Listed firms	2002-2006
Alves (2011a)	Earnings management	Single country	Non-financial listed firms	2002-2007
Alves (2012)	Earnings management	Single country	Non-financial listed firms	2003-2010
Alves (2014)	Earnings management	Single country	Non-financial listed firms	2003-2010
Alves and Mendes (2004)	Financial performance	Single country	Listed firms	1998-2001
Alves and Vicente (2013)	Earnings management	Multi-country	Non-financial listed firms	1997-2009
Alves, Couto and Francisco (2016)	Executive compensation	Single country	Listed firms	2002-2011
Alves, Martins and Ferreira (2009)	Executive compensation	Single country	Listed firms	2003
Barros and Nunes (2007)	Executive compensation	Single country	Non-profit organizations	2002
Beuselinck, Blanco and Lara (2017)	Earnings management	Multi-country	Listed firms	2002-2007
Carvalho, Rodrigues and Branco (2017)	Information disclosure	Single country	Non-profit organizations	2012
Costa, Oliveira, Rodrigues and Craig (2013)	Information disclosure	Single country	Listed firms	2006-2011
Cunha and Mendes (2017)	Information disclosure	Single country	Non-financial listed firms	2005-2011
Cunha and Rodrigues (2018)	Information disclosure	Single country	Non-financial listed firms	2005-2011
Dias, Rodrigues and Craig (2017)	Information disclosure	Single country	Listed firms	2011
Felício and Rodrigues (2014)	Financial performance	Multi-country	Listed firms	2004-2006
Félix and David (2019)	Financial performance	Single country	Portuguese association of family firms	2006-2014
Fernandes (2008)	Executive compensation	Single country	Listed firms	2002-2004
Ferraz, Lopes and Kopliku (2018)	Financial performance	Multi-country	Non-financial listed firms	2014
Gulamhussen and Guerreiro (2009)	Financial performance	Single country	Financial listed firms	1996-2004
Gulamhussen and Santa (2015)	Financial performance and corporate risk	Multi-country	Financial listed firms	2006
Isidro and Gonçalves (2011)	Earnings management	Single country	Listed firms	2005-2009
Lisboa (2016)	Earnings management	Single country	Listed firms	2003-2015
Lisboa and Esperança (2010)	Financial performance	Single country	Listed firms	2002-2008
Lopes and Reis (2019)	Financial performance	Multi-country	Listed firms	2010-2013
Lopes and Rodrigues (2007)	Information disclosure	Single country	Listed firms	2001
Lopes, Ferraz and Martins (2016)	Financial performance	Multi-country	Non-financial listed firms	2014
Madaleno and Vieira (2018)	Corporate risk	Single country	Non-financial listed firms	2008-2017
Martins, Morais, Isidro and Laureano (2018)	Information disclosure	Single country	Non-financial listed firms	2001-2009
Miralles-Marcelo, Miralles-Quirós and Lisboa (2014)	Financial performance	Multi-country	Listed firms	1999-2008
Oliveira, Azevedo and Silva (2019)	Information disclosure	Multi-country	Listed and non-listed financial firms	2011
Oliveira, Rodrigues and Craig (2011)	Information disclosure	Single country	Listed and non-listed non-financial firms	2005
Oliveira, Serrasqueiro and Mota (2018)	Information disclosure	Multi-country	Non-financial listed firms	2011
Pacheco (2019)	Financial performance	Single country	Non-financial and non-listed firms	2011-2016
Pereira and Esperança (2015)	Executive compensation	Single country	Listed and non-listed firms	non-defined
Pereira and Filipe (2015)	Financial performance	Single country	Listed and non-listed financial firms	2007-2011
Pereira and Filipe (2018)	Financial performance	Single country	Listed and non-listed financial firms	2012-2014
Rodrigues, Tejedo-Romero and Graig (2016)	Information disclosure	Single country	Listed firms	2007-2011
Sá, Neves and Góis (2017)	Corporate risk	Single country	Non-financial listed firms	2008
Saona, Muro, San Martín and Baier-Fuentes (2019)	Earnings management	Multi-country	Listed firms	2006-2016
Schwab, Werbel, Hofmann and Henriques (2016)	Financial performance	Single country	Listed and non-listed financial firms	1985-2000
Vieira (2014)	Corporate risk	Single country	Listed firms	1999-2010
Vieira (2016)	Financial performance	Single country	Non-financial listed firms	1999-2011
Vieira (2016a)	Earnings management	Single country	Listed firms	1999-2011
Vieira (2017)	Financial performance	Single country	Non-financial listed firms	1999-2014
Vieira (2018)	Financial performance	Single country	Non-financial listed firms	2002-2013
Vieira, Neves and Dias (2019)	Financial performance	Single country	Non-financial listed firms	2010-2015

Figure 1. Evolution of publications related to Portuguese Corporate Governance
Source: Own elaboration, based on Scopus and Web of Science databases

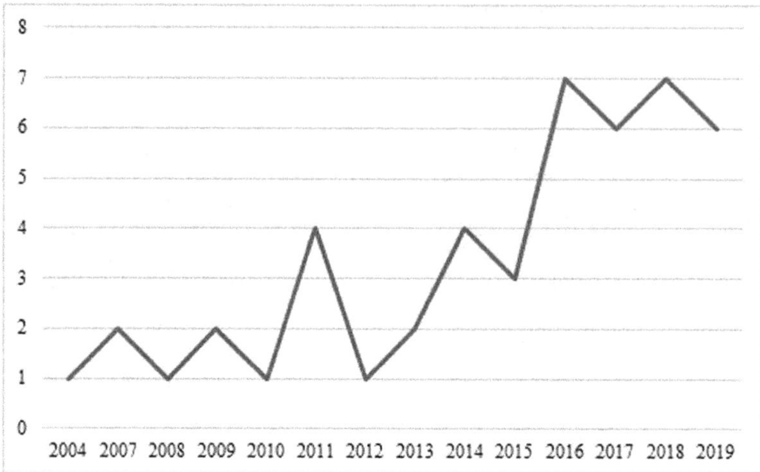

Figure 2. Research Topics
Source: Own elaboration, based on Scopus and Web of Science databases

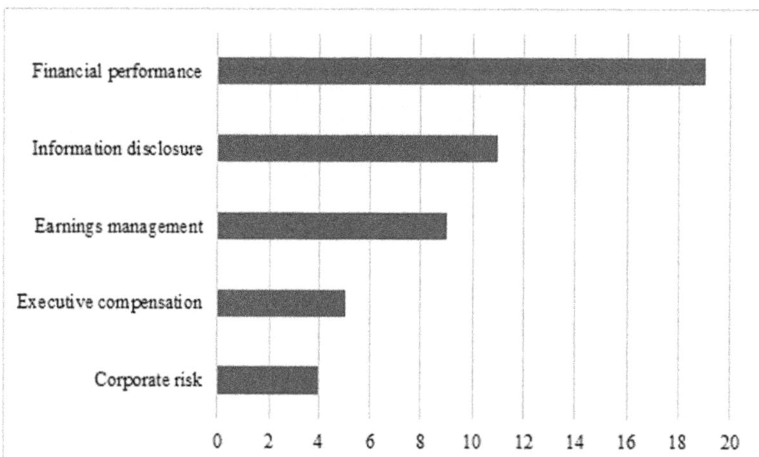

Figure 3. Sample of listed and non-listed firms
Source: Own elaboration, based on Scopus and Web of Science databases

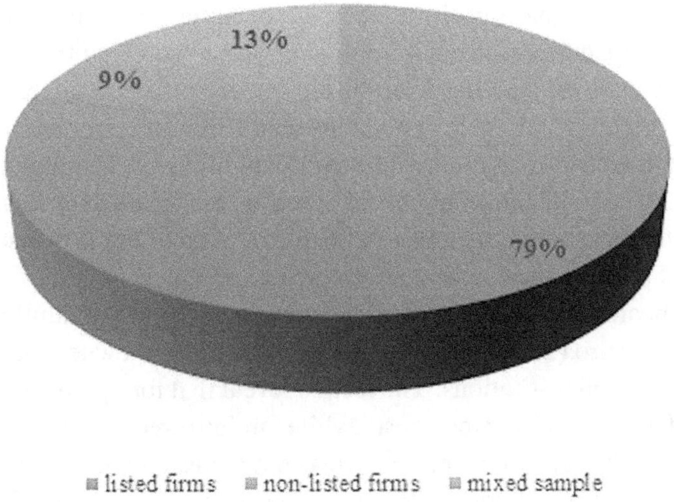

Figure 4. Sample of financial and non-financial firms
Source: Own elaboration, based on Scopus and Web of Science databases

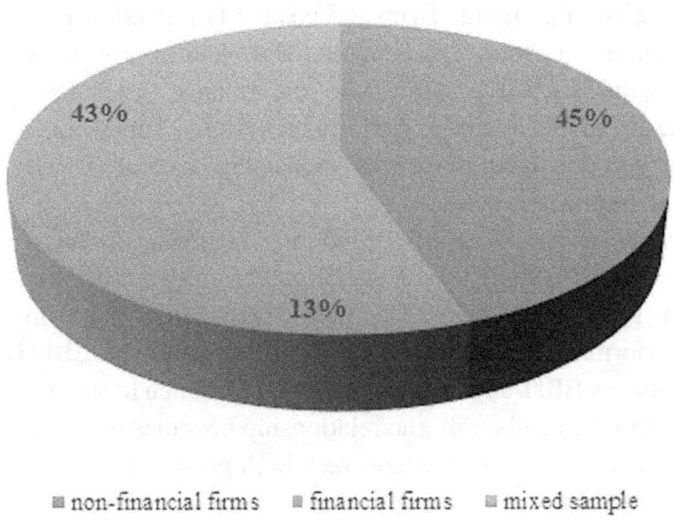

Corporate Governance Effects on Firms' Financial Performance

As we previously mentioned, Alves and Mendes (2004) were the first to study the effects of corporate governance mechanisms on firm performance. They provide evidence that the compliance of corporate recommendations does not have a systematic effect on firm excess returns. In a subsequent study, Alves (2011) document a detrimental effect of board size on firm performance and an incremental effect of the CEO non-duality on the total shareholder returns. Also using a sample of financial and non-financial listed firms, Felício and Rodrigues (2014) analyze the relationship between corporate governance mechanisms and performance of Portuguese and U.K. firms. The authors find out that there is an inverted "U-shape" association between board independence and financial performance of Portuguese firms, measured by Tobin's Q. Besides, they document a positive linear association between a dual leadership structure (CEO is different from the Chairperson) and Tobin's Q, Return on Equity (ROE) and MTB. Lopes, Ferraz and Martins (2016) investigate the relationship between diverse governance mechanisms and firm performance of Portuguese and Spanish non-financial firms and only report a significant positive association between the fraction of busy directors and firm turnover. Using a similar sample, Ferraz, Lopes and Kopliku (2018) conclude that only board size is a significant determinant of performance. In this case, the higher is the board size the lower is the ROE. Vieira (2017) investigates the relationship between debt policy and performance among family firms and argues for a negative influence of short and long-term debt and board independence on the performance (ROA) of family and non-family firms.

Gulamhussen and Guerreiro (2009) analyze the effects of foreign ownership and board foreignness on the performance of financial institutions. The results reveal that foreign ownership contributes to the reduction of the ratios of operational and total costs, while foreign directors' presence on boards decreases the ratio on net income and the ratio of operational costs but increases the ratio of total costs. Lisboa and Esperança (2010) study the effect of corporate ownership structure on the performance of Portuguese financial and non-financial listed firms and argue for a positive contribution of ownership concentration on firm performance. However, when considered only the effect of the three largest shareholders, no association is found. Miralles-Marcelo, Miralles-Quirós and Lisboa (2014) study performance differences between family and non-family firms, taking into account the Portuguese and the Spanish stock markets. The authors conclude that family firms are positively related to ROA, but negatively related to Tobin's Q. The associations are stronger for smaller and older family firms and, when family firms hold these characteristics, they have at least the same performance as non-family firms. Also, they find out that family CEOs are negatively related to performance (ROA, Tobin's Q). Vieira (2016) studies the Portuguese stock market and document that firms' ownership structure is irrelevant to market performance measured by share returns.

More recently, Vieira, Neves and Dias (2019) find mixed evidence in the role of CEO ownership on firm performance. Pacheco (2019) studies the association of family power on the financial performance of non-listed SME firms in the wine sector. The author reports a positive linear association between family power and firm performance, measured by ROA, the ratio between EBITDA and total assets (REBITDA), and the ratio between EBIT and total assets (REBIT). When he analysis one of the components of family power (family presence on board), the relationship becomes non-linear and with a "U-shape" form, meaning that companies with very low and very high presence of family directors on board are the ones with better performance.

Pereira and Filipe (2015) also investigate some determinants of Portuguese banks' performance and conclude that boards with more members with academic degrees on business and economics obtain better performance. Later on, Pereira and Filipe (2018) report robust findings that directors holding degrees from prestigious foreign universities impact positively on the financial performance of the banking industry.

Gulamhussen and Santa (2015) analyze the relationship between gender diversity (board of directors, supervisory board and audit committee), firm performance, and corporate risk-taking using a multi-country sample of financial firms. In what concerns firms' performance, the authors report that board gender diversity, in all the considered boards and committees, is positively associated with bank's performance, measured by Tobin's Q, ROE, and Return on Assets (ROA). Schwab, Werbel, Hofmann and Henriques (2016) conclude for a cubic relationship between gender diversity, in all management levels, and listed and non-listed financial firms' performance. This result indicates that lower levels of gender diversity decrease firm performance, but when this diversity increases until a certain level, the performance increases, turning again detrimental with very high levels of gender diversity. Veira (2018) also support the idea that gender diversity is incremental to firm performance of family firms. Additionally, the author reports the same beneficial effect of ownership for family firms while board gender diversity is detrimental to the performance of non-family firms. Félix and David (2019) study the relationship between board gender diversity and family firms' performance. The authors conclude that board gender diversity is positively associated with family firms' performance, measured by variation of sales, business volume over total assets, and variation of business volume. In addition, the authors document that company size and firm age are also important variables to explain family firms' performance.

Lopes and Reis (2019) document that risk committees have a contingent effect on firm performance. While the existence of a risk committee in non-financial firms is positively valued by the market, the market penalizes firms holding risk committees that report contingent liabilities.

Corporate Governance Effects on Firms' Information Disclosure Practices

In what concerns corporate information disclosure, we organize Portuguese research in six different topics: (1) Accounting disclosure (Carvalho, Rodrigues & Branco, 2017; Lopes & Rodrigues, 2007); (2) Corporate governance disclosure (Cunha & Rodrigues, 2018; Cunha & Mendes, 2017); (3) Corporate Social Responsibility disclosure (Dias, Rodrigues & Craig, 2017; Oliveira, Azevedo & Silva, 2019); (4) Intellectual Capital disclosure (Martins, Morais, Isidro & Laureano, 2018; Rodrigues, Tejedo-Romero & Graig, 2016); (5) Risk-related disclosure (Oliveira, Serrasqueiro & Mota, 2018; Oliveira, Rodrigues & Craig, 2011); CEO communication (Costa, Oliveira, Rodrigues & Craig, 2013).

Lopes and Rodrigues (2007) study the determinants of financial instruments disclosure in Portuguese listed companies. The authors report that larger listed financial firms, audited by one of the BIG5[3], are the ones that present a higher degree of financial instruments disclosure. The authors document a positive but non-significant association between board independence and information disclosure. Carvalho et al. (2017) analyze the determinants of the Voluntary Disclosure Index (VDI), specifically voluntary accounting information, of Portuguese non-profit organizations (NPOs). The authors conclude that NPOs' board structure have no impact on information disclosure.

The second group of research is related to the Corporate Governance Disclosure (CGD) index. Using the same database, Cunha and Rodrigues (2018) and Cunha and Mendes (2017) investigate the determinants of CGD of Portuguese non-financial firms. They conclude that firm size, foreign investor ownership, the board size, growth opportunities, board independence, external audit quality and degree of internationalization have a significant and positive influence on the corporate governance disclosure level, while an opposite effect is associated with ownership concentration, unitary leadership structure, and debt.

In relation to Corporate Social Responsibility Disclosure (CSRD), Dias et al. (2017) document that non-financial listed larger companies, with more visibility to the consumers, are associated with high levels of CSRD. In the same vein, corporate board structures with larger and more independent boards in which there is a dual leadership structure (CEO is a different person from the Chairman) are more prone to disclosure information. Concomitantly, Oliveira et al. (2019), using a multi-country sample of financial firms, confirm that countries with more robust banking systems, industry self-regulation, and the organization's commitments in maintaining a dialogue with relevant stakeholders, are crucial elements in the increase of CSRD. In contradiction with authors' expectations, they find that the countries with less robust banking systems and with weaker legal environments also positively promote higher levels of CSRD.

Rodrigues et al. (2016) and Martins et al. (2018) explore the influence of boards of directors on listed companies' voluntary intellectual capital disclosure index (ICDI). They prove that IC disclosures are found to increase with company size and industry type (Martins et al., 2018; Rodrigues et al, 2016). Rodrigues et al. (2016) also document that dual corporate governance models, listing on sustainability indexes and increases in board size up to a maximum point (beyond which disclosures decrease), are determinants of high ICDI. In the opposite pole, ICDI is reduced by CEO duality and board independence. Contrary to Rodrigues et al. (2015), Martins et al. (2018) do not find any significant effect of CEO duality and board independence on ICDI.

Oliveira et al. (2011), using a sample of Portuguese non-financial listed and non-listed firms, investigate the determinants of corporate risk-related disclosures (RRD). They find out that firm size, leverage, board independence, environmental sensitivity, and listing status improves the level of RRD. Oliveira et al. (2018) expand their initial work to Spanish firms and restricted the analysis to non-financial firms. The authors report that firm size is a robust predictor of RRD and board independence is especially relevant to non-financial risk type disclosure. Besides, they argue that stronger legal environments are inhibitors of RRD and do not confirm the previous finding related to the relevance of environmental sensitivity in the increase of RRD.

In what concerns CEO communication, Costa et al. (2013) document that corporate governance mechanisms are not relevant to determine the publication of CEO letters. However, firms more profitable, belonging to the financial sector, with a higher number of subsidiaries and audited by a BIG4 company, are more likely to publish CEO letters.

Corporate Governance Effects on Firms' Earnings Management Practices

Alves (2011a) investigate the effect of board structure on earnings management practices, using a sample of Portuguese non-financial listed firms. She reports a "U-shaped" relationship between board size and discretionary accruals and a positive role of the fraction of non-executive directors in its decreasing. Alves (2012) expanded her initial database and analyze the implications of stock options grants on earnings management. The author documents that managers holding stock options are more likely to engage in management earnings. In addition, the author reports that firms with larger boards and a higher number of board meetings reduce earnings management practices. In the same vein, and using the same sample, Alves (2014) find out that firms with more independent boards engage less in earnings management practices. Vieira (2016a) contradicts these findings and argues for a detrimental effect of board independence in the level of earnings management practices, especially for non-family firms.

Alves and Vicente (2013) study the relationship between corporate governance models and earnings management, in Portuguese and Brazilian non-financial listed firms. The results show that firms with the Latin governance model engage less in discretionary accruals than firms with different governance models. Moreover, firms that move from the Latin governance model do not generally decrease their levels of earnings management. In a different perspective, Isidro and Gonçalves (2011) examine the role of CEO on earnings management practices and conclude that older CEOs, CEOs with management or finance background, and CEOs that accumulate the Chairman position, are more prone to manage earnings.

Lisboa (2016) and Beuselinck, Bianco and Lara (2017) investigate firm ownership as determinants of earnings management practices. Lisboa (2016) document that this type of practices is higher in family firms that in non-family firms. Beuselink et al. (2017) conclude that foreign ownership benefits reporting quality but only when foreign shareholders are domiciled in high regulated markets and when firms have foreign institutional investors.

Using a sample of European listed firms, Saona, Muro, San Martín and Baier-Fuentes (2019) study the relationship between board gender diversity and earnings management. The results present evidence that a higher board gender diversity mitigates earnings management practices.

Corporate Governance Effects on Firms' Executive Compensation

Barros and Nunes (2007) investigate the CEO pay of Portuguese NPOs. The authors report a considerable number of determinants of CEO pay that are associated with firm performance, board characteristics and individual characteristics. Among board characteristics, the investigation finds evidence that board size, the fraction of inside directors, external directors nominated by the CEO, external directors with more than 65 years and external directors with political connections are positively associated with CEO pay. In opposition, CEO duality is detrimental to total CEO remuneration. In terms of CEO characteristics, education, age and performance-related pay promote higher levels of CEO pay.

Fernandes (2008) analyze the effects of board independence on executives' payment and concludes for a positive association, meaning that firms with more independent boards pay higher executive salaries, with and a higher fixed component. Pereira and Esperança (2015) analyze the determinants of the other slice of executive remuneration (variable component) of top Portuguese executives, in listed and non-listed firms. The major determinants considered are related to executive demographic characteristics (age and education), executive contract (tenure), firm performance (ROE and sales growth), and firm characteristics (e.g.: listed or not, productivity, size, location, activity sector). The authors conclude that executive education, a firm be listed in the Portuguese stock market, and a firm is located in the Lisbon region, are promoters of higher levels of variable executive compensation. In an opposite pole, firms' productivity contributes to the decrease of this form of remuneration. No significant relationship between CEO age, financial performance and variable compensation is reported.

Alves, Martins and Ferreira (2009) study the determinants of stock options attribution and report that firm size and equity held by managers are positively associated with stock options attribution. Alves, Couto and Francisco (2016) analyze the relationship between financial performance and total CEO compensation of listed firms. The authors document a positive association between Total Shareholder Returns (TSR) and CEO payment. However, firm performance only explains less than five percent of the variance in the total of CEO remuneration. The authors reveal that other determinants than firm performance (CEO characteristics and corporate governance mechanisms) help to explain better the variation of the dependent variable. The results reveal that CEO age, the number of directors on the remuneration committee, and the fraction of foreign directors, are positively associated with the increase of CEO compensation, while CEO education, CEO duality, and the fraction of independent directors, have an opposite effect.

Table 2. Summary of results

Dependent Variables	Independent Variables	Type of Association	Studies
Group of measures related to financial performance	Board independence	Inverted "U-Shape"	Felício, et al. (2014)
		(-)	Vieira (2017)
	Board size	(-)	Alves (2011); Ferraz et al. (2018)
	Busy directors	(+)	Lopes, et al. (2016)
	CEO non-duality	(+)	Alves (2011); Felício and Rodrigues (2014)
	CEO Ownership	(+/-)	Vieira, et al. (2019)
	Directors' degrees in business and economics	(+)	Pereira, et al. (2015)
	Directors' degrees from prestigious foreign universities	(+)	Pereira and Filipe (2018)
	Family CEO	(-)	Miralles-Marcelo, et al. (2014)
	Family ownership	(+/-)	Miralles-Marcelo, et al. (2014)
	Family directors	"U-Shape"	Pacheco (2019)
	Female directors	(+)	Fėlix and David (2019); Gulamhussen and Santa (2015)
		Cubic	Schwab, et al. (2016)
		(+/-)	Vieira (2018)
	Foreign directors	(-)	Gulamhussen and Guerreiro (2009)
	Ownership concentration	(+/-)	Lisboa and Esperança (2010)
		Non-significant	Vieira (2016)
	Risk Committee	(+/-)	Lopes and Reis (2019)
Group of measures related to information disclosure	Board independence	Non-significant	Lopes and Rodrigues (2007); Martins, et al. (2018)
		(+)	Cunha and Rodrigues (2018); Dias, et al. (2017); Rodrigues, et al. (2016); Oliveira, et al. (2011); Oliveira, et al. (2018)
	Board size	(+)	Cunha and Rodrigues (2018); Dias, et al. (2017)
	CEO duality	(-)	Cunha and Rodrigues (2018); Dias, et al. (2017); Rodrigues, et al. (2016)
		Non-significant	Martins, et al. (2018)
	Foreign ownership	(+)	Cunha and Rodrigues (2018)
	Inside directors	Non-significant	Carvalho, et al. (2017)
	Ownership concentration	(-)	Cunha and Rodrigues (2018)
	Remunerated directors	Non-significant	Carvalho, et al. (2017)
	Remunerated CEO	Non-significant	Carvalho, et al. (2017)
Group of measures related to earnings management	Board independence	(-)	Alves (2014)
		(+)	Vieira (2016a)
	Board size	"U-Shape"	Alves (2011)
		(-)	Alves (2012)
	CEO age	(+)	Isidro and Gonçalves (2011)
	CEO duality	(+)	Isidro and Gonçalves (2011)
	CEO with a degree in business or finance	(+)	Isidro and Gonçalves (2011)
	Family firms	(+)	Lisboa (2016)
	Female directors	(-)	Saona, et al. (2019)
	Foreign ownership	(+/-)	Beuselinck, et al. (2017)
	Latin governance model	(-)	Alves and Vicente (2013)
	Managers stock options	(+)	Alves (2012)
	Non-executive directors	(-)	Alves (2011)
	Number of board meetings	(-)	Alves (2012)

continued on following page

Table 2. Continued

Dependent Variables	Independent Variables	Type of Association	Studies
Group of measures related to executive compensation	Board independence	(+)	Fernandes (2008)
		(-)	Alves, et al. (2016)
	Board size	(+)	Barros and Nunes (2007)
	CEO age	(+)	Alves, et al. (2016); Barros and Nunes (2007)
		Non-significant	Pereira and Esperança (2015)
	CEO duality	(-)	Alves, et al. (2016); Barros and Nunes (2007)
	CEO education	(+)	Barros and Nunes (2007)
		(-)	Alves, et al. (2016)
	CEO performance -related pay	(+)	Barros and Nunes (2007)
	Foreign directors	(+)	Alves, et al. (2016)
	Inside directors	(+)	Barros and Nunes (2007)
	Managers ownership	(+)	Alves, et al. (2009)
	Number of directors on the remuneration committee	(+)	Alves, et al. (2016)
	Outside directors, nominated by the CEO, older than 65 years	(+)	Barros and Nunes (2007)
	Outside directors with political connections	(+)	Barros and Nunes (2007)
	Top executives education	(+)	Pereira and Esperança (2015)
Group of measures related to corporate risk	Board independence	(+)	Sá, et al. (2017); Vieira (2014)
	Busy directors	(-)	Sá, et al. (2017)
	Female directors	(-)	Gulamhussen and Santa (2015)
	Non-executive directors	(-)	Sá, et al. (2017)
	Ownership concentration	(+)	Sá, et al. (2017)

Corporate Governance Effects on Firms' Risk-Taking Policies

Vieira (2014) study the impact of board independence and ownership on risk-taking policies of listed firms. The author argues for a detrimental effect of board independence on market and operational risks for non-family firms.

Gulamhussen and Santa (2015) analyze the relationship between gender diversity, firm performance, and corporate risk-taking using a multi-country sample of financial firms. In what concerns corporate risk-taking, the authors report that board gender diversity is negatively associated with a wide range of risk measures (loan loss provisions, loan loss reserves, impaired loans, and Z-score). Using a sample of non-financial listed firms, Madaleno and Vieira (2018) examine whether there are differences in risk and volatility between Family Firms and non-Family listed Firms. The authors find no differences in the liquidity-volatility relationship between firm groups. Sá, Neves and Góis (2017) analyze the effect of different corporate governance mechanisms on corporate risk, of non-financial listed firms, in a time-frame of 24 months, being the reference middle point, the date of the bankruptcy on Lemon Brothers (September, 15th of 2008). Their findings suggest that board independence, as perceived by Portuguese regulatory authorities and higher levels of ownership concentration are detrimental to firm risk, while financial markets reward firms with higher levels of non-executive directors and board busyness.

Summary of the Findings

This section presents a summary of the findings reported by research devoted to the study of corporate governance in the Portuguese context. Table 2 describes the results and the studies that support them.

In what concerns the corporate governance mechanisms effects on firm performance, it is possible to conclude that firms with busy directors within their boards, with a dual leadership structure and whose directors' education is in the business and economics fields and in prestigious foreign universities reveal a higher firm performance. In opposition, firms with larger boards, with foreign directors within their boards and with family CEOs present a poorer performance. In addition, there is mixed evidence on the effects of the board independence, the presence of family directors on the board, the CEO and family ownership, the ownership concentration, the existence of a risk committee and the board gender diversity on firm performance.

In relation to firms' information disclosure, it can be concluded that firms with larger boards, higher levels of board independence and foreign ownership provide more information to shareholders and to the markets. In the opposite pole, firms with a unitary leadership model and with higher levels of ownership concentration are more opaque.

Different corporate governance mechanisms impact differently on firms' earnings management practices. Literature shows that these practices are higher in family firms and when managers hold stock options. In addition, firms with unitary leadership structures (CEO duality), with older CEOs and with CEOs whose academic background is in business or in finance also promote those type of practices. On the other side, firms adopting the Latin governance model, with a higher presence on non-executive and women directors on their boards and with a greater frequency of board meetings engage less in earnings management practices. In terms of board independence, board size and foreign ownership results still inconclusive.

Research in the Portuguese context shows that board independence and top executives' age and education are not robust promoters of an increase of executives' compensation. While firms with unitary leadership structures pay less to their executives, firms with larger boards, with larger remuneration committees, and with more foreign directors pay higher levels of compensation. In the same vein, organizations with more outside directors nominated by the CEO and with more outside political directors increase executive compensation. Similar benefits are associated to firms with more inside directors and with higher levels of managerial ownership.

Lastly, firms engage in more risk-taking activities when there are strong levels of ownership concentration and when their boards have higher levels of independence. More conservative risk-taking policies are associated to firms with more non-executive directors, busier directors and more female directors.

CONCLUSION

In this investigation it was performed a literature review on the corporate governance mechanisms effects on Portuguese firms and NPO's, between 2004 and 2019. Research on Portuguese corporate governance has been increasing over the last decade and covers a different number of organization types, namely, financial and non-financial listed and non-listed firms and NPO's. The preferred topic of researchers is firm performance and the ones with least attention are firm risk-taking and executive compensation. Literature shows that, in Portugal, the corporate governance mechanisms most studied as antecedents to firms' outputs are the board independence, board size, leadership structure and different types of ownership. Concomitantly, it is not possible to highlight any corporate governance characteristic universally beneficial to organizations.

Based on this study, it is possible to identify some avenues for future research. First, in terms of directors' characteristics, the effects of gender and nationality diversity on firm outputs are considerable understudied in almost all main topics of corporate governance research. Second, there are very few studies on the governance determinants of firms' risk policies and firms' remuneration plans. Third, since the majority of research focus on listed firms, more studies on private firms, cooperatives and NPO's are needed. Fourth, based on Table 2, it is also possible to provide several more specific future research lines, for example, as a result of the mixed evidence related to the benefits of higher levels of board independence, the benefits of larger and more diverse boards and the benefits of managerial ownership.

ACKNOWLEDGMENT

This work was financially supported by the research unit on Governance, Competitiveness and Public Policy (UIDB/04058/2020), funded by national funds through FCT - Fundação para a Ciência e a Tecnologia.

REFERENCES

Alves, C., & Mendes, V. (2004). Corporate Governance Policy and Company Performance: The Portuguese case. *Corporate Governance*, *12*(3), 290–301. doi:10.1111/j.1467-8683.2004.00370.x

Alves, C., & Vicente, E. F. R. (2013). Does the Latin model of corporate governance perform worse than other models in preventing earnings management? *Applied Financial Economics*, *23*(21), 1663–1673. doi:10.1080/09603107.2013.844322

Alves, P., Couto, E. B., & Francisco, P. M. (2016). Executive pay and performance in Portuguese listed companies. *Research in International Business and Finance*, *37*, 184–195. doi:10.1016/j.ribaf.2015.11.006

Alves, S. (2011). The association between executive stock options and corporate performance: Evidence from Portugal. *International Journal of Business Governance and Ethics*, *6*(2), 203–223. doi:10.1504/IJBGE.2011.039969

Alves, S. (2011a). The effect of the board structure on earnings management: Evidence from Portugal. *Journal of Financial Reporting and Accounting*, *9*(2), 141–160. doi:10.1108/19852511111173103

Alves, S. (2012). Executive stock options and earnings management in the portuguese listed companies. *Revista de Contabilidad*, *15*(2), 211–235. doi:10.1016/S1138-4891(12)70043-2

Alves, S. (2014). The Effect of Board Independence on the Earnings Quality: Evidence from Portuguese Listed Companies. *Australasian Accounting. Business and Finance Journal*, *8*(3), 23–44.

Alves, S., Martins, J., & Ferreira, C. (2009). Determinants of executive stock options: Portuguese evidence. *Corporate Ownership & Control*, *7*(2), 260–268. doi:10.22495/cocv7i2c2p2

Barros, C. P., & Nunes, F. (2007). Governance and CEO pay and performance in non-profit organizations. *International Journal of Social Economics*, *34*(11), 811–827. doi:10.1108/03068290710826404

Beuselinck, C., Blanco, B., & Lara, J. M. G. (2017). The Role of Foreign Shareholders in Disciplining Financial Reporting. *Journal of Business Finance & Accounting*, *44*(5&6), 558–592. doi:10.1111/jbfa.12239

Carvalho, A. O., Rodrigues, L. L., & Branco, M. C. (2017). Factors Influencing Voluntary Disclosure in the Annual Reports of Portuguese Foundations. *Voluntas*, *28*(5), 2278–2311. doi:10.100711266-017-9883-8

CMVM. (1999). *Recomendações da CMVM sobre o Governo das Sociedades Cotadas*. https://www.cmvm.pt/pt/Legislacao/Legislacaonacional/C%C3%B3dGoverno%20das%20Sociedades/AnexosGovSoc/Pages/99_indice.aspx

CMVM. (2007). *Recomendações da CMVM sobre o governo das sociedades cotadas*. https://www.cmvm.pt/pt/Legislacao/Legislacaonacional/Recomendacoes/Pages/Recomendacoes.aspx?pg

CMVM. (2010). *Consolidação de fontes normativas e do código de governo das sociedades*. https://www.cmvm.pt/pt/Legislacao/Legislacaonacional/Recomendacoes/Pages/Recomendacoes.aspx?pg

CMVM. (2010a). *Recomendações da CMVM sobre o governo das sociedades cotadas*. https://www.cmvm.pt/pt/Legislacao/Legislacaonacional/Recomendacoes/Pages/Recomendacoes.aspx?pg

CMVM. (2013). *Recomendações da CMVM sobre o Governo das Sociedades*. https://www.cmvm.pt/pt/Legislacao/Legislacaonacional/Recomendacoes/Pages/Recomendacoes.aspx?pg

Costa, G. A., Oliveira, L. C., Rodrigues, L. L., & Craig, R. (2013). Factors associated with the publication of a CEO letter. *Corporate Communications*, *18*(4), 432–450. doi:10.1108/CCIJ-07-2012-0045

Cunha, V., & Rodrigues, L. L. (2018). Determinants of Structure of Corporate Governance Disclosure in Portugal. *RBGN-. Revista Brasileira de Gestão de Negócios*, *20*(3), 338–360. doi:10.7819/rbgn.v0i0.3359

Cunha, V. L. M., & Mendes, S. M. D. (2017). Financial Determinants of Corporate Governance Disclosure: Portuguese Evidence. *Athens Journal of Business and Economics*, *3*(1), 21–35. doi:10.30958/ajbe.3.1.2

Decreto-Lei nº 76-A/2006, Diário da República, 1ª série - A, Nº 63, 29 de março de 2006.

Dias, A., Rodrigues, L. L., & Craig, R. (2017). Corporate Governance Effects on Social Responsibility Disclosures. *Australasian Accounting. Business and Finance Journal*, *11*(2), 3–22.

Felício, J. A., & Rodrigues, R. (2014). Study on the influence of governance mechanisms on performance: Evidence of nonlinear relationships of listed companies in different contexts. *Corporate Ownership & Control*, *11*(2), 429–445. doi:10.22495/cocv11i2c5p1

Fėlix, E. G. S., & David, D. S. T. (2019). Performance of family-owned firms: The impact of gender at the management level. *Journal of Family Business Management*, *9*(2), 228–250. doi:10.1108/JFBM-10-2018-0051

Fernandes, N. (2008). EC: Board compensation and firm performance: The role of "independent" board members. *Journal of Multinational Financial Management*, *18*(1), 30–44. doi:10.1016/j.mulfin.2007.02.003

Ferraz, D. P., Lopes, I. T., & Kopliku, A. (2018). Can board diversity and choice of auditor enhance profitability? *International Journal of Business Performance Management*, *19*(3), 289–306. doi:10.1504/IJBPM.2018.092757

Gulamhussen, M. A., & Guerreiro, L. (2009). The influence of foreign equity and board membership on corporate strategy and internal cost management in Portuguese banks. *Management Accounting Research*, *20*(1), 6–17. doi:10.1016/j.mar.2008.10.006

Gulamhussen, M. A., & Santa, S. F. (2015). Female directors in bank boardrooms and their influence on performance and risk-taking. *Global Finance Journal*, *28*, 10–23. doi:10.1016/j.gfj.2015.11.002

IPGC. (2018). *Código de Governo das Sociedades*. https://cgov.pt/images/ficheiros/2018/codigo_de_governo_das_sociedades_ipcg_vf.pdf

Isidro, H., & Gonçalves, L. (2011). Earnings management and CEO characteristics in Portuguese firms. *Corporate Ownership & Control*, *9*(1), 86–95. doi:10.22495/cocv9i1art5

Jensen, M. C., & Meckling, W. H. (1976). Theory of the firm: Managerial behavior, agency costs and ownership structure. *Journal of Financial Economics*, *3*(4), 305–360. doi:10.1016/0304-405X(76)90026-X

Lisboa, I. (2016). Impact of financial crisis and family control on earning management of Portuguese listed firms. *European Journal of Family Business*, *6*(2), 118–131. doi:10.1016/j.ejfb.2017.06.002

Lisboa, I., & Esperança, J. P. (2010). Ownership structure and performance: Evidence from Portugal. *Corporate Ownership & Control*, *7*(3), 25–32. doi:10.22495/cocv7i3p2

Lisboa, I., Guilherme, M. C., & Teixeira, N. (2020). Corporate governance practices in Portugal. *Corporate Law & Governance Review*, *2*(1), 42–54. doi:10.22495/clgrv2i1p4

Lopes, A. I., & Reis, L. (2019). Are provisions and contingent liabilities priced by the market? An exploratory study in Portugal and the UK. *Meditari Accountancy Research*, *27*(2), 228–257. doi:10.1108/MEDAR-09-2017-0212

Lopes, I. T., Ferraz, D. P., & Martins, M. M. (2016). The influence of diversity on boards profitability: An overview across Iberian non-financial listed companies. *Corporate Ownership & Control*, *13*(2), 454–460. doi:10.22495/cocv13i2c2p6

Lopes, P. T., & Rodrigues, L. L. (2007). Accounting for financial instruments: An analysis of the determinants of disclosure in the Portuguese stock exchange. *The International Journal of Accounting*, *42*, 25-56.

Madaleno, M., & Vieira, E. (2018). Volatility analysis of returns and risk: Family versus nonfamily firms. *Quantitative Finance and Economics*, *2*(2), 348–372. doi:10.3934/QFE.2018.2.348

Martins, M. M., Morais, A. I., Isidro, H., & Laureano, R. (2018). Intellectual Capital Disclosure: The Portuguese Case. *Journal of the Knowledge Economy*, *9*(4), 1224–1245. doi:10.100713132-016-0412-6

Miralles-Marcelo, J. L., Miralles-Quirós, M. M., & Lisboa, I. (2014). The impact of family control on firm performance: Evidence from Portugal and Spain. *Journal of Family Business Strategy*, *5*(2), 156–168. doi:10.1016/j.jfbs.2014.03.002

Oliveira, J., Rodrigues, L. L., & Craig, R. (2011). Risk-related disclosures by non-finance companies: Portuguese practices and disclosure characteristics. *Managerial Auditing Journal*, *26*(9), 817–839. doi:10.1108/02686901111171466

Oliveira, J., Serrasqueiro, R., & Mota, S. N. (2018). Determinants of risk reporting by Portuguese and Spanish non-finance companies. *European Business Review*, *30*(3), 311–339. doi:10.1108/EBR-04-2017-0076

Oliveira, J. S., Azevedo, G. M. C., & Silva, M. J. P. C. (2019). Institutional and economic determinants of corporate social responsibility disclosure by banks: Institutional perspectives. *Meditari Accountancy Research, 27*(2), 196–227. doi:10.1108/MEDAR-01-2018-0259

Pacheco, L. (2019). Performance vs. Family Ownership and Management: The Case of Portuguese Wine Firms. *Entrepreneurial Business and Economics Review, 7*(3), 7–24. doi:10.15678/EBER.2019.070301

Pereira, I. N., & Esperança, J. P. (2015). Top executive compensation in less developed capital markets. *Corporate Governance, 15*(1), 122–133. doi:10.1108/CG-11-2014-0128

Pereira, V. M. M., & Filipe, J. A. B. (2015). Measuring the Board's Members Effect on Banks' Performance: An Application to Portugal. *International Journal of Latest Trends in Finance and Economic Sciences, 20*(10), 1–16.

Pereira, V. M. M., & Filipe, J. A. B. (2018). Quality of Board Members' Training and Bank Financial Performance: Evidence from Portugal. *International Journal of Economics and Business Administration, 6*(3), 47–79.

Regulamento da CMVM nº 10/2001, Diário da República, 2ª série Nº 222, 18 de novembro de 2005.

Regulamento da CMVM nº 1/2007, Diário da República, 2ª série - Nº 224, 21 de novembro de 2007.

Regulamento da CMVM nº 1/2010, Diário da República, 2ª série - Nº 21, de 1 de fevereiro de 2010.

Regulamento da CMVM nº 4/2013, Diário da República, 2ª série - Nº 147, de 1 de agosto de 2013.

Regulamento da CMVM nº 7/2001, Diário da República, 2ª série - Nº 299, 28 de dezembro de 2001.

Report, C. (1992). The *Financial aspects of Corporate Governance*. Retrieved from: https://ecgi.global/sites/default/files//codes/documents/cadbury.pdf

Rodrigues, L. L., Tejedo-Romero, F., & Graig, R. (2016). Corporate governance and intellectual capital reporting in a period of financial crisis: Evidence from Portugal. *International Journal of Disclosure and Governance, 14*(1), 1–29. doi:10.1057/jdg.2015.20

Sá, T. M., Neves, E. D., & Góis, C. G. (2017). The influence of corporate governance on changes in risk following the global financial crisis: Evidence from the Portuguese stock market. *The Journal of Management and Governance, 21*(4), 841–878. doi:10.100710997-016-9361-5

Saona, P., Muro, L., San Martín, P., & Baier-Fuentes, P. (2019). Board of director's gender diversity and its impact on earnings management: An empirical analysis for select European firms. *Technological and Economic Development of Economy, 25*(4), 634–663. doi:10.3846/tede.2019.9381

Schwab, A., Werbel, J. D., Hofmann, H., & Henriques, P. L. (2016). Managerial Gender Diversity and Firm Performance: An Integration of Different Theoretical Perspectives. *Group & Organization Management, 41*(1), 5–31. doi:10.1177/1059601115588641

Vieira, E., & Neiva, J. (2019). Corporate Governance Board of Directors and Firm Performance in Portugal. In Handbook of Board of Directors and Company Performance: An International Outlook. Virtus Interpress.

Vieira, E. S. (2014). Corporate Risk in Family Businesses Under Economic Crisis. *Innovar (Universidad Nacional de Colombia)*, *24*(53), 61–73. doi:10.15446/innovar.v24n53.43909

Vieira, E. S. (2016). Investor sentiment and share returns: Evidence on family firms. *Academia (Caracas)*, *29*(1), 65–83. doi:10.1108/ARLA-08-2015-0234

Vieira, E. S. (2016a). Earnings Management in Public Family Firms under Economic Adversity. *Australian Accounting Review*, *26*(2), 190–207. doi:10.1111/auar.12096

Vieira, E. S. (2017). Debt policy and firm performance of family firms: The impact of economic adversity. *International Journal of Managerial Finance*, *13*(3), 267–286. doi:10.1108/IJMF-03-2016-0062

Vieira, E. S. (2018). Board of directors characteristics and performance in family firms and under the crisis. *Corporate Governance: The International Journal of Business in Society*, *18*(1), 119–142. doi:10.1108/CG-01-2017-0010

Vieira, E. S., Neves, M. E., & Dias, A. G. (2019). Determinants of Portuguese firms' financial performance: Panel data evidence. *International Journal of Productivity and Performance Management*, *68*(7), 1323–1342. doi:10.1108/IJPPM-06-2018-0210

Xie, E., Reddy, K. S., & Liang, J. (2017). Country-specific determinants of cross-border mergers and acquisitions: A comprehensive review and future research directions. *Journal of World Business*, *5*(2), 127–183. doi:10.1016/j.jwb.2016.12.005

KEY TERMS AND DEFINITIONS

Corporate Governance: Firm's governance bodies.

Directors: Members of the Board of Directors and remaining committees.

Earnings Management: Accounting practices related to accruals manipulation.

Executive Compensation: Remuneration of the Executive Directors.

Information Disclosure: Level of information supplied by firms to markets and shareholders.

Performance: Firms' profitability.

Risk: Level of exposure to uncertain future events that may damage firms' financial stability and profitability.

ENDNOTES

1. No studies were found in 2020, between January, 1st and July, 1st.
2. From the Web of Science database only two indexes were taking into account: Social Sciences Citation Index (SSCI); and Emerging Sources Citation Index (ESCI).
3. Arthur Andersen, PricewaterhouseCoopers, Deloitte Touche Tohmatsu, Ernst and Young and KPMG.

Chapter 9
The Social Responsibility of the Firm:
A Corporate Governance Perspective

Alvaro Nascimento
https://orcid.org/0000-0001-5570-8039
Catolica Porto Business School, Universidade Católica Portuguesa, Portugal

ABSTRACT

This chapter pursues a normative approach to corporate governance, bridging economic theory on the nature of the firm and corporate management strategy. It intends to show that from a welfare economics perspective there is room for improvement if governments are willing to revisit the legal framework and redesign the institutional boundaries of the firm. In concrete, echoing concerns being put forward by the World Economic Forum and other international organisations, it is proposed that the social accountability of the modern corporation and its institutional boundaries should be revisited on legal grounds. A new role for top management is advanced in the context of principal-agent theory.

INTRODUCTION

The usually stakeholder-shareholder rhetoric of opposites is a false dichotomy. When managers take into consideration other stakeholders' interests, they are not acting against rewarding owners of capital with a fair financial return given the risks. Neither, when undertaking a holistic approach to the firm, they are necessarily sacrificing productive efficiency. A new definition of corporation is needed. One that does not contradict profit maximisation but encompasses the way organisations adapt to social and technological ever-changing environments.

A combination of theories explaining the boundaries of the firm, and how the modern corporation is organised internally is needed to shed some light on how resources and capabilities interact with each other, and help managers to take better decisions, while delivering optimal performance. The emphasis on shareholder value is a simplistic representation of a complex mesh of social relationships having the firm as stage, that one cannot but agree.

DOI: 10.4018/978-1-7998-7596-3.ch009

Financial investors are being cursed for extreme income inequalities and economic instability. As a result, internationally, corporate governance codes of best practices mirror OECD (2020) guidelines on board independence and diversity, and large companies gradually adapt governing structures and strategies to achieve broader economic objectives. The World Economic Forum preaches a shift from the dominant shareholder value maximisation to responsible capitalism, fostering the theme of 'purpose' as to motivate stakeholders around a common social and environmental goal[1]. In the news, Larry Fink, Chairman and CEO of BlackRock, pressures chief executives to have a sense of purpose, and achieve company's full potential.[2]

Technology and social norms play a pivotal role in the way corporations organise themselves. Uber and corporations alike are weaving a new mesh of relationships, directing the use resources in completely new ways, highly unthinkable before. Platform capitalism is challenging the institutional view of the firm and its boundaries as defined by existing norms. For many, volatile market relationships are substituting stable and long-lasting contracts with suppliers and customers, having implications for management, regarding sustainability and firm survival.

One needs an overarching theory that links concepts such as agency theory, transaction costs, asymmetric information, stewardship theory and human relationships: i.e., what one could label freely as "economics old school", on philosophical and normative tradition. The economic and legal definition of a corporation is as much a matter of academic curiosity as it has nonnegligible implications for strategic management, but also for competition policy, regulation and corporate governance issues alike.

The rest of the paper is organised as follows. Next section presents briefly the theoretical background, before moving into a critical review of transaction costs economics and the nature of the firm. Then, we introduce the market value of the firm concept, supporting the generally adopted capital market practice of corporate managers as agents of shareholders and acting on their only interest. Section four is about how shareholder primacy fails to represent adequately the modern corporation, and the merit of stakeholder and stewardship theories. The firm is presented as a social vehicle, with its own internal set of rules and regulations, paving the way to discuss the governance of the corporation (in section 5). Suggestions and recommendations regarding stakeholder representation and the role of management are offered. Section 6 concludes.

THE NATURE OF THE FIRM

Without controversy one can say the firm is a social arrangement for production. The seminal view on the nature of the firm proposed by Coase (1937) perceives the firm as a nexus of contracts and offers one of the most influential contributions to corporate governance. Transaction costs, used to draw a dividing line between the firm and the market, opens a role for managers which Williamson (1973, 1975), Holmstrom (1977) and Hart (1995), among many others, explored. The cost of setting up a hierarchical structure to coordinate production has to be analysed vis-a-vis the costs of trading in the market.

In a recent paper, Kay (2019) argues that economic theory fails to account for a correct representation of the firm, missing the very social nature of the corporation, and the fact that a stakeholder approach is currently dominant in corporate strategy. Yet, if Kay (2019) is correct, it is puzzling why we do not see more corporations concerned with social welfare and taking all stakeholders' views into consideration. Quite likely, the principal-agent theory introduced by Jensen and Meckling (1976) still dominates the financial world, explaining much of what one sees as corporate behaviour.

In his critique, Kay (2019) says that both corporate management and corporate governance are seen as principal-agent problems, to be resolved with appropriate incentives. But the nature of the firm and the scope of the problem managers are expected – and empowered – to solve is well beyond this narrow perspective. The transactions cost paradigm pioneered by Coase (1937) and Williamson (1973) endorses a biased view of the firm, focusing on shareholder value maximisation, implicitly assuming that financial markets are dominant when it comes to define a role for top management.

Empirical studies show that firm-level performance is linked to the organisation goals, its complexity, not to mention the procedures to solve conflicting views and interests. Partially underpinning this idea, Alfaro et al. (2019: 38) say that understanding how complex corporations work is increasingly important, and a multidimensional approach is needed to both illuminate interdependencies, that are crucial for understanding functioning, and guide organisation design.

Exploring the applicability of transaction cost economics, Alfaro et al. (2018: 39) show that firms integrate suppliers just to achieve better coordination over production decisions: managers can reallocate decision making to or from suppliers that the firm "owns". Firm-boundaries and allocation of power to make decisions regarding the use of assets and resources are intrinsically linked. "Supply assurance" is a rationale for integration. It is not about forcing the supplier to provide the input, but rather to ensure it is suited for use in production in a timely manner and obeying required specifications (e.g., quantity and quality).

When firms are unable to reach cooperation, and delegation is not feasible, a merger is likely to follow, particularly if the producer needs to control the provision of an essential input, or idiosyncratic asset as Coase (1937) refers. When value chains become global and parts are crafted everywhere, coordination becomes essential for production, except when input specification is not of surmount importance and suppliers are easily substituted. Generic inputs can be found in the market, in a competitive trading environment.

Alfaro et al (2018) are not as much interested in explaining strategic management as understanding the boundaries of the firm and the main differences between vertical integration and delegation. Recent empirical research shows that they are not truly alternatives, and their interrelatedness must be considered when analysing firm boundaries from an institutional and organisational perspective, in order to generate new insights for corporate governance.

Management power does not exist because of delegated property rights only. There is the authority over production decisions as it is with the power to allocate control. Integration is not necessarily associated with hierarchical rigidities. On contrary, it might come with re-allocation of decision rights across the firm, in a manner that is very close to outsourcing, except to the property of the assets. Some companies just cross the boundary and are willing to disintegrate parts of the supply chain, in exchange of cooperation from suppliers.

In real world, managers take into consideration suppliers' capabilities and their ability to cooperate with the firm and jointly achieve strategic goals. Not all corporations vertically integrate operations for competitiveness. On a globalised world, firms scan suppliers wherever they are to contract production and develop firm-specific products and services together. Cooperation, rather than a simplistic view of competition, is needed both when managers think about resources for production, and markets to place final goods and services.

Firms pursue strategies based on their capabilities and resources. Production is organised as to deliver goods and services with distinctive features to their customers. Cooperation with upstream suppliers might be required to achieve this goal, particularly when the input characteristics cannot be fully specified ex-ante, or when preventing specific developments to be made available to competitors. Because contracting is incomplete and property rights cannot be uniquely and clearly assigned, control has to be distributed between the firm and its supplier to achieve the desired coordination.

The model of the corporation as a nexus of contracts fails to capture the real nature and historical evolution of the firm and should be proclaimed dead (Kay, 2019). One sees firms breaching implicit contracts, such as tax avoidance schemes or excessive management rewards, amongst others, without penalties either from governments or the community. Concluding, transaction costs economics is of little use to lay the foundations of the firm, and a stakeholder approach, such as the one advocated by Freeman (1984) should be used instead.

On his contributions to strategic management, Freeman (1984) adopts a stakeholder approach to the firm and adds that one cannot see the world of business separate from ethics and politics, otherwise, models will do a poor job and fail in explaining the world. When insisting separating the two, stakeholder theory becomes ethical only, instead of a unique and holist business theory, able to explain how corporations interact with markets and its stakeholders. One needs new models to describe value creation from trade and corporate organisations.

Though apparently myopic, one can argue that Coase's (1937) theoretical framework is still valid to analyse the scope and boundaries of the firm, as long as transaction cost economics is defined to encompass both explicit and implicit contracting. A plethora of formal and informal rules shape the relationships of the firm with a myriad of stakeholders. Considering relationships as contracts, formal and informal, they are incomplete because of both uncertainty and bounded rationality, and its enforceability is dependent not only on formal institutions – such as courts of law – but also on society – its values and its moral.

Coase's transaction cost economics has been upgraded since his seminal work back in 1937.[3] Yet, the core has not changed much. A proof of this is empirical evidence of firms continuously moving their boundaries in response to an ever-changing institutional environment. Advances in information and communication technologies made market coordination more effective and less costly without dispute. Corporations are nowadays able to outsource operations to the international arena and operate globally, otherwise a move difficult to achieve, if not impossible. Value chains are global and more exposed to systemic risks and contagion, as COVID-19 pandemics show.

The importance of enquiring into the complexities of production systems taking a step away from classical economics is acknowledged by Loasby (2015). The author suggests that Coases' conceptual innovation was, contrary to mainstream economic reasoning at the time, the need to compare the cost of market transactions with internal management or, otherwise, the cost of planning. Coase's argument was ingenious: transactions in firms as well as in markets are not costless. The novelty is about finding the roots of these costs and link them to institutional frictions that exist in society.

A micro theoretical approach is needed, where institutions matter and the governing power rules how property rights are assigned amongst constituencies that meet and act together at the corporation level. A task which in turn is consistent with Adam Smith's central principle of 'economic progress through the interaction of competition and division of labour', and Marshall's warning that 'return is a continuous process of organizational change and improving knowledge'.

Loasby (2015: 248-250) reasons that market equilibria are – necessarily and desirably – local and temporary, while the main activity of a firm is to run a business. Markets incur in costs because agents need to invest to discover equilibrium, in a trial-and-error process. Any non-equilibrium trade leads to a redistribution of income between agents, and suboptimal allocation of resources is expected. It is odd, he argues, that in general equilibrium models such searching is neglected. If one asks why markets exist, a reasonable conclusion is that firms and markets are alternative and competitive institutional arrangements to direct the use of resources in the economy.[4]

Coase's marked contrast between markets and firms is to be rhetorically effective and should not prevent from completely understanding the complexities of industrial organisation, and its functioning. The suppression of price is not the distinctive feature between markets and internal management. Though prices do not exist explicitly, there are other means to weight costs and benefits. Quoting Richardson (1998: 57):

as Voltaire said of God, if prices did not exist, we should have to invent them, and in the design of intellectual arrangements of the firm, this is what we in fact do.

The purpose of the organization and operation of the industry is to deliver progress, which is more important than efficient allocation. Firms are decision making systems, and neither the set of products nor the methods of production are given. Every firm is different and cannot be coordinated simply by giving instructions. Therefore, markets do not exist naturally and have to be created by the application of human cognition and capabilities (Loasby, 2015).

Figure 1. A schematic representation of the nature of the firm

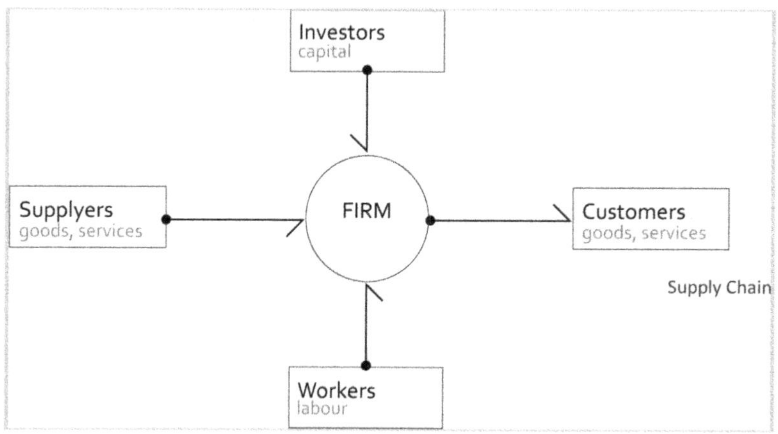

Upon this brief review, a schematic representation of the firm is proposed in figure 1. Corporations exchange goods and services with several stakeholders through markets. One can think of these markets as places where firms contract to buy economic inputs – labour, capital – that are used in the production. Goods and services obtained are sold to other firms and end users. This further implies that raw materials, components and services produced by others are also used in production. Usually, each individual firm has operations related to part of the supply chain only, not necessarily its entirety.

Briefly, stakeholders can be arranged in four different groups: suppliers, customers, workers and investors. The first two can be thought as a stylized representation of the (positioning of the) firm in the value chain, and the other two reveals the relationship with the markets for inputs, i.e., the classical production function. Any of them interact with the firm through a series of exchange transactions supported on a range of diverse contracts, more or less formal. Contracting is not always formal, particularly when the costs of doing so are prohibitively high, undermine competitiveness – from the point of view of the firm – and hinder economic efficiency – from the social planner perspective.

In real world not all coordination is achieved through the price mechanism. If one looks inside the firm, one acknowledges that resource allocation does not respond do market prices, but because they are ordered so by management. Economists reckon the importance of firm organisation and management for long. Microeconomic models have incorporated entrepreneurial and organisational skills as factors of production, which has encouraged research into management practices, just do discover that they matter for productivity, competitiveness and, ultimately, corporate finance.[5]

Business firms have their own internal markets, using non-transparent and discriminatory rules and procedures to dictate resource allocation. In doing so they compare its performance against alternatives outside. If a superior solution is found externally, they outsource resource allocation – production as to speak – as to remain competitive and survive its competitors. Several questions follow, which are central to discuss corporate governance and management: who has the power to set the rules, how are they chosen, and what determines its enforcement?

For many transactions, buyers can evaluate the quality of the goods and services which are delivered against payment. In other cases, trust allows trades to be arranged with minimal formal documentation. As transaction cost economics suggests, when contract enforcement is not difficult, markets are superior to hierarchies, and firms outsource production. On the contrary, vertical integration emerges when transaction costs are high.

Labour and capital markets are usually subject to a high degree of formality. Contracts are written between the firm and both workers and investors, allowing the firm to use their resources – labour and capital – with a given degree of discretion. Because of bounded rationality and asymmetric information, parties need institutions able to enforce the contracts and solve conflicts of interest rooted on states of nature that are not anticipated, and for which the existing clauses does not offer a way out.

Using this theoretical concept of firm, the size and scope of corporations depends on how efficient they are in making goods and services at the lowest possible cost. To a certain extent, how they are able to smoothly coordinate the production process. Strategically, the success and survival of the firm depends on its competitiveness – i.e., ability to outpace its rivals – which is grounded not only on economies of scale and scope, but also in its ability to reduce transaction costs. The theory can explain vertical integration, as well as conglomerates where economies of scope are a source of competitive advantage.

Two important questions stem from Coase's (1937) pioneering approach, which have implications for corporate governance and economic policy. The first, is whether one can reconcile his views with the theoretically profit maximising black box, i.e., a firm that achieves allocative and economic efficiency according to the orthodox representation. The second, given the first is true, is under which restrictions should firms behave in order to achieve a socially desirable outcome, using the answer to this as the ground to develop a corporate governance framework grounded on both economic theory and law.

Representing the corporation as a nexus of contracts raises the question of knowing to whose benefit should it be managed? Classical economics postulates the firm is a profit maximiser, assuming implicitly that the owners of capital interests should be addressed primarily. In real world, law gives shareholders the right to control the corporation, allowing them to nominate managers, who are expected to act on their behalf.

In fact, transaction cost economics is originally founded on a shareholders' perspective of the firm and, because of that, there is a reasoning bias flawing conclusion. However, one must argue that cutting on transaction costs – e.g., vertically integrate and achieve synergies – does not translate necessarily into increasing the financial value of the firm – i.e., the value to the owners of capital. There is more complexity in the firm than classical corporate finance valuation models are able to capture.

The financial approach to corporate governance is rooted on the principal agent problem and focus on the need to protect investors from moral hazard and adverse selection arising on asymmetric information between managers – who oversight the contracts – and owners – financing firms' assets. Under this framework, corporate social responsibility (CSR) is ad-hoc to the model, used opportunistically to maximise firm value through reducing the cost of financing. Empirical results about the relationship between CSR and corporate financial performance are mixed, but the majority suggest the link is there, though not much is said about the social impact of CSR practices.

Figure 2. Managers oversight of firms' contracts with stakeholders

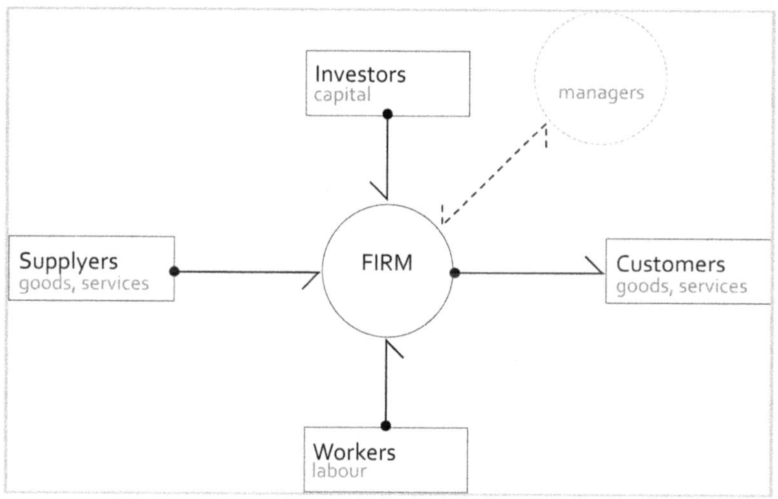

Profit maximisation is frequently at odds with the interests of other stakeholders, be them either workers, suppliers or customers. In order to maximise profits, the firm has either to reduce the costs of production or increase revenues from sales. It is not difficult to think of circumstances when stakeholders have conflicting interests and different perspectives on how the firm should be run. The manager is in the difficult position of having to choose an equilibrium, despite its subordination to shareholders, because all stakeholders are important for the firm to exist.

Coase's model cannot be seen in opposition to Kay's views, and it is suited to accommodate Freeman's (2010) stakeholder approach also. The firm is an entity entering in exchanges and transacting with several constituencies, through binding contracts. Intuitively, implicit contracts are difficult to enforce when informal norms and values are looser or inconsistent with individual behaviour and society's moral. This is consistent with Deakin (2012) and Kay (2019), who propose a broad social perspective of transactions costs economics, suggesting that society is of tantamount importance as technology.

Corporations are, to a certain extent, equivalent to public goods, and there are well founded reasons to believe that its contribution to society can be enhanced if a more holistic approach is taken. Deakin (2012) suggests the corporation is commons, while Kay (2019) blames capital markets myopic view for the most recent financial crises. To complete the argument, in real world there are a number of corporate boards where the approach is already beyond the principal-agent theory prescription.

Having said that, one needs to reread Coase's transaction cost approach, taking the view not from the perspective of shareholders, but from the perspective of the firm itself. Particularly, one should measure the costs from a survival perspective, that means knowing the role corporations perform in society, offering individuals access to goods and services at the lowest effort, both in the short and long run. Firms hire managers proposed by shareholders to act on behalf of the whole organisation.[6]

THE VALUE OF THE FIRM

Corporate Finance is responsible for using Coase (1937) transaction cost economics and introducing the value of the firm from the perspective of financial investors.[7] The value of the firm draws on the existence of an objective function to be maximised and a performance criterion to choose among alternative policy options, and against which managers performance can be assessed. Most economists would agree that such criterion should be maximisation of the long-term market value of the firm, rooted in 200 years of research in economics and finance, says Jensen (2001: 8).

Managers are hired as agents to maximise firm's (financial) value and benefit the principal. The intuition behind this goal is that firms need to borrow funds to acquire capital, in order to set up production. Managers are guardians of this financial investment, ensuring that the firm meets the conditions agreed on its use and pays the promised rate of return, considering risks involved (Jensen and Meckling, 1976; Davis et al., 1997; Jensen, 2001).

Such financial bias underlies shareholders prominence when it comes to corporate governance. Contractually, they are residual claimants of the firm, and ultimate bearers of business risk. Being given the power to nominate the management board, they are in a privileged position to reap benefits at expenses of the remaining stakeholders. This leaves clear the importance of managers and the difficult role they play in the firm. Whose interests are they expected to address first and mostly?

One can, however, argue that if markets for inputs are competitive and all stakeholders are at equilibrium with the corporation, maximising the value of the firm provides the right incentives for managers to improve on the terms of the relationships with them all, envisioning long term success – 'enlightened value maximisation', in Jensen (2001) words. When facing market failures, the answer is not to ask the corporation to maximise something other than profits, but rather to empower an authority with decision rights able to eliminate them – i.e., the State in its ruling function.[8] This implies that no moral judgement is expected from the corporation, other than pursuing the growth of shareholders' wealth.

When managers are distinct from equity owners, there is room for them to act either on their self-interest, or on behalf of other stakeholders. Corporate governance in such a financial context is just about the principal-agent problem, and the need to align managers and shareholders' interests, preventing deviations from the single value maximisation objective. The default is to defend the interest of shareholders first, while having all other constituencies committed to the success of the company.

At first sight, the financial value of the firm is in sharp contrast with stakeholder theory, according to which, managers should make decisions taking into consideration the interests of all corporations' stakeholders. They should take account not only of financial claimants, but also employees, customers, communities, and many other constituencies. Jensen (2001) argues stakeholder theory offers too many and diverse value propositions, failing to specify the trade-offs among competing interests, leaving managers with an impossible mission to accomplish.

One cannot but agree that shareholders expect managers to understand how customers, employees and suppliers interact with the firm, and how they react when respective market conditions and other environmental variables change. Freeman and McVea (2001: 16) say on this respect:

It matters less that management understands that "shareholders-in-general" expect steady dividend growth. It matters more that we understand that our shareholders expect us to increase internal investment as fast as possible because they invested expecting us to be "first to market" with the next generation product. Good strategic management, according to this approach, emerges from the specifics rather than descending from the general and theoretical.

Showing the contrast between these competing theories is unreal, Jensen (2001: 9) mentions 'enlightened value maximisation and its reciprocal 'enlightened stakeholder theory'. Moral and judgmental values are critical for managing the firm when stakeholders have diverse interests, and to achieve effectiveness one needs all of them sharing the same set of rules and beliefs. It becomes clear the social nature of the firm, which can be simplistically pictured as a "small state within the State".

The dominant financial view of the firm as a nexus of contracts is shallow, ignores its social role and presents the corporation as an empty shell (Kay, 2019). The focus of the organization is presented as economic efficiency only, rather than any social and political goals. Managers do not derive power from the owners of the means of production. They find themselves facing different stakeholders, who benefit from the firm, each with its unique perspective and using its own metrics of value. This suggests also competing definitions of value, one for each constituency, such as it is the "customer value" widely used in strategic marketing (Slater, 1997).

Stakeholders can then be presented as competing for managers whom, themselves, have their own interests and hold the power to choose whom to represent when acting within the firm. The power within the organisation is likely to be with those stakeholders who own the most idiosyncratic asset, i.e., the resources that the corporation needs most – and cannot live without them – dictate how top management behaves and to who is willing to pay respect.

In most strategic management and marketing books customers are key for companies, giving them a purpose. From time to time they are elevated to be the constituency that most benefits from the corporation, accessing a wide range of products at very low prices.[9] That is to say, managers are facing a game, where value created – whatever it means – is to be shared with all stakeholders, and the distribution rule has to be defined. Sustainability is achieved as long as the firm is able to strike the right balance, i.e., a distribution of value that is considered fair by all and entices them to trade with the corporation in the long run.

Again, Jensen (2001) does not dismiss the stakeholder argument entirely. Maximising the value of the firm does not mean holding shareholders in higher regard than other constituencies, or other stakeholders. The problem, he suggests, should not be framed this way. The real issue is to know if the corporation is able to make the best use of scarce resources in the economy. This is a problem of firm behaviour and corporate governance. Not whether a particular class of stakeholders should gather more benefits than another.

THE FIRM AS A SOCIAL VEHICLE

The successful corporation is able to exploit economies of scale and scope while creating resilience to uncertainty. Indivisibilities in production – of technological nature – and exposure to risks – because of unanticipated shocks – require cooperation between individuals and explain why the firm exists. Individuals pursuing self-interest, in Adam Smith (1759, 1776) terms, find labour division increases productivity and reduces the effort needed to produce goods and services, while the burden of negative shocks is better addressed collectively. Kay (2019) says the total exceeds the sum of the parts.

One can thus propose the firm is a social vehicle, an agreement among individuals to share pooled costs and benefits, and face risks together. If continuity – i.e., sustainability – is the goal, individuals have to commit to a sharing rule, which allocates costs and benefits to each one. Sharing rules are contracts – both formal and informal – that need enforcement. Managers´ role can be defined as to oversee and enforce distribution of value within the firm, and because of that they need to understand the position of the company vis-à-vis its stakeholders.

The corporation exists because it fulfils a role in society, which cannot be divorced from the social and technological context. It is a cooperative venture and to a certain extent, the value created by the firm can be regarded as an economic rent, which is made possible by the collective action of its stakeholders (Kay, 2019: 11).[10]

What is certain is that the assertion that the value added created in a business is in its entirety the property of the stockholders is a position which would fundamentally undermine the factors which give rise to that value added in the first place – and in practice has. It is not, however, possible to calculate – even if it were appropriate to do so – what distribution of economic rent would maximise the net present value of current and future returns to shareholders. There is no basis for any claim that creating value for all stakeholders necessarily maximises shareholder value. It might, or it might not, and we shall never know.

This functional approach to the firm offers a value chain perspective on production. It places firms as nodes of a complex network, attempting to efficiently articulate flows of goods and services with others, through markets. It is an interconnected system where goods and services "travel" from one firm to another, until they reach final destination, i.e., consumption. In each of these nodes goods and services are assembled in a planned process. Not all firms deal with end consumers, and just because of that one could argue that governance structures might differ, among many other reasons.

Several authors argue corporations are "open systems", part of a large network.[11] They cannot be conceived in isolation, as self-standing entities, and external links are part of the organisation. Under this systems perspective, problems can only be solved collectively by all stakeholders, in such a way to optimize the network. Individual solutions are likely to be suboptimal. That implies firms should not be autonomous entities. A caveat, however, as the interests of the firm and those of the network do not always converge, and self-government is necessary for the company to exist.

Refusing firms' autonomy is in clear contrast to what they do in real world. Corporations keep a degree of power, allowing interactions to be brought within their scope. Each firm is a decision-making entity, in direct relationship with its stakeholders, who bear a stake in the success of the corporation. Therefore, as node of a complex network, it shows both cooperative and competitive behaviours towards its constituencies.

The firm as a social entity has borders bounded by the markets where products and services are bought and sold, including the resources and final goods used within the organisation according to privately chosen rules, i.e., an internal code of conduct. At least, market participants are the firm's stakeholders. When markets are competitive, people agree voluntarily to contract with the firm. Each contract is a claim, better described as comprising three key elements: quantity, price, and risk.

Recognizing that firms compete with markets, allows one to better understand what makes them successful, and how different stakeholders are made accountable and rewarded by the contracts they sign. Coase's construct is powerful but needs to be adjusted in order to accommodate the concept of a corporation that goes beyond its legal boundaries, taking into account cultural, social and technological considerations. Both explicit and implicit contracts – existing in parallel – determine the boundaries of the firm.[12]

Continuity and survival of the firm depends on how the contracts are intrinsically coherent. For example, if one stakeholder transfers risk to the firm, sustainability requires other stakeholders to accept bearing it. Parties engaged in the exchange do not have to agree on quantity and prices only. Risk cannot be detached from the contract. It arises from either external contingencies or induced moral hazard and adverse selection behaviour. The whole set of contracts has to find balance on the three attributes: price, quantity and risk: in essence, no risk should be left without owner.

The corporation is endowed with an intangible asset of culture that determines business performance and ultimately its success. Theoretically, past experience and implicit contracts – i.e., corporate culture – explain the distinctive behaviour of firms with the same set of explicit contracts. Implicit contracts are within the reach of the construct proposed by Coase (1937), who argues that stakeholders transact with the firm. The point is that they are loose and costly to enforce, particularly when values and social norms are time changing.

Corporate culture plays a role not only the way corporations are organised, but also on their size, performance, and relationships with its constituencies (Davis et al, 1997). Bloom et al (2012) collected information about management practices in firms across the world to conclude that social capital as proxied by trust increases firm's productivity. Decentralization and power delegation change from country to country, and also across multinationals when home origins are diverse. Based on a large international data sample, Bloom et al. (2012:1664):

We find that the level of trust prevalent in the country where the multinational is headquartered has a strong positive correlation with decentralization in the affiliate's foreign location: for example, in California, a multinational affiliate from Sweden (a high-trust country) would typically be more decentralized than a multinational affiliate from France (a relatively low-trust country).

Similarly, Freeman and Evan (1990) support that transaction cost economics can be used to approach the firm from a stakeholder perspective, rather than the narrow shareholder perspective in mainstream finance. Many stakeholders hold relationships that are specific to the firm, and should be treated accordingly by managers, depending on how easily they can be replaced in the market or are able to influence the business of the corporation.[13]

The firm embodies a risk sharing agreement, beyond simple productive efficiency, and this feature is present in Coase's transactions cost economics. When risk is brought into the equation one just needs to revisit the model, allowing stakeholders to transact with the firm in a way that they might benefit or be harmed from uncertainty. Each contract stipulates a quantity, a price and a level of risk. Risks are many and diverse, ranging from strategic to operational, and the corporation has to be managed and prepared to withstand all shocks.[14]

Should markets be complete – i.e., no information asymmetry, unbounded rationality – and there is a price for risk, which parties use to decide on accepting or unloading the burden of uncertainty.[15] This is the competitive markets classical paradigm. The role for managers in a corporation is diminished, as there is no room for social judgment. Only technical decisions are needed, i.e., how to combine inputs in the most productive way. Managers just have to allocate risks to the counterparties who values it most – i.e., those requiring the lowest reward.

In such a theoretical and ideal world, the corporation interacts with its stakeholders through competitive markets, trading quantities at prices that reflect the economic social cost. The sustainability of the firm requires that all stakeholders are balanced at market equilibrium prices and quantities. Each stakeholder buys and sells goods and services to the corporation and bears the corresponding risks from trading (see figure 3). In a complete information setup, everyone knows and accepts the risks arising from its contract.

Figure 3. The Firm and its markets

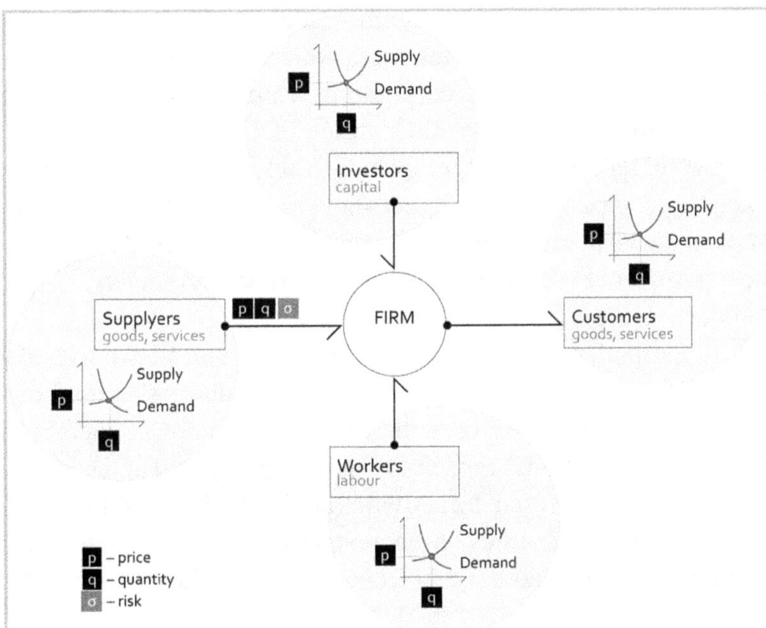

Such a construction does not imply a unique representation for the firm. There are many alternative organisational structures to choose from, depending on how risks are shared. For example, it might happen that workers are willing to accept a variable compensation, depending on the success of the corporation, while in other cases, they only accept fixed remuneration contracts. Each implies a different distribution of risks. In the first case, equity owners face less risks, and require a lower return, and the corporation is likely to be funded with interest rate bonds, all the rest constant.

A problem arises when markets are incomplete because of asymmetric information and bounded rationality. Asymmetric information, on one hand, allows for adverse selection and moral hazard, as each party is likely to behave opportunistically. Managers can relocate risks designing contracts that take advantage of their superior information. On the other hand, because one cannot devise all possible future states of nature, uncertainty replaces risk, and judgment needs to be used when reality moves outside the envisioned range.

If markets are incomplete, managers have the power to rebalance interests within the firm and play a crucial role in stating equilibrium conditions. But do they have the responsibility of ensuring that the social cost equals the social benefit? If the answer is yes, this implies they should act not on shareholders' best interest, but rather be independent and committed to drive markets to the optimal solution, such as if they are vested with the power of a social planner.[16]

Accepting a functional lens, markets and firms are social organisations competing against each other, and transparency is the most prominent distinguishing feature: firms are opaque, while markets are transparent. Coase (1937) wrote that the company is a nexus of contracts underlying buying and selling of property rights over resources and, one can add, giving management the power of discretion to use and direct them to achieve a pre-established goal: maximise the value of the firm in mainstream finance or, equivalently, maximise profits in classical economic theory.

For reasons not discussed here, contemporaneous market imbalances undermine the future of the modern corporation, as mounting social and environmental concerns seem to be nowhere in stakeholders' selfish behaviour. There are no self-enforcing moral values in the markets where the firm contracts and trades resources, goods and services. The corporation seems not reunited with society, because the latter lacks representation in the current stakeholder structure.

One cannot resolve market failures asking companies to act voluntarily (Jensen, 2001). Those trying to do so, will be replaced by competitors who do not show any commitment or civic sympathy towards social goals. At most, their survival upon acting this way requires not only a redistribution of economic rents – harming some constituencies – but also a likely welfare loss to society, as resources are diverted away from its most productive use.

Stakeholder theory supports that the interests of all constituencies have to be taken into consideration, adding to the specification of the objective function, i.e., managers' commitment to the long-term value of the firm. Deakin (2012: 339) proposes the firm[17] as commons, where different stakeholders hold interests. The firm has organisational capacity (combining physical and cognitive resources) and it should not be exploited, but rather nurtured. Its activities are likely to affect third parties, both positively and negatively.[18] Moreover, the legal features of the modern corporation already grant managers power and independency to organise the business freely from any stakeholders and constituencies, including shareholders:

The idea of the commons better describes the legal structure of the business enterprise than does the shareholder primacy model: the firm's various stakeholders have overlapping property claims in relation to its assets, including rights of access, withdrawal, management, exclusion and alienation. Furthermore, as in a common, the right of alienation is not the most salient right in a corporation.

THE GOVERNANCE OF THE CORPORATION

The problem of shareholder value maximisation reflects the way shareholders wield power at the board, and to whom are managers accountable. The corporation seems stripped of its social role just because political and legal institutions empower financial markets and allow shareholders to control the use of capital and, at a later stage, offer managers financial rewards if they succeed in deploying the most lucrative options. This is partly a result of the growing shareholder influence before the crisis, and the excessive risk-taking incentives to management boards (Deakin, 2012 and Davis et al., 1997).

Yet, value maximisation is neither a strategy, nor a purpose, nor shareholders should not rank higher than any other constituency. Value is just a measurement scale against which performance is judged and success evaluated. As financial markets are usually short sighted and fail to understand the full implication of firm's policies, a long-term perspective is needed, one that gives people structure to understand what value means and how to achieve it, engaging everyone (Jensen, 2001).

In recognizing the stakeholder nature of the firm, there are two questions one needs to answer: firstly, how is power allocated to stakeholders; and secondly, how does each constituency exercise its power. In particular, how do financial market investors fail to take into proper consideration both the social cost and the social benefit. Should fund managers, for instance, be concerned with firm social impact? Should the contracting of managers be done differently?

A legally standing fiduciary duty of management towards shareholders is common in most jurisdictions, if not at least in practice. Principal-agent theory, on one hand, holds that managers behave opportunistically and imply an agency loss, which can only be mitigated if the right incentives are put in place, such as internal controls and compensation schemes. However, it forgets, on the other hand, that non-financial motivators are equally important, such as advocated by stewardship theory (Donaldson and Davis, 1991; and Davis et al., 1997).

In both cases, the empowerment of management structures rests mostly on shareholders, whom might have a myopic view of the problem. Because firms need to adapt and if they are expected to survive, enacting social responsibility of the corporation in law – to be enforced in courts – is probably the route, if shareholders fail to voluntarily make the choice. The same conciliatory way seems to be present in Kay (2019:11):

If our economy could really be described by production functions in which homogenous capital and labour come together to create standardised products in competitive markets under conditions of constant returns to scale, there would be no need for the corporate economy. Corporations exist because these assumptions are not fulfilled, and the successful corporation is one that creates rents through distinctive combinations of idiosyncratic factors.

One needs to pay close attention to the assumptions underlying the model. What drives corporate behaviour are stakeholders and not shareholders alone (Kay, 2019). Emphasis must be placed on the group, not the individual. Using Freeman (1984) concept, stakeholders are those without whose support the organisation ceases to exist, and as such managers should derive power from them all, providing there exists a trade-off rule to weight conflicting interests.[19]

It is easy to mistake the stakeholder paradigm to assess corporate performance with a call for social responsibility of the firm, or business ethics. There is no such thing. The firm is just a reflexion of the social environment and as Friedman (1984), corporations should not have ethics. Instead, individuals – who are stakeholders of corporations – should adopt behaviours in accordance to their beliefs and culture. For instance, consumers might refrain from buying supplies from corporations that follow practices they disagree with.

Without individual commitment, the environmental, social and governance agenda (ESG), and corporate social responsibility (CSR) translate in a proliferation of self-congratulatory practices showing that firms are friendly to communities where they operate and to the environment and still make money. Implicitly preserving the restrictive shareholder value proposition, and not endorsing the true concerns of most stakeholders, because their power is not properly recognized. A holistic approach is needed if managers' strategic decision-making problem is to address every constituency interests.

Managers are not expected to undertake actions that replace politics and politicians in defining and meeting the social good. Corporations are not universal representations of society, and managers are not vested to operate outside the interests of firms' most direct stakeholders. It is up to governments to define the least social goals to be met, be it either income distribution or environmental targets, amongst others. Managers should be independent and take a distant approach – as they are able to – refraining from assuming the pain of any particular stakeholder. Otherwise, they end up with a corporation that meets interests according to what mainstream politics requires at each moment in time.[20]

If corporate governance is both to respond to the success – and sustainability – of the business firm, the stakeholder approach[21] is the one that best characterizes the modern corporation and able to offer the right answers to fast changing environments. The stakeholder approach to strategy, rooted in Freeman (1984), is most promising when traditional frameworks are unable to offer adequate solutions, and is particularly useful when managers face difficulties finding new directions in periods of turbulence and change, as pointed out by Freeman and McVea (2001: 14):

We propose that as the business world becomes ever more turbulent, interconnected and as the boundaries between firms, industries and our public and private lives become blurred, a stakeholder approach has more and more to tell us about both values and value creation.

Managers have to devise methods to articulate the interests of a myriad of different stakeholders, understand the goals and concerns of those who carry on a relationship with the firm, be it employees, suppliers, customers, lenders and, not the least, the society. This way, management structures are well beyond the principal agent paradigm, and resemble more stewardship theory, where managers act for reputation, forming a coalition aiming at the success of the corporation.

If the survival of the firm is envisioned, then the interests of key stakeholders must be taken into account and incorporated into its purpose. Constituencies must be engaged in an integrated and coherent fashion, continuously assessing the balance of power, and adapting corporate actions to deliver the value requested by each stakeholder, while everyone is committed to the success of the corporation. Firm boundaries become elastic, as participation in the network changes in reaction to shifts in stakeholders' preferences and technology, as well as new institutional arrangements.

Under this paradigm, how can the value of the corporation be a representation of successful management? Not placing managers as uniquely mirroring the owners of equity capital – but committing them to the continuity and survival of the firm – raises the issue about how to measure management and business performance. Freeman and McVea (2001: 13) reject the single objective function:

To the contrary, a stakeholder approach rejects the very idea of maximizing a single objective function as a useful way of thinking about management strategy. Rather, stakeholder management is a never-ending task of balancing and integrating multiple relationships and multiple objectives.

Yet, trade-offs between competing goals should not be forgotten, and have to be continuously assessed. Managers have to identify and focus attention on concrete stakeholders, those which are most specific to the firm. To a certain extent these are the ones which can exercise more market power when contracting with the firm, eliciting higher transaction costs if not included within the boundaries of the firm and under management control as proposed by Coase (1937).

Managers must find a way to satisfy multiple stakeholders at the same time, knowing that firm strategy distributes 'benefits' and 'harms' to the various stakeholders. There are not all-time winners, and one just have to find combinations that ensure the firm gathers long term support from all constituencies. When this is not feasible anymore, innovation is needed to redraw the boundaries of the firm.

CONCLUSION

Normative theories of business search for the philosophical foundations and advocate that corporations should obey by the social contract, arguing that firms do not have ends, but their only purpose is to serve the stakeholders' wellbeing. This can be interpreted as business ethics, when establishing that firms have a moral obligation for which they are accountable, and should act fairly when trading with stakeholders, while preserving the system network. The purpose of the organization and operation of the industry is to deliver progress, which is more important than just efficient allocation (Robinson, 1933).

Advocating a functional perspective of the firm implies a holistic view that has implications for corporate governance design and, ultimately, management practices. Firms are centres of conscious power in an ocean (markets) of unconscious cooperation. Coordination takes place through a series of exchange transactions, using prices as information signals. In a perfect and complete world, production could be done without organisation, leaving technology alone to explain firms' existence and reserving a minor role for management. But Eden is biblical only, and managers existence is required on earth!

There is a variety of corporation concepts, reflecting different cultures and social environments, some enacted in statutory and legal frameworks, some present in management practices. The US corporation is quite different from the Japanese and the German models. It prizes shareholder value, while the others give more power to workers and suppliers, albeit in distinctive ways. Still a nexus of contracts, the firm transacts with stakeholders through formal and informal codes, not only legally written contracts. These embody rules of power distribution amongst stakeholders, which need a common goal and require effort in different proportions from all participants.

Finding the common goal and striking the balance is what top management is expected to do. This paper challenges the classical principal-agent approach and explores a broad and widespread view of corporate governance. It brings contemporaneous political concerns about the role of the firm for social cohesion and economic development – traditionally under CSR – and the emerging ESG (environmental, social and governance) initiative on sustainability, led by the World Economic Forum, and now being proposed in many jurisdictions.

Platform capitalism is emerging everywhere. Big firms are established as network facilitators, weaving relationships between producers and consumers – Uber, Airbnb, Booking, Facebook, are examples amongst many others. As the size range stretches – from small to large firms – gaps and discontinuities show up, suggesting a dual corporation system. One obvious question is what should be the mandate for managers of new enterprises? Should they, because of network externalities and systemic risks, be subject to distinct – more demanding, probably – corporate governance obligations? And, what about firms' commitment to social responsibility, should it be mandatory by law?

One feel compelled to ask who are the legitimate owners of the firm? This is probably the most urgent key point when discussing corporate governance. Or alternatively, is there any illegitimate stakeholder? Managers that play a stakeholder approach should be able to identify the relative power of each group's interest and act accordingly. In practice, managers performance is measured using financial indicators. When financial figures are able to demonstrate the corporation's social performance, this should not be viewed as a problem. The issue arises however when there is a gap between financial and social performance, as documented by recent financial crisis.

All stakeholders place a constraint on the operations and the management of the firm. That does not mean that managers have just to understand and accept the limits they observe and continue developing strategies that address shareholders' value maximisation. On contrary, all stakeholders are central to firms' performance and benefiting all is a consequence rather than a measure of its success. If non-equity stakeholders are seen just as a constraint, corporate social responsibility emerges as a damage control response, as a means to achieve positive reputation towards activist groups, with shallow effects.

From a broad perspective, corporate governance means good management practices, and the full understanding of the firm as a social institution, and its role in the community. Evidence shows that companies with best practices outperform those that do not. One can also argue that if markets are efficient and complete, financial returns will be harmed if the company fails to account for all groups' interests. Unethical behaviour can have high costs and undermine firms' profitability, in the long run at least. But because complete and efficient markets is not real world, when bringing the top management to the drawing board, one must think about having the main stakeholders represented, with power to influence the business firm decisions.

Not all stakeholders are equally important. Prioritizing is a matter of strategic choice, rather than simply assessing their strength based on economic and political power. Successful corporations pursue paths that are unique, depending on how they perspective the long run. They identify the most critical stakeholders and develop strategies to address their concerns. They focus on trust and how mutual interests shape management behaviour within the corporation, facilitating better resource allocation and growth.

In a closing remark, corporate governance might imply new legislation, a renewed charter for corporations, centred around risk sharing and market power mitigation, where accountability might need to be taken beyond firms' traditional borders, and be legally enforced as such. A caveat about justice, because framing the problem this way does not imply firms should have social concerns about welfare distribution. When choosing between competing Pareto optimal equilibria based on judgment, this is not necessarily that of the firm, but the society.

REFERENCES

Alfaro, L., Bloom, N., Conconi, P., Fadinger, H., Legros, P., & Newman, A. (2018). *Come Together: Firm Boundaries and Delegation*. HBS Working Paper, 18-051.

Barney, J. B. (1990). The Debate Between Traditional Management Theory and Organizational Economics: Substantive Differences or Intergroup Conflict? *Academy of Management Review*, *15*(3), 382–393. doi:10.5465/amr.1990.4308815

Bloom, N., Sadun, R., & Van Reenen, J. (2012). The Organization of Firms Across Countries. *The Quarterly Journal of Economics, 127*(4), 1663–1705. doi:10.1093/qje/qje029

Clarkson, M. (1995). A Stakeholder Framework for Analysing and Evaluating Corporate Social Performance. *Academy of Management Review, 20*(1), 92–117. doi:10.5465/amr.1995.9503271994

Coase, R. H. (1937). The Nature of the Firm. *Economica, 4*(16), 386–405. doi:10.1111/j.1468-0335.1937.tb00002.x

Davis, J. H., Schoorman, F. D., & Donaldson, L. (1997). Toward a Stewardship Theory of Management. *Academy of Management Review, 22*(1), 20–47. doi:10.5465/amr.1997.9707180258

Deakin, S. (2012). The Corporation as Commons: Rethinking Property Rights, Governance and Sustainability in the Business Enterprise. *Queen's Law Journal, 37*(2), 339–381.

Donaldson, L. (1990). The Ethereal Hand: Organizational Economics and Management Theory. *Academy of Management Review, 15*(3), 369–381. doi:10.5465/amr.1990.4308806

Donaldson, L., & Davis, J. H. (1991). Stewardship Theory: CEO Governance and Shareholder Returns. *Australian Journal of Management, 16*(1), 49–65. doi:10.1177/031289629101600103

Donaldson, T., & Dunfee, T. (1999). *Ties that Bind: A social contracts approach to business ethics.* HBS Press.

Freeman, R. E. (1984). *Strategic Management: A Stakeholder Approach.* Cambridge University Press.

Freeman, R. E., & McVea, J. (2001). *A Stakeholder Approach to Strategic Management.* Darden Business School Working Paper, 01-02. doi:10.2139srn.263511

Hart, O. (1995). *Firms, Contracts, and Financial Structure.* Clarendon Press. doi:10.1093/0198288816.001.0001

Holmström, B. (1977). *On Incentives and Control in Organizations* (Unpublished PhD dissertation). Stanford University, Palo Alto, CA.

Jensen, M. C. (2001). Value Maximization, Stakeholder Theory, and the Corporate Objective Function. *Journal of Applied Corporate Finance, 14*(3), 8–21. doi:10.1111/j.1745-6622.2001.tb00434.x

Jensen, M. C., & Meckling, W. H. (1976). Theory of the Firm: Managerial Behaviour, Agency Costs and Ownership Structure. *Journal of Financial Economics, 3*(4), 305–360.

Jensen, M. C., & Meckling, W. H. (1994). The Nature of Man. *Journal of Applied Corporate Finance, 7*(2), 4–19. doi:10.1111/j.1745-6622.1994.tb00401.x

Jones, T. M., & Wicks, A. C. (1999). Convergent Stakeholder Theory. *Academy of Management Review, 24*(2), 206–221. doi:10.5465/amr.1999.1893929

Jones. (1995). Instrumental Stakeholder Theory. *Academy of Management Review, 24*, 92–117.

Kay, J. (2019). The Concept of the Corporation. *Business History, 61*(7), 1129–1143. doi:10.1080/00076791.2018.1509956

Kirzner, I. (1973). *Competition and Entrepreneurship*. University of Chicago Press.

Loasby, B. J. (2015). Ronald Coase's Theory of the Firm and the Scope of Economics. *Journal of Institutional Economics*, *11*(2), 245–264. doi:10.1017/S1744137414000265

Marshall, A. (1920). *Principles of Economics*. Macmillan.

OECD. (2015). *G20/OECD Principles of Corporate Governance*. OECD Publishing. doi:10.1787/9789264236882-

Phillips, R. (1997). Stakeholder Theory and a Principle of Fairness. *Business Ethics Quarterly*, *7*(1), 51–66. doi:10.2307/3857232

Slater, S. F. (1997). Developing a Customer Value-Based Theory of the Firm. *Journal of the Academy of Marketing Science*, *25*(2), 162–167. doi:10.1007/BF02894352

Smith, A. (1759). *The Theory of Moral Sentiments*. Retrieved: http://metalibri.wikidot.com/title:theory-of-moral-sentiments:smith-a

Smith, A. (1776). *An Inquiry into the Nature and the Causes of the Wealth of Nations*. Retrieved: http://metalibri.wikidot.com/title:an-inquiry-into-the-nature-and-causes-of-the-wealth-of

Williamson, O. (1973). Markets and Hierarchies: Some Elementary Considerations. *The American Economic Review*, *63*(2), 316–325.

KEY TERMS AND DEFINITIONS

Business Ethics: It describes how moral principles and values impact managers' decision making when facing ethical dilemmas and controversial situations – i.e., differentiating right from wrong, or good from bad.

Corporate Governance: System of internal rules, practices and processes to govern the corporation, defining power and accountability, and enabling managers to deal with the challenges of running a company – from setting goals to decision making – while balancing the interests of all stakeholders.

Corporate Strategy: Articulated action set, describing how managers use resources and develop capabilities to achieve chosen corporate goals.

CSR: Corporate Social Responsibility (CSR) defines how corporations self-commit to sustainability and integrate social and environmental concerns in its strategic goals and management practices.

Enterprise Risk Management: Theoretical framework to incorporate risk definitions and concepts in management practices, from corporate strategy to operations systems, aiming at preventing and mitigating adverse situations and to minimise losses.

ESG: Environmental, Social, and Governance (ESG) comprises a set of standards meant to measure the social and environmental impact of a company; the argument being that business performance should be assessed on factors other than simply the financial return on investment.

Principal Agent: Firms are not always managed by the owners of capital, and when this is the case managers are contracted as professionals (agents) to act on behalf of the proprietors (principal).

Shareholder Value: In stock markets, shareholders are usually taken as privileged stakeholders to whose benefit should the firm be managed; accordingly, managers should pursue shareholder value maximization.

Stakeholders: A stakeholder is a party who has an interest in a firm and can either affect or be affected by its business; firms have an array of stakeholders with diverse and often conflicting interests.

Transaction Cost Economics: The term "transaction costs" is credited to Coase and is meant to represent the cost of contracting and combining resources in production. As there are multiple and alternative modes of production, each incurring in different costs, preference should be given to the most economical one.

ENDNOTES

1 WEF (2019). Davos Manifesto 2020. Retrieved: https://www.weforum.org/agenda/2019/12/davos-manifesto-2020-the-universal-purpose-of-a-company-in-the-fourth-industrial-revolution/ | accessed: 30/11/2020.

2 BlackRock Seeks to Regain Lost ground in Climate Fight, *Financial Times*, January 14, 2020. Retrieved from: https://www.ft.com/content/36282d86-36e4-11ea-a6d3-9a26f8c3cba4 | accessed: 30/11/2020.

3 I thank an anonymous referee this remark and for pointing out Loasby (2015) paper as one of the latest contributions in the field.

4 See also Marshall (1920) about the choice between firms and markets as organizational forms. Taking this step allows one to recognize that the standard concept of (production) function is a meagre representation of real-world firms and needs to be enhanced with Kirzner's (1973) differentiated knowledge and entrepreneurship.

5 See Marshall (1920) and Kirzner (1973), amongst others.

6 Although voted by shareholders to exercise power, the legal practice requires managers to work on behalf of the entire organization, and its conduct must obey blurred and ill-defined principles of equity and sustainability.

7 Firms should pursue strategies that are cost efficient and increase revenues. Mergers and Acquisitions, outsourcing and joint ventures have their merits assessed on its ability to generate synergies: i.e., decrease costs of production (mostly economies of scale and scope), and increase revenues and profits.

8 This solution to be effective needs, however, ability to identify and define remedies that address the problem properly. Empirical evidence shows this not to be always the case. There are regulatory failures and institutional frictions, preventing the best outcome from being achieved.

9 Most emerging start-up businesses share this feature of benefiting consumers, offering them with goods and services at expenses of other stakeholders, who burden the cost of keeping the firm afloat. Particularly, during the early stage, shareholders are willing to accept losses on their investment while acquiring a relevant market position. That does not mean however that the corporation is harming shareholders, as long as they are aware that they expect to achieve a sustainable return in the long run, as long as the start-up cycle is over.

10 When joining efforts, there are economies of scale and production increases at a faster pace than the cost of resources used. The rent comes from the fact, that in the group it is possible to reduce

individual effort keeping aggregate production constant, as compared to the case where each individual alone is a productive unit.

11 Freeman (1984: 37), root systems theory in the contributions of Barnard (1938) and Ackoff (1974).

12 The firm is accountable not only for its legal obligations, but it must obey informal norms and existing traditions also. The case of Uber being ordered by courts to classify drivers as employees instead of independent contractors for health insurance and compensation purposes illustrates the case.

13 Individuals are stakeholders of the firm in various forms: a worker is many times a customer and a taxpayer also, and because of that has different interests in the firm. Successful managers are able to take into consideration multi-level relationships.

14 Risk can take various forms: goods and services provided by suppliers might be defective, sick workers do not show up for work, and unsatisfied customers have the right to return the products, or simply walk away if they stop liking offers available.

15 One can find an equivalent for this in Jensen's (2001) argument that 'value maximisation maximises social welfare'.

16 Jensen (2001) argues market failures should be resolved with appropriate public policies, outside the boundaries of the firm.

17 Deakin (2012) makes a distinction between firm and corporation, the latter being first and foremost a legal mechanism, a principal-agent device that allows businesses to operate in contemporary market economies.

18 Deakin (2012) sees the firm as having capacity to absorb, control and diffuse the risks to society – i.e., externalities.

19 Otherwise, argues Jensen (2001), one risks confusion, conflict, and inefficiency due to lack of focus.

20 For example, repudiate shareholders' interests to address environmental sustainability or social equality issues in replacement, making valid Jensen's (2001) argument that stakeholder theory collects the support of managers, only to escape control.

21 Freeman (1984: 5) defines stakeholder as any group or individual who is affected by or can affect the achievement of an organization's objectives.

Chapter 10
How Different Corporate Governance and Corporate Social Responsibility Impact Earnings Management:
Eastern and Western European Countries

Susana Callao
University of Zaragoza, Spain

José Ignacio Jarne
University of Zaragoza, Spain

David Wroblewski
University of Zaragoza, Spain

ABSTRACT

Nowadays, companies increasingly focus on corporate concerns as they are in need of the detecting and controlling management activities in order to improve good business practices, objectivity, and integrity. This research addresses the question of the role of corporate governance and corporate social responsibility in earnings management. Previous studies confirmed that both mechanisms play an important role in limiting earnings management. In this context, the objective of the study is to test whether the effectiveness of both in constraining earnings management is the same or vary within the Eastern and Western Europe. By analyzing a sample of 1,339 firms from three developing Eastern European countries and three Western European countries over the period of 2010–2018, the findings confirm the positive impact of corporate social responsibility on the quality of the earnings. Additionally, the analysis shows that corporate governance is more effective in controlling earnings management in Western European countries.

DOI: 10.4018/978-1-7998-7596-3.ch010

INTRODUCTION

Corporate governance is directly involved in monitoring managers' decisions, as the good corporate governance serves as an effective mechanism to alleviate the opportunistic behaviors of management and to improve a company's reporting quality. At the same time, firms with poor corporate governance are more vulnerable to managerial opportunism and EM (e.g. Francis and Wilson, 1988; Klein, 2002; Xie, Davidson and DaDalt, 2003; Cornett, Marcus and Tehranian, 2008; Jaggi, Leung and Gul, 2009; Mishra and Malhotra, 2016; among others).

Seemingly, firms that are socially responsible are more ethical in their reporting behaviors less likely to manipulate their earnings numbers. In other words, EM occurs less often in companies with a strong commitment to social responsibility, as corporate social responsibility (CSR) boosts transparency and reduces the number of opportunities to manage earnings (e.g. Shleifer, 2004; Bansal, 2005; Prior, Surroca and Tribo, 2008; Chih, Shen and Kang, 2008; Gao and Zhang, 2015; Kim, Park and Wier, 2012, among others).

Nevertheless, the literature also strikes differences in the practices in corporate governance and CSR within the different countries, economies or included within the firms in the same environment. Corporate governance will be different because firms may perform differently depending on the environment, because the range of the governance control devices may be different, etc. The degree of CSR adoption may be different because the level of economic development of the country influences, because local community relations change, relationships with suppliers and customers change, including culture may change, etc.

Boards dominated by outsiders are arguably in a better position to monitor and control managers by being more independent of the firm's managers, and bringing a greater breadth of experience to the firm (Brickley, Coles, and Terry, 1994; Byrd and Hickman, 1992; Weissbach, 1998; Cornett, Marcus and Tehranian, 2008). However, in other environments some authors point out opposite results. Osma and Noguer (2007), for example, show that reductions in the proportion of independent directors on the board are associated with a lower level of EM. They clarify the inefficiency of simply adding numerous independent directors to the board for improving the quality of information and reduction of EM.

In this research, considering the existence of the differences in terms of the mechanisms of corporate governance and CSR disclosure between Eastern and Western economies, the principal objective is to test whether the effectiveness of both mechanisms in constraining earnings management is the same or vary within these two blocks of countries.

The study contributes to the EM literature at least in two important ways. First, the research responds about the differences in effectiveness of corporate governance and CSR for controlling EM in Eastern and Western European countries.

Second, the study contributes by verifying the existence of EM in firms from emerging Eastern European countries. Therefore, present research may also give insights to the literature of developing Eastern European countries in terms of the effectiveness of the mechanism of corporate governance and CSR in limiting EM.

The study focuses on three developing Eastern European countries (Poland, Hungary, and the Czech Republic) and three Western European countries (Germany, Spain and France) during the period from 2010 to 2018. Four research hypotheses have been tested with a methodology based on discretionary accruals.

The remainder of this research is organized in the following manner. First, the study presents a review of the literature on the EM in connection to corporate governance and corporate social responsibility. Next, the focus is on the CSR in Eastern European countries and on corporate governance in that countries. Following, the sample selection is presented and the methodology employed is explained. Then, the results are discussed. Finally, the final remarks are pointed out and some implications for further studies are shown.

EARNINGS MANAGEMENT IN CONNECTION TO CORPORATE GOVERNANCE AND CSR

EM is an essential topic of considerable interest to academics and practitioners in literature over the last 20 years. Many studies are focusing on this phenomenon from different perspectives. Growing literature recently for example, describes different mechanisms (investor protection, ownership, legal enforcement, audit quality), which may determine variations in EM activities in the firm (Leuz, Nanda and Wysocki, 2003; Roychowdhury, 2006; Cohen and Zarowin, 2010; Banko*et al.*, 2013; Li, Selover and Stein, 2011; Mindzak and Zeng, 2018). Present study focuses on two of them: corporate governance and corporate social responsibility. Bergstresser and Philippon (2006) mentioned that corporate governance and corporate social responsibility are two distinct constructs widely used to explain EM. Additionally, broad literature regarding these two mechanisms and EM, show similarities recognizing the effectiveness in reducing EM, as the pressure from corporate governance as well as, corporate social responsibility implies practices towards improving a company's reporting quality.

1. Corporate Social Responsibility and Earnings Management

Corporate Social Responsibility (CSR) is defined as a business commitment to give contribution to sustainable economic development beyond the requirements of law in order to improve the business itself and the development of the environment (Waryanto, 2010). In particular, customers, investors, and other stakeholders increasingly require transparency about all dimensions of a firm, including the accuracy and transparency of financial reporting, etc.

According to Li and Zhang (2010), the main motivation of a company in implementing corporate social responsibility is to create a positive image for public. Atkins (2006) claims that "being socially responsible" for the firm is "being transparent" in its financial statements by disclosing reliable and relevant information. The firm that makes an effort in implementing CSR and resources is able to constrain EM in order to comply with stakeholder's ethical expectations. Kim, Park and Wier (2012) confirm that firms actively engaged in socially responsible activities are more reliable and transparent and have a better quality of financial reporting. It is because firms conducting business based on corporations and trust have incentives to commit to ethical behavior (Malik, 2015; Brammer and Millington, 2005), which includes more transparent financial reporting (Chih, Shen and Kang, 2008; Kim and Venkatachalam, 2011).

Additionally, the implementation of CSR can improve the company's performance as its reputation and competitiveness increase (Ayu and Zulfia, 2018). It gives a positive value in terms of financial aspect, brand image, as mentioned, and the sustainability of those companies (Kim and Venkatachalam, 2011).

Therefore, financial transparency and accountability are fast becoming principles of corporate social responsibility that reduce the extent to which insiders abuse their information advantage over outsiders

(Chih, Shen and Kang, 2008). Socially responsible firms incur less EM manipulations by being more responsible in preparing financial statements. Indeed, ethics are motivating managers to be honest and trustworthy since this behavior is benefit for the firm (Kim, Park and Wier, 2012). In this regard, Shleifer (2004) interprets that earnings manipulation occurs less often in corporations with a strong commitment to social responsibility. CSR augments transparency and reduces the number of opportunities to manage (Chih, Shen and Kang, 2008).

Similarly, Gelb and Strawser (2001) state that firms that engage in socially responsive activities provides more informative and extensive disclosures compared with companies that are less focused on advancing social goals. Therefore, these arguments lead to the first hypothesis (in alternative form):

Hypothesis One: Corporate social responsibility is negatively associated with the level of EM.

In other words, firms with poor corporate social responsibility activities have more opportunities to engage in EM. Alternatively, it is expected that socially responsible firms have low incentive to manage earnings.

2. Corporate Governance and Earnings Management

The separation of ownership and control in modern corporations creates a demand for monitoring or governance mechanisms (Jensen and Meckling, 1976; Becht, Jenkinson and Mayer, 2005). Corporate governance mechanisms are directly involved in monitoring managers' decisions, as the good corporate governance serves as an effective mechanism to alleviate the opportunistic behaviors of management and to improve a company's reporting quality (Klein, 2002; Xie, Davidson and DaDalt, 2003; Jaggi, Leung and Gul, 2009; Berkman, Cole and Fu, 2009; Mishra and Malhotra, 2016, among others).

While there are different governance mechanisms such as outside directors, institutional shareholders, shareholder rights, investor protection laws, corporate control markets, monitoring mechanisms such as: external auditors, board of directors, institutional shareholders, which shapes the actions of the managers (e.g., Denis, Denis and Sarin, 1997; Ahn and Walker, 2007; Bauguess *et al.*, 2009), dividend decisions (Brav*et al.*, 2005).

Nevertheless, the majority of studies agree that corporate governance constrain EM. A better quality of governance mechanisms increases the efficiency of the supervision of management, and consequently limits the discretionary behaviour regarding EM (Xue and Hong, 2016). Chung, Firth and Kim (2002), Park and Shin (2004), Berkman, Cole and Fu (2009), Chen *et al.* (2006), Chi-Keung (2013), among others, confirm that corporate governance reduces the extent of EM practices. Therefore, firms with poor corporate governance are more vulnerable to managerial opportunism and EM (Francis and Wilson, 1988; Cornett, Marcus and Tehranian, 2008). Therefore, the second hypothesis, stated in its alternative form, is as follows:

Hypothesis Two: Corporate governance quality is negatively associated with EM, meaning that mechanisms of corporate governance are effective in constraining EM.

CORPORATE SOCIAL RESPONSIBILITY IN EMERGING COUNTRIES

Corporate Social Responsibility (CSR) has only a short past in the former socialist countries of Eastern Europe, but it is observed a growing demand for CSR in the recent years. The political, economic, historical and cultural backgrounds of society all have an impact on these requirements. Arraiano and Hategan (2019) examined the stage of CSR in Central and Eastern European Countries members of the European Union, in accordance with Global Reporting Initiative which is consistent with globally recognized criteria worldwide, in the period 2002-2018. They updated analysis of topical CSR and showing that there is an evolution of reporting practices which has improved over the last years for the emerging Eastern European countries. Nevertheless, their overall conclusion was that there is still much to be done, but the trend is rising and the companies have understood that CSR can only bring benefits. The quality of the reports published in the last years is rising and more and more companies have reported according to general standards (Arraiano and Hategan, 2019).

Petera, Wagner and Knorova (2016) conducted a study on perception and interpretation of sustainability in Eastern European companies. They explained that sustainability reporting was a relatively new topic for respondents, but its importance is increasing. Simeonov and Stefanova (2015) pointed out that the future development of CSR in Eastern European countries depends on the ability of the public policies to develop and implement an updated CSR strategy, also on the ability of the companies, the institutions and civil society to collaborate at strategic level.

Steurer and Konrad (2009) suggest that there is a gap in economic development between the Western and Eastern EU countries, which is also a gap in CSR activities. Other study, with similar line of investigation, showed that the governments in the Western European countries are promoting CSR more intense than East governments and found that public policies reinforce CSR (Steurer, Martinuzzi and Margula, 2012).

Therefore, in emerging Eastern European there is an increasing awareness of corporate social responsibility. It is observed growing concerns of the awareness of CSR, and the types of CSR activities carried out by companies and the transparency of the information in the sustainability reports. Nevertheless, the managers of companies from the countries of this region have not yet understood the advantages of adopting this strategy in their management. Therefore, again it is expected differences in EM between companies from Eastern and Western European countries conditioned by the differences in CSR. It is because the brake exerted by the CSR on EM will be less effective in firms from Eastern countries.

Therefore, the third hypothesis, stated in its alternative form, is as follows:

Hypothesis Three: Corporate social responsibility is less effective in limiting EM in Eastern European countries comparing to Western European countries.

CORPORATE GOVERNANCE IN EMERGING COUNTRIES

In transitional economies, the internal structure of firms has been changing radically all over the years, and it has been the center of attention. For anyone who is familiar with the corporate governance environments that have developed in recent years in other markets, the corporate governance picture in the Eastern European region looks still markedly different. Following it is explained some main difference in terms of the corporate governance.

First, the key reason for this is the relatively short histories of the Eastern European countries as market economies. In the late 1980s and early 1990s the unexpected upheaval and revolution in Eastern European countries changed them from the centrally run economies into market driven societies (Brouthers and Lamb, 1995). Therefore, the Eastern European countries barely carry 30 years of market-oriented economies. They are growing, but they are still not at the same level of Western European countries.

Second, there is an absence of powerful investor groups across the region (Allen and Overy, 2010). OECD Report (2010) related to corporate governance and the financial crisis indicates that the transparency towards shareholders and the public was less relevant in Eastern European markets due to the absence of concerted investor pressure that in Western European economies.

Moreover, markets in the Eastern European region largely lack the sort of investor-driven guidelines and codes of practice that are such an important source of corporate governance regulation in more mature economies. The key reference points for corporate governance in this region therefore tend to be the minimum standards prescribed by law rather than any higher standards required by investors (Allen and Overy, 2010).

Furthermore, the ownership and control are very concentrated in these countries and, as a result, the main agency conflicts arise between controlling shareholders and minority shareholders rather than between shareholders and firm managers (Berglof and Pajuste, 2003).

Additionally, recent international surveys and reports have also focused the spotlight upon the importance of corporate governance in the recession and post-recession era, where the recent European Commission study on monitoring and enforcement of corporate governance practices in members of the European Union also noted that certain European requirements relating to (for example) the existence of independent board members had been less closely followed in Eastern European member states with a more recent corporate governance tradition (European Commission, 2016[1]).

Besides, the privatization process of the firms from the emerging countries has offered a natural process for choosing an incentive-compatible corporate governance framework. In other words, privatization has enabled and spurred these firms to search for a governance framework that is in the interest of the main stakeholders of the firm, but it is still dissimilar in comparison to other European countries (Klapper et al., 2006).

Likewise, the state-driven nature of corporate governance regulation in the Eastern European economies also means that there is a far greater importance attached to sanctions for breaches of proper corporate governance. This tendency is probably most pronounced for example in Poland, where members of the management board can also find themselves liable for the company's tax liabilities where enforcement against the company has been ineffective (Allen and Overy, 2010). Examples of strict rules and severe liability in the Eastern European countries must be set against the background in which practice does not always correspond to the legal rules. In recent years there is a perception that executives have flouted not only good corporate governance but legal rules. Eastern European countries have moved down the transparency indices. However, compliance with corporate governance rules is set to become increasingly important in further years as regulatory enforcement improves regulations (Allen and Overy, 2010).

Therefore, the fourth hypothesis, stated in its alternative form, is:

Hypothesis Four: Corporate governance is less effective in controlling EM practices in Eastern European countries than in Western European countries.

In other words, it is expected differences in EM between companies from Eastern and Western European countries conditioned by different quality of corporate governance. The effective corporate governance mechanism of Western European countries will better control EM that in firms from Eastern European countries.

SAMPLE AND METHODOLOGY

Sample and Analysis Period

The sample comprises companies from six European countries: three Western European countries: France, Spain and Germany; and three developing Eastern European countries: Poland, Hungary, and the Czech Republic.

These countries are selected from the following reasons. First, economic statistics reveal that both three Western and three Eastern European countries are leading countries from each part of Europe (see data for Gross Domestic Product, interest rate, inflation rate, among others[2]). At the same time, macroeconomic statistics show that developing Eastern European countries are still not at the same economic level as Western European countries. It may be observed important differences between the blocs of Eastern and Western Europe, especially in terms of the existing still economic gap between the two parts of Europe.

Second, all six European countries are European Union members. The European Union membership has created a significant influence and pressure on relations between Eastern and Western European countries. Therefore, it may have also an important effect on the earnings manipulation.

Third, the selected countries represent two distinct legal traditions in Europe: French code law (France and Spain), German code law (Germany, and Eastern European countries) (LaPorta*et al.,* 1998; Funken, 2003; Jaakko and Tapani, 2005; Deakin, 2008; Bernitz, 2010). Different legal traditions recognize different sources of law and thus prescribe different theories and methods for the administration of the companies. Literature confirms that different legal traditions have a significant influence on corporate governance and definitely, on the existence and scope of EM (see for example, La Porta *et al.,* 1997; Ball, Kothari and Robin, 2000; Leuz, Nanda and Wysocki, 2003; Daske and Gebhardt, 2006, among others).

The analysis covers the period of 2010 to 2018. There area total of 1,026 companies from three Western European countries; and 313 companies from Eastern European countries. Therefore, the total sample includes 1,339 listed firms, which make up 12,051 firm-year observations (Table 1). The data were collected using the Eikon trading platform for financial analysis provided by Refinitiv, formerly Thomson Reuters Worldscope Fundamentals database.

Table 1. Sample selection procedure

	France	Spain	Germany	Poland	Czech R.	Hungary	Total
Total number of firms available in data base	763	221	560	680	16	38	2,278
Incomplete data (missing data)	(240)	(126)	(160)	(393)	(9)	(19)	(947)
Total sample firms	523	95	400	287	7	19	1,331
Number of observations	4,707	855	3,600	2,583	63	171	11,979

The descriptive statistics and frequencies of some of the variables that characterize the sample are shown in Table 2 and Table 3.

Methodology. Model Specification

In order to test four hypotheses examining of the possible connection between both: corporate social responsibility and practices of corporate governance, and EM, the linear regression of the following model has been run:

$$absDA_{it}=\beta_0 + \beta_1 logSOC_{it} + \beta_2 logGOV + \beta_3 Block_i \text{ x } logSOC_{it} + \beta_4 Block_i \text{ x } logGOV_{it}$$

$$+\beta_5 LIQ_{it} + \beta_6 SOL_{it} + \beta_7 ROA_{it} + \beta_8 logA_{it} + \beta_9 SECTOR_{it} + \beta_{10} OWNERSHIP_{it} \quad (1)$$

Table 2. Descriptive statistics of continuous variables for companies in the sample

		Mean	Std. Deviation	Max	Min
Total assets (thousands €)	East	558,059.62	2,153,363.24	26,834,612.00	2.53
	West	5,737,262.16	24,996,987.11	448,025,000.00	14.00
Net income (thousands €)	East	22,194.86	137,962.71	2,544,594.88	-1,336,530.00
	West	163,190.46	825,495.14	21,717,000.00	-9,289,000.00
Board Size	East	9.85	4.59	23.00	5.00
	West	13.30	0.27615	26.00	3.00
Board strucutre (% independent)	East	32.81	22.27	100.00	0.00
	West	46.49	26.77	0.00	100.00

The dependent variable, $absDA_{it}$, is the absolute value of discretionary accruals for company *i* in period *t* and it is used as a proxy of EM.

Independent variables are:

- *logSOC* is defined as the logarithm of the social pillar score for company *i* in period *t*, obtained from Eikon database. This score is one of the three pillar scores (environmental, E; social, S; and

Table 3. Frequencies of discrete variables

			%
Ownership	East	Public	23.00
		Private	77.00
	West	Public	2.40
		Private	97.60
Sector	East	1	13.20
		2	3.70
		3	7.50
		4	24.10
		5	42.70
		6	8.80
	West	1	19.80
		2	9.80
		3	8.70
		4	27.80
		5	27.20
		6	6.70

Sector codes: 1. Technology & Telecommunications; 2. Health Care; 3. Real Estate; 4. Consumer Discretionary; 5. Industrials & Basic materials; 6. Energy

Source: The author

corporate governance, G) in the calculation of ESG Scores designed by Thomson and Reuters to transparently and objectively measure a company´s relative ESG performance, commitment and effectiveness across different themes related to environmental, social and corporate governance practices, based on company-reported data. It is used as a measure of the corporate social responsibility, that is, it measures the quality of the relationships between the firm and employees, customers and the society. It is composed of seven sub-categories: human rights, community, product responsibility, employment quality, training and development, diversity and opportunity, and health and safety.

- *logGOV* is defined as logarithm of governance pillar score for company *i* in period *t*, obtained from Eikon database. The corporate governance score reflects the company´s commitment and effectiveness towards following best practice corporate governance principles. It is used as a measure of the corporate governance quality. This governance pillar is composed of five categories: board functions, board structure, compensation policy, shareholders policy, and vision-and-strategy.
- *Block x logSOC* is the product between Block (dichotomous variable which takes a value of 1 if the company is from the Eastern European country and a value of 0 when the company is from a Western European country) and *logSOC*.
- *Block x logGOV* is the product between Block (dichotomous variable which takes a value of 1 if the company is from the Eastern European country and a value of 0 when the company is from a Western European country) and *logGOV*.

Finally, sixcontrol variables have been included:

- *LIQ* variable is the liquidity ratio for company *i* in period *t*, which it is defined as the quotient between the current assets and current liabilities (data from Eikon).
- *SOL* variable is the solvency ratio for company *i* in period *t*, which it is defined as the quotient between the total assets and total liabilities (data from Eikon).
- *ROA* variable is the return-on-assets for company *i* in period *t*, which it is defined as the quotient between the operating profits and total assets (data from Eikon).
- *logA* is defined as the logarithm of total assets for company *i* in period *t*, obtained from Eikon database. It is a measure of the size of the company (data from Eikon).
- *SECTOR* is the industrial sector to which the company *i* belongs (data from Eikon).
- *OWNERSHIP* is a variable which indicate if the company *i* is mainly state-owned or privately owned (data from Eikon).

Dependent Variable. Measurement of Earnings Management

The study uses a methodology based on accruals to detect and estimate the discretionary part of accruals. Accruals are defined as the part of revenues and expenses that do not imply collections and payments, and are indirectly calculated as the difference between profit and operating cash flows. Total accruals are composed of non-discretionary accruals *(NDA),* which are the part of accruals that are difficult to manipulate, and discretionary accruals *(DA),* which are easier to manipulate; therefore, *TA* = *NDA* + *DA*.

Since the discretionary and non-discretionary components of accruals are not directly observable, the study used the model employed in Dechow, Sloan and Sweeney (1995)[3], which is the most popular accrual model pointed out by the EM literature, see for example, study of Callao, Jarne and Wroblewski (2017). They revised 195 papers, and they confirmed that this model was applied in almost 30% of the studies. In this study, it is used this model in cross sectional version to estimate the DA:

$$\frac{TA_{it}}{A_{it-1}} = \alpha_0 \frac{1}{A_{it-1}} + \alpha_1 \frac{\Delta REV_{it} - \Delta REC_{it}}{A_{it-1}} + \alpha_2 \frac{PPE_{it}}{A_{it-1}} + \varepsilon_{it} \qquad (2)$$

where

- TA_{it} represents the total accruals for company *i* in period *t*, which were calculated based on the difference between earnings (E) and cash flow from operations (CFO): $TA_{it} = E_{it} - CFO_{it}$.
- ΔREV_{it} represents the change in revenues for company *i* in period *t* compared to *t-1*.
- ΔREC_{it} represents the change in receivables for company *i* in period *t* compared to *t-1*.
- PPE_{it} represents the property, plants and equipment of company *i* in period *t*.
- A_{it-1} represents the total assets of company *i* in period *t-1,* which it is used as a deflator to prevent heteroscedasticity problems.
- e_{it} is the error term for company *i* in period *t*.

Having estimated the parameters of equation *(2)*, the study applied the values obtained to predict discretionary accruals for the 2010–2018 study period. The prediction error is interpreted as the discretionary part of accruals, defined in equation *(3)*:

$$\frac{DA_{it}}{A_{it-1}} = \frac{TA_{it}}{A_{it-1}} - \left(\alpha_0 \frac{1}{A_{it-1}} + \alpha_1 \frac{\Delta REV_{it} - \Delta REC_{it}}{A_{it-1}} + \alpha_2 \frac{PPE_{it}}{A_{it-1}} + \varepsilon_{it}\right) \quad (3)$$

where, DA_{it} are discretionary accruals for firm *i* in period *t*, and a_0, a_1, and a_2 are the estimated values of αi.

The coefficients of the variables were estimated by maximum likelihood using an ordinary least squares regression. The results are shown in Table 4.

$$\frac{TA_{it}}{A_{it-1}} = \alpha_0 \frac{1}{A_{it-1}} + \alpha_1 \frac{\Delta REV_{it} - \Delta REC_{it}}{A_{it-1}} + \alpha_2 \frac{PPE_{it}}{A_{it-1}} + \varepsilon_{it}$$

Table 4. Results of ordinary least squares regression

	Variables	Unstandardized Coefficients		t	Significance
		B	Std. Error		
East	(Constant)	-.030	.004	-6.513	.000
	(ΔREV-ΔREC)/A	.150	.001	137.727	.000
	PPE/A	-.041	.007	-5.652	.000
West	(Constant)	-.035	.001	-19.816	.000
	(ΔREV-ΔREC)/A	.067	-.0002	2784.106	.000
	PPE/A	-.004	.0004	-1044.30	.000

ΔREV_{it} represents the change in revenues for company *i* in period *t* compared to *t-1*.
ΔREC_{it} represents the change in receivables for company *i* in period *t* compared to *t-1*.
PPE_{it} represents the property, plants and equipment of company *i* in period *t*.
A_{it-1} represents the total assets of company *i* in period *t-1*

In the equation (1), the absolute value of discretionary accruals ($absDA_{it}$) were used to measure the magnitude of EM without regard to its sign.

Independent and Control Variables. Measurement of Effect of Corporate Governance and CSR on Earnings Management

Two groups of **independent variables** were included. First, two variables (logSOC and logGOV) to measure the direct effect of corporate social responsibility and corporate governance on the EM have been incorporated. Secondly, two variables (*Block x logSOC* and *Block x logGOV)* have been included to assess potential differences in the effectiveness of CSR and corporate governance in controlling EM between the companies from East and West of Europe.

logSOC and logGOV Variables

The research includes these two variables to measure the effect of corporate social responsibility and corporate governance on the EM. Both variables represent indexes ESG (Environment, Social, and Governance) that are available from Thomson Reuters incorporated in Eikon database. The ESG indexes evaluate different dimensions including the management, shareholders, corporate social responsibility strategy, workforce, human rights, community, product responsibility, resource use, emissions and innovation based on company-reported non-financial information from publicly available data, such as sustainability reports, financial reports, and company websites (Thomson Reuters, 2019).

In detail, the social pillar examines factors including employment quality, health and safety issues, training, diversity, human rights, community involvement and product responsibility. On the other hand, the corporate governance pillar examines factors including board structure, compensation policy, board functions, financial and operational transparency, shareholder rights and vision and strategy (Thomson Reuters, 2013).

As an example of studies, this database was also considered in the study of Kim, Park and Wier (2012), Tangjitprom (2013), Velte (2016), Garcia, Mendes-Da-Silva and Orsato (2017), Miralles-Quirós, Miralles-Quirós and Gonçalves (2018), Aouadi and Marsat (2018), Burgos, Lee and Tsai (2019), Borralho *et al.* (2019), among others. Moreover, Eikon Thomson Reuters ESG indexes have extended coverage, including the developed and emerging markets.

In terms of the predicted sign it is expected for both variables a negative predicted sign according to the first two hypotheses. Socially responsible firms behave ethical, trustworthy and honest, so these firms are less likely to engage in EM. Regarding second variables, the effective corporate governance mechanism improves the quality of financial reporting and in effect will mitigate EM.

Block x logSOC and Block x logGOV Variables

The research includes these two variables to evaluate how CSR and corporate governance operate as a brake on EM in companies from Eastern and Western European countries. Both variables are constructed as a product of the *logSOC* or *logGOV* and dichotomus variables which takes a value of 1 if the company is from the Eastern European country and a value of 0 when the company is from a Western European country. In this way it is investigated the impact of CSR and corporate governance on the quality of financial information in developed and in developing countries, and differences between them.

In terms of the predicting signs, it is expected positive relationship for both variables, which is according to the third and fourth hypothesis. Companies from Western European countries have much more effective corporate governance mechanism, and they implemented better the CSR instruments than their counterparts from Eastern European countries; therefore, it may be observed greater effectiveness of EM control.

Finally, six **control variables** have been included: three economic and financial ratios (liquidity ratio, solvency ratio and return-on-assets) and size, industrial sector, and ownership.

Table 5 shows the predicted signs of the variables in the model.

Table 5. Predicted sign of the variables' coefficients

Variable	Expected Sign
Dependent variable:	
absDA	
Independent variables:	
logSOC	–
logGOV	–
Block x logSOC	+
Block x logGOV	+
Control variables	
LIQ	–
SOL	–
ROA	–
logA	–
SECTOR	+/–
OWNERSHIP	–

absDA is absolute value of discretionary accruals; *logSOC* is a logarithm of the social pillar score; *logGOV* is a logarithm of governance pillar score; *Block x logSOC* is the product between *logSOC* variable and dichotomous variable which takes a value of 1 if the company is from the Eastern European country and a value of 0 when the company is from Western European country; *Block x logGOV* is the product between *logGOV* variable and dichotomous variable which takes a value of 1 if the company is from the Eastern European country and a value of 0 when the company is from Western European country; *LIQ* is liquidity ratio; *SOL* is solvency ratio; *ROA* is return-on-assets; *logA* is the logarithm of total assets and measures the size of the company; *SECTOR* (dichotomous variables S1 to S5) indicate the industrial sector to which company belongs; *OWNERSHIP* is a dichotomous variable which takes a value of 1 if the company is state-owned and value 0 when it privately owned.

Source: The author

The ratios reflect the economic and financial situation of the firms and their general performance which could be a reason to manipulate their earnings. It is expected a negative sign of the variables indicating that better economic and financial situation of the firms less EM is expected, as previous researchers have demonstrated that managers tend to engage in EM to meet predicted profit margins, to beet financial forecasts, to match certain economic results, etc. (e.g. DeFond and Jiambalvo, 1994; Guidry, *et al.*, 1999; Kasznik, 1999; Bharath*et al.,* 2008; Elayan*et al.*, 2008; Chou *et al.*, 2009; Razza-quee*t al.*, 2016; Ding *et al.*, 2018). Therefore, companies that look healthy financially they appeal less to EM activity, as confirmed literature.

The size of the companies, measured by the logarithm of total assets, may also influence the earnings management. Larger companies are more visible and are followed by more analysts, which may slow down the earnings management. Therefore, the expected sign of the coefficient is negative.

Respect to the industrial sector, is considered through the variable SECTOR. In the sample there are companies belonging to six industrial sectors, so we introduce five dichotomous variables (S1 to S5) into the model. Thus, S1 is equal to 1 if the company belongs to sector 1 and is equal to 0 if it belongs to any other sector, proceeding in the same way with the variables S2 to S5. Literature has shown that the sector influences manipulation, although we are not able to predict the expected sign of the coefficient, since we do not know which sectors are more prone to manipulation.

Finally, the ownership variable is a dichotomous variable that adopts value 1 when the company is mainly state-owned and value 0 when it is mainly privately owned. Since the management of state-owned companies is assumed to be more controlled, we expect the coefficient to be negative.

RESULTS

Descriptive Statistics

Table 6 reports the descriptive statistics for the continuous variables in equation (1) and the frequencies for categorical variables are shown in Table 3. The mean value of absolute values of discretionary accruals is slightly higher in firms from Eastern European countries rounding 0.0774. In firms from Western Europe the mean is 0.0624.

Table 6. Descriptive statistics of the variables in equation (1)

		Mean	Std. Deviation	Max	Min
absDA	East	0.07740	0.08146	0.45191	0.00004
	West	0.06244	0.07014	0.45271	0.00001
logSOC	East	1.43714	0.34494	1.94330	0.04922
	West	1.76297	0.25325	1.99224	0.13988
logGOV	East	1.60661	0.22119	1.93992	0.95665
	West	1.63023	0.27615	1.97991	-0.08619
LIQ	East	1.80789	1.36607	10.53622	0.00000
	West	1.86622	1.34837	10.92523	-4.23793
SOL	East	2.63650	1.65058	10.76130	0.00084
	West	2.13646	1.31467	10.81375	-10.52632
ROA	East	0.03417	0.08673	0.53803	-0.29947
	West	0.03212	0.09191	0.57331	-0.30399
logA	East	5.74668	0,90069	7.42870	0.40312
	West	6.75870	1,12191	8.65130	1.14613

absDA is absolute value of discretionary accruals; *logSOC* is a logarithm of the social pillar score; *logGOV* is a logarithm of governance pillar score; *Block x logSOC* is the product between *logSOC* variable and dichotomous variable which takes a value of 1 if the company is from the Eastern European country and a value of 0 when the company is from Western European country; *Block x logGOV* is the product between *logGOV* variable and dichotomous variable which takes a value of 1 if the company is from the Eastern European country and a value of 0 when the company is from Western European country; *LIQ* is liquidity ratio; *SOL* is solvency ratio; *ROA* is return-on-assets; *logA* is the logarithm of total assets and measures the size of the company.

Source: The author

The mean value of the logarithm of the CSR score is 1.43 and 1.76 for Eastern and Western European companies respectively. In terms of the mean value of the logarithm of the corporate governance score is also slightly higher in Western European firms comparing to their Eastern counterparts, 1.60 to 1.63. The mean of liquidity ratio in firms from West of Europe is again slightly higher than in Eastern

European companies, 1.866 to 1.807. The mean value of solvency ratio is a little higher this time in Eastern European firms, 2.636. In Western European firms the mean of solvency ratio is 2.136. Finally, the mean value of ROA is almost exactly the same in both blocks of European firms, rounding 0.03.

Correlation Analysis

Table 7 exhibits correlations analysis among continuous variables employed in this investigation. Results unveil that social pillar score and corporate governance score are moderate positively correlated. Nevertheless, other variables do not show important correlations.

Table 7. Correlation analysis

	absDA	*logSOC*	*logGOV*	*LIQ*	*SOL*	*ROA*	*logA*
absDA	1						
logSOC	-.139**	1					
logGOV	-.102**	.466**	1				
LIQ	.027**	-.132**	-.088**	1			
SOL	-.004	.114**	.139**	.082**	1		
ROA	-.168**	.013	-.031	.011	.032**	1	
logA	-.293**	.301**	.357**	.027**	.004	-.168**	1

absDA is absolute value of discretionary accruals; *logSOC* is a logarithm of the social pillar score; *logGOV* is a logarithm of governance pillar score; *Block x logSOC* is the product between *logSOC* variable and dichotomous variable which takes a value of 1 if the company is from the Eastern European country and a value of 0 when the company is from Western European country; *Block x logGOV* is the product between *logGOV* variable and dichotomous variable which takes a value of 1 if the company is from the Eastern European country and a value of 0 when the company is from Western European country; *LIQ* is liquidity ratio; *SOL* is solvency ratio; *ROA* is return-on-assets; *logA* is the logarithm of total assets and measures the size of the company.

** Correlation significant at 0.01.

Source: The author

Given the correlation of social pillar score and governance pillar score, which are the two main research variables, a regression is run where one of the correlated variables is an independent variable, and the other one is a dependent variable (equation 4):

$$\log SOC_{it} = \chi_0 + \chi_1 \log GOV_{it} + \varepsilon_{it} \quad (4)$$

The dependent variable is logarithm of the social pillar score for company *i* in period *t* (log*SOC*), and independent variable is logarithm of governance pillar score of the firms for company *i* in period *t* (log*GOV*).

ε_{it} describes the residual part of social pillar score which is not explained by the independent variable (log*GOV*). Therefore, to avoid the correlation within the log*SOC* and *logGOV* variables, the research replaces in the new regression model the log*SOC* variable by the residual part of this variable (res*SOC*), not explained by the independent variable (log*GOV*). Hence, the new model is as follows:

$$absDA_{it}=\beta_0 + \beta_1\ resSOC_{it} + \beta_2 logGOV + \beta_3 Block_i \times resSOC_{it} + \beta_4 Block_i \times logGOV_{it}$$

$$+\beta_5 LIQ_{it} + \beta_6 SOL_{it} + \beta_7 ROA_{it} + \beta_8 logA_{it} + \beta_9 SECTOR_{it} + \beta_{10} OWNERSHIP_{it} \quad (5)$$

The dependent variable, $absDA_{it}$, is the absolute value of discretionary accruals for company *i* in period *t* and it is used as a proxy of EM, the dependent variable.

Independent variables are:

- *resSOC* represents the residual part of the variable *logSOC* for company *i* in period *t*. It is used as a measure of the corporate social responsibility.
- *logGOV* is defined as logarithm of governance pillar score of the firms for company *i* in period *t*. It is used as a measure of the corporate governance quality.
- *Block x resSOC* is the product between Block (dichotomous variable which takes a value of 1 if the company is from the Eastern European country and a value of 0 when the company is from a Western European country) and *resSOC*.
- *Block x logGOV* is the product between Block (dichotomous variable which takes a value of 1 if the company is from the Eastern European country and a value of 0 when the company is from a Western European country) and *logGOV*.

and three control variables:

- *LIQ* variable is the liquidity ratio for company *i* in period *t*, which it is defined as the quotient between the current assets and current liabilities.
- *SOL* variable is the solvency ratio for company *i* in period *t*, which it is defined as the quotient between the total assets and total liabilities.
- *ROA* variable is the return-on-assets for company *i* in period *t*, which it is defined as the quotient between the operating profits and total assets.
- *logA* is defined as the logarithm of total assets for company *i* in period *t*, obtained from Eikon database. It is a measure of the size of the company (data from Eikon).
- *SECTOR* is the industrial sector to which the company *i* belongs (data from Eikon). Five dichotomous variables (S1 to S5) have been included into the model to consider the six different industrial sectors.
- *OWNERSHIP* is a variable which indicate if the company *i* is mainly state-owned or privately owned (data from Eikon).

Regression Results

Table 8 presents the results of the regression (5).

$$absDA_{it}=\beta_0 + \beta_1\ resSOC_{it} + \beta_2 logGOV + \beta_3 Block_i \times resSOC_{it} + \beta_4 Block_i \times logGOV_{it}$$

$$+\beta_5 LIQ_{it} + \beta_6 SOL_{it} + \beta_7 ROA_{it} + \beta_8 logA_{it} + \beta_9 SECTOR_{it} + \beta_{10} OWNERSHIP_{it}$$

Table 8. Results of ordinary least squares regression

Variables	Unstandardized Coefficients		Standardized Coefficients	t	Significance
	B	Std. Error	Beta		
(Constant)	.154	.017		9.293	.000
resSOC	-.019	.008	-.086	-2.414	.016
logGOV	-.013	.006	-.064	-2.201	.028
Block x resSOC	.011	.016	.026	.694	.488
Block x logGOV	.012	.003	.125	3.487	.001
LIQ	-.003	.002	-.053	-1.440	.150
SOL	.000	.002	.008	.206	.837
ROA	-.090	.019	-.131	-4.698	.000
logA	-.012	.002	-.176	-5.402	.000
S1	.005	.005	.036	.957	.339
S2	-.012	.006	-.070	-2.066	.039
S3	.042	.034	.033	1.268	.205
S4	.012	.005	.115	2.692	.007
S5	-.009	.004	-.084	-2.024	.043
OWNERSHIP	-.016	.007	-.069	-2.350	.019
F-value	10.225*				

absDA is absolute value of discretionary accruals; *resSOC* is residual part of the variable *logSOC social pillar score;logGOV* is a logarithm of governance pillar score; *Block x resSOC* is the product between *resSOC* variable and dichotomous variable which takes a value of 1 if the company is from the Eastern European country and a value of 0 when the company is from Western European country; *Block x logGOV* is the product between *logGOV* variable and dichotomous variable which takes a value of 1 if the company is from the Eastern European country and a value of 0 when the company is from Western European country; *LIQ* is liquidity ratio; *SOL* is solvency ratio; *ROA* is return-on-assets; *logA* is the logarithm of total assets and measures the size of the company; *S1 to S5* are dichotomous variables representing the industrial sector to which company belongs; *OWNERSHIP* is a dichotomous variable which takes a value of 1 if the company is state-owned and value 0 when it privately owned.

*Significant at 1%

Source: The author

The coefficient on the *logGOV* variable is negative and significant (-0.013), according to the prediction. This means that the better the corporate governance practices in a company, the lower its level of EM. Consequently, as expected, corporate governance plays an important role in monitoring managers' activities in European companies. Corporate governance mechanisms reflect the ability to improve quality of financial reports and show the ability to restrict managers' discretional behavior.

The coefficient on the *resSOC* variable is negative and significant (-0.019), which is also consistent with the prediction. It indicates the positive impact of corporate social responsibility on the quality of the earnings. In other words, more socially responsible firms show lower level of EM activity.

Therefore, in terms of the evaluation of the effect of corporate governance and CSR on the EM practice, it may be confirmed the effectiveness of the control exercised by both mechanisms in order to limit EM (the first and second hypothesis). With higher strength of the issue of those company's practices, the lower discretionary accruals intensity is observed. As commented Rahim (2013), both mechanisms are complementary and exercise intensity and pressure on firms. Winberg and Randolph (2004) also agree that both mechanisms are closely linked, even sometimes confused with each other.

In relation to the incidence of corporate social responsibility in EM conditioned by the differences in CSR between Eastern and Western Europe, *Block x resSOC* variable, it can be confirmed a positive sign (β_3 = 0.011) but it is not significant. Therefore, it cannot be verified the third hypothesis.

The interaction between *Block* and *logGOV* shows positive and significant coefficient (β_4 = 0.012) indicating that corporate governance mechanism as a control measure for EM, is significantly reduced in companies located in Eastern European countries. In a company located in Eastern countries the effectiveness of corporate governance is smaller ($\beta_4 > 0$) compared to firms from Western countries.

Indeed, in companies belonging to countries from Western area EM is lower (-0.013, that is β_2) that in the companies from Eastern area (-0.001, that is $\beta_2 + \beta_4$). Therefore, it is confirmed that companies from Western European countries show corporate governance mechanism more effective in mitigate EM than their counterparts from emerging Eastern European countries. Consequently, firms from countries with the higher levels of corporate governance are associated with less EM activity.

In regard to control variables, all of them, except liquidity and solvency ratios, are significant. The coefficient of *ROA*. *logA* and *OWNERSHIP* is negative, as it was predicted, indicating that the better the economic situation, the more size and state-owned, the less EM. The sector is also important. The results show that companies belonging to S2 or S5 manage earnings less than companies belonging to the other sectors.

FUTURE RESEARCH DIRECTIONS

Although the present study has filled some gaps in EM literature, there are further issues to investigate. Future studies might increase the scope of research objects by extending the study including some other firm's macro factors to provide a more comprehensive picture of the results of the study.

This study contemplates on the data from ESG reports provided by an independent rating company which limits this study from the inclusion of missing indexes of some firms within the Eastern European countries.

Finally, it would be also useful to conduct the analysis using the sample of other developing countries in order to know whether the European evidence is unique.

CONCLUSION

Corporate governance and corporate social responsibility have become a buzzword all over the world and this is no different in Eastern Europe. The present study explored the relationship between EM and both: corporate social responsibility and practices of corporate governance.

Based on the sample of three emerging European countries (Poland, Hungary, and the Czech Republic) and three Western European countries (France, Spain and Germany), within the period of 2010 to 2018, the present research conducted a comparative study, as comparative study may reveal similarities or differences between both markets, and help to illustrate links between both parts of Europe.

First, the results indicate that better the corporate governance practices in a company, the lower its level of EM. Therefore, as expected, there is a direct relation of the impact of corporate governance mechanisms in monitoring managers' activities in European companies. Corporate governance mechanisms reflect the ability to reduce discretionary accruals practice.

Second, it is also confirmed the positive impact of corporate social responsibility on the quality of the earnings. More socially responsible firms show lower level of EM activity in companies from all European countries. Therefore, the findings show that both mechanisms act as a brake on EM, with its effectiveness limited in those organizations managers' activities.

Third, it is verified the existence of the differences in EM conditioned by the dissimilar corporate governance mechanisms of the firms within the different European countries. In detail, companies from emerging European countries show less effective corporate governance in controlling EM comparing to the Western European firms, as they have worst developed corporate governance frameworks. In other words, companies located in countries with lower corporate governance index, the brake on EM is lower. As explained Osma and Noguer (2007), the inefficiency of structures and instrument may not provide adequate ability to respond.

REFERENCES

Ahn, S., & Walker, M. (2007). Corporate governance and the spinoff decision. *Journal of Corporate Finance, 13*(1), 76–93. doi:10.1016/j.jcorpfin.2006.03.001

Allen & Overy. (2010). *Corporate governance in Central and Eastern Europe.* Available at: www.allenovery.com

Aouadi, A., & Marsat, S. (2018). Do ESG Controversies Matter for Firm Value? Evidence from International Data. *Journal of Business Ethics, Springer, 151*(4), 1027–1047. doi:10.100710551-016-3213-8

Arraiano, I., & Hategan, C. (2019). The Stage of Corporate Social Responsibility in EU- CEE Countries. *European Journal of Sustainable Development, 8*(3), 340–353. doi:10.14207/ejsd.2019.v8n3p340

Atkins, B. (2006). Corporate social responsibility: Is it "irresponsibility"? *Corporate Governance Advisor, 14*, 28–29.

Ayu, C., & Zulfia, K. (2018). The Effect of Good Corporate Governance and Earnings Management to Corporate Social Responsibility Disclosure. *Academy of Accounting and Financial Studies Journal, 22*(1), 45–61.

Ball, R., Kothari, S., & Robin, A. (2000). The effect of international institutional factors on properties of accounting earnings. *Journal of Accounting and Economics, 29*(1), 1–51. doi:10.1016/S0165-4101(00)00012-4

Banko, J., Frye, M., Wang, W., & Whyte, A. (2013). Earnings Management and Annual General Meetings: The Role of Managerial Entrenchment. *Financial Review, 48*(2), 259–282. doi:10.1111/fire.12003

Bansal, P. (2005). Evolving sustainably: A longitudinal study of corporate sustainable development. *Strategic Management Journal, 26*(3), 197–218. doi:10.1002mj.441

Bauguess, S., Moeller, S., Schlingemann, F., & Zutter, C. (2009). Ownership structure and target returns. *Journal of Corporate Finance*, *15*(1), 48–65. doi:10.1016/j.jcorpfin.2008.09.002

Becht, M., Jenkinson, T., & Mayer, C. (2005). Corporate governance: An assessment. *Oxford Review of Economic Policy*, *21*(2), 155–163. doi:10.1093/oxrep/gri009

Berglof, E., & Pajuste, A. (2003). *Emerging Owners, Eclipsing Markets? Corporate Governance in Central and Eastern Europe. Corporate Governance and Capital Flows in a Global Economy*. Oxford University Press.

Bergstressera, D., & Phililippon, T. (2006). CEO incentives and earnings management. *Journal of Financial Economics*, *80*(3), 511–529. doi:10.1016/j.jfineco.2004.10.011

Berkman, H., Cole, R., & Fu, L. (2009). Expropriation through loan guarantees to related parties: Evidence from China. *Journal of Banking & Finance*, *33*(1), 141–156. doi:10.1016/j.jbankfin.2007.11.001

Berniz, U. (2010). What is Scandinavian Law? Concept, Characteristics, Future. *Stockholm Institute for Scandianvian Law*, *1957*, 13–29.

Bharath, S., Sunder, J., & Sunder, S. (2008). Accounting quality and debt contracting. *The Accounting Review*, *83*(1), 1–28. doi:10.2308/accr.2008.83.1.1

Borralho, J., Gallardo, D., Hernández-Linares, R., & Paiva, I. (2019). Earnings Management and Corporate Social Responsibility. Family and non-family firms. *Workshop 1 al qual opta participar: "Agenda 2030 para el desarrollo sostenible: colaboración público-privada"*, 1-22.

Brammer, S., & Millington, A. (2005). Corporate reputation and philanthropy: An empirical analysis. *Journal of Business Ethics*, *61*(1), 29–44. doi:10.100710551-005-7443-4

Brav, A., Graham, J., Harvey, C., & Michaely, R. (2005). Payout policy in the 21st century. *Journal of Financial Economics*, *77*(3), 483–527. doi:10.1016/j.jfineco.2004.07.004

Brickley, J., Coles, J., & Terry, R. (1994). Outside directors and the adoption of poison pills. *Journal of Financial Economics*, *35*(3), 371–390. doi:10.1016/0304-405X(94)90038-8

Brouthers, L., & Lamb, C. Jr. (1995). National Ideology, Public Policy, and the Business Environment: A Contingency Approach to Economic Reform in Hungary, Poland and Eastern Europe. *International Business Review*, *4*(3), 355–372. doi:10.1016/0969-5931(95)00014-Q

Burgos, E., Lee, J., & Tsai, F. (2019). Doing Good with Creative Accounting? Linking Corporate Social Responsibility to Earnings Management in Market Economy. Country and Business Sector Contexts. *Sustainability, MDPI. Open Access Journal*, *11*(17), 1–20.

Byrd, J., & Hickman, K. (1992). Do outside directors monitor managers? Evidence from tender offer bids. *Journal of Financial Economics*, *32*(2), 195–222. doi:10.1016/0304-405X(92)90018-S

Callao, S., Jarne, J., & Wroblewski, D. (2017). Detecting earnings management investigation on different models measuring earnings management for emerging Eastern European countries. *International Journal of Research*, *5*(11), 222–259.

Chen, G., Firth, M., Gao, D., & Rui, O. (2006). Ownership structure, corporate governance, and fraud: Evidence from China. *Journal of Corporate Finance*, *12*(3), 424–448. doi:10.1016/j.jcorpfin.2005.09.002

Chi-Keung, M. (2012). Corporate governance and earnings management: A survey of literature. *Journal of Applied Business Research*, *29*, 2.

Chih, H., Shen, C., & Kang, F. (2008). Corporate Social Responsibility, Investor Protection, and Earnings Management: Some International Evidence. *Journal of Business Ethics*, *79*(1), 179–198. doi:10.100710551-007-9383-7

Chou, D., Wang, C., Chen, S., & Tsai, S. (2009). Earnings management and the long run underperformance of firms following convertible bond offers. *Journal of Business Finance & Accounting*, *36*(1-2), 73–98. doi:10.1111/j.1468-5957.2008.02120.x

Chung, R., Firth, M., & Kim, J. (2002). Institutional monitoring and opportunistic earnings management. *Journal of Corporate Finance*, *8*(1), 29–48. doi:10.1016/S0929-1199(01)00039-6

Cohen, D., & Zarowin, P. (2008). Economic Consequences of Real and Accrual-Based Earnings Management Activities. New York University.

Cornett, M., Marcus, A., & Tehranian, H. (2008). Corporate governance and pay-for-performance: The impact of earnings management. *Journal of Financial Economics*, *87*(2), 357–373. doi:10.1016/j.jfineco.2007.03.003

Daske, H., & Gebhardt, G. (2006). International financial reporting standards and experts' perceptions of disclosure quality. *Abacus*, *42*(3-4), 3–4, 461–498. doi:10.1111/j.1467-6281.2006.00211.x

Deakin, S. (2008). Legal origin, juridical form and industrialization in historical perspective: The case of the employment contract and the joint-stock company. *Socio-economic Review*, *7*(1), 35–65. doi:10.1093er/mwn019

Dechow, P., Sloan, R., & Sweeney, A. (1995). Detecting Earnings Management. *The Accounting Review*, *70*(2), 193–225.

DeFond, M., & Jiambalvo, J. (1994). Debt covenant violation and manipulation of accruals. *Journal of Accounting and Economics*, *17*(1-2), 145–176. doi:10.1016/0165-4101(94)90008-6

Denis, D., Denis, D., & Sarin, A. (1997). Agency problems, equity ownership, and corporate diversification. *The Journal of Finance*, *52*(1), 135–160. doi:10.1111/j.1540-6261.1997.tb03811.x

Ding, R., Li, J., & Wu, Z. (2018). Government affiliation, real earnings management, and firm performance: The case of privately held firms. *Journal of Business Research*, *83*, 138–150. doi:10.1016/j.jbusres.2017.10.011

Doing Business Database. (n.d.). www.doingbusiness.org

Elayan, F., Li, J., & Meyer, T. (2008). Accounting irregularities, management compensation structure and information asymmetry. *Accounting and Finance*, *48*(5), 741–760. doi:10.1111/j.1467-629X.2008.00266.x

European Commission. (2016). https://ec.europa.eu

Francis, J., & Wilson, E. (1988). Audit change: A test of theories relating to agency costs and auditor differentiation. *The Accounting Review*, *64*, 663–682.

Funken, K. (2003). *The best of both worlds: the trend towards convergence of the civil law and the common law system.* University of Munich School of Law.

Gao, L., & Zhang, J. (2015). Firms' earnings smoothing, corporate social responsibility. *Journal of Corporate Finance*, *32*, 108–127. doi:10.1016/j.jcorpfin.2015.03.004

Garcia, A., Mendes-Da-Silva, W., & Orsato, R. (2017). Sensitive industries produce better ESG performance: Evidence from emerging markets. *Journal of Cleaner Production*, *150*, 135–147. doi:10.1016/j.jclepro.2017.02.180

Gelb, D., & Strawser, J. (2001). Corporate social responsibility and financial disclosure: An alternative explanation for increased disclosure. *Journal of Business Ethics*, *33*(1), 1–13. doi:10.1023/A:1011941212444

Guidry, F., Leone, A., & Rock, S. (1999). Earnings-based bonus plans and earnings management by business-unit managers. *Journal of Accounting and Economics*, *26*(1-3), 113–142. doi:10.1016/S0165-4101(98)00037-8

Jaakko, H., & Tapani, J. (2005). Germanic and Nordic Fraud: A Comparative Look Under the Surface of Commonalities. *Global Jurist Advances*, *5*(2), 2–14.

Jaggi, B., Leung, S., & Gul, F. (2009). Family control, board independence and earnings management: Evidence based on Hong Kong firms. *Journal of Accounting and Public Policy*, *28*(4), 281–300. doi:10.1016/j.jaccpubpol.2009.06.002

Jensen, M., & Meckling, W. (1976). Theory of the firm: Managerial behavior, agency costs, and ownership structure. *Journal of Financial Economics*, *3*(4), 305–360. doi:10.1016/0304-405X(76)90026-X

Kasznik, R. (1999). On the association between voluntary disclosure and earnings management. *Journal of Accounting Research*, *37*(1), 57–81. doi:10.2307/2491396

Kim, I., & Venkatachalam, M. (2011). Are sin stocks paying the price for accounting sins? *Journal of Accounting, Auditing & Finance*, *26*(2), 415–442. doi:10.1177/0148558X11401222

Kim, Y., Park, M., & Wier, B. (2012). Is earnings quality associated with corporate social responsibility? *The Accounting Review*, *87*(3), 761–796. doi:10.2308/accr-10209

Klapper, L., Laeven, L., & Rajan, R. (2006). Entry regulation as a barrier to entrepreneurship. *Journal of Financial Economics*, *82*(3), 591–629. doi:10.1016/j.jfineco.2005.09.006

Klein, A. (2002). Audit Committee, Board of Director characteristics, and earnings management. *Journal of Accounting and Economics*, *33*(3), 375–400. doi:10.1016/S0165-4101(02)00059-9

La Porta, R., Lopez-de-Silanes, F., Shleifer, A., & Vishny, R. (1998). Law and finance. *Journal of Political Economy*, *106*(6), 1113–1155. doi:10.1086/250042

Leuz, C., Nanda, D., & Wysocki, P. (2003). Earnings management and investor protection: An international comparison. *Journal of Financial Economics*, *69*(5), 505–527. doi:10.1016/S0304-405X(03)00121-1

Li, S., Selover, D., & Stein, M. (2011). "Keep silent and make money": Institutional patterns of earnings management in China. *Journal of Asian Economics*, *22*(5), 369–382. doi:10.1016/j.asieco.2011.06.003

Li, W., & Zhang, R. (2010). Corporate Social Responsibility, Ownership Structure and Political Interference: Evidence from China. *Journal of Business Ethics*, *96*(4), 631–645. doi:10.100710551-010-0488-z

Malik, M. (2015). Value-enhancing capabilities of CSR: A brief review of contemporary literature. *Journal of Business Ethics*, *127*(2), 419–438. doi:10.100710551-014-2051-9

Mindzak, J., & Zeng, T. (2018). The impact of pyramid ownership on earnings management. *Asian Review of Accounting*, *26*(2), 208–224. doi:10.1108/ARA-11-2016-0130

Miralles-Quirós, M., Miralles-Quirós, J., & Gonçalves, V. (2018). The value relevance of environmental, social, and governance performance: The Brazilian case. *Sustainability*, *10*(3), 574. doi:10.3390u10030574

Mishra, M., & Malhotra, A. (2016). Earnings Management Practices in Indian Companies: A Cross-Sectional Analisis. *Journal of Modern Accounting and Auditing*, *12*(6), 295–305. doi:10.17265/1548-6583/2016.06.001

Osma, G., & Noguer, B. (2007). The Effect of the Board Composition and its Monitoring Committees on Earnings Management: Evidence from Spain. *Corporate Governance*, *15*(6), 1413–1430. doi:10.1111/j.1467-8683.2007.00654.x

Park, Y., & Shin, H. (2004). Board composition and earnings management in Canada. *Journal of Corporate Finance*, *10*(3), 431–457. doi:10.1016/S0929-1199(03)00025-7

Petera, P., Wagner, J., & Knorová, K. (2016). Perception and interpretation of sustainability among the largest corporations established in the Czech Republic. *Acta Universitatis Agriculturae et Silviculturae Mendelianae Brunensis*, *64*(3), 1053–1065. doi:10.11118/actaun201664031053

Prior, D., Surroca, J., & Tribo, J. (2008). Are socially responsible managers really ethical? Exploring the relationship between earnings management and corporate social responsibility. *Corporate Governance*, *16*(3), 160–177. doi:10.1111/j.1467-8683.2008.00678.x

Rahim, M. (2013). Legal Regulation of Corporate Social Responsibility: A Meta-Regulation Approach of Law for Raising CSR in a Weak Economy. Berlin: Springer.

Razzaque, R., Ali, M., & Mather, P. (2016). Real earnings management in family firms: Evidence from an emerging economy. *Pacific-Basin Finance Journal*, *40*, 237–250. doi:10.1016/j.pacfin.2015.12.005

Report, O. E. C. D. (2010). *The OECD Principle of Corporate Governance*. The Organization for Economic Cooperation and Development.

Roychowdhury, S. (2006). Management of earnings through the manipulation of real activities that affect cash flow from operations. *Journal of Accounting and Economics*, *42*, 335–370. doi:10.1016/j.jacceco.2006.01.002

Shleifer, A. (2004). *Does Competition Destroy Ethical Behavior?* Harvard University. doi:10.3386/w10269

Simeonov, S., & Stefanova, M. (2015). Corporate Social Responsibility in Bulgaria: The Current State of the Field. In S. Idowu, R. Schmidpeter, & M. Fifka (Eds.), *Corporate Social Responsibility in Europe. United in Sustainable Diversity* (1st ed., pp. 313–332). Springer. doi:10.1007/978-3-319-13566-3_17

Steurer, R., & Konrad, A. (2009). Business–society relations in Central-Eastern and Western Europe: How those who lead in sustainability reporting bridge the gap in corporate (social) responsibility. *Scandinavian Journal of Management, 25*(1), 23–36. doi:10.1016/j.scaman.2008.11.001

Steurer, R., Martinuzzi, A., & Margula, S. (2012). Public policies on CSR in Europe: Themes, instruments, and regional differences. *Corporate Social Responsibility and Environmental Management, 19*(4), 206–227. doi:10.1002/csr.264

Tangjitprom, N. (2013). The role of corporate governance in reducing the negative effect of earnings management. *International Journal of Economics and Finance, 5*(3), 213–220. doi:10.5539/ijef.v5n3p213

Thomson Reuters. (2019). *Thomson Reuters ESG Scores*. https://www.refinitiv.com

Thomson Reuters Corporate Responsibility Ratings (TRCRR). (2013). *Rating and Ranking Rules and Methodologies*. https://financial.thomsonreuters.com

Trading Economics Database. (n.d.). www.tradingeconomics.com

Velte, P. (2016). Women on management board and ESG performance. *Journal of Global Responsibility, 7*(1), 98–109. doi:10.1108/JGR-01-2016-0001

Waryanto, E. (2010). *Pengaruh Karakteristik Good Corporate Governance terhadap Luas Pengungkapan Corporate Social Responsibility di Indonesia. Skripsi*. Universitas Diponegoro.

Weisbach, M. (1998). Outside directors and CEO turnover. *Journal of Financial Economics, 20*, 431–460. doi:10.1016/0304-405X(88)90053-0

Winberge, D., & Randolph, P. (2004). *Corporate Social Responsibility: What every In-House Council Should Know.* ACC Docket, 72. World Bank Database. www.worldbank.org/

World Economic Forum Database. (n.d.). www.weforum.org

World Investment Report. (n.d.). https://unctad.org/en/

Xie, B., Davidson, W. III, & Da Dalt, P. (2003). Earnings management and corporate governance: The roles of the board and the audit committee. *Journal of Corporate Finance, 9*(3), 295–316. doi:10.1016/S0929-1199(02)00006-8

Xue, S., & Hong, Y. (2016). Earnings management, corporate governance and expense stickiness. *China Journal of Accounting Research, 9*(1), 41–58. doi:10.1016/j.cjar.2015.02.001

KEY TERMS AND DEFINITIONS

Comparative Studies: The studies which reveal similarities or differences between different markets, countries, aspects of companies, etc. They help to illustrate links and dissimilarities between these different elements.

Corporate Governance: It is an internal mechanism of the company which includes policies, processes, and people. This mechanism is directly involved in monitoring managers' decisions. It serves to improve a company's reporting quality, and at the same time, it serves as an effective mechanism to alleviate the opportunistic behaviors of management.

Corporate Social Responsibility: It is defined as company's integration into social and environmental concerns. Being socially responsible indicates business actions which lead to contribution to a sustainable economic development by the firm beyond the requirements of law in order to improve the business itself and the development of the environment.

Discretionary Accruals: Defined as the part of total accruals, which are not directly observable, and they are easily to manipulate by the company.

Earnings Management: A purposeful intervention in the external financial reporting, to reach earnings targets. This action may take place without violating accounting regulation. It takes benefits from a possibility to make certain choices in policy and accounting system. This action can lead, but not necessary, to mislead stakeholders into believing certain financial information.

Emerging Economies/Developing Countries: They are characterized by a rapid economic growth. They are in current state of development. Nevertheless, they are still not at the same level of developed countries.

Quality of the Reporting Earnings: It shows the value of business by analyzing detailed aspects of the reporting financial reports. High quality reporting earnings indicates the transparency and efficiency of the supervision of management to avoid misleading investors.

ENDNOTES

1 https://ec.europa.eu.

2 See data: World Bank database (www.worldbank.org/), World Economic Forum database (www.weforum.org), World Investment Report (https://unctad.org/en/), Trading Economics database (www.tradingeconomics.com), European Commission (http://ec.europa.eu), Doing Business database (www.doingbusiness.org).

3 In literature this model is called: modified Jones model.

Chapter 11
Corporate Governance and Company Performance:
A Comparative Analysisi Across Sectors in Portugal

Eleonora Santos
https://orcid.org/0000-0003-4693-0804
Centre of Applied Research in Management and Economics (CARME), Portugal

Jacinta Moreira
ESTG, Instituto Politécnico de Leiria, Portugal

Neuza Ribeiro
https://orcid.org/0000-0002-1228-2522
Centre of Applied Research in Management and Economics (CARME), Portugal

ABSTRACT

The assessment of the implementation of the corporate governance practices is important because it contributes to the efficient use of resources and, thus, increases corporate performance. However, the practice of CG in Portugal is below European standards due to several issues related to weak legal protection, concentrated ownership structures, and limited information transparency. Using a panel data of 17 firms listed on PSI20, this chapter investigates the impact of the internal CG mechanisms on corporate performance, in 2014-2018. Results show that the size of the audit committee impacts positively on firm performance. However, the number of independent members of audit committee decreases corporate performance in firms operating in services, and ownership of related parties increases corporate performance. Also, fewer leveraged firms are likely to exhibit better performances. This research provides understanding of the relationships between internal mechanisms of CG and corporate performance by comparing results across groups of sectors.

DOI: 10.4018/978-1-7998-7596-3.ch011

INTRODUCTION

The main objective of firms is to maximize their value, which depends on their organizational structure. However, when there is separation of ownership and control of a large company, agency problems arise (see for example, Fama, 1980; Fama & Jensen, 1983; Morck & Yeung, 2003; Abatino & Dari-Mattiacci, 2020; Li et al., 2020) and risk sharing between principals (owners) and agents (other stakeholders) (Abe et al., 2020; Zaid et al., 2020).

The main source of this problem is asymmetric information, enabling managers to acquire an advantage over shareholders in accessing information (Boone et al., 2019) and, therefore, being able to take advantage of the flexibility of accounting principles and rules for the disclosure of results. In particular, managers of listed companies may attempt to increase their salaries and bonuses at the expense of shareholders profit has been subject to discussion in the literature (Crossan, 2011). This problem entails an agency cost for the principal, which, if not properly restricted, can affect the potential for value creation and compromise the company's sustainability (Nuber et al., 2020).

Since corporate finance focuses on maximizing value in the decision-making process, resolving the agency's problems involves adopting incentive policies and aligning interests (for example, remuneration, indebtedness and profit sharing) (Borah et al., 2020; Carlson & Bussin, 2020). However, the development of the capital markets has motivated a strong debate about the structure and control of listed companies. Additionally, the financial scandals of some international companies have raised Corporate Governance (CG) issues, namely with regard to accountability, business with related parties and composition and functioning of the management body, the audit committee and the role of the board in the performance of listed companies (Soltani & Maupetit, 2015; Resende, 2017).Thus, there is a need to study the extent to which CG systems fulfill their role in corporate management. In this context, some studies show that the sensitivity between certain control mechanisms (for example, indebtedness and remuneration policies) and corporate performance depends on the type of majority shareholder (Unite et al., 2008). On the other hand, in countries where the labor market is poorly developed and with a high concentration of ownership, as is the case in Portugal, a greater number of non-executive directors on the board of directors would motivate the alignment of interests (Azevedo, 2013). However, because no CG system is perfect, agency problems are not solved solely by defining ownership and the administrative structure typical of each CG paradigm (Schulze et al., 2001; Dalton et al., 2003).

Therefore, the analysis of the impact of internal CG mechanisms on corporate performance is crucial in the context of agency problems.

CG is the system that controls and manages the company's activities and is composed of people, policies and processes necessary to achieve shareholders' expectations with integrity, respect, transparency and responsibility (Dewi, 2020). The purpose of the CG is, therefore, that companies be managed and managed for the benefit of all shareholders and not just in the interests of some.

CG can be considered a model that favors an environment of trust by giving the board of directors the mission of protecting the interests of shareholders and, at the same time, maximizing the value of companies (Crowther & Sefi, 2011), balancing the relationships between management and shareholders (Santos, 2009).

Good CG practices require reconciliation of CG mechanisms to minimize agency costs and allow for an efficient allocation of resources (Lal, 2019). As a result, companies with a higher level of adoption of the best CG practices have greater value creation (Danoshana & Ravivathani, 2019; Mertzanis et al., 2019). The high requirements and standards imposed by international markets oblige listed companies to apply these principles mainly following a legislative and regulatory basis. Thus, the concept of CG is strongly present in companies listed on Euronext Lisbon. Indeed, the Securities Market Commission (CMVM), aims to provide, through a set of recommendations, an optimization of the performance of companies and contribute to a balanced composition of the interests of shareholders (CMVM, 2013). In fact, since 1999, the CMVM has published recommendations for good CG practices, having undergone some changes over the years in order to make companies increasingly attractive to investors and markets.

However, the practice of CG in Portugal is below European standards and Portuguese companies still have a long way to go before international markets feel confident in investing in Portugal (Heidrick & Struggles, 2003). This can be explained, at least in part, by the fact that the majority of companies listed in Portugal are controlled by families (Tierno, 2014). In addition, since there is weak legal protection for investors in Portugal, concentrated ownership structures (Silva, 2017), capital markets that are still insufficient to pressure corporate behavior and limited information transparency, the role of the CG is crucial to resolve agency problems (Filho & Alves, 2018).

On the other hand, many empirical studies confirm many of the patterns predicted by new trade theories that explain the heterogeneity of companies (for example, Bernard et al., 2012). Thus, assessments for the KM are crucial to determine the efficiency and effectiveness of KM practices, and the heterogeneity of companies must be understood in an analysis framework at the sector level (Aiello et al., 2015). Hence, based on a quantitative methodology and using a sample of 17 companies listed on EURONEXT (PSI20), for the period 2014-2018, this chapter investigates the relationship between the internal mechanisms of corporate governance and the performance of companies in Portugal. Firm financial reports from the SABI database are used to build a panel data set and test Tobin's Q against a set of explanatory variables, such as size, leverage and ownership. Subsequently, the company's performance is compared across sectors, in order to draw conclusions and recommend sector policy measures on KM.

To the best of authors' knowledge, this study is the first to examine the impact of internal CG mechanisms on the business performance of PSI-20 companies in Portugal, for the 2014-2018 period.

The first section of the chapter is devoted to the literature review on the internal Corporate Governance mechanisms. In the second part of the chapter, the methodology for conducting the study is presented and explained, after the goals being set and the statistical data collection and analysis are described. In the third part, the results obtained from the application of the method of analysis are presented and critically analysed. In conclusion, some remarks on recommendations and implications are presented.

BACKGROUND

Internal Mechanisms of Corporate Governance

There are several aspects of firms' ownership, board, capital and compensation structure that can work as effective governance mechanisms or devices, the internal mechanisms of CG. For example, managerial ownership may alleviate agency costs due to the separation of ownership and control (Jensen & Meckling, 1976). Since managers become residual claimants, a higher ownership stake by insiders may help to align different interests and, thus, managerial ownership is regarded as one major internal governance mechanism that mitigates the agency problem between managers and shareholders.

Corporate board of directors (Musteen et al., 2010; Oh et al., 2019) and the Audit Committee are also regarded as other important internal governance mechanisms (Beasley et al., 2009; Dhaliwal et al.,

2010). Furthermore, debt integrates significant monitoring, signaling and renegotiation features that can alleviate agency conflicts between managers and external investors (Mishra, & Dasgupta, 2019; Vijayakumaran & Vijayakumaran, 2019).

A large body of empirical studies has exploited the impact of at least one of the following four internal mechanisms on firms' performance.

Board Governance-The board characteristics, such as composition, size and leadership structure, play a key role on firms' management (Musteen et al., 2010; Oh et al., 2019).

Regarding composition, researchers are not consensual on whether a company should have more insiders than the outsiders or vice versa. Yet, CG practices worldwide suggest that an independent member should be included on the board. The inclusion of independent directors may allow to reduce the agency cost because they turn the monitoring and the strategic planning of the board more effective (Duru et al., 2016; Agrawal & Nasser, 2019). However, there is not much empirical evidence in the literature supporting the idea that independent members improve firm performance (Iwu-Egwuonwu & Chibuike, 2012). Some studies, such as DeAndreas et al. (2005), Chaghadari and Chaleshtori (2011) and Kajola (2008) could not find a significant relationship between board independency and firm performance. However, Omware et al. (2020) found that board independence, level of education of board members, gender diversity, and ethnic composition positively influence the financial performance of commercial banks.

Concerning board size, a large and varied board of directors (BD) may increase board performance, regarding knowledge and skills. Nevertheless, a large board may face problems regarding group dynamics, turning the board less effective (Van den Berghe & Levrau, 2004). Thus, some studies (e.g., Suntraruk, 2009; Chaghadari & Chaleshtori, 2011; Shao, 2019) found no association between board size and firm performance; other studies (e.g., Jaafar & El Shawa, 2009; and Omware & Jagongo, 2020) found that the size of the board is positively associated with the firm performance.

The greater the size of the BD, the lower the involvement of that board in firm strategic decisions (Kouloukoui et al., 2019). For example, García-Ramos and García-Olalla (2011) found a negative effect of board size on firm performance in founder-led family companies. Also, in a study for Vietnam, Vo and Phan (2013) found a negative link between board size and firm performance.

Thus, the results of studies on the relationship between the size of the boards of directors and firm performance are inconclusive and do not elucidate the optimal number of members in order that firm could be efficient. Some authors point out the advantages of small-sized boards of directors such as a lower likelihood of disagreement, lack of cohesion and individual demotivation (Rodrigues, 2012).

As regards board leadership, Agency Theory endorses separation of the roles of CEO and chairperson on the board, therefore reducing the control of management on the board; while the Stewardship Theory supports a structure where the CEO also assists as the chairperson, to increase the trust and the motivation of the board. Hence, mixing results are found in studies analysing the relationship between the board leadership structure and firm performance. For example, Hussain et al. (2019) find that firms with a high presence of family related directors exhibit superior accounting profitability. Li and Patel (2019) find a negative link between more generalist CEO experience and firm performance, which is alleviated with longer CEO tenure. Shao (2019) finds that CEO duality has a significantly negative effect on firm performance. Finally, Yoo et al. (2020) find that poorly performing firms are more likely to appoint multiple CEOs and adopt shared leadership.

Based on the above arguments the first two hypotheses are as follows:

H1: There is a significant relationship between the Board of Directors' size and corporate performance

H2: There is a positive relationship between the number of independent directors and corporate performance

Audit Committee-Audit committee (AC) effectiveness depends on four determinants: composition, authority, resources and diligence (DeZoort et al., 2002; Krishnan, 2005; Beasley et al., 2009; Dhaliwal et al., 2010). It is argued that a larger AC has greater authority and organizational status (Braiotta, 2000) and a wider knowledge base (Karamanou & Vafeas, 2005). However, if the AC becomes too, it can suffer from diffusion of responsibility (Karamanou & Vafeas, 2005). According to DeZoort et al. (2002), a team of 3-6 members should be independent, financially literate, have objectivity and integrity and be willing to work as a team.

Though literature provides an extensive discussion of the AC size and firm performance relationship, the results are still inconclusive. For example, Agency theory advocates propose that if the committee size is too big, the performance is expected to be poor.

Some studies in developed countries (Bauer et al., 2009; Reddy et al., 2010) reported a positive relationship; as well as some of those conducted in the developing countries (Heenetigala & Armstrong, 2011; Obiyo & Lenee, 2011; Al-Matari et al., 2012).

The independence of the AC is also regarded as crucial in the literature. Marzuki et al. (2019) investigated the relationship between AC characteristics and the propensity of committing fraud among Malaysian firms. Based on a matched-pair sample of 64 observations for the years 2002–2014, they found limited evidence to suggest that audit committee characteristics matters. Also, the study of Ferdinand and Santosa (2019) investigates the impact of AC characteristics on the fraudulent financial statements reports in retail companies listed on the Indonesia Stock Exchange, for 2012-2016. Results shows that AC characteristics do not have significant effect on the fraudulent financial statements report.

Founded on previous literature, the next two hypotheses are formulated as follows:

H3: There is a positive relationship between the size of Audit Committee and corporate performance
H4: There is a positive relationship between the number of independent members of AC and corporate performance

Leverage- Financial leverage is another internal instrument of CG that increases firm performance (Mishra & Dasgupta, 2019; Vijayakumaran & Vijayakumaran, 2019). The debt-equity composition may increase the monitoring activities by outsiders. Nonetheless, on one hand, it is a potential device to discipline management that having commitment to pay debt. On the other hand, while debt offers tax advantages, too much debt increases the bankruptcy risk. Thus, literature of the disciplining role of leverage is mixed (Sarkar & Sarkar, 2008). Using data from 130 non-financial firms, for 2012-2015 and Multiple Regression, Khan et al (2019) analysed the link between CG (board size, outside directors) and firm performance (Tobin's Q). The authors used financial leverage as an interaction term. Results showed that the interaction effect of leverage exerted a significant impact between CG and firm performance. For China, Vijayakumaran and Vijayakumaran (2019) also found a positive association between leverage and firm performance.

Based on the evidence presented above, the following hypothesis is formulated:

H5: There is a significant relationship between leverage and corporate performance.

Ownership-Majority shareholders have a greater incentive to monitor managers and greater power to defend and reinforce their interests (Thomsen & Conyon, 2012). Firms with several owners can have a very positive cost / benefit ratio. They will have more transaction costs associated with contracts, and thus benefit from the monitoring and advisory services that shareholders will be encouraged to provide (Sauerwald et al., 2019). Ownership of independent institutions and individuals by ensuring management to perform in the best interest of the shareholders, may contribute to better monitoring and, therefore, to increase output and firm value (Dau et al., 2020). On the other hand, some aspects of management ownership will rise the management's sense of belonging to the company which inspires the managers to run the company optimally (Fahlenbrach & Stulz, 2009).

Grounded on above mentioned arguments, the following hypothesis state that:

H6: There is a positive relationship between unrelated parties' ownership and corporate performance
H7: There is a positive relationship between block outsider ownership and corporate performance
H8: There is a positive relationship between management ownership and corporate performance
H9: There is a negative relationship between related parties' ownership and corporate performance

DATA AND METHODOLOGY

In this paper, the sample is composed of 17 PSI-20 firms. PSI-20 (Portuguese Stock Index) aggregates the 20 largest companies listed on the Portuguese stock exchange, Euronext Lisbon. Thus, it is the main reference index of the Portuguese capital market.

This research focus on testing the impact of internal CG mechanisms on corporate performance of listed firms in Portugal. Governance factors concern the company's leadership and culture, such as the board accountability and structure, executive remuneration, internal audits, risk profile, quality of management and the level at which they include social and environmental performance in the strategic decisions for the company. These factors also include level of transparency on reporting and even of bribery and corruption.

Because firms in the sample are listed on EURONEXT LISBON, they are subject to stock exchange's rules and regulations. In other words, these firms must comply with a set of requirements, which function as critical success factors: • they have systematically systematized their business model, in order to be clear to investors which are the company's drivers, the path they have already taken and the outlined strategy. • the company's evolution prospects must clearly and consistently show a strategy for growth and consolidation of an appreciation trend. • the management and control structure must follow the best standards in the market. • there must be a clear perception of the company's value, regardless of the valuation method used. • the existence of previous (and positive) experience with the capital market is a plus. Thus, the accounting practices effective in these firms and, therefore, their performance measures should be reasonably consistent.

The data were collected for the last 5 years available (2014-2018) and the sample was selected based on the availability of financial reports on SABI database. SABI provides firms' financial reports necessary to investigate the relationship between CG and firm performance.

Due to the small number of observations that poses problems with estimation by sectors, the sample was divided only by two groups: 1) including companies producing paper, cork, telecommunications and IT; and 2) construction, energy, trade, food and beverages and banking. The criterium was to group holdings that operate in the manufacturing sector and in services sector. Simulations with other combinations of industries were not possible due to insufficient number of observations or nonsignificant results.

A set of indicators were used to compare the financial and economic performance of the two groups of sectors, which are turnover, assets, ROE, ROA, Liquidity and debt-to-equity.

Profitability ratios are a good approach to measure corporate performance, because profitability means the ability of a company to earn a profit. Profitability is critical both for shareholders and creditors because profits allow for dividends and funds for covering debts. Examples include return on equity (ROE), return on assets (ROA), cash return on assets, return on debt, return on retained earnings, return on revenue, risk-adjusted return, return on invested capital, and return on capital employed. This paper employs the two first measures.

The ROE measures the ability of a firm to generate profits from the shareholders' investments, i.e., the financial profitability. The calculation formula is as follows:

Return on Equity (ROE) = Net Profit After Taxes/Equity (1)

This ratio shows how much profit is generated by 1 Euro of shareholders' equity. In other words, it measures how effectively money from shareholders is being used for the generation of profits. In view of this, a high value of the ROE is desirable because that would mean efficient usage of investors' funds.

The ROA measures the economic profitability and can be used as an indicator of a firm's effort of minimizing the assets, which are not taking part in the process of generation returns. The formula is:

Return on Assets (ROA) = Net Profit After Taxes / Total Assets (2)

Liquidity ratios measure firms' ability to pay off current debt obligations without raising external capital and its margin of safety through the calculation of metrics, including the current ratio, quick ratio, and operating cash flow ratio. This paper uses the current liquidity ratio measured as

Current Liquidity Ratio= Current Assets/ Current Liabilities (3)

This ratio measures a firm's capacity to pay off its current liabilities (payable within one year) with its current assets (cash, accounts receivable and inventories), to evaluate the coverage of short-term debts in an emergency. The higher the ratio, the better the firm's liquidity position.

This analysis may be internal or external. Internal analysis involves comparing previous time periods to current operations; while external analysis involves comparing the liquidity ratios of one firm or a group of firms to another firm or group of firms. This ratio is useful to compare the firm's strategic positioning concerning its competitors when creating standard goals.

Financial leverage ratios (also known as equity or debt ratios) compare the overall debt load of a firm with the assets or equity. This shows how much of the firm assets belong to the shareholders rather than creditors. When shareholders own a majority of the assets, the firm is said to be less leveraged; conversely, when creditors own a majority of the assets, the firm is considered highly leveraged and the firm is regarded as riskier for lenders. The most common is the debt ratio, that shows how many assets the firm must sell in order to pay off all its liabilities, and it is calculated as

Debt Ratio= Total Liabilities/Total Assets (4)

This ratio helps investors and creditors to analyze the overall debt burden on the firm as well as the firm's ability to pay off the debt in the future.

In group 1, the paper industry shows the best performance in all indicators, except regarding debt-to-equity, in which the communications industry shows the best performance, i.e., displays a lower level of indebtedness. In group 2, the sector of Electricity & Gas show the best performance regarding turnover, level of assets and liquidity; the sector of construction shows the best financial performance (ROE); while the sector of Food & Beverages shows the best economic performance (ROA) and firms operating in Retail Trade show the lowest percentage of debt-to equity.

The worst performances in group 1 are shown in communications (regarding ROE, ROA and assets); paper (liquidity and financial indebtedness); and the sectors of cork and communications (regarding turnover). In group 2, the worst performances are verified in retail trade, as regards turnover, ROE, ROA and liquidity. Not surprisingly, the sector of financial services is the most indebted; while the sector of Food & Beverages displays the lowest level of assets. The combined analysis of the two groups suggests that:

- In general, the sectors with the best performance are paper (group 1) and electricity and gas (group 2).
- However, some paper producing companies show lower levels of liquidity and therefore resort more to external indebtedness.
- The worst performance belongs to companies operating in communications (group 1), and in retail trade (group 2).
- The communications sector is the least indebted, perhaps because it has the lowest level of assets. On the other hand, as it has less turnover, this may explain, in part, the fact that it presents a worse performance in terms of economic and financial profitability.
- In the retail sector, there is less indebtedness. This fact, combined with a lower turnover, justifies the lower liquidity and may explain, in part, the worse economic and financial profitability (measured by ROA and ROE, respectively).
- Electricity and gas companies exhibit the highest level of investment (as measured by the assets) and the highest turnover, which explain the greater liquidity.
- The lower level of investments in the Food & Beverages services sector may explain its better economic profitability.
- The only company operating in the construction sector has the best financial profitability.
- The financial services sector has, as already mentioned, the highest level of external debt.

Comparing the economic and financial performance between groups, group 1 exhibits greater liquidity, less indebtedness and therefore better financial profitability; while group 2 shows higher turnover and investment and, therefore, better economic profitability.

The intra-industry analysis of corporate performance in 2018 shows that:

- In the paper industry, Navigator is the largest company (both in terms of turnover and number of employees) and holds a bigger asset structure. However, in terms of liquidity, Semapa leads the industry. However, concerning economic and financial profitability (ROA and ROE), Altri shows a better performance.
- In the telecommunications industry, the company NOS leads in terms of assets and financial profitability. The company Novabase shows a lower level of indebtedness and greater liquidity.

However, Pharol, being larger in terms of number of employees, displays worse performances regarding turnover, assets and economic and financial profitability.

- In the energy sector, EDP - Energias de Portugal presents a better performance in terms of turnover, assets, and liquidity. The highest level of indebtedness suggests that EDP resorted to external financing to acquire assets (investment). On the other hand, the company Galp Energia shows the worst performance in terms of liquidity.
- Finally, in retail trade, Sonae Capital displays the worst performance regarding turnover. However, this company also had a lower level of indebtedness compared to its rivals. In contrast, Sonae Indústria shows the worst economic and financial profitability, as well as lower liquidity, compared to its competitors.

Data distribution, presented on Figure 1., shows that half of variables follow a log-normal distribution.

Panel data estimation has been subject of several studies. However, most of them focus on the estimation, disregarding the efficiency and consistency issues. Since that, in real world, the exact value of the population is not known, estimators are used to infer the value of an unknown parameter in statistical models. Conventional panel estimators such as fixed or random effects are said to result in misleading inference and even become inconsistent estimators (Phillips & Sul, 2007; Sarafidis & Robertson, 2009). The most common estimators in panel data are Generalized Least Square (GLS) and Feasible Generalized Least Square (FGLS). However, it can only be implemented when the number of time periods (T) is greater than or equal to the number of cross-sections (N), which is not the case in the present study. An additional problem is that FGLS estimator is known to underestimate SEs in finite samples, often severely (Reed & Ye, 2009).

GLS estimators, on the other hand, are more efficient than those obtained in a simpler model neglecting unobserved factors. Thus, GLS is regarded as producing an optimal unbiased estimator of β (Musau et al., 2015).

The econometric model for multiple regressions is as follows:

$$Q=\beta_0+\beta_1 BDS+\beta_2 IBD+\beta_3 ACS+\beta_4 IDAC+\beta_5 S+\beta_6 LEV$$

$$+\beta_7 IO+\beta_8 IOUP+\beta_9 IORP+\beta_{10} BLOCK+\varepsilon i \qquad (5)$$

Where Q is Tobin's q, BDS is the size of BD, IBD is the number of independent members in BD, ACS is the size of AC, IDAC is the number of independent members in AC, S is the firm size, LEV is Leverage, IO is insider ownership, IOUP is the institutional ownership, unrelated parties, IORP is the institutional ownership, related parties and BLOCK is the Outsider ownership (individual) with ownership more than 5%.

Following Kiel and Nicholson (2003) and Darmawati et al. (2004), the CG effectiveness is analysed using Tobin's Q. A value greater than 1, suggests a high market value for the company's asset and growth.

Adapting the methodology of Chung and Pruitt (1994), Tobin's Q is:

Figure 1. Data distribution
Multiple regressions using GLS and a test of the endogenous problem (Durbin Wu-Hausman Test) were conducted (see Table A1 in the Appendix)

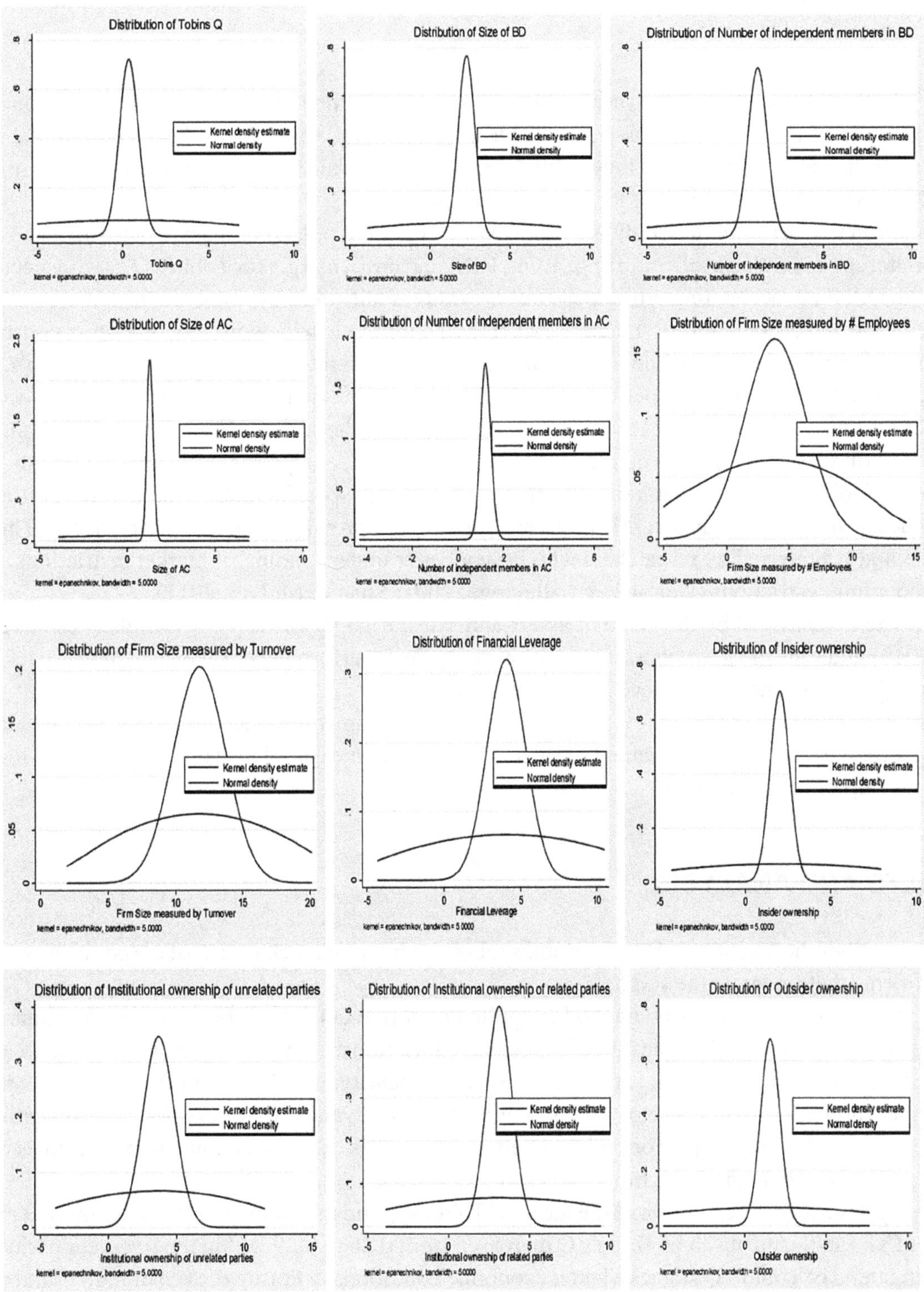

$$Tobin's\,Q = \frac{Market\,Value\,of\,Asset}{Book\,Value\,of\,Asset} = \frac{VCOMS + STDEBT + LTDEBT - ADJ}{TOTASST}$$

Where VCOMS is the price of the firm's common stock multiplied by the number of shares outstanding at the close of the year (December 31), STDEBT is the book value of the firm's current liabilities, LTDEBT is the value of the firm's long-term debt, ADJ is the Value of the firm's net short-term assets and TOTASST is the book value of the firm's total assets.

A question that arises in this study is to know which measure of the company's performance is more appropriate: an accounting profit ratio (e.g., ROE, ROA and profit margin) or Tobin's Q? Two aspects must be considered: First, accounting profit measures are traditionally used by accountants that are restrained by accounting and accountability standards; whereas Tobin's Q is widely used by investors constrained by their perceptions. Second, while accounting profit ratios are retrospective measures; Tobin's Q is a prospective measure of corporate performance. In this context, the first measures are affected by accounting practices and emphasize management achievements; while the second measure reveals the value that investors attribute to a company's tangible and intangible assets, comparing cost flows with cash-flows. The use of Tobin's Q also supports the idea that markets favor specific features on boards, particularly independence and professional qualifications as a means of improving corporate performance. Thus, the latter method is preferred by researchers who have a better understanding of market restrictions, rather than accounting restrictions (Demsetz & Villalonga, 2001; Shan & McIver, 2011).

Firm size is measured by the value of assets and sales, if larger firms possess higher resources (Ho et al., 2019) and thus greater opportunities for a strong firm performance. Likewise, larger sales cause growth and better chances to achieve higher performances.

Bearing in mind the literature review on the internal mechanisms of CG, it is expected that all independent variables are positively related to firm performance (measured by Tobin's Q), except leverage and ownership of related parties.

RESULTS AND ANALYSIS

Table 2 describes the basic statistics of variables related to internal mechanisms of corporate governance in 17 of firms that integrate the PSI20.

The three-sigma rule of thumb method is applied to define outliers. Table 2 shows that none of the variables log-transformed falls outside of 3 standard deviations. As the study employs panel data it is expected that the result will not be affected by multicollinearity, which was confirmed by the application of the Variance Inflation Factor. According to tests, VIF values were less than 10, indicating the absence of a multicollinearity error problem between variables. Thus, all explanatory variables can be used in panel data set at the same time.

Figure 2 describes the evolution of the mean of Tobin's Q and the variables related to internal mechanisms of CG. Firstly, the mean of Tobin's Q increased from 0.26 to 0.29 within the five-year period. The increasing trend of Tobin's Q suggests better economic conditions in Portugal, even though its maximum has decreased from 1.38 in 2014 to 1.09 in 2018. The decreasing trend in the leverage also supports this conclusion. The statistics show that the mean value of leverage decreased from 4.33 in 2015 to 4.03 in 2018 while the maximum leverage also decreased from 5.51 to 5.32 in 2014-2018.

Table 1. Variables, data sources and expected sign

Variable		Expected Sign	Data Source
BDS: Size of BD	Number of members of BD	+	CG Report
IBD: Number of independent members in BD	Number of independent members of BD	+	CG Report
ACS: Size of AC	Number of members of AC	+	CG Report
IDAC: Number of independent members in AC	Number of independent members of AC	+	CG Report
S: Firm Size	Turnover, Number of employees	+	CG Report
LEV: Financial Leverage	Total Liabilities/Total Assets	-	SABI
IO: Insider ownership	Number of individuals inside the company	+	CG Report
IOUP: Institutional ownership, unrelated parties	Number of institutions which have no relationship with the company	+	CG Report
IORP: Institutional ownership, related parties	Number of institutions which have relationship with the company (such as parent or subsidiary companies)	-	CG Report
BLOCK: Outsider ownership > 5%	Number of individuals outside the company with shares >5%	+	CG Report

Table 2. Descriptive Statistics

Variables	Obs	Mean	Std.Dev.	Min	Max	Skew.	Kurt.
Tobin's Q	70	.371	.552	0	1.792	1.058	2.674
Size BD	85	2.294	.52	1.099	3.178	-.537	2.743
# Indep. BD	71	1.293	.558	0	2.996	.128	3.371
Size AC	85	1.304	.176	1.099	1.946	.43	3.521
# Indep. AC	85	1.223	.228	.693	1.609	-.613	3.193
Size (# Employees)	85	3.889	2.47	0	9.308	.888	2.953
Size (Turnover)	79	11.794	1.964	6.962	15.122	-.416	2.554
Leverage	77	4.076	1.245	.693	5.517	-1.24	4.143
Insider Ownership	75	2.045	.565	.693	2.944	-.313	2.04
Unrelated Parties	85	3.69	1.15	1.099	6.516	.238	3.54
Related Parties	85	3.155	.779	1.099	4.511	-.872	3.819
Outsider Ownership	85	1.582	.587	0	2.639	-.236	2.762

Figure 2. Evolution of Tobin's q, firm size and ownership, 2014-2018
Notes- values in logs. Source: Authors' elaboration based on data from SABI database.

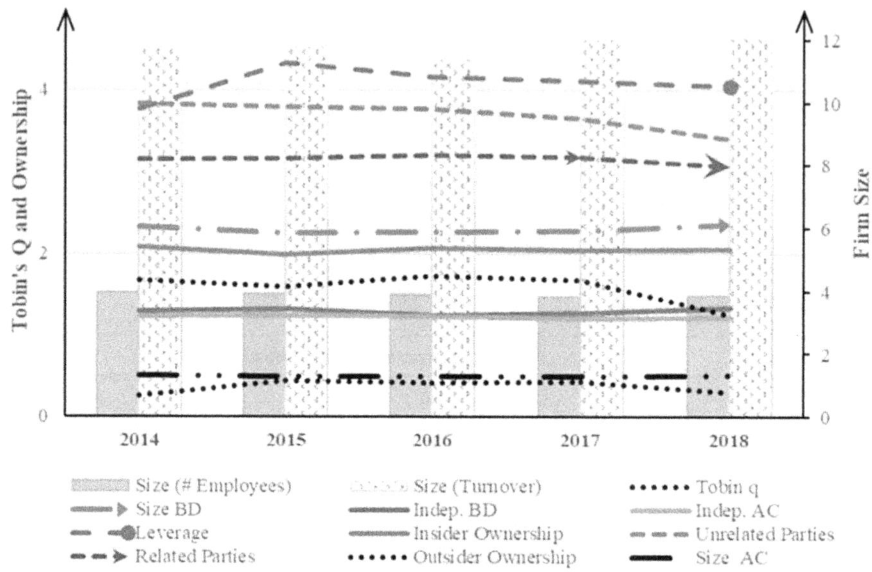

Regarding the ownership of the 17 of PSI20 companies, it was mainly composed of unrelated parties, i.e., with no business relationship with the company, although the average share of ownership of this type of institutions decreased from 90% to 76% in 2014-2018. Similarly, the average share of ownership of institution that had business relationships with the company (related parties) decreased from 30% to 26% in the same period. In addition, whereas insider ownership remained stable, the outsider ownership experienced an uneven evolution, decreasing in the last two years.

Concerning the Board of Directors and the Audit Committee, the size of BD and AC remained steady over the period 2014-2018. The number of independent members of the BD is roughly the same as the one concerning AC, and both remained stable around an average of 4, in the period analyzed. The share of independent members of BD is on average 36% while in the AC, around 94% of the members are independent. The average value for the variables that proxy company size (# employees and turnover) remained stables in the five-year period, respectively around 4 and 12. Overall, the figures related to board governance of the Portuguese companies show that most of the companies complied with the best practice. However, there are still companies that did not have any independent members of Board of directors, despite the requirement of corporate governance regulations.

Using the Generalized Least Square estimator in Stata 13.0 the results are shown in Table 3. The R-square in Table 3 of the model indicates that 77.47% of variance in company performance can be explained by the model.

Table 3. Regression results using GLS for the whole sample, 2014-2018

Size BD	-0.469
	(-0.97)
# Indep. BD	0.231
	(0.98)
Size AC	1.332*
	(2.42)
# Indep. AC	-0.711
	(-1.84)
Size (# Employees)	0.0373
	(0.69)
Size (Turnover)	0.0699
	(1.13)
Leverage	-0.373***
	(-4.93)
Insider Ownership	0.170
	(0.52)
Unrelated Parties	0.0990
	(1.08)
Related Parties	0.111
	(1.09)
Outsider Ownership	-0.280*
	(-2.04)
_cons	0.368
	(0.27)
N	46

Notes- Statistics in parentheses * $p<0.05$, ** $p<0.01$, *** $p<0.001$
Furthermore, with the acceptance of a significant level of 5%, the F-statistic suggests the overall model is significant ($P<0.05$).

Turning to the significance of each independent variable, the t-statistic suggests that the size of Audit Committee, leverage and outsider ownership with more that 5% are significant in explaining companies' performance proxied by Tobin's Q. In particular 1% increase in size of AC increases company performance by 1.3% ($p<0.05$), confirming H3.

The hypothesis H5 is also confirmed, 1% increase in leverage decreases Tobin's Q by nearly 0.4% ($p<0.001$). Furthermore, 1% increase in outsider ownership, with more that 5%, decreases company performance by 0.3% ($p<0.05$). The impact of the remaining variables is not significant on Tobin's Q.

The analysis of Table 4 shows that in group 1 (holding companies operating in paper, cork, telecommunications and IT sectors) the only significant impact on companies' performance is from ownership of related parties. In particular, and contrary to what was expected, 1% increase in ownership of related parties increases Tobin's Q in 0.9% ($p<0.01$).

Table 4. Results by groups of sectors using GLS for 2014-2018

	Group 1	Group 2
Size BD	-1.284	0.290
	(-0.91)	(0.61)
# Indep. BD	0.204	-0.335
	(0.36)	(-1.24)
Size AC	-0.308	0.374
	(-0.34)	(1.04)
# Indep. AC	0.301	-2.268***
	(0.45)	(-7.60)
Size (# Employees)	-0.247	0.0965**
	(-1.48)	(2.92)
Size (Turnover)	-0.0588	-0.0404
	(-0.63)	(-0.98)
Leverage	-0.468	-0.227***
	(-0.86)	(-4.45)
Insider Ownership	0.179	-0.148
	(0.25)	(-0.51)
Unrelated Parties	0.0625	-0.197**
	(0.12)	(-2.89)
Related Parties	0.927**	0.275***
	(2.65)	(4.04)
Outsider Ownership	-0.276	-0.0650
	(-1.11)	(-0.72)
_cons	2.738	3.789***
	(1.16)	(4.31)
N	17	29

Notes- Statistics in parentheses * $p<0.05$, ** $p<0.01$, *** $p<0.001$

However, in group 2 (holding companies operating in energy, trade and banking sectors) there are several internal mechanisms of CG that impact significantly and positively on companies' performance, namely the ownership of related parties (0.3; $p<0.01$). Therefore, hypothesis H9 does not hold. Control variable, firm size (measured by the number of employees) has a significantly positive (0.1, $p<0.01$) effect on corporate performance of companies operating in services (Group 2).

Other CG mechanisms impact negatively and significantly on Group 2 performance, such as the number of independent members of AC (-2.3, $p<0.01$), leverage (-0.2, $p<0.01$) and ownership of unrelated parties (-0.197, $p<0.01$). In this case, hypothesis H5 is confirmed, but H4 and H6 do not hold. Thus, companies in the services sector should restrain the number of independent members of AC and reduce leverage as well as ownership of unrelated parties.

In order to test the homogeneity / heterogeneity between the 2 groups of industries, we use in the same regression an interaction term Z that assumes value 0 in group 1 and value 1 in group 2. The results are now shown in Table 5.

Table 5. Results by groups of sectors using GLS with interaction between groups, 2014-2018

	Group 1	Group 2
Size BD	-1.500	1.865
	(-1.81)	(1.95)
# Indep. BD	0.152	-0.509
	(0.43)	(-1.03)
Size AC	-0.417	0.878
	(-0.74)	(1.34)
# Indep. AC	0.319	-2.532***
	(0.74)	(-4.45)
Size (# Employees)	-0.240*	0.333**
	(-2.22)	(2.89)
Size (Turnover)	-0.0735	0.0416
	(-1.33)	(0.61)
Leverage	-0.514	0.281
	(-1.49)	(0.80)
Insider Ownership	0.250	-0.441
	(0.55)	(-0.79)
Unrelated Parties	0.117	-0.305
	(0.34)	(-0.86)
Related Parties	0.915***	-0.642**
	(4.03)	(-2.65)
Outsider Ownership	-0.271	0.216
	(-1.68)	(1.10)
_cons		3.437***
		(3.85)

Notes- N=46. Statistics in parentheses * $p<0.05$, ** $p<0.01$, *** $p<0.001$

These results (i.e, regression models with different intercepts and slopes) suggest that the two groups of companies are heterogeneous.

Considering that corporate performance (measured by Tobin's q) is 3.437 in the absence of the internal CG mechanisms for group 2 of companies and zero for group 1, it appears that group 2 shows a better performance. On the other hand, the effects of the number of independent members in the AC (-2,532, $p <0.001$) and the number of related parties (-0,642, $p <0.01$), on the performance of group 2 of companies, are significantly negative; while in group 1, the impact of related parties (0.915, $p <0.001$)

on corporate performance is significantly positive. Hence, the hypothesis H4 does not hold and H9 holds only for companies in Group 2. The remaining hypotheses do not hold.

Company size (measured by the number of employees) has a significant effect on corporate performance in both groups. However, in Group 1, the impact is negative (-0.240, p <0.05) and it is positive (0.333, p <0.01) in group 2.

To sum-up, the interaction of the 2 groups of companies reveal that: in the manufacturing industry the internal mechanisms of CG appear to be more important to increase the value of the firms, when compared to the performance of firms operating in services. In the manufacturing, smaller firms (i.e, with a lower number of employees) appear to increase more their value than larger firms; while in services, companies employing more workers have more opportunities to increase their value. It appears that AC in companies operating in the services sector should have a small number of independent members in order to maximize the value of the companies. In manufacturing, ownership of related parties is beneficial to companies in the sense that help to increase the value of the firms. However, this kind of ownership appears to be harmful in the case of the services sector.

Comparing the results of table 5 (whole sample with interaction between groups) with Table 3 (whole sample with no interaction), the results on the significant negative impact of leverage on corporate performance are confirmed. On the other hand, the cross- analysis of tables 5 and 4 (separate regressions for groups 1 and 2), the significance and sign of the impacts of the number of independent members in the AC and firm size (measured by the number pf employees) on corporate performance of firms in Group 2 are confirmed. However, the model with group interactions shows a much lower magnitude for the impact of firm size. Also, the impact of ownership from Related Parties on corporate performance of Group 1 is confirmed. On the other hand, the sign of the impact of this mechanism on corporate performance of Group 2 is now the opposite, turning positive.

Discussion- Results for the whole sample confirm the expected sign and significance of the impacts of AC size and leverage on corporate performance. Positive impacts are due to the size of AC (in line with the studies of Jaafar & El Shawa, 2009; and Omware & Jagongo, 2020), company size (measured by the number of employees) and ownership of related parties; while mechanisms with negative impact on firm performance are leverage, and ownership of unrelated parties and outsiders with shares over 5% as well as the number of independent members of AC.

The findings do not support the study of DeZoort et al. (2002) ssuggesting an independent AC increases the effectiveness of the role of the AC, leading to better company performance.

The analysis by groups of firms only confirms the expected sign for the impact of leverage. This last result means that firms with higher debt-to-equity ratios experience greater difficulties to deliver higher profits and, thus, show a worse performance when compared to firms less leveraged. Two reasons can explain these results. First, high leverage may decrease demand for the firm's products and/or increase production costs, as stakeholders' expectations towards firm's viability are adversely affected (Merika et al., 2007). Moreover, the CG of highly leveraged firms may be affected by aggressive business strategies of less leveraged competitors (Bolton & Scharfstein, 1990). The results for leverage contradict the studies of Khan et al (2019) and Vijayakumaran and Vijayakumaran (2019) who found a positive association between leverage and firm performance.

Regarding the role of board size and the number of its independent members, this analysis could not find significant evidence to support the theory suggesting that BD (size and independence) are determinant factors of company performance.

Previous studies (Adams & Mehran, 2005; Kula, 2005), also failed to detect the relationship between board size and company performance. In addition, this study could not find evidence of the role of firm size (measured by turnover) and insider ownership on companies' performance. Results are not significant and mixed.

Finally, the study suggests that in Portuguese case, the ownership of related parties is more effective in increasing companies' performance than the ownership of unrelated parties and outsiders. These results find some support in the work of Seddon (2019) which suggests that management ownership raises the management's sense of belonging to the company which stimulates the managers to run the company optimally. This idea could be also extensive to related parties.

The results on the negative impact of unrelated parties and outsiders' ownership contradicts the conclusions of Dau et al. (2020) arguing that ownership of independent institutions and individuals ensure management to perform in the best interest of the shareholders and, thus, may contribute to better monitoring, increase output and firms' value.

CONCLUDING REMARKS AND IMPLICATIONS

The scandals of the financial sector in Portugal as well as the financial crisis, showed the weaknesses of internal control, supervisory bodies and external audit. Thus, CG models must be more effective regarding internal control structures, management and supervisory bodies.

In addition, literature review raises questions about the real effectiveness of some control mechanisms (Alves & Mendes, 2003), because some measures appear to exert an opposite effect on the corporate performance. Indeed, results of previous studies that analyze the impact of CG on corporate performance are mixed due to differences in definitions, measures of variables and periods of analysis, which suggests the needs for further investigation (Shank et al., 2013; Steigenberger, 2014).

In the first part of this chapter, CG practices in Portuguese companies was analyzed and literature of internal mechanisms of corporate governance was presented. The results point that Portuguese listed companies are increasingly aware of the need to comply with the good CG practices.

Subsequently, this chapter tested whether there is a significant relationship between internal CG mechanisms and PSI20 companies' performance in Portugal. The results suggest that, among the internal mechanisms of CG analyzed, the size of the AC is the main determinant factor of companies' performance that has a positive impact. Indeed, a 1% increase in the size of the AC increases Tobin's Q in 1.3%. By contrast, the independent members of the AC are the main factor that impacts negatively and significantly on companies' performance, a 1% increase in the number of independent members decreases Tobin's Q in 2.3%. The ownership of related parties is also an important internal mechanism of CG that impacts on corporate performance. Firm size measured by the number of employees is also found to impact significantly on corporate performance.

Concerning the role of board size and the number of independent members, this analysis could not find significant evidence to support the theory suggesting that BD (size and independence) are determinant factors of company performance. Also, the study could not find evidence of the role of firm size (measured by turnover) and insider ownership on companies' performance.

Regarding implications, the implementation of other internal CG mechanisms, namely the ownership of related parties, would contribute to the valuation of companies, especially those related to the manufacturing industry that integrate the PSI20 index.

In the services sector, one way to increase the company's value is to reduce the number of independent AC members. Although the analysis suggests that there was an increasing responsiveness of companies to comply with good CG practices; nevertheless, it was found that there are still a few companies which do not have independent commissioners. Since the code for CG practices is compulsory for listed companies, it is regulators' responsibility in imposing the regulations in order to increase the market confidence. However, in the current framework of general concern about the stability of the financial system, an emerging question is whether the (optimal) CG principles for non-financial companies should be extended to financial companies. This becomes relevant in a context of different challenges and limitations according to the nature of the companies, that is, financial and non-financial. First, traditionally, the focus of CG is on "equity governance", that is, conflicts of interest between owners and managers and / or between majority and minority shareholders (Dewatripont & Tirole, 1994). At stake is the monitoring structure for conflicting interests. This can, nevertheless, constitute a very limiting view for financial companies whose demand for financing efficiently faces agency distortions (Heremans, 2007). Second, in financial companies, due to the opacity of the accounting items, there is a greater likelihood of information asymmetry that results in a management control bias translated into the difficulty in monitoring the behaviour of managers. In addition, in the context of systemic externalities (e.g., external shocks that lead to increased risks) that raise special concerns about the solvency and stability of financial companies, many debtors are not monitoring experts. On the contrary, in non-financial companies, creditors are often financial companies themselves who have the experience and power to monitor debtors. Thirdly, especially in financial companies, where product opacity exists, majority shareholders may have the incentive and power to transfer wealth to other members, thus abusing small (more dispersed) shareholders. Fourthly, shareholders have an incentive to take the company to take excessive risks, with the expectation of earning marginal returns. This moral hazard problem is more serious in financial companies because there the high proportion of debt in total liabilities and, therefore, the high leverage, facilitate the transfer of risk by shareholders (Tirole, 2006).

These findings contribute to the literature and the understanding of the influence of AC attributes such as size on the corporate performance. Furthermore, this study provides managers, stakeholders and policy makers with a better understanding of the various features of the AC that could be incorporated in future policy formulation in order to safeguard investments and protect the interest of various stakeholders and enhance the flow of capital and foreign direct investment into companies and the economy in general.

Overall, and since that sectoral performance is heterogeneous, this chapter provides significant insights for the understanding of the relationships between internal mechanisms of CG and firm performance in Portugal, by focusing on the internal mechanisms and comparing the results across groups of sectors.

Regarding l*imitations and future research,* the study focused only on 17 companies listed on PSI20, therefore its conclusions cannot be generalized to other companies operating in Portugal.

The attributes examined include size and independence of BD and AC, leverage and ownership. Future studies could examine other attributes such as the number of meetings and the internal process of the AC, as well as personal characteristics of the directors. Furthermore, the study used secondary data while future studies could use primary data or a combination of primary and secondary data. The study only examined the period 2014-2018, while future research could focus on the impact of CG on corporate performance in recent years. Finally, since CG practices focus on formal mechanisms (for example, legislation), they are considered as the part of the organizational structure that is publicly exposed (Thomsen & Conyon, 2012). However, formal mechanisms are sometimes less important in the process of implementing good KM practices, since most intra-organizational behaviors are influenced by informal mechanisms (for example, social norms, ethics and company reputation).Future avenues of research could include the analysis of the impact of informal mechanisms of CG on corporate performance.

ACKNOWLEDGMENT

This research is financed by National Funds of the FCT – Portuguese Foundation for Science and Technology within the project «UIDB/04928/2020».

REFERENCES

Abatino, B., & Dari-Mattiacci, G. (2020). Agency problems and organizational costs in slave-run businesses. *Roman Law and Economics: Institutions and Organizations, I*, 23. doi:10.1093/oso/9780198787204.003.0010

Abe, P. O., Ajayi-Owoeye, A. E., & Adegbie, F. F. (2020). IFRS Disclosures and Protection of Shareholders' Interests in Nigerian Quoted Firms. *European Journal of Business and Management Research, 5*(5). Advance online publication. doi:10.24018/ejbmr.2020.5.5.579

Adams, R. B., & Mehran, H. (2005, August). Corporate performance, board structure and its determinants in the banking industry. *EFA 2005 Moscow Meetings*. 10.2139srn.302593

Agrawal, A., & Nasser, T. (2019). Blockholders on boards and CEO compensation, turnover and firm valuation. *Quarterly Journal of Finance, 9*(3). doi:10.1142/S2010139219500101

Aiello, F., Pupo, V., & Ricotta, F. (2015). Firm Heterogeneity in TFP, sectoral innovation and location. Evidence from Italy. *International Review of Applied Economics, 29*(5), 579–607. doi:10.1080/02692171.2015.1016408

Al-Matari, Y. A., Al-Swidi, A. K., & Bt Fadzil, F. H. (2012). Audit committee effectiveness and performance of Saudi Arabia listed companies. *Wulfenia Journal, 19*(8), 169–188.

Bauer, R., Eichholtz, P., & Kok, N. (2009). Corporate governance and performance: The Reit Effect. *Financial Management, 38*(1), 1–29.

Beasley, M., Carcello, J., Hermanson, D., & Neal, T. (2009). The audit committee oversight process. *Contemporary Accounting Research, 1*(1), 65–122. doi:10.1506/car.26.1.3

Bernard, A. B., Jensen, J. B., Redding, S. J., & Schott, P. K. (2012). The empirics of firm heterogeneity and international trade. *Annual Review of Economics, 4*(1), 283–313. doi:10.1146/annurev-economics-080511-110928

Bolton, P., & Scharfstein, D. S. (1990). A theory of predation based on agency problems in financial contracting. *The American Economic Review*, 93–106.

Borah, N., James, H. L., & Park, J. C. (2020). Does CEO inside debt compensation benefit both shareholders and debtholders? *Review of Quantitative Finance and Accounting, 54*(1), 159–203. doi:10.100711156-018-00786-0

Braiotta, L. Jr. (2000). Advice on Audit Committees. *Internal Auditor*, *57*(1), 19–19.

Carlson, C., & Bussin, M. H. (2020). Relationship between executive pay and company financial performance in South African state-owned entities. *SA Journal of Human Resource Management*, *18*, 11. doi:10.4102ajhrm.v18i0.1211

Chaghadari, M. F., & Chaleshtori, G. N. (2011). *Corporate Governance and Firm Performance*. Paper presented at the International Conference on Sociality and Economics Development, Singapore.

CMVM. (2013). *Relatório Anual sobre o Governo das Sociedades Cotadas em Portugal 2012. Comissão do Mercado de Valores Mobiliários*. Lisboa: CMVM. http://www.cmvm.pt/CMVM/Estudos/Em%20Arquivo/Documents/RGS_2012.pdf

Crossan, K. (2011). The effects of a separation of ownership from control on UK listed firms: An empirical analysis. *Managerial and Decision Economics*, *32*(5), 293–304. doi:10.1002/mde.1535

Dalton, D., Daily, C., Certo, S., & Roengpitya, R. (2003). Metaanalysis of financial performance and equity: Fusion or confusion? *Academy of Management Journal*, *46*(1), 13–26. doi:10.5465/30040673

Danoshana, S., & Ravivathani, T. (2019). The impact of the corporate governance on firm performance: A study on financial institutions in Sri Lanka. *SAARJ Journal on Banking & Insurance Research*, *8*(1), 62–67. doi:10.5958/2319-1422.2019.00004.3

Darmawati, D., Khomsiyah, K., & Rahayu, R. G. (2004). *Hubungan Corporate Governance dan Kinerja Perusahaan*. Simposium Nasonal Akuntansi VII Denpasar Bali.

Dau, L. A., Moore, E. M., & Kostova, T. (2020). The impact of market based institutional reforms on firm strategy and performance. Review and extension. *Journal of World Business*, *55*(4), 101073. doi:10.1016/j.jwb.2020.101073

DeAndreas, P., Azofra, V., & Lopez, F. (2005). Corporate Boards in OECD Countries: Size, Composition, Functioning and Effectiveness. *Corporate Governance*, *13*(2), 197–210. doi:10.1111/j.1467-8683.2005.00418.x

Dewatripont, M., & Tirole, J. (1994). *The Prudential Regulation of Banks*. MIT Press.

Dewi, R. S. (2020). The Application of Good Corporate Governance (GCG) Through the Implementation of Quality Management System At PT. CS. *Journal of Accounting and Finance Management*, *1*(1), 24–37. doi:10.38035/jafm.v1i1.8

DeZoort, F. T., Hermanson, D. R., Archambeault, D. S., & Reed, S. A. (2002). Audit Committee Effectiveness: A Synthesis of the Empirical Audit Committee Literature. *Journal of Accounting Literature*, *21*, 38–75.

Dhaliwal, D., Naiker, V., & Navissi, F. (2010). The Association Between Accruals Quality and the Characteristics of Accounting Experts and Mix of Expertise on Audit Committees. *Contemporary Accounting Research*, *27*(3), 787–827. doi:10.1111/j.1911-3846.2010.01027.x

Duru, A., Iyengar, R. J., & Zampelli, E. M. (2016). The dynamic relationship between CEO duality and firm performance: The moderating role of board independence. *Journal of Business Research*, *69*(10), 4269–4277. doi:10.1016/j.jbusres.2016.04.001

Fahlenbrach, R., & Stulz, R. M. (2009). Managerial ownership dynamics and firm value. *Journal of Financial Economics*, *92*(3), 342–361. doi:10.1016/j.jfineco.2008.06.005

Fama, E. F. (1980). Agency problems and the theory of the firm. *Journal of Political Economy*, *88*(2), 288–307. doi:10.1086/260866

Fama, E. F., & Jensen, M. C. (1983). Separation of ownership and control. *The Journal of Law & Economics*, *26*(2), 301–325. doi:10.1086/467037

Ferdinand, R., & Santosa, S. (2019). Factors that Influence Fraudulent Financial Statements in Retail Companies-Indonesia. *Journal of Applied Accounting and Finance*, *2*(2), 99–109. doi:10.33021/jaaf.v2i2.548

García-Ramos, R., & García-Olalla, M. (2011). Board characteristics and firm performance in public founder-and nonfounder-led family businesses. *Journal of Family Business Strategy*, *2*(4), 220–231. doi:10.1016/j.jfbs.2011.09.001

Heenetigala, K., & Armstrong, A. (2011). The impact of corporate governance on firm performance in an unstable economic and political environment: Evidence from Sri Lanka. *Conference on financial markets and corporate governance, 13*, 1-17.

Heidrick & Struggles. (2003), Is Your Board Fit for the Global Challenge? Third annual survey conducted by Heidrick & Struggles. Chicago, IL: Academic Press.

HeremansD. (2007). Corporate governance issues for banks: a financial stability perspective. doi:10.2139srn.1024693

Ho, F. N., Wang, H. M. D., Ho-Dac, N., & Vitell, S. J. (2019). Nature and relationship between corporate social performance and firm size: A cross-national study. *Social Responsibility Journal*, *15*(2), 258–274. doi:10.1108/SRJ-02-2017-0025

Hussain, H. I., Ali, A., Thaker, H. M. T., & Ali, M. (2019). Firm Performance and Family Related Directors: Empirical Evidence from an Emerging Market. *Contemporary Economics*, *13*(2), 187–204.

Iwu-Egwuonwu, D., & Chibuike, R. (2012). Does Corporate Governance Enhance Firm Performance? An Empirical Literature Evidence. *Romanian Statistical Review Supplement*, *60*(1), 53–56.

Jaafar, A., & El-Shawa, M. (2009). Ownership concentration, board characteristics and performance: Evidence from Jordan. *Research in Accounting in Emerging Economies*, *9*, 73–95. doi:10.1108/S1479-3563(2009)0000009005

Jensen, M. C., & Meckling, W. H. (1976). Theory of the firm: Managerial behavior, agency costs and ownership structure. *Journal of Financial Economics*, *3*(4), 305–360. doi:10.1016/0304-405X(76)90026-X

Kajola, S. O. (2008). Corporate governance and firm performance: The case of Nigerian listed firms. European Journal of Economics. *Finance and Administrative Sciences*, *14*(14), 16–28.

Karamanou, I., & Vafeas, N. (2005). The association between corporate boards, audit committees, and management earnings forecasts: An empirical analysis. *Journal of Accounting Research*, *43*(3), 453–486. doi:10.1111/j.1475-679X.2005.00177.x

Khan, S. N., Yaseen, M. N., Mustafa, F., & Abbasi, S. (2019). The Interaction Effect of Financial Leverage on the Relationship Between Board Attributes and Firm Performance; Evidence of Non-financial Listed Companies of Pakistan. *Journal of Accounting and Finance in Emerging Economies*, *5*(1), 115–122. doi:10.26710/jafee.v5i1.681

Kiel, G. C., & Nicholson, G. J. (2003). Board composition and corporate performance: How the Australian experience informs contrasting theories of corporate governance. *Corporate Governance*, *11*(3), 189–205. doi:10.1111/1467-8683.00318

Kouloukoui, D., de Oliveira Marinho, M. M., da Silva Gomes, S. M., de Jong, P., Kiperstok, A., & Torres, E. A. (2020). The impact of the board of directors on business climate change management: Case of Brazilian companies. *Mitigation and Adaptation Strategies for Global Change*, *25*(1), 127–147. doi:10.100711027-019-09864-7

Krishnan, J. (2005). Audit committee quality and internal control: An empirical analysis. *The Accounting Review*, *80*(2), 649–675. doi:10.2308/accr.2005.80.2.649

Kula, V. (2005). The impact of the roles, structure and process of boards on firm performance: Evidence from Turkey. *Corporate Governance*, *13*(2), 265–276. doi:10.1111/j.1467-8683.2005.00421.x

Lal, P. (2019). Agency costs, corporate governance and the Fiji Sugar Corporation. *Pacific Economic Bulletin*, *21*(2), 70–93.

Li, S., Fu, H., Wen, J., & Chang, C. P. (2020). Separation of ownership and control for Chinese listed firms: Effect on the cost of debt and the moderating role of bank competition. *Journal of Asian Economics*, *67*, 101179. doi:10.1016/j.asieco.2020.101179

LiZ. F.PatelS.RamaniS. (2019). The role of mutual funds in corporate social responsibility. doi:10.2139srn.3366100

Marzuki, M. M., Haji-Abdullah, N. M., Othman, R., Abdul Wahab, E. A., & Harymawan, I. (2019). Audit committee characteristics, board diversity, and fraudulent financial reporting in Malaysia. *Asian Academy of Management Journal*, *24*(2), 143–167. doi:10.21315/aamj2019.24.2.7

Merika, A., Syriopoulos, T., & Negakis, C. (2007). Highly leveraged firms and corporate performance in distressed industries. European Journal of Economics. *Finance and Administrative Sciences*, *8*, 93–101.

Mertzanis, C., Basuony, M. A., & Mohamed, E. K. (2019). Social institutions, corporate governance and firm-performance in the MENA region. *Research in International Business and Finance*, *48*, 75–96. doi:10.1016/j.ribaf.2018.12.005

Mishra, S., & Dasgupta, R. (2019). Cross-impact of leverage and firm performance: Developed vs frontier bank-based economies. *Managerial Finance*, *45*(8), 982–1000. doi:10.1108/MF-09-2018-0435

Morck, R., & Yeung, B. (2003). Agency problems in large family business groups. *Entrepreneurship Theory and Practice*, *27*(4), 367–382. doi:10.1111/1540-8520.t01-1-00015

Musau, V. M., Waititu, A. G., & Wanjoya, A. K. (2015). Modeling panel data: Comparison of GLS estimation and robust covariance matrix estimation. *American Journal of Theoretical and Applied Statistics*, *4*(3), 185–191. doi:10.11648/j.ajtas.20150403.25

Musteen, M., Datta, D. K., & Kemmerer, B. (2010). Corporate reputation: Do board characteristics matter? *British Journal of Management*, *21*(2), 498–510.

Nuber, C., Velte, P., & Hörisch, J. (2020). The curvilinear and time-lagging impact of sustainability performance on financial performance: Evidence from Germany. *Corporate Social Responsibility and Environmental Management*, *27*(1), 232–243. doi:10.1002/csr.1795

Obiyo, O. C., & Lenee, L. T. (2011). Corporate governance and firm performance in Nigeria. *IJEMR*, *1*(4), 1–12.

Oh, W. Y., Chang, Y. K., & Jung, R. (2019). Board characteristics and corporate social responsibility: Does family involvement in management matter? *Journal of Business Research*, *103*, 23–33. doi:10.1016/j.jbusres.2019.05.028

Omware, I. M., Atheru, G., & Jagongo, A. (2020). Corporate governance and financial performance of selected commercial banks listed at Nairobi Securities Exchange in Kenya. *International Academic Journal of Economics and Finance*, *3*(5), 75–91.

Reddy, K., Locke, S., & Scrimgeour, F. (2010). The efficacy of principle-based corporate governance practices and firm financial performance: An empirical investigation. *International Journal of Managerial Finance*, *6*(3), 190–219. doi:10.1108/17439131011056224

Reed, W. R., & Ye, H. (2011). Which panel data estimator should I use? *Applied Economics*, *43*(8), 985–1000. doi:10.1080/00036840802600087

Rodrigues, E. N. (2012). *Corporate Governance: A Relação entre As Características do Conselho de Administração e o Desempenho das Empresas na Euronext Lisbon* (Doctoral dissertation). Instituto Superior de Economia e Gestão.

Sarkar, J., & Sarkar, S. (2008). Debt and corporate governance in emerging economies Evidence from India 1. *Economics of Transition*, *16*(2), 293–334. doi:10.1111/j.1468-0351.2008.00307.x

Sauerwald, S., Heugens, P. P., Turturea, R., & Van Essen, M. (2019). Are all private benefits of control ineffective? Principal–Principal benefits, external governance quality, and firm performance. *Journal of Management Studies*, *56*(4), 725–757. doi:10.1111/joms.12420

Schulze, W. S., Lubatkin, M. H., Dino, R. N., & Buchholtz, A. K. (2001). Agency relationships in family firms: Theory and evidence. *Organization Science*, *12*(2), 99–116. doi:10.1287/orsc.12.2.99.10114

Shao, L. (2019). Dynamic study of corporate governance structure and firm performance in China. *Chinese Management Studies*, *13*(2), 299–317. doi:10.1108/CMS-08-2017-0217

Suntraruk, P. (2013). An empirical analysis on the association between corporate governance rating and firms' characteristics: Evidence from MAI Thailand. *International Journal of Academic Research in Business & Social Sciences*, *3*(12), 732–744. doi:10.6007/IJARBSS/v3-i12/488

Thomsen, S., & Conyon, M. (2012). Stakeholder governance in Scandinavia. In S. Thomsen & M. Conyon (Eds.), *Corporate Governance: Mechanisms and Systems*. McGraw Hill.

Tierno, M. V. (2014). *Corporate governance and portuguese listed companies' performance* (Doctoral dissertation). Instituto Superior de Economia e Gestão.

Tirole, J. (2006). *The Theory of Corporate Finance*. Princeton University Press.

Van den Berghe, L. A., & Levrau, A. (2004). Evaluating boards of directors: What constitutes a good corporate board? *Corporate Governance*, *12*(4), 461–478. doi:10.1111/j.1467-8683.2004.00387.x

Vijayakumaran, S., & Vijayakumaran, R. (2019). Corporate governance and capital structure decisions: Evidence from Chinese listed companies. Journal of Asian Finance. *Economics and Business*, *6*(3), 67–79.

Vo, D., & Phan, T. (2013). Corporate governance and firm performance: Empirical evidence from Vietnam. *Journal of Economic Development*, *7*(1), 62–78.

Yoo, S. W., Lee, G., Shin, J. E., & Kim, J. (2020). Firm performance and the adoption of a co-CEO structure: Evidence from Korea. *Asia Pacific Journal of Management*, 1–18. doi:10.100710490-020-09713-1

Zaid, M. A., Abuhijleh, S. T., & Pucheta-Martínez, M. C. (2020). Ownership structure, stakeholder engagement, and corporate social responsibility policies: The moderating effect of board independence. *Corporate Social Responsibility and Environmental Management*, *27*(3), 1344–1360. doi:10.1002/csr.1888

KEY TERMS AND DEFINITIONS

Agency Cost: Agency costs correspond to an internal expense of the company, resulting from wrong or ineffective actions by an internal agent.

Agency Problem: The agency problem results from a conflict-of-interest characteristic of any relationship where one of the parties acts to maximize its benefit.

Audit Committee: Internal governance mechanism.

Board of Directors: Internal governance mechanism.

Corporate Governance Report: Corporate governance reports provide guidelines that guarantee stakeholders that companies are committed to good corporate governance and that they comply with all applicable laws and regulations.

Corporate Performance: Corresponds to the correct execution of administrative, financial and market functions, reflecting on the company's financial performance.

Financial Company: Corresponds to an institution or organization that provides loans to individuals and companies.

Firm Size: Company size measured in number of employees.

Independent Member: Member who does not have a relevant relationship with the company, is not part of its team, nor participates in the day-to-day of the company.

Insider Ownership: Corresponds to the total number of shares held by insiders (shareholders who own more than 5% of the corporation or an executive or director of the company) divided by the total number of shares outstanding.

Internal Mechanism: Corporate or inner mechanism.

Related Party: Person or entity that is related to the reporting entity.
Unrelated Party: Person or entity that is not related to the reporting entity.

APPENDIX

Table 6. DWH Test results

Variable	Coefficient	t-Statistics	p-Value
Size BD	.3562147	1.17	0.176
# Indep. BD	.4831822	1.31	0.184
Size AC	.1343853	3.52	0.016
# Indep. AC	.7541365	1.28	0.195
Size (# Employees)	.2898246	2.63	0.013
Size (Turnover)	.6315431	1.15	0.168
Leverage	-.3780452	-2.63	0.013
Insider Ownership	.4813427	1.35	0.183
Unrelated Parties	.4783489	2.63	0.019
Related Parties	.8349457	2.71	0.013
Outsider Ownership	-.6361649	-1.35	0.179

Notes-Variables in logs. Source: Own analysis in STATA 13.0.

Chapter 12
Corporate Governance Mechanisms and Firm Performance in a Young Stock Exchange:
The Case of I&M Bank, Rwanda

Pierre Sindambiwe
University of Rwanda, Rwanda

Samuel Mutarindwa
University of Rwanda, Rwanda

ABSTRACT

This chapter aimed at assessing the contribution of a bank's listing to its governance and performance. Using a single case study, it collected data on bank governance, performance, and stability over the period 2009-18. Findings show that listing improved I&M Bank's internal governance in particular soon after it listed on the Rwanda Stock Exchange in 2008. Its board's independence, size, and ownership showed significant changes soon after it listed and listing improved its performance as well as stability through governance. A change in both the board's size and independence significantly reduced the bank's non-performing loans and increased the bank's resilience (Z-score) and lending.

INTRODUCTION

With a case of a young stock market in a developing country context, this study contributes to the debate on corporate governance by exploring how listing either constrains or improves the corporate governance mechanisms, as well as their effects on a firm's performance. The chapter sheds light on the changes happening in the governance and performance of a bank during its earlier stages of listing. By focusing on a specific case of a bank in Rwanda, the chapter understands how corporate governance mechanisms

DOI: 10.4018/978-1-7998-7596-3.ch012

change with listing requirements on a young stock market. I&M Bank listed on the stock exchange which too is in its infancy in Rwanda. Therefore, the bank did not have any benchmark in the country. All financial institutions must comply with the external corporate governance policy imposed by the Central Bank. However, a successful listing requires additional governance policies specific to the listing process. Therefore, a listing firm has more pressure from the stock exchange if it wants to list. Coping with external pressures of complying with the Central Bank's policies and internal pressures to meet stock market governance requirements may bring changes in internal corporate governance mechanisms leading to an impact on a firm's performance and stability. This paper focuses on changes in corporate governance mechanisms as a result of complying with listing requirements.

It is known that firms, banks, and countries adopt corporate governance mechanisms in response to pressures from international markets and inter-governmental organizations, mostly channeled through reforms imposed by the World Bank (Adu-Amoah, Tsamenyi & Mensah Onumah, 2008; Chanda, Burton & Dunne, 2017; Kun Liew, 2008; Jain, Aguilera & Jamali, 2017). Therefore, banks establish and improve their governance mechanisms as a response to external pressures. Further, in developing countries, extant corporate mechanisms are imposed by different bodies which were adopted from western governance systems for improving the working environment of local firms and regulators (Tsamenyi & Uddin, 2008). It is also known that for a young stock market, listing firms must comply with certain corporate governance mechanisms established by the stock market. For the sake of staying on the stock market, newly listed firms make more efforts to comply with the stock market's corporate governance requirements. In such a situation instead of responding to external pressures to comply with certain corporate governance mechanisms, firms try and improve their corporate governance mechanisms to be accepted on a stock market and for continuing to operate on the stock market. These corporate governance mechanisms are not only external to a firm's usual practices but are also new to both the country and the firm since the stock market is new in the countery, Rwanda. This is problematic because literature shows that corporate governance mechanisms are normally embedded within a country's social-political system (Alawattage & Wickramasinghe, 2008; Mahadeo, Soobaroyen & Hanuman, 2012). Moreover, less developed countries operate under structural conditions which are very different from those in developed countries, the way things like power relationships and intra-organizational power are treated when it comes to corporate governance in countries like Ghana (Gesiye Angaye & Gwilliam, 2008) and Egypt (Kamal Hassan, 2008). It is also known that corporate governance mechanisms in developing countries with their weak judicial systems and enforcement in capital markets, expectedly lead to the adopted governance mechanisms not working (Tsamenyi & Uddin, 2008). This is also connected with ownership being concentrated in families and family linkages with external economic, social, and political actors.

However, little is known about how compliance with corporate governance guidelines affects a firm's performance. Existing literature focuses on well-established stock markets and not on newly listed firms.

Before joining a stock market, a firm has to follow corporate mechanisms imposed by the Central Bank. However, after a firm joins a stock market, more mechanisms are added, and it is in a firm's interests to comply with both the Central Bank and the stock market's regulations. What is missing is the evaluation of the effect that complying with corporate governance has on a firm's performance and whether there is an improvement, a deterioration, or a stagnation in a firm's performance due to these governance mechanisms. In other words, does listing improve internal governance and/or a firm's performance? How does improving internal governance affect the performance of a recently listed firm? Researchers also want to know the changes happening in a firm's corporate governance mechanisms as a result of adopting listing requirements and how these changes affect a firm's stability and performance. Unfortunately, literature on corporate governance and its adoption in developing countries does not provide a coherent account of corporate governance in the context of emerging economies (Tsamenyi & Uddin, 2008). It is important to know this because there exists a gap in our understanding of how the concepts of corporate governance like accountability and transparency, are being applied in a developing country's context.

For evaluating the relationship between improved corporate governance due to a listing and a recently listed firm's performance this paper does a case study of a recently listed bank in Rwanda. Researcher can use a single or multiple-cases for a study of a particular phenomenon (Eisenhardt, 1989; Stake, 1995; Yin, 1994). However, if a case represents a certain phenomenon of interest, it is used as an instrumental and a single case to understand something more than the case itself (Stake, 1995). This is the reason why the authors chose I&M Bank as a single case. The case study in this paper follows the first six years of I&M's listing and makes a series of observations about improvements, deterioration, or stagnation in its performance due to the changes in its governance mechanisms. Through curves, these observations help us describe and visualize how the corporate governance mechanisms changed over the period of observation, as well as their effect on I&M's performance following compliance with the listing requirements of a young stock market. The relationships are observed with descriptive statistics with a focus on the bank's internal governance (board structure in terms of size, board's independence, and ownership in terms of percentage of shareholding), risk-taking, bank stability (non-performing loans – NPLs, growth in loans, and stability represented by the Z-score), and performance (ROE- return on equity and ROA- return on assets).

The chapter has both academic and policy implications. The paper sheds light on the changes happening to the governance and performance of a bank during its earlier stage of listing.

Understanding if changes in internal governance affect the performance of a recently listed bank is important because all banks are subject to compliance with the Central Bank's governance policies, but all banks are not listed. Therefore, comparing and contrasting banks that are listed with those that are not listed can help our understanding of corporate governance and listing. This will help practitioners understand the benefits or disadvantages of listing, other than immediate bond or stock transaction deals.

At a policy level, the findings of the chapter can serve as a marketing tool for the young stock market of Rwanda to attract banks based on internal governance's benefits of listing. Even when not trading on the stock market, being listed can push banks to comply with both the Central Bank and the stock market's regulations and see their internal governance mechanisms, stability, and performance improving thus helping them decide whether to stay listed or delist, if necessary.

The preceding section introduced the paper by showing the importance of the phenomenon under study. The rest of this paper is organized as follows. The following section provides a literature review of studies on corporate governance of banks and their implications for banks' performance. Another section discusses the data sources, methods used for data collection, variables' measurements, and the approaches used in the data analysis. Another section discusses the results and the last section gives the conclusion and provides some implications for policy and practice.

Literature Review

The relationship between corporate governance and a firm's performance after listing is extensively documented in literature. For instance, Ntim's (2009) study of South-African listed firms found that there was a positive and significant association between the quality of firms' internal corporate governance structures and their financial performance. Similarly, Fauzi and Locke (2012) investigated the role of a board's structure and the effect of ownership structure on firms' performance of New Zealand's listed firms. Their study found that the board of directors, board committees, and managerial ownership had a significant positive impact on firm performance while non-executive directors, female directors on the board, and block-holder ownership lowered s firm's performance. However, in addition to the effect of some governance variables, Filatotchev, Lien, and Piesse (2005) and Moche (2014) did not find any effect of family control on the performance of listed family-owned businesses.

Chen, Li, and Lin (2007) investigated corporate governance issues related to changes in ownership, regulation effects, and performance in newly listed firms in China and concluded that on average, their performance in terms of profitability, sales, and employee productivity improved as compared to the pre-listing period. However, this improvement did not come immediately after listing. Balatbat, Taylor, and Walter (2004) and Huang and Song (2005) examined the ownership structure and corporate governance attributes of Australian and Chinese listing firms respectively and their relation with post-listing performance and found that the operating performance of a firm typically deteriorated over the first few years post-listing. Positive effects of the listing on performance came after the 4th year of listing (Balatbat et al., 2004).

Board and Ownership Structure as Central Corporate Governance Mechanisms

Chancharat and Chancharat (2019) show how board and ownership structures influenced listed firms' performance in Thailand. According to Baysinger and Butler (1985), corporate governance mechanisms inform us about how and who owns and manages a firm. The board's composition and ownership structure are concerned with concentration or separation of ownership and a firm's control or management. This role of corporate governance is all about making a distinction between rights and responsibilities among owners or shareholders and other stakeholders, including the board of directors, managers, outside creditors, auditors, and regulators. The board of directors is an influential governance mechanism which has the power to hire, regulate, compensate, fire the management, and mediate in conflicts between owners (principal – principal) or between owners and directors (principal-agency) (Baysinger & Butler, 1985). The board of directors overseas, compensates, approves, and monitors strategic changes in operations as well as management, a mechanism that reduces agency conflict between managers, majority and minority shareholders (González & García-Meca, 2014).

Baysinger and Butler (1985) maintain that there is no point discussing the board without discussing its composition. They identified three different sections that composed a good and balanced board of directors with significant and different affiliations, roles performed, experience, and strong connectivity with the firm's management. These three components are the executive, monitoring, and instrumental components. The first category is *executive components* which includes members with exposure and managerial know-how in the core business, who provide expertise and decision-making support to the management and help in formulating and implementing strategies. Executive directors may come from CEOs, division heads, subsidiary managers, founder's kin, employees, retired employees, or other decision-makers affiliated with a firm. The second category of *monitoring components* is composed of those outside members who have no current employment or psychological link with the management except being on the board and giving objective and independent views on the firm's costs and operations. These are public and/or professional directors, private investors, or independent decision-makers. They are called independent directors because they are not financially dependent on the managers. Being independent, boads monitor and inform about the managers' behavior and allegiance to the plans and shareholders' interests. They ratify managers' decisions and provide additional advisory services. These two categories play a role in advising, monitoring, and disciplining the management, including hiring the CEO and firing them if necessary. The third category is *instrumental components*, which is composed of those who are appointed for mission beyond advising, controlling, or disciplining management, but for their individual wisdom to inspire the management in decision-making. The instrumental component includes people with expertise in domains like law, finance, consultancy, and interdependent decision-making who able to help a firm expand its links with other stakeholders. For Baysinger & Butler (1985),the board's composition does not affect changes in a firm's performance a lot over time, authorities. Howener, in the developing countries, the governance system pushes listed firms to increase the top management's ownership while reducing the size of the board to improve corporate governance and dual CEOs take advantage of the small board in Egypt for (Kholeif, 2008).

Board Independence

The debate on board structure is very divided. Some studies prefer a board dominated by outsiders, while others do not find it significant. Studies also find the link between the board's independence and a firm's performance to be both negative and positive (Kajola, 2008) depending on different contexts. Some studies suggest that the monitoring component should exceed 50 percent, a generally accepted level for democratic decision-making (Baysinger & Butler, 1985). Darko, Aribi, and Uzonwanne (2016) show that female representation on the board is significantly and positively related to a firm's performance. They found that the board's independence and frequency of audit committee meetings had a negative significant relationship with a firm's performance. The pros and cons of a board dominated by outsiders, or non-executive directors, are illustrated by Haniffa and Hudaib (2006), who state that outsiders bring their expertise, prestige, and contacts that influence the quality of directors' decision making and lead to an improvement in a firm's performance on the one hand while, on the other hand, this kind of a structure may lead to excessive monitoring and asphyxiate strategic action. Some studies have found a negative relationship between the number of outsiders on the board and a firm's performance, while others have found a significant positive relationship between the two (Ehikioya, 2009).

Chancharat and Chancharat (2019) show that a board's independence is significantly related to corporate performance, especially a negatively significant impact on the performance measure return on assets (ROA). Bekiris (2013) concluded that firms with a higher external block-holder shareholdings have independent boards.

Board Size

Several studies show that board size is negatively related with the CEO turnover or corporate performance, like the case of Chen (2015) while other studies show that any board size should be fit to execute the monitoring, controlling, and decision-making roles in any company (Monks & Minow, 1995). However, small boards are found to be more effective while they become more symbolic. Theyslow decision making and are easily controllable by the CEO (Haniffa & Hudaib, 2006). Costs and agency problems also increase as a board becomes bigger (Chen, 2015). On average, a good size for a board is about seven to nine members (Baysinger & Butler, 1985); and seven to eight members (Jensen, 1993) with a greater proportion of outsiders or non-management directors who are known for their independence from firm management (Chen, 2015). Counting the three components made of two members at least plus the CEO suggests that a minimum size of the board is seven as per Baysinger and Butler (1985). However, due to complexities, some firms are likely to have larger boards and depend more on external contractual outsourcing, for instance, larger firms (Pfeffer, 1972) or firms with a greater scope of operations (Boone, Field, Karpoff & Raheja, 2007; Coles, Daniel & Naveen, 2008). However, as stated by Ehikioya (2009), even though the number of board members is believed to influence a firm's performance, people are divided on whether a small or a bigger board is better when it comes to a firm's performance.

Investigating the relationship between ownership structure and the board's structure of listed companies in sub-Saharan African countries, Munisi, Hermes, and Randøy (2014) found that ownership concentration, managerial ownership and foreign ownership were negatively associated with board size. And, the board size is negatively correlated with board independence and managerial ownership (Bekiris, 2013).

According to Uadiale (2010), there is strong positive association between board size, outside directors and corporate financial performance. However, other studies find that a board's size has an insignificant impact on performance (Arouri, Hossain & Muttakin, 2014; Tomar & Bino,2012).

CEO Duality

Both agency and stewardship theories are in dispute about the dual role of a CEO as the CEO and the chairperson of the board. There is CEO duality when the CEO is also simultaneously the chairman of the board. In that case, there is a concentration of power in one individual (Haniffa & Hudaib, 2006). Some authors found that it would be good to separate these two roles while others found that the CEO and the chairman of the board being the same person had no significant impact on a firm's performance.

Proponents of stewardship theory argue that role duality helps enhance decision making and promotes a swift implementation of operational decisions without the interference of the board (Lin, 2005; Haniffa & Hudaib, 2006). However, proponents of the agency theory claim that the CEO and the chairman of the board being the same person compromises the board's independence and may lead to shareholders interests' being at risk of conflict when the board fails to oversee the management as expected (Hashim & Devi, 2008). A CEO performing a dual role also means that there is a risk of opportunistic behavior of reporting biased information in reports or dominating decision making (Kamran & Shah, 2014; Kholeif, 2008). Therefore, separation of the two roles may provide better checks and balances of the management's performance (Hashim & Devi, 2008; Haniffa & Hudaib, 2006) and protection of stakeholders' interests (Ehikioya, 2009).

However, literature is divided on this aspect. While some studies consider separating the role of the CEO and chairman of the board as significant, others do not find any significance between role duality and corporate governance (Hashim & Devi, 2008; Kholeif, 2008).

In relation to a firm's performance, Bekiris (2013) found that firms having a CEO who is also the chairman of the board are likely to have smaller block-holder ownership and fewer outside directors. Arouri, Hossain, and Muttakin (2014) found that governance variables such as board size and CEO duality had a less significant impact on a firm's performance. On the contrary, according to Uadiale (2010), there was a negative association between a firm's performance in terms of ROE and CEO duality.

Board Meetings

Every country or firm have regulations stipulating the frequency of board meetings as well as general conditions like tenure, recruitment, and experience required for members. See for example, Kholeif

(2008) on Egypt, or Hashim & Devi (2008) on Malaysia. The board of directors has the power to hire and fire and compensate the management, and it works at a certain intervals, sometimes regular or irregular intervals (Baysinger & Butler,1985). In fact, determining the optimum board size and independence is not enough as one also needs to determine the frequency of its meetings (González & García-Meca, 2014). A number of studies support regular and increased number of board meetings being associated with a firm's performance because members spend much time on important matters compared to those boards which meet less frequently (Tauringana, Kyeyune & Opio, 2008). According to Hashim and Devi (2008), a high frequency of board meetings increases potential problem identification and timely problem solving that facilitate decision making, for instance, ratifying final reports on time.

Considering the board structure's components listed earlier and their effect on a firm's operations, stability, and performance, the following proposition is made:

Proposition 1: A change in board structure is associated with changes in both the stability and performance of a listed bank

Ownership Concentration

Corporate ownership means what share of a firm belongs to the founder's family, institutions like pension funds and the government, other corporations, and other different stakeholders like individuals (Baysinger & Butler 1985). A board's control mechanisms come from the right of ownership that a person, a group of people, or an institution has over a firm. So, the starting point is ownership. Monitoring powers come from ownership. Such powers to control a firm depend on several ownership structures such as whether the ownership is held: (1) by the management or by outsiders (managerial ownership), (2) whether you are the main, majority, or minority shareholder (ownership concentration and/or dispersion), and (3) whether you are an individual, family, or an institution owning the firm. Hence equal attention is paid to these three dimensions of ownership structure in this paper because they have the ability to affect the monitoring expected from the board.

According to Baysinger and Butler (1985), ownership is closely held if it exceeds 10 percent otherwise it is widely held or dispersed, but statistics differ according to the context of a research. For instance, a 5 percent ownership of the voting shares gives a person a position on the board.

Arouri, Hossain, and Muttakin (2014) show that the extent of the ownership, either family ownership, foreign ownership, or institutional ownership has a significant and positive association with a firm's performance. Mang'Unyi (2011) confirms that there esist a significant difference between type of ownership and financial performance and a firm's ownership structure and corporate governance practices. And, the author states that firms with foreign-ownership had a slightly better performance than domestically-owned firms.

Managerial Ownership – Inside and Outside Ownership

As stated by Hashim and Devi (2008), both inside and outside directors or board members can have a certain degree of ownership, which also changes the required degree of monitoring. So, it is important to investigate the magnitude of insider and outsider ownership of a board and the management's performance separately.

In case managers have shares, there will be no need for intense monitoring if the management's ownership increases. Inside ownership reduces the expected role of outside board members for monitoring. As the proportion of insiders increases, both shareholders and managerial interests are closed. Shareholders let managers run a firm if their interests are aligned, and, hence principal-agency conflicts are reduced and discretionary behavior decreases because managers' opportunistic behavior is constrained by insider ownership, which is also, according to González & García-Meca (2014), known as the convergence of interests hypothesis. Of course, high insider ownership also leads to personal decision-making by the managers.

Inversely, more outside directors mean more effective monitoring and this has a positive impact on firm performance and accuracy of financial statements (Hashim & Devi, 2008). Such excessive control is needed because as per the agency theory, when managers are not the owners then they do not have an equity stake in a firm and their self-interest prevails over shareholders' interests which puts maximizing corporate value at risk (González & García-Meca, 2014). It is also believed that ownership concentration or larger shareholding increases monitoring, reduces managers' opportunistic behavior, increases the value of firms, and contributes to the goal of shareholders' wealth maximization (González & García-Meca, 2014). Nevertheless, such domination by a large number of shareholders, even though protecting a firm's value, comes with the risk of expropriating minority shareholders' interests (González & García-Meca, 2014).

Uadiale (2010), found a negative relationaship between the firm's financial performance and a directors' stockholding.

Family Ownership

Literature is divided into family ownership and corporate governance. Some authors salute a family's ability to reduce agency conflict because of its reputation, but others see families as accentuating agency conflict.

For some authors supporting family firm governance, family ownership has a positive impact on corporate behavior (González & García-Meca, 2014) as the long-term tenure of business owners builds trust with outside stakeholders like suppliers and lenders which is based on the owner family's reputation (Anderson & Reeb, 2003). Even though reputation is attached to the founder-manager, it is conveyed and sustained by his heirs with their long-term orientation. A family's reputation and long-term orientation of its members prevent them from acting in an opportunistic way (Ali, Chen & Radhakrishnan, 2007; Wang, 2006), which contributes to the firm's wealth maximization in the long term. However, this is possible and beneficial for both family and minority shareholders in an environment with proper minority shareholders' protection.

Another school of thought believes that family firms have a low level of professional managers, a lower proportion of independent directors, and greater CEO duality, which reduces the effectiveness of independent directors (González & García-Meca, 2014; Jaggi, Leung & Gul, 2007). A high proportion of family members on the board does not guarantee good governance in Malaysian firms (Haniffa & Cooke, 2002). Connelly, Limpaphayom, and Nagarajan (2012) investigated the relationship between the corporate governance and the ownership structure in Thailand and concluded that family ownership made controlling families use governance practices to their advantage. It also discussed the agency conflict between owners, where majority shareholders exploited the information asymmetry and possibly expropriated minority shareholders, or simply took action that benefitted them to the detriment of minority shareholders in what is known as Type II agency conflicts (Connelly et al., 2012; Fama & Jensen, 1983; González & García-Meca, 2014). Such behavior is observed in Hong Kong's family firms where the managerial ownership is used in literature as a proxy for family ownership (Ng, 2005) and it is very likely to be seen in many other developing countries with poor shareholder protection (Porta, Lopez-de-Silanes & Shleifer, 1999) where legal rights and investor protection are weak (Connelly et al., 2012).

Institutional Ownership

Munisi, Hermes, and Randøy (2014) discussed how government ownership is positively associated with the proportion of outside directors as opposed to relationship between the ownership concentration and the proportion of outside directors. Tomar and Bino (2012) show that banks having the institutional majority ownership have the best performance and that any increase in the managers and board members' ownership percentages, automatically, banks become more efficient.

Institutional investments are an important force in protecting minority shareholders' interests, and therefore, an increase in institutional investors' shareholding brings a powerful ingredient to corporate governance (Hashim & Devi, 2008). Institutional investors are common in capital market participation (Ahmad & Omar, 2016). Institutional investors' shareholding helps mitigate principal-principal agency problems, especially between controlling owners and minority shareholders, like selling shares at prevailing prices (Chung, Firth & Kim, 2005; González & García-Meca, 2014). Institutional investors prevent CEOs from becoming the sole policymakers, even in a case of CEO duality (Kholeif, 2008). They help prevent managers' opportunistic behavior of providing wrong information and reports or acting in their own interests to the detriment of the shareholders (Chung, Firth & Kim, 2005; Espinoza, de la Fuente Mella, Palavecinos & Riffo, 2014; González & García-Meca, 2014; Wan Hussin & Ibrahim, 2003). For instance, in Latin America, institutional investors, especially pension funds, provide capital and influence many changes in laws and practices that result in protecting minority shareholders in the capital market (Iglesias, 1999).

However, institutional investors are known for supporting myopic investments led by managers' short-term view and actions rather than long term investments like family ownership (Abdullah,1999) since, in most cases, institutional investors have access to insider information at the same level as the CEO (Kholeif, 2008). In the study, institutional ownership and ownership concentration are used interchangeably.

In the beginning, the chapter talked about imported corporate governance mechanisms. Considering the role of FDI in today's business, all these ownership modes, that is, family, managerial or institutional ownership, can be both local or foreign.

Considering the components of the ownership structure (managerial ownership, ownership concentration, family ownership, foreign ownership, and institutional ownership) and their effect on a board's composition and functioning, and a firm's performance, the following proposition is made:

Proposition 2: A change in ownership structure is associated with changes in both the stability and performance of a listed bank

METHODOLOGY

Sources of Data

I&M Bank's annual reports and financial statements are the only sources of data. Specifically, data on ownership, board composition, and financial performance from the bank's annual reports is used in this study. I&M Bank was selected as it is the only listed bank that listed ten years ago (2009 to 2018).

Research Design

This study uses one case study design. This approach was chosen for its suitability (Stake, 1995) in gaining an in-depth understanding of banks' corporate governance structures and mechanisms and relating them to their performance and risk-taking/stability. Case studies help researchers gain deep and contextual understanding of the case or pheonomen under study in real-ife circumstances. Yin (1994; 2003) notes that they can be vital in situations where separating the pheonomen under study and its context are not clearly separable. This study relied on published data from I&M bank's financial statements available on its website.

Research Approach: Quantitative Design

Data collected from the annual reports was analyzed following a quantitative approach. Descriptive tables and graphs were generated using the STATA software for the period 2009-18. The study could not generate regression results to relate the variables as the number of observations was very small as only one bank was studied.

MEASUREMENT OF VARIABLES

Board Composition and Attributes*

This study used three board variables namely; the size of the board, the independence of the board and the level of separation of duties of CEO and chairpersons of the board (CEO duality) as was previously been used other studies (e.g., Andres & Vallelado, 2008;; De Haan & Vlahu, 2016; Mutarindwa, Schäfer & Stephan, 2020). Board size is the total number of members sitting on the bank's board.. The independence of the board is measured by considering the proportion of non-executive external and independent members to total board members sitting on the bank's board. CEO duality measures the extent to which the board's chairman also serve the dual role of the bank's CEO. This study uses dummy variables to measure CEO duality. A value of 1 denotes CEO duality and otherwise.

Bank Ownership

This study follows De Haan and Vlahu (2016) for measuring bank ownership. Ownership concentration measures the extent to which a bank is closely or widely held. A dummy variable of 1 is given to a closely held ownership and 0 to dispersed ownership. A closely held firm is one in which some owners own more than 10 percent of the entire shareholding. Second and related to this, the percentage of ownership is used as a measure of the extent of ownership.

Lastly, the study measures the origins of majority shareholders. A dummy variable of 1 is given to foreign shareholders and 0 to domestic ones.

Financial Performance and Risk-Taking

This paper uses several proxies of financial performance namely Return on Assets (ROA), Return on Equity (ROE), and lending. ROA and ROE are computed from I&M Bank's balance sheet and income statement figures of I&M Bank annual reports for the period 2009-18. Values of the bank's lending are readily available in the bank's financial statements (balance sheet).

Bank risk-taking/resilience is measured using two variables namely the percentage of loan defaults or Non-Performing Loans (NPL) and Z-scores. NPL is the ratio of loan defaults to all the loans given to customers over the period of study. These figures are available in the bank's financial statements. Z-score is measured as:

$$\text{Z-score} = \text{ROA} + \text{Equity ratio/Std.dev of ROA}$$

The equity ratio is computed by dividing equity by the bank's total assets. Figures for this ratio are obtained from the bank's balance sheets for the period 2009-18.

Other Variables Used

This study also uses other bank variables. First, total assets are used as a measure of the bank's size. Second, this study uses the variable listing, which denotes that the bank is listed on the domestic exchange. A dummy variable of 1 is used for the time that the bank has been listed and 0 before it was listed.

DISCUSSION OF RESULTS

Presentation of the Case Study: I &M Bank (Rwanda) Limited

Company Profile

According to I&M Bank's annual reports, the bank started operations in 1963 as Banque Commerciale du Rwanda (BCR) or Rwanda Commercial Bank headquartered in capital Kigali. The bank was fully owned by the Government of Rwanda, with a capital of RFW 15 million. Following the government's policy of relinquishing its stake in major state parastatals in the 1990s, a decision was taken in 2004 to privatize BCR and it was acquired by Actis Group, a private equity firm with 80 percent ownership. In 2007, BCR was registered on the Rwanda Capital Market Authority over the counter market, and it floated a 10-year mortgage bond in 2009 to finance its products portfolio. In July 2012, BCR was sold to a consortium of investors, including I&M Bank from Kenya, the European Investment -DEG, and PROPARCO. This acquisition led to 80 shareholders of the consortium. Following the acquisition, BCR was changed to I&M Bank (Rwanda) Limited. In 2017, I&M Bank (Rwanda) Limited listed again on the Rwanda Stock Exchange and quoted its shares in the same year.

Key Activities and Results

According to the 2018 annual report, I&M Bank (Rwanda) Limited's core business is accepting deposits (savings, current, and recurring) from individuals, householders, and enterprises; providing liquidity for the financing needs of various stakeholders, and giving loans. The bank is also actively involved in digital banking both domestically and internationally. The bank's total net income after tax stood at USD 4.6 million as of September 2019, and its total assets were USD 344.6 million as of September 2019. The bank employs 300 employees. Headquartered in Kigali, the bank operates 14 branches nation-wide, seven in the capital city and seven in countryside provinces.

Descriptive Results

Table 1 provides the descriptive statistics of the variables used in this study using means and standard deviations.

Table 1. Descriptive statistics of the variables used

Variable	Obs	Mean	Std. Dev.	Min	Max
Board Independence	6	6.33	1.21	4	7
Boardsize	6	8.5	0.83	7	9
CEO duality	9	0	0	0	0
Equity ownership	9	0	0	0	0
Family ownership	9	0	0	0	0
Foreign ownership	9	1	0	1	1
Percentage of ownership	9	84.1	79	79	80
Government ownership	6	0	0	0	0
Institutional ownership	9	1	0	1	1
Lending	6	11.35	25.04	-24.96	38.1
Listing	10	1	0	1	1
Log (Total assets)	7	137 229	30 269	107 522	191 900
NPL	7	14	11.33	2.94	27.52
ROA	10	2.92	1.05	0.89	4.17
ROE	10	22.3	5.94	11	30.5
Z-Score	7	3.31	1.2	1.59	5.13

Source: (the authors, 2021)

Table 1 summarizes statistics for the variables used. Six members are non-executive independent board members. The bank's board had about nine members during the period of study. The results also show that throughout the study period, the roles of the chair of the board and that of the CEO were separate. On average, institutional shareholders owned a majority stake in the bank with an average of 84 percent stake implying that the bank was closely held. The results also show that the average size of the bank as proxied by total assets is 137. 229 million USD. NPL is on average 14 percent of the total loans to customers. The average return on assets was 2.92 percent, whereas the average return on equity was 22.3 percent. The bank was highly resilient, with an average Z-score of 3.32.[1] The average lending for the bank was 11.35 million RWF.

Main Results

This section discusses results pertaining to corporate governance structure and mechanisms at I&M Bank. Specifically, it discusses the ownership structure of the bank and its specific implications for the bank's corporate governance and performance. It also discusses internal governance (size, independence and CEO duality) and relates them to the bank's financial results over time.

Shareholding and Corporate Governance

To date, the shareholding of the bank is: BCR Investment Company owns most of the shares (79.2 percent). The rest of the shares are owned by minority investors owning less than 10 percent of the total shareholding, implying that the bank is closely held. The shareholding structure has remained the same over time. The shareholding structure of the bank is given in Table 2.

Table 2. Shareholding structure of I&M bank

Shareholders	Percentage
1. BCR Investment Company	79.22
2. Private Investors	0.17
3. ESOP (I&M Bank Employees	0.99
4. The KIBO Fund II LLC	7.22
5. Nile Holding Company for Development and Investment	2.45
6. AGDF Corporate Trust LTD	2.11
7. Rwanda Social Security Board	1.94
8. Dyer & Blair Investment Bank Ltd	0.86
9. Rwanda Mountain Tea	0.73
9. GA Insurance LTD	0.45

Source: I&M Bank Annual Report (2018).

Table 3 shows that major institutional investors owned more about 80 percent of the shares and the rest of the shareholders owned less than 20 percent of the shares. In corporate governance for banks this has two-sided implications. The first is that this structure helped minority shareholders as there was active supervision and monitoring of managerial behavior by the majority shareholders given the size of their investments in the bank (Fama & Jensen, 1983). On the other hand, it may imply that majority investors can expropriate minority investors by conniving and investing in risky and unproductive investments, which may ruin the company (Haw, Ho, Hu & Wu, 2010).

A review of the bank's annual reports shows that minority investors were protected through a constant supply of and access to information about the bank's performance and stock market information. Shareholders also participated in the Annual General Assembly and have voting rights. The bank operates an Investor Relations office that engages with shareholders by handling their claims and informing them of the bank's policies and activities. The office also informs shareholders about the regulations and the bank's compliance and communicates financial reports to them.

Internal Governance, Bank Stability, and Performance

This section discusses the findings on the impacts of ownership and corporate governance structure and on the bank's stability and performance. It also illustrates internal corporate governance (board size, independence, and CEO duality) influenced the bank's financial results over time (Figure 1).

Figure 1. Internal governance
Source: (the authors, 2021)

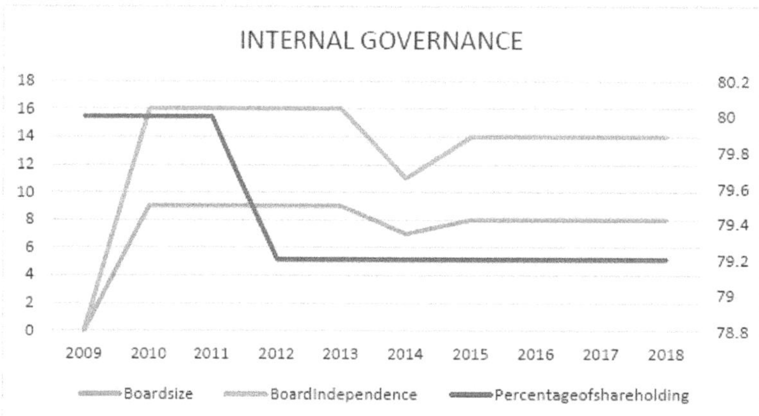

On average, six members[2] were non-executive board members and the roles of the chairman of the board and the CEO were separate. On average, the bank's board had about nine members during the period of study showing that I &M Bank had an optimum board size, with 7-9 members on its board during the time of the study. This board size allowed adequate board independence from the bank's management (Chen, 2015).

However, during 2013-14 and 2014-15, there were changes in the board's composition. In light of Proposition 1 Figure 2 shows how both bank stability and performance between 2013 and 2015 changed direction. The growth in loans stopped and dropped as compared to 2013. Before 2013, non-performing loans had been cut down considerably, but this stopped in 2013, and this negative move turned positive in 2015. The same trend was observed in bank stability (represented by Z-scores). Similarly, the peak of the bank's performance in both ROE and ROA was reached in 2013 which continued to drop slightly till 2018. One can conclude that these negative changes in the bank's stability and performance were related to the changes in its board structure between 2013 and 2015. Hence, one can confirm the first proposition that changes in the board's structure positively increased a listed bank's performance and stability.

Figure 1 also shows that BCR had 80 percent ownership of I&M Bank before 2011 which changed to 79.2 percent in 2012 and remained constant during the period of study, that is till 2018. I&M Bank is not privately or family-owned; it is owned by institutional investors. Institutional shareholders have owned a majority stake in the bank over time and have remained unchanged (see Table 1).

In light of the second proposition, Figure 2 shows how bank stability and performance changed direction between 2013 and 2015. While these changes had to do with the board's structure they were also because of changes in shareholding in 2012. Recall that the shareholding is closely held, making it responsible for subsequent changes in board structure and their effect on both the bank's stability and performance.

These negative changes in the bank's stability and performance are related to the changes in shareholding in 2012. Figures 1 and 2 confirm the second proposition that a change in ownership is positively associated with changes in both the stability and performance of a listed bank.

Figure 2. Performance, Risk-taking, and bank stability
Source: (the authors, 2021)

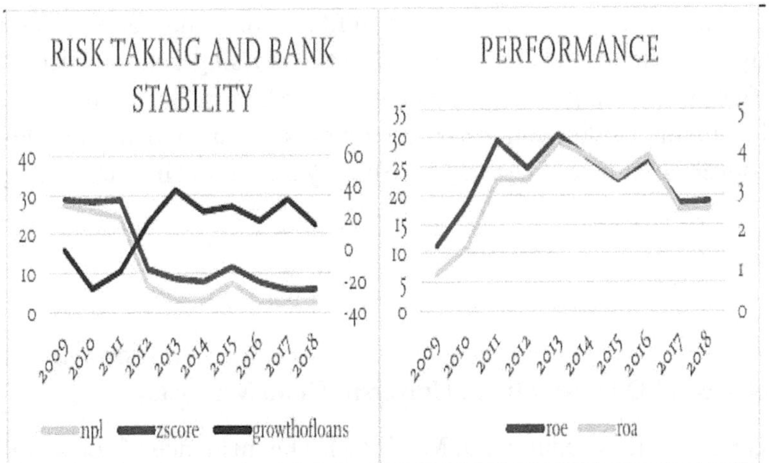

I&M Bank's non-performing loans were 14 percent of the total loans given to customers. The average return on assets was 2.92 percent, whereas average return on equity was 22.3 percent. The bank was highly resilient, with an average Z-score of 3.32 and average lending for the bank was 11-35. It was only the changes in 2013-15 which were highly associated with the board and ownership structure of the bank.

CONCLUSION

This paper established the contribution of a bank's listing to its governance and performance. Using a single case study, it collected data on bank governance, performance, and stability over the period 2009-18.

Findings show that listing improved I&M Bank's internal governance in particular soon after it listed on the Rwanda Stock Exchange in 2008. Its board's composition(size and independence), and ownership showed significant changes soon after it listed and listing improved its performance as well as stability through governance. A change in both the board's size and independence significantly reduced the bank's non-performing loans, and increased the bank's resilience (Z-score) and lending.

This paper has both academic and policy implications. Its use of a young stock market in a developing country contributes to the empirical corporate governance literature by exploring how listing either constrains or improves corporate governance mechanicms as well as its effect on a bank's performance. The paper also sheds light on the changes that happened to I&M Bank's governance and performance during the earlier stages of listing.

This paper has some policy implications as well. Listing can add more strength to corporate governance of banks than what is provided by central banks as it (listing) requires firms to adhere to stock market guidelines that protect minority investors.

FUTURE RESEARCH DIRECTIONS

One potential limitation of the study is the sample size as this did not help us do a robust analysis of the results. In addition, some of the variables discussed in literature could not be used in the methodology and subsequent analysis of the results. This was a result of missing data on such variables. Future researches could benefit by using a larger sample of banks over a long period of time with more time-variant explanatory variables. Future studies can also focus on cross-country bank samples which necessitate introducing country-level variables as these might be highly influential in determining bank-level effects.

REFERENCES

Abdullah, S. N. (1999). *The role of corporate governance and ownership structure on accounting earnings quality* (Unpublished PhD Dissertation). Universiti Utara Malaysia.

Adu-Amoah, A., Tsamenyi, M., & Onumah, J. M. (2008). The influence of social and political relations on corporate governance systems: The case of rural banks in Ghana. *Research in Accounting in Emerging Economies*, *8*(1), 311–334. doi:10.1016/S1479-3563(08)08011-0

Ahmad, S., & Omar, R. (2016). Basic corporate governance models: A systematic review. *International Journal of Law and Management*, *58*(1), 73–107. doi:10.1108/IJLMA-10-2014-0057

Alawattage, C., & Wickramasinghe, D. (2008). Appearance of accounting in a political hegemony. *Critical Perspectives on Accounting*, *19*(3), 293–339. doi:10.1016/j.cpa.2006.08.006

Ali, A., Chen, T. Y., & Radhakrishnan, S. (2007). Corporate disclosures by family firms. *Journal of Accounting and Economics*, *44*(1), 238–286. doi:10.1016/j.jacceco.2007.01.006

Anderson, R. C., & Reeb, D. M. (2003). Founding-family ownership and firm performance: Evidence from the S&P 500. *The Journal of Finance*, *58*(3), 1301–1328. doi:10.1111/1540-6261.00567

Angaye, P. E. G., & Gwilliam, D. (2008). Corporate governance in infancy and growth– an interview-based study of the development of governance and corporate regulation in Nigeria. *Research in Accounting in Emerging Economies*, *8*, 359–407.

Arouri, H., Hossain, M., & Muttakin, M. B. (2014). Effects of board and ownership structure on corporate performance: Evidence from GCC countries. *Journal of Accounting in Emerging Economies*, *4*(19), 117-130.

Balatbat, M. C., Taylor, S. L., & Walter, T. S. (2004). Corporate governance, insider ownership and operating performance of Australian initial public offerings. *Accounting and Finance*, *44*(3), 299–328. doi:10.1111/j.1467-629x.2004.00114.x

Baysinger, B. D., & Butler, H. N. (1985). Corporate governance and the board of directors: Performance effects of changes in board composition. *Journal of Law Economics and Organization*, *1*(1), 101–124.

Bekiris, F.V. (2013). Ownership structure and board structure: are corporate governance mechanisms interrelated? *Corporate Governance*, *13*(4), 352-364. doi:10.1108/CG-02-2011-0013

Boone, A. L., Field, L. C., Karpoff, J. M., & Raheja, C. G. (2007). The determinants of corporate board size and composition: An empirical analysis. *Journal of Financial Economics*, *85*(1), 66–101. doi:10.1016/j.jfineco.2006.05.004

Chancharat, S., & Chancharat, N. (2019). Board Structure, Ownership Structure, and Performance of Thai Listed Companies. *Australasian Accounting. Business and Finance Journal*, *13*(3), 53–70.

Chanda, S., Burton, B., & Dunne, T. (2017). The nature and potential of corporate governance in developing countries: Zambian perceptions. *Accounting, Auditing & Accountability Journal*, *30*(6), 1257–1287. doi:10.1108/AAAJ-08-2015-2208

Chen, L., Li, S., & Lin, W. (2007). Corporate governance and corporate performance: Some evidence from newly listed firms on Chinese stock markets. *International Journal of Accounting. Auditing and Performance Evaluation*, *4*(2), 183–197. doi:10.1504/IJAAPE.2007.015233

Chen, T. (2015). Institutions, board structure, and corporate performance: Evidence from Chinese firms. *Journal of Corporate Finance*, *32*, 217–237. doi:10.1016/j.jcorpfin.2014.10.009

Chung, R., Firth, M., & Kim, J. B. (2005). Earnings management, surplus free cash flow, and external monitoring. *Journal of Business Research*, *58*(6), 766–776. doi:10.1016/j.jbusres.2003.12.002

Coles, J. L., Daniel, N. D., & Naveen, L. (2008). Boards: Does one size fit all? *Journal of Financial Economics*, *87*(2), 329–356. doi:10.1016/j.jfineco.2006.08.008

Connelly, J. T., Limpaphayom, P., & Nagarajan, N. J. (2012). Form versus substance: The effect of ownership structure and corporate governance on firm value in Thailand. *Journal of Banking & Finance*, *36*(6), 1722–1743. doi:10.1016/j.jbankfin.2012.01.017

Darko, J., Aribi, Z. A., & Uzonwanne, G. C. (2016). Corporate governance: the impact of director and board structure, ownership structure and corporate control on the performance of listed companies on the Ghana stock exchange. *Corporate Governance: The International Journal of Business in Society*, *16*(2), 259-277.

De Andres, P., & Vallelado, E. (2008). Corporate governance in banking: The role of the board of directors. *Journal of Banking & Finance, 32*(12), 2570–2580. doi:10.1016/j.jbankfin.2008.05.008

Ehikioya, B. I. (2009). Corporate governance structure and firm performance in developing economies: evidence from Nigeria. *Corporate Governance: The International Journal of Business in Society, 9*(3), 231-243.

Eisenhardt, K. M. (1989). Building theories from case study research. *Academy of Management Review, 4*(4), 532–549. doi:10.5465/amr.1989.4308385

Espinoza, R. A. C., de la Fuente Mella, H. A., Palavecinos, B. S., & Riffo, P. A. D. (2014). Revelación de información en las empresas bursátiles chilenas: El efecto de la propiedad de los inversionistas institucionales y el nivel de endeudamiento. *Estudios Gerenciales, 30*(131), 190–199. doi:10.1016/j.estger.2014.04.008

Fama, E. F., & Jensen, M. C. (1983). Separation of ownership and control. *The Journal of Law & Economics, 26*(2), 301–325. doi:10.1086/467037

Fauzi, F., & Locke, S. (2012). Board structure, ownership structure and firm performance: A study of New Zealand listed-firms. *Asian Academy of Management Journal of Accounting and Finance, 8*(2), 43-67. http://hdl.handle.net/10289/7793

Filatotchev, I., Lien, Y. C., & Piesse, J. (2005). Corporate governance and performance in publicly listed, family-controlled firms: Evidence from Taiwan. *Asia Pacific Journal of Management, 22*(3), 257–283. doi:10.100710490-005-3569-2

González, J. S., & García-Meca, E. (2014). Does corporate governance influence earnings management in Latin American markets. *Journal of Business Ethics, 121*(3), 419–440.

Haniffa, R., & Hudaib, M. (2006). Corporate governance structure and performance of Malaysian listed companies. *Journal of Business Finance & Accounting, 33*(7-8), 1034–1062.

Haniffa, R. M., & Cooke, T. E. (2002). Culture, corporate governance and disclosure in Malaysian corporations. *Abacus, 38*(3), 317–349.

Hashim, H. A., & Devi, S. (2008). Board characteristics, ownership structure and earnings quality: Malaysian evidence. *Research in Accounting in Emerging Economies, 8*(97), 97–123.

Haw, I. M., Ho, S. S., Hu, B., & Wu, D. (2010). Concentrated control, institutions, and banking sector: An international study. *Journal of Banking & Finance, 34*(3), 485–497.

Huang, G., & Song, F. M. (2005). The financial and operating performance of China's newly listed H-firms. *Pacific-Basin Finance Journal, 13*(1), 53–80.

Iglesias, A. (1999). Economic impact of pension reforms in Chile. In *International Conference "Universal Pension Funds Systems"* (pp. 19-20). Academic Press.

Jaggi, B., Leung, S., & Gul, F. A. (2007). *Board independence and earnings management in Hong Kong firms: Some evidence on the role of family ownership and family board control.* Working Paper. Department of Accounting and Information System, Rutgers University.

Jain, T., Aguilera, R. V., & Jamali, D. (2017). Corporate stakeholder orientation in an emerging country context: A longitudinal cross industry analysis. *Journal of Business Ethics*, *143*(4), 701–719.

Jensen, M. C. (1993). The modern industrial revolution, exit, and the failure of internal control systems. *The Journal of Finance, 48*(3), 831-880.

Kajola, S. O. (2008). Corporate governance and firm performance: The case of Nigerian listed firms. *European Journal of Economics, Finance and Administrative Sciences, 14*(14), 16-28.

Kamal Hassan, M. (2008). The corporate governance inertia: the role of management accounting and costing systems in a transitional public health organization. In Corporate Governance in Less Developed and Emerging Economies (pp. 409-454). Academic Press.

Kamran, K., & Shah, A. (2014). The impact of corporate governance and ownership structure on earnings management practices: Evidence from listed companies in Pakistan. *The Lahore Journal of Economics*, *19*(2), 27–70.

Kholeif, A. (2008). CEO duality and accounting-based performance in Egyptian listed companies: A re-examination of agency theory predictions. In *Corporate governance in less developed and emerging economies* (pp. 65–96). Emerald Group Publishing Limited.

La Porta, R., Lopez-de-Silanes, F., & Shleifer, A. (1999). Corporate ownership around the world. *The Journal of Finance*, *54*(2), 471–517.

Liew, P. K. (2008). The (Perceived) roles of corporate governance reforms in Malaysia: The views of corporate practitioners. *Corporate governance in less developed and emerging economies*, 455-482.

Lin, Y. F. (2005). Corporate governance, leadership structure and CEO compensation: Evidence from Taiwan. *Corporate Governance*, *13*(6), 824–835.

Mahadeo, J. D., Soobaroyen, T., & Hanuman, V. O. (2012). Board composition and financial performance: Uncovering the effects of diversity in an emerging economy. *Journal of Business Ethics*, *105*(3), 375–388.

Mang'Unyi, E. E. (2011). Ownership structure and Corporate Governance and its effects on performance: A case of selected Banks in Kenya. *International Journal of Business Administration*, *2*(3), 2.

Moche, S. W. (2014). *Corporate governance and firm performance of listed family- owned firms in Kenya* (Doctoral dissertation).

Monks, R., & Minow, N. (1995). *Corporate governance*. Basil Blackwell.

Munisi, G., Hermes, N., & Randøy, T. (2014). Corporate boards and ownership structure: Evidence from Sub-Saharan Africa. *International Business Review*, *23*(4), 785–796.

Mutarindwa, S., Schäfer, D., & Stephan, A. (2020). Central banks' supervisory guidance on corporate governance and bank stability: Evidence from African countries. *Emerging Markets Review*.

Ng, C. Y. (2005). An empirical study on the relationship between ownership and performance in a family-based corporate environment. *Journal of Accounting, Auditing & Finance*, *20*(2), 121–146.

Ntim, C. G. (2009). *Internal corporate governance structures and firm financial performance: evidence from South African listed firms* (Doctoral dissertation). University of Glasgow.

Pfeffer, J. (1972). Size and composition of corporate boards of directors: The organization and its environment. *Administrative Science Quarterly*, 218–228.

Stake, R. E. (1995). The art of case study research. *Sage (Atlanta, Ga.)*.

Tauringana, V., Kyeyune, M. F., & Opio, P. J. (2008). Corporate governance, dual language reporting and the timeliness of annual reports on the Nairobi stock exchange. *Research in Accounting in Emerging Economies*, *8*(1), 13–37.

Tomar, S., & Bino, A. (2012). Corporate governance and bank performance: Evidence from Jordanian banking industry. *Jordan Journal of Business Administration*, *153*(655), 1–40.

Tsamenyi, M., & Uddin, S. (2008). Introduction to corporate governance in less developed and emerging economies. *Research in Accounting in Emerging Economies*, *8*(1), 1–11.

Uadiale, O. M. (2010). The impact of board structure on corporate financial performance in Nigeria. *International Journal of Business and Management*, *5*(10), 155–166.

Wan Hussin, W. N., & Ibrahim, M. A. (2003). Striving for quality financial reporting. *Akauntan Nasional*, *16*(3), 18–24.

Wang, D. (2006). Founding family ownership and earnings quality. *Journal of Accounting Research*, *44*(3), 619–656.

Yin, R. K. (1994). Case study research: Design and methods. Academic Press.

Yin, R. K. (2003). *Case study research: Design and methods* (3rd ed.). Sage.

KEY TERMS AND DEFINITIONS

Bank Stability: Is the absence of banking crises measured in terms of the z-score.

Board Structure: The two structures of the board, that is the management board, and the supervisory board that composing one board governing the organization but having different roles.

Internal Governance: The firm's formal set of structures, communication lines, procedures and rules.

Listed Bank: A bank that trades its shares or bonds on a stock market.

Ownership Structure: A legal form that the owner chose for the business, which can differ as the business grows.

Post-Listing Performance: The companies' status of performance in a period after the first IPO. The period definition may vary depending on the circumstances of the research.

Stockmarket: A physical place or virtual arrangement where regular activities of buying, selling, and issuance of shares of publicly held companies take place.

ENDNOTES

* Some board variables such as the number of bank's board meetings, gender, and board committees were not available in the annual reports and are therefore not included in the analysis section.

1 The standard minimum Z-score is equal to 1.

2 No data on board size and independence available for 2009.

APPENDIX

Table 3. Variable description

Variable	Description	Source of Data
Ownership concentration	Variable measuring with dummies 1 and 0. Value 1 shows majority shareholding of more than or equal to 10% of shares and 0 otherwise.	Annual reports
Percentage	Percentage of ownership of the first biggest shareholder	Annual reports
Institutional ownership	Variable measuring with dummies 1 and 0. Value 1 denotes if majority shareholder is an institutional investor, 0 otherwise.	Annual reports
Foreign/domestic owners	Variable measuring with dummies 1 and 0. Value 1 denotes majority owners are foreign and 0 if they are domestic shareholders	Annual reports
Board size	Number of bank's board members.	Annual reports
CEO duality	Variable measuring with dummies 1 and 0. Value 1 indicates that CEO is the bank's chairperson and 0 otherwise.	Annual reports
Board independence	Non-board ownership (board members with 0 ownership in the bank)	Annual reports
ROA	Return on average assets ratio	Annual reports
ROE	Return on average equity ratio expressed in percentage	Annual reports
NPL ratio	Impaired loans/gross loans	Annual reports
Bank size (Logtotalassets)	Measure of bank's size by taking the natural logarithim of its total assets	Annual reports
Z-scores	Calculated as: ROA + Equity ratio/ Standard deviation of ROA	Annual reports
Equity ratio	Total equity/ Total assets	Annual reports

Source: (the authors, 2021)

Chapter 13
Investigating the Relationship of Corporate Cash Holdings, Corporate Governance, and Firm Performance in Malaysia

Kiarash Ehtiat Karrahemi
https://orcid.org/0000-0001-5542-5223
Universiti Teknologi Malaysia, Malaysia

Siti Zaleha Abdul Rasid
Universiti Teknologi Malaysia, Malaysia

Rohaida Basiruddin
Universiti Teknologi Malaysia, Malaysia

Maizaitulaidawati Md Husin
https://orcid.org/0000-0002-2789-8274
University of Business and Technology, Saudi Arabia

ABSTRACT

Current practice shows that firms throughout the world are in favor of high cash holdings; yet, they are still performing well. This situation contradicts the agency and free cash flow theories, which suggest that excessive cash may increase agency costs and lower firm performance. The purpose of this study is to examine the relationship between corporate governance, cash holdings, and firm performance. Five thousand four hundred twenty observations were conducted, and a balanced panel data analysis was performed. The results indicate that corporate governance has a significant impact on cash holdings, corporate governance has a significant impact on firm performance, and cash holding has a significant impact on a firm's performance. The findings of this study do not show any evidence to support the agency and free cash flow theories among non-financial Malaysian firms listed on Bursa Malaysia. Thus, this study contributes to the finance and accounting literature by gaining a better understanding of firm performance indicators in Malaysia, specifically.

DOI: 10.4018/978-1-7998-7596-3.ch013

INTRODUCTION

According to CNN Money (2015), Apple Inc., one of the most valuable and successful companies in the world, had kept $203 billion in cash in 2015. This was a rise in value from $178 billion in 2014, making it the first firm in the world to ever cross $200 billion in cash reserves. Besides, in the 2015 Moody's Investors Service report, Apple was reported to have raised its cash reserves by $138 billion since 2009. All these figures show the significance of cash reserves (also known as cash holdings) to the profitability and success of a firm. This new trend of cash holdings, however, cannot be explained by conventional theories. From the agency theory perspective, high cash holdings will lead to the deterioration of firm performance (Al-Najjar and Clark, 2017; Abid and Lodhi, 2015; Jensen, 1986; Jensen and Meckling, 1979).

Cash holding is one of the essential means to control the agency issue and can be employed as a substitute for corporate governance to mitigate agency conflict (Mikkelson and Partch, 2003; Opler et al., 1999). In Asia, corporate governance has been a concern and is often regarded as a weak link in firm performance (Zabri et al., 2016; Tam and Tan, 2007; Singham, 2003). Since the inception of agency theory by Jensen and Meckling (1979) and Jensen (1986), quite a several studies have investigated the relationship between corporate governance, cash holding, and firm performance. However, these studies failed to examine the combination of these parameters altogether. Most of the previous research fell short on assessing the relationship between crucial explanatory variables of corporate governance and cash holdings (Alves and Pinho, 2012; Bansal and Sharma, 2016; Bigelli and Sánchez-Vidal, 2012; Bruynseels et al., 2016; Chen and Chuang, 2009; Dittmar and Mahrt-Smith, 2007; Kuan et al., 2011; Kusnadi, 2011).

Furthermore, the association between the board of directors' and the chairman's expertise with firm performance has not been thoroughly investigated. In addition, studies on this topic reported contradictory results, were limited to small sample sizes, and have been identified as not having enough experimental variables to represent the corporate governance, economic environment, political and regulatory systems of countries together with the corporate governance mechanisms, business risk and nature of industries (Bruinshoofd and de Haan, 2005; Chen, 2008; Ittner et al., 2003). In this study, the missing part of this puzzle is addressed. The economic environment is controlled by choosing samples from a homogenous dataset at a stable range of time within one country. Although similar studies have been conducted within the same context (e.g., Kusnadi, 2011; Zabri et al., 2016), most of them employed a limited number of observations. This study thus provides comprehensive evidence on the relationship between corporate cash holding, corporate governance, and firm performance.

LITERATURE REVIEW

Malaysian Code on Corporate Governance

Malaysian Code on Corporate Governance (MCCG) introduced in 2000 is comprised of a set of best practices anchored on accountability and transparency aimed to strengthen the corporate culture (Securities Commission of Malaysia, 2017). The introduction of MCCG is also aimed to promote ethical behavior, improve accountability and transparency, develop sustainability, eliminate inefficiency, and abolish corporate fraud among Malaysian firms. To ensure that the MCCG remains relevant and is aligned with globally-recognized best practices and standards, it is reviewed periodically by a group of experts.

The recommendation set out in MCCG is divided into three parts. The first part is onboard leadership and effectiveness, which outlines a company board's responsibilities, composition, and remuneration. The second part of the MCCG outlines the effective audit and risk management of a firm, which includes requirements for the audit committee as well as risk management and internal control framework. In the last part of the MCCG, the outline of integrity in corporate reporting and meaningful relationships with stakeholders is provided (Securities Commission of Malaysia, 2017).

Underlying Theories

The free cash flow theory stresses that firms' excessive cash is the main reason behind managers' and shareholders' conflict. A high volume of cash holdings in firms encourages managers to pursue self-interest ambitions and eventually exploit firms' financial resources (Jensen, 1986). Therefore, Jensen (1986) suggested that firms keep low cash holdings to mitigate agency issues. Such a paradox can be solved through accurate monitoring of managers' behavior and controlling the firms' fund allocation, which can only be achieved through a stout corporate governance mechanism. Therefore, strong corporate governance neutralizes the negative effect of agency conflict and transaction costs on firm performance and gives managers access to the optimum level of cash (Jensen, 1986, 1993).

Myers and Majluf (1984) and Coase (1937), on the other hand, developed the pecking order and transaction cost theory, which is in favor of high cash holdings in a firm. According to Myers and Majluf (1984), high corporate cash holdings aid managers in dealing with forthcoming investment opportunities. It also increases firms' flexibility and adaptability in volatile markets and provides a cheaper source of funds, which eventually leads to lower operational costs and better firm performance. However, there will be a rise in agency costs as a side effect of having a high cash holdings ratio. Similar to Jensen's theory (1986), the pecking order and transaction cost theories suggest that firms improve their corporate governance to reduce agency costs (Dittmar and Mahrt-Smith, 2007; Harford et al., 2012; Kalcheva and Lins, 2007). Consistent with the pecking order and transaction costs theories, the trade-off theory suggests that keeping higher cash holdings is more advantageous due to market volatility, investment opportunities, and lower cost of transactions (Opler et al., 1999).

Relationship Between Corporate Governance and Firm Performance

Walker (2009) defined corporate governance as "the role of corporate governance is to protect and advance the interest of shareholders through setting the strategic direction of a company and appointing and monitoring capable management to achieve this". Many studies have found that corporate governance can directly (or indirectly) influence firm performance via waste of capital (Deb, et al., 2017; Jensen, 1986; Jensen and Meckling, 1979; John et al., 2008; Shleifer and Vishny, 1997) and changing cost of capital (Garmaise and Liu, 2005; Habib, 2005; Jensen and Meckling, 1979; Lombardo and Pagano, 2006). According to Jensen (1986), robust corporate governance reduces managers' access to free cash flow, which leads to higher efficiency in a firm's operations. Consequently, it reduces the waste of capital, which eventually leads to better firm performance. Likewise, John et al. (2008) and Shleifer and Wolfenzon (2002) claimed that corporate governance alters the diversion of cash flow, which leads to operational efficiency. Further, Shleifer and Vishny (1997), in line with Jensen and Meckling (1979) stated that efficient operation eliminates the waste of capital, which indirectly improves firm performance and future value. Similarly, Chen et al. (2012) and Owusu and Weir (2018) reported that strong corporate governance is an effective method to reduce agency costs.

One of the critical advantages of robust corporate governance is its ability to diminish information asymmetry (Habib, 2005; Cui et al., 2018; Cai et al., 2015). A firm with a low level of information asymmetry has better value and more robust corporate governance (Cai et al., 2015; Han et al., 2014)). Robust corporate governance provides two significant benefits which eventually lead to better firm performance; first, reduction in monitoring cost by investors (Mohan and Chandramohan, 2018; Habib, 2005; Jensen and Meckling, 1979; Lombardo and Pagano, 2006) and second, reduction in the cost of capital (Habib, 2005). Although systematic risks can alter firm performance, Lombardo and Pagano (2006) and Garmaise and Liu (2005) argued that stout corporate governance could directly affect and diminish the systematic risk. Such an effect can lead to a reduction of market risk, decrease the cost of capital, and improve firm performance (Garmaise and Liu, 2005). Based on the discussion above, it can be recapitulated that corporate governance can affect firm performance through various means such as information asymmetry (Habib, 2005), monitoring cost by investors (Habib, 2005; Jensen and Meckling, 1979; Lombardo and Pagano, 2006), systematic risk (Garmaise and Liu, 2005; Lombardo and Pagano, 2006), market risk (Garmaise and Liu, 2005), efficient operations (Shleifer and Vishny, 1997), waste of capital (Jensen and Meckling, 1979), free cash flow (Jensen, 1986), and diversion of cash flow (John et al., 2008; Shleifer and Wolfenzon, 2002).

The consensus on the association between corporate governance and firm performance is for firms with more robust corporate governance to have higher firm performance and value. Even though some studies reported mixed results (Larcker et al., 2005), most of the research on the relationship between corporate governance and firm performance reported a significant positive relationship (Bhagat and Brian, 2019; Garmaise and Liu, 2005; Habib, 2005; Jensen, 1986; Jensen and Meckling, 1979; John et al., 2008; Shleifer and Vishny, 1997; Shleifer and Wolfenzon, 2002; Velnampy, 2013). A majority of recently published studies are also in favor of the positive relationship between corporate governance and firm performance (Aggarwal et al., 2014; Ammann et al., 2013; Andreou et al., 2014; Claessens and Yurtoglu, 2013; Daily and Dalton, 2015; Francis et al., 2015; Krafft et al., 2014; Kumar and Zattoni, 2013; Miller et al., 2013). Therefore, based on the existing literature, this study is going to take strong corporate governance as a sign of better firm performance. Therefore, the following hypothesis was formed.

H1 There is a positive relationship between corporate governance and firm performance.

Relationship Between Corporate Governance and Corporate Cash Holdings

Cash holdings are one of the firms' internal sources of funds and are mainly accumulated from the firm's return earnings and operational profit (Chen et al., 2012). It can be in the form of firms' cash holdings (liquid assets) and non-liquid assets (Bigelli and Sánchez-Vidal, 2012; Kuan et al., 2011).

Much research has been conducted on the relationship between corporate governance and corporate cash holdings (Jebran et al., 2019; Kwan and Lau, 2019; Dittmar and Mahrt-Smith; 2017; Ittner et al., 2003; Chen and Chuang; 2009). However, these studies had reported mixed results. For instance, Opler et al. (1999) stated that high cash holdings do not necessarily lead to lower firm performance; managers often hold cash as a precautionary motive and do not necessarily allocate them for investments. Mikkelson and Partch (2003) remarked that there is no association between a high level of cash holdings and poor corporate governance. They even suggested that extra cash holdings do not bring about agency conflict but rather increase a firm's value. Kusnadi (2011) remarked that firms with weak corporate governance tend to have higher cash holdings compared to well-governed firms. Similarly, Harford et al. (2012) suggested that firms keep less visible cash holdings as excessive cash holdings attract activist shareholders' attention, which eventually can threaten managers' positions and weakens firm governance.

However, recent studies have demonstrated that firms prefer to keep a large number of cash holdings (Bates et al., 2009; Garcia-Teruel et al., 2011; Kahle and Stulz, 2013; Kalcheva and Lins, 2007; Martínez-Sola et al., 2013). According to a report by Global Vintage Database, the largest firms around the world keep 1.5 trillion dollars of cash, which equals 9% of their assets' book value. In the United States, the cash holdings of large firms are equal to 13% of their assets (Dittmar and Mahrt-Smith, 2007). The same goes for French and British firms (Guney et al., 2003; Saddour, 2006). These figures show that firms throughout the world are in favor of high cash holdings. Thus, the following hypothesis was formulated.

H2 There is a positive relationship between corporate governance and corporate cash holdings.

Relationship Between Corporate Cash Holdings and Firm Performance

Most studies on the association between cash holdings and firm performance back the agency and free cash flow theories originated by Jensen (1986). There are two schools of thought; the first group is based on the agency and free cash flow theories, which are in favor of lower free cash flow and thus suggest firms to keep lower cash holdings. The second group, on the other hand, is in favor of the pecking order, transaction costs, resource dependency, and stewardship theories, whereby they believe that free cash flow has the potential to boost corporate performance by providing a cheaper source of funds for managers to deal with investment opportunities. They also believe that the availability of internal funds for managers increases their flexibility to deal with more investment opportunities in a more efficient manner. Hence, they are in favor of higher cash holdings in a firm. For example, Alnori (2020) and Doan (2020) found that the proportion of cash holding had a positive impact on the firm performance.

Trends in corporate cash holdings studies show that a majority of recent studies are in favor of higher cash holdings. This is also because the findings of this group are by far nearer to the reality of firms' behavior today. For instance, in the last decade, American, French and British firms kept 10% to 13% of their assets' book value as cash and its equivalents (Guney et al., 2003; Saddour, 2006). These figures have increased since then, and it seems that the growing trend is going to be continued (Bates et al., 2009; Garcia-Teruel et al., 2011; Kahle and Stulz, 2013; Kalcheva and Lins, 2007; Martínez-Sola et al., 2013). Therefore, the below hypothesis was postulated.

H3 There is a positive relationship between corporate cash holdings and firm performance.

THEORETICAL FRAMEWORK

The proposed relationships between the variables are illustrated in Figure 1. The corporate governance is measured using nine variables (size of the board of directors, board of directors independence, board of directors meeting frequency, board of directors financial expertise, size of audit committee, audit committee independence, audit committee meeting frequency and audit committee financial expertise).

Figure 1. Theoretical framework

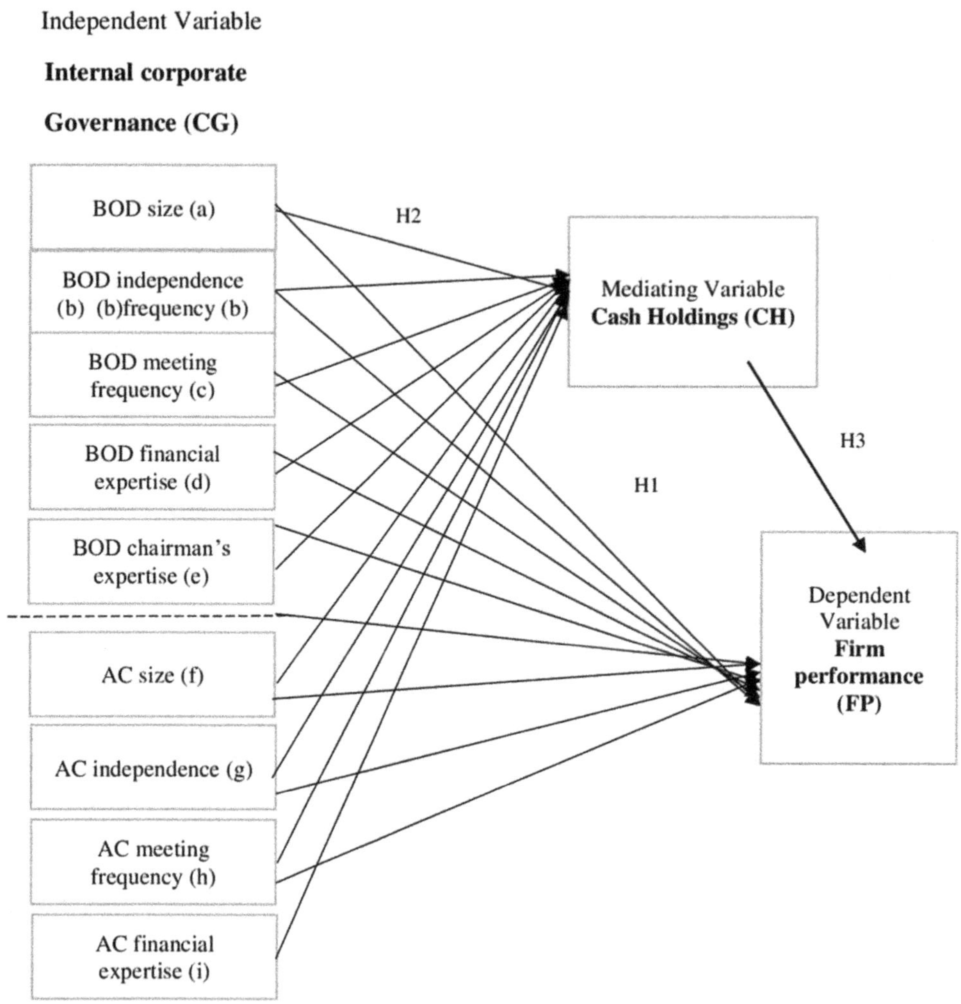

METHODOLOGY

Data in the form of annual reports were collected from 542 non-financial Malaysian firms listed on Bursa Malaysia. Samples for a period of 10 years (from 2003 to 2012) were collected, amounting to 5420 observations. The number of observations is relatively large and sufficient for this study (Fauzi et al., 2012; Yusoff and Alhaji, 2012). One important reason for choosing 2012 as the last year for data collection is the fact that the MCCG was last reviewed in 2012. To prevent problems concerning the corporate governance index in the data collection process, a handful of most related and representative variables were handpicked and individually tested. As a prudential step, financial firms were excluded from data analysis since they do not possess characteristics (such as having an item that can represent what 'annual sales' can work for non-financial firms), which makes them non-comparable with non-financial firms. The same practice was also employed previously by Bruynseels et al. (2016), Elzahar and Hussainey (2012), and Ismail (2016). The theoretical framework was analyzed using multivariate regressions. The balanced panel data set was selected and analyzed using Stata 13.1. Stata is a robust and comprehensive data analysis software that can handle sophisticated tests for panel datasets (Rasbash et al., 2000). Panel data is formed by a series of observations on a cross-section of firms (or countries, people, etc.) for a specific duration (Baltagi, 2009; Hsiao, 2014). Panel data was chosen due to its ability to (i) handle larger data sets at a higher degree of freedom and less collinearity among independent variables; (ii) control individual heterogeneity; (iii) provide better identification and estimation of the effects; and (iv) provide more predictive power for individual outcomes compared to cross-section or time-series (Baltagi, 2009).

DATA ANALYSIS

Descriptive Statistics

Table 1 shows the descriptive analysis for corporate governance, cash holdings, firm performance, and proxies along with control variables. Based on the table, the mean and median of the board of director size are 7.597 and 7, respectively, while the average number of independent and non-executive directors is 3.207. According to the MCCG, at least half of a firm's board must be comprised of independent directors. This implies that firms in Malaysia comply with the regulations set by the MCCG. Data also shows that the firms conducted 5.318 board meetings on average, therefore fulfilling the MCCG's requirement of a minimum of 4 meetings a year. However, few firms fall short of the mentioned requirements. For example, Astino Berhad and Pansar held no board meetings in the years 2003 and 2008, respectively (LRBM, 2014). The data also shows that the average number of financially expert directors on the board is only 0.315. This implies that only one out of three boards of directors of firms have financial expertise. The average number of auditors in the audit committee is 3.348, which is slightly higher than MCCG's (2000) suggestion of 3 members.

The average number of independent auditors in the audit committee is 0.642, meeting the LRBM's requirement of at least a half-independent audit committee. However, these figures fall short when it comes to countries with strong corporate governance like the U.S, which requires every auditor in the audit committee to be independent.

In this study, the audit committee meeting was calculated as a dummy variable to check for the requirement of four minimum audit committee meetings per year. Based on the result, 98.4% of the firms meet the mentioned requirement. The mean for the audit committee's financial expertise is 0.462, implying that more than half of the auditors in the audit committees in Malaysia do not have the required financial expertise. Nonetheless, the requirements of this study on financial expertise are stricter and only limited to auditors with accounting or finance academic degrees or related qualifications such as ACCA, CPA, and CIMA. The mean for cash holdings is 0.122, which illustrates that public-listed Malaysian firms tend to keep cash at about 12% of the book value of their assets.

Correlation Matrix

Table 2 demonstrates the correlation matrix of all variables used in this study. The table shows correlation coefficients between variables. Each cell in the table shows the correlation between two variables. Based on the table, all variables are moderately correlated and are clear from the multicollinearity problem.

Table 1. Descriptive statistics

Variable	Mean	Median	Standard Deviation	Min	Max	Skewness	Kurtosis
BSIZE	7.597	7.000	1.972	3.000	17.000	0.703	3.961
BIND	3.207	3.000	0.939	1.000	7.000	0.806	3.751
BMEET	5.318	5.000	1.991	0.000	27.000	3.329	23.838
BFEX	0.315	0.286	0.143	0.000	1.000	0.684	3.820
BCFEX	0.135	0.000	0.341	0.000	1.000	2.142	5.590
ACSIZE	3.348	3.000	0.627	1.000	8.000	1.636	6.506
ACIND	0.642	1.000	0.480	0.000	1.000	-0.591	1.349
ACMEET	0.984	1.000	0.127	0.000	1.000	-7.610	58.916
ACFEX	0.462	0.333	0.200	0.000	1.000	0.402	3.083
CH	0.122	0.082	0.122	0.001	0.730	1.785	6.734
ROA	0.065	0.059	0.161	-1.956	1.983	-0.443	45.238
ROE	0.087	0.092	0.252	-1.861	2.727	0.668	31.745
LNA	12.741	12.591	1.481	0.046	18.452	0.044	7.581
LEV	0.393	0.385	0.206	0.003	0.975	0.237	2.405
NWC	0.222	0.208	0.289	-1.602	1.718	-0.828	8.776
QR	1.919	1.070	2.893	0.003	24.950	4.379	26.636
SG	0.106	0.070	0.359	-0.991	1.976	1.318	7.583
B	1.012	0.985	0.576	-2.585	3.987	0.371	4.401
DE	0.946	0.627	1.070	0.003	8.959	3.033	15.676
DIV	0.605	1.000	0.489	0.000	1.000	-0.429	1.184

Return On Asset (ROA) =Earnings before interest, taxes, depreciation and amortization divided by net operating asset (Total asset minus cash and equivalents); Board Of Director's Size (BSIZE) = Total number of directors on the board; Board Of Director's Independence (BIND) = Number of independent and non-executive directors on the board; Board Of Director's Meeting Frequency (BMEET) = Number of board of directors' meetings in a year; Board Of Director Financial Expertise (BFEX) = Percentage of board members with professional accounting or finance qualification; Board Of Directors' Chairman's Expertise (BCFEX) = 1 if the chairman of the board is a financial expert and 0 if otherwise; Audit Committee Size (ACSIZE) = Total number of auditors on the audit committee; Audit Committee Independence (ACIND) = 1 if the number of independent and non-executive auditors in audit committee is at least 3 persons and 0 if otherwise; Audit Committee Meeting Frequency (ACMEET) = 1 if the number of audit committee meetings in a year is minimum 4 and 0 if otherwise; Audit Committee Financial Expertise (ACFEX) = The percentage of auditors with professional accounting or finance qualification on the audit committee; Cash Holdings (CH) = Total cash and equivalents to total asset; Size (LNA) = Natural logarithm of total assets; Leverage (LEV) = Total debt divided by total assets; Sales Growth (SG) = Sales of year t minus Sales of year (t-1) divided by sales of year t; Beta (B) = Systematic risk of portfolio compared to the market; Net Working Capital (NWC) = Current assets minus current liabilities; Quick Ratio (QR) = Current assets minus inventories divided by current liabilities; Debt equity Ratio (DE) = Total debt divided by total equity; Dividend dummy (DIV) = 1 if firm pays dividends 0 otherwise.

Table 2a. Correlation matrix

	BSIZE	BIND	BMEET	BFEX	BCFEX	ACSIZE	ACIND	ACMEET	ACFEX
BSIZE	1								
BIND	0.4995***	1							
BMEET	0.0794***	0.1546***	1						
BFEX	-0.2186***	-0.0846***	0.0671***	1					
BCFEX	-0.0202	0.0168	0.0207	0.2072***	1				
ACSIZE	0.3564***	0.3432***	0.1089***	-0.0431***	0.0297**	1			
ACIND	0.2794***	0.5032***	0.0374***	-0.0499***	-0.028**	0.3551***	1		
ACMEET	0.0060	-0.0055	0.0403***	0.0153	0.0212	0.0115	0.0124	1	
ACFEX	-0.0164	-0.0297**	0.0305**	0.4743***	-0.0042	-0.1833***	-0.0236*	0.0248*	1
CH	0.0654***	0.0574***	0.0298**	0.0337**	0.0442***	0.0776***	0.0613***	0.0291**	0.0027
ROA	0.1188***	0.0652***	-0.0673***	-0.0159	-0.0007	0.0903***	0.0623***	0.0243*	-0.0374***
LNA	0.3582***	0.3258***	0.2073***	-0.0077	0.0493***	0.2***	0.1605***	0.0647***	-0.0244*
LEV	0.0489***	0.0435***	0.1057***	0.0373***	0.0273**	0.0118	0.0150	0.0285**	0.0476***
NWC	0.0150	-0.0344**	-0.0949***	-0.023*	0.0056	0.0269**	0.04***	-0.0108	-0.0214
QR	-0.0333**	-0.0316**	-0.0321**	-0.01	0.0583***	0.0405***	-0.0055	0.0177	-0.0162
SG	0.0436***	0.0095	-0.0303**	-0.0253*	-0.0012	0.0191	0.0056	-0.011	-0.0007
B	-0.0216	0.0355***	0.1034***	0.0684***	0.0779***	-0.0159	-0.0079	0.023*	0.0589***

Table 2b. Correlation matrix (continued)

	CH	ROA	LNA	LEV	NWC	QR	SG	B
CH	1							
ROA	0.3409***	1						
LNA	0.0092	0.1754***	1					
LEV	-0.3745***	-0.1056***	0.2392***	1				
NWC	0.4358***	0.2395***	-0.0483***	-0.4535***	1			
QR	0.5635***	0.1491***	-0.1236***	-0.4944***	0.4188***	1		
SG	-0.0038	0.1533***	0.0719***	0.057***	0.0229*	-0.0198	1	
B	-0.0616***	-0.0887***	0.1437***	0.095***	-0.0772***	-0.0666***	0.0063	1

Return On Asset (ROA) =Earnings before interest, taxes, depreciation, and amortization divided by net operating asset (Total asset minus cash and equivalents); Board Of Director's Size (BSIZE) = Total number of directors on the board; Board Of Director's Independence (BIND) = Number of independent and non-executive directors on the board; Board Of Director's Meeting Frequency (BMEET) = Number of board of directors' meetings in a year; Board Of Director Financial Expertise (BFEX) = Percentage of board members with professional accounting or finance qualification; Board Of Directors' Chairman's Expertise (BCFEX) = 1 if the chairman of the board is independent and 0 if otherwise; Audit Committee Size (ACSIZE) = Total number of auditors on the audit committee; Audit Committee Independence (ACIND) = 1 if the number of independent and non-executive auditors in audit committee is at least 3 persons and 0 if otherwise; Audit Committee Meeting Frequency (ACMEET) = 1 if the number of audit committee meetings in a year is minimum 4 and 0 if otherwise; Audit Committee Financial Expertise (ACFEX) = The percentage of auditors with professional accounting or finance qualification on the audit committee; Cash Holdings (CH) = Total cash and equivalents to total asset; Size (LNA) = Natural logarithm of total assets; Leverage (LEV) = Total debt divided by total assets; Sales Growth (SG) = Sales of year t minus Sales of year (t-1) divided by sales of year t; Beta (B) = Systematic risk of portfolio compared to the market; Net Working Capital (NWC) = Current assets minus current liabilities; Quick Ratio (QR) = Current assets minus inventories divided by current liabilities.

RESULTS AND DISCUSSION

Firm Performance and Corporate Governance

Table 3 demonstrates the regression results for firm performance and corporate governance. The R-squared and adjusted R-squared between firm performance and corporate governance are 9.9% and 9.7%, respectively. Based on the table, a board of directors' size, a board of director's financial expertise, audit committee size, number of audit committee meetings, sales growth, and firm size are reported to have a positive and significant correlation with firm performance.

The significant relationship between a board of directors and firm performance implies that firms with a higher number of members on their board of directors tend to have a higher return on assets and performance. Although larger board size in some studies is associated with weaker corporate governance (Abbott et al., 2006; Jensen, 1993), quite many studies found that larger board size can show great performance and governance ability (Rahman and Ali, 2006).

The positive and significant correlation between sales growth, a board of directors' financial expertise, number of audit committee meetings, audit committee size and firm size on firm performance implies that firms with higher growth in their annual sales (Lumpkin and Dess, 2001), the higher number of financial experts as a board of directors (Lin and Hwang, 2010), the higher number of audit committee meetings (Abbott et al., 2000; Abbott et al., 2004; Raghunandan and Rama, 2007[REMOVED HYPERLINK FIELD][REMOVED HYPERLINK FIELD]), the higher number of auditors in audit committee (Chen and Zhou, 2007; Lin and Hwang, 2010) and bigger firm size (Aldamen et al., 2012; Brick and Chidambaran, 2010; Francis et al., 2012) tend to record better performance.

Board independence and board chairman's financial expertise have been found to have no significant relationship with firm performance. This implies that the number of independent directors on the board does not affect the performance of firms in Malaysia. Although previous studies recorded a relationship between board independence (Jensen and Meckling, 1979; Liu et al., 2015; Tulung and Ramdani, 2018) and board chairman's financial expertise with firm performance, this study's findings suggest that there is not enough evidence to accept such an association.

This study also found that there is not enough evidence to prove the association between the audit committee's financial expertise and the audit committee's independence with firm performance. Further justification for this result is that firms with a higher number of independent auditors in their audit committee do not necessarily record better performance (Agrawal and Chadha, 2005; Barber et al., 2007; Rahmat et al., 2009).

Leverage and the number of board meetings showed a significant negative association with firm performance. This implies that firms with lower debt to asset ratio (Aldamen et al., 2012; Brick and Chidambaran, 2010; Francis et al., 2012) and lower number of board meetings tend to show better performance. Although it is uncommon for board meetings to be negatively associated with corporate performance, results remained steady throughout the ten years of this study except for 2006, 2007, and 2011 which showed no relation. The level of significance (1% with a coefficient of -0.007) also illustrates the sturdy reliability of the outcome. However, there is evidence of mixed results in previous studies. Brick and Chidambaran (2010), for instance, suggested that the number of board meetings does not merely and necessarily represent the quality of the board of directors and their activities. Adams (2005), on the other hand, found that board meetings increase the level of pressure and the unnecessary costs borne by meeting fees; these thus reduce the efficiency of board monitoring.

Table 3. Multivariate regression for firm performance and corporate governance

Variable	2003	2004	2005	2006	2007	2008	2009	2010	2011	2012	Pooled
Intercept	-0.073	-0.122	-0.238	-0.228	-0.209	-0.347	-0.195	-0.266	-0.182	-0.151	-0.204
	(-0.950)	(-1.240)	(-2.77)***	(-2.9)***	(-2.24)**	(-5.08)***	(-2.9)***	(-3.29)***	(-1.71)*	(-1.32)	(-7.91)***
BSIZE	0.009	0.006	0.009	0.006	0.004	0.001	0.005	0.002	0.002	0.003	0.004
	(2.180)**	(1.260)	(2.010)**	(1.340)	(0.870)	(0.410)	(1.510)	(0.430)	(0.390)	(0.720)	(3.07)***
BIND	-0.016	-0.002	-0.019	-0.007	-0.010	-0.006	-0.002	-0.004	-0.008	0.006	-0.005
	(-1.540)	(-0.190)	(-1.840)*	(-0.680)	(-0.960)	(-0.800)	(-0.260)	(-0.490)	(-0.880)	(0.620)	(-1.590)
BMEET	-0.011	-0.008	-0.009	-0.003	-0.003	-0.008	-0.007	-0.006	0.000	-0.017	-0.007
	(-3.27)***	(-1.820)*	(-2.40)**	(-0.930)	(-0.770)	(-2.89)***	(-2.57)***	(-1.99)**	(0.090)	(-4.78)***	(-6.55)***
BFEX	0.118	-0.013	0.157	0.006	0.128	0.071	-0.027	-0.019	0.015	-0.069	0.035
	(1.960)**	(-0.180)	(2.570)***	(0.100)	(1.900)*	(1.470)	(-0.580)	(-0.420)	(0.260)	(-1.270)	(1.940)**
BCFEX	0.012	0.018	-0.044	-0.005	0.025	-0.023	0.011	0.002	0.012	-0.023	-0.002
	(0.560)	(0.700)	(-2.090)**	(-0.240)	(1.080)	(-1.390)	(0.680)	(0.120)	(0.600)	(-1.150)	(-0.270)
ACSIZE	-0.018	0.009	0.015	-0.002	0.003	0.014	0.023	0.013	0.036	0.031	0.009
	(-1.530)	(0.630)	(1.220)	(-0.160)	(0.220)	(1.400)	(2.080)**	(1.140)	(2.29)**	(2.090)**	(2.41)***
ACIND	0.009	-0.007	0.011	0.010	0.024	-0.007	-0.005	0.017	0.019	-0.001	0.007
	(0.540)	(-0.350)	(0.620)	(0.590)	(1.280)	(-0.540)	(-0.370)	(1.250)	(1.110)	(-0.070)	(1.280)
ACMEET	0.008	-0.025	0.020	0.016	0.130	0.046	0.012	0.094	0.025	-0.123	0.027
	(0.180)	(-0.450)	(0.400)	(0.370)	(2.320)**	(1.000)	(0.300)	(1.480)	(0.310)	(-1.350)	(1.640)*
ACFEX	-0.059	-0.021	-0.049	0.024	-0.112	-0.012	0.031	-0.004	-0.040	0.044	-0.020
	(-1.480)	(-0.460)	(-1.200)	(0.620)	(-2.460)**	(-0.370)	(0.970)	(-0.110)	(-0.980)	(1.080)	(-1.620)
LNA	0.023	0.020	0.023	0.025	0.016	0.035	0.017	0.023	0.016	0.029	0.023
	(4.53)***	(3.24)***	(4.38)***	(4.84)***	(2.62)***	(7.88)***	(3.82)***	(5.28)***	(2.80)***	(5.26)***	(14.2)***
LEV	-0.135	-0.084	-0.152	-0.101	-0.111	-0.134	-0.056	-0.104	-0.163	-0.125	-0.116
	(-4.24)***	(-2.140)**	(-4.57)***	(-3.08)***	(-2.93)***	(-4.73)***	(-2.01)**	(-3.70)***	(-4.52)***	(-3.55)***	(-11.09)***
SG	0.017	0.052	0.067	0.046	0.065	0.082	0.077	0.072	0.115	0.053	0.064
	(0.750)	(2.79)***	(3.75)***	(2.51)**	(3.16)***	(4.91)***	(4.59)***	(4.53)***	(5.26)***	(2.94)***	(10.99)***
B	-0.038	-0.038	-0.004	-0.029	-0.009	-0.040	-0.025	-0.030	-0.025	-0.036	-0.026
	(-2.34)**	(-2.34)**	(-0.260)	(-2.24)**	(-0.680)	(-4.27)***	(-2.58)***	(-3.44)***	(-2.130)**	(-3.0)***	(-7.18)***
No Obs	542	542	542	542	542	542	542	542	542	542	5420
R^2	0.106	0.074	0.129	0.096	0.081	0.238	0.113	0.141	0.124	0.148	0.099
Adj R^2	0.084	0.052	0.107	0.074	0.058	0.219	0.091	0.120	0.102	0.127	0.097

1) *** are significant at $p<0.01$, ** are significant at $p<0.05$ and * are significant at $p<0.10$
2) Coefficient (t-statistics).

Beta was found to have a negative and significant association with firm performance, which means that firms with lower systematic risk record better performance (Aldamen et al., 2012; Francis et al., 2012).

Cash Holdings and Corporate Governance

Table 4 shows the relationship between cash holdings and corporate governance. The R-squared and adjusted R-squared are 38.7% and 38.5%, respectively. Nevertheless, the minimum R-squared belongs to the year 2007, which is 34%, and the maximum belongs to the year 2003 with 47.2%. Nine out of 13 variables showed significant correlations with corporate governance and cash holdings.

Board size, board independence, number of board meetings, board's financial expertise, number of an audit committee meeting, and firm size are found to have positive and significant correlations with cash holdings. This implies that higher number of directors (Adkins, 2011; Kuan et al., 2011), the higher number of independent directors (Kuan et al., 2011; Davidson et al., 2005; Rahman and Muhamad, 2013), the higher number of board meetings, the higher number of financially expert directors, higher number of audit committee meetings (Benjamin and Ehtiatkar Rahemi, 2013), and larger firm size (Chen and Chuang, 2009; Kuan et al., 2011) are associated with stronger corporate governance which eventually gives the shareholders the needed confidence to keep higher cash in the firm.

Networking capital and quick ratio also showed a significant positive relationship with cash holdings. This means that firms with higher net working capital (Bigelli and Sánchez-Vidal, 2012; Chen, 2008; Kuan et al., 2011; Morellec et al., 2013) and more liquidity power (Cohen and Li, 2013) have a higher rate of cash holdings.

This study also found that the board chairman's financial expertise, independence of audit committee, firm size, and financial expertise are among the corporate governance proxies that showed no signs of relation to cash holdings. This means that there is not enough evidence to prove any association between all of the variables with the amount of money a firm keeps.

Leverage is significantly and negatively associated with cash holdings. This implies that firms with a higher ratio of debt to total assets tend to keep less cash (Chen, 2008; Kuan et al., 2011; Morellec et al., 2013). This is especially true when the firm's policy is to finance itself with external sources like risky debt rather than use its internal sources such as earnings.

Firm Performance and Cash Holdings

Table 5 shows the relationship between firm performance and cash holdings. According to the table, there is a significant positive relationship between firm performance and cash holdings with a relatively large coefficient number of 0.425. This implies that firms with higher cash holdings record better performance. This result is also consistent with the pecking order theory, which suggests having a higher cash holdings ratio. Besides, this finding is also consistent with research done by Gregory and Wang (2013) and Mikkelson and Partch (2003).

Firm size and sales growth were found to have a positive and significant correlation with firm performance. This result implies that firms that are bigger (Aldamen et al., 2012; Brick and Chidambaran, 2010; Francis et al., 2012) and record higher sales growth (Lumpkin and Dess, 2001) have better chances of performing better. Leverage and beta, on the other hand, were found to have a significant negative relationship with firm performance. The result implies that firms with high debt

Table 4. Multivariate regression for cash holdings and corporate governance

Variable	2003	2004	2005	2006	2007	2008	2009	2010	2011	2012	Pooled
Intercept	0.011	-0.028	-0.091	-0.084	-0.052	-0.098	-0.027	-0.143	-0.173	-0.004	-0.061
	(0.240)	(-0.550)	(-1.800)*	(-1.87)*	(-0.950)	(-1.88)*	(-0.530)	(-2.28)**	(-2.57)***	(-0.050)	(-3.72)***
BSIZE	0.002	0.001	0.000	0.002	0.004	0.004	0.003	0.008	0.005	0.007	0.003
	(0.610)	(0.390)	(-0.050)	(0.840)	(1.290)	(1.550)	(1.240)	(2.84)***	(1.830)*	(2.480)**	(3.78)***
BIND	0.003	0.006	0.006	0.006	0.001	0.005	0.011	-0.004	-0.005	-0.005	0.003
	(0.430)	(0.990)	(1.030)	(1.110)	(0.170)	(0.830)	(1.94)*	(-0.660)	(-0.960)	(-0.820)	(1.85)*
BMEET	0.000	0.004	0.004	0.004	0.003	0.004	0.003	0.002	0.002	0.002	0.003
	(0.210)	(1.860)*	(1.640)	(2.26)**	(1.200)	(2.05)**	(1.240)	(0.920)	(1.000)	(0.730)	(4.41)***
BFEX	0.032	0.062	0.041	0.087	0.108	0.013	-0.008	0.008	0.057	0.065	0.052
	(0.850)	(1.700)*	(1.120)	(2.56)**	(2.77)***	(0.350)	(-0.220)	(0.230)	(1.660)*	(1.940)*	(4.64)***
BCFEX	-0.005	0.001	0.003	0.012	0.006	0.016	0.003	0.002	-0.012	-0.008	0.001
	(-0.400)	(0.060)	(0.250)	(1.070)	(0.450)	(1.230)	(0.270)	(0.140)	(-1.000)	(-0.650)	(0.35)
ACSIZE	0.000	0.004	0.011	0.001	-0.001	0.005	0.010	0.011	0.014	-0.005	0.001
	(0.010)	(0.610)	(1.550)	(0.190)	(-0.120)	(0.620)	(1.190)	(1.220)	(1.430)	(-0.590)	(0.49)
ACIND	0.004	0.005	0.002	-0.001	-0.001	-0.003	-0.004	0.008	0.011	-0.001	0.005
	(0.390)	(0.430)	(0.150)	(-0.110)	(-0.130)	(-0.280)	(-0.360)	(0.790)	(1.050)	(-0.130)	(1.51)
ACMEET	0.013	0.022	0.039	0.035	0.022	0.041	-0.036	0.048	0.053	-0.075	0.019
	(0.500)	(0.760)	(1.290)	(1.410)	(0.670)	(1.180)	(-1.180)	(0.980)	(1.070)	(-1.340)	(1.81)*
ACFEX	0.020	0.002	-0.001	-0.048	-0.057	0.000	0.043	0.017	0.005	0.017	-0.005
	(0.800)	(0.070)	(-0.040)	(-2.09)**	(-2.15)**	(0.000)	(1.74)*	(0.700)	(0.200)	(0.700)	(-0.620)
LNA	0.001	0.000	0.004	0.005	0.005	0.002	0.003	0.007	0.007	0.007	0.004
	(0.170)	(0.060)	(1.130)	(1.670)*	(1.370)	(0.730)	(0.860)	(2.140)**	(2.030)**	(2.140)**	(4.19)***
LEV	-0.045	-0.053	-0.054	-0.057	-0.049	-0.004	-0.058	-0.058	-0.021	0.006	-0.047
	(-1.97)**	(-2.29)**	(-2.37)**	(-2.60)***	(-1.76)*	(-0.150)	(-2.14)**	(-2.110)**	(-0.740)	(0.220)	(-5.96)***
NWC	0.078	0.088	0.065	0.055	0.070	0.095	0.108	0.108	0.153	0.182	0.094
	(5.46)***	(5.92)***	(4.65)***	(4.00)***	(3.64)***	(4.9)***	(5.58)***	(5.510)***	(7.77)***	(9.380)***	(17.87)***
QR	0.021	0.017	0.018	0.021	0.019	0.021	0.016	0.017	0.020	0.016	0.019
	(13.92)***	(11.53)***	(12.0)***	(13.37)***	(9.9)***	(10.59)***	(8.9)***	(8.84)***	(10.32)***	(9.38)***	(34.59)***
No Obs	542	542	542	542	542	542	542	542	542	542	5420
R^2	0.472	0.406	0.406	0.450	0.340	0.365	0.371	0.379	0.416	0.405	0.387
Adj R^2	0.459	0.391	0.391	0.437	0.323	0.349	0.356	0.364	0.402	0.391	0.385

1) *** are significant at $p<0.01$, ** are significant at $p<0.05$ and * are significant at $p<0.10$
2) Coefficient (t-statistics)

(Aldamen et al., 2012; Bauer et al., 2010; Brick and Chidambaran, 2010; Francis et al., 2012) and higher beta (Aldamen et al., 2012; Francis et al., 2012) tend to have lower performance due to the volatility of their business. This connotes that firms with a higher proportion of debt in their capital structure tend to perform lower than their counterparts, therefore suggesting that firms should implement their internal funds rather than employ external sources.

Table 5. Multivariate regression for firm performance and cash holdings

Variable	2003	2004	2005	2006	2007	2008	2009	2010	2011	2012	Pooled
Intercept	-0.167	-0.191	-0.216	-0.236	-0.145	-0.301	-0.163	-0.189	-0.158	-0.313	-0.211
	(-2.9)***	(-2.7)***	(-3.5)***	(-4.1)***	(-2.24)**	(-6.09)***	(-3.44)***	(-4.47)***	(-2.91)***	(-5.59)***	(-12.16)***
CH	0.348	0.322	0.390	0.365	0.616	0.205	0.256	0.504	0.647	0.578	0.425
	(6.44)***	(4.75)***	(6.59)***	(6.29)***	(10.03)***	(4.21)***	(5.23)***	(11.17)***	(12.38)***	(10.540)***	(24.160)***
LNA	0.019	0.020	0.020	0.022	0.012	0.032	0.017	0.016	0.012	0.025	0.020
	(4.21)***	(3.59)***	(4.32)***	(4.94)***	(2.31)**	(8.15)***	(4.24)***	(4.55)***	(2.58)***	(5.44)***	(14.09)***
LEV	-0.054	-0.020	-0.073	-0.018	0.034	-0.099	0.002	0.020	0.007	-0.002	-0.021
	(-1.620)	(-0.480)	(-2.1)**	(-0.540)	(0.90)	(-3.37)***	(0.070)	(0.730)	(0.200)	(-0.050)	(-1.97)**
SG	0.028	0.053	0.067	0.043	0.067	0.080	0.078	0.068	0.107	0.046	0.064
	(1.280)	(2.89)***	(3.83)***	(2.44)**	(3.52)***	(4.85)***	(4.7)***	(4.81)***	(5.64)***	(2.720)***	(11.59)***
B	-0.038	-0.037	-0.006	-0.027	-0.017	-0.041	-0.026	-0.025	-0.015	-0.035	-0.026
	(-2.41)**	(-2.39)**	(-0.430)	(-2.22)**	(-1.54)	(-4.55)***	(-2.68)***	(-3.12)***	(-1.490)	(-3.23)***	(-7.45)***
No Obs	542	542	542	542	542	542	542	542	542	542	5420
R2	0.136	0.099	0.159	0.152	0.199	0.241	0.133	0.288	0.303	0.244	0.176
Adj R2	0.128	0.090	0.151	0.144	0.192	0.234	0.125	0.281	0.297	0.237	0.175

1) *** are significant at $p<0.01$, ** are significant at $p<0.05$ and * are significant at $p<0.10$
2) Coefficient (t-statistics)

CONCLUSION

This study investigates the relationship between corporate governance, cash holdings, and firm performance. Data were drawn from 542 non-financial Malaysian public firms in 10 years, starting from 2003 to 2012. The panel data were analyzed using Ordinary Least Square (OLS) regression. Based on the findings, corporate governance and firm performance are positively correlated; this finding is consistent with previous studies (Aldamen et al., 2012; Alm and Winberg, 2016; Bansal and Sharma, 2016; Bhagat and Brian, 2019; Bruynseels et al., 2016; Rahman and Ali, 2006). Cash holdings and firm performance are also found to be positively and significantly correlated (Alnori, 2020; Doan, 2020; Ehtiat Karrahemi et al., 2016; Gregory and Wang, 2013; Kumar, 2016; Mikkelson and Partch, 2003). Finally, cash holdings and corporate governance also showed a significant positive association consistent with the findings of Adkins (2011), Bruynseels et al. (2016), Ehtiat Karrahemi et al. (2016), Kuan et al. (2011) and Noman et al., (2019). In line with the pecking order, transaction cost, resource dependency, and stewardship theories, the findings of this study suggest that to record better performance, firms should have higher cash holdings and strong corporate governance. The results of this study offer several practical implications. First, the backbone of firms should create a strategy to allow and maintain higher cash holdings. By doing so, firms can efficiently cope with the market and have more flexibility with investment opportunities; these two steps reduce transaction costs and consequently improve firm performance. Second, policymakers should introduce a guiding principle on the appropriate level of cash holdings for firms in the same industry as a benchmark. Third, as positive firm performance is connected with dividend and bonus payments, the stakeholders and stockholders of a firm as well as the wider community will, directly and indirectly, benefit from higher cash holdings and strong corporate governance.

REFERENCES

Abbott, L. J., Park, Y., & Parker, S. (2000). The effects of audit committee activity and independence on corporate fraud. *Managerial Finance*, *26*(11), 55–68. doi:10.1108/03074350010766990

Abbott, L. J., Parker, S., & Peters, G. F. (2004). Audit committee characteristics and restatements'. *Auditing*, *23*(1), 69–87. doi:10.2308/aud.2004.23.1.69

Abbott, L. J., Parker, S., & Peters, G. F. (2006). Earnings management, litigation risk, and asymmetric audit fee responses. *Auditing*, *25*(1), 85–98. doi:10.2308/aud.2006.25.1.85

Abid, S. F., & Lodhi, S. (2015). Impact of changes in reserve requirement on banks profitability: A case of commercial banks in Pakistan. *European Journal of Business and Management*, *7*(31), 1–6.

AdamsR. B. (2005) What Do Boards Do? Evidence From Board Committee and Director Compensation Data. Evidence From Board Committee and Director Compensation Data. https://ssrn.com/abstract=397401

Adkins, L. C. (2011). *Using Stata For Principles Of Econometrics*. Wiley Global Education.

AggarwalR.SchloetzerJ. D.WilliamsonR. (2014) Economic Consequences of Corporate Governance Mandates for Poorly Governed Firms, Available at SSRN 891411.

Agrawal, A., & Chadha, S. (2005). Corporate governance and accounting scandals. *The Journal of Law & Economics*, *48*(2), 371–406. doi:10.1086/430808

Al-Najjar, B., & Clark, E. (2017). Corporate governance and cash holdings in MENA: Evidence from internal and external governance practices. *Research in International Business and Finance*, *39*, 1–12. doi:10.1016/j.ribaf.2016.07.030

Aldamen, H., Duncan, K., Kelly, S., McNamara, R., & Nagel, S. (2012). Audit committee characteristics and firm performance during the global financial crisis. *Accounting and Finance*, *52*(4), 971–1000. doi:10.1111/j.1467-629X.2011.00447.x

Alm, M., & Winberg, J. (2016). *How Does Gender Diversity on Corporate Boards Affect the Firm Financial Performance?: An Empirical Investigation of Swedish OMX- listed Firms*. University of Gothenburg.

Alnori, F. (2020). Cash holdings: Do they boost or hurt firms' performance? Evidence from listed non-financial firms in Saudi Arabia. *International Journal of Islamic and Middle Eastern Finance and Management*, *13*(5), 919–934. doi:10.1108/IMEFM-08-2019-0338

Alves, S., & Pinho, C. (2012). Executive stock options: A panel data analysis of determinants in Portugal. *International Journal of Economics and Accounting*, *3*(2), 148–164. doi:10.1504/IJEA.2012.048048

Ammann, M., Oesch, D., & Schmid, M. M. (2013). Product market competition, corporate governance, and firm value: Evidence from the EU area. *European Financial Management*, *19*(3), 452–469. doi:10.1111/j.1468-036X.2010.00605.x

Andreou, P. C., Louca, C., & Panayides, P. M. (2014). Corporate governance, financial management decisions and firm performance: Evidence from the maritime industry. *Transportation Research Part E, Logistics and Transportation Review*, *63*, 59–78. doi:10.1016/j.tre.2014.01.005

Baltagi, B. H. (2009). *A Companion to Econometric Analysis of Panel Data*. John Wiley and Sons.

Bansal, N., & Sharma, A. K. (2016). Audit committee, corporate governance and firm performance: Empirical evidence from India. *International Journal of Economics and Finance*, *8*(3), 103. doi:10.5539/ijef.v8n3p103

Barber, N., Ghiselli, R., & Deale, C. (2007). Assessing the relationship of CEO compensation and company financial performance in the restaurant segment of the hospitality industry. *Journal of Foodservice Business Research*, *9*(4), 65–82. doi:10.1300/J369v09n04_05

Bates, T. W., Kahle, K. M., & Stulz, R. M. (2009). Why do US firms hold so much more cash than they used to? *The Journal of Finance*, *64*(5), 1985–2021. doi:10.1111/j.1540-6261.2009.01492.x

Benjamin, S. J., & Ehtiatkar Rahemi, K. (2013). A test of audit committee characteristics and free cash flows. *Corporate Ownership and Control*, *10*(2), 611–626. doi:10.22495/cocv10i2c3art4

Bhagat, S., & Brian, B. (2019). Corporate governance and firm performance: The sequel. *Journal of Corporate Finance*, *58*, 142–168. doi:10.1016/j.jcorpfin.2019.04.006

Bigelli, M., & Sánchez-Vidal, J. (2012). Cash holdings in private firms. *Journal of Banking & Finance*, *36*(1), 26–35. doi:10.1016/j.jbankfin.2011.06.004

Brick, I. E., & Chidambaran, N. (2010). Board meetings, committee structure, and firm value'. *Journal of Corporate Finance*, *16*(4), 533–553. doi:10.1016/j.jcorpfin.2010.06.003

Bruinshoofd, A., & de Haan, L. (2005). *Financing the New Economy: are ICT Firms Really That Different?* De Nederlandsche Bank.

Bruynseels, L., Krishnamoorthy, G., & Wright, A. (2016). *The Association Between Audit Committee Chair Characteristics And Earnings Management*. Academic Press.

CaiJ.LiuY.QianY.YuM. (2015) Information Asymmetry and Corporate Governance, Available at SSRN: https://ssrn.com/abstract=1082589

Chen, C. X., Lu, H., & Sougiannis, T. (2012). The agency problem, corporate governance, and the asymmetrical behavior of selling, general, and administrative costs. *Contemporary Accounting Research*, *29*(1), 252–282. doi:10.1111/j.1911-3846.2011.01094.x

Chen, K. Y., & Zhou, J. (2007). Audit committee, board characteristics, and auditor switch decisions by andersen's clients. *Contemporary Accounting Research*, *24*(4), 1085–1117. doi:10.1506/car.24.4.2

Chen, Y. R. (2008). Corporate governance and cash holdings: Listed new economy versus old economy firms. *Corporate Governance*, *16*(5), 430–442. doi:10.1111/j.1467-8683.2008.00701.x

Chen, Y.-R., & Chuang, W.-T. (2009). Alignment or entrenchment? corporate governance and cash holdings in growing firms. *Journal of Business Research*, *62*(11), 1200–1206. doi:10.1016/j.jbusres.2008.06.004

Claessens, S., & Yurtoglu, B. B. (2013). Corporate governance in emerging markets: A survey. *Emerging Markets Review*, *15*, 1–33. doi:10.1016/j.ememar.2012.03.002

Coase, R. H. (1937). The nature of the firm. *Economica*, *4*(16), 386–405. doi:10.1111/j.1468-0335.1937.tb00002.x

CohenD.LiB. (2013) Why Do Firms Hold Less Cash? Why Do Firms Hold Less Cash, Available at SSRN: https://ssrn.com/abstract=2440794

Cui, J., Jo, H., & Na, H. (2018). Does corporate social responsibility affect information asymmetry? *Journal of Business Ethics*, *148*(3), 549–572. doi:10.100710551-015-3003-8

Daily, C. M., & Dalton, D. R. (2015). Corporate governance in the small firm: Prescriptions for CEOs and directors. *Journal of Small Business Strategy*, *5*(1), 57–68.

Davidson, R., Goodwin-Stewart, J., & Kent, P. (2005). Internal governance structures and earnings management. *Accounting and Finance*, *45*(2), 241–267. doi:10.1111/j.1467-629x.2004.00132.x

Deb, P., David, P., & O'Brien, J. (2017). When is cash good or bad for firm performance? *Strategic Management Journal*, *38*(2), 436–454. doi:10.1002mj.2486

Dittmar, A., & Mahrt-Smith, J. (2007). Corporate governance and the value of cash holdings. *Journal of Financial Economics*, *83*(3), 599–634. doi:10.1016/j.jfineco.2005.12.006

Doan, T. (2020). The effect of cash holdings on firm performance: Evidence from Vietnam listed firms. *Accounting*, *6*(5), 721–726. doi:10.5267/j.ac.2020.6.012

Ehtiat Karrahemi, K., Abdul Rasid, S. Z., & Basiruddin, R. (2016). Cash holdings and corporate governance: An empirical study on Malaysian publicly listed companies. *Afro-Asian Journal of Finance and Accounting*, *6*(4), 305–317. doi:10.1504/AAJFA.2016.080520

Elzahar, H., & Hussainey, K. (2012). Determinants of narrative risk disclosures in UK interim reports. *The Journal of Risk Finance*, *13*(2), 133–147. doi:10.1108/15265941211203189

Fauzi, F., Hewa-Wellalage, N., & Locke, S. (2012). The global financial crisis' impact on short-term performance of IPO: The case study of New Zealand firms' IPOs. *Asian Journal of Finance and Accounting*, *4*(2), 180–198. doi:10.5296/ajfa.v4i2.1829

Francis, B., Hasan, I., & Wu, Q. (2015). Professors in the Boardroom and Their Impact on Corporate Governance and Firm Performance. *Financial Management*, *44*(3), 547–581. doi:10.1111/fima.12069

Francis, B. B., Hasan, I., & Wu, Q. (2012) *Do Corporate Boards Affect Firm Performance? New Evidence from the Financial Crisis.* Bank of Finland Research Discussion Paper.

Garcia-Teruel, P. J., Martinez-Sola, C., & Martinez-Solano, P. (2011). Corporate cash holdings and firm value. *Applied Economics*, *45*(2), 161–170.

GarmaiseM. J.LiuJ. (2005) Corruption, Firm Governance, and the Cost of Capital. https://ssrn.com/abstract=644017 doi:10.2139srn.644017

Gregory, A., & Wang, Y.-H. (2013). Cash acquirers: Can free cash flow, debt and institutional ownership explain long-run performance? *Review of Behavioural Finance*, *5*(1), 35–57. doi:10.1108/RBF-02-2013-0010

GuneyY.OzkanA.OzkanN. (2003) Additional International Evidence on Corporate Cash Holdings, Available at SSRN: https://ssrn.com/abstract=406721.2003 doi:10.2139srn.406721

HabibA. 2005. Information Risk and the Cost of Capital: Review of the Empirical Literature. https://ssrn.com/abstract=722781 doi:10.2139srn.722781

Han, S. H., Kim, M., Lee, D. H., & Lee, S. (2014). Information asymmetry, corporate governance, and shareholder wealth: Evidence from unfaithful disclosures of Korean listed firms. *Asia-Pacific Journal of Financial Studies*, *43*(5), 690–720. doi:10.1111/ajfs.12064

Harford, J., Mansi, S. A., & Maxwell, W. F. (2012). Corporate Governance and Firm Cash Holdings in the US. In Corporate Governance (pp. 107-138). Springer.

Hsiao, C. (2014). *Analysis of Panel Data, 54*. Cambridge University Press. doi:10.1017/CBO9781139839327

Ismail, R. (2016). Impact of liquidity management on profitability of Pakistani firms: A case of KSE-100 index. *International Journal of Innovation and Applied Studies*, *14*(2), 304.

Ittner, C. D., Lambert, R. A., & Larcker, D. F. (2003). The structure and performance consequences of equity grants to employees of new economy firms. *Journal of Accounting and Economics*, *34*(1), 89–127. doi:10.1016/S0165-4101(02)00088-5

Jebran, K., Chen, S., Tauni, M. Z., & Ahmad, H. (2019). Corporate governance, ultimate owner, and target cash holdings: Evidence from China. *SAGE Open*, *9*(4), 1–12. doi:10.1177/2158244019894293

Jensen, M. C. (1986). Agency costs of free cash flow, corporate finance, and takeovers. *The American Economic Review*, 323–329.

Jensen, M. C. (1993). The modern industrial revolution, exit, and the failure of internal control systems. *The Journal of Finance*, *48*(3), 831–880. doi:10.1111/j.1540-6261.1993.tb04022.x

Jensen, M. C., & Meckling, W. H. (1979). *Theory of the Firm: Managerial Behavior, Agency Costs, and Ownership Structure*. Springer.

John, K., Litov, L., & Yeung, B. (2008). Corporate governance and risk-taking. *The Journal of Finance*, *63*(4), 1679–1728. doi:10.1111/j.1540-6261.2008.01372.x

Kahle, K. M., & Stulz, R. M. (2013). Access to capital, investment, and the financial crisis. *Journal of Financial Economics*, *110*(2), 280–299. doi:10.1016/j.jfineco.2013.02.014

Kalcheva, I., & Lins, K. V. (2007). International evidence on cash holdings and expected managerial agency problems. *Review of Financial Studies*, *20*(4), 1087–1112. doi:10.1093/rfs/hhm023

Krafft, J., Qu, Y., Quatraro, F., & Ravix, J.-L. (2014). Corporate governance, value and performance of firms: New empirical results on convergence from a large international database. *Industrial and Corporate Change*, *23*(2), 361–397. doi:10.1093/icc/dtt007

Kuan, T. H., Li, C. S., & Chu, S. H. (2011). Cash holdings and corporate governance in family-controlled firms. *Journal of Business Research*, *64*(7), 757–764. doi:10.1016/j.jbusres.2010.07.004

Kumar, P., & Zattoni, A. (2013). Corporate governance, board of directors, and firm performance'. *Corporate Governance*, *21*(4), 311–313. doi:10.1111/corg.12032

Kumar, S. (2016). Corporate governance and firm performance in Indian listed IT companies. *Corporate Governance*, *2*(10), 219–230.

Kusnadi, Y. (2011). Do corporate governance mechanisms matter for cash holdings and firm value? *Pacific-Basin Finance Journal*, *19*(5), 554–570. doi:10.1016/j.pacfin.2011.04.002

Kwan, J. H., & Lau, W. Y. (2019). The Effects of Country-Level Governance and Corporate Cash Holdings: Evidence from Hospitality Firms in ASEAN-5. *Humanities (Washington)*, *7*(3), 123–140. doi:10.18488/journal.73.2019.73.123.140

Larcker, D., Richardson, S., & Tuna, A. (2005). *How important is corporate governance?* SSRN Working Paper.

Lin, J. W., & Hwang, M. I. (2010). Audit quality, corporate governance, and earnings management: A meta-analysis. *International Journal of Auditing*, *14*(1), 57–77. doi:10.1111/j.1099-1123.2009.00403.x

Liu, Y., Miletkov, M. K., Wei, Z., & Yang, T. (2015). Board independence and firm performance in China. *Journal of Corporate Finance*, *30*, 223–244. doi:10.1016/j.jcorpfin.2014.12.004

Lombardo, D., & Pagano, M. (2006). *Legal Determinants of the Return on Equity, Corporate and Institutional Transparency for Economic Growth in Europe*. SSRN Working Paper.

LRBM. (2014). Kuala Lumpur Stock Exchange (KLSE) Listing Requirements 2001. Kuala Lumpur, Malaysia: LRBM.

Lumpkin, G. T., & Dess, G. G. (2001). Linking two dimensions of entrepreneurial orientation to firm performance: The moderating role of environment and industry life cycle. *Journal of Business Venturing*, *16*(5), 429–451. doi:10.1016/S0883-9026(00)00048-3

Martínez-Sola, C., García-Teruel, P. J., & Martínez-Solano, P. (2013). Corporate cash holding and firm value. *Applied Economics*, *45*(2), 161–170. doi:10.1080/00036846.2011.595696

Mikkelson, W. H., & Partch, M. M. (2003). Do persistent large cash reserves hinder performance? *Journal of Financial and Quantitative Analysis*, *38*(2), 275–294. doi:10.2307/4126751

Miller, D., Breton-Miller, I. L., & Lester, R. H. (2013). Family firm governance, strategic conformity, and performance: Institutional vs. strategic perspectives. *Organization Science*, *24*(1), 189–209. doi:10.1287/orsc.1110.0728

MohanA.ChandramohanS. (2018) Impact of Corporate Governance On Firm Performance: Empirical Evidence from India, Available at SSRN: https://ssrn.com/abstract=3133491

Morellec, E., Nikolov, B., & Zucchi, F. (2013). *Competition, cash holdings, and financing decisions.* Swiss Finance Institute Research Paper, 13-72.

Myers, S. C., & Majluf, N. S. (1984). Corporate financing and investment decisions when firms have information that investors do not have. *Journal of Financial Economics*, *13*(2), 187–221. doi:10.1016/0304-405X(84)90023-0

Noman, M., Din, B. H., & Mustafa, F. (2019). The influence of corporate governance on cash holdings; Empirical evidence from Jordan. *Asian Journal of Multidisciplinary Studies*, *7*(3), 1–5.

Opler, T., Pinkowitz, L., Stulz, R., & Williamson, R. (1999). The determinants and implications of corporate cash holdings. *Journal of Financial Economics*, *52*(1), 3–46. doi:10.1016/S0304-405X(99)00003-3

Owusu, A., & Weir, C. (2018). Agency costs, ownership structure and corporate governance mechanisms in Ghana. *International Journal of Accounting. Auditing and Performance Evaluation*, *14*(1), 63–84. doi:10.1504/IJAAPE.2018.089414

Raghunandan, K., & Rama, D. V. (2007). Determinants of audit committee diligence. *Accounting Horizons*, *21*(3), 265–279. doi:10.2308/acch.2007.21.3.265

Rahman, A. H. A., & Muhamad, S. F. (2013). Corporate governance and firms cash holding in Malaysia. *Proceeding of the International Conference on Social Science Research*, 1236-1247.

Rahman, R. A., & Ali, F. H. M. (2006). Board, audit committee, culture and earnings management: Malaysian evidence. *Managerial Auditing Journal*, *21*(7), 783–804. doi:10.1108/02686900610680549

Rahmat, M. M., Iskandar, T. M., & Saleh, N. M. (2009). Audit committee characteristics in financially distressed and non-distressed companies. *Managerial Auditing Journal*, *24*(7), 624–638. doi:10.1108/02686900910975350

Rasbash, J., Browne, W., Goldstein, H., Yang, M., Plewis, I., & Healy, M. (2000). *A User's Guide to MLwiN*. University of Bristol.

Saddour, K. (2006). *The determinants and the value of cash holdings: Evidence from French firms.* Cahier De Recherche n. 6.

Securities Commission of Malaysia. (2017). *Malaysian Code on Corporate Governance*. Available at https://www.sc.com.my/api/documentms/download.ashx?id=70a5568b-1937-4d2b-8cbf-3aefed112c0a

Shleifer, A., & Vishny, R. W. (1997). A survey of corporate governance. *The Journal of Finance*, *52*(2), 737–783. doi:10.1111/j.1540-6261.1997.tb04820.x

Shleifer, A., & Wolfenzon, D. (2002). Investor protection and equity markets. *Journal of Financial Economics*, *66*(1), 3–27. doi:10.1016/S0304-405X(02)00149-6

Singham, K. (2003). Corporate governance in Malaysia. *Bond L. Rev.*, *15*, i.

Tam, O. K., & Tan, M. G. S. (2007). Ownership, governance and firm performance in Malaysia'. *Corporate Governance*, *15*(2), 208–222. doi:10.1111/j.1467-8683.2007.00555.x

TulungJ. E.RamdaniD. (2018) Independence, Size and Performance of the Board: An Emerging Market Research. https://ssrn.com/abstract=3133857 doi:10.22495/cocv15i2c1p6

Velnampy, T. (2013). Corporate governance and firm performance: A study of Sri Lankan manufacturing companies. *Journal of Economics and Sustainable Development*, *4*(3), 228–235.

Walker, D. (2009). *A review of corporate governance in UK banks and other financial industry entities.* Academic Press.

Yusoff, W. F. W., & Alhaji, I. A. (2012). Corporate governance and firm performance of listed companies in Malaysia. *Trends and Development in Management Studies*, *1*(1), 43–65.

Zabri, S. M., Ahmad, K., & Wah, K. K. (2016). Corporate governance practices and firm performance: Evidence from top 100 public listed companies in Malaysia. *Procedia Economics and Finance*, *35*, 287–296. doi:10.1016/S2212-5671(16)00036-8

KEY TERMS AND DEFINITIONS

Board of Directors: An elected group of individuals that represent shareholders.

Cash Holdings: Liquidity and the retention of cash in a company.

Corporate Governance: The system of rules, practices, and processes by which a company is directed and controlled.

Firm Performance: Stability or healthiness of a company.

Chapter 14
Accounting Conservatism and Corporate Governance: Firm-Level Evidence From Turkey

Ahmet Özcan
Adana Alparslan Türkeş Science and Technology University, Turkey

ABSTRACT

In this chapter, the impacts of corporate governance mechanisms on accounting conservatism are examined by using a sample that includes 85 non-financial firms quoted in Borsa Istanbul during the years of 2013 to 2018. The results of empirical analysis indicate that board size, board independency, institutional ownership, and firm size are positively related with accounting conservatism. However, leverage is negatively related with accounting conservatism, while there is no statistically significant association between CEO duality and accounting conservatism. This chapter contributes to limited literature on the association between accounting conservatism practices and corporate governance in the emerging market.

INTRODUCTION

Accounting conservatism, a prominent feature of financial information, is one of the critical issues in the economic environment. Conservatism, one of the most important accounting principles, influences financial reporting process in many ways (Basu, 1997). Accounting conservatism improves the reliability of financial statements by constraining firm managements' opportunistic behavior (Ball and Shivakumar, 2006; Watts, 2003; Mora and Walker, 2015). Additionally, accounting conservatism significantly decreases agency problems within the firm and protects creditors from bad management.

The optimal level of accounting conservatism enhances the quality of financial market participants' decisions. Watts (2003) stated that regulations massively influence accounting conservatism. To save the interests of creditors and investors, standard setting bodies may push firms to adopt more conservative accounting practices (Bushman and Piotroski, 2006).

DOI: 10.4018/978-1-7998-7596-3.ch014

The presence of accounting conservatism leads to a decrease in the net profit and total assets. Accounting conservatism enables firms to defer the recognition of positive economic transactions until the realization and recognize negative economic transactions when anticipated.

In today's business environment, management incentives play a pivotal role in financial reporting policies. Lewitt (1998) stated that certain management incentives may lead distortions in firms' financial statements and corporate scandals. The concerns related to management incentives have led the call for the well-established corporate governance mechanisms. Corporate governance mechanisms can be used to effectively mitigate managerial opportunism.

Corporate governance has important effects on the quality of financial statements. Firms having effective corporate governance mechanisms adopt more accounting conservatism (García et al., 2007; Beekes et al., 2004; Ahmed and Henry, 2012). Additionally, cultural values, social norms and macroeconomic structure are important factors shaping corporate governance standards in the business environment.

In the developed economies, the impacts of corporate governance on accounting conservatism have been well documented. However, there are few research studies that aim to analyze the impacts of corporate governance on accounting conservatism in the developing economy. Thus, the finding of the present chapter is prominent as it reveals the impacts of corporate governance on accounting conservatism in the developing economy using a multivariate model.

The rest of the book chapter is structured as follows. Second section discusses literature review and hypotheses development. Third section reveals research design. The results of empirical analysis are discussed in the fourth section. The final section concludes the chapter and provides suggestions for further studies.

LITERATURE REVIEW AND HYPOTHESES DEVELOPMENT

In this section of the chapter, literature review and hypotheses development are presented. The investigation of impacts of corporate governance on accounting conservatism practices needs further investigation. The empirical results of previous studies are inconclusive. The majority of studies that investigate the impacts of corporate governance on accounting conservatism are guided by agency theory.

Agency problems emerge between firm management and shareholders. In the modern business environment, the controlling shareholders tend to pursue their own self-interests. This leads to serious agency problems. As the interests of controlling shareholders and minority shareholders differ, the agency conflicts are likely to occur within the firm.

Corporate governance mechanisms have a critical role in solving these problems (Mohammad et al., 2017). Corporate governance mechanisms can constrain firms' management opportunism. The ownership structure in Turkey and other emerging economies is highly concentrated. Agency problems frequently emerge within firms operating in developing economies. Information asymmetry among controlling shareholders and minority shareholders prompts accounting conservatism practices (LaFond and Watts, 2008).

According to the agency theory, the appointment of independent board members can decrease agency problems through monitoring the firm management's actions (Fama, 1980; Jensen and Meckling, 1976). In the competitive economic environment, the independent board members are strongly needed on the board of firms to effectively monitor the actions of management.

Regulatory bodies (Capital Markets Board and Banking Regulation and Supervision Agency) in Turkey encourage firms to hire more independent board members in the board of directors. The presence of outside board members contributes to the greater transparency and accountability. When non-independent directors dominate board of directors, the firm management is likely to adopt aggressive accounting practices. Suleiman (2014), Kukah et al. (2016) and Beekes et al. (2004) state that a high percentage of independent board members induces accounting conservatism practices, claiming that the higher percentage of independent board members can prominently alleviate the firm management's opportunistic behavior. Hence, the following hypothesis is proposed.

H1: There is a positive relationship between the level of accounting conservatism and percentage of independent board members.

There are opposing views on the relationship between board size and accounting conservatism practices. Some previous studies claim that small-sized boards are much more effective than large-sized boards. Ahmed et al. (2006) found that there is an inverse relationship between board size and the effectiveness of monitoring activities. Firms that have large-sized boards tend to suffer from coordination problems among board members (Jensen, 1993). It is worth noting that board size is one of the factors affecting corporate governance mechanisms. In today's competitive economic environment, boards should have members from diverse backgrounds to effectively conduct their operations (Mishra and Jhunjhunwala, 2013). Larger board size positively influences board diversity. Ahmed and Duellman (2007) stated that high board diversity results in greater specialization. Thus, the greater specialization within board of directors can enhance the effectiveness of monitoring activities. Taken as a whole, large-sized board significantly boosts the monitoring activities' effectiveness, resulting in high-level of accounting conservatism practices. Thus, the second hypothesis is formulated as follows.

H2: There is a positive relationship between the level of accounting conservatism and board size.

Fama and Jensen (1983) asserted that the separation of duties in the firm is likely to increase the effectiveness of monitoring mechanisms. Chi et al. (2009) argued that CEO duality leads to agency problems and information asymmetry between firm management and stockholders. The chairman of the board is the head of board. The chairman of the board is responsible for recruiting, sacking and assessing the performance of CEO. Hence, the performance of CEO cannot be accurately assessed when the same person occupies both the position of CEO and chairman of the board. Klein (2002) purported that CEO duality can increase the likelihood of managerial opportunism. Krishnan and Vivanathan (2008) found that CEO duality is a sign of weak corporate governance and negatively associated with accounting conservatism. Based on prior literature, the present chapter claims that CEO duality result in less accounting conservatism practices and formulates the following hypothesis.

H3: There is a negative relationship between the level of accounting conservatism and CEO duality.

After the financial liberalization policies implemented in 1980s, Turkish financial markets succeed to grab the attention of institutional investors around the world. Currently, institutional investors have huge impacts on Turkish financial markets. Institutional investors played a vital role in the governance of firms. Institutional investors give high prominence to the accuracy and reliability of financial statements disclosed by firms. Institutional investors have significant abilities to effectively monitor and affect the decisions of the firm management and are much more capable of communicating with firm management than individual investors. The high level of institutional ownership can constrain managerial opportunism (Nesbitt, 1994; Hartzell and Starks, 2003). Kaplan and Minton (1994) advocated that institutional ownership can contribute to decrease agency problems within the firm. The prior literature supported the statement that institutional investors demand more conservative accounting practices. Hence, the last hypothesis is formulated as follows.

H4: There is a positive relationship between the level of accounting conservatism and institutional ownership.

RESEARCH DESIGN

Sample Selection

This section provides details about sample selection process. The sample of this study consists of 85 non-financial firms listed on Borsa Istanbul (BIST) 100 index over the period from 2013 to 2018. The data of sample firms are collected through annual reports and website of public disclosure platform (www.kap.org.tr).

In this book chapter, firms operating in financial industry are excluded from the sample since the specific regulations adopted by these firms may influence their level of accounting conservatism practices. Moreover, the exclusion of financial firms enables us to compare the empirical results of this study with those of previous studies.

Table 1 shows sample selection process and industry classifications of sample firms. The final sample used in this study includes 85 firms. Sample firms operate in eleven different industries, implying a broad distribution of industries. According to table 1, 31.7% of sample firms are operating in manufacturing industry.

Empirical Model and Variables

In this part of the book chapter, the empirical model and variables are presented. In the selection of independent variables, the present chapter follows Nasr and Ntim (2018), Lim (2011), Chi et al. (2009) and García Lara et al. (2007). The use of relevant variables significantly enhances the quality of empirical results. Control variables are included to invigorate the empirical model. The control variables used in the empirical model are leverage and firm size. Highly-leveraged firms are likely to suffer from the conflicts between bondholders and shareholders. These conflicts considerably influence the level of accounting conservatism (Ahmed and Duellman, 2007).

Large-sized firms are more likely to employ conservative accounting policies in order to diminish political costs (Watts and Zimmerman, 1990). Contrarily, Khan and Watts (2009) assert that large-sized firms does not suffer from high information asymmetry and hence less demand for conservative accounting practices. Table 2 presents the definition and measurement of variables employed in the empirical analysis.

Table 1. Sample Selection and Industry Classifications

Panel A		
Number of firms quoted in BIST 100	100	
Excluding		
Financial firms	15	
Final sample	85	
Panel B	**Number of Firms**	**Percentage**
Manufacturing	27	31.7
Consumer goods	10	11.7
Technology	8	9.4
Petroleum and Chemical	6	7
Construction	6	7
Beverage and Food	6	7
Transportation	6	7
Health Care and Sport	5	5.8
Energy	5	5.8
Mining	4	4.7
Textile	2	2.3
Total	85	100

Table 2. The Definition and Measurement of Variables

Variable	Definition	Measurement
Dependent Variable		
CONS	Accounting conservatism	Book-to-market ratio measure of conservatism based on Beaver and Ryan (2000).
Independent Variables		
BIND	Board independency	Percentage of independent board members
BSIZE	Board size	Total number of board members
CEODUAL	CEO duality	A dummy variable that takes the value 1 when CEO occupies the position of head of the board, zero otherwise.
INSTOWN	Institutional ownership	The percentage of a firm's common stock owned by institutional investors
Control Variables		
LEV	Leverage	The ratio of total debt to total assets
SIZE	Firm size	The natural log of total assets

The model developed by Beaver and Ryan (2000) is employed to measure the level of accounting conservatism. Beaver and Ryan's (2000) measure of conservatism is based on market data. In this chapter, book-to-market ratio measure of conservatism based on Beaver and Ryan (2000) is multiplied by negative one for the ease of interpretation. According to model developed by Beaver and Ryan (2000), there is a positive relationship between the level of accounting conservatism accounting practices and firm growth. Beaver and Ryan (2000) stated that the market value is significantly higher than book value in the long run when the firm employs conservative accounting practices. In other words, firms that employ conservative accounting practices tend to have a lower book to market ratio due to understatement of book value of equity. The empirical model consists of four different independent variables and two control variables. To test research hypotheses, the following fixed effects regression model is created.

$$CONS_{it} = \beta_0 + \beta_1 BIND + \beta_2 BSIZE + \beta_3 CEODUAL$$
$$+\beta_4 INSTOWN + \beta_5 LEV + \beta_6 SIZE + \varepsilon_{it}$$

EMPIRICAL ANALYSIS

Descriptive Statistics and Correlation Analysis

This section is devoted to present descriptive statistics and correlation analysis. Table 3 shows descriptive statistics of empirical variables. For independent variables, on average, 33.2 percent of directors are independent. The descriptive statistics show that average board size is 7.226. Moreover, 55.8 percent of sample firms separate the positions of CEO and head of board, a lower percentage than that disclosed by firms operating in the United States, 62.2 percent (Enache and García-Meca, 2019). Even though there is no clear recommendation of Capital Markets of Board for the separation of CEO and head of board, CEO duality in sample firms is not high. The average institutional ownership is 0.595, ranging from 0.05 to 0.82. The standard deviation of 0.22 reveals that the ownership of sample firms exhibits considerable variation. The average leverage ratio is 0.543, with the range being 0.09-0.74, suggesting that some sample firms rely more on debt financing. The natural log of total assets is between 4.87 and 11.160, with the average being 8.837, implying that the sample includes relatively large-sized firms.

Table 3. Descriptive Statistics

Variable	Obs.	Mean	Std. Dev.	Min	Max
CONS	510	0.117	0.094	-0.14	0.234
BIND	510	0.332	0.049	0.15	0.400
BSIZE	510	7.226	1.792	6	15
CEODUAL	510	0.442	0.497	0	1
INSTOWN	510	0.595	0.220	0.05	0.820
LEV	510	0.543	0.207	0.09	0.740
SIZE	510	8.837	1.348	4.87	11.160

Notes: All variable definitions are presented in Table 2.

Table 4 shows the correlations among research variables. The problem of multicollinearity exists when the correlation among variables exceeds 0.80 (Kumari, 2008). As shown in table 4, none of the correlation coefficients is above 0.80. The results indicate that accounting conservatism is significantly positively correlated with board independency, institutional ownership, leverage and size. Generally speaking, the correlation coefficients among variables align with agency theory.

Table 4. Pearson Correlations

Variables	CONS	BIND	BSIZE	CEODUAL	INSTOWN	LEV	SIZE
CONS	1						
BIND	0.68***	1					
BSIZE	-0.02	-0.13***	1				
CEODUAL	0.05	0.05	-0.09*	1			
INSTOWN	0.73***	0.76***	-0.13***	0.05	1		
LEV	0.61***	0.69***	-0.09**	0.14***	0.71***	1	
SIZE	0.68***	0.77***	-0.15***	-0.02	0.70***	0.75***	1

Notes: All variable definitions are presented in Table 2. ***, ** and * indicate statistical significance at the 1%, 5% and 10% levels, respectively.

The Results of Regression Analysis

This section presents the results of empirical analysis. Fixed effects regression model is used to analyze the relationship between accounting conservatism and predictor variables. Fixed effects regression model in the studies of accounting conservatism has been employed by Beekes et al. (2004), Enache and García-Meca (2019) and Ahmed and Duellman (2007). Table 5 reports the results of fixed effects regression analysis.

Table 5. Regression Results

	Coefficient	t-Statistic
BIND	0.388***	2.79
BSIZE	0.004***	2.75
CEODUAL	0.014	1.49
INSTOWN	0.262***	4.87
LEV	-0.188***	-4.37
SIZE	0.018**	2.34
Constant	-0.258***	-4.74
Observations	3570	
R-squared	50.76	
Prob> chi2	0.000	

Notes: All variable definitions are presented in Table 2. ***, ** and * indicate statistical significance at the 1%, 5% and 10% levels, respectively.

The coefficient on board independency is positive and statistically significant at the 1% level, suggesting that boards dominated by independent directors are likely to adopt conservative accounting practices. Another possible explanation is that independent directors demand more conservative accounting policies so as to decrease agency conflicts within the firm. This finding is consistent with those of Nasr and Ntim (2018), Kukah et al. (2016) and Beekes et al. (2004). Hypothesis 1 that there is a positive relationship between the level of accounting conservatism and percentage of independent board members is accepted.

Table 5 indicates a statistically significant positive relationship between accounting conservatism and board size, consistent with Ahmed and Henry (2012). This result implies that firms with a large-sized board tend to employ conservative accounting policies. In a firm with a large-sized board, board members have great opportunity to specialize in a specific area. The greater specialization prominently bolsters the effectiveness of monitoring activities. Hypothesis 2 that there is a positive relationship between the level of accounting conservatism and board size is accepted.

The coefficient on CEO duality is not negative and statistically significant in the empirical model. This result supports the findings of García et al. (2007) and Chi et al. (2009). As the CEO occupies the position of head of the board, the level of accounting conservatism policies adopted by the sample firm is increased. This finding can be explained by the view that when CEO who occupies the position of head of the board tends to adopt conservative accounting policies to eliminate problems arising from weak governance system. Hypothesis 3 that there is a negative relationship between the level of accounting conservatism and CEO duality is rejected.

The results of regression analysis indicate that there is a positive and statistically significant relationship between accounting conservatism and institutional ownership. In today's business environment, institutional ownership is one of the important monitoring mechanisms. This finding suggests that as institutional ownership rises, the firm management is more inclined to adopt conservative reporting policies. Hypothesis 4 that there is a positive relationship between the level of accounting conservatism and institutional ownership is accepted.

The coefficients on control variables (leverage and firm size) are statistically significant in the empirical model. The results of regression analysis indicate that low-leveraged firms demand more conservative accounting policies. This result supports the notion that highly-leveraged sample firms may adopt aggressive accounting policies to report better financial position than actual. This finding contradicts previous research (Ahmed and Henry, 2012; Ahmed et al., 2002; Rodríguez, 2010).

According to table 5, there is a positive association between accounting conservatism and firm size, which supports the findings of Lim (2011) who asserted that large-sized firms adopt more conservative accounting policies to eliminate agency problems. It is worth mentioning that 50.76% variation in accounting conservatism is explained by predictor variables and the empirical model is statistically significant (Prob>chi2= 0.000).

CONCLUSION

Conservatism is among the important qualitative characteristics of financial statements. Accounting conservatism enables firms to report losses more quickly than gains. Timely recognition of operating losses enables firms to speed up corrective measures when needed. Accounting conservatism practices deter the management to exaggerate financial performance of the firm. This is because accounting conservatism practices require greater verification before reporting gains and losses. Do and Nabar (2019) stated that accounting conservatism enables firms' management to focus on value-adding activities.

As the world economy is becoming much more globalized than before, corporate governance practices rapidly evolve to satisfy the needs of firms. In the current business environment, corporate governance mechanisms have substantial influences over accounting policy choice. Corporate governance mechanisms are viewed as an important tool that can prominently mitigate agency conflicts between shareholders and firm management.

This chapter aims to contribute to the existing literature on the interaction between corporate governance and accounting conservatism. In the present book chapter, multivariate model is established to analyze the impacts of corporate governance measures on accounting conservatism practices. Also, two control variables, leverage and firm size, are added to the model in order to capture the impacts of omitted variables.

Employing a sample that consists of 3570 firm-year observations over five-year period 2013-2018, this chapter concluded that board independency, board size, institutional ownership, leverage and firm size are statistically significant related with accounting conservatism practices. Conversely, no statistical significant relationship is found between accounting conservatism and CEO duality. Taken together, this chapter shed more light on previous studies by producing evidence that well-established corporate governance mechanisms considerably enhance accounting conservatism.

This chapter enables financial market participants and standard setting bodies to deeply understand the relation between corporate governance and accounting conservatism. Future studies can use more sophisticated statistical models to comprehensively analyze the impacts of corporate governance mechanisms on accounting conservatism. Additionally, future studies can concentrate on the impacts of accounting conservatism on economic environment, cost of capital and credit ratings.

REFERENCES

Ahmed, A. S., Billings, B. K., Morton, R. M., & Stanford-Harris, M. (2002). The role of accounting conservatism in mitigating bondholder-shareholder conflicts over dividend policy and in reducing debt costs. *The Accounting Review*, *77*(4), 867–890. doi:10.2308/accr.2002.77.4.867

Ahmed, A. S., & Duellman, S. (2007). Accounting conservatism and board of director characteristics: An empirical analysis. *Journal of Accounting and Economics*, *43*(2-3), 411–437. doi:10.1016/j.jacceco.2007.01.005

Ahmed, K., & Henry, D. (2012). Accounting conservatism and voluntary corporate governance mechanisms by Australian firms. *Accounting and Finance*, *52*(3), 631–662. doi:10.1111/j.1467-629X.2011.00410.x

Ahmed, K., Hossain, M., & Adams, M. B. (2006). The effects of board composition and board size on the informativeness of annual accounting earnings. *Corporate Governance*, *14*(5), 418–431. doi:10.1111/j.1467-8683.2006.00515.x

Ball, R., & Shivakumar, L. (2006). The role of accruals in asymmetrically timely gain and loss recognition. *Journal of Accounting Research*, *44*(2), 207–242. doi:10.1111/j.1475-679X.2006.00198.x

Basu, S. (1997). The conservatism principle and the asymmetric timeliness of earnings. *Journal of Accounting and Economics*, *24*(1), 3–37. doi:10.1016/S0165-4101(97)00014-1

Beaver, W. H., & Ryan, S. G. (2000). Biases and lags in book value and their effects on the ability of the book-to-market ratio to predict book return on equity. *Journal of Accounting Research*, *38*(1), 127–148. doi:10.2307/2672925

Beekes, W., Pope, P., & Young, S. (2004). The link between earnings timeliness, earnings conservatism and board composition: Evidence from the UK. *Corporate Governance*, *12*(1), 47–59. doi:10.1111/j.1467-8683.2004.00342.x

Bushman, R. M., & Piotroski, J. D. (2006). Financial reporting incentives for conservative accounting: The influence of legal and political institutions. *Journal of Accounting and Economics*, *42*(1-2), 107–148. doi:10.1016/j.jacceco.2005.10.005

Cano-Rodríguez, M. (2010). Big auditors, private firms and accounting conservatism: Spanish evidence. *European Accounting Review*, *19*(1), 131–159. doi:10.1080/09638180902989426

Chi, W., Liu, C., & Wang, T. (2009). What affects accounting conservatism: A corporate governance perspective. *Journal of Contemporary Accounting and Economics*, *5*(1), 47–59. doi:10.1016/j.jcae.2009.06.001

Do, C., & Nabar, S. (2019). Macroeconomic effects of aggregate accounting conservatism: A cross-country analysis. *Journal of International Financial Management & Accounting*, *30*(1), 83–107. doi:10.1111/jifm.12093

Enache, L., & García-Meca, E. (2019). Board composition and accounting conservatism: The role of business experts, support specialist and community influentials. *Australian Accounting Review*, *29*(1), 252–265. doi:10.1111/auar.12279

Fama, E. F. (1980). Agency problems and the theory of the firm. *Journal of Political Economy*, *88*(2), 288–307. doi:10.1086/260866

Fama, E. F., & Jensen, M. C. (1983). Separation of ownership and control. *The Journal of Law & Economics*, *26*(2), 301–325. doi:10.1086/467037

García Lara, J. M., Osma, B. G., & Penalva, F. (2007). Board of directors' characteristics and conditional accounting conservatism: Spanish evidence. *European Accounting Review*, *16*(4), 727–755. doi:10.1080/09638180701706922

Hartzell, J. C., & Starks, L. T. (2003). Institutional investors and executive compensation. *The Journal of Finance*, *58*(6), 2351–2374. doi:10.1046/j.1540-6261.2003.00608.x

Jensen, M. C. (1993). The modern industrial revolution, exit, and the failure of internal control systems. *The Journal of Finance*, *48*(3), 831–880. doi:10.1111/j.1540-6261.1993.tb04022.x

Jensen, M. C., & Meckling, W. H. (1976). Theory of the firm: Managerial behavior, agency costs and ownership structure. *Journal of Financial Economics*, *3*(4), 305–360. doi:10.1016/0304-405X(76)90026-X

Kaplan, S. N., & Minton, B. A. (1994). Appointments of outsiders to Japanese boards: Determinants and implications for managers. *Journal of Financial Economics*, *36*(2), 225–258. doi:10.1016/0304-405X(94)90025-6

Khan, M., & Watts, R. L. (2009). Estimation and empirical properties of a firm-year measure of accounting conservatism. *Journal of Accounting and Economics*, *48*(2-3), 132–150. doi:10.1016/j.jacceco.2009.08.002

Klein, A. (2002). Audit committee, board of director characteristics, and earnings management. *Journal of Accounting and Economics*, *33*(3), 375–400. doi:10.1016/S0165-4101(02)00059-9

Krishnan, G. V., & Visvanathan, G. (2008). Does the SOX definition of an accounting expert matter? The association between audit committee directors' accounting expertise and accounting conservatism. *Contemporary Accounting Research*, *25*(3), 827–858. doi:10.1506/car.25.3.7

Kukah, M. A., Amidu, M., & Abor, J. Y. (2016). Corporate governance mechanisms and accounting information quality of listed firms in Ghana. *African Journal of Accounting. Auditing and Finance*, *5*(1), 38–58.

Kumari, S. S. (2008). Multicollinearity: Estimation and elimination. *Journal of Contemporary Research in Management*, *3*(1), 87–95.

Lafond, R., & Watts, R. L. (2008). The information role of conservatism. *The Accounting Review*, *83*(2), 447–478. doi:10.2308/accr.2008.83.2.447

Levitt, A. (1998). Speech by SEC Chairman: The numbers game. Remarks delivered at the NYU Center for Law and Business, New York, NY.

Lim, R. (2011). Are corporate governance attributes associated with accounting conservatism? *Accounting and Finance*, *51*(4), 1007–1030. doi:10.1111/j.1467-629X.2010.00390.x

Mishra, R. K., & Jhunjhunwala, S. (2013). *Diversity and the effective corporate board*. Academic Press.

Mohammed, N. F., Ahmed, K., & Ji, X. D. (2017). Accounting conservatism, corporate governance and political connections. *Asian Review of Accounting*, *25*(2), 288–318. doi:10.1108/ARA-04-2016-0041

Mora, A., & Walker, M. (2015). The implications of research on accounting conservatism for accounting standard setting. *Accounting and Business Research*, *45*(5), 620–650. doi:10.1080/00014788.2015.1048770

Nasr, M. A., & Ntim, C. G. (2018). Corporate governance mechanisms and accounting conservatism: Evidence from Egypt. *Corporate Governance: The International Journal of Business in Society*, *18*(3), 386–407. doi:10.1108/CG-05-2017-0108

Nesbitt, S. L. (1994). Long-term rewards from shareholder activism: A study of the "CalPERS effect. *Journal of Applied Corporate Finance*, *6*(4), 75–80. doi:10.1111/j.1745-6622.1994.tb00251.x

Suleiman, S. (2014). Corporate governance mechanisms and accounting conservatism. *Journal of Management Policies and Practices*, *2*(2), 113–127.

Watts, R. L. (2003). Conservatism in accounting part I: Explanations and implications. *Accounting Horizons*, *17*(3), 207–221. doi:10.2308/acch.2003.17.3.207

Watts, R. L., & Zimmerman, J. L. (1990). Positive accounting theory: A ten year perspective. *The Accounting Review*, *65*(1), 131–156.

Chapter 15
Why Malaysian Companies Are Involved in Related Party Transactions (RPT) in the Context of Corporate Governance (CG)

Suleman Sherali Kamwani
College of Business Administration, Department of Accounting and Finance, A' Sharqiyah University, Oman

Sofri B. Yahya
Universiti Sains Malaysia, Malaysia

ABSTRACT

The regulations related to corporate governance mechanisms such as the sensitivity of pay and performance of chief executive officers, board characteristics, and watches outside of those that are well connected in related party transactions (RPTs)in Malaysia are struggling from the monitoring and enforcement of good corporate governance. The primary aims of this study are to investigate the gap that exists in Malaysian company failures due to appropriate related party transactions and to evaluate the impact of good corporate governance on shareholders' confidence in related party transaction (RPTs) disclosures from the Malaysian Accounting Standards Board (MASB) of regulations. In the year 2000, a study was done by Claessens that examined the data of 236 Malaysian public organizations. The study found the dominancy of a large block of shareholders in organizations in addition to weak institutional structures. This chapter focuses on the usage of related party transactions undertaken to benefit Malaysian companies which have led to financial reporting disclosure information.

DOI: 10.4018/978-1-7998-7596-3.ch015

Figure 1. Related party transactions

INTRODUCTION

The objective of corporate governance is to maximize shareholder values legally and ethically and to ensure transparency and equity foreach stakeholder including the community, investors, vendors, employees, customers, and the government. Nevertheless, the function of corporate governance priorities is to ensure quality in the process of financial reporting disclosure. Ultimately, it is hard to separate corporate governance from related party transactions (RPTs), which are mandatory requirements for companies to follow according to Internal Accounting Standard (IAS) 24. According to the IAS 24 standard, related party transactions must disclose all information and transactions (resources and services) between a subsidiary and its parent company—otherwise, either the ultimate controlling parties or the senior parents, whichever is responsible for generating the financial statement must be disclosed (Standard, 2009).

There are numerous instances of harsh related party transactions around the world in emerging markets and developed countries (Hashim, 2014). Related party transactions attracted global attention when mega organizations such as world.com and Enron declined in early the 2000. Subsequently, scholars began to examine corporate governance from numerous perspectives (Pizzo, 2009). Then, statuary bodies were initiated to imply rules and regulations through financial reporting disclosures to resolve the problem. There are many best practices employed around the world in line with guidelines such as the Sarbanes Oxley and Cadbury reports. Moreover, the accessible literature found chief executive officer performance sensitivity and certain board characteristics to be helpful to corporate governance mechanisms for better management of agency problems, and additionally, huge shareholder possession or high leverage plays a corporate governance role in the management of serious agency problems. Therefore, the sole objective of this paper is to recognize the gap which is a failure in Malaysian companies' corporate governance due to related party transactions. The accomplishment of the study objectives; I intended for develop a framework to reduce manipulation of related party transaction earnings management and also to identify quality drivers for strengthening shareholders' confidence in related party transaction disclosure.

Figure 1 displays the related party transaction occurrence from the beginning of purchasing materials, goods, properties, and executive services by decision-makers with the sellers and suppliers to ensure that profits distributed throughout the related parties.

Figure 2. Organization types in a related party

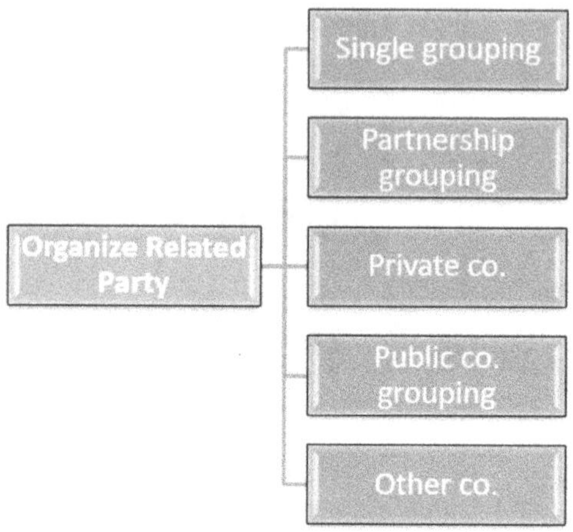

Figure 2 shows that all types of organizations have to be very organized to be involved in related party transactions

BACKGROUND

Importance of Corporate Governance and Related Party Transactions

Corporate governance mechanisms must be able to identify the conflicts in related party transactions ahead of the related parties' attempts at such transactions. Moreover, corporate governance must be accountable to stakeholders, and each party should act in their self-interest and not be subject to any pressure or duress from the other party. Besides, corporate governance should not seize and transfer wealth from a prevailing company to another organization; rather, there should be a boost in worth through corporate governance. Therefore, if corporate governance is performed well, it is easy to control negative experiences, and the board of directors and/or a professional team can assist in improving and controlling the efficiency of the transactions (Saleh, 2005). Chen and Chien showed that corporate governance can lessen the negative effects of related party transactions on business performance (Chen, 2007). Also, Cheung disputed whether the stakeholder could accurately predict the impact of related party transactions value to the firm (Cheung, 2009). Cheung understood that it is a signal of poor corporate governance when the outcome reduces the organizational valuation of those engaged in such transactions (Cheung, 2006). According to the relevant literature, related party transactions have always reflected multifaceted business events between organizations and their directors or managers. According to Johnstone and Bedard (2004) and the American Institute of Certified Public Accountants (AICPA) (2001), in public accounting practice, related party transactions are one of the potential areas for audit risk (Johnstone, 2004). In

2009, the productivity commission commenced an investigation into the current Australian regulatory framework focusing solely on the remuneration of directors and executives (Gul, 2002).

Relationship Between Corporate Governance and Financial Reporting Disclosure

Financial reporting disclosure links the professionals involved in corporate governance. Moreover, it is the communication channel between the organization and other stakeholders for the evaluation of the performance of the entire accounting period. In the principal, corporate governance handles integrity in financial reporting. According to Arleen R. Thomas and Kim M. Gibson, auditors, and top/middle-level management handle ensuring integrity in financial reporting of the organization (Gibson, 2003). According to Sloan, the performance of the company manager is reflected by the financial reporting information, which is main the attraction for management interest (Sloan, 2001).

Motivation or Psychological Reasons why Malaysian Companies are Involved in Related Party Transactions

Johnson et al. revealed several Malaysian examples of expropriation of wealth by controlling organizational stakeholders upon minority stakeholders, and this includes the allocation of assets to new organizations where most of the stake holders control and withdraws cash through questionable transactions (Chan, 2010). With the amendment of the Companies Act of 1965 in 2007 in Malaysia, the rules related to related party transactions became stricter (Malaysia, Incorporating the latest amendment - Act A1299, 2007). However, it is clear from recently reported transactions that there are weaknesses in the rules which may be exploited by the majority (controlling) stakeholders to the disadvantage of minority stakeholders. In Malaysia, the legislation that underlies corporate governance is the Companies Act of 1965 which has been changed about 35 times since its introduction (Salim, 2011). In March 1999, a high-level finance committee published a document revealing a massive loss of confidence by investors in the Malaysian capital market because of abusive corporate behavior involving related party transactions. This was probably due to a few stakeholders controlling and influencing companies as well as the ineffective implementation of the law. As a result, in the year 2000, the finance committee issued a corporate governance code(Governance, 2000). One of the recommendations of this code was that the board of directors should organize an audit committee based on the majority independently responsible for related party transactions within groups or organizations (Saleh, 2007). The corporate governance code was not enforceable by law; therefore, on December 17, 2007, Malaysia implemented a corporate law reform committee to change the organizational legislation in line with the best practices in other parts of the world.

The theory of planned behavior highlights the physiological reasons behind the expropriation of minority shareholder benefits through related party transactions by Malaysian family-owned enterprises (Chrisman, 2003). It was found that while 62.7% of Malaysian public organizations are family-owned enterprises, 28.3% are controlled by only 15 families. In the year 2005, Pearson and Ensley revealed that family members' involvement within the management teams of firms could inspire a high sense of connection to management, encourage solid abilities and beliefs, and foster ahigh degree of agreement on the strategic direction of firms and less negative conflict (Miller, 2006). In 2005, Carney suggested that family-owned organizations should be run and controlled through an efficient and effective governance system instead of through meanness and personalism (Radhakrishnan, 2007).

Nevertheless, more than half of public organizations are family proprietorships, and this shows great dominancy in the Malaysian territory (Claessens, 2000). This pattern has been observed in Thailand, Hong Kong, Singapore, and other East Asian countries. Importantly, family-owned companies' physiological beliefs are useful regarding related party transactions via the family-owned organization. They are based on the guess that people act according to their values in the effort to fulfill their needs. Therefore, the human schools of thought that concentrate on psychological factors and characteristics connected with free enterprise have always been given a high degree of importance—for example, risk-taking, locus of control, achievement, self-confidence, ambiguity tolerance (Begley, 1987; Brännback, 2009), and innovativeness (Schumpeter, 1934, 2008).

In 2005, Connie et al. revealed the significant role of the entrepreneurial personality highlighted in the vital areas of interest (Rauch, 2000). There is a study based on 133 Malaysian small businesses which shows that an enormous number had a rather low motivation for achievement (Radzi, 2017). As well as being a psychological trait, it is a significant ingredient of motivational achievement in entrepreneurial success. This characteristic seemed to be missing in Malaysian local entrepreneurs. Malaysian studies showed the negative features which contributed to the low level of accomplishment motivation. For example, Malaysians do not agree with taking an intermediate risk. Nevertheless, risk taking is another quality highly encouraged among entrepreneurs. Given a task that is difficult and important with a 50% chance of failure in comparison to an assignment that is not difficult but important, 47% would rather not try it. The results show that approximately one-half of people are not happy with taking an intermediate risk with equivalent chances of failure and success (Albaity, 2012).

Atkinson suggested that individuals have a strong aspiration to get success with high achievement while those with short accomplishment motivations are inclined to avoid failure (Atkinson, 1984). The strong reason for avoiding failure is that it is an added undesirable character which is an addition towards low motivation, and Malaysians have more negative attitudes connected with losing or failure; therefore, the association is stronger for family-owned businesses than non-family firms (Albaity, 2012). This finding reveals that related party transactions carried out by family firms are more likely to be used strategically for taking minority shareholder benefits (Munir, 2013). The second reason for related party transactions in Malaysia is the motivation to extract benefits from minority shareholders and transfer them to family ownership (Group, 2019).

According to studies by Villalonga and Amit, family entrepreneurs are likely to relate to declining values because entrepreneurs in these organizations are accustomed to taking benefits from minority stakeholders (Villalonga & Amit, 2006). Moreover, agency theory is also relevant in this outcome, which suggests that managers use more benefits than perquisites, which damages the organizational stakeholders (Jensen, 1976; Kuek, 2015). Apparently, both the concept of tunneling and agency theory suggests that related party transactions help to transfer profits and wealth from organizational funds to managers, thereby leading to the exploitation of minority shareholders (La Porta, 2002a). Studies show the market point of view about the expropriation of minority stakeholders' interests through related party transactions.

In 1997, financial crises in Asia revealed that related party transactions were an abusive practice within Asian countries for three reasons (Hashim, 2013; Lemmon, 2001):

1. The association-based business system and corporation governance offered a faultless environment in Asian countries for controlling stakeholders to profit at the cost of the organization's financial

health. Organizations sold assets at extremely low prices and bought the assets back at inflated prices, and the assets were then offered by the organizations to their controlling stakeholders on conditions far better than the market price.

2. The major risk of offensive related party transactions occurred where controlling stakeholders owned private interests outside the listed organizations, e.g., in Asian countries.
3. The legal implementation in East Asian counties was inappropriate. There is another finding of the managerial motivation to get incentives behind the diverse kinds of related party transaction disclosure. Means and Berele's theory of principal agency conflict revealed in 1932 that related party transactions were harmful to organizations economically.

Besides, market reactions show that related party transactions relate to lower market values (Bertrand, 2002; Wong, 2003; Cheung, 2006; Gordon, 2004). There is a sign in the market of the expropriation of the benefits of minority shareholders (Fana &Wong, 2002). In the year 2000, Johnson et al. innovated the tunneling concept in the context of transferring profits and assets out of an organization for the benefit of those who control them (Chan, 2010). This practice proposes that managers may be part of transactions related to both the concepts of tunneling and agency theory which help to transfer money or profits from company funds into managers' hands for the expropriation of minority stockholders' profits (Kuek, 2015.La Porta, 2002b).

How My Topic Has Relevance in Malaysian Practices

Malaysia, as one of the countries that cannot escape from the corporate governance problem, is always looking for improvement in corporate governance to get stakeholder confidence. The term 'corporate governance' appeared after the crises in Asian countries which focused attention on the weaknesses of Malaysian corporate governance practices (Abdullah, 2004). Numerous scandals have come up such as those related to the Malaysian airline system, technology resource industries, Bumiputera Malaysian finance, and others.

In the long term, people are always linked with related party transactions that are well connected in corporate governance. Moreover, related party disclosures and corporate governance are always used to communicate with external parties about companies' earnings management (Munir, 2011). Governance failures influence the financial reporting which is showed in annual accounts by organizations. Therefore, corporate governance failures themselves will result in financial reporting disclosure failures as well.

LITERATURE REVIEW

Related Party Transactions in the Context of the Accounting Practices in Malaysia, i.e., the Accounting Standard and Other Laws and Regulations That Govern This Issue

The Malaysian Accounting Standards Board (MASB) is the governing body in Malaysia. It acts through the Financial Reporting Foundation (FRF), which handles the resolution and issuance of accounting standards that are helpful in the preparation of financial statements for submission to regulatory bodies in Malaysia (Board, FRF MASB, 2020). These bodies can be the Registrar of Companies, Bank Negara

Malaysia, or the Securities Commission. The Financial Reporting Foundation (FRF) in Malaysia helps the functions of the Malaysian Accounting Standards Board (MASB), conducts assessments of the performance of the MASB, and has responsibility for all financing preparations for MASB operations (Liew, 2007; Board, FRF MASB, 2020).

Proposed Revised Related Party Transaction Standard by the Malaysian Accounting Standards Board (MASB)

On April 30, 2010, the MASB proposed a revised standard for related party transactions that were applicable for annual periods beginning on or after January1, 2012(MASB, 2012). This was just a reflection of the International Accounting Standard (IAS) 24 issued by the International Accounting Standard (IAS) in November of 2009. The purpose of the MASB was to introduces a simpler definition of related party transactions (Board, FRF MASB, 2020). The proposal drafted by the MASB recommended a limited exemption from government-related party disclosures on the condition that the transaction is significant collectively or individually among government-related entities (Board, FRF MASB, 2020). Previously, the board did not recognize state-owned entities in transactions of financial statement disclosures.

Related Party Transaction Disclosure From Malaysia Accounting Standards Board (MASB)

The purpose of related party disclosures from the perspective of the MASB is not unlike that of the International Accounting Standard (IAS 24) related party transaction standard (http://www.masb.org.my/pages.php?id=91, 2020). In Malaysia and other parts of the world, related party transaction standards look to ensure that organizations' financial statements include the disclosures necessary to determine whether their profits or losses and financial positions may have been affected by the existence of related parties and by outstanding balances and transactions with such parties. Related party transaction associations are a standard feature of business and commerce, and so, organizations often carry out a part of their actions through joint ventures, associates, and subsidiaries.

An organization's ability to affect the operating and financial policies of the investee derives from the existence of joint control, control, or substantial influence. Related party transaction association could affect the financial position and profit or loss of an organization. There is a possibility of related parties having differences in dealing with unrelated parties, e.g., business transactions could favor the producer dealing with the related parties compared to unrelated parties. Also, related party transactions can potentially influence the financial position or profit and loss even if the related party transaction does not happen. For example, a subsidiary could dismiss an association with a trading partner. On contrary, one party could cease acting due to the high influence of another. Therefore, there are instructions by the parents to subsidiaries not to be involved in research and development. There are reasons connected with the outstanding balance, knowledge of related party transactions, and relationships that could affect assessments of an organization's risk, opportunities, and operations by the user of financial statements.

Related Party Transaction Amendments Proposed by Bursa Malaysia Securities Berhad (BMSB)

According to Bursa Malaysia Securities Berhad (BMSB), the purpose of the related party transaction requirement is to make sure that the related party cannot exploit its power to help itself or people associated with it and damage the shareholders and listed issuers. To secure the interests of minority shareholders, BMSB agreed on the description of what or who constitutes the related party and what amounts to a related party transaction. BMSB defines related party transactions in the context of the organization, major shareholders, directors, or persons associated with major directors or shareholders (Malaysia B., 2015). A related party transaction is described as a "transaction entered into by the listed issuer of its subsidiaries which involves the interest, direct or indirect, of a related party" (Malaysia B., 2015). The existing framework of related party transactions on listed issuers may be unintentionally enforced and represent a costly and a hefty compliance burden, particularly in the areas of theoretical conflicts of interest that do not pose any risk to shareholders (Wei, 2014).

Main Market Listing Current Monetary Threshold in Related Party Transaction Disclosures

The percentage and monetary threshold requirement defined by the Main Market Listing Requirement (MMLR) specifies what is a minor risk to shareholders and listed issuers according to the related party transaction framework (Malaysia B., 2020a). It says that if the value of the transaction is more than Malaysian Ringgit MYR 500,000, the listed issuer will have to follow the related party transaction requirements under the Main Market Listing Requirement (MMLR) (Malaysia B., 2020a).

Figure 3. Related party transaction disclosure from Bursa Malaysia.

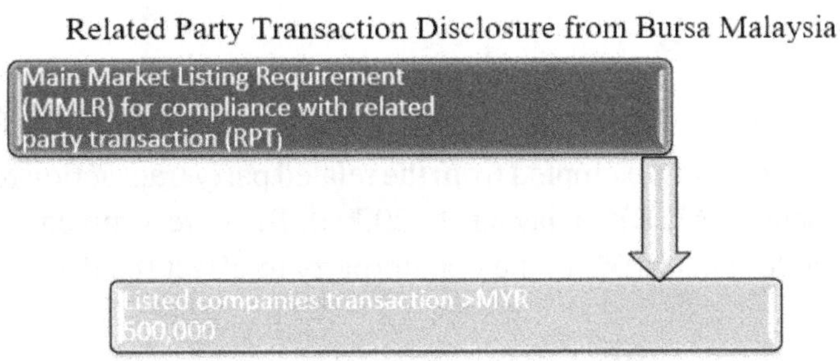

Figure 3 shows that Bursa Malaysia is an official regulator for the Malaysian capital market and that all the listed companies must follow the main market listing requirement for the compliance of related party transactions (those greater than MYR 500,000) (Malaysia B., 2015).

Bursa Malaysia is the frontline regulator of the Malaysian capital market and has to support a fair and orderly market in the securities and derivatives that are traded through its facilities.

Bursa Malaysia Securities Proposes the Role of Related Party Transaction Advisers

At present, the Main Market Listing Requirement (MMLR) allows the practice of both advisers on the condition that if the related party transaction is 5% or more, a principal adviser will be appointed, and if the related party transaction is 25% or more, an independent adviser will be appointed to go with the principal adviser. This applies in all conditions of reasonable and fair transactions to protect minority shareholders (Malaysia B., 2020b). Busra studied the role of both advisers and proposed allowing only the principal adviser to have the responsibility to make sure that transactions are carried out on commercial terms at an arm's length basis.

Waiver From Common Directorship

The Main Market Listing Requirement (MMLR) presently waives off less than 1% related party transactions, stopping common directorship in the subsidiaries or listed issuer and another person (Malaysia B., 2020c). It is proposed that this policy should be more relaxed less than 5%, and this is supported by the industry based on Bursa's informal consultation given in November 2013.

Exemption on Buying and Selling Target Company

The Main Market Listing Requirement (MMLR) exempts buying and selling from subsidiaries/listed issuers from or to non-related parties with an interest in the target company (another company) if the related party transaction holds less than 5% within the target company (Malaysia B., 2002d). Busra recommends enhancing the target company-related party shareholding threshold from lower than 5% to less than 10%.

Exemption on Counterparty

If there is no relationship between a subsidiary and its listed issuer, transactions having lower than a 5% shareholding threshold are presently exempted from the related party transaction requirement of the Main Market Listing Requirement (MMLR)(Malaysia B., 2020e). Busra recommends increasing this threshold from lower than 5% to less than 10% in the counterparty to affect the decision of the counterparty.

Removal of Interest in Investee Organization

At present, the discarding of interest by the related party (RP) major shareholder of the investee company is exempted from the related party transaction requirement if the person associated with the related party transaction and major shareholder both are not a part, agent, or initiator of the said disposal (Malaysia B., 2002). Busra suggests enlarging the present exemption to add transactions where the listed securities disposal in the investee company is not influenced by Busra.

Role of Malaysian Auditors in Related Party Transactions

The International Standards on Auditing also deal with related party transactions as a part of auditors' responsibilities to deal with the transactions according to auditing standards. It increases how the International Standard of Auditing (ISA) 315,1, (ISA) 330,2, and (ISA) 2403 standards can be applied in the context of finding the risk associated with the material misstatement of transactions and related party (RP) relationships. However, several related party transactions are working in the routine course of business. But in some circumstances, related party transactions increase the risk of material misstatement in financial statements unrelated to party transactions (Malaysia B. N., 2013). Auditors in Malaysia have the responsibility to always keep an eye on the related party transaction requirements related to the discourse in financial statements which enable financial statement users to understand the actual and/or possible effects on the financial statements. Therefore, the financial reporting framework has developed such requirements, and auditors should perform audit procedures to assess, identity, and address the risks of material misstatement arising from an organization's failure to properly account for or reveal related party transactions.

Companies May Take Related Party Transactions to Their Advantage

The latest dishonors in the corporate sector show that organizations have used related party tractions for profit through the controlling of shareholders', directors', and other business affiliates' involvement in undisclosed business affairs, and through complex and diverse transactions among the parties and a firm. Related party transactions offer opportunities to use organizational resources to deliver power to managers with enticements to implement earning management (Gordon, 2004). Wong and Jian (2008) argued that certain corporate Chinese groups use related party transactions for their benefit by managing their earnings before issuing new equity or to stop delisting (Wong, 2008). Moreover, the internal and external users of a financial statement have confidence in aggressive accounting practices by the companies to enhance or degrade earnings appropriately (McNichols, 2002; Sherman, 2001). Therefore, related party transactions are a difficult focus for auditors, which is one of the reasons for organizations to restate financial reports (Office, 2003). According to a report published by Gordon and Henry, earnings management, and certain related-party transactions help organizations to fix financing avenues to adjust for abnormal accruals (Gordon, 2006.Dechow, 2002). Nevertheless, corporate scandals have highlighted the complications of recognizing related party transactions and relationships by auditors who are influenced by fraud or illegal earnings management (Dechow, 1995). Also, there are three main reasons why auditors have difficulty in tracing related party transactions: 1) such transactions are very rarely identifiable as related party transaction; 2) auditors are mainly dependent on the main owner and management to recognize related party transactions and related parties; and 3) it is never easy to trace related party transactions through internal control of the company.

Throughout the investigation, the context arises of related party transaction usage by Malaysian companies like that of two non-executive independent directors of Transmile Bhd taking up real estate and sales transactions when the outcome harms the minority stakeholders (Ng, 2012). Busra Malaysia media revealed one case in 2012 of a related party transaction that involved a group of eight KNM directors that have been highly criticized. In this case, Blue Fire Capital Group proposed the idea of an organization controlled by the managing director of the KNM group himself who would buy the whole business, and this was not revealed in the disclosure of material information, which is the offer of condition. The directors accepted the announcement and charged a fine of Malaysian Ringgit MYR 200,000 for this offense. According to the Edge report, related party transactions are the major reason for accounting irregularities at Patimas Computer Bhd (Market, 2013). This company showed inflated revenue through fabricated entries for sales, and these few transactions generated a conflict of interest as they involved a person with directorship power in four different organizations who was also attached to the Ptimas director (Market, Patimas to be delisted from Bursa on Friday, 2014). The Malaysian auditing firm UHY Advisors (KL) Sdn. Bhd found that there was no declaration of such association for these transactions (International, 2018). In the global scenario, several incidents were associated with multinational companies using related party transactions for their huge benefit. Enron, like many other companies, used special purpose entities (SPE) to take up hedge and capital risks. Special purpose entities (SPE) use related party transactions to develop limited partnerships with outside parties (Thomas, 2002).

Moreover, through the use of special-purpose entities (SPE), an organization can enhance returns on assets and leverage without showing it in the balance sheet and then borrow enormous funds from a monetary institution to buy assets or conduct other corporate business without assets and debts showing up on the organization's financial statements. Tycon International Ltd is alleged to have engaged in accounting fraud worth billions of dollars. Among several malpractices, the company used related party transactions for its benefit. Tycon Ltd did not show in its annual reports the related party transactions of its high-ranked management or certain executive indebtedness and executive compensation. Finally, the company also inaccurately reported certain bonuses for the highest-ranked executives, thereby dropping the cost of those bonuses from its operating expenses. The company also disregarded the anti-bribery provisions of the Foreign Corrupt Practices Act when agents or employees belonging to subsidiary Earth Tech Brazil Ltd made payments to Brazilian officials for keeping the business of Tyco Ltd (Commission, 2006).

The Managerial Implication for Corporate Governance Through Related Party Transactions

There are often conflicts of interest seen among shareholders and organization managers. Do related party transactions stand for a couple of alternative views based on economic theory, which are an efficient transactional view and conflict of interest view? There is no harm in managers adopting an efficient transactional view through related party transactions to fulfill the economic needs of a company to set up faith and exchange confidential information. Effective transactions address the economic demands of an organization by enabling it to buy ability and skills from non-executive directors and offer financial incentives to reduce conflict of interest, minimize monitoring costs, and motivate employees (family relatives) as a part of their job packages rather than increase the shareholders' value appropriately. Nevertheless, the general feeling of government officials and auditors is doubtful about fair transactions between related parties. On the contrary, the conflict-of-interest view of related party transactions sees it as a potential threat to shareholders' benefits. This has been revealed with organizations such as Tyco and Adelphia. To overcome high agency costs, an organization can enhance the analysis of such transactions by spending more on monitoring related to unrelated third-party transactions appropriately. Moreover, managers need to follow related party transaction disclosure policies and follow an approval process involving independent members of corporate governance or a board audit committee. This implies that the contractual non-executive director's services/goods are detached from the directorship.

Variables That May Explain Such Practices

Here author focus on two variables, culture (dependent variable) and corruption (independent variable), in the context of related party transaction usage by Malaysian companies. Several scholars from different fields of research have agreed that distinguishing the culture of a society influences a wider diversity in social phenomena (House, 2002; Hofstede, 1983). Organizational behavior has revealed that culture and value are intensely influenced by personal behavior (The relationship between culture and corruption: A cross-national study, 2009). Moreover, cultural scopes may influence the individual paradigm of ethical conditions; therefore, differences in national culture are anti expected to affect dishonesty. This segment of research focuses on the cultural dimensions concerning Malaysian territorial enterprises.

To understand the cultural dimensions that may affect the corruption level is dangerous to national and organizational effectiveness (Davis, 2003) and also, for directing international business abroad (Park, 2003). The earlier study revealed that national-level culture (way of doing business) is a significant factor that may reflect corruption and has not been investigated in different parts of the world (Davis, 2003). As a dependent variable, "corruption" is precisely what it sounds like. It is something that depends on other factors. When searching for a relationship between two things, is it recognize what makes the dependent variable changes in the way it does. Related party transaction usage by entities for their benefit is due to diverse physiological reasons the case of Malaysian companies, and it is considered as a partial exercise and dishonesty by the company's official (Development, 2001). Transparency International describes corruption as the misappropriation of public power for private benefits and involving such methods as illegal and non-ethical standards. Few researchers describe corruption from a behavioral paradigm as the public abasement for personal benefit (Park, 2003).

Svensson in 2005 highlighted that corruption can be a reaction to either harmful or beneficial directions (Corruption, 2005). Corruption has always reacted to generous rules when a single person initiates bribes to ignore harmful conduct or avoid penalties when enforcement of rules is incomplete. Moreover, Ashour (2006) categorized the supporting factors of corruption into the economic structure, cultural infrastructure, and state political infrastructure; therefore, corruption is a result of a country's economic and structural policy, political and legal aspects, globalization, human development, and the role of the institution (Bontis, 2009).

Relationship Between Corruption and National Culture Dimensions

Corruption uncertainty avoidance and uncertainty avoidance are part of the cultural dimension relevant to the way a single person reacts to an uncertain situation (Ethics, 2002). It is argued by Getz and Volkema (2001) that in extraordinary uncertainty avoidance culture, the public desires organizations with healthily established standards, policies, rules, and procedures. This desire and these conditions may encourage corruption (Getz, 2001a). Moreover, a few scholars have argued that bureaucratic structures reward managers for unethical behavior. The cultural and social direction set the boundaries in behavior for an individual to work via a comfortable channel to carryout personal objectives (Getz, 2001b). To follow this direction, one might pay or offer bribes and become involved in similar dishonest dealing such as persuading officials to accept bribes. Once this unethical pattern is implemented, it serves as a guide for everyone to continue and no one breaks out of this pattern so as not to create uncertainty (Getz, 2001c). There is a positive relationship between corruption and uncertainty avoidance; in the case of a high level of uncertainty avoidance, the public is inclined to not be as corrupt and more anxious about standing behind procedures and rules (Seleim, 2009).

Individual Corruption and Collectivism

The meaning of individual collectivism is based on the bonding between families and close friends within small groups. In this scenario, close friends and family members have a high expectancy of one another, as is the case within Malaysian territory enterprise culture. In such a scenario, public individuals can bypass legal procedures and rules to pursue their expectations. However, it is common to recommend family members or close friends in promotion, recruiting, and most importantly, in giving rewards (House, 2001). Such societies concentrate on individualism as people look after their immediate families, set personal goals instead of group goals, take part alone in activities, engage in public thinking with rationality, and set differences between 'out' groups and 'in' groups (Healy, 2004). According to Gelfand et al., in 2004, the GLOBE Project highlighted that collectivism of within-group practices and values is negatively and significantly connected with accomplishments in basic science. Individuals in these societies put group reliability over efficiency, tend to build close social networks, and have a solid belief in making group decisions (Woolsey, 2003). It has been found that 62.7% of Malaysian public organizations are family-owned enterprises and that Malaysians trust in their family groups. This is one of the significant reasons such organizations use related party transactions to their benefit (Maury, 2006). Network-related and collectivist culture reveals that families and friends are always strengthening relationships that might help prohibited transactions (Getz, 2001). Consequently, connections between families might motivate corruption (Wiseman, 1998).

What Are the Elements of Financial Reporting Disclosure?

National standard-setters such as the International Accounting Standards Board (IASB) and the Financial Accounting Standards Board (FASB) encourage motivated financial statement aims. There are several elements in financial reporting disclosure such as related party transaction information about accounting policies, income statements, cash flow statements, and balance sheets (International Financial Reporting Standard, IFRS framework 1). The lesson learned from accounting scandals that the expectation for financial reporting to fulfill the hopes of stakeholders results in an expectation gap and underlies illegal practices.

Established Findings in Related Party Transactions and Corporate Governance

Adam Smith said that when public money is involved, "it cannot be expected that the managers would watch over it with the same anxious vigilance as they would watch over their own and [that] negligence and profusion, therefore, must always prevail, more or less, in the management of the affairs of such accompany"(Smith).Financial reporting changes covering more than two decades include the pre-and post-Malaysian Accounting Standards Board (MASB) periods and the emergence of the International Financial Reporting Standard (IFRS). Before the formation of the Malaysian Accounting Standards Board (MASB), organizations followed accounting standards set up by the Malaysian Institute of Accountants (MIA)and the Malayan Association of Certified Public Accountants (MACPA), both of which ran under the umbrella of the International Accounting Standards Committee (IASC).In the pre-Malaysian Accounting Standards Board (MASB) period from 1993 to 1998 in Malaysia (Accountant, 2018)there was no obligatory requirement to follow accounting standards. Instead, organizations were bound to follow the Companies Act of 1965 and reporting directions from Bursa Malaysia, the Securities Commission, or relevant authorities. It was expected that organizations would voluntarily show their accounts and financial positions to stakeholders. Interestingly, during this reporting period conventional assets (properties, plants, equipment, etc.) were recognized and measured at the historical cost. The post-Malaysian Accounting Standards Board (MASB) period lasted from 1999 to 2005. This body was set up through the Financial Reporting Act 1997. It had independent authority to issue and develop financial reporting standards. The International Financial Reporting Standard(IFRS) convergence period started in 2006. This period also saw the start of non-current asset recognition for selling purposes, for which outcome the income statement shows obligatory accrued expenses and losses of assets that arise from the provision. Many Malaysian reports do not focus on the International Financial Reporting Standard (IFRS) adaptation and instead generally concentrate on financial reporting relevance in value and accounting numbers such as cash flow value relevance, intangible assets, etc. I found a report issued in 2009 by Kadri Aziz and Muhd, a Malaysia International Financial Reporting Standard (IFRS) adaptation with the value relevance. The report concentrates only on real estate industry reporting through the International Financial Reporting Standard (IFRS) (Kadri, 2009). There are a lot of efforts that have been made in the convergence of financial reporting. Several countries have adopted the International Financial Reporting Standard (IFRS) such as China, Australia, and the EU countries in 2005. Also, the US Financial Accounting Standards Board (FASB) started the convergence with the International Accounting Standards Board (IASB). Consequently, an MOU was signed in 2006 between the US GAAP and the International Financial Reporting Standard (IFRS). Another MOU was signed between the International Accounting Standard Board (IASB) andJapan'saccountingboardfortheharmonizationofaccountingstandar ds. Organizations needed a program that was centrally based, could watch and measure internal controls very efficiently and had in-line configuration between the three components of outside reporting, inside controls, and corporate governance. Several companies have corporate governance teams organized to meet the requirement in financial reporting. The teams, therefore, are very energetic in multiple areas of organizational activity to make sure that the organization has been working together as a whole. To become part of the corporate governance team, an accountant along with directors can play an important role in every area. According to, accounting exploitation related to related party transaction resources can be transferred among stakeholders, resulting in some gains and losses to others (Lo, 2010). Moreover, this exploitation creates a huge information asymmetry in line with reduced confidence within the firm and distorts financial statements. Therefore, Shan (2009) saw that the necessity to show proper information about related party transactions is a significant aspect of protecting minority shareholders' rights, which is an expectation of good corporate governance (Fooladi, 2011). According to Gordon (2004), financial statements can protect shareholder interest by showing necessary information which helps shareholders to estimate the effects of transactions (Gordon, 2004). Consequently, corporate governance needs the executive and board of directors to strictly support related party disclosure and watch organizations for any potential stakeholder interest.

In 1997, Shleifer and Vishny defined corporate governance of suppliers of investment to organizations to ensure a return on their investment (Shleifer, 1997). Most importantly, the significance of corporate governance arises in an organization due to the distance between managers and stakeholders (Epps, n.d.). According to Abdullah (2004), the distance between control and ownership causes the inefficiency of stakeholders to control managerial actions (Abdullah, 2004). In the early 1980s, McCullers and Schroeder discussed agency theory about the self-dealing of individuals who wanted to maximize their expected interest and who were in a position to do so, which led to opposition among those who were interested (Schroeder, 1983). Furthermore, Judge (2003) discussed agency perspective about a group or person of managerial responsibility and development of a system to better strengthen a managerial quality of performance which avoids offending and stops the opportunistic attitude of agents to ensure that they can generate the best rate of return for the owners. According to Bursa Malaysia Securities Berhad (BMSB) (2008), regulations related to related party transactions are reflected in the Bursa Malaysia listing requirement. Part E of the requirement demands that an organization make an urgent announcement when entering into an exchange of transactions along with relevant information. Organizations that undertake a 5% related party transaction of net tangible assets needed a circular along with relevant information to shareholders and ask for approval at a general meeting. Furthermore, the organization should appoint a neutral advisor whose duty it is to figure out decide the transactions are reasonable and fair as they relate to the shareholders, and also to advise minority shareholders whether they should vote in support of the transactions. In the case of transactions reflecting more than 25% of net tangible assets, organizations should also appoint a main adviser along with an independent adviser. A director with any direct or indirect interest must be careful with the board and vote on relevant resolutions about party transactions. According to the listing requirement, shareholder approval requires repeated related party transactions such as the revenue of trading nature, which is important in the day-to-day operation of an organization (Malaysia B., 2020f).

FUTURE RESEARCH DIRECTIONS

There are cultural & financial reasons for this gap in our knowledge about the parties involved in corporate governance failures due to related party transactions. This particular research extends from our findings and would benefit from being investigated includes the following examples.

To get started, an in-depth investigation of how related party transactions turn out to be committed to thorough failure of corporate governance and how to influence skeptical shareholders' involvement would be helpful. The research could investigate factors mutually associated with corporate governance failures and the impact of good corporate governance on shareholders' confidence and value creation.

More methodological focus on historical research to compare financial reporting disclosure of different companies (pre-and-post-MASB and in convergence with IFRS) and corporate governance practices (past and present).

Toward further development of research that could lead to a full cost-benefit analysis of related party transactions in research would be advantageous. Nevertheless, while methodologically challenging, it would be helpful to conduct longer-term studies that sought to calculate the impact of related party transactions on corporate governance, such as key indicators that shows the shareholder confidence in related party transaction disclosure and indicators of corporate governance failure in Malaysia.

It would also, be helpful to assess the related party transactions for scandalized insolvent companies and then separate the related party transitions into four categories: the minor party involved, the major party involved, number of transactions (if disclosed), and type of transaction.

Finally, author identified an important question after data collection had finished: How does good corporate governance help Malaysian companies to achieve shareholders' confidence in financial performance?

CONCLUSION

High eminence related to related party transaction disclosure empowers the market to find the worth of securities and other shares appropriately. Also, prompt presentation of financial information reflects an organization's economic condition which is a part of corporate governance. Moreover, these directions strengthen the inactive monitoring of executive management by those who do not have rights of control. Also, the use of an added new data set of culture classification confirms the significance of a cultural perspective in explaining corruption. The contribution of this research study is in differentiating between values and cultural practices. The results of this study also add to the growing base of literature on corruption and reveal the usefulness of the dimensions reported (2004, 2002) by House et al. Forecasting organizations' corruptive practices by focusing on cultural differences is significant for international and multinational companies.

REFERENCES

Abdullah, S. (2004, December 1). Board composition, CEO duality and performance among Malaysian listed companies. Corporate Governance. *International Journal (Toronto, Ont.)*, 47–59.

Abdullah, S. N. (2004). Board, composition, CEO duality and performance among Malaysian listed companies. *The international Journal of Business in Society*, *4*, 47.

Accountant, M. I. (2018). *International standard on Auditing Related Parties*. MIA, ISA.

Agnes, W. Y., & Lo, R. M. (2010, April). Can corporate governance deter management from manipulating earnings? Evidence from related-party sales transactions in China. *Journal of Corporate Finance*, *16*(2), 225–235.

Ahmed Seleim, N. B. (2009). The relationship between. *Journal of Intellectual Capital*, *10*, 168.

Albaity, M. (2012). Behavioural Finance and Malaysian Culture. *International Business Research*, *5*(11), 65–74.

Ashiq Alia, T.-Y. C. (2007). Corporate disclosures by family firms. *Journal of Accounting and Economics*, *8*. https://citeseerx.ist.psu.edu/viewdoc/download?doi=10.1.1.1078.2478&rep=rep1&type=pdf

Atkinson, J. M. J. H. (1984). Structures of social action. Cambridge University Press.

Begley, D. B. (1987). Psychological characteristics associated with performence in entrepreneurial firms and smaller businesses. *Journal of Business Venturing*, *2*(1), 79–93.

Board, M. A. (2020). *FRF MASB*. Retrieved from Financial Reporting Standards: http://www.masb.org.my/pages.php?id=91

Bontis, C. B. (2009, January 16). The relationship between culture and corruption: A cross-national study. *Journal of Intellectual Capital*, *10*(1).

Brännback, A. L. (2009). *Understanding the entrepreneurial mind: Opening the black box*. International Studies in Entrepreneurship.

Chan, W. (2010). Expropriation through related party transactions: the position in Malaysia. *IABR & ITLC Conference Proceedings*, 1-11.

Chen, C. C. (2007). *Monitoring mechanism, corporate governance, and related party transactions.* Academic Press.

Cheung, P. R. (2006, November). Tunneling, propping, and expropriation: Evidence from connected party transactions in Hong Kong. *Journal of Financial Economics*, *82*(2), 343–386.

Cheung, Y. L. Y. Q. (2009, May). Buy high, sell low: How listed firms price asset transfers in related party transactions. *Journal of Banking & Finance, 33*(5), 914-924. Retrieved from https://www.sciencedirect.com/science/article/abs/pii/S0378426608002318

Chrisman, J. J. J. C. (2003). *Current trends and future directions in family business management studies: Toward a theory of the family firm.* Coleman white paper series.

Claessens, S. D. (2000). The separation of ownership and control in East Asian corporations. *Journal of Financial Economics*, *58*(1-2), 81–112.

Commission, U. s. (2006). *SEC Brings Settled Charges Against Tyco International Ltd. Alleging Billion Dollar Accounting Fraud*. US SECP.

Davis, J. R. (2003, April). Perceptions of country corruption: Antecedents and outcomes. *Journal of Business Ethics*, *43*, 275–288.

Dechow, P. M. R. S. (1995, April). Detecting earnings management. *The Accounting Review, 70*(2), 193-225. Retrieved from https://www.jstor.org/stable/248303?seq=1

Dechow, P. M. I. D. (2002). The quality of accruals and earnings. *The Accounting Review, 77*(1), 35-39. Retrieved from https://meridian.allenpress.com/accounting-review/article-abstract/77/s-1/35/53276

Development, O. f.-o. (2001). *The private sector fights corruption*. OECD.

Epps, R. W. (2008). Do institutional shareholder services (ISS) corporate governance ratings reflect a company's operating performance? *Critical Perspectives on Accounting*, *19*(8), 1135–1148.

Ethics, J. o. (2002). Culture and international anti-corruption agreements in Latin America. *Journal of Business Ethics*, *37*, 413–422.

Fana & Wong. (2002, August). Corporate ownership structure and the informativeness of accounting earnings in East Asia. *Journal of Accounting and Economics*, *33*(3), 401–425.

Fooladi, M. Z. S. (2011). Corporate governance and disclosure of related party transactions. In 2nd International Conference on Business and Economic Research (pp. 1392-1405). ICBER.

Getz, R. V. (2001, March 1). Culture, perceived corruption, and economics: A model of predictors and outcomes. *Business & Society*, *40*(1), 1–24.

Getz, A-KA, R. V. (2001, March 1). Culture, perceived corruption, and economics: A model of predictors and outcomes. *Business & Society*, *40*(1), 1–24.

Gibson, A. R. (2003). Management Is Responsible, Too. *Journal of Accountancy*.

Gordon, E. H. (2004). Related party transactions and corporate governance. *Advances in Financial Economics*, 9.

Gordon, E. A. E. H. (2006). Related party transactions: associations with corporate governance and firm value. *EFA 2004 Maastricht Meeting*, 1-59.

Governance, F. C. (2000). *Malaysian Code on Corporate Governance, March 2000*. Malaysian Government.

Group, M. s. (2019, August). *MSWG*. Retrieved from Encouraging Minority Shareholder Activism: http://www.mswg.org.my/news/encouraging-minority-shareholder-activism

Gul, F. A. S. L. (2002, January 1). Audit quality, management ownership, and the informativeness of accounting earnings. *SAGE Journals, 17*(1), 25-49. Retrieved from https://journals.sagepub.com/doi/abs/10.1177/0148558X0201700102

Hashim, A. M. (2013). The Breadth and Depth of Related Party Transactions. *International Journal of Trade, Economics and Finance, 4*, 388. Retrieved from https://www.researchgate.net/profile/Hafiza_Hashim/publication/272909338_The_Breadth_and_Depth_of_Related_Party_Transactions_Disclosures/links/558f5f6608ae1e1f9baceaba/The-Breadth-and-Depth-of-Related-Party-Transactions-Disclosures.pdf

Hashim, A. M. (2014, April 2). Accounting Irregularities in Related Party Transactions. International Journal of Trade. *Economics and Finance*, *5*, 181.

Healy, H. B. (2004, August 18). Individualism and collectivism. *Industrial Relations*, *35*(5).

Hofstede, G. (1983, June 1). The Cultural Relativity of Organizational Practices and Theories. *Journal of International Business Studies*, *14*, 75–89.

House, M. J. (2001, October). Project GLOBE: An introduction. *Applied Psychology*, *50*(4), 489–505.

House, M. J. (2002). Understanding cultures and implicit leadership theories across the globe: An introduction to project GLOBE. *Journal of World Business*, *37*(1), 3–10.

International. A. s. (2018). ASI Final Assessment Report. Malaysia: ASI.

Jensen, MC, W. M. (1976, October). Theory of the firm: Managerial behavior, agency costs and ownership structure. *Journal of Financial Economics*, *3*(4), 305–360.

Johnstone, J. B. (2004, July 29). Audit firm portfolio management decisions. *Journal of Accounting Research*, *42*(4), 659–690.

Kadri, M. I. (2009). Value relevance of book value and earnings: Evidence from two different financial reporting regimes. *The Journal of Finance*, *7*(1), 1–16.

Kuek, C. Y. (2015, June). Shareholder activism through exit and voice mechanisms in Malaysia: A comparison with the Australian experience. *Research Gate*, *26*(2), 1–179.

Kuek, C. Y. (2015, June). *Shareholder activism through exit and voice mechanisms in Malaysia: A comparison with the Australian experience*. Research Gate.

La Porta, R. F. L.-d.-S. (2002, June). Investor protection and corporate valuation. *The Journal of Finance*, *57*(3), 1147-1170. Retrieved from https://onlinelibrary.wiley.com/doi/full/10.1111/1540-6261.00457

Lemmon, M. L. K. L. (2001, April). Ownership structure, corporate governance, and firm value: Evidence from the East Asian financial crisis. *The Journal of Finance, 58*(4), 1445-1468. Retrieved from https://deepblue.lib.umich.edu/bitstream/handle/2027.42/39777/wp393.pdf?sequence=3

Liew, P. (2007, September). Corporate governance reforms in Malaysia: The key leading players' perspectives. *International Review (Steubenville, Ohio), 15*(5), 724–740. https://d1wqtxts1xzle7.cloudfront.net/52122942/Corporate_Governance_Reforms_in_Malaysia20170312-15935-kkvki3.pdf?1489326252=&response-content-disposition=inline%3B+filename%3DCorporate_Governance_Reforms_in_Malaysia.pdf&Expires=1605775918&Signature=WouDsU

Malaysia. L. O. (Incorporating latest amendment - Act A1299 /2007). ACT 125, COMPANIES ACT 1965 (REVISED - 1973), Incorporating the latest amendment - Act A1299 /2007. Malaysian Government. Malaysia: Malaysian government.

Malaysia, B. (2015a). *Related party transaction requirements, main market listing requirements. Busra Malaysia.* Busra Malaysia. Retrieved from https://www.bursamalaysia.com/sites/5bb54be15f36ca0af339077a/content_entry5ce3b5005b711a1764454c1a/5ce3c84a5b711a13e3b4bbfa/files/MainApp2_RPT-final_22Jan2015_.pdf?1570701456

Malaysia, B. (2015b, October). *Main market listing requirement.* Retrieved 2020, from Transactions: http://asklisting.bursamalaysia.com:8080/MainLR/Pages/MainChapter10.aspx

Malaysia, B. (2020). *Bursa Malaysia.* Retrieved from Listing on Bursa Malaysia: https://www.bursamalaysia.com/listing/why_bursa_malaysia/your_listing_destination

Malaysia, B. (n.d.a). *Bursa Malaysia.* Retrieved from Listing on Bursa Malaysia: https://www.bursamalaysia.com/listing/why_bursa_malaysia/your_listing_destination

Malaysia, B. (n.d.b). *Related party transaction requirements.* Retrieved from Main Market Listing Requirements: https://www.bursamalaysia.com/sites/5bb54be15f36ca0af339077a/content_entry5ce3b5005b711a1764454c1a/5ce3c84a5b711a13e3b4bbfa/files/MainApp2_RPT-final_22Jan2015_.pdf?1570701456

Malaysia, B. N. (2013). *Guidelines on related party.* Bank Negara Malaysia.

Marianne Bertrand, P. M. (2002, February). Ferreting out tunneling: An application to Indian business groups. *The Quarterly Jounral of Economics, 117*(1), 121-148.

Market, T. E. (2013). *Patimas audit reveals irregularities.* Academic Press.

Market, T. E. (2014, March 19). *Patimas to be delisted from Bursa on Friday.* Retrieved from Patimas to be delisted from Bursa on Friday: https://www.theedgemarkets.com/article/patimas-be-delisted-bursa-friday

MASB. (2012). *First-time Adoption of Malaysian Financial.* Retrieved from http://masb.org.my/article.php?id=270

Maury, B. (2006, January). Family ownership and firm performance: Empirical evidence from Western European corporations. *Journal of Corporate Finance, 12*(2), 321–341. https://www.sciencedirect.com/science/article/pii/S0929119905000404

McNichols, M. F. (2002). Discussion of the Quality of Accruals and Earnings: The Role of Accrual Estimation Errors. *The Accounting Review*, *77*(1), 61–69. https://aaapubs.org/doi/10.2308/accr.2002.77.s-1.61

Miller, I. L.-M. (2006, March). *Family governance and firm performance: Agency, stewardship, and capabilities*. SAGE.

Morck, R. B. Y. (2003, October). Agency problems in large family business groups. *SAGE, 27*(4), 367-382. Retrieved from https://journals.sagepub.com/doi/abs/10.1111/1540-8520.t01-1-00015

Munir, R. G. (2011). Related party transactions, family firms and firm performance: Some Malaysian evidence. *Corporate Governance Conference*.

Ng, B. S. (2012). Corporate governance: Golden parachute for minority shareholders. *Business (Atlanta, Ga.)*.

Office, U. S. (2003, June). *By the Comptroller General of the United States*. Retrieved from Government Auditing Standards, 2003 Revision: https://www.gao.gov/assets/80/76730.pdf

Park, H. (2003, June 17). Determinants of corruption: A cross-national analysis. *Multinational Business Review*, *11*(2).

Pizzo, M. (2009, July 31). *Related Party Transactions in Corporate Governance*. Retrieved from https://papers.ssrn.com/sol3/papers.cfm?abstract_id=1441173

Radhakrishnan, A. A.-Y. (2007). Corporate disclosures by family firms. *Journal of Accounting and Economics*, *3*. https://citeseerx.ist.psu.edu/viewdoc/download?doi=10.1.1.1078.2478&rep=rep1&type=pdf

Radzi, M. N. (2017, June 30). The impact of internal factors on small business success: A case of small enterprises under the FELDA scheme. *Asian Academy of Management*, *22*(1), 27–55.

Rauch, M. F. (2000). *Psychological approaches to entrepreneurial success: A general model and an overview of findings*. Academic Press.

Sa'adiah Munir, N. M. (2013). Family ownership, related-party. *Asian Academy*, *9*(1), 129–153.

Saleh, N. M. T. I. (2005). Earnings management and board characteristics: Evidence from Malaysia. *Jurnal Pengurusan, 4*, 77-103. Retrieved from http://103.219.237.47/pengurusan/article/viewFile/1455/1265

Saleh, N. M. T. I. (2007, April 3). Audit committee characteristics and earnings management: Evidence from Malaysia. *Asian Review of Accounting, 15*(2), 147-163. Retrieved from https://www.emerald.com/insight/content/doi/10.1108/13217340710823369/full/html

Salim, M. R. (2011). *Corporate governance in Malaysia: the macro and micro issues*. Handbook on International Corporate Governance.

Schroeder, M. a. (1983). *Accounting Theory: Text and Readings* (Vol. 58). Pro Quest.

Schumpeter, J. (2008). The Theory of Economic Development: An Inquiry into Profits, Capital, Credit, Interest and the Business Cycle. *Journal of Comparative Research*.

Sherman, S. Y. (2001). Tread lightly through these accounting minefields. *Harvard Business*, 1-8.

Shleifer, R. V. (1997, June). A survey of corporate governance. *The Journal of Finance*, *52*(2), 737–783.

Sloan, R. (2001). Financial accounting and corporate governance: A discussion. *Journal of Accounting and Economics*, *32*(1-3), 335–347.

Smith, A. (n.d.). *93-adam-smith-the-wealth-of-nations-on-joint-stock-companies*. Retrieved from http://media.bloomsbury.com/rep/files/primary-source-93-adam-smith-the-wealth-of-nations-on-joint-stock-companies.pdf

Standard, I. A. (2009, November 1). *IAS 24 — Related Party Disclosures*. Retrieved from Deloitte: https://www.iasplus.com/en/standards/ias/ias24

The relationship between culture and corruption: A cross-national study. (2009, January 16). *Journal of Intellectual Capital, 10*(1), 165-184.

Thomas, W. (2002). The Rise and Fall of Enron. *Journal of Accountancy*.

Villalonga, R. A. (2006, May 2). How do family ownership, control and management affect firm value? *Journal of Financial Economics*, *80*(2), 385–417.

Wei, T. S. (2014, June 30). *SKRINE*. Retrieved 2020, from Proposed Amendments to Related Party Transactions: https://www.skrine.com/insights/newsletter/june-2014/proposed-amendments-to-related-party-transactions

Wiseman, L. G.-M. (1998, January 1). A behavioral agency model of managerial risk taking. *Academy of Management Journal*, *23*(1), 133–153.

Wong, M. J. (2008, September 20). *Propping through related party transactions*. Springer. Retrieved from https://link.springer.com/article/10.1007/s11142-008-9081-4

Wong, T. J. M. J. (2003). Earnings management and tunneling through related party transactions: Evidence from Chinese corporate groups. In *EFA 2003 Annual Conference Paper* (pp. 1-44). Academic Press.

Woolsey, D. R. (2003, March). The use of tv in teaching physiology and anatomy: 1956. *Academic Medicine*, *78*(3), 264.

ADDITIONAL READING

Cottingham, J., & Hussey, R. (2001). Related party transactions: A case study of standard setting in the UK. In *Contemporary Issues in Accounting Regulation* (pp. 105–118). Springer.

Dell, G. (2018). *Exporting Corruption: Progress Report 2018: Assessing Enforcement of the OECD Anti-Bribery Convention*. Transparency International.

Enriques, L., & Tröger, T. H. (Eds.). (2019). *The Law and Finance of Related Party Transactions*. Cambridge University Press.

Galani, A., & Rehn, N. (2010). Related Party Transactions: Empowering Boards and Minority Shareholders to Prevent Abuses. *Nat'l L. Sch. India Rev.*, *22*, 29.

Lo, A. W., Wong, R. M., & Firth, M. (2010). Can corporate governance deter management from manipulating earnings? Evidence from related-party sales transactions in China. *Journal of Corporate Finance*, *16*(2), 225–235. doi:10.1016/j.jcorpfin.2009.11.002

Romashchenko, I. (2020). *Related Party Transactions and Corporate Groups: When Eastern Europe Meets the West*. Kluwer Law International BV.

Shan, Y. G. (2019). Do corporate governance and disclosure tone drive voluntary disclosure of related-party transactions in China? *Journal of International Accounting, Auditing & Taxation*, *34*, 30–48.

Utama, C. A., & Utama, S. (2014). Corporate governance, size and disclosure of related party transactions, and firm value: Indonesia evidence. *International Journal of Disclosure and Governance*, *11*(4), 341–365.

KEY TERMS AND DEFINITIONS

BMSB: Busra Malaysia Securities Berhad is the main securities exchange in Malaysia. Besides equities trading, BMSB provides for shariah-compliant trading and trading in derivatives markets as well.

Corruption: The deceitful or falsified conduct by those in power, usually involving in corruption.

Dominance of Shareholders: A majority shareholder is an entity or person that controls and owns more than fifty percent of a company's outstanding shares.

Family-Owned Organization: A family business is a commercial organization in which decision-making is prejudiced by the intergenerational family member; particularly those related by blood, who can influence the vision of the business and the readiness to pursue distinctive goals.

Financial Reporting Disclosure: A financial statement disclosure will correspond to pertinent information that is not included in the financial statement s itself to a company's shareholders.

International Financial Reporting Standard: A set off common rules so that financial statements can be transparent, reliable, and similar to around the world.

MASB: Malaysian Accounting Standard Board is an organization that is responsible to prepare a framework for Malaysian financial reporting. This framework is accompanied by all the relevant parties working in the standard-setting process liaise with an independent standard-setting structure.

Minority Stakeholders: A less than fifty percent stock ownership or partnership in an organization.

National Level Culture: It refers to precise characteristics and norms such as Malaysian national culture, values, traditions, and behaviors.

Chapter 16
Analysis of Investment Decision Making in Private Hospitals:
Qualitative Study of the Process of Investment

Isabel Cristina Panziera Marques
University of Beira Interior, Portugal

Zélia Serrasqueiro
University of Beira Interior, Portugal

Fernanda Nogueira
University of Lisbon, Portugal

ABSTRACT

This study seeks to define a model outlining the importance of private hospital managers' competences the profile role of the manager private hospital the process and the relationship with analyses for investment decision making in private hospitals in order to orient future work to improve contribute to health institutions' performance. Qualitative interviews were held in Brazil and Canada, analysed through the conventional content analysis method, and coded using NVivo 11. A model of analysis for investment decision making is proposed and can be used to improve resource allocation and hospital performance. The results point out the importance of a multidisciplinary management training of managers that makes contributes to good an efficient use of resources and that contributes to maintains quality in patient care, including with regard to investment and financing of hospitals where performance analysis contributes to decision making.

INTRODUCTION

The manager's involvement is considered an important factor in planning, analyses and decisions on investment in hospitals. The hospital is a complex organisation making active use of human resources,

DOI: 10.4018/978-1-7998-7596-3.ch016

capital, technology and knowledge, with hospital governance playing a fundamental role in the context it is part of, related to the specific type of service — healthcare provision (De Pourcq et al., 2018). Hospital governance refers to the complex set of checks and balancing that determine the decision-making of hospital governance organs leading to global functioning and effective performance through defining its mission, objective-setting and operational support (Moll et al., 2009; Eeckloo et al., 2004), allowing integrated access to support and monitor all the hospital's activities, including clinical performance (Torres et al., 2018).

The initial level of financing is the main way to reduce the weight of the project's risks in private hospitals (Akintoye & Chinyio, 2005). Definition of the risk found here is observed in different contexts, such as risks that affect institutions' financial performance (Ch & Jola, 2017; Kuntz et al., 2016; Ngo et al., 2016; Stathopoulos & Voulgaris, 2016) and the volatility of companies' stock return (Jizi & Nehme, 2017), as well as risks associated with organisational decision-making on investments and agency costs due to withholding information (Hsu et al., 2019; Shan et al., 2018; Thaiyalnayaki & Divakara, 2018;Ouyang & Hilsenrath, 2017). In 2009, the Regional Committee of the World Health Organisation (WHO, 2009) for the Eastern Mediterranean emphasized the importance of management and leadership in hospitals due to being a significant part of the health system and representing from 70% to 80% of health costs. Good management practices have been adopted as a way for hospitals to create value and improve health results (Bloom et al., 2009). Managers in the area of health, particularly, need to cope with a much greater number of challenges, difficult decision-making and problem-solving linked to strategic thinking (Toygar & Akbulut, 2013).

Understanding the factors affecting the adoption of better management practices is fundamental for improved performance. A hospital's specific characteristics can affect the quality of best management practices, such as size, the complexity of care, staff qualifications and skills, health teams' autonomy and capacities, managers' communication skills, and the organisational hierarchy that can orient reforms in medical care, destined to provide high quality health services in hospitals (Holá et al., 2020; Agarwal et al., 2016). The manager's role continues to grow in importance, as the healthcare sector evolves and is concentrated more on managing the population and relations with those making payments and suppliers in the community (Stark, 2020; Bankston & Birmingham, 2015; Toygar & Akbulut, 2013).

The great majority of national health systems have major financing problems, due mostly to the changing demographic paradigm and the introduction of new technology which result in continuously increasing expenditure. Therefore, states are forced to adopt rigorous policies to contain the growth in expenses, and the one with greatest impact on the efficiency of healthcare provision is improvement of the hospital financing model. Considering the absence of an ideal financing model, the models must constantly be discussed so as to evaluate whether more efficient alternatives exist and give greater sustainability to health systems and greater quality in providing healthcare to the population. In the private hospital sector, profit is essential and sometimes a small added value does not require major investment (Lüleci et al., 2015). According to Siskou et al. (2008), increased private expenditure on health and the sector's development are associated with increased demand for services and the lack of public resources and financing, leading the private sector to fill the gap through increased investment (Fernandes & Nunes, 2016). Managers can improve the efficiency, effectiveness, response capacity and sustainability of health services, whether public or private (Kakemam & Dargahi, 2019; Pillay, 2010), but various studies indicate difficulties for public hospital managers in decision-making on investment due to a wide range of budget restrictions and insufficient government transfers that impede the planning of improvements (Diaconu et al., 2020; Gordon et al., 2020; Pericleous, Amin & Goeree, 2019).

The efficiency scores of private hospitals, many of them specialized, are better than many public hospitals, due to efficient use of resources, infrastructure and good financing choices for new investment (Cunha et al., 2019; Gandhi & Sharma, 2018). However, as far as we know, few studies have focused on investment decisions and performance analysis for decision-making in private hospitals.

According to the World Health Organisation (2020), hospitals are complex and vulnerable institutions that depend on crucial support and supplies, and which in normal working conditions tend to work at almost full capacity. In this context, even a modest increase in patient volume can overload a hospital beyond its functional reserve. Well-established partnerships with local authorities, service providers, suppliers, transport companies and other organisations are necessary to ensure the continuity of essential services. The lack of equipment and critical supplies can limit access to necessary care and have a direct impact on healthcare provision (WHO, 2020).

This current study is an exploratory study seeking to develop a model for outlining the role of the managers of private hospitals in Brazil and Canada, through qualitative analysis of interviews to identify the specific factors influencing decision-making on investment. These countries were chosen due to the differences and similarities in the National Health Systems (Attachment 1). Concerning Brazil, it could be thought that the country's similarities with Canada, such as its large size and the same economic system – capitalism –, could have a decisive influence on the organisation of services, due to the effects created in geographical accessibility to services and in financing, for example (Santos & Melo, 2018). In Brazil, according to the Computing Department of the Single Health System (Datasus, 2019), of the 6.702 hospitals registered in the country, 63,67% are private (4.267 hospitals) and correspond to 63,55% (260.695) of beds available, with the density of beds per 1.000 inhabitants, in 2019, being 1,95. The *Canadian Institute for Health Information* (CIHI, 2018) states there are 1.417 hospitals distributed over the Canadian provinces, with 3 hospital beds per 1.000 inhabitants), a total of 71.412 beds in 2017-2018 (CIHI, 2018).

Due to the growing number of private hospitals, there is an opportunity for research related to processes of decision-making on investment. For Gandhi and Sharma (2018), the increased demand for medical and hospital services, and for better services with greater value for money, leads to growth in the number of private hospitals, partly due to how they are managed in terms of resource use to generate income, and in terms of agility of service, without the patient being subjected to long waiting lists.

The remainder of this paper is structured as follows. Section 2 presents the methodology used. The results are presented in Section 3. Section 4 discusses the results, and finally, Section 5 presents the conclusion.

METHODS

This study used the open qualitative interview to produce insights into managers' real experience. The semi-structured interview design joined the narratives, giving managers the chance to speak about their own experiences or concerns and inducing a definition of their managerial involvement.

An administrative, or financial, director was interviewed in Brazil, a country with a national health system in which public and private services co-exist, being semi-decentralized and inspired on the British model. A comparison was then made with a financial director of a Canadian hospital, a country with universal public health insurance, completely decentralized, and different from European national health systems and the American and Brazilian models. The interviews were conducted in May 2020, at the height of the pandemic caused by Covid-19, which made access to hospital managers more difficult. The hospitals involved in the study were selected according to the classification criteria of the National Register of Health Establishments of the Single Health System and DataSUS (2019), as presented in Figure 1. Using the Brazilian classification allows comparison between the two countries, due to having the simplest format, applicable to identifying any hospital unit regarding characterisation (financial objective, type of care, size and ownership regime).

Figure 1.

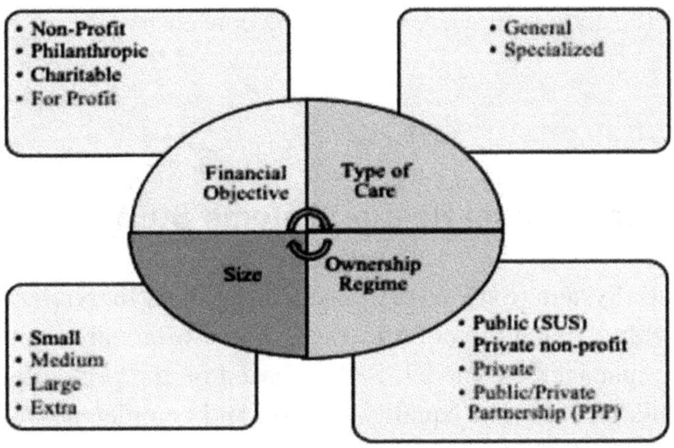

Table 1 shows the limitation of hospitals approached as being private, medium or large and that serve patients who need procedures of high or medium complexity. The hospitals were chosen partly because of the relatively good perception of their performance and functioning as regards service provision.

Table 1. Hospital characteristics for data collection.

Type of Administration (1)	Hospital Size (2)		Complexity of Care (3)	
Private	Medium	50 to 149 beds	Medium	Intensive Therapy, Surgery and Anaesthetics and Mother and Child Care
	Large	150 or more beds	High	Characteristics of medium complexity plus Radiotherapy, Chemotherapy and Chronic Renal Disease

Source: Adapted from the National Register of Health Establishments (CNES, 2019) of the Single Health System (SUS), Ministry of Health (MS), Brazil.

The interview script was drawn up from the literature review and piloted with a respondent in each country so that the language could be adapted to make understanding clearer and easier. The interviews were held in the interviewee's mother tongue (English or Portuguese) face-to-face or via Skype and varied between 60 and 80 minutes, 70 minutes on average, were transcribed word-for-word and respondents' identities were hidden prior to data analysis.

The data were analysed inductively using a conventional content analysis method (Hsieh & Shannon, 2005). The sub-set of interview transcriptions was studied and an "open code" book was developed in NVivo 11 to look for common points in interviews, which involved placing data extracts in a themed grouping procedure (Nowell et al., 2017; Braun & Clarke, 2006). The name of the hospital group was coded to ensure anonymity, with the Brazilian administrative director being described as "G BR" and the Canadian financial director as "G CAN". The main topics arising from the interview content included governance in health, manager competences, performance assessment, investment and financing. The topics were refined in specific matters to be sufficiently broad to include the set of ideas contained in the texts. Some topics were stratified in sub-topics (nodes), with a view to organising the findings. The emerging topics added to the code book were assessed by consensus.

RESULTS

Characterisation of the National Health Systems Studied

In Brazil, the Single Health System (SHS) is organised in regional, hierarchical networks and operates throughout the country with a single direction in each sphere of government (Brazil, 1990 – Federal Law nº 8.080). As for the management model, SHS is based on the principle of universality (ensured access for the whole population), equity (equality of care) and completeness (health actions that cover all the individual's needs), involving the action of a variety of public and private organisations (Paim et al., 2011). It has incomplete and participated decentralized management, with a model of financing shared between the three federal spheres of government (42% Union, 26% State and 31% Municipal), defined in the public budget, paid for through taxation, according to the size of the population, their epidemiological needs and the organisation of actions and services, and transferred to local authorities on a *per capita* basis (Almeida, 2001).

Five basic principles govern the organisation and financing of the healthcare system in Canada: i) public administration of the provincial insurance plan, on a non-profit basis; ii) comprehensive coverage, which means providing all necessary hospitalization services as well as remedies, tests and diagnoses, out-patient treatment and nursing services at home; iii) universal service, extended to all those legally resident in the country; iv) portability of benefits, meaning continued coverage even in other provinces; and v) accessibility, which is the provision of all necessary medical resources without imposing any financial barrier (*Canada Health Act*, 1985). These requirements are monitored by the National Department of Health and Well-Being as conditions for the substantial federal subsidy. Medical, hospital and out-patient insurance programmes are administered by the provinces, but according to legal conditions established by the federal government. The Canadian health system is based on ten public insurance schemes with different characteristics according to the ten provinces and three territories with powers delegated by parliament. There are also private hospitals, managed by foundations or similar structures, and also provide services to the whole population, being paid by the government. The main source of resources is the provinces, with an important (but decreasing) part coming from the Federal Government. The municipal contribution is almost non-existent, unlike the Brazilian model. Private health insurance cannot compete in the range of services available in the public network but can compete in the supplementary benefit market for private rooms, expenses on medicine, aesthetic surgery, care at home, dental treatment and optician services. The *Canada Health Act* of 1984 does not directly prevent private delivery or private insurance for publicly assured services, but there are financial disincentives to doing so. Attachment I presents the main characteristics of the national health systems of Brazil and Canada. The focused coding process, extracted from the interviews, describes the nodes presented in Figure 2, the results being shown as follows.

Figure 2.

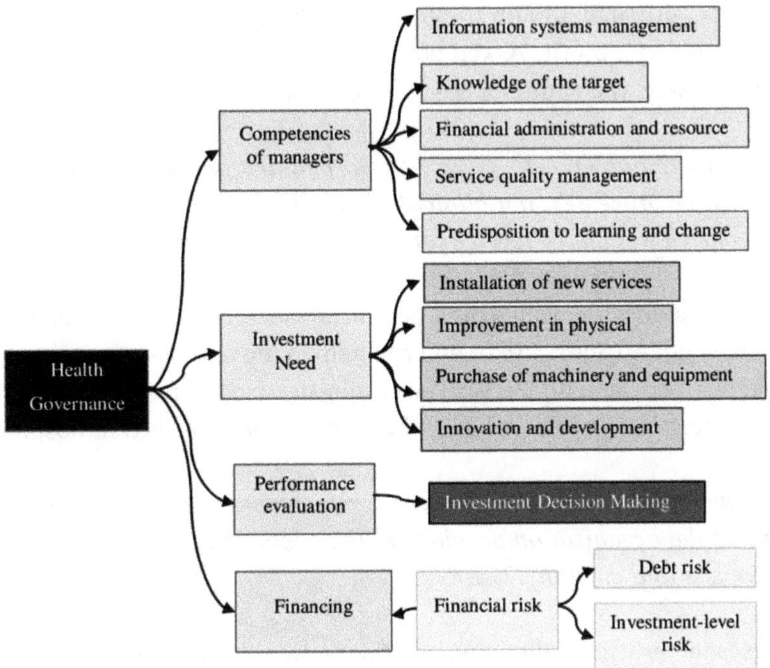

Hospital Characteristics, Managers' Profile and Competences

The training of health administrators reflects the concern with the leadership capacity (Chanes, 2006) that supports the organizational strategy (Sherafat et al., 2019), however, health leadership requires some attributes in order to be able to practice it. For Kemp (2005) such elements, as the basis for the training of health managers, are the clarity of objectives (Carsen & Xia, 2006), the identification of motivational factors in the organization's view (Sherafat et al., 2019), communication (Paim et al., 2011), decentralized decision-making (Diaconu et al., 2020), the establishment of relational links (Pillay, 2010), transformational leadership (Shan et al., 2018) and innovation (Lüleci et al., 2015). The hospital organization is seen as a unique institution where the flows of decision-making processes can sometimes constitute one of the factors that generate conflicts (Zhu et al., 2019), especially since the contracting between doctors and directors is fragile, possibly due to the fact that the doctor who assists the patient has little involvement in management issues, putting assistance actions in the foreground.

The Brazilian hospital studied is situated in Rio Grande do Norte, in the North-East region of Brazil, was inaugurated 20 ago and is considered large in size (more than 150 beds). It specializes in cardiology and kidney transplant, characterised as being of high complexity and has an average of 6,3 employees per bed. Hospital performance is accompanied every six months through a set of indicators that can compare private Brazilian hospitals aiming for strategic resource management. The hospital has a shareholder group formed of 15 doctors and the board of administration, which manages the institution, formed of an administrator and three directors, all the latter being doctors: Administrative, Financial and Medical, all being over 60 years old. The hierarchy in charge of the hospital is established at the top of the organisational chart in the form of shared power with the Board of Directors. As for their basic qualifications, only the interviewee, the administrative director, has a Post-Graduate in Health, the others having clinical skills, although all aim to provide the hospital with guidance and vision regarding service provision and making a profit. Asked about the directing body's need for training in Hospital Management, the interviewee, the administrative director, says:

Directors should have minimum knowledge of how to manage people, resources, computer systems, clinical and administrative processes, but clinical knowledge is imperative; even if the organisation's objective is profit, in our view, quality service for the patient predominates. (G BR).

The manager's role becomes relevant as the healthcare sector focuses on managing the population and relations with stakeholders (Stark, 2020) and can help in the response capacity and sustainability of health services (Kakemam & Dargahi, 2019). The administrative director was asked what competences and responsibilities are relevant and desirable in the professional involved in hospital management:

Knowledge about financial administration, resource management; the ability to recognize and manage the quality services the organisation provides to the community; willingness to learn and change; leadership, pro-activeness and empathy. G BR).

Table 2 summarises the profile of directors and the particularities of the hospitals studied.

In Canada, the hospital chosen is located in Ontario. It has existed for 97 years, provides highly complex services, is specialized in the treatment of cancer, emergency medicine and geriatrics, and considered large in size having 442 beds (4,2 employees per bed). It has been awarded Exemplary Standing by Accreditation Canada, with evaluation every two years. The interviewee is male, between 45 and 59 years old, and is the executive vice-president, of finances and the financial director. He joined the hospital in 2019 to orient the organisation's financial sustainability and provide financial and operational leadership in redeveloping the premises, which included doubling the size of the emergency department and opening new operating theatres. As the main strategy, he says it is his job to lead the work of strategic consultancy and change for health sector clients, focusing on digital health. As for assessment of the hospital's performance, he highlights that the indicators are implemented at all levels of the organisations, from the front line team to the Administration Council. Monitoring and tracking of data is through the Balanced Scorecard. Each indicator provides information at three-monthly intervals, called report quarters. Each indicator is defined and explained. The most recent score is provided, together with an explanation of how the hospital compares with other similar ones, when available. Finally, the actions taken for continuous improvement of performance are described. As for training in Hospital Management among members of the directing body, the interviewee highlights:

Table 2. Characteristics of hospitals and profile of directors.

	Country	Brazil	Canada
Hospital characteristics	Year of inauguration	2000	1923
	Number of beds	162	442
	Classification according to complexity of service	High	High
	Number of employees	1.028	1.856
	General or specialized hospital	Specialized	Specialized
	Is there a set of indicators for performance assessment that can be compared internally and with other institutions?	Yes	Yes
Manager profile	Gender		
	Male	X	X
	Female		
	Age group		
	Up to 24 years		
	25 to 34 years;		
	35 to 44 years;		
	45 to 59 years;		X
	60 years or over.	X	
	Professional Category	Doctor	Economist
	Basic training (degree) and length of service	"Medicine, with Post-Graduate in Health; 41 years of experience"	"Economics, Computer Science; 37 years of experience. Post-Graduate in Hospital Management."
	Post occupied and for how long (in years)	"Administrative Director for 12 years"	"Executive vice-president, finance and financial director, for 2 years"

It is fundamental. Management involves different competences. In the field of health, the range should be even greater due to the complexity of these institutions. Knowledge of strategies, management of change, innovation, sustainability are fundamental examples that a hospital manager should have (G CAN).

For the financial director, the most important characteristics and desirable knowledge for a hospital manager are:

Competence in managing information systems; knowledge of the target population as regards socio-demographic, behavioural factors; knowledge about financial administration, resource management; the ability to recognise and manage quality services that the organisation provides the community with; willingness to learn and change. The competences result from the combination of technical knowledge, aptitude and behaviours; in this context I highlight negotiation and pro-activeness (G CAN).

Governance in Health

Extending to the health sector, the literature on the topic of governance is diversified and covers corporate, integrated, hospital and clinical governance. The expression "Corporate Governance" aims to conceptualize a system in which a company's shareholders "govern", i.e., take responsibility for their company (MacVane Phipps, 2020; Steinberg, 2003). Other definitions appear in the literature, such as those of a normative nature saying they are "institutional arrangements that govern relations between shareholders (or other groups) and firms' administration" (Lethridge, 1997, p. 210), or the set of practices that aim to improve an institution's performance, protecting all stakeholders, such as investors, employees and creditors, facilitating access to capital, the definition of the Securities and Exchange Commission (SEC, 2002).

The World Health Organisation (WHO, 1998a) considers that a more wide-ranging and specific definition should be established when discussing the health context. As such, it approves the definition presented in the document "*Health for All (HFA) in the 21st Century*" as the system through which a society organises and manages the matters of various sectors and partners in order to achieve its objectives and reinforces this emphasizing that good governance for health means allowing the participation of all concerned about formulating and developing policies, programmes and practices that lead to equitable and sustainable health systems. In this context, governance in health emerges as a new paradigm to solve health systems' problems and has an increasingly influential role in developing these systems (Shepheard et al., 2019; Sakellarides, 2003). Addressing governance in health includes the interaction between different society actors (State, civil society and private sector) (Gordon et al., 2020) and the government's changing role in social environments (Fleet et al., 2017).

Integrated governance is explained as the set of systems and processes through which health organisations orient, direct and check their functions, in order to achieve organisational goals, safety and service quality (Zhu et al., 2019; Kennedy et al., 2017; Deighan et al., 2004). Administrative bodies include citizen and patient involvement in their decisions, and these should be considered in the light of their global impact on the community (Helmers & Harper, 2019; Deighan & Bullivant, 2006). This approximation aims to associate the principles of good governance in health with the principles of business governance and clinical governance.

As for hospital governance, this is defined by Fidler (2010) as the use of institutions, rules and formal and informal processes by states, inter-governmental institutions and non-state actors to cope effectively with the challenges for health that require collective cross-border action. Clinical governance was introduced for the first time in 1997 in the UK's National Health Service (NHS), as a strategy to modernize and improve the quality of the health system (HSC, 1999). It is based on the Model of Excellence of the European Foundation for Quality Management (EFQM) guided by the principles of Total Quality and forms a point of reference to structure, evaluate and improve the quality of organisations (Gualtieri et al., 2020; Uddin et al., 2020; Jiang et al., 2012; Degeling, 2006; Allen, 2000; Roland & Backer, 1999), highlighting the fundamental principles of excellence: results-oriented, customer-oriented, leadership and coherence of objectives, process and activity management, collaborator development and involvement, learning, innovation and continuous improvement, development of partnerships and social responsibility (Smits & Champagne, 2020; Chen et al., 2020). The major contribution of the model of Clinical Governance was to bring the clinical decision to the managerial and organisational context (Price et al., 2020; Spigelman & Rendalls, 2015).

Table 3 reflects the understanding of the managers of the hospitals studied regarding the subject of governance.

Table 3. Qualitative quotations from directors on the perception of governance.

Origin	Quotation From the Interview
Perception of corporate, hospital, clinical and integrated governance.	
G BR	"To a certain extent, corporate governance and hospital governance have the same format; both represent similar ways, for top administration, to manage relations with those involved (both internal and external) in processes. Integrated management (clinical and corporate) aims to minimize the risks involving patients (safety), and the risks associated with organisational decision-making on investment."
G CAN	"Corporate management concerns shareholders, their relations with stakeholders and how processes are managed. Clinical governance refers to how patient treatment is carried out by the multi-disciplinary team. I believe that hospital governance is in fact a mediation between administrative and clinical processes aiming for alignment in order to achieve better institutional performance. Then, we reach integrated governance, which as I see it, includes the other types."
Is there a Board of Directors that decides on questions of investment, financing and other matters? How is this Board formed? Is nursing management involved?	
G BR	"Yes, the Board is formed of shareholder representatives (3): medical, administrative and financial directors (all doctors) and an administrator, but nursing management is not included. We recommend doctors' participation in the Board as we consider cost control important; a lot of wastage or badly used resources can arise from the doctor's pen."
G CAN	"There is an Administration Council and an Executive Team. The Council is formed of the president of the administration council, the vice-president, treasurer and secretary. As for management of nursing services, the director belongs to the Council and her services cover academic professional practice, clinical operations, quality, patient safety, corporate risk management, information technology, sustainability and operational readiness, besides strategic initiatives for clinical, administrative and academic change."
Communication and dissemination of information within the institution. How is this carried out?	
G BR	"Through monthly meetings with all managers, a WhatsApp group and e-mail".
G CAN	"There are different weekly meetings, in various areas of the whole hospital complex. Then, every month, the main resolutions and initiatives are passed to the Administration Council by the executive leaders."
How is the institution's capital formed? Is it formed of Open or Closed Capital (company status)?	
G BR	"Closed. Company".
G CAN	"This is a Foundation with the founders' own capital, and is financed, mainly by the province of Ontario, according to the budgets established by both. We encourage companies to involve their employees in charitable donations, through compatible donation programmes, holding fund-raising events or donating a percentage of their income. Corporate sponsoring of events also allows companies to demonstrate leadership and commitment to supporting the hospital."

G BR = Director in Brazil; G CAN = Director in Canada

Hospital Financing and Investment

In the study by Sopper et al. (1995), the authors state that financing models implemented in the last decades have led to adopting mechanisms of cost control and risk management favouring the appearance of new forms of hospital action regarding the costing of services provided, with consequent changes in the management process. For Barbosa (2003), the manager's role in hospital institutions requires knowledge and articulation, since the pressures they come under are different from those felt by managers in other organisations, due to the cultural aspect of dissociation between patient care and the economic and financial aspects of management. In this context, governance models can influence the formation of capital structure. Financial leverage and capital structure are closely linked to the concepts related to capital cost and also to decisions regarding the capital budget (Campos, 2008). Morlock and Alecxander

(1986) indicate that corporate administration councils tend to have greater influence on the hospital's budgetary matters than on other types of decisions in the hospital context.

Decision-making on hospital investment is influenced by health systems' characteristics, namely in terms of health insurance, financing methods and reimbursement (Wernz et al., 2014). In the competitive environment, hospitals understand that an important way to handle the competition is by attracting patients through (i) installing new services that can extend care to a wide range of patients (Navarro et al., 2017; Xue et al., 2008), (ii) investing in improved premises so that, allied with good service quality, this can convey service organisation (Abedi et al., 2019), (iii) provide modern equipment that helps diagnosis and therapy (Shamayleh et al., 2020) and extends the institution's technological facilities (not considering equipment for substitution after depreciation), and (iv) investment in Innovation and Development (I&D) to allow increasingly good use of scarce resources, improving institutions' performance (Fasterholdt et al., 2017).

The preference of how to finance activities has a high impact on the types of projects aimed for, as well as on the parties involved (Turner et al., 2015). These decisions are highly complex and can be influenced by agency costs (Myers 1977; Jensen & Meckling 1976), asymmetric information (Myers 1984; Myers & Majluf 1984), product/input interactions (Sarig, 1998) and considerations of corporate control (Turner, 2014; Jensen 1986). Capital structure is also clearly influenced by historical indices and projected financial performance (Lemmon et al., 2008).

For privately owned hospitals, the use of leverage has the potential to increase the returns for shareholders, as long as the return on assets is greater than the cost of the debt. These hospitals depend more heavily on debt as a source of funding for their long-term financial operations, and therefore on their capital structure, mainly due to the capacity to take advantage of a number of tax shields that reduce their tax obligations and increase their profitability. Turner et al. (2015) indicate that private hospital company managers should consider compensatory tax benefits and bankruptcy costs when deciding on adjustments to their current capital structure. Privately owned hospitals have a greater tax incentive to use debt in their capital structure, but greater use of debt puts hospitals at a higher financial risk.

According to Becker and Koch (2006), hospitals should accept the concept of allocation as a dominant strategy, i.e., hospitals often invest significantly in one line or category of service. Hospitals that invest in certain types of service lines, such as surgery, image, oncology, orthopaedics or neurosurgery, are found to have a very good performance, and although the diversification strategy tends to mitigate the risks regarding money owed, it is also relevant for hospitals to focus on one line of service or specialization where they can become known and recognised as a key supplier in their community and stand out as the supplier of choice. Essentially, they should develop some specific reason for their existence, as sources of income change and the competition develops.

According to Hai et al. (2020), in analysing an investment, the types of sources of risks are designated to influence the percentage participation in financing, i.e., the economic risk connected to the level of debt that affects the availability of resources to make the total investment, the financial risk associated with stability, the construction risk due to the size and complexity of the project and the market risk through the length of the concession and the variety of services granted. Table 4 shows quotations from the managers interviewed regarding financing and hospital investment.

Table 4. Directors' qualitative quotations regarding investment.

Origin	Quotation From the Interview
How are investment opportunities identified? What investments have been made in the last 5 years?	
G BR	"They are identified by market demands and technological developments in the field of health. Opportunities to improve internal processes and the increasing demand for health services are always observed. **Extensions to structures**: increased number of beds (35 more beds); **Acquisition** of a new tomograph (due to increased patient demand); in terms of **I&D**, specific hospital costing software was acquired. A **new service** is projected (unannounced due to being strategic)."
G CAN	"In-depth studies are elaborated, by different departments, to analyse the needs of the general population. The need to maintain the quality of service, as well as observation, arising from studies made internally in the institution, of increased demand for certain services provided. **Physical premises**: modernization of the emergency department, extending the operating theatres, Intensive Care Unit, main areas for out-patients and a new hospitalization unit; **Equipment**: new emergency vehicles, increased reserve of surgical equipment, integrated equipment to monitor patients in intensive care. **I&D**: service innovation; advanced training for Human Resources."
What are the main limitations to investment and what are the sources of resources (types of financing) used when deciding on investment regarding the hospital's projects? In the case of using External Capital as the source of finance, how is the risk of failing to meet the hospital's commitments to creditors dealt with?	
G BR	"The main limitation is the low net profit margin. Normally, we prefer to use own capital when we decide to invest, and as a last resort, we turn to banks and promoters. When it is necessary to use outside capital, we seek medium-term financing so that the new investment can start to generate income and in that way help to cover the funding."
G CAN	"I wouldn't say limitations, but rather the capacity to decide what investments can produce greater financial results and at the same time meet the needs of the population we aim to serve. As sources of resources, we have donations, bank loans, government transfers. Sources of finance: the hospital is exposed to a variety of financial risks, including credit risk, liquidity risk and market risk, and therefore, it adopted a structure of integrated risk management. Credit risk is attributed principally to its accounts to be received. The hospital is exposed to this risk in the case of non-payment by patients for uninsured services provided to non-resident patients. That risk is common to hospitals that are obliged to provide patients with care, irrespective of their ability to pay for the services provided. The hospital administers liquidity risk with anticipation of capital, investment and financing of activities and maintaining lines of credit to ensure it has enough funds available to cover current and foreseeable financial needs. The hospital is also exposed to the risk of the interest rate on its long-term debt and has tried to mitigate this risk through a swap of interest rates, which effectively corrects the interest rates of a part of the long-term debt."
To determine the amount of capital necessary for new investments, does the institution contrast short-term financial needs with medium and long-term needs? Does the institution have and follow a strategic plan (for 3, 5 years)? Is the time for a return on investment estimated? Is an analysis made of the investment's economic-financial viability?	
G BR	"According to the investment, it contrasts medium-term financing needs. The country's economic instability and the group's focus on equity as the source of finance do not allow long-term debt". "Yes; five-year planning, looking to fulfil goals to achieve objectives". "The time for return on investment is always assessed; our projects are analysed so as not to jeopardize payment of the debt taken on, instalments".
G CAN	"It contrasts; however, there's the relation between the size of the investment and the availability of capital. Depending on this factor, short or medium and long-term investment is chosen, always analysing the interest rates for bank finance. The institution's planning is always long-term. We have a multi-disciplinary team focused on these studies and accompaniment." "For some investment projects, the time for return is important and influences the decision to invest or not. We always check the economic-financial viability. Analysing financial, market and liquidity risks lets us grow with more security."

G BR = Director in Brazil; G CAN = Director in Canada

Performance Analyses and Investment Decision-Making

Managing performance is one of the essential components for any organisation, and so to be aware of the conformity and quality of its activities, an organisation needs an efficient, accurate assessment system that lets managers control, monitor and improve the quality of healthcare and the organisation's performance (Lin et al., 2013). Resources provided by different methods to assess performance, such as coverage, comparability, measurability and compatibility with objectives, give advantages such as identifying opportunities for improvement, improved quality of health, efficiency and responsibility, contributing to decision-making, transparency and justification of decisions for interested parties (Nsamzinshuti et al., 2014). Measuring performance is a continuous challenge for managers and beneficiaries, and at the present time, also plays a vital role in organisations' success.

Table 5. Directors' qualitative quotations regarding performance analyses for investment decision-making.

Origin	Quotation From the Interview
Types of analyses made.	
G BR	"BSC – *Balanced Scorecard* (performance measurement tool); *Lean Six Sigma* (practice of product and process improvement); ERM (*Enterprise Risk Management*), PDCA Cycle (*Plan – Do – Check – Act)* for internal processes."
G CAN	"BSC – *Balanced Scorecard* (performance measurement tool); *Lean Six Sigma* (practice of product and process improvement); ERM (*Enterprise Risk Management*); GRC (*Governance, Risk and Compliance),* PDCA Cycle (*Plan – Do – Check – Act).*"
Use of a costing method to determine the results of patient care.	
G BR	"Yes, implementation of software that carries out activity-based costing (ABC method). This method provides analyses of the costs of clinical or surgical hospitalization, and also information about the costs of procedures by medical specialization or surgical team, which facilitates monitoring of where resources are being consumed."
G CAN	"Even if a product or piece of information does not have a price on it, it certainly has a cost and this is determined in all areas, by different methods; there is a department dealing with these activities."
How are the risks of new investments assessed?	
G BR	"We always assess the market demand, the sustainability of the chain and the quality/efficiency of competitors".
G CAN	"Regarding future situations, nobody can be sure that a given event will occur. As a project's forecast cash-flow is a future event, it can be the amount foreseen or some other. At present, we use two methods: sensitivity analysis and scenario creation."

G BR = Director in Brazil; G CAN = Director in Canada

Strategic administration of hospital resources involves different aspects, such as the creation and share of knowledge (Kaper et al., 2020), which can lower the cost of medicine (Mohan et al., 2019), increase customer satisfaction (Sherafat et al., 2019), improve service cycle times (Neves et al., 2019), reduce the pressure on professionals (Luo et al., 2019) and generate services of excellence (Kulkarni et al., 2019). Today, the use of indicators in integrated information systems has improved hospitals' financial results, promoting transparency in actions (Salampessy et al., 2019). Monitoring through indicators can contribute to improved quality, productivity and a low cost of health services, when combined with other management tools and aligned with the organisational strategy (Comendeiro-Maaløe et al., 2019). Management of hospital performance is a multi-dimensional question, each dimension having its own meaning. Based on evidence, the indicators depend on the assessment model used, the objective of the assessment and the opinions of the executive managers and participants in the study. Selection of the most appropriate indicators is therefore the key to a wide-ranging system of performance assessment (Pourmohammadi et al., 2018). Measuring performance is a continuous challenge for managers, and today it also plays a vital role in organisations' success when analysed for investment decision-making.

Table 5 outlines the types of performance analyses made by the hospitals studied here, and the approach to assessing the risk of new investment.

DISCUSSION

The directors' perception of the concepts of governance are consistent and show a broad understanding, especially when mentioning the inter-relation between the clinical and administrative parts of hospital management, which are complementary, each having different focuses, such as quality healthcare for patients (clinical) and appropriate management of administrative processes and relations between stakeholders.

As for the guidelines from the Direction, it is understood that cost control is essential to keep the hospital profitable, maintaining patient satisfaction. It was mentioned that for an effective hospital direction, the medical team's participation is necessary (Alexander et al., 1986). Regarding the small size of the council, in the case of Brazil, this also implies that essential decisions related to administrative and clinical matters can be taken promptly. The fact that Nursing Services management is not part of the Direction concerns the control and decision-making power of members, the majority of whom are doctors, owners and founders of the hospital. In Canada, the composition seems more heterogeneous. Formed of the administration council, executive team and with the participation of the director of Nursing Services, which provides the council with knowledge and information from the hospital's main internal specialists, and consequently, the knowledge and experience of these professionals gives the council competence to monitor and lead administration more effectively (Abor, 2015).

Hospitals are complex organisations arising from a wide range of processes and interests that need different administrative aspects and management tools (Barbosa, 2003). An important question has been raised in recent decades concerning the hospital manager's training, whether this individual should be a doctor or not. For Chanes (2006), the administrator's general training can affect understanding of the applicability of the concepts of administration to this segment (health), causing delay in the hospital's decision-making. On the other hand, having an excellent doctor in charge of a hospital is no guarantee of better management, as understanding the factors affecting the adoption of best management practices is fundamental for improved hospital results. In this study, both types of actors are observed in management: a doctor and an economist, and in this context, it is not possible to conclude on which one manages the institution better. Besides basic training, relevant aspects such as capacities and skills can be developed. Doctors are increasingly occupying positions of leadership/management in health organisations (Carsen & Xia, 2006) and many leaders who are doctors can have skills, qualities or management approaches that have a positive effect on the quality of the hospital and the value of the care provided (Tasi et al., 2019). Hospitals that wish to improve clinical and financial performance through having more doctors in leadership positions need to converge on selecting and developing leaders who are strong strategists (Huhs et al., 2019), socially qualified and accepted by clinical colleagues (Van de Riet et al., 2019).

Regarding investment needs, apart from substitution of machines and equipment, i.e., through breakage or depreciation, hospitals are always seeking to extend their technological facilities, implementing new services that add value to their patient care and consequently increase the hospital's income, as well as enlarging the physical premises, as in the case of increasing the number of beds, keeping the focus on the importance of innovation and development (I&D). New interventions need greater development in relation to the cost-benefit, value of the investment and the training necessary to provide certain technology (Lesmana et al., 2017). In this sequencing, the possibilities of financing are central points. For Morse (2008), the amount of capital to be raised should be carefully assessed to have the right amount necessary at the various stages of development. It is very important to know at what stage to ask for additional funding, because the risks involved in a business vary in degree according to the different stages of business growth (Morse, 2008). In most cases, business failure is attributed to bad management and can be related to inappropriate financing and bad planning of business finances. The financial director in Canada is concerned about the financial risks in greater detail than the administrative director in the Brazilian hospital. The latter says he seeks to balance the expenditure on bank finance for investment with the income this produces. On the other hand, in the Canadian hospital, concern is found not only about the type of investment, but also with the credit, liquidity and market risks, leading the direction to adopt an integrated risk management structure. Both hospitals have medium or long-term strategic planning, but in Brazil, the economic and political instability influences medium and short-term financing, whereas in the Canadian hospital, planning is always long-term and counts on a multi-disciplinary team that constantly assesses investment projects, analysing financial, market and liquidity risks so that they can grow more securely. One relevant aspect is the number of employees per hospital bed, with this being greater in the Brazilian hospital (6,3 employees/bed, having 162 beds) than in the Canadian hospital (4,2 employees/bed, having 442 beds), which supposedly may reflect positively on the Brazilian case, with better care for patients, and in the Canadian case may express more adjusted processes leading to savings on staff expenditure. The employee/bed figures found demonstrate there is no pre-established standard as this can vary between 3,5 and 5,0 (Hunger & Weelen, 2002; Ibáñez et al., 2001), and according to these authors, only the Canadian hospital comes within this range.

Therefore, hospitals' performance analysis is crucial and decisive in decision-making on investment. Both hospitals studied use BSC – *Balanced Scorecard*, *Lean Six Sigma*, ERM (*Enterprise Risk Management*) among other indicators, to accompany and analyse the evolution of their processes before making decisions on investments. Hospitals present complex, vital services that consume a significant part of financial resources in the health sector in developed and developing countries (Markazi-Moghaddam et al., 2016; Mohammadkarim et al., 2011). Performance management is one of the essential components for any organisation, and therefore, to be aware of the conformity and quality of its activities, an organisation needs an efficient, accurate assessment system to enable managers to control, monitor and improve the quality of health services and organisational performance (Lin et al., 2013). Resources provided by different methods of performance assessment, such as coverage, comparability, measurability and compatibility with objectives give advantages such as identifying opportunities for improvement, improved quality of health, efficiency and responsibility, a contribution to decision-making, transparency and a justification of decisions for interested parties (Nsamzinshuti et al., 2014). Measuring performance is a constant challenge for managers and beneficiaries, and today, it also plays a vital role in organisations' success. Based on the qualitative analyses made, a model to integrate the involvement and competences of hospital managers in private institutions in Brazil and Canada is proposed, to identify the specific factors influencing decision-making on investment. This is shown in Figure 3.

Figure 3.

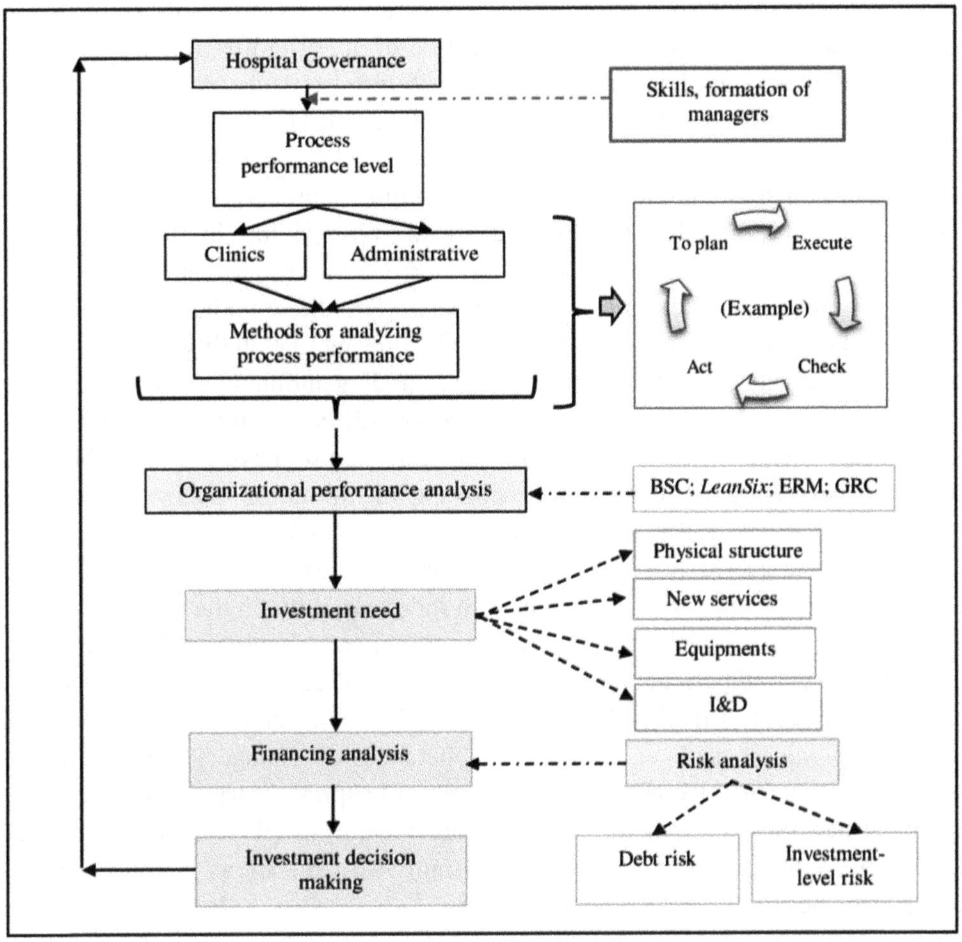

CONCLUSION

This research aims to fill a relevant gap in the literature concerning the importance of private hospital managers' competences in investment decisions through a study carried out in Brazil and Canada. In qualitative analysis, using NVivo 11, interviews were held with administrative and/or financial directors. Important elements emerge in the subject of governance in health through understanding the differentiation between corporate, hospital, clinical and integrated governance.

Raising the question of who should manage a hospital, a doctor or a professional specializing in management, the best scenario is found to be that in which hospital management can count on experienced clinicians with vision and managerial skills, and where the direction includes a technical team (accountant, economist, administrator and others) who understand the processes of patient care, as they complement each other and tend to govern the hospital with a greater capacity for resource application, without sacrificing quality in patient care, intervening coherently even in questions related to hospitals' investment and financing.

In this context, performance analysis takes the centre stage by providing resources produced through different methods of assessment, such as coverage, comparability, measurability and compatibility with objects. These bring advantages such as the identification of opportunities for improvement, improved quality of health, efficiency and responsibility, a contribution to decision-making, transparency and justifying decisions to interested parties (Nsamzinshuti et al., 2014).

Different forms of investing in the hospital sector correspond to technology and innovation, changes in process management, extending infrastructure and installing new services, acquiring new equipment, among other aspects, and reflect that investment can lead to innovation, improved efficiency and cost reduction, as long as the costs, financing and benefits of decisions are evaluated.

Health systems come under great pressure from costs. The directors believe that the financial resources spent should contribute to increasing the added value and the quality of the services provided.

Governance in the private hospital sector is crucial to understanding how the sector can be efficient and effective in providing healthcare. However, there are different groups of private hospitals and management approaches can also differ. This study was carried out in two important hospitals in Brazil and Canada and in interpreting the findings, we recognise this limitation, thus we cannot generalize the results here obtained. However, this study allows to outline a model for future research. Moreover, future quantitative research is suggested, involving representative samples of private hospitals in these two and more countries, where it is hoped to be conclude with more certainty on the deepen our understanding about the topic of management, performance, decision-making and investment in private hospitals. This study is one of the few to compare the importance of managers' competences for investment decision-making in private hospitals in Brazil and Canada. We apply the principal-agent relations lens to reveal how investment decisions are made and how the competences of managers influence these decisions. By contributing a manager involvement model specific to hospitals, various intra-hospital teams can work to implement new interventions for greater involvement of employees, middle management and directors in institutional management and in this way improve organisations' performance, outlining the importance of private hospital managers' competences.

REFERENCES

Abedi, G., Malekzadeh, R., Moosazadeh, M., Abedini, E., & Hasanpoor, E. (2019). Nurses' perspectives on the impact of marketing mix elements (7Ps) on patients' tendency to kind of hospital. *Ethiopian Journal of Health Sciences*, *29*(2), 223–230. PMID:31011270

Abor, P. A. (2015). The effects of health governance and ownership structure on the performance of hospitals in Ghana. *Int J Law Manag.*, *5*(2), 107–140. doi:10.1108/IJLMA-04-2014-0031

Agarwal, R., Green, R., Agarwal, N., & Randhawa, K. (2016). Management practices in australian healthcare: Can NSW public hospitals do better? *Journal of Health Organization and Management*, *30*(3), 331–353. doi:10.1108/JHOM-01-2015-0016 PMID:27119390

Akintoye, A., & Chinyio, E. (2005). Private finance initiative in the healthcare sector: Trend and risk assessment. *Engineering, Construction, and Architectural Management*, *12*(6), 601–616. doi:10.1108/09699980510634155

Alexander, J. A., Morrisey, M. A., & Shortell, S. M. (1986). Effects of competition, regulation and corporatization on hospital-medical relations. *Journal of Health and Social Behavior, 27*(3), 220–235. doi:10.2307/2136743 PMID:3772060

Allen, P. (2000). Accountability for clinical governance: Developing collective responsibility for quality in primary care. *BMJ (Clinical Research Ed.), 321*(7261), 608–611. doi:10.1136/bmj.321.7261.608 PMID:10977839

Almeida, M. H. T. (2001). Federalism, democracy and government in Brazil: Ideas, hypotheses and evidence. *Brazilian Journal of Bibliographic Information in Social Sciences. BBI, 51*, 13–34.

Bankston White, C., & Birmingham, J. (2015). Case management directors: How to manage in a transition-focused world: Part 2. *Professional Case Management, 20*(3), 115–127. PMID:25700135

Barbosa, A. P. (2003). *Corporate Governance in Non-Profit Hospitals: A study of the corporate leadership profile in eleven Brazilian hospitals* (Doctoral Thesis). EAESP/FGV. Retrieved from http://bibliotecadigital.fgv.br/dspace;/handle/10438/2578

Becker, S., & Koch, E. (2006). Hospitals and health systems: The best of times and the worst of times. *Journal of Health Care Finance, 32*(3), 1–7. PMID:18975727

Bloom, N., Van Reenen, J., Propper, C., & Seiler, S. (2009). *Management practices in hospitals.* Health, Econometrics and Data Group (HEDG) Working Papers 09/23, HEDG, c/o Department of Economics, University of York.

Braun, V., & Clarke, V. (2006). Using thematic analysis in psychology. *Qualitative Research in Psychology, 3*(2), 77–101. doi:10.1191/1478088706qp063oa

Brazil. (1990). *Law No. 8,080, of September 19, 1990. Provides for the conditions for the promotion, protection and recovery of health, the organization and functioning of the corresponding services and provides other measures.* Available at http://www.planalto.gov.br/ccivil_03/leis/l8080.htm

Campos, C. (2008). *Comparison of Pecking Order and Trade-off Theories: Evidence Based on Brazilian Listed Companies.* Presbyterian University Graduate Program in Business Administration Mackenzie. São Paulo. Retrieved from http://tede.mackenzie.br/jspui/handle/tede/720

Canada. Canada Health Act. Minister of Justice. (1985). Available at: https://laws.justice.gc.ca/PDF/C-6.pdf

Canadian Institute for Health Information (CIHI). (2018). Available at: https://www.cihi.ca/en/acess-data-and-reports

Carsen, S., & Xia, C. (2006). The physician as leader. *McGill Journal of Medicine, 9*(1), 1Y2.

Ch, F. N., & Jola, S. P. (2017). Bank health level analysis using rbbr in financial services sector - case in Indonesia stock exchange. *International Journal of Economic Research, 14*, 181–192.

Chanes, M. (2006). The challenges in training leading health managers. *The World of Health Sao Paulo, 30*(2), 326–333.

Chen, H., Hou, C., Zhang, L., & Li, S. (2020). Comparative study on the strands of research on the governance model of international occupational safety and health issues. *Safety Science*, *122*, 122. doi:10.1016/j.ssci.2019.104513

Chen, Z., Song, Y., Yu, J., & Wang, I. (2014). Differential development strategies of aged care support and continuity services in China, Japan and Australia. *Journal of Clinical Gerontology & Geriatrics*, *5*(2), 36–41. doi:10.1016/j.jcgg.2014.02.004

Comendeiro-Maaløe, M., Ridao-López, M., Gorgemans, S., & Bernal-Delgado, E. (2019). A comparative performance analysis of a renowned public private partnership for health care provision in spain between 2003 and 2015. *Health Policy (Amsterdam)*, *123*(4), 412–418. doi:10.1016/j.healthpol.2018.11.009 PMID:30554791

Cunha, C. L. F., Moreira, J. P. L., Oliveira, B. L. C. A., Bahia, L., & Luiz, R. R. (2019). Private health plans and the health of workers in Brazil [Planos privados de saúde e a saúde dos trabalhadores do Brasil]. *Collective Science & Health*, *24*(5), 1959–1970. PMID:31166528

De Pourcq, K., De Regge, M., Van den Heede, K., Van de Voorde, C., Gemmel, P., & Eeckloo, K. (2018). Hospital networks: How to make them work in belgium? facilitators and barriers of different governance models. *Acta Clinica Belgica: International Journal of Clinical and Laboratory Medicine*, *73*(5), 333–340. doi:10.1080/17843286.2018.1457196 PMID:29595095

Degeling, P. (2006). Realising the developmental potential of clinical governance. *Clinical Chemistry and Laboratory Medicine*, *44*(6), 688–691. doi:10.1515/CCLM.2006.120 PMID:16729853

Deighan, M., & Bullivant, J. (2006). *Integrated Governance Handbook - A handbook for executives and non-executives in healthcare organisations*. Department of Health. London.

Deighan, M., Cullen, R., & Moore, R. (2004) The development of integrated governance. *Debate (the voice of NHS management)*, (4).

Department of Informatics of the Unified Health System - DataSUS. (2019). Available at: http://www.cns.org.br/links/D_SETOR_DATES.htm

Diaconu, K., Falconer, J., Vidal, N., O'May, F., Azasi, E., Elimian, K., Bou-Orm, I., Sarb, C., Witter, S., & Ager, A. (2020). Understanding fragility: Implications for global health research and practice. *Health Policy and Planning*, *35*(2), 235–243. doi:10.1093/heapol/czz142 PMID:31821487

Dlugosz, Z. (2011). Population ageing in Europe. *Procedia: Social and Behavioral Sciences*, *19*(1), 47–55. doi:10.1016/j.sbspro.2011.05.106

Eeckloo, K., Herck, G. V., Hulle, C. V., & Vleugels, A. (2004). From Corporate Governance to Hospital Governance. Authority, transparency and accountability of Belgian non-profit hospitals' board and management. *Health Policy (Amsterdam)*, *68*(1), 1–15. doi:10.1016/j.healthpol.2003.07.009 PMID:15033548

Fasterholdt, I., Krahn, M., Kidholm, K., Yderstræde, K. B., & Pedersen, K. M. (2017). Review of early assessment models of innovative medical technologies. *Health Policy (Amsterdam)*, *121*(8), 870–879. doi:10.1016/j.healthpol.2017.06.006 PMID:28701260

Feierstein, M. (2012). *Planet Ponzi – How Politicians and Bankers Stole Your Future: What Happens Next, How You can Survive*. Transworld Publishers/Bantam.

Fernandes, A. C., & Nunes, A. M. (2016). Hospitals and the public-private combination in the portuguese health system [Os hospitais e a combinação público-privado no sistema de saúde português]. *Acta Medica Portuguesa, 29*(3), 217–223. doi:10.20344/amp.6712 PMID:27285098

Fidler, D. (2010). *The challenges of global health governance*. Council on Foreign Relations.

Fleet, R., Dupuis, G., Fortin, J., Gravel, J., Ouimet, M., Poitras, J., & Légaré, F. (2017). Rural emergency care 360°: Mobilising healthcare professionals, decision-makers, patients and citizens to improve rural emergency care in the province of quebec, canada: A qualitative study protocol. *BMJ Open, 7*(8), e016039. doi:10.1136/bmjopen-2017-016039 PMID:28819068

Gandhi, A. V., & Sharma, D. (2018). Technical efficiency of private sector hospitals in Índia using data envelopment analysis. *Benchmarking, 25*(9), 3570–3591. doi:10.1108/BIJ-06-2017-0135

Gordon, D., McKay, S., Marchildon, G., Sacha Bhatia, R., & Shaw, J. (2020). Collaborative governance for integrated care: Insights from a policy stakeholder dialogue. *International Journal of Integrated Care, 20*(1), 3. doi:10.5334/ijic.4684 PMID:32089655

Gualtieri, G., Traverso, S., Pozza, A., Ferretti, F., Carabellese, F., Gusinu, R., & Coluccia, A. (2020). Clinical risk management in high-security forensic psychiatry residences. protecting patients and health professionals: Perspectives and critical issues of the law 81/2014. *La Clinica Terapeutica, 171*(2), e97–e100. PMID:32141478

Hai, V. D., Trung, L. H. P., Hung, P. M., Hung, D. V., Ngoc, P. P., Hung, P. D., Dan, C. Q., & Vi, T. Q. (2020). Design of noninvasive hemodynamic monitoring equipment using impedance cardiography. *IFMBE Proceedings, 69*, 3-9. 10.1007/978-981-13-5859-3_1

Health Services Circular (HSC). (1999). *Clinical Governance. Quality in the new NHS*. Available at http://www.dh.gov.uk/prod_consum_dh/groups/dh_digitalassets/@dh/@en/documents/digitalasset/dh_40120 43.pdf

Helmers, R. A., & Harper, C. M. (2019). The mayo clinic model of clinical integration. *Health Care, 7*(3). PMID:29970294

Hilmola, O., & Henttu, V. (2016). Transportation costs do matter: Simulation study from hospital investment decision. *Journal of Modelling in Management, 11*(2), 560–584. doi:10.1108/JM2-10-2013-0053

Holá, J., Moravcová, M., & Hlaváčková, E. (2020). Communication competency: The topic of lifelong learnifor nurse managers in hospitals [Komunikační kompetence: Téma celoživotního vzdělávání všeobecných sester manažerek v nemocnicích]. *Kontakt, 22*(1), 33–39. doi:10.32725/kont.2019.053

Hsieh, H., & Shannon, S. E. (2005). Three approaches to qualitative content analysis. *Qual Health Res., 15*, 1277-1288.

Hsu, G. C. M., Clarkson, P., & Ouyang, A. X. (2019). Do biotechnology and health-care firms have poorer continuous disclosure practices as reflected in ASX queries? *Accounting Research Journal, 32*(2), 88–112. doi:10.1108/ARJ-12-2015-0152

Huhs, E., Gliebe, W., & Sendlhofer, G. (2019). Qualitative analysis of lean management in healthcare: Perspectives of Austrian and swiss experts [Qualitative Analyse zu Lean Management im Gesundheitswesen: Sichtweisen österreichischer und Schweizer Experten]. *Zeitschrift für Evidenz, Fortbildung und Qualität im Gesundheitswesen, 143*, 8–14. doi:10.1016/j.zefq.2019.05.003 PMID:31153810

Hunger, J. D., & Wheelen, L. T. (2002). *Strategic management: principles and practices*. Reichmann e Afffonso.

Ibáñez, N. (2001). Social health organizations: the model in the State of São Paulo. *ABRASCO, 6*(2).

Jensen, M., & Meckling, W. T. (1976). Theory of the firm: Managerial behavior, agency cost, and ownership structure. *Journal of Financial Economics*, *3*(4), 305–360. doi:10.1016/0304-405X(76)90026-X

Jensen, M. C. (1986). Agency costs of free cash flow, corporate finance, and takeovers. *The American Economic Review*, *76*(2), 323–329.

Jiang, H. J., Lockee, C., & Fraser, I. (2012). Enhancing board oversight on quality of hospital care: An agency theory perspective. *Health Care Management Review*, *37*(2), 144–153. doi:10.1097/HMR.0b013e3182224237 PMID:21712722

Jizi, M. I., & Nehme, R. (2017). Board gender diversity and firms' equity risk. *Equality, Diversity and Inclusion*, *36*(7), 590–606. doi:10.1108/EDI-02-2017-0044

Kakemam, E., & Dargahi, H. (2019). Competencies gap in hospital management in Tehran, Iran: A cross-sectional survey. *Journal of Health Management*, *21*(4), 451–464. doi:10.1177/0972063419884412

Kaper, M. S., Reijneveld, S. A., van Es, F. D., de Zeeuw, J., Almansa, J., Koot, J. A. R., & de Winter, A. F. (2020). Effectiveness of a comprehensive health literacy consultation skills training for undergraduate medical students: A randomized controlled trial. *International Journal of Environmental Research and Public Health*, *17*(1), 81. doi:10.3390/ijerph17010081 PMID:31861918

Kennedy, M., Elcock, M., Ellis, D., & Tall, G. (2017). Pre-hospital and retrieval medicine: Clinical governance and workforce models. *EMA -. Emergency Medicine Australasia*, *29*(4), 467–469. doi:10.1111/1742-6723.12776 PMID:28378954

Klemp, G. Jr. (2005). *Leadership skills. Nursing administration and leadership: theory and practice*. Artmed.

Knickman, J. R., & Snell, E. K. (2002). The 2030 problem: Caring for ageing baby boomers. *Health Services Research*, *37*(4), 849–884. doi:10.1034/j.1600-0560.2002.56.x PMID:12236388

Kulkarni, S. S., Barnato, A. E., Rosengart, M. R., Fischhoff, B., Angus, D. C., Yealy, D. M., Wallace, D. J., & Mohan, D. (2019). Does preexisting practice modify how video games recalibrate physician heuristics in trauma triage? *The Journal of Surgical Research*, *242*, 55–61. doi:10.1016/j.jss.2019.04.013 PMID:31071605

Kuntz, L., Pulm, J., & Wittland, M. (2016). Hospital ownership, decisions on supervisory board characteristics, and financial performance. *Health Care Management Review*, *41*(2), 165–176. doi:10.1097/HMR.0000000000000066 PMID:25978002

Lemmon, M. L., Roberts, M. R., & Zender, J. F. (2008). Back to the beginning: Persistence and the cross-section of corporate capital structure. *The Journal of Finance*, *63*(4), 1575–1608. doi:10.1111/j.1540-6261.2008.01369.x

Lesmana, C. R. A., Gani, R. A., Hasan, I., Sulaiman, A. S., & Lesmana, L. A. (2017). Therapeutic interventional endoscopic ultrasound based on rare cases in indonesia: A single-center experience in unselected patients. *Case Reports in Gastroenterology*, *11*(1), 72–77. doi:10.1159/000456606 PMID:28611556

Lethbridge, E. (1997). Corporate governance. *BNDES Journal*, *4*, 209–231.

Lin, Q. L., Liu, L., Liu, H. C., & Wang, D. J. (2013). Integrating hierarchical balanced scorecard with fuzzy linguistic for evaluating operating room performance in hospitals. *Expert Systems with Applications*, *40*(6), 1917–1924. doi:10.1016/j.eswa.2012.10.007

Lüleci, N. E., Gemlik, H. N., Bektas, G., & Manioglu, Y. (2015). The awareness of experience innovation and an application in private hospitals. *JPMA. The Journal of the Pakistan Medical Association*, *65*(10), 1108–1111. PMID:26440843

Luo, L., Li, J., Liu, C., & Shen, W. (2019). Using machine-learning methods to support health-care professionals in making admission decisions. *The International Journal of Health Planning and Management*, *34*(2), e1236–e1246. doi:10.1002/hpm.2769 PMID:30957270

MacVane Phipps, F. (2020). Challenges of 21st-century health governance. *International Journal of Health Governance*, *25*(1), 12–18. doi:10.1108/IJHG-12-2019-0080

Markazi-Moghaddam, N., Arab, M., Ravaghi, H., Rashidian, A., Khatibi, T., & Zargar Balaye Jame, S. A. (2016). Knowledge Map for Hospital Performance Concept: Extraction and Analysis: A Narrative Review Article. *Iranian Journal of Public Health*, *45*(7), 843–854. PMID:27516990

Mohammadkarim, B., Jamil, S., Pejman, H., Seyyed, M. H., & Mostafa, N. (2011). Combining multiple indicators to assess hospital performance in Iran using the Pabon Lasso Model. *The Australasian Medical Journal*, *4*(4), 175–179. doi:10.4066/AMJ.2011.620 PMID:23393508

Mohan, D., Wallace, D. J., Kerti, S. J., Angus, D. C., Rosengart, M. R., Barnato, A. E., Yealy, D. M., Fischhoff, B., Chang, C-C., & Kahn, J. M. (2019). Association of practitioner interfacility triage performance with outcomes for severely injured patients with fee-for-service medicare insurance. *JAMA Surgery, 154*(12).

Moll, M. C., Decavel, F., & Merlet, C. (2009). A quality evaluation tableau for health institutions: An educational tool [Tableau de bord d'évaluation du système qualité des pôles en établissement de santé: un outil pédagogique.]. *Recherche en Soins Infirmiers*, *98*, 19–27. doi:10.3917/rsi.098.0019 PMID:19947122

Morlock, L. L., & Alexander, J. (1986). Models of Governance in Multi Hospital Systems Implications for Hospital and System-Level Decision. *Making. Medical Care*, *24*(2). PMID:3796079

Morse. (2008). Entrepreneurs: Generating cash in a credit crunch. *Ivey Business Journal Online, 72*(6), 1.

Myers, S. C. (1977). Determinants of corporate borrowing. *Journal of Financial Economics*, *5*(2), 147–175. doi:10.1016/0304-405X(77)90015-0

Myers, S. C. (1984). The capital structure puzzle. *The Journal of Finance, 39*(3), 575–592. doi:10.2307/2327916

Myers, S. C., & Majluf, N. S. (1984). Corporate financing and investment decisions when firms have information that investors do not have. *Journal of Financial Economics, 13*(2), 187–221. doi:10.1016/0304-405X(84)90023-0

Navarro, T. M., Durán, F. M., & Santos, J. L. (2017). A regional competitiveness index for Spain [Un índice de competitividad regional para España]. *Revista De Estudios Regionales, 109*, 67–94.

Neves, J. B., Shepherd, S., Cullen, D., Powles, T., Aitchison, M., & Tran, M. G. B. (2019). Performance and cost of a renal cancer specialist multidisciplinary team meeting: Results from 1500 discussions. *Journal of Clinical Urology, 12*(4), 314–319. doi:10.1177/2051415819829309

Ngo, A., Duong, H., & Chen, A. (2016). The Effects of Covenant Violations on the Underpricing of Seasoned Equity Offerings and the Implied Cost of Equity Capital. *The Quarterly Journal of Finance, 06*(01), 1–33. doi:10.1142/S2010139216400036

Nowell, L. S., Norris, J. M., White, D. E., & Moules, N. J. (2017). Thematic analysis: seeking to meet the reliability criteria. *Int J Qual Meth., 16*(1).

Nsamzinshuti, A., Van Elslande, C., & Alassane, N. B. (2014). Managing hospital efficiency and effectiveness: Designing a hospital performance measurement system. *Proceedings of 2nd IEEE International Conference on Logistics Operations Management, GOL 2014*, 188-200. 10.1109/GOL.2014.6887440

Ouyang, W., & Hilsenrath, P. E. (2017). Merger & Acquisition and Capital Expenditure in Health Care. INQUIRY. *The Journal of Health Care Organization, Provision, and Financing, 54*, 004695801769227. doi:10.1177/0046958017692275

Paim, J., Travassos, C., Almeida, C., Bahia, L., & MacInko, J. (2011). The brazilian health system: History, advances, and challenges. *Lancet, 377*(9779), 1778–1797. doi:10.1016/S0140-6736(11)60054-8 PMID:21561655

Pericleous, L., Amin, M., & Goeree, R. (2019). The value and consequences of using public health technology assessments for private payer decision-making in Canada: One size does not fit all. *Journal of Medical Economics, 22*(5), 478–487. doi:10.1080/13696998.2019.1582535 PMID:30757934

Pillay, R. (2010). The skills gap in hospital management: A comparative analysis of hospital managers in the public and private sectors in South Africa. *Health Services Management Research, 23*(1), 30–36. doi:10.1258/hsmr.2009.009015 PMID:20150608

Pourmohammadi, K., Hatam, N., Shojaei, P., & Bastani, P. (2018). A comprehensive map of the evidence on the performance evaluation indicators of public hospitals: A scoping study and best fit framework synthesis. *Cost Effectiveness and Resource Allocation, 16*(1), 64. doi:10.118612962-018-0166-z PMID:30534009

Price, T., Tredinnick-Rowe, J., Walshe, K., Tazzyman, A., Ferguson, J., Boyd, A., Archer, J., & Bryce, M. (2020). Reviving clinical governance? A qualitative study of the impact of professional regulatory reform on clinical governance in healthcare organisations in england. *Health Policy (Amsterdam)*, *124*(4), 446–453. doi:10.1016/j.healthpol.2020.01.004 PMID:32044153

Roland, M., & Baker, R. (1999). *Clinical governance: a practical guide for primary care teams*. University of Manchester. Available at http://www. npcrdc.ac.uk/Publications/HANDBOOK%20CLINICAL%20 GOVERNANCE.pdf

Sakellarides, C. (2003). Health governance in a global post modern world - when Beauty meets the Beast. *Humanitas. Humanidades Médicas*, *1*(3), 91–100.

Salampessy, B. H., Bijlsma, W. R., Van Der Hijden, E., Koolman, X., & Portrait, F. R. M. (2019). On selecting quality indicators: Preferences of patients with breast and colon cancers regarding hospital quality indicators. *BMJ Quality & Safety*, *29*(7), 576–585. doi:10.1136/bmjqs-2019-009818 PMID:31831636

Santos, J. C., & Melo, W. (2018). Comparative Health Study: Primary Health Care Models in Brazil, Canada and Cuba. *Interinstitutional Journal of Psychology*, *11*(1), 79–98.

Sarig, O. H. (1998). The effect of leverage on bargaining with a corporation. *Financial Review*, *33*(1), 1–16. doi:10.1111/j.1540-6288.1998.tb01603.x

Securities and Exchange Commission (SEC). (2002). Available at http://www.cvm.gov.br

Shamayleh, A., Awad, M., & Farhat, J. (2020). IoT based predictive maintenance management of medical equipment. *Journal of Medical Systems*, *44*(4), 72. doi:10.100710916-020-1534-8 PMID:32078712

Shan, C. M., Razak, N. H. A., & Ali, A. B. I. (2018). The impact of board of directors' characteristics and remuneration on companies' performance in Malaysia. *Indian Journal of Public Health Research & Development*, *9*(11), 1220–1221. doi:10.5958/0976-5506.2018.01625.X

Shepheard, J., Lapiz, E., Read, C., & Jackson, T. J. (2019). Reconciling hospital-acquired complications and CHADx+ in victorian coded hospital data. Health Information Management. *Journal of the Health Information Management Association of Australia*, *48*(2), 76–86. doi:10.1177/1833358318770282 PMID:29690788

Sherafat, A., Vaezi, A., Vafaeenasab, M., Ehrampoush, M., Fallahzadeh, H., & Tavangar, H. (2019). Responsibility-evading performance: The experiences of healthcare staff about triage in emergency departments: A qualitative study. *Iranian Journal of Nursing and Midwifery Research*, *24*(5), 379–386. doi:10.4103/ijnmr.IJNMR_217_18 PMID:31516525

Siskou, O., Kaitelidou, D., Papakonstantinou, V., & Liaropoulos, L. (2008). Private health expenditure in the greek health care system: Where truth and the myth begins. *Health Policy (Amsterdam)*, *88*(2-3), 282–293. doi:10.1016/j.healthpol.2008.03.016 PMID:18486985

Smits, P., & Champagne, F. (2020). Governance of health research funding institutions: An integrated conceptual framework and actionable functions of governance. *Health Research Policy and Systems*, *18*(1), 22. doi:10.118612961-020-0525-z PMID:32070372

Soper, M. R., Stallmeyer, J. M., Bopp, K. D., & Wood, M. B. (1995). Balancing the Triad: Cost Containment, Quality of Service, and Quality of Care in Managed Care Systems. National Center for Managed Health Care Administration, University of Missouri.

Spigelman, A. D., & Rendalls, S. (2015). Clinical governance in Australia. *Clinical Governance*, *20*(2), 56–73. doi:10.1108/CGIJ-03-2015-0008

Stark, P. (2020). Advancing complex case management competencies in a health care system. *Professional Case Management*, *25*(1), 19–25. doi:10.1097/NCM.0000000000000361 PMID:31764712

Stathopoulos, K., & Voulgaris, G. (2016). The Impact of Investor Horizon on Say-on-Pay Voting. *British Journal of Management*, *27*(4), 796–818. doi:10.1111/1467-8551.12172

Steinberg, H. (2003). *The Human Dimension of Corporate Governance*. People.

Tasi, M. C., Keswani, A., & Bozic, K. J. (2019). Does physician leadership affect hospital quality, operational efficiency, and financial performance? *Health Care Management Review*, *44*(3), 256–262. doi:10.1097/HMR.0000000000000173 PMID:28700509

Thaiyalnayaki, M., & Divakara Reddy, G. (2018). A brief analysis on dividend payout vs promoters share in corporate firms. *Indian Journal of Public Health Research & Development*, *9*(2), 19–24. doi:10.5958/0976-5506.2018.00084.0

Torres, J. A., Leal, M. D. C., Domingues, R. M. S. M., Esteves-Pereira, A. P., Nakano, A. R., Gomes, M. L., Figueiró, A. C., Nakamura-Pereira, M., De Oliveira, E. F. V., Ayres, B. V. D. S., Sandall, J., Belizán, J. M., & Hartz, Z. (2018). Evaluation of a quality improvement intervention for labour and birth care in brazilian private hospitals: A protocol. *Reproductive Health*, *15*(1), 194. doi:10.118612978-018-0636-y PMID:30477517

Toygar, S. A., & Akbulut, Y. (2013). An assessment of the decision making and problem-solving skills of hospital administrators. *International Journal of Healthcare Management*, *6*(3), 168–176. doi:10.1179/2047971913Y.0000000035

Turner, J. (2014). Predicting long-term debt in the healthcare sector. Saarbrucken, Germany: Scholars' Press.

Turner, J. S., Broom, K., Elliot, M., & Lee, J. (2015). A comparison of capital structure: The use of debt in investor owned and not-for-profit hospitals. *Journal of Health Care Finance*, *41*(4).

Uddin, S., Mori, Y., & Shahadat, K. (2020). Private management and governance styles in a japanese public hospital: A story of west meets east. *Social Science & Medicine*, *245*, 245. doi:10.1016/j.socscimed.2019.112719 PMID:31838335

van de Riet, M. C. P., Berghout, M. A., Buljac-Samardžić, M., van Exel, J., & Hilders, C. G. J. M. (2019). What makes an ideal hospital-based medical leader? three views of healthcare professionals and managers: A case study. *PLoS One*, *14*(6), e0218095. doi:10.1371/journal.pone.0218095 PMID:31185051

Wernz, C., Zhang, H., & Phusavat, K. (2014). International study of technology investment decisions at hospitals. *Industrial Management & Data Systems*, *114*(4), 568–582. doi:10.1108/IMDS-10-2013-0422

World Health Organization (WHO). (1998a). *Health for All in the 21st Century*. World Health Organization. Available in: https://apps.who.int/iris/bitstream/handle/10665/55721/WHSQ_1998_51__p3-6_eng.pdf?sequence=1&isAllowed=y

World Health Organization (WHO). (2009). *Who are health managers: Case studies from three African countries*. Human Resources for Health Observer - Issue No. 1. Geneva, Switzerland: World Health Organization. Available in: https://www.who.int/hrh/resources/hrh_observer/en/

World Health Organization (WHO). (2020). *Regional Office for Europe. Hospital Readiness Checklist for COVID 19*. Available in: http://www.euro.who.int/_data/assets/pdf_file/0010/430210/Hospital-Readiness-Checklist.pdf?ua=1

Xue, Y., Liang, H., & Boulton, W. (2008). Information technology governance information technology investment decision process: The impact of investment characteristics, external environment, and internal context. *Management Information Systems Quarterly*, *32*(1), 67–96. doi:10.2307/25148829

Zhu, L., Peng, Z., Liu, L., & Ling, S. (2019). Combining resource, structure and institutional environment: A configurational approach to the mode selection of the integrated healthcare in county. *International Journal of Environmental Research and Public Health*, *16*(16), 2975. doi:10.3390/ijerph16162975 PMID:31430889

APPENDIX

Table 6. Main similarities and differences between the Unified Health System (SUS), Brazil and Canadian Health Care (CHC), Canada.

Country	System/ year of institution/ regulating body	Health system reform	Organisation	Directives	Private sector participation and the relation with the public sector	Management model (predominant system)	Financing model	Co-payment and reimbursement	Treatment model	Organisation of the health system (relevant points)
Brazil	Single Health Service (SUS)/ (1988)/ National Health Agency (ANS)	1990s: containing expenditure with rationalisation of supply through focusing policies on the basic health package; encouraging private insurance; decentralizing services to the local level; financial cuts in health. It is the State's duty to ensure the population's health. This is based on principles of social justice, on the idea that the health system should protect the most vulnerable citizens and act universally. Human health from an integral perspective, including promotion, prevention and rehabilitation. Co-existence of public and private service. Inspired by the British model.	The SUS is organised in regionalized and hierarchical networks and operates throughout Brazil, with single direction in each sphere of government.	Regionalized and hierarchical network and with incomplete decentralization directives, with single direction in each sphere of government (Federal Law n. 8.080/1990).	According to Art. 199 of the Federal Constitution of 1988, private institutions can participate in the SUS, in a complementary way, following the latter's directives. Law no 9.565, of 1998, created the Supplementary National Health Agency (ANS), which must control, assess and supervise the procedures of private health services. In Brazil, private initiative can cover the same health services as the SUS, and in practice, has a great coverage, mainly in relation to out-patient treatment. Law no 8.080/90 also establishes that the SUS can sign agreements or public law contracts with private bodies, in order to ensure treatment for the population.	Universality, integrity and equity, and social control as the directing axis of health actions. The SUS has incomplete and participated decentralized management, with the aim of fulfilling, on the State's behalf, the responsibility for the protection of individual and collective health.	Mutually binding financing, decentralized between the three spheres of government (42% Federal, 26% State and 31% Municipal), defined in the public budget, arises from the public sector through taxes collected from the population, according to the size of the population, their epidemiological needs and the organisation of actions and services and transferred to local authorities following a per capita criterion.	No charge for use at the moment of healthcare provision	Family Health Strategy (ESF) is a structuring axis of the process of reorganising the health system, based on Primary Healthcare (APS). Access to care at home, care for women and children's health, especially in low-risk pre-maternity and childcare, and special care for the elderly and those with chronic illnesses.	* Decree no 2.488/11 determines that work should be carried out with the support of Family Health Support Centres (Nasf), created in order to increase the coverage and effectiveness of primary care initiatives.
Canada	Canadian Health Care (CHC)/ (1984)/ In Canada there is no universal regulatory system or for the various professions, and Health comes under State or regional jurisdiction.	The Canadian Health Decree (1984) establishes five decisive programmes: public administration, coverage, universality, portability and accessibility. All Canadian health plans are directed by the provinces. Each locality has autonomy to establish its rules, forms of adhesion, hospitals and planning deemed most pertinent. With Parliament's approval of the Canada Health Act, Canadian society established the principles unifying provinces and territories' health plans.	The National Health Insurance Programme is called Medicare and exists to ensure Canadian citizens' access to hospital services, doctors and medicine. Canadian Medicare can be described as an interlinked set of ten provincial health insurance plans and three territorial ones. It is the federal government's responsibility to set and administer the system's principles and national norms. In health systems' organisation, the role attributed to the general practitioner is that of controlling access to specialists and hospital admissions.	Services are structured according to specializations and complexity. Primary health care is based on the experience that healthcare, well-being and quality of life are influenced by economic, cultural and physical situations and spiritual beliefs.	Private health insurance must not compete in the domain of services available in the public network, but can compete in the market of supplementary benefits for private rooms, expenditure on medicine, aesthetic surgery, care at home and dental treatment. The private segment is dominant only in actions not considered of great relevance for sanitary authorities, such as: dentistry, aesthetic surgery, eye medication and optician services. In Canada, the private health plan sector can be divided in five categories: life assurance, residential and accident insurance, religious or philanthropic societies, non-profit societies and employers.	Since the1970s, the Canadian health system has been characterised predominantly as public, providing universal, wide-ranging coverage. Decentralization: since the origin of the Confederation in 1867, health is the responsibility of the provinces and territories. The effective decentralization of the Canadian health system is due to three main factors: (1) finance and service provision are the responsibility of the provinces and territories; (2) doctors are not civil servants; and (3) the presence of regional health authorities, which make detailed plans of health services for defined populations. It is considered one of the most decentralized in the world, since the provinces and territories have great autonomy to develop their local systems, each province/territory having its own Ministry of Health.	The system is defined as public or national insurance and financed by taxation shared between federal and provincial governments. The federal government finances the provinces through fiscal transfers depending on provincial/territorial governments' adhesion to standards the former establishes through Canada Health and Social Transfers. Finance for health comes from taxation. Hospitals are private entities, i.e., they are not public institutions, although their employees are paid by the government and their income also comes from the government. In practice, therefore, they operate as State institutions.	Co-payment of medicine, dentistry, false teeth (OECD, 2016).	Canadian provinces and territories must satisfy five principles: (1) Public administration, (2) Coverage, (3) Universality, (4) Accessibility, and (5) Portability.	* Canada has no employed doctors, with the majority working in private consultancies (they are paid for services provided on presentation of their fees directly to the provincial/territorial health insurance plan for payment); * Ninety five per cent of Canadian hospitals operate as private non-profit entities and are administered by community boards of directors, philanthropic organisations or local authorities. * Management and provision of health services is the responsibility of each province/territory, which establishes its priorities, finances and allocates resources among the regions, grants licences, registers and pays workers and sends financial resources to hospitals, controls costs and assesses the medical treatment provided, related services and certain aspects of public health.

Chapter 17
Executive Women and Firm Economic Value

Inês Lisboa
https://orcid.org/0000-0003-2802-2589
School of Technology and Management, CARME, Polytechnic of Leiria, Portugal

João Teodósio
https://orcid.org/0000-0002-7877-1564
School of Management and Technology, Polytechnic Institute of Santarém, Portugal

ABSTRACT

This study analyses the relationship between gender diversity on the board of directors' executive roles and the firm economic value. Based on a sample of Portuguese non-financial listed firms, between 2010 and 2018, results show that executive female contribute to decrease the firm economic value-added, and CEO gender diversity to decrease market value added, while no impact is found to traditional performance measures. Since the presence of women on the board of Portuguese firms is still scarce, female presence is not seen as relevant to add value to firms. These results are pioneer since previous studies found no impact of female presence on boards on value added measures. Moreover, findings show the relevance of value-added measures to analyze performance and singularities compared to profitability measures.

INTRODUCTION

Research on the gender diversity effects on firm performance has around four decades. According to Zahra and Pearce (1989)'s literature review, only two studies on the relationship of the board of directors' demographic characteristics and firm performance were published to that date. While Provan (1980) document a non-significant association between the fraction of male directors on board and firm performance, Zahra and Stanton (1988) also report similar effects regarding board ethnical diversity. Since Provan (1980)'s findings research on board gender diversity and firm performance was almost two decades in hibernation, until Burke and Mattis' edition of the *Women on Corporate Boards of Directors: International Challenges and Opportunities*, published in 2000.

DOI: 10.4018/978-1-7998-7596-3.ch017

Following Burke and Mattis (2000)'s suggestions and Burke (2000)'s findings of a positive association between the presence of women on the board of directors and firms' assets, revenues and profit margins, Erhardt, Werbel and Shrader (2003) analyze how the fraction of white and non-white women in the executive boards of U.S. firms interact with firm performance. The authors conclude for the incremental effect of board diversity on firms' return on assets (ROA) and return on investment (ROI). In a similar study, Carter, Simkins and Simpson (2003) find that U.S. boards with higher diversity in terms of gender and race are promoters of higher values of Tobin's Q. In opposition, and still within the U.S. context, Adams and Ferreira (2009) document that firms, on average, perform worse when they have female directors on the board. However, the authors document that this effect is contingent to the protection of shareholders rights. The detrimental effect of gender diversity is captured in firms where there are stronger shareholders' rights, but when shareholders' rights are weaker, the impact of female representation on board become positive.

Outside the U.S. context, Rose (2007) investigates the association between female board representation and performance of firms listed on the Copenhagen Stock Exchange. The author concludes for a non-association of board gender diversity and firm performance measured by Tobin's Q. In the author's perspective, this absence of diversity effects on firm performance, when compared to the results obtained in the U.S. context, may the explained due to the socialization process between female and male directors, which leads to the adoption of the behaviors from traditional board members.

Strøm, D'Espallier and Mersland (2014) investigate the effect of female leadership in the performance of microfinance institutions (MFI), over 73 countries, and conclude that MFI with female directors on the CEO and Chairperson positions present better financial performance when compared to those managed by males. The theoretical reasoning presented by the authors to support these findings is related to the customers' profile and with internal governance mechanisms. That is, firms with female leaders perform better because most customers are women and, as such, female directors are more aware and are more sensitive to the customers' needs. In addition, firms managed by female present weaker corporate governance mechanisms, which means that they have less oversight. Also using a multi-country sample, Terjesen, Couto and Francisco (2016) document women directors' effectiveness on firm performance using accounting and market measures.

Research on the female board representation impact on firm performance measured by indicators of added value, such as economic added value (EVA), cash value added (CVA) and market value added (MVA) is rare. According to our literature review, only three studies address this specific issue. Al Mamun, Yasser, Entebang, Nathan and Rahman (2013) analyze the relationship between board gender diversity on the EVA of a subsample of Pakistani listed firms. The authors conclude for an insignificant effect of gender diversity on firm performance. Later, Yasser, Al Mamun and Seamer (2017) and Yasser, Al Mamun and Rodrigs (2017) using all Pakistani listed firms reach to the same conclusion, that is, female directors have no direct impact on EVA.

Based on a sample of 35 Portuguese non-financial listed firms, between 2010 and 2018, our results demonstrate that executive woman contributes to a decrease of firm economic value added, and CEO gender diversity to a decrease in market value added. Portugal is a small-size country, with civil law and low protection of investors. Moreover, female representativeness on board is still scarce, which can explain results due to the difficulties of woman to be accepted and recognized by the market.

The contributions of the research are twofold: Firstly, we analyze the female executive effects on firm value added with other measure than the CEO gender dummy used by Al Mamun *et al.* (2013), namely, the fraction of female executive directors over total executive directors. With this alternative measure, we provide new evidence to the literature by capturing gender influence on other executive positions than de CEO. Secondly, and to the best of our knowledge, with the use of a sample of Portuguese non-financial listed firms, we are the first to provide information on the gender effects on firm value added, in the European context.

The remaining of the chapter is organized as follows: Section 2, presents de literature review and the hypotheses under investigation; Section 3, presents the methodology of the study; Section 4 describes and discusses the results and; Section 5, presents robustness tests, and section 6 concludes.

LITERATURE REVIEW

Corporate Governance and Firm Value

Literature on the effect of corporate governance mechanisms on firm economic value has call some attention to researchers. Coles, McWilliams and Sem (2001) investigate the relationship between corporate governance and the value of U.S. listed firms. They report a positive association between CEO duality and EVA, and a detrimental effect of board independence on MVA. In addition, the authors report a non-significant relationship between board independence, CEO ownership and directors' ownership and firm performance. Adjaoud, Zeghal and Andaleeb (2007) investigate the relationship between board quality and firm performance in the Canadian context. The authors report a positive association between the quality of corporate governance (e.g.: board independence, CEO non-duality, the existence of a compensation and audit committees) and value performance measured by EVA and MVA. Al Mamun, Yasser, Rahman, Wickramasinghe and Nathan (2014) investigate the Malaysian listed firms and conclude that the size and independence of the audit committee contributes to the increase of firms' economic value. Mirsharafoddini *et al.* (2014) also conclude that the existence of an internal audit committee increases firm value in the Iranian context. Moreover, the authors document an incremental effect of CEO duality, while board size and board independence have no effect on EVA.

El Mir and Seboui (2008) document that CEO duality, CEO tenure, managerial ownership and board size decrease firm value (difference between created shareholder value and EVA) while more independent boards, with more experts in finance, are incremental to firm value. In opposition, Pham, Suchard and Zein (2011) study the Australian non-financial listed firms and conclude for a non-significant association between board size, board independence and different measures of ownership and firm value measured by the ratio between EVA and total assets. Al Mamun *et al.* (2013) also find a non-significant association between board size and the economic value of Pakistani listed firms. More recently, Zhang and Aboud (2019), using a sample of Chinese listed banks, conclude for a non-significant association between board size and board independence and bank's economic value.

Bayrakdaroglu, Ersoy and Citak (2012) investigate the impact of a number of corporate governance mechanisms on firms' value. Using a sample of Turkish firms, the results indicate a positive effect of CEO duality on EVA, MVA and CVA. In addition, the authors find that ownership concentration have a positive effect on CVA but is detrimental to EVA, while foreign ownership promotes the increase of EVA. Board size and managers' ownership have no influence on the value of corporations.

Pamburai, Chamisa, Abdulla and Smith (2015) study the impact of corporate governance on the performance of South African listed firms and conclude for a negative effect of board size on EVA.

Concomitantly, they report a non-significant association between the fraction of independent and non-executive directors and the number of board meetings on firm value.

Shakina, Barajas and Molodchik (2017) investigate the association between intangible assets and EVA and document a positive association between directors' qualifications and firm value. This finding is in line with Athanassakos (2007) that reports the same association between directors' background on accounting and finance and EVA for Canadian firms. A similar association between directors' expertise on finance and EVA is reported by Upadhyay, Bhargava and Faircloth (2014). The latter authors also document a negative association between the number of committees, the board independence and the board business and EVA. In addition, they report that the combination of a higher number of board committees with a larger board is beneficial to firm value, while CEO non-duality has no significant effect. Yasser, Al Mamun and Seamer (2017) also conclude for a beneficial effect of board size, board minority representation, institutional and foreign ownership and firm value.

Krismiaji, Purwantini and Prabhata (2019) investigate the effect of earnings management and corporate governance on EVA. The authors find that while accruals earnings management have a positive effect on EVA, real earnings management have an opposite effect. In addition, results demonstrate that the effect of governance index on EVA is contingent to the type of earnings management.

In conclusion, literature indicates that the existence of audit committees and its greater independence favors firm economic value. Similarly, there is a consensus on the incremental effect of board directors' financial expertise in firm value. Research on the remaining corporate governance mechanisms effects on firm value presents mixed evidence. Nevertheless, it seems that the majority of the studies conclude for a beneficial effect of a unitary leadership structure (CEO and the Chairperson are the same person) and a non-significant effect of board size and board independence on firms' economic value added.

Board Gender Diversity and Firm Performance

Research on women directors' impact on firm performance is extensive and encapsulates a wide range of theoretical foundations. In a recent meta-analysis, Post and Byron (2015) identified some frameworks used by research to explain board gender diversity effects on firm performance, namely, and among others, agency theory and upper echelons theory. Agency theory addresses the existent conflicts between managers and shareholders and its costs (Jensen & Meckling, 1976). One of its major premises is that outside directors' presence on the boards is beneficial to the protection of the shareholders' interests. Carter, *et al.* (2003) following this theoretical reasoning analyzed the association between female directors and firm value and document that board gender diversity is incremental to firm performance. Alternatively, upper echelons theory (Hambrick, 2007; Hambrick & Mason, 1984) suggests that directors differ in their cognitive frames and that diversity impacts on firm performance. Based on these assumptions, Post and Bryon (2015) proved that board diversity improves accounting performance but not market performance.

Dezö and Ross (2012) study the relationship between women presence on the top management team (TMT) and firm performance in the U.S. context. The authors argue that women directors are beneficial to firm performance but only when firms are focus on innovation. Perryman, Fernando and Tripathy (2016) find out that board gender diversity increases the performance and decreases the risk of non-financial and non-utility firms, without any contingency. Using a sample of Chinese firms, Liu, Wei and Xie (2014) argue for the positive effects of female representation on board to firm performance, being the effect of executive female stronger than when female serve as independent directors.

Moving to the European context, Joecks, Pull and Vetter (2013) report that incremental effects on performance only occur when female representation is greater than 30%. Martín-Ugedo and Minguez-Vera (2014) document a linear association between women presence on board and firm performance of Spanish SMEs. Martín-Ugedo, Minguez-Vera and Rossi (2019) analyze the Spanish and Italian contexts and conclude that while the total sample reveals a positive significant effect of women directorships and firm performance, when the sample is divided by country, the results hold for Spain but turns negative to Italy. Bennouri, Chtioui, Nagati and Nekhili (2018) investigate the French context and argue that female directorships benefit firm performance measured by the accounting indicators return on assets (ROA) and return on equity (ROE) but not firms' market performance, measured by Tobin's Q.

In relation to research focused on Portuguese firms, Schwab, Werbel, Hofmann and Henriques (2016) analyse the Portuguese banking industry, between 1985 and 2000, and conclude for a cubic relationship between gender diversity, in all management levels, and listed and non-listed financial firms' performance. This result indicates that lower levels of gender diversity decrease firm performance, but when this diversity increases until a certain level, the performance increases, turning again detrimental with very high levels of gender diversity. Vieira (2018) support the idea that gender diversity is incremental to firm performance of family firms but is detrimental to the performance of non-family firms. Félix and David (2019) study the relationship between board gender diversity and family firms' performance. The authors conclude that board gender diversity is positively associated with family firms' performance, measured by variation of sales, business volume over total assets, and variation of business volume. Madaleno, Vieira and Teodósio (2019) study the effect of board gender diversity on the Portuguese and Spanish main stock markets and conclude for a non-significant association between different measures of gender diversity and accounting performance. However, the influence of women directors on market performance is more complex. While female Chief Financial Officer (CFO) and the fraction of women on the board of directors and committees contribute to the increase of firm market performance, when both measures are analysed separately, the combination of a female CFO and a higher fraction of women directors becomes detrimental to market performance.

Literature on the gender impact on firm performance measured by value added indicators is very scarce. Al Mamun *et al.* (2013) analyze the effect of board gender diversity on firm economic value in Pakistan. Results reveal no significant association between CEO gender, women presence on board and the fraction of women over total directors and EVA. Also using a Pakistani sample of listed firms, Yasser, Al Mamun and Rodrigs (2017) and Yasser, Al Mamun and Seamer (2017) report no association between board gender diversity and EVA.

Since it was not possible to find studies that investigate the impact of board gender diversity on firms' value added in the South European context, we postulate our hypotheses on the base of the literature findings using alternative accounting and market performance measures. Grounded on agency and upper echelons theories, we expect that:

Hypothesis 1 – There will be a positive association between executive women and firm economic value added.

Hypothesis 2 – There will be a positive association between executive women and firm market value added.

SAMPLE, VARIABLES AND METHODOLOGY

Sample

This investigation analyzes non-financial listed firms from Euronext Lisbon. Financial and accounting data was collected from SABI database (from Bureau Van Dijk); information about risk free premium was taken from Pordata database; unlevered beta and market risk premium were gathered from Damadoran website. Finally, corporate governance information was taken from the individual annual report of each firm per year. We kept only firms for which we have obtained data to calculate corporate governance variables, namely gender, since it is the focus of our work. Our final sample is composed of 35 Portuguese listed firms.

Most studies on this thematic focus on large size countries as U.S., China, Europe, calling the need to explore smaller countries to understand the similarities and main differences. Moreover, Portugal presents cultural specificities in terms of masculinity that literature reveals to be an important environmental determinant of financial corporate policies. Women still remain underrepresented as top managers or even in board of directors in Portugal. In 2018, Teodósio and Lisboa (2020) found that, in Portugal, women represent around 11% of the members of the board of directors. This fact makes relevant to understand the impact of female presence on boards on value-performance measures.

Regarding the period analyzed it starts in 2010, since is the year when accounting information standards has changed in Portugal, and it ends in 2018, which is the more recent year with information available.

Variables

To measure firms performance, we use measures of value creation, namely the **Economic Value Added - EVA** (Adjaoud *et al.*, 2007; Athanassakos, 2007; Coles *et al.*, 2001; Pham *et al.*, 2011; Yasser, Al Mamun and Seamer, 2017; Yasser, Al Mamun and Rodrigs, 2017; Zhang and Aboud, 2019) and the **Market Value Added - MVA** (Bayrakdaroglu *et al.*, 2012; Lee and Kim, 2009; Narang and Kaur, 2014).

There is no universal measure of performance. Most studies use accounting and market measures as both have advantages and disadvantages. While accounting measures can be subject to earnings management, market measures depend on investors' expectations and can be influence by information asymmetries (Vieira, Neves and Dias, 2019). Thus, using both measures allow to detect singularities catch by each and corroborate results. Moreover, most works use traditional measures such as Return on Assets, Return on Equity and Tobin's Q (e.g. Erhardt et al., 2003, Carter et al., 2003, Rose, 2007, Adams and Ferreira, 2009). This study uses value creation measures, less used variables, to contribute to knowledge expansion. Additionally, Krismiaji *et al.* (2019) argue that value creation measures are more accurate measures of financial performance because they show not only if the firm is generating earnings but also if the earnings are enough to cover the cost of financing the capital invested.

EVA was introduced by Stern Stewart Management Service and shows the amount (in monetary units) of the difference between net operating profit after taxes and the cost of capital employed (both cost of debt and cost of equity). This variable (an accounting variable) is more related with shareholders wealth and company's value (Adjaoud *et al.*, 2007). To calculate EVA the following formula was used:

$$EVA_t = NOPAT_t - WACC_t \times Capital\,invested_{t-1}$$

With:

NOPAT – net operating profit after taxes (net operating profit deducted from income taxes)

WACC – weight average cost of capital $= k_E \times \frac{E}{E+D} + k_D \times (1-t) \times \frac{D}{E+D}$

k_E – cost of equity $= r_f + \beta_e \times (r_m - r_f)$

r_f – risk-free premium, usually measured as the 10-year T-bond as a proxy

β_e – levered beta; company's sensitiveness to market risk-premium $= \beta_u \times \left[1 + (1-t) \times \frac{D}{E}\right]$

β_u – unlevered beta for the industry
k_D – cost of debt
E – equity
D – debt (liabilities)
t – income tax (%)
Capital invested – Equity + long-term liabilities
t – period analyzed

A positive EVA means that the company is able to create value to shareholders, while a negative value predicts value destruction (Al Mamun *et al.*, 2013). As EVA is a value in euro, we have divided EVA by total assets, following Pham *et al.* (2011).

The other value-performance variable - MVA shows the value added by the market since it is the excess of market value of capital over the book value of capital (Tan, Zhang and Ma., 2011). This is a long-term market performance measure.

$$MVA = Market\,Value - Book\,Value$$

A positive MVA signals that investors believe that the firm value is greater than its accounting value, it means, that company is creating value for shareholders, while a negative MVA suggests that the company's value has been damaged. We used MVA per share.

As independent variables we use board gender variables, and other corporate governance variables and company's financial variables as control variables.

In the group of board gender variables, we include CEO Gender (**CEOG**) - dummy variable which is 1 if the CEO is a woman, and zero otherwise (Al Mamun *et al.*, 2013; Conyon and He, 2017; Yasser, Al Mamun and Seamer, 2017; Yasser, Al Mamun and Rodrigs, 2017; Madaleno *et al.*, 2019; Teodósio and Lisboa, 2020), and percentage of executive woman (**EW**) – ratio of the number of executive women divided by the total number of executive members (Madaleno *et al.*, 2019; Teodósio and Lisboa, 2020).

To control for other impacts of corporate governance characteristics that might influence the firm performance we also included: CEO duality (**CEOD**) – dummy variable which is 1 if the CEO and the Chairperson are the same person (Coles *et al.*, 2001; DeFeo *et al.*, 2010; Bayrakdaroglu *et al.*, 2012; Mirsharafoddini *et al.*, 2014; Aubert et al., 2017); board size (**BS**) – number of members on the board of directors (DeFeo, Nikbakht and Spieler, 2010; Pham *et al.*, 2011; Bayrakdaroglu *et al.*, 2012; Al Mamun *et al.*, 2013; Mirsharafoddini *et al.*, 2014; Upadhyay *et al.*, 2014; Pamburai *et al.*, 2015; Conyon and He, 2017; Ilaboya and Ashafoke, 2017; Yasser, Al Mamun and Seamer, 2017; Yasser, Al Mamun and Rodrigs, 2017; Zhang and Aboud, 2019); and percentage of independent members (**IND**) – number of independent members divided by the total members of the board (Pham *et al.*, 2011; Upadhyay *et al.*, 2014; Pamburai *et al.*, 2015; Zhang and Aboud, 2019). These measures help to understand the structure and quality of firms' corporate governance. Finally, we also include firm characteristics as control variables since it may impact the firm performance. Vieira et al. (2019) argue that firm specific characteristics, as are decided by the firm managers, are crucial for every company and as a consequence to its performance. The following variables were included: leverage (**LEV**) – liabilities divided by total assets (Martani & Saputra, 2009; DeFeo *et al.*, 2010; Pham *et al.*, 2011; Bayrakdaroglu *et al.*, 2012; Choi, Sul & Min., 2012; Upadhyay *et al.*, 2014; Pamburai *et al.*, 2015; Conyon and He, 2017; Yasser, Al Mamun and Seamer, 2017; Yasser, Al Mamun and Rodrigs, 2017; Krismiaji *et al.*, 2019; Singh *et al.*, 2019); firm size (**SIZE**) – natural logarithm of total assets (Coles *et al.*, 2001; Martani & Saputra, 2009; DeFeo *et al.*, 2010; Pham *et al.*, 2011; Bayrakdaroglu *et al.*, 2012; Choi *et al.*, 2012; Narang and Kaur, 2014; Upadhyay *et al.*, 2014; Pamburai *et al.*, 2015; Perryman *et al.*, 2016; Conyon and He, 2017; Yasser, Al Mamun and Seamer, 2017; Yasser, Al Mamun and Rodrigs, 2017; Costa *et al.*, 2019; Krismiaji *et al.*, 2019; Singh *et al.*, 2019; Zhang and Aboud, 2019); firm age (**AGE**) – natural logarithm of the firm years of working activity (Martani & Saputra, 2009; Choi *et al.*, 2012; Narang and Kaur, 2014; Perryman *et al.*, 2016; Conyon and He, 2017; Yasser, Al Mamun and Seamer, 2017; Yasser, Al Mamun and Rodrigs, 2017).

Models

To analyze the impact of female executive on firm performance, the following regression model was tested:

$$Performance_{i,t} = \alpha + \beta_n \times \sum Gender\,Variables_{i,t} + \alpha_p \times \sum Governance\,Control\,Variables_{i,t} + \gamma_l \times \sum Firm\,Control\,Variables_{i,t} + U_i + V_i + \varepsilon_{i,t}$$

Where n represents the number of gender variables (n = 1, … 4); p the number of corporate control variables (p = 1, …, 3), l the number of financial control variables (l = 1, … 3); i is the firm analyzed and t the year study. U_i represents the fixed effect to firms, V_i the fixed effect to years and $\varepsilon_{i,t}$ the error term.

The model is estimated using OLS and OLS with fixed and random effects estimators. The F-statistic and the Hausman test are then conducted to decide which model is more accurate. Results are present in table 3.

RESULTS

Table 1 shows the summary statistics of the presented variables namely: mean, maximum, minimum, standard deviation, skewness and kurtosis.

Table 1. Summary statistics

	EVA/A	MVA p/ Share	CEOG	EW	CEOD	BS	IND	LEV	Ln(A)	Ln(Age)
Mean	-0.421	-0.048	0.071	0.092	0.509	9.060	0.200	0.431	19.817	3.444
Median	-0.065	-0.415	0.000	0.000	1.000	8.000	0.200	0.448	19.521	3.611
Maximum	0.333	13.733	1.000	1.000	1.000	23.000	0.778	0.948	23.907	5.263
Minimum	-9.412	-11.087	0.000	0.000	0.000	2.000	0.000	0.001	14.879	0.693
Std. Dev.	1.542	3.593	0.258	0.192	0.501	4.563	0.200	0.228	1.667	0.772

Analyzing Table 1 the following facts emerge: 1) in mean, Portuguese listed firms are not generating value added, since EVA and MVA are negative, but not all firms exhibit the same performance. While some firms present a high value added others have a negative one (the standard deviation is high). This fact can be explained due to the fact that, between 2011 and 2014, Portugal faced economic and financial assistance with several austerity measures applied by Troika.

With regards to female presence on the board, it is more an exception than a reality. In 2012, the European Commission has proposed that women should have a presence of 40% in non-executive positions in public firms in 2020 (European Commission, 2012). Although, in Portugal, in mean, only 7% of the firms in the sample have gender diversity in CEO positions. Adams and Ferreira (2009: 291) argue that the percentage of "female directors in Australia, Canada, Japan, and Europe is estimated to be 8.7%, 10.6%, 0.4%, and 8.0%, respectively". This conclusion is confirmed to Portugal, who exhibit a low presence of women as CEO. With regards to the percentage of female executives, in mean they represent less than 10% of the total executive members.

The CEO is also the chairman of the board in 51% of the firms in the sample, showing the prevalence of a singular leadership structure. In mean, there are 9 members in the board of directors, but the difference among firms is considerable. On average, 20% of the board members are independent, but some companies do not have any independent member on the board. These numbers show that the recommendation of corporate governance is not followed since at least every firm should have one third of independent members (recommendation number III. 4, IPCG, 2018).

Finally, around 43% of total assets are financed through liabilities, suggesting that listed firms are not to indebt. Although, the difference in the sample is also high, with some companies too indebtedness (leverage is almost 100%), while others finance almost all assets with equity. The firm size is similar to firms in the sample, but regarding to age, one company has only 2 years while other more than 194, suggesting some differences with regards to background knowledge.

Table 2 shows the correlation matrix.

Table 2. Correlation matrix

	EVA/A	MVA p/ Share	CEOG	EW	CEOD	BS	IND	LEV	Ln(A)	Ln(Age)
EVA/A	1									
MVA p/ share	-0.011	1								
CEOG	-0.027	-0.139 **	1							
EW	-0.089	-0.066	0.697 ***	1						
CEOD	-0.021	-0.061	-0.224 ***	-0.177	1					
BS	-0.013	0.218 ***	-0.100 *	-0.064	-0.481 ***	1				
IND	-0.057	0.185 ***	0.050	0.025	-0.246 ***	0.334 ***	1			
LEV	-0.075	-0.105 *	-0.265 ***	-0.192 ***	0.016	0.228 ***	0.151 **	1		
Ln(A)	0.011	0.327 ***	-0.015	-0.061	-0.300 ***	0.713 ***	0.414 ***	0.038	1	
Ln(Age)	-0.082	-0.089	-0.126 **	-0.052	-0.037	-0.098 *	0.089	-0.022	-0.064	1

CEO gender is negatively correlate with firm market value added, suggesting that financial investors do not perceive female CEO as a positive sign of the firm performance. Board size, percentage of independent members and firm' size are positively correlated with MVA per share, while leverage is negatively correlated. The increase in the size of the board allow the control of opportunistic behaviors by managers, which is enforced by the presence of independent members. Moreover, large-size firms can easily increase performance since turnover increases, leading to an increase in profits. Additionally, these firms have less information asymmetries and thus, financial investors prefer to invest in these firms. Finally, more indebt firms have additional costs (financial costs), which increase its risk and reduce its performance. Moreover, these firms will have difficulties in accept new growth opportunities due to the lack of financial source.

The other performance variable, economic value added, does not seem statistically correlated with any independent variable. Results also show that firms with female CEO exhibit higher presence of women on the board of directors and have a dual leadership structure. Moreover, female CEO are associated with younger and less indebted firms. The number of executive woman on the board is also negatively correlated with leverage, suggesting that women presence impacts on firms' capital structure.

The results of the estimation of the proposed model are presented in Table 3.

Results show a negative association between executive women and firm economic value added, contrary to postulate in hypothesis 1. This relation is only relevant when other variables are added since in a univariate analysis (correlation matrix) this relation is not forecast. This finding is new to the literature since previous studies, as Al Mamun *et al.* (2013), Yasser, Al Mamun and Rodrigs (2017) and Yasser, Al Mamun and Seamer (2017), analyzing Pakistan, found no association between women presence on the board and EVA. Although it confirms the results of Schwab *et al.* (2016), who analyze the Portuguese banking industry, and show that to lower levels of gender diversity firm performance decreases. While most of previous studies, using traditional performance measures, confirm that women work as a monitoring effect to managers, this control does not seem sufficient to add economic value to the firm. None of the other variables included in the model are relevant to explain economic value added, showing the singularity of this variable when compared to traditional performance measures.

Table 3. Regression results

	EVA/A		MVA p/Share	
	I	II	I	II
C	-0.359 ***	-0.538	0.028	-8.520
CEOG	0.466	0.226	-2.535 **	-1.143 *
EW	-0.109 *	-1.053 *	1.138	-0.006
CEOD	-	-0.253	-	-0.054
BS	-	-0.028	-	-0.002
IND	-	-0.650	-	-1.086
LEV	-	-0.227	-	-0.152
Ln(A)	-	0.068	-	0.118
Ln(Age)	-	-0.158	-	1.901 **
Adjusted R^2	0.34%	0.07%	1.40%	85.24%
Hausman test	0.562	0.262	0.497	15.748 **
	Random effects	Random effects	Random effects	Fixed effects

Analyzing firm performance though market value added measure, results show that CEO gender diversity contributes to decrease firm performance. Previous studies analyzing performance through value added measures did not find any association (Madaleno *et al.*, 2019). Concomitantly, our findings contradict the results of other studies who analyze performance using traditional measures (see e.g. Martín-Ugedo and Minguez-Vera, 2014, Bennouri *et al.*, 2018). In Portugal, firms who have female as CEO are not perceive by the market to have higher performance. Moreover, none of the other governance variables are relevant to explain market value added. In the correlation matrix, a positive effect of board size and independent members on MVA is founded, but in the multivariate analysis these effects disappear, suggesting that they are capture by other control variables. Finally, older firms exhibit higher market value-added since investors have more information about those firms.

ROBUSTNESS ANALYSIS

To validate previous results and to compare with the ones found by studies using traditional measures, the same model was estimated using Return on Assets (ROA), Return on Equity (ROE) and Tobin's Q as proxies of performance. Results are shown in the Table 4.

Table 4 results prove that using traditional measures of performance, executive women have no impact on performance, confirming the results found by Madaleno *et al.* (2019). Conclusions suggest that the presence of women as CEO or other executive positions do not impact firm profitability. Moreover, analyzing the correlation between traditional performance variables and the board of directors size a positive impact is suggested (results send upon request). When adding other control variables this association disappears.

Table 4. Additional regression results

	ROA	ROE	Tobin's Q
C	-2.183 ***	-4.818 ***	-0.518
CEOG	-0.021	-0.023	-0.077
EW	-0.012	-0.053	0.063
CEOD	0.008	-0.008	-0.092
BS	0.003	0.007	0.007
IND	-0.007	-0.022	-0.083
LEV	-0.122 ***	-0.348 ***	-0.416 **
Ln(A)	0.103 ***	0.227 ***	0.013
Ln(Age)	0.059	0.129	0.269 **
Adjusted R^2	43.94%	34.65%	1.09%
Hausman test	31.179 ***	25.733 ***	6.363
	Fixed Effects	Fixed Effects	Random effects

Less indebted and larger firms exhibit higher profitability, while less indebted and older firms present higher values of Tobin's Q. This conclusion proves that financial investors have higher expectations to older firms due to its experience and knowledge. These findings were also found by Vieira *et al.* (2019)

Finally, traditional measures of performance and MVA per share are positively and significantly correlated, while no relation is founded to EVA.

CONCLUSION

This chapter aims to analyze the impact of female executive on firm performance. Analyzing a sample of Portuguese non-financial listed firms over the period between 2010 and 2018, main results show that executive females do not add economic value to firms, and CEO gender diversity has a negative impact in market value added. Few firms on the sample have women as CEO, which can explain the negative impact on performance. Therefore, women presence on boards can cause divergence of opinion with men, which can weak corporate governance. Diverse firms add women to boards due to the pressure of gender equality, but women are still not recognized as an efficient member. Moreover, using traditional performance measures as ROA, ROE and Tobin's Q, results show that female presence has no impact on performance. Thus, conclusions show the relevance to analyze performance through another measures than profitability or market-based measures.

Findings are not only relevant to literature, since we extend previous findings, giving new insights that can be explored in future researches, but also to practice and to governance. Results show that gender diversity is still scarce in Portuguese firms suggesting that top positions are still assured by males. Moreover, women in top positions have not the same recognizing and opportunities than those given to men, showing the need to change this opinion. To governance, this study contributes to increase the debate about gender equality, since Portugal is far from others European countries, where women presence on board is higher. Finally, to practice since results show managers which determinants are more relevant to increase firm performance.

STUDY LIMITATIONS AND FUTURE RESEARCH DIRECTIONS

The proposed aims were accomplished. Although, as all studies, this investigation is not without limitations. First, we analyze a singular country. If for one side it allows us to explore into detail this sample and understand better this country, the number of observations is scarce and female presence on boards is still an exception which can cause inferences in results. Therefore, to future research we suggest expanding this study to other countries, especially European ones, where no studies analyzing the impact of female executives on firm value added exist, to corroborate results. Most of studies that focus on corporate governance and gender diversity on performance focus on traditional measures, such as ROA and Tobin's Q. Economic value measures, such as EVA and MVA are more accurate measures of financial performance since they show not only if the firm is generating earnings but also if these earnings are enough to cover the cost of financing the capital invested.

Moreover, the period analyzed (2010-2018) cover a recession period in Portugal. From 2010 till 2014 several austerity measures were imposed to companies and individuals to surpass the country economic deficit. In mean, the firm economic value is negative, which can be justified due to this crisis. Thus, the sample can be divided into two to understand if the period analyzed has some impacts in the findings.

Third, the impact of female was measured using two alternative variables: CEO gender diversity and percentage of executive female over total executives. Other measures can be used as the specific role of each directorship type or even if executive female is a family member of the firm or an independent member.

Additionally, the difference between family and non-family firms could be addressed or even difference between large and small-size firms. Finally, additional measures as industry control, macroeconomic variables could be used to increment the prediction value of the model.

ACKNOWLEDGMENT

This research was supported by National Funds of the FCT – Portuguese Foundation for Science and Technology within the project [UIDB/04928/2020].

REFERENCES

Adams, R. B., & Ferreira, D. (2009). Women in the boardroom and their impact on governance and performance. *Journal of Financial Economics*, *94*(2), 291–309. doi:10.1016/j.jfineco.2008.10.007

Adjaoud, F., Zeghal, D., & Andaleeb, S. (2007). The effect of board's quality on performance: A study of Canadian firms. *Corporate Governance*, *15*(4), 623–635. doi:10.1111/j.1467-8683.2007.00592.x

Al Mamun, A., Yasser, Q. R., Entebang, H., Nathan, T. M., & Rahman, M. A. (2013). Gender diversity and economic performance of firms: Evidences from emerging market. *Journal of Economic Development, Management, IT, Finance, and Marketing*, *5*(2), 100–110.

Athanassakos, G. (2007). Value-based management, EVA and stock price performance in Canada. *Management Decision*, *45*(9), 1397–1411. doi:10.1108/00251740710828663

Bayrakdaroglu, A., Ersoy, E., & Citak, L. (2012). Is There a Relationship Between Corporate Governance and Value-based Financial Performance Measures? A Study of Turkey as an Emerging Market. *Asia-Pacific Journal of Financial Studies*, *41*(2), 224–239. doi:10.1111/j.2041-6156.2012.01071.x

Bennouri, M., Chtioui, T., Nagati, H., & Nekhili, M. (2018). Female board directorship and firm performance: What really matters? *Journal of Banking & Finance*, *88*, 267–291. doi:10.1016/j.jbankfin.2017.12.010

Burke, R. J. (2000). Company Size, Board Size and the Numbers of Women Corporate Directors. In R. Burke & M. Mattis (Eds.), *Women on Corporate Boards of Directors: Women International Challenges and Opportunities* (pp. 157–167). Kluwer Academic Publishers. doi:10.1007/978-90-481-3401-4_11

Burke, R. J., & Mattis, M. C. (2000). Women on Corporate Boards of Directors: Where do We Go from Here? In R. Burke & M. Mattis (Eds.), *Women on Corporate Boards of Directors: Women International Challenges and Opportunities* (pp. 3–10). Kluwer Academic Publishers. doi:10.1007/978-90-481-3401-4_1

Carter, D. A., Simkins, B. J., & Simpson, W. G. (2003). Corporate Governance, Board Diversity and Firm Value. *Financial Review*, *38*(1), 33–35. doi:10.1111/1540-6288.00034

Choi, H. M., Sul, W., & Min, S. K. (2012). Foreign board membership and firm value in Korea. *Management Decision*, *50*(2), 207–233. doi:10.1108/00251741211203533

Coles, J. W., McWilliams, V. B., & Sen, N. (2001). An examination of the relationship of governance mechanisms to performance. *Journal of Management*, *27*(1), 23–50. doi:10.1177/014920630102700102

Conyon, M. J., & He, L. (2017). Firm performance and boardroom gender diversity: A quantile regression approach. *Journal of Business Research*, *79*, 198–211. doi:10.1016/j.jbusres.2017.02.006

Costa, L., Sampaio, J. D. O., & Flores, E. S. (2019). Diversidade de Gênero nos Conselhos Administrativos e sua Relação com Desempenho e Risco Financeiro nas Empresas Familiares. *Revista de Administração Contemporânea*, *23*(6), 721–738. doi:10.1590/1982-7849rac2019180327

DeFeo, R., Nikbakht, E., & Spieler, A. C. (2010). Corporate governance and the use of EVA compensation. *Corporate Ownership and Control*, *8*(1), 37–48. doi:10.22495/cocv8i1p3

Dezö, C. L., & Ross, D. G. (2012). Does female representation in top management improve firm performance? a panel data investigation. *Strategic Management Journal*, *33*(9), 1072–1089. doi:10.1002mj.1955

El Mir, A., & Seboui, S. (2008). Corporate governance and the relationship between EVA and created shareholder value. *Corporate Governance*, *8*(1), 46–58. doi:10.1108/14720700810853392

Erhardt, N. L., Werbel, J. D., & Shrader, C. B. (2003). Board of Director Diversity and Firm Financial Performance. *Corporate Governance*, *11*(2), 102–111. doi:10.1111/1467-8683.00011

European Commission. (2012). *Women on Boards: Commission proposes 40% objective*. Retrieved from: https://ec.europa.eu/commission/presscorner/detail/en/IP_12_1205

Félix, E. G. S., & David, D. S. T. (2019). Performance of family-owned firms: The impact of gender at the management level. *Journal of Family Business Management*, *9*(2), 228–250. doi:10.1108/JFBM-10-2018-0051

Hambrick, D. C. (2007). Upper echelons theory: An update. *Academy of Management Review*, *32*(2), 334–343. doi:10.5465/amr.2007.24345254

Hambrick, D. C., & Mason, P. A. (1984). Upper echelons: The organization as a reflection of its top managers. *Academy of Management Review*, *9*(2), 193–206. doi:10.5465/amr.1984.4277628

Ilaboya, J., & Ashafoke, T. (2017). Board Diversity and Firm Performance in Nigeria. *International Journal of Management, Accounting and Economics*, *4*(10).

Jensen, M. C., & Meckling, W. H. (1976). Theory of the firm: Managerial behavior, agency costs and ownership structure. *Journal of Financial Economics*, *3*(4), 305–360. doi:10.1016/0304-405X(76)90026-X

Joecks, J., Pull, K., & Vetter, K. (2013). Gender Diversity in the Boardroom and Firm Performance: What Exactly Constitutes a "Critical Mass?". *Journal of Business Ethics*, *118*(1), 61–72. doi:10.100710551-012-1553-6

Krismiaji, P. M., & Prabhata, A. (2019). Corporate Governance, Earnings Management, and Economic Value Added Indonesian Evidence. *KnE Social Sciences*, 182-199.

Lee, S., & Kim, W. G. (2009). EVA, refined EVA, MVA, or traditional performance measures for the hospitality industry? *International Journal of Hospitality Management*, *28*(3), 439–445. doi:10.1016/j.ijhm.2009.01.004

Liu, Y., Wei, Z., & Xie, F. (2014). Do women directors improve firm performance in China? *Journal of Corporate Finance*, *28*, 169–184. doi:10.1016/j.jcorpfin.2013.11.016

Madaleno, M., Vieira, E. S., & Teodósio, J. P. (2019). Corporate Female Leadership Effects Considering PSI20 and IBEX35 Companies' Performance. In Handbook of Research on Women in Management and the Global Labor Market (pp. 280-301). IGI Global. doi:10.4018/978-1-5225-9171-9.ch014

Martani, D., & Saputra, Y. E. (2009). The impact of corporate governance to the economic value added listed company in BEI 2003-2004. *China-USA Business Review*, *8*(3), 26–40.

Martín-Ugedo, J. F., & Minguez-Vera, A. (2014). Firm Performance and Women on the Board: Evidence from Spanish Small and Medium-Sized Enterprises. *Feminist Economics*, *20*(3), 136–162. doi:10.1080/13545701.2014.895404

Martín-Ugedo, J. F., Minguez-Vera, A., & Rossi, F. (2019). Female directors and firm performance in Italian and Spanish listed firms Does masculinity matter? *Academia (Caracas)*, *32*(3), 411–436. doi:10.1108/ARLA-06-2018-0124

Mirsharafoddini, H. S., Farhani, M. G., Hajiha, Z., Yahaghi, E., Honarvar, M. S., Khodaverdi, E., Behnood, V., & Tousi, E. F. (2014). Characteristics of Board of directors and creating Economic Value Added: Evidence from Iran. *International Journal of Current Research and Academic Review*, *2*(3), 149–162.

Narang, S., & Kaur, M. (2014). Impact of firm-specific attributes on shareholder value creation of Indian companies: An empirical analysis. *Global Business Review*, *15*(4), 847–866. doi:10.1177/0972150914543422

Pamburai, H., Chamisa, E., Abdulla, C., & Smith, C. (2015). An analysis of corporate governance and company performance: A South African perspective. *South African Journal of Accounting Research*, *29*(2), 115–131. doi:10.1080/10291954.2015.1006482

Perryman, A. A., Fernando, G. D., & Tripathy, A. (2016). Do gender differences persist? An examination of gender diversity on firm performance, risk, and executive compensation. *Journal of Business Research*, *69*(2), 579–586. doi:10.1016/j.jbusres.2015.05.013

Pham, P. K., Suchard, J. A., & Zein, J. (2011). Corporate governance and alternative performance measures: Evidence from Australian firms. *Australian Journal of Management*, *36*(3), 371–386. doi:10.1177/0312896211413035

Post, C., & Byron, C. (2015). Women on boards and firm financial performance: A meta-analysis. *Academy of Management Journal*, *58*(5), 1546–1571. doi:10.5465/amj.2013.0319

Provan, K. G. (1980). Board power and organizational effectiveness among human service agencies. *Academy of Management Journal*, *23*, 221–236. PMID:10247028

Rose, C. (2007). Does female board representation influence firm performance? The Danish evidence. *Corporate Governance*, *15*(2), 404–413. doi:10.1111/j.1467-8683.2007.00570.x

Schwab, A., Werbel, J. D., Hofmann, H., & Henriques, P. L. (2016). Managerial Gender Diversity and Firm Performance: *An Integration of Different Theoretical Perspectives. Group & Organization Management*, *41*(1), 5–31. doi:10.1177/1059601115588641

Shakina, E., Barajas, A., & Molodchik, M. (2017). Bridging the gap in competitiveness of Russian companies with intangible bricks. *Measuring Business Excellence*, *21*(1), 86–100. doi:10.1108/MBE-03-2016-0017

Singh, A. K., Singhania, S., & Sardana, V. (2019). Do Women on Boards affect Firm's Financial Performance? Evidence from Indian IPO Firms. *Australasian Accounting. Business and Finance Journal*, *13*(2), 53–68.

Strøm, R. Ø., D'Espallier, B., & Mersland, R. (2014). Female leadership, performance, and governance in microfinance institutions. *Journal of Banking & Finance*, *42*, 60–75. doi:10.1016/j.jbankfin.2014.01.014

Tan, Q. M., Zhang, N., & Ma, M. Z. (2011, September). Empirical investigation on EVA and accounting performance measures: Evidence from China stock market. In *2011 IEEE 18th International Conference on Industrial Engineering and Engineering Management* (pp. 2054-2057). IEEE.

Teodósio, J., & Lisboa, I. (2020). Board gender diversity and Capital Structure: the case of Portuguese listed firms. *International Conference on Management, Technology and Tourism: Social Value Creation*.

Terjesen, S., Couto, E. B., & Francisco, P. M. (2016). Does the presence of independent and female directors impact firm performance? A multi-country study of board diversity. *The Journal of Management and Governance, 20*(3), 447–483. doi:10.100710997-014-9307-8

Upadhyay, A. D., Bhargava, R., & Faircloth, S. D. (2014). Board structure and role of monitoring committees. *Journal of Business Research, 67*(7), 1486–1492. doi:10.1016/j.jbusres.2013.07.017

Vieira, E. S. (2018). Board of directors characteristics and performance in family firms and under the crisis. Corporate Governance. *The International Journal of Business in Society, 18*(1), 119–142.

Vieira, E. S., Neves, M. E., & Dias, A. G. (2019). Determinants of Portuguese firms' financial performance: Panel data evidence. *International Journal of Productivity and Performance Management, 68*(7), 1323–1342. Advance online publication. doi:10.1108/IJPPM-06-2018-0210

Yasser, Q. R., Al Mamun, A., & Rodrigs, M. (2017). Impact of board structure on firm performance: Evidence from an emerging economy. *Journal of Asia Business Studies, 11*(2), 210–228. doi:10.1108/JABS-06-2015-0067

Yasser, Q. R., Al Mamun, A., & Seamer, M. (2017). Do corporate boards affect firm performance? New evidence from an emerging economy. *International Journal of Productivity and Performance Management, 66*(6), 724–741. doi:10.1108/IJPPM-06-2015-0085

Zahra, S., & Pearce, J. II. (1989). Boards of Directors and Corporate Financial Performance: A Review and Integrative Model. *Journal of Management, 15*(2), 291–344. doi:10.1177/014920638901500208

Zahra, S. A., & Stanton, W. W. (1988). The implications of board of directors' composition for corporate strategy and value. *International Journal of Management, 5*, 229–236.

Zhang, J., & Aboud, A. (2019). Determinants of economic value added (EVA) in Chinese listed banks. *Asian Review of Accounting, 27*(4), 595–613. doi:10.1108/ARA-11-2018-0216

KEY TERMS AND DEFINITIONS

CEO Duality: When the CEO and the Chairperson are the same person.

Economic Value Measures: Financial performance measures, which show not only if the firm is generating earnings but also if the earnings are enough to cover the cost of financing the capital invested.

Executive Woman: Female director in executive positions.

Female CEO: The CEO is a woman.

Gender Diversity: Diversity of gender (female and male) on the board of directors.

Compilation of References

Abatino, B., & Dari-Mattiacci, G. (2020). Agency problems and organizational costs in slave-run businesses. *Roman Law and Economics: Institutions and Organizations, I*, 23. doi:10.1093/oso/9780198787204.003.0010

Abbott, L. J., Parker, S., & Peters, G. F. (2004). Audit committee characteristics and restatements'. *Auditing, 23*(1), 69–87. doi:10.2308/aud.2004.23.1.69

Abbott, L. J., Parker, S., & Peters, G. F. (2006). Earnings management, litigation risk, and asymmetric audit fee responses. *Auditing, 25*(1), 85–98. doi:10.2308/aud.2006.25.1.85

Abbott, L. J., Park, Y., & Parker, S. (2000). The effects of audit committee activity and independence on corporate fraud. *Managerial Finance, 26*(11), 55–68. doi:10.1108/03074350010766990

Abdelkarim, N., & Zuriqi, K. (2020). Corporate governance and earnings management: Evidence from listed firms at palestine Palestine exchange. *Asian Economic and Financial Review, 10*(2), 200–217. doi:10.18488/journal.aefr.2020.102.200.217

Abdullah, S. N. (1999). *The role of corporate governance and ownership structure on accounting earnings quality* (Unpublished PhD Dissertation). Universiti Utara Malaysia.

Abdullah, S. N. (2004). Board, composition, CEO duality and performance among Malaysian listed companies. *The international Journal of Business in Society, 4*, 47.

Abdullah, S. (2004, December 1). Board composition, CEO duality and performance among Malaysian listed companies. Corporate Governance. *International Journal (Toronto, Ont.)*, 47–59.

Abedi, G., Malekzadeh, R., Moosazadeh, M., Abedini, E., & Hasanpoor, E. (2019). Nurses' perspectives on the impact of marketing mix elements (7Ps) on patients' tendency to kind of hospital. *Ethiopian Journal of Health Sciences, 29*(2), 223–230. PMID:31011270

Abe, P. O., Ajayi-Owoeye, A. E., & Adegbie, F. F. (2020). IFRS Disclosures and Protection of Shareholders' Interests in Nigerian Quoted Firms. *European Journal of Business and Management Research, 5*(5). Advance online publication. doi:10.24018/ejbmr.2020.5.5.579

Abeyratna, G., & Power, D. (2002). The post-announcement performance of dividend-changing companies: The dividend-signalling hypothesis revisited. *Accounting and Finance, 42*(2), 131–151. doi:10.1111/1467-629X.00071

Abid, S. F., & Lodhi, S. (2015). Impact of changes in reserve requirement on banks profitability: A case of commercial banks in Pakistan. *European Journal of Business and Management, 7*(31), 1–6.

Abor, P. A. (2015). The effects of health governance and ownership structure on the performance of hospitals in Ghana. *Int J Law Manag., 5*(2), 107–140. doi:10.1108/IJLMA-04-2014-0031

Accountant, M. I. (2018). *International standard on Auditing Related Parties*. MIA, ISA.

Achleitner, A., Günther, N., Kaserer, C., & Siciliano, G. (2014). Real earnings management and accrual based earnings management in family firms. *European Accounting Review*, *23*(3), 431–461. doi:10.1080/09638180.2014.895620

Adams, R. B., & Mehran, H. (2005, August). Corporate performance, board structure and its determinants in the banking industry. *EFA 2005 Moscow Meetings*. 10.2139srn.302593

AdamsR. B. (2005) What Do Boards Do? Evidence From Board Committee and Director Compensation Data. Evidence From Board Committee and Director Compensation Data. https://ssrn.com/abstract=397401

Adams, R. B., & Ferreira, D. (2009). Women in the boardroom and their impact on governance and performance. *Journal of Financial Economics*, *94*(2), 291–309. doi:10.1016/j.jfineco.2008.10.007

Adiguzel, H. (2013). Corporate governance, family ownership and earnings management: Emerging market evidence. *Accounting and Finance Research*, *2*(4), 17–33. doi:10.5430/afr.v2n4p17

Adjaoud, F., Zeghal, D., & Andaleeb, S. (2007). The effect of board's quality on performance: A study of Canadian firms. *Corporate Governance*, *15*(4), 623–635. doi:10.1111/j.1467-8683.2007.00592.x

Adkins, L. C. (2011). *Using Stata For Principles Of Econometrics*. Wiley Global Education.

Adu-Amoah, A., Tsamenyi, M., & Onumah, J. M. (2008). The influence of social and political relations on corporate governance systems: The case of rural banks in Ghana. *Research in Accounting in Emerging Economies*, *8*(1), 311–334. doi:10.1016/S1479-3563(08)08011-0

Aganin, A., & Volpin, P. (2002). The history of corporate ownership in Italy. In R. A. Morck (Ed.), *A history of corporate governance around the World* (pp. 325–365). The University of Chicago Press.

Agarwal, R., Green, R., Agarwal, N., & Randhawa, K. (2016). Management practices in australian healthcare: Can NSW public hospitals do better? *Journal of Health Organization and Management*, *30*(3), 331–353. doi:10.1108/JHOM-01-2015-0016 PMID:27119390

AggarwalR.SchloetzerJ. D.WilliamsonR. (2014) Economic Consequences of Corporate Governance Mandates for Poorly Governed Firms, Available at SSRN 891411.

Agnes, W. Y., & Lo, R. M. (2010, April). Can corporate governance deter management from manipulating earnings? Evidence from related-party sales transactions in China. *Journal of Corporate Finance*, *16*(2), 225–235.

Agrawal, A., & Nasser, T. (2019). Blockholders on boards and CEO compensation, turnover and firm valuation. *Quarterly Journal of Finance, 9*(3). doi:10.1142/S2010139219500101

Agrawal, A., & Chadha, S. (2005). Corporate governance and accounting scandals. *The Journal of Law & Economics*, *48*(2), 371–406. doi:10.1086/430808

Aguilera, R. V., Judge, W. Q., & Terjesen, S. A. (2018). Corporate governance deviance. *Academy of Management Review*, *43*(1), 87–109. doi:10.5465/amr.2014.0394

Agustia, D., Muhammad, N. P. A., & Permatasari, Y. (2020). Earnings management, business strategy, and bankruptcy risk: Evidence from Indonesia. *Heliyon*, *6*(2), e03317. doi:10.1016/j.heliyon.2020.e03317 PMID:32055735

Ahmad, S., & Omar, R. (2016). Basic corporate governance models: A systematic review. *International Journal of Law and Management*, *58*(1), 73–107. doi:10.1108/IJLMA-10-2014-0057

Ahmed Seleim, N. B. (2009). The relationship between. *Journal of Intellectual Capital*, *10*, 168.

Ahmed, A. S., Billings, B. K., Morton, R. M., & Stanford-Harris, M. (2002). The role of accounting conservatism in mitigating bondholder-shareholder conflicts over dividend policy and in reducing debt costs. *The Accounting Review, 77*(4), 867–890. doi:10.2308/accr.2002.77.4.867

Ahmed, A. S., & Duellman, S. (2007). Accounting conservatism and board of director characteristics: An empirical analysis. *Journal of Accounting and Economics, 43*(2-3), 411–437. doi:10.1016/j.jacceco.2007.01.005

Ahmed, K., & Henry, D. (2012). Accounting conservatism and voluntary corporate governance mechanisms by Australian firms. *Accounting and Finance, 52*(3), 631–662. doi:10.1111/j.1467-629X.2011.00410.x

Ahmed, K., Hossain, M., & Adams, M. B. (2006). The effects of board composition and board size on the informativeness of annual accounting earnings. *Corporate Governance, 14*(5), 418–431. doi:10.1111/j.1467-8683.2006.00515.x

Ahn, S., Denis, D. J., & Denis, D. K. (2006). Leverage and investment in diversified firms. *Journal of Financial Economics, 79*(2), 317–337. doi:10.1016/j.jfineco.2005.03.002

Ahn, S., & Walker, M. (2007). Corporate governance and the spinoff decision. *Journal of Corporate Finance, 13*(1), 76–93. doi:10.1016/j.jcorpfin.2006.03.001

Aiello, F., Pupo, V., & Ricotta, F. (2015). Firm Heterogeneity in TFP, sectoral innovation and location. Evidence from Italy. *International Review of Applied Economics, 29*(5), 579–607. doi:10.1080/02692171.2015.1016408

Ajina, A., & Habib, A. (2017). Examining the relationship between earning management and market liquidity. *Research in International Business and Finance, 42*, 1164–1172. doi:10.1016/j.ribaf.2017.07.054

Akintoye, A., & Chinyio, E. (2005). Private finance initiative in the healthcare sector: Trend and risk assessment. *Engineering, Construction, and Architectural Management, 12*(6), 601–616. doi:10.1108/09699980510634155

Al Mamun, A., Yasser, Q. R., Entebang, H., Nathan, T. M., & Rahman, M. A. (2013). Gender diversity and economic performance of firms: Evidences from emerging market. *Journal of Economic Development, Management, IT, Finance, and Marketing, 5*(2), 100–110.

Al-Absy, M. S. M., Ismail, K. N. I. K., & Chandren, S. (2019). Corporate governance mechanisms, whistle-blowing policy and real earnings management. *International Journal of Financial Research, 10*(6), 265–282. doi:10.5430/ijfr.v10n6p265

Al-Absy, M. S. M., Ku Ismail, K. N. I., & Chandren, S. (2019). Audit committee chairman characteristics and earnings management: The influence of family chairman. *Asia-Pacific Journal of Business Administration, 11*(4), 339–370. doi:10.1108/APJBA-10-2018-0188

Alam, N., Ramachandran, J., & Nahomy, A. H. (2020). The impact of corporate governance and agency effect on earnings management – A test of the dual banking system. *Research in International Business and Finance, 54*, 101242. Advance online publication. doi:10.1016/j.ribaf.2020.101242

Alawattage, C., & Wickramasinghe, D. (2008). Appearance of accounting in a political hegemony. *Critical Perspectives on Accounting, 19*(3), 293–339. doi:10.1016/j.cpa.2006.08.006

Albaity, M. (2012). Behavioural Finance and Malaysian Culture. *International Business Research, 5*(11), 65–74.

Al-Bassam, W. M., Ntim, C. G., Opong, K. K., & Downs, Y. (2018). Corporate boards and ownership structure as antecedents of corporate governance disclosure in Saudi Arabian publicly listed corporations. *Business & Society, 57*(2), 335–377. doi:10.1177/0007650315610611

Aldamen, H., Duncan, K., Kelly, S., & McNamara, R. (2020). Corporate governance and family firm performance during the global financial crisis. *Accounting and Finance, 60*(2), 1673–1701. doi:10.1111/acfi.12508

Aldamen, H., Duncan, K., Kelly, S., McNamara, R., & Nagel, S. (2012). Audit committee characteristics and firm performance during the global financial crisis. *Accounting and Finance*, *52*(4), 971–1000. doi:10.1111/j.1467-629X.2011.00447.x

Alexander, J. A., Morrisey, M. A., & Shortell, S. M. (1986). Effects of competition, regulation and corporatization on hospital-medical relations. *Journal of Health and Social Behavior*, *27*(3), 220–235. doi:10.2307/2136743 PMID:3772060

Alfaro, L., Bloom, N., Conconi, P., Fadinger, H., Legros, P., & Newman, A. (2018). *Come Together: Firm Boundaries and Delegation*. HBS Working Paper, 18-051.

Al-Gamrh, B., Izah, K. N., Ismail, K., & Al-Dhamari, R. (2018). The role of corporate governance strength in crisis and non-crisis times. *Applied Economics*, *50*(58), 6263–6284. doi:10.1080/00036846.2018.1489513

Al-Haddad, L., & Whittington, M. (2019). The impact of corporate governance mechanisms on real and accrual earnings management practices: Evidence from jordan. *Corporate Governance*, *19*(6), 1167–1186. doi:10.1108/CG-05-2018-0183

Ali, A., Chen, T. Y., & Radhakrishnan, S. (2007). Corporate disclosures by family firms. *Journal of Accounting and Economics*, *44*(1-2), 238–286. doi:10.1016/j.jacceco.2007.01.006

Ali, M. S., & Hashmi, S. H. (2018). Impact of institutional ownership on stock liquidity: Evidence from Karachi Stock Exchange, Pakistan. *Global Business Review*, *19*(4), 939–951. doi:10.1177/0972150918772927

Al-Jaifi, H. A. (2017). Ownership Concentration, Earnings Management and Stock Market Liquidity: Evidence from Malaysia. *Corporate Governance: The International Journal of Business in Society*, *17*(3), 490–510. doi:10.1108/CG-06-2016-0139

Allen & Overy. (2010). *Corporate governance in Central and Eastern Europe*. Available at: www.allenovery.com

Allen, P. (2000). Accountability for clinical governance: Developing collective responsibility for quality in primary care. *BMJ (Clinical Research Ed.)*, *321*(7261), 608–611. doi:10.1136/bmj.321.7261.608 PMID:10977839

Al-Matari, Y. A., Al-Swidi, A. K., & Bt Fadzil, F. H. (2012). Audit committee effectiveness and performance of Saudi Arabia listed companies. *Wulfenia Journal*, *19*(8), 169–188.

Almeida, M. H. T. (2001). Federalism, democracy and government in Brazil: Ideas, hypotheses and evidence. *Brazilian Journal of Bibliographic Information in Social Sciences. BBI*, *51*, 13–34.

Alm, M., & Winberg, J. (2016). *How Does Gender Diversity on Corporate Boards Affect the Firm Financial Performance?: An Empirical Investigation of Swedish OMX- listed Firms*. University of Gothenburg.

Al-Najjar, B., & Clark, E. (2017). Corporate governance and cash holdings in MENA: Evidence from internal and external governance practices. *Research in International Business and Finance*, *39*, 1–12. doi:10.1016/j.ribaf.2016.07.030

Alnori, F. (2020). Cash holdings: Do they boost or hurt firms' performance? Evidence from listed non-financial firms in Saudi Arabia. *International Journal of Islamic and Middle Eastern Finance and Management*, *13*(5), 919–934. doi:10.1108/IMEFM-08-2019-0338

Al-Okaily, J., BenYoussef, N., & Chahine, S. (2020). Economic bonding, corporate governance and earnings management: Evidence from UK publicly traded family firms. *International Journal of Auditing*, *24*(2), 185–204. doi:10.1111/ijau.12186

Aluchna, M. (2016). Applying corporate governance in Europe. In G. Aras (Ed.), *Global Perspectives on Corporate Governance and CSR* (pp. 47–71). Routledge.

Alves, C., & Mendes, V. (2004). Corporate Governance Policy and Company Performance: The Portuguese case. *Corporate Governance*, *12*(3), 290–301. doi:10.1111/j.1467-8683.2004.00370.x

Alves, C., & Vicente, E. F. R. (2013). Does the Latin model of corporate governance perform worse than other models in preventing earnings management? *Applied Financial Economics*, *23*(21), 1663–1673. doi:10.1080/09603107.2013.844322

Alves, P., Couto, E. B., & Francisco, P. M. (2016). Executive pay and performance in Portuguese listed companies. *Research in International Business and Finance*, *37*, 184–195. doi:10.1016/j.ribaf.2015.11.006

Alves, S. (2011). The association between executive stock options and corporate performance: Evidence from Portugal. *International Journal of Business Governance and Ethics*, *6*(2), 203–223. doi:10.1504/IJBGE.2011.039969

Alves, S. (2011a). The effect of the board structure on earnings management: Evidence from Portugal. *Journal of Financial Reporting and Accounting*, *9*(2), 141–160. doi:10.1108/19852511111173103

Alves, S. (2012). Executive stock options and earnings management in the portuguese listed companies. *Revista de Contabilidad*, *15*(2), 211–235. doi:10.1016/S1138-4891(12)70043-2

Alves, S. (2012). Ownership structure and earnings management: Evidence from Portugal. *Australasian Accounting. Business and Finance Journal*, *6*(1), 57–74.

Alves, S. (2014). The Effect of Board Independence on the Earnings Quality: Evidence from Portuguese Listed Companies. *Australasian Accounting. Business and Finance Journal*, *8*(3), 23–44.

Alves, S., Martins, J., & Ferreira, C. (2009). Determinants of executive stock options: Portuguese evidence. *Corporate Ownership & Control*, *7*(2), 260–268. doi:10.22495/cocv7i2c2p2

Alves, S., & Pinho, C. (2012). Executive stock options: A panel data analysis of determinants in Portugal. *International Journal of Economics and Accounting*, *3*(2), 148–164. doi:10.1504/IJEA.2012.048048

Alzoubi, E. S. S. (2016). Audit quality and earnings management: Evidence from Jordan. *Journal of Applied Accounting Research*, *17*(2), 170–189. doi:10.1108/JAAR-09-2014-0089

Alzoubi, E. S. S. (2018). Audit quality, debt financing, and earnings management: Evidence from jordan. *Journal of International Accounting, Auditing & Taxation*, *30*, 69–84. doi:10.1016/j.intaccaudtax.2017.12.001

Amihud, Y. (2002). Illiquidity and stock returns: Cross-section and time-series effects. *Journal of Financial Markets*, *5*(1), 31–56. doi:10.1016/S1386-4181(01)00024-6

Ammann, M., Oesch, D., & Schmid, M. M. (2013). Product market competition, corporate governance, and firm value: Evidence from the EU area. *European Financial Management*, *19*(3), 452–469. doi:10.1111/j.1468-036X.2010.00605.x

Anderson, R. C., Mansi, S. A., & Reeb, D. M. (2003). Founding family ownership and the agency cost of debt. *Journal of Financial Economics*, *68*(2), 263–285. doi:10.1016/S0304-405X(03)00067-9

Anderson, R. C., & Reeb, D. M. (2003). Founding-family ownership and firm performance: Evidence from the S&P 500. *The Journal of Finance*, *58*(3), 1301–1327. doi:10.1111/1540-6261.00567

Andreou, P. C., Louca, C., & Panayides, P. M. (2014). Corporate governance, financial management decisions and firm performance: Evidence from the maritime industry. *Transportation Research Part E, Logistics and Transportation Review*, *63*, 59–78. doi:10.1016/j.tre.2014.01.005

Andries, A. M., Balutel, D., Ihnatov, I., & Ursu, S. G. (2020). The nexus between corporate governance, risk taking, and growth. *PLoS One*, *15*(2), 1–24. doi:10.1371/journal.pone.0228371 PMID:32017781

Angaye, P. E. G., & Gwilliam, D. (2008). Corporate governance in infancy and growth– an interview-based study of the development of governance and corporate regulation in Nigeria. *Research in Accounting in Emerging Economies*, *8*, 359–407.

Ansari, I. F., Goergen, M., & Mira, S. (2014). The determinants of the CEO successor choice in family firms. *Journal of Corporate Finance*, *28*, 6–25. doi:10.1016/j.jcorpfin.2013.12.006

An, Z., Li, D., & Yu, J. (2016). Earnings management, capital structure, and the role of institutional environments. *Journal of Banking & Finance*, *68*, 131–152. doi:10.1016/j.jbankfin.2016.02.007

Aouadi, A., & Marsat, S. (2018). Do ESG Controversies Matter for Firm Value? Evidence from International Data. *Journal of Business Ethics, Springer*, *151*(4), 1027–1047. doi:10.100710551-016-3213-8

Aouni, B., Martel, J. M., & Hassaine, A. (2009). Fuzzy goal programming model: An overview of the current state-of-the art. *Journal of Multi-Criteria Decision Analysis*, *16*(5-6), 149–161. doi:10.1002/mcda.448

Arioglu, E. (2020b). *Upper Echelons Theory, Conservative Chairmen and Informative Earnings Management*. Available at: https://www.researchgate.net/profile/Emrah_Arioglu/publication/343657293_Upper_Echelons_Theory_Conservative_Chairmen_and_Informative_Earnings_Management/links/5f39367192851cd302faa29f/Upper-Echelons-Theory-Conservative-Chairmen-and-Informative-Earnings-Management.pdf

Arioglu, E. (2020a). The affiliations and characteristics of female directors and earnings management: Evidence from Turkey. *Managerial Auditing Journal*, *35*(7), 927–953. doi:10.1108/MAJ-07-2019-2364

Arouri, H., Hossain, M., & Muttakin, M. B. (2014). Effects of board and ownership structure on corporate performance: Evidence from GCC countries. *Journal of Accounting in Emerging Economies*, *4*(19), 117-130.

Arraiano, I., & Hategan, C. (2019). The Stage of Corporate Social Responsibility in EU- CEE Countries. *European Journal of Sustainable Development*, *8*(3), 340–353. doi:10.14207/ejsd.2019.v8n3p340

Arthur, N., Tang, Q., & Lin, Z. (2015). Corporate accruals quality during the 2008–2010 Global Financial Crisis. *Journal of International Accounting, Auditing & Taxation*, *25*, 1–15. doi:10.1016/j.intaccaudtax.2015.10.004

Arya, A., Glover, J. C., & Sunder, S. (2003). Are unmanaged earnings always better for shareholders? *Accounting Horizons*, *17*(s-1), 111–116. doi:10.2308/acch.2003.17.s-1.111

Ascioglu, A., Hegde, S. P., Krishnan, G. V., & McDermott, J. B. (2012). Earnings management and market liquidity. *Review of Quantitative Finance and Accounting*, *38*(2), 257–274. doi:10.100711156-010-0225-9

Astami, E. W., Rusmin, R., Hartadi, B., & Evans, J. (2017). The role of audit quality and culture influence on earnings management in companies with excessive free cash flow – Evidence from the Asia-Pacific region. *International Journal of Accounting and Information Management*, *25*(1), 21–42. doi:10.1108/IJAIM-05-2016-0059

Athanassakos, G. (2007). Value-based management, EVA and stock price performance in Canada. *Management Decision*, *45*(9), 1397–1411. doi:10.1108/00251740710828663

Atkins, B. (2006). Corporate social responsibility: Is it "irresponsibility"? *Corporate Governance Advisor*, *14*, 28–29.

Atkinson, J. M. J. H. (1984). Structures of social action. Cambridge University Press.

Attig, N., Chen, R., El Ghoul, S., Guedhami, O., Kwok, C., & Pittman, J. (2020). Are insiders equal? evidence from earnings management in closely held east asian firms. *Research in International Business and Finance*, *54*, 101243. Advance online publication. doi:10.1016/j.ribaf.2020.101243

Ayedh, A. M., Fatima, A. H., & Mohammad, M. H. S. (2019). Earnings Management in Malaysian Companies during the Global Financial Crisis and the Coincidental Effect of IFRS Adoption. *Australasian Accounting, Business, and Finance Journal*, *13*(1), 4-26. doi:10.14453/aabfj.v13i1.2

Aygun, M., Ic, S., & Sayim, M. (2014). The Effects of corporate ownership structure and board size on earnings management: Evidence from Turkey. *International Journal of Business and Management*, *9*(12), 123–132. doi:10.5539/ijbm.v9n12p123

Ayu, C., & Zulfia, K. (2018). The Effect of Good Corporate Governance and Earnings Management to Corporate Social Responsibility Disclosure. *Academy of Accounting and Financial Studies Journal*, *22*(1), 45–61.

Bahramara, S., Sheikhahmadi, P., Damavandi, M. Y., Shafie-Khah, M., Osório, G. J., & Catalão, J. P. (2018, June). Strategic Behavior of a Distribution Company in the Wholesale Energy Market: A Risk-Based Stochastic Bi-Level Model. In *2018 IEEE International Conference on Environment and Electrical Engineering and 2018 IEEE Industrial and Commercial Power Systems Europe (EEEIC/I&CPS Europe)* (pp. 1-6). IEEE. 10.1109/EEEIC.2018.8493872

Bainbridge, S. (2006). Director Primacy and Shareholder Disempowerment. *Harvard Law Review*, *119*(6), 1735–1758.

Baker, T. A., Lopez, T. J., Reitenga, A. L., & Ruch, G. W. (2019). The influence of CEO and CFO power on accruals and real earnings management. *Review of Quantitative Finance and Accounting*, *52*(1), 325–345. doi:10.100711156-018-0711-z

Balatbat, M. C., Taylor, S. L., & Walter, T. S. (2004). Corporate governance, insider ownership and operating performance of Australian initial public offerings. *Accounting and Finance*, *44*(3), 299–328. doi:10.1111/j.1467-629x.2004.00114.x

Ball, R., Kothari, S., & Robin, A. (2000). The effect of international institutional factors on properties of accounting earnings. *Journal of Accounting and Economics*, *29*(1), 1–51. doi:10.1016/S0165-4101(00)00012-4

Ball, R., Robin, A., & Wu, J. (2003). Incentives versus standards: Properties of accounting income in four East Asian countries. *Journal of Accounting and Economics*, *36*(1-3), 235–270. doi:10.1016/j.jacceco.2003.10.003

Ball, R., & Shivakumar, L. (2005). Earnings quality in UK private firms: Comparative loss recognition timeless. *Journal of Accounting and Economics*, *39*(1), 83–128. doi:10.1016/j.jacceco.2004.04.001

Ball, R., & Shivakumar, L. (2006). The role of accruals in asymmetrically timely gain and loss recognition. *Journal of Accounting Research*, *44*(2), 207–242. doi:10.1111/j.1475-679X.2006.00198.x

Baltagi, B. H. (2009). *A Companion to Econometric Analysis of Panel Data*. John Wiley and Sons.

Banderlipe, M. R. S. (2009). The impact of selected corporate governance variables in mitigating earnings management in the Philippines. *DLSU Business & Economics Review*, *19*(1), 17–27. doi:10.3860/ber.v19i1.1110

Bange, M. M., & De Bondt, W. F. (1998). R&D budgets and corporate earnings targets. *Journal of Corporate Finance*, *4*(2), 153–184. doi:10.1016/S0929-1199(98)00006-6

Banko, J., Frye, M., Wang, W., & Whyte, A. (2013). Earnings Management and Annual General Meetings: The Role of Managerial Entrenchment. *Financial Review*, *48*(2), 259–282. doi:10.1111/fire.12003

Bankston White, C., & Birmingham, J. (2015). Case management directors: How to manage in a transition-focused world: Part 2. *Professional Case Management*, *20*(3), 115–127. PMID:25700135

Bansal, N., & Sharma, A. K. (2016). Audit committee, corporate governance and firm performance: Empirical evidence from India. *International Journal of Economics and Finance*, *8*(3), 103. doi:10.5539/ijef.v8n3p103

Bansal, P. (2005). Evolving sustainably: A longitudinal study of corporate sustainable development. *Strategic Management Journal*, *26*(3), 197–218. doi:10.1002mj.441

Barber, N., Ghiselli, R., & Deale, C. (2007). Assessing the relationship of CEO compensation and company financial performance in the restaurant segment of the hospitality industry. *Journal of Foodservice Business Research*, *9*(4), 65–82. doi:10.1300/J369v09n04_05

Barbosa, A. P. (2003). *Corporate Governance in Non-Profit Hospitals: A study of the corporate leadership profile in eleven Brazilian hospitals* (Doctoral Thesis). EAESP/FGV. Retrieved from http://bibliotecadigital.fgv.br/dspace;/handle/10438/2578

Bard, J. F. (1984). Optimality conditions for the bilevel programming problem. *Naval Research Logistics Quarterly, 31*(1), 13–26. doi:10.1002/nav.3800310104

Bard, J. F. (1991). Some properties of the bilevel programming problem. *Journal of Optimization Theory and Applications, 68*(2), 371–378. doi:10.1007/BF00941574

Barney, J. B. (1990). The Debate Between Traditional Management Theory and Organizational Economics: Substantive Differences or Intergroup Conflict? *Academy of Management Review, 15*(3), 382–393. doi:10.5465/amr.1990.4308815

Barontini, R., & Caprio, L. (2006). The effect of family control on firm value and performance: Evidence from Continental Europe. *European Financial Management, 12*(5), 689–723. doi:10.1111/j.1468-036X.2006.00273.x

Barros, C. P., & Nunes, F. (2007). Governance and CEO pay and performance in non-profit organizations. *International Journal of Social Economics, 34*(11), 811–827. doi:10.1108/03068290710826404

Bar-Yosef, S., & Prencipe, A. (2013). The Impact of Corporate Governance and Earnings Management on Stock Market Liquidity in a Highly Concentrated Ownership Capital Market. *Journal of Accounting, Auditing & Finance, 28*(3), 292–316. doi:10.1177/0148558X13492591

Basu, S. (1997). The conservatism principle and the asymmetric timeliness of earnings. *Journal of Accounting and Economics, 24*(1), 3–37. doi:10.1016/S0165-4101(97)00014-1

Bates, T. W., Kahle, K. M., & Stulz, R. M. (2009). Why do US firms hold so much more cash than they used to? *The Journal of Finance, 64*(5), 1985–2021. doi:10.1111/j.1540-6261.2009.01492.x

Bauer, R., Eichholtz, P., & Kok, N. (2009). Corporate governance and performance: The Reit Effect. *Financial Management, 38*(1), 1–29.

Bauguess, S., Moeller, S., Schlingemann, F., & Zutter, C. (2009). Ownership structure and target returns. *Journal of Corporate Finance, 15*(1), 48–65. doi:10.1016/j.jcorpfin.2008.09.002

Bayrakdaroglu, A., Ersoy, E., & Citak, L. (2012). Is There a Relationship Between Corporate Governance and Value-based Financial Performance Measures? A Study of Turkey as an Emerging Market. *Asia-Pacific Journal of Financial Studies, 41*(2), 224–239. doi:10.1111/j.2041-6156.2012.01071.x

Baysinger, B. D., & Butler, H. N. (1985). Corporate governance and the board of directors: Performance effects of changes in board composition. *Journal of Law Economics and Organization, 1*(1), 101–124.

Beasley, M. (1996). An empirical analysis of the relation between the board of director composition and financial statement fraud. *The Accounting Review, 71*(4), 443–464.

Beasley, M. S., & Salterio, S. E. (2001). The relationship between board characteristics and voluntary improvements in audit committee composition and experience. *Contemporary Accounting Research, 18*(4), 539–570. doi:10.1506/RM1J-A0YM-3VMV-TAMV

Beasley, M., Carcello, J., Hermanson, D., & Neal, T. (2009). The audit committee oversight process. *Contemporary Accounting Research, 1*(1), 65–122. doi:10.1506/car.26.1.3

Beaver, W. H., & Ryan, S. G. (2000). Biases and lags in book value and their effects on the ability of the book-to-market ratio to predict book return on equity. *Journal of Accounting Research, 38*(1), 127–148. doi:10.2307/2672925

Becht, M., Jenkinson, T., & Mayer, C. (2005). Corporate governance: An assessment. *Oxford Review of Economic Policy, 21*(2), 155–163. doi:10.1093/oxrep/gri009

Becker, C. L., DeFond, M. L., Jiambalvo, J., & Subramanyam, K. R. (1998). The Effect of Audit Quality on Earnings Management. *Contemporary Accounting Research, 15*(1), 1–24. doi:10.1111/j.1911-3846.1998.tb00547.x

Becker, S., & Koch, E. (2006). Hospitals and health systems: The best of times and the worst of times. *Journal of Health Care Finance, 32*(3), 1–7. PMID:18975727

Bedard, J. C., & Johnstone, K. M. (2004). Earnings manipulation risk, corporate governance risk, and auditors' planning and pricing decisions. *The Accounting Review, 79*(2), 277–304. doi:10.2308/accr.2004.79.2.277

Beekes, W., Pope, P., & Young, S. (2004). The link between earnings timeliness, earnings conservatism and board composition: Evidence from the UK. *Corporate Governance, 12*(1), 47–59. doi:10.1111/j.1467-8683.2004.00342.x

Begley, D. B. (1987). Psychological characteristics associated with performence in entrepreneurial firms and smaller businesses. *Journal of Business Venturing, 2*(1), 79–93.

Bekiris, F.V. (2013). Ownership structure and board structure: are corporate governance mechanisms interrelated? *Corporate Governance, 13*(4), 352-364. doi:10.1108/CG-02-2011-0013

Belcredi, M., & Enriques, L. (2014). *Institutional investor activism in a context of concentrated ownership and high private benefits of control: The case of Italy.* ECGI, law working paper, No. 225.

Belcredi, M., Bozzi, S., & Di Noia, C. (2013). Board elections and shareholders activism: The Italian experiment. In M. Belcredi & G. Ferrarini (Eds.), *Boards and shareholders in European listed companies*. Cambridge University Press. doi:10.1017/CBO9781139629126.008

Bellman, R. E., & Zadeh, L. A. (1970). Decision-making in a fuzzy environment. *Management Science, 17*(4), B-141–B-164. doi:10.1287/mnsc.17.4.B141

Ben Amar, A., & Chakroun, S. (2018). Do dimensions of corporate social responsibility affect earnings management?: Evidence from france. *Journal of Financial Reporting and Accounting, 16*(2), 348–370. doi:10.1108/JFRA-05-2017-0033

Benjamin, S. J., & Ehtiatkar Rahemi, K. (2013). A test of audit committee characteristics and free cash flows. *Corporate Ownership and Control, 10*(2), 611–626. doi:10.22495/cocv10i2c3art4

Benkraiem, R. (2008). The influence of institutional investors on opportunistic earnings management. *International Journal of Accounting. Auditing and Performance Evaluation, 5*(1), 89–106. doi:10.1504/IJAAPE.2008.020195

Ben-Nasr, H., Boubaker, S., & Rouatbi, W. (2015). Ownership structure, control contestability, and corporate debt maturity. *Journal of Corporate Finance, 35*, 265–285. doi:10.1016/j.jcorpfin.2015.10.001

Bennouri, M., Chtioui, T., Nagati, H., & Nekhili, M. (2018). Female board directorship and firm performance: What really matters? *Journal of Banking & Finance, 88*, 267–291. doi:10.1016/j.jbankfin.2017.12.010

Benyasrisawat, P. (2019). Firm attributes, earnings management, and anti-corruption activities in thai-listed firms. *Afro-Asian Journal of Finance and Accounting, 9*(4), 439–458. doi:10.1504/AAJFA.2019.102982

Berger, P. G., Ofek, E., & Yermack, D. L. (1997). Managerial entrenchment and capital structure decisions. *The Journal of Finance, 52*(4), 1411–1438. doi:10.1111/j.1540-6261.1997.tb01115.x

Berglof, E., & Pajuste, A. (2003). *Emerging Owners, Eclipsing Markets? Corporate Governance in Central and Eastern Europe. Corporate Governance and Capital Flows in a Global Economy.* Oxford University Press.

Bergstressera, D., & Phililippon, T. (2006). CEO incentives and earnings management. *Journal of Financial Economics, 80*(3), 511–529. doi:10.1016/j.jfineco.2004.10.011

Berkman, H., Cole, R., & Fu, L. (2009). Expropriation through loan guarantees to related parties: Evidence from China. *Journal of Banking & Finance, 33*(1), 141–156. doi:10.1016/j.jbankfin.2007.11.001

Bernard, A. B., Jensen, J. B., Redding, S. J., & Schott, P. K. (2012). The empirics of firm heterogeneity and international trade. *Annual Review of Economics, 4*(1), 283–313. doi:10.1146/annurev-economics-080511-110928

Berniz, U. (2010). What is Scandinavian Law? Concept, Characteristics, Future. *Stockholm Institute for Scandianvian Law, 1957*, 13–29.

Betz, M., O'Connell, L., & Shepard, J. M. (1989). Gender differences in proclivity for unethical behavior. *Journal of Business Ethics, 8*(5), 321–324. doi:10.1007/BF00381722

Beuselinck, C., Blanco, B., & Lara, J. M. G. (2017). The Role of Foreign Shareholders in Disciplining Financial Reporting. *Journal of Business Finance & Accounting, 44*(5&6), 558–592. doi:10.1111/jbfa.12239

Beuselinck, C., Cascino, S., Deloof, M., & Vanstraelen, A. (2019). Earnings Management within Multinational Corporations. *The Accounting Review, 94*(4), 45–76. doi:10.2308/accr-52274

Bhagat, S., & Brian, B. (2019). Corporate governance and firm performance: The sequel. *Journal of Corporate Finance, 58*, 142–168. doi:10.1016/j.jcorpfin.2019.04.006

Bharath, S., Sunder, J., & Sunder, S. (2008). Accounting quality and debt contracting. *The Accounting Review, 83*(1), 1–28. doi:10.2308/accr.2008.83.1.1

Bhattacharya, N., Ecker, F., Olsson, P. M., & Schipper, K. (2012). Direct and mediated associations among earnings quality, information asymmetry, and the cost of equity. *The Accounting Review, 87*(2), 449–482. doi:10.2308/accr-10200

Bhundia, A. (2012). A comparative study between free cash flows and earnings management. *Business Intelligence Journal, 5*(1), 123–129.

Bialas, W. F., & Karwan, M. H. (1984). Two-level linear programming. *Management Science, 30*(8), 1004–1020. doi:10.1287/mnsc.30.8.1004

Bianchi, M., & Bianco, M. (2006). *Italian corporate governance in the last 15 years: From pyramids to coalitions?* ECGI, finance working paper, No. 144.

Bianchi, M., Ciavarella, A., Novembre, V., & Signoretti, R. (2011). Comply or explain: Investor protection through the italian corporate governance code. *Journal of Applied Corporate Finance, 23*(1), 107–121. doi:10.1111/j.1745-6622.2011.00319.x

Bigelli, M., & Sánchez-Vidal, J. (2012). Cash holdings in private firms. *Journal of Banking & Finance, 36*(1), 26–35. doi:10.1016/j.jbankfin.2011.06.004

Bloom, N., Van Reenen, J., Propper, C., & Seiler, S. (2009). *Management practices in hospitals.* Health, Econometrics and Data Group (HEDG) Working Papers 09/23, HEDG, c/o Department of Economics, University of York.

Bloom, N., Sadun, R., & Van Reenen, J. (2012). The Organization of Firms Across Countries. *The Quarterly Journal of Economics, 127*(4), 1663–1705. doi:10.1093/qje/qje029

Board, M. A. (2020). *FRF MASB*. Retrieved from Financial Reporting Standards: http://www.masb.org.my/pages.php?id=91

Bolton, P., & Scharfstein, D. S. (1990). A theory of predation based on agency problems in financial contracting. *The American Economic Review*, 93–106.

Bontis, C. B. (2009, January 16). The relationship between culture and corruption: A cross-national study. *Journal of Intellectual Capital, 10*(1).

Boone, A. L., Field, L. C., Karpoff, J. M., & Raheja, C. G. (2007). The determinants of corporate board size and composition: An empirical analysis. *Journal of Financial Economics, 85*(1), 66–101. doi:10.1016/j.jfineco.2006.05.004

Borah, N., James, H. L., & Park, J. C. (2020). Does CEO inside debt compensation benefit both shareholders and debtholders? *Review of Quantitative Finance and Accounting, 54*(1), 159–203. doi:10.100711156-018-00786-0

Borokhovich, K. A., Bricker, R. J., & Simkins, B. J. (2000). An analysis of finance journal impact factors. *The Journal of Finance, 55*(3), 1457–1469. doi:10.1111/0022-1082.00254

Borralho, J., Gallardo, D., Hernández-Linares, R., & Paiva, I. (2019). Earnings Management and Corporate Social Responsibility. Family and non-family firms. *Workshop 1 al qual opta participar: "Agenda 2030 para el desarrollo sostenible: colaboración público-privada"*, 1-22.

Bose, S., Khan, H. Z., Rashid, A., & Islam, S. (2018). What drives green banking disclosure? An institutional and corporate governance perspective. *Asia Pacific Journal of Management, 35*(2), 501–527. doi:10.100710490-017-9528-x

Braiotta, L. Jr. (2000). Advice on Audit Committees. *Internal Auditor, 57*(1), 19–19.

Brammer, S., & Millington, A. (2005). Corporate reputation and philanthropy: An empirical analysis. *Journal of Business Ethics, 61*(1), 29–44. doi:10.100710551-005-7443-4

Brännback, A. L. (2009). *Understanding the entrepreneurial mind: Opening the black box.* International Studies in Entrepreneurship.

Braun, V., & Clarke, V. (2006). Using thematic analysis in psychology. *Qualitative Research in Psychology, 3*(2), 77–101. doi:10.1191/1478088706qp063oa

Brav, A., Graham, J., Harvey, C., & Michaely, R. (2005). Payout policy in the 21st century. *Journal of Financial Economics, 77*(3), 483–527. doi:10.1016/j.jfineco.2004.07.004

Brazil. (1990). *Law No. 8,080, of September 19, 1990. Provides for the conditions for the promotion, protection and recovery of health, the organization and functioning of the corresponding services and provides other measures.* Available at http://www.planalto.gov.br/ccivil_03/leis/l8080.htm

Brick, I. E., & Chidambaran, N. (2010). Board meetings, committee structure, and firm value'. *Journal of Corporate Finance, 16*(4), 533–553. doi:10.1016/j.jcorpfin.2010.06.003

Brickley, J., Coles, J., & Terry, R. (1994). Outside directors and the adoption of poison pills. *Journal of Financial Economics, 35*(3), 371–390. doi:10.1016/0304-405X(94)90038-8

Brockman, P., & Chung, D. Y. (2003). Investor Protection and Firm Liquidity. *The Journal of Finance, 58*(2), 921–937. doi:10.1111/1540-6261.00551

Brouthers, L., & Lamb, C. Jr. (1995). National Ideology, Public Policy, and the Business Environment: A Contingency Approach to Economic Reform in Hungary, Poland and Eastern Europe. *International Business Review, 4*(3), 355–372. doi:10.1016/0969-5931(95)00014-Q

Bruinshoofd, A., & de Haan, L. (2005). *Financing the New Economy: are ICT Firms Really That Different?* De Nederlandsche Bank.

Bruynseels, L., Krishnamoorthy, G., & Wright, A. (2016). *The Association Between Audit Committee Chair Characteristics And Earnings Management*. Academic Press.

Buckmaster, D. (1997). Antecedents of Modern Earnings Management Research: Income smoothing in literature, 1954–1965. *The Accounting Historians Journal, 24*(1), 75–91. doi:10.2308/0148-4184.24.1.75

Buckmaster, D. (2001). *Development of the Income Smoothing Literature 1893–1998: A Focus on the United States*. Elsevier Science Ltd.

Buertey, S., Sun, E., Lee, J. S., & Hwang, J. (2020). Corporate social responsibility and earnings management: The moderating effect of corporate governance mechanisms. *Corporate Social Responsibility and Environmental Management, 27*(1), 256–271. doi:10.1002/csr.1803

Burgos, E., Lee, J., & Tsai, F. (2019). Doing Good with Creative Accounting? Linking Corporate Social Responsibility to Earnings Management in Market Economy. Country and Business Sector Contexts. *Sustainability, MDPI. Open Access Journal, 11*(17), 1–20.

Burgstahler, D. C., Hail, L., & Leuz, C. (2006). The importance of reporting incentives: Earnings management in European private and public firms. *The Accounting Review, 81*(5), 983–1016. doi:10.2308/accr.2006.81.5.983

Burkart, M., Panunzi, F., & Shleifer, A. (2003). Family firms. *The Journal of Finance, 58*(5), 2167–2201. doi:10.1111/1540-6261.00601

Burke, R. J. (2000). Company Size, Board Size and the Numbers of Women Corporate Directors. In R. Burke & M. Mattis (Eds.), *Women on Corporate Boards of Directors: Women International Challenges and Opportunities* (pp. 157–167). Kluwer Academic Publishers. doi:10.1007/978-90-481-3401-4_11

Burke, R. J., & Mattis, M. C. (2000). Women on Corporate Boards of Directors: Where do We Go from Here? In R. Burke & M. Mattis (Eds.), *Women on Corporate Boards of Directors: Women International Challenges and Opportunities* (pp. 3–10). Kluwer Academic Publishers. doi:10.1007/978-90-481-3401-4_1

Burns, N., Kedia, S., & Lipson, M. (2010). Institutional ownership and monitoring: Evidence from financial misreporting. *Journal of Corporate Finance, 16*(4), 443–455. doi:10.1016/j.jcorpfin.2010.06.001

Bushee, B. J. (1998). The influence of institutional investors on myopic R&D investment behavior. *The Accounting Review, 73*(3), 305–333.

Bushman, R. M., & Piotroski, J. D. (2006). Financial reporting incentives for conservative accounting: The influence of legal and political institutions. *Journal of Accounting and Economics, 42*(1-2), 107–148. doi:10.1016/j.jacceco.2005.10.005

Byrd, J., & Hickman, K. (1992). Do outside directors monitor managers? Evidence from tender offer bids. *Journal of Financial Economics, 32*(2), 195–222. doi:10.1016/0304-405X(92)90018-S

Cai, J. (2013). Does corporate governance reduce the overinvestment of free cash flow? Empirical evidence from China. *Journal of Finance and Investment Analysis, 2*(3), 97–126.

CaiJ.LiuY.QianY.YuM. (2015) Information Asymmetry and Corporate Governance, Available at SSRN: https://ssrn.com/abstract=1082589

Callao, S., Jarne, J., & Wroblewski, D. (2017). Detecting earnings management investigation on different models measuring earnings management for emerging Eastern European countries. *International Journal of Research, 5*(11), 222–259.

Campbell, F. B. F. (1896). *The theory of the national and international bibliography: with special reference to the introduction of system in the record of modern literature*. Library Bureau.

Campos, C. (2008). *Comparison of Pecking Order and Trade-off Theories: Evidence Based on Brazilian Listed Companies.* Presbyterian University Graduate Program in Business Administration Mackenzie. São Paulo. Retrieved from http://tede.mackenzie.br/jspui/handle/tede/720

Canada. Canada Health Act. Minister of Justice. (1985). Available at: https://laws.justice.gc.ca/PDF/C-6.pdf

Canadian Institute for Health Information (CIHI). (2018). Available at: https://www.cihi.ca/en/acess-data-and-reports

Candler, W., & Townsley, R. (1982). A linear two-level programming problem. *Computers & Operations Research, 9*(1), 59–76. doi:10.1016/0305-0548(82)90006-5

Cano-Rodríguez, M. (2010). Big auditors, private firms and accounting conservatism: Spanish evidence. *European Accounting Review, 19*(1), 131–159. doi:10.1080/09638180902989426

Caplan, D. H., Dutta, S. K., & Marcinko, D. J. (2019). Unmasking the fraud at toshiba. *Issues in Accounting Education, 34*(3), 41–57. doi:10.2308/iace-52429

Carlson, C., & Bussin, M. H. (2020). Relationship between executive pay and company financial performance in South African state-owned entities. *SA Journal of Human Resource Management, 18*, 11. doi:10.4102ajhrm.v18i0.1211

Carsen, S., & Xia, C. (2006). The physician as leader. *McGill Journal of Medicine, 9*(1), 1Y2.

Carter, D. A., Simkins, B. J., & Simpson, W. G. (2003). Corporate Governance, Board Diversity and Firm Value. *Financial Review, 38*(1), 33–35. doi:10.1111/1540-6288.00034

Carvalho, A. O., Rodrigues, L. L., & Branco, M. C. (2017). Factors Influencing Voluntary Disclosure in the Annual Reports of Portuguese Foundations. *Voluntas, 28*(5), 2278–2311. doi:10.100711266-017-9883-8

Cascino, S., Pugliese, A., Mussolino, D., & Sansone, C. (2010). The influence of family ownership on the quality of accounting information. *Family Business Review, 23*(3), 246–265. doi:10.1177/0894486510374302

Cengiz, S., Dilsiz, M. Ş., & Aslanoğlu, S. (2016). Kar Dağıtım Politikasının Kazanç Yönetimi Uygulamaları Üzerindeki Etkisi. *Muhasebe ve Finansman Dergisi*, (70), 39–54. doi:10.25095/mufad.396677

Cengiz, S., Gör, Y., & Terzi, S. (2016). Kurumsal Yönetim ve Kazanç Yönetimi Arasındaki İlişki: Borsa İstanbul'da İşlem Gören Şirketler Üzerine Uygulama. *Uluslararası Yönetim İktisat ve İşletme Dergisi, 30*, 756–770.

Chaghadari, M. F., & Chaleshtori, G. N. (2011). *Corporate Governance and Firm Performance.* Paper presented at the International Conference on Sociality and Economics Development, Singapore.

Chakraborty, D. (1995). *Optimization in imprecise and uncertain environment* (Doctoral dissertation, Ph. D. Thesis). Department of Mathematics, IIT Kharagpur.

Chakraborty, D. (2002). Redefining chance-constrained programming in fuzzy environment. *Fuzzy Sets and Systems, 125*(3), 327–333. doi:10.1016/S0165-0114(00)00133-0

Chakraborty, D. (2015). Solving geometric programming problems with fuzzy random variable coefficients. *Journal of Intelligent & Fuzzy Systems, 28*(6), 2493–2499. doi:10.3233/IFS-141528

Chamberlain, T. W., Butt, U. R., & Sarkar, S. (2014). Accruals and Real Earnings Management Around Debt Covenant Violations. *International Advances in Economic Research, 20*(1), 119–120. doi:10.100711294-013-9422-3

Chan, W. (2010). Expropriation through related party transactions: the position in Malaysia. *IABR & ITLC Conference Proceedings*, 1-11.

Chancharat, S., & Chancharat, N. (2019). Board Structure, Ownership Structure, and Performance of Thai Listed Companies. *Australasian Accounting. Business and Finance Journal, 13*(3), 53–70.

Chanda, S., Burton, B., & Dunne, T. (2017). The nature and potential of corporate governance in developing countries: Zambian perceptions. *Accounting, Auditing & Accountability Journal, 30*(6), 1257–1287. doi:10.1108/AAAJ-08-2015-2208

Chanes, M. (2006). The challenges in training leading health managers. *The World of Health Sao Paulo, 30*(2), 326–333.

Chatchawanchanchanakij, P., Arpornpisal, C., & Jermsittiparsert, K. (2019). The role of corporate governance in creating a capable supply chain: A case of Indonesian Tin industry. *International Journal of Supply Chain Management, 8*(3), 855–864.

Chen, C. C. (2007). *Monitoring mechanism, corporate governance, and related party transactions*. Academic Press.

Chen, C. X., Lu, H., & Sougiannis, T. (2012). The agency problem, corporate governance, and the asymmetrical behavior of selling, general, and administrative costs. *Contemporary Accounting Research, 29*(1), 252–282. doi:10.1111/j.1911-3846.2011.01094.x

Chen, G., Firth, M., Gao, D., & Rui, O. (2006). Ownership structure, corporate governance, and fraud: Evidence from China. *Journal of Corporate Finance, 12*(3), 424–448. doi:10.1016/j.jcorpfin.2005.09.002

Chen, H., Hou, C., Zhang, L., & Li, S. (2020). Comparative study on the strands of research on the governance model of international occupational safety and health issues. *Safety Science, 122*, 122. doi:10.1016/j.ssci.2019.104513

Chen, H., Jory, S., & Ngo, T. (2020). Earnings management under different ownership and corporate governance structure: A natural experiment with master limited partnerships. *The Quarterly Review of Economics and Finance, 76*, 139–156. doi:10.1016/j.qref.2019.05.005

Chen, K. Y., Elder, R. J., & Hung, S. (2010). The investment opportunity set and earnings management: Evidence from the role of controlling shareholders. *Corporate Governance, 18*(3), 193–211. doi:10.1111/j.1467-8683.2010.00793.x

Chen, K. Y., & Zhou, J. (2007). Audit committee, board characteristics, and auditor switch decisions by andersen's clients. *Contemporary Accounting Research, 24*(4), 1085–1117. doi:10.1506/car.24.4.2

Chen, L., Li, S., & Lin, W. (2007). Corporate governance and corporate performance: Some evidence from newly listed firms on Chinese stock markets. *International Journal of Accounting. Auditing and Performance Evaluation, 4*(2), 183–197. doi:10.1504/IJAAPE.2007.015233

Chen, T. (2015). Institutions, board structure, and corporate performance: Evidence from Chinese firms. *Journal of Corporate Finance, 32*, 217–237. doi:10.1016/j.jcorpfin.2014.10.009

Chen, X., Cheng, Q., & Wang, X. (2015). Does increased board independence reduce earnings management? Evidence from recent regulatory reforms. *Review of Accounting Studies, 20*(2), 899–933. doi:10.100711142-015-9316-0

Chen, X., Sun, Y., & Xu, X. (2016). Free cash flow, over-investment and corporate governance in China. *Pacific-Basin Finance Journal, 37*, 81–103. doi:10.1016/j.pacfin.2015.06.003

Chen, Y. R. (2008). Corporate governance and cash holdings: Listed new economy versus old economy firms. *Corporate Governance, 16*(5), 430–442. doi:10.1111/j.1467-8683.2008.00701.x

Chen, Y.-R., & Chuang, W.-T. (2009). Alignment or entrenchment? corporate governance and cash holdings in growing firms. *Journal of Business Research, 62*(11), 1200–1206. doi:10.1016/j.jbusres.2008.06.004

Chen, Z., Song, Y., Yu, J., & Wang, I. (2014). Differential development strategies of aged care support and continuity services in China, Japan and Australia. *Journal of Clinical Gerontology & Geriatrics*, *5*(2), 36–41. doi:10.1016/j.jcgg.2014.02.004

Cheung, P. R. (2006, November). Tunneling, propping, and expropriation: Evidence from connected party transactions in Hong Kong. *Journal of Financial Economics*, *82*(2), 343–386.

Cheung, Y. L. Y. Q. (2009, May). Buy high, sell low: How listed firms price asset transfers in related party transactions. *Journal of Banking & Finance, 33*(5), 914-924. Retrieved from https://www.sciencedirect.com/science/article/abs/pii/S0378426608002318

Cheung, W. M., & Jiang, L. (2016). Does free cash flow problem contribute to excess stock return synchronicity? *Review of Quantitative Finance and Accounting*, *46*(1), 123–140. doi:10.100711156-014-0464-2

Ch, F. N., & Jola, S. P. (2017). Bank health level analysis using rbbr in financial services sector - case in Indonesia stock exchange. *International Journal of Economic Research*, *14*, 181–192.

Chih, H., Shen, C., & Kang, F. (2008). Corporate Social Responsibility, Investor Protection, and Earnings Management: Some International Evidence. *Journal of Business Ethics*, *79*(1), 179–198. doi:10.100710551-007-9383-7

Chi-Keung, M. (2012). Corporate governance and earnings management: A survey of literature. *Journal of Applied Business Research*, *29*, 2.

Chi, W., Liu, C., & Wang, T. (2009). What affects accounting conservatism: A corporate governance perspective. *Journal of Contemporary Accounting and Economics*, *5*(1), 47–59. doi:10.1016/j.jcae.2009.06.001

Choi, H. M., Sul, W., & Min, S. K. (2012). Foreign board membership and firm value in Korea. *Management Decision*, *50*(2), 207–233. doi:10.1108/00251741211203533

Chou, D., Wang, C., Chen, S., & Tsai, S. (2009). Earnings management and the long run underperformance of firms following convertible bond offers. *Journal of Business Finance & Accounting*, *36*(1-2), 73–98. doi:10.1111/j.1468-5957.2008.02120.x

Chou, J. S., Ongkowijoyo, C. S., Ngo, N. T., & Chen, S. Y. (2020). Evolutionary bi-level model for optimizing ticket fares and operations profit of Taiwan high-speed rail. *Research in Transportation Business & Management*, *37*, 100548. doi:10.1016/j.rtbm.2020.100548

Chrisman, J. J. J. C. (2003). *Current trends and future directions in family business management studies: Toward a theory of the family firm.* Coleman white paper series.

Chrisman, J. J., Chua, J. H., & Litz, R. A. (2004). Comparing the agency costs of family and non-family firms: Conceptual issues and exploratory evidence. *Entrepreneurship Theory and Practice*, *28*(4), 335–354. doi:10.1111/j.1540-6520.2004.00049.x

Chua, J. H., Chrisman, J. J., & Sharma, P. (1999). Defining the family business by behaviour. *Entrepreneurship Theory and Practice*, *23*(4), 19–39. doi:10.1177/104225879902300402

Chung, C. Y., Hwang, J. H., Kim, D., & Liu, C. (2018). When institutions passively curb earnings management: Evidence from the korean market. *Finance Research Letters*, *25*, 274–279. doi:10.1016/j.frl.2018.02.033

Chung, H., Elder, J., & Kim, J. C. (2010). Corporate governance and liquidity. *Journal of Financial and Quantitative Analysis*, *45*(2), 265–291. doi:10.1017/S0022109010000104

Chung, H., Sheu, H. J., & Wang, J. L. (2009). Do firms' earnings management practices affect their equity liquidity? *Finance Research Letters*, *6*(3), 152–158. doi:10.1016/j.frl.2009.03.003

Chung, R., Firth, M., & Kim, J. B. (2002). Institutional monitoring and opportunistic earnings management. *Journal of Corporate Finance*, *8*(1), 29–48. doi:10.1016/S0929-1199(01)00039-6

Chung, R., Firth, M., & Kim, J.-B. (2005). Earnings management, surplus free cash flow, and external monitoring. *Journal of Business Research*, *58*(6), 766–776. doi:10.1016/j.jbusres.2003.12.002

Ciftci, I., Tatoglu, E., Wood, G., Demirbag, M., & Zaim, S. (2019). Corporate governance and firm performance in emerging markets: Evidence from Turkey. *International Business Review*, *28*(1), 90–103. doi:10.1016/j.ibusrev.2018.08.004

Claessens, S. D. (2000). The separation of ownership and control in East Asian corporations. *Journal of Financial Economics*, *58*(1-2), 81–112.

Claessens, S., & Yurtoglu, B. B. (2013). Corporate governance in emerging markets: A survey. *Emerging Markets Review*, *15*, 1–33. doi:10.1016/j.ememar.2012.03.002

Clarkson, M. (1995). A Stakeholder Framework for Analysing and Evaluating Corporate Social Performance. *Academy of Management Review*, *20*(1), 92–117. doi:10.5465/amr.1995.9503271994

Cline, B. N., Walkling, R. A., & Yore, A. S. (2018). The consequences of managerial indiscretions: Sex, lies, and firm value. *Journal of Financial Economics*, *127*(2), 389–415. doi:10.1016/j.jfineco.2017.11.008

CMVM. (1999). *Recomendações da CMVM sobre o Governo das Sociedades Cotadas*. https://www.cmvm.pt/pt/Legislacao/Legislacaonacional/C%C3%B3dGoverno%20das%20Sociedades/AnexosGovSoc/Pages/99_indice.aspx

CMVM. (2007). *Recomendações da CMVM sobre o governo das sociedades cotadas*. https://www.cmvm.pt/pt/Legislacao/Legislacaonacional/Recomendacoes/Pages/Recomendacoes.aspx?pg

CMVM. (2010). *Consolidação de fontes normativas e do código de governo das sociedades*. https://www.cmvm.pt/pt/Legislacao/Legislacaonacional/Recomendacoes/Pages/Recomendacoes.aspx?pg

CMVM. (2010a). *Recomendações da CMVM sobre o governo das sociedades cotadas*. https://www.cmvm.pt/pt/Legislacao/Legislacaonacional/Recomendacoes/Pages/Recomendacoes.aspx?pg

CMVM. (2013). *Recomendações da CMVM sobre o Governo das Sociedades*. https://www.cmvm.pt/pt/Legislacao/Legislacaonacional/Recomendacoes/Pages/Recomendacoes.aspx?pg

CMVM. (2013). *Relatório Anual sobre o Governo das Sociedades Cotadas em Portugal 2012. Comissão do Mercado de Valores Mobiliários*. Lisboa: CMVM. http://www.cmvm.pt/CMVM/Estudos/Em%20Arquivo/Documents/RGS_2012.pdf

Coase, R. H. (1937). The Nature of the Firm. *Economica*, *4*(16), 386–405. doi:10.1111/j.1468-0335.1937.tb00002.x

Cobb, J. A. (2019). Managing the conflicting interests of workers and shareholders: Evidence from pension-assumption manipulations. *Industrial & Labor Relations Review*, *72*(3), 523–551. doi:10.1177/0019793918789155

Cohen, D., & Zarowin, P. (2008). Economic Consequences of Real and Accrual-Based Earnings Management Activities. New York University.

CohenD.LiB. (2013) Why Do Firms Hold Less Cash? Why Do Firms Hold Less Cash, Available at SSRN: https://ssrn.com/abstract=2440794

Coles, J. L., Daniel, N. D., & Naveen, L. (2008). Boards: Does one size fit all? *Journal of Financial Economics*, *87*(2), 329–356. doi:10.1016/j.jfineco.2006.08.008

Coles, J. W., McWilliams, V. B., & Sen, N. (2001). An examination of the relationship of governance mechanisms to performance. *Journal of Management*, *27*(1), 23–50. doi:10.1177/014920630102700102

Collins, D. W., Gong, G., & Hribar, P. (2003). Investor sophistication and the mispricing of accruals. *Review of Accounting Studies*, *8*(2-3), 251–276. doi:10.1023/A:1024417513085

Comendeiro-Maaløe, M., Ridao-López, M., Gorgemans, S., & Bernal-Delgado, E. (2019). A comparative performance analysis of a renowned public private partnership for health care provision in spain between 2003 and 2015. *Health Policy (Amsterdam)*, *123*(4), 412–418. doi:10.1016/j.healthpol.2018.11.009 PMID:30554791

Commission, U. s. (2006). *SEC Brings Settled Charges Against Tyco International Ltd. Alleging Billion Dollar Accounting Fraud*. US SECP.

Connelly, J. T., Limpaphayom, P., & Nagarajan, N. J. (2012). Form versus substance: The effect of ownership structure and corporate governance on firm value in Thailand. *Journal of Banking & Finance*, *36*(6), 1722–1743. doi:10.1016/j.jbankfin.2012.01.017

Conyon, M. J., & He, L. (2017). Firm performance and boardroom gender diversity: A quantile regression approach. *Journal of Business Research*, *79*, 198–211. doi:10.1016/j.jbusres.2017.02.006

Corbetta, G., & Salvato, C. (2004). Self-serving or selfactualizing? Models of man and agency costs in different types of family firms. *Entrepreneurship Theory and Practice*, *28*(4), 355–362. doi:10.1111/j.1540-6520.2004.00050.x

Cornett, M., Marcus, A., & Tehranian, H. (2008). Corporate governance and pay-for-performance: The impact of earnings management. *Journal of Financial Economics*, *87*(2), 357–373. doi:10.1016/j.jfineco.2007.03.003

Costa, G. A., Oliveira, L. C., Rodrigues, L. L., & Craig, R. (2013). Factors associated with the publication of a CEO letter. *Corporate Communications*, *18*(4), 432–450. doi:10.1108/CCIJ-07-2012-0045

Costa, L., Sampaio, J. D. O., & Flores, E. S. (2019). Diversidade de Gênero nos Conselhos Administrativos e sua Relação com Desempenho e Risco Financeiro nas Empresas Familiares. *Revista de Administração Contemporânea*, *23*(6), 721–738. doi:10.1590/1982-7849rac2019180327

Crossan, K. (2011). The effects of a separation of ownership from control on UK listed firms: An empirical analysis. *Managerial and Decision Economics*, *32*(5), 293–304. doi:10.1002/mde.1535

Crowther, D., & Seifi, S. (2011). Corporate governance and risk management. *Ventus Publishing*, *58*, 2–16.

Cui, J., Jo, H., & Na, H. (2018). Does corporate social responsibility affect information asymmetry? *Journal of Business Ethics*, *148*(3), 549–572. doi:10.100710551-015-3003-8

Cunha, C. L. F., Moreira, J. P. L., Oliveira, B. L. C. A., Bahia, L., & Luiz, R. R. (2019). Private health plans and the health of workers in Brazil [Planos privados de saúde e a saúde dos trabalhadores do Brasil]. *Collective Science & Health*, *24*(5), 1959–1970. PMID:31166528

Cunha, V. L. M., & Mendes, S. M. D. (2017). Financial Determinants of Corporate Governance Disclosure: Portuguese Evidence. *Athens Journal of Business and Economics*, *3*(1), 21–35. doi:10.30958/ajbe.3.1.2

Cunha, V., & Rodrigues, L. L. (2018). Determinants of Structure of Corporate Governance Disclosure in Portugal. *RBGN -. Revista Brasileira de Gestão de Negócios*, *20*(3), 338–360. doi:10.7819/rbgn.v0i0.3359

Currie, R. R., & Pandher, G. S. (2011). Finance journal rankings and tiers: An active scholar assessment methodology. *Journal of Banking & Finance*, *35*(1), 7–20. doi:10.1016/j.jbankfin.2010.07.034

D'Mello, R., & Miranda, M. (2010). Long-term debt and overinvestment agency problem. *Journal of Banking & Finance, 34*(2), 324–335. doi:10.1016/j.jbankfin.2009.07.021

Daily, C. M., & Dalton, D. R. (2015). Corporate governance in the small firm: Prescriptions for CEOs and directors. *Journal of Small Business Strategy, 5*(1), 57–68.

Dalton, D., Daily, C., Certo, S., & Roengpitya, R. (2003). Metaanalysis of financial performance and equity: Fusion or confusion? *Academy of Management Journal, 46*(1), 13–26. doi:10.5465/30040673

Damak, S. T. (2018). Gender diverse board and earnings management: Evidence from French listed companies. *Sustainability Accounting. Management and Policy Journal, 9*(3), 289–312.

Dang, T. L., Faff, R., Luong, H., & Nguyen, L. (2019). Individualistic cultures and crash risk. *European Financial Management, 25*(3), 622–654. doi:10.1111/eufm.12180

Dang, T. L., Nguyen, T. H., Tran, N. T. A., & Vo, T. T. A. (2018). Institutional ownership and stock liquidity: International evidence. *Asia-Pacific Journal of Financial Studies, 47*(1), 21–53. doi:10.1111/ajfs.12202

Danoshana, S., & Ravivathani, T. (2019). The impact of the corporate governance on firm performance: A study on financial institutions in Sri Lanka. *SAARJ Journal on Banking & Insurance Research, 8*(1), 62–67. doi:10.5958/2319-1422.2019.00004.3

Dao, B. T. T., & Ngo, H. A. (2020). Impact of corporate governance on firm performance and earnings management a study on vietnamese non-financial companies. *Asian Economic and Financial Review, 10*(5), 480–501. doi:10.18488/journal.aefr.2020.105.480.501

Darko, J., Aribi, Z. A., & Uzonwanne, G. C. (2016). Corporate governance: the impact of director and board structure, ownership structure and corporate control on the performance of listed companies on the Ghana stock exchange. *Corporate Governance: The International Journal of Business in Society, 16*(2), 259-277.

Darmawati, D., Khomsiyah, K., & Rahayu, R. G. (2004). *Hubungan Corporate Governance dan Kinerja Perusahaan.* Simposium Nasonal Akuntansi VII Denpasar Bali.

Daske, H., & Gebhardt, G. (2006). International financial reporting standards and experts' perceptions of disclosure quality. *Abacus, 42*(3-4), 3–4, 461–498. doi:10.1111/j.1467-6281.2006.00211.x

Dau, L. A., Moore, E. M., & Kostova, T. (2020). The impact of market based institutional reforms on firm strategy and performance. Review and extension. *Journal of World Business, 55*(4), 101073. doi:10.1016/j.jwb.2020.101073

Davidson, R., Goodwin-Stewart, J., & Kent, P. (2005). Internal governance structures and earnings management. *Accounting and Finance, 45*(2), 241–267. doi:10.1111/j.1467-629x.2004.00132.x

Davis, J. R. (2003, April). Perceptions of country corruption: Antecedents and outcomes. *Journal of Business Ethics, 43*, 275–288.

Davis, J. H., Schoorman, F. D., & Donaldson, L. (1997). Toward a stewardship theory of management. *Academy of Management Review, 22*(1), 20–47. doi:10.5465/amr.1997.9707180258

De Andres, P., & Vallelado, E. (2008). Corporate governance in banking: The role of the board of directors. *Journal of Banking & Finance, 32*(12), 2570–2580. doi:10.1016/j.jbankfin.2008.05.008

De Poli, M., & De Gioia Carabellese, P. (2017). The minority directors in the corporate governance of EU listed institutions: A chimaera or a possibility? *Maastricht Journal of European and Comparative Law, 24*(1), 43–62. doi:10.1177/1023263X17693187

De Pourcq, K., De Regge, M., Van den Heede, K., Van de Voorde, C., Gemmel, P., & Eeckloo, K. (2018). Hospital networks: How to make them work in belgium? facilitators and barriers of different governance models. *Acta Clinica Belgica: International Journal of Clinical and Laboratory Medicine*, *73*(5), 333–340. doi:10.1080/17843286.2018.1457196 PMID:29595095

Deakin, S. (2008). Legal origin, juridical form and industrialization in historical perspective: The case of the employment contract and the joint-stock company. *Socio-economic Review*, *7*(1), 35–65. doi:10.1093er/mwn019

Deakin, S. (2012). The Corporation as Commons: Rethinking Property Rights, Governance and Sustainability in the Business Enterprise. *Queen's Law Journal*, *37*(2), 339–381.

DeAndreas, P., Azofra, V., & Lopez, F. (2005). Corporate Boards in OECD Countries: Size, Composition, Functioning and Effectiveness. *Corporate Governance*, *13*(2), 197–210. doi:10.1111/j.1467-8683.2005.00418.x

Debnath, N. C., Patnaik, B. C. M., & Satpathy, I. (2019). Female directorship and real earnings management in bangladesh: Towards an analytical assessment. *Management Science Letters*, *9*(11), 1723–1740. doi:10.5267/j.msl.2019.6.018

Deb, P., David, P., & O'Brien, J. (2017). When is cash good or bad for firm performance? *Strategic Management Journal*, *38*(2), 436–454. doi:10.1002mj.2486

Dechow, P. M. I. D. (2002). The quality of accruals and earnings. *The Accounting Review, 77*(1), 35-39. Retrieved from https://meridian.allenpress.com/accounting-review/article-abstract/77/s-1/35/53276

Dechow, P. M. R. S. (1995, April). Detecting earnings management. *The Accounting Review, 70*(2), 193-225. Retrieved from https://www.jstor.org/stable/248303?seq=1

Dechow, M. P., Sloan, R. G., & Sweeney, A. P. (1995). Detecting earnings management. *The Accounting Review*, *70*(2), 193–225.

Dechow, P. M., & Dichev, I. D. (2002). The quality of accruals and earnings: The role of accruals estimation error. *The Accounting Review*, *77*(1), 35–39. doi:10.2308/accr.2002.77.s-1.35

Dechow, P. M., Sloan, R. G., & Sweeney, A. P. (1995). Detecting Earnings Management. *The Accounting Review*, *70*(2), 193–225. https://www.jstor.org/stable/248303

Dechow, P., Ge, W., & Schrand, C. (2010). Understanding earnings quality: A review of the proxies, their determinants and their consequences. *Journal of Accounting and Economics*, *50*(2-3), 344–401. doi:10.1016/j.jacceco.2010.09.001

Dechow, P., Sloan, R., & Sweeney, A. (1996). Causes and consequences of earnings manipulation: An analysis of firms subject to enforcement actions by the SEC. *Contemporary Accounting Research*, *13*(1), 1–36. doi:10.1111/j.1911-3846.1996.tb00489.x

Decreto-Lei nº 76-A/2006, Diário da República, 1ª série - A, Nº 63, 29 de março de 2006.

DeFeo, R., Nikbakht, E., & Spieler, A. C. (2010). Corporate governance and the use of EVA compensation. *Corporate Ownership and Control*, *8*(1), 37–48. doi:10.22495/cocv8i1p3

DeFond, M. L., & Jiambalvo, J. (1994). Debt covenant violation and manipulation of accruals. *Journal of Accounting and Economics*, *17*(1-2), 145–176. doi:10.1016/0165-4101(94)90008-6

Degeling, P. (2006). Realising the developmental potential of clinical governance. *Clinical Chemistry and Laboratory Medicine*, *44*(6), 688–691. doi:10.1515/CCLM.2006.120 PMID:16729853

Deighan, M., Cullen, R., & Moore, R. (2004) The development of integrated governance. *Debate (the voice of NHS management),* (4).

Deighan, M., & Bullivant, J. (2006). *Integrated Governance Handbook - A handbook for executives and non-executives in healthcare organisations*. Department of Health. London.

Demsetz, H., & Villalonga, B. (2001). Ownership structure and corporate performance. *Journal of Corporate Finance*, *7*(1), 209–233. doi:10.1016/S0929-1199(01)00020-7

Demski, J. S. (1998). Performance measure manipulation. *Contemporary Accounting Research*, *15*(3), 261–285. doi:10.1111/j.1911-3846.1998.tb00560.x

Denis, D., Denis, D., & Sarin, A. (1997). Agency problems, equity ownership, and corporate diversification. *The Journal of Finance*, *52*(1), 135–160. doi:10.1111/j.1540-6261.1997.tb03811.x

Department of Informatics of the Unified Health System - DataSUS. (2019). Available at: http://www.cns.org.br/links/D_SETOR_DATES.htm

Development, O. f.-o. (2001). *The private sector fights corruption*. OECD.

Dewatripont, M., & Tirole, J. (1994). *The Prudential Regulation of Banks*. MIT Press.

Dewi, R. S. (2020). The Application of Good Corporate Governance (GCG) Through the Implementation of Quality Management System At PT. CS. *Journal of Accounting and Finance Management*, *1*(1), 24–37. doi:10.38035/jafm.v1i1.8

Dezö, C. L., & Ross, D. G. (2012). Does female representation in top management improve firm performance? a panel data investigation. *Strategic Management Journal*, *33*(9), 1072–1089. doi:10.1002mj.1955

DeZoort, F. T., Hermanson, D. R., Archambeault, D. S., & Reed, S. A. (2002). Audit Committee Effectiveness: A Synthesis of the Empirical Audit Committee Literature. *Journal of Accounting Literature*, *21*, 38–75.

Dhaliwal, D., Naiker, V., & Navissi, F. (2010). The Association Between Accruals Quality and the Characteristics of Accounting Experts and Mix of Expertise on Audit Committees. *Contemporary Accounting Research*, *27*(3), 787–827. doi:10.1111/j.1911-3846.2010.01027.x

Diaconu, K., Falconer, J., Vidal, N., O'May, F., Azasi, E., Elimian, K., Bou-Orm, I., Sarb, C., Witter, S., & Ager, A. (2020). Understanding fragility: Implications for global health research and practice. *Health Policy and Planning*, *35*(2), 235–243. doi:10.1093/heapol/czz142 PMID:31821487

Dias, A., Rodrigues, L. L., & Craig, R. (2017). Corporate Governance Effects on Social Responsibility Disclosures. *Australasian Accounting. Business and Finance Journal*, *11*(2), 3–22.

Dimitrasa, A. I., Kyriakoua, M. I., & Iatridis, G. (2015). Financial crisis, GDP variation and earnings management in Europe. *Research in International Business and Finance*, *34*, 338–354. doi:10.1016/j.ribaf.2015.02.017

Ding, R., Li, J., & Wu, Z. (2018). Government affiliation, real earnings management, and firm performance: The case of privately held firms. *Journal of Business Research*, *83*, 138–150. doi:10.1016/j.jbusres.2017.10.011

Dittmar, A., & Mahrt-Smith, J. (2007). Corporate governance and the value of cash holdings. *Journal of Financial Economics*, *83*(3), 599–634. doi:10.1016/j.jfineco.2005.12.006

Dlugosz, Z. (2011). Population ageing in Europe. *Procedia: Social and Behavioral Sciences*, *19*(1), 47–55. doi:10.1016/j.sbspro.2011.05.106

Doan, T. (2020). The effect of cash holdings on firm performance: Evidence from Vietnam listed firms. *Accounting*, *6*(5), 721–726. doi:10.5267/j.ac.2020.6.012

Do, C., & Nabar, S. (2019). Macroeconomic effects of aggregate accounting conservatism: A cross-country analysis. *Journal of International Financial Management & Accounting*, *30*(1), 83–107. doi:10.1111/jifm.12093

Doing Business Database. (n.d.). www.doingbusiness.org

Donaldson, L. (1990). The Ethereal Hand: Organizational Economics and Management Theory. *Academy of Management Review*, *15*(3), 369–381. doi:10.5465/amr.1990.4308806

Donaldson, L., & Davis, J. H. (1991). Stewardship Theory: CEO Governance and Shareholder Returns. *Australian Journal of Management*, *16*(1), 49–65. doi:10.1177/031289629101600103

Donaldson, T., & Dunfee, T. (1999). *Ties that Bind: A social contracts approach to business ethics*. HBS Press.

Duru, A., Iyengar, R. J., & Zampelli, E. M. (2016). The dynamic relationship between CEO duality and firm performance: The moderating role of board independence. *Journal of Business Research*, *69*(10), 4269–4277. doi:10.1016/j.jbusres.2016.04.001

Eeckloo, K., Herck, G. V., Hulle, C. V., & Vleugels, A. (2004). From Corporate Governance to Hospital Governance. Authority, transparency and accountability of Belgian non-profit hospitals' board and management. *Health Policy (Amsterdam)*, *68*(1), 1–15. doi:10.1016/j.healthpol.2003.07.009 PMID:15033548

Ehikioya, B. I. (2009). Corporate governance structure and firm performance in developing economies: evidence from Nigeria. *Corporate Governance: The International Journal of Business in Society, 9*(3), 231-243.

Ehtiat Karrahemi, K., Abdul Rasid, S. Z., & Basiruddin, R. (2016). Cash holdings and corporate governance: An empirical study on Malaysian publicly listed companies. *Afro-Asian Journal of Finance and Accounting*, *6*(4), 305–317. doi:10.1504/AAJFA.2016.080520

Eisenhardt, K. M. (1989). Agency theory: An assessment and review. *Academy of Management Review*, *14*(1), 57–74. doi:10.5465/amr.1989.4279003

Eisenhardt, K. M. (1989). Building theories from case study research. *Academy of Management Review*, *4*(4), 532–549. doi:10.5465/amr.1989.4308385

El Diri, M., Lambrinoudakis, C., & Alhadab, M. (2020). Corporate governance and earnings management in concentrated markets. *Journal of Business Research*, *108*, 291–306. doi:10.1016/j.jbusres.2019.11.013

El Mir, A., & Seboui, S. (2008). Corporate governance and the relationship between EVA and created shareholder value. *Corporate Governance*, *8*(1), 46–58. doi:10.1108/14720700810853392

Elayan, F., Li, J., & Meyer, T. (2008). Accounting irregularities, management compensation structure and information asymmetry. *Accounting and Finance*, *48*(5), 741–760. doi:10.1111/j.1467-629X.2008.00266.x

El-Helaly, M., Shehata, N. F., & El-Sherif, R. (2018). National corporate governance, GMI ratings and earnings management: A country level study. *Asian Review of Accounting*, *26*(3), 373–390. doi:10.1108/ARA-07-2017-0124

Elzahar, H., & Hussainey, K. (2012). Determinants of narrative risk disclosures in UK interim reports. *The Journal of Risk Finance*, *13*(2), 133–147. doi:10.1108/15265941211203189

Enache, L., & García-Meca, E. (2019). Board composition and accounting conservatism: The role of business experts, support specialist and community influentials. *Australian Accounting Review*, *29*(1), 252–265. doi:10.1111/auar.12279

Enriques, L. (2009). *Modernizing Italy's corporate governance institutions: mission accomplished?* ECGI Law Working Paper, n. 123.

Epps, R. W. (2008). Do institutional shareholder services (ISS) corporate governance ratings reflect a company's operating performance? *Critical Perspectives on Accounting*, *19*(8), 1135–1148.

Erhardt, N. L., Werbel, J. D., & Shrader, C. B. (2003). Board of Director Diversity and Firm Financial Performance. *Corporate Governance*, *11*(2), 102–111. doi:10.1111/1467-8683.00011

Erkens, D. H., Hung, M., & Matos, P. (2012). Corporate governance in the 2007-2008 financial crisis: Evidence from financial institutions worldwide. *Journal of Corporate Finance*, *18*(2), 389–411. doi:10.1016/j.jcorpfin.2012.01.005

Espinoza, R. A. C., de la Fuente Mella, H. A., Palavecinos, B. S., & Riffo, P. A. D. (2014). Revelación de información en las empresas bursátiles chilenas: El efecto de la propiedad de los inversionistas institucionales y el nivel de endeudamiento. *Estudios Gerenciales*, *30*(131), 190–199. doi:10.1016/j.estger.2014.04.008

Ethics, J. o. (2002). Culture and international anti-corruption agreements in Latin America. *Journal of Business Ethics*, *37*, 413–422.

European Commission. (2012). *Women on Boards: Commission proposes 40% objective*. Retrieved from: https://ec.europa.eu/commission/presscorner/detail/en/IP_12_1205

European Commission. (2016). https://ec.europa.eu

Ezzine, H., & Olivero, B. (2013). Evolution of corporate governance during the recent financial crises. *The International Journal of Business and Finance Research*, *7*(1), 85–100.

Fahlenbrach, R., & Stulz, R. M. (2009). Managerial ownership dynamics and firm value. *Journal of Financial Economics*, *92*(3), 342–361. doi:10.1016/j.jfineco.2008.06.005

Fakhfakh, I., & Jarboui, A. (2020). Audit certification, earnings management and risk governance: A moderated-mediation analysis. *Journal of Financial Reporting and Accounting*, *18*(2), 277–299. doi:10.1108/JFRA-01-2019-0015

Fama, E. F. (1980). Agency problems and the theory of the firm. *Journal of Political Economy*, *88*(2), 288–307. doi:10.1086/260866

Fama, E., & Jensen, M. (1983). Separation of ownership and control. *The Journal of Law & Economics*, *26*(2), 321–325. doi:10.1086/467037

Fana & Wong. (2002, August). Corporate ownership structure and the informativeness of accounting earnings in East Asia. *Journal of Accounting and Economics*, *33*(3), 401–425.

Fasterholdt, I., Krahn, M., Kidholm, K., Yderstræde, K. B., & Pedersen, K. M. (2017). Review of early assessment models of innovative medical technologies. *Health Policy (Amsterdam)*, *121*(8), 870–879. doi:10.1016/j.healthpol.2017.06.006 PMID:28701260

Fauzi, F., & Locke, S. (2012). Board structure, ownership structure and firm performance: A study of New Zealand listed-firms. *Asian Academy of Management Journal of Accounting and Finance*, *8*(2), 43-67. http://hdl.handle.net/10289/7793

Fauzi, F., Hewa-Wellalage, N., & Locke, S. (2012). The global financial crisis' impact on short-term performance of IPO: The case study of New Zealand firms' IPOs. *Asian Journal of Finance and Accounting*, *4*(2), 180–198. doi:10.5296/ajfa.v4i2.1829

Feierstein, M. (2012). *Planet Ponzi – How Politicians and Bankers Stole Your Future: What Happens Next, How You can Survive*. Transworld Publishers/Bantam.

Felício, J. A., & Rodrigues, R. (2014). Study on the influence of governance mechanisms on performance: Evidence of nonlinear relationships of listed companies in different contexts. *Corporate Ownership & Control*, *11*(2), 429–445. doi:10.22495/cocv11i2c5p1

Félix, E. G. S., & David, D. S. T. (2019). Performance of family-owned firms: The impact of gender at the management level. *Journal of Family Business Management*, *9*(2), 228–250. doi:10.1108/JFBM-10-2018-0051

Ferdinand, R., & Santosa, S. (2019). Factors that Influence Fraudulent Financial Statements in Retail Companies-Indonesia. *Journal of Applied Accounting and Finance*, *2*(2), 99–109. doi:10.33021/jaaf.v2i2.548

Fernandes, A. C., & Nunes, A. M. (2016). Hospitals and the public-private combination in the portuguese health system [Os hospitais e a combinação público-privado no sistema de saúde português]. *Acta Medica Portuguesa*, *29*(3), 217–223. doi:10.20344/amp.6712 PMID:27285098

Fernandes, N. (2008). EC: Board compensation and firm performance: The role of "independent" board members. *Journal of Multinational Financial Management*, *18*(1), 30–44. doi:10.1016/j.mulfin.2007.02.003

Fernandez, R. (2011). *Explaining the decline of the Amsterdam financial centre: Globalizing finance and the rise of a hierarchical inter-city network* (PhD Thesis). University of Amsterdam, The Netherlands.

Fernandez, V. (2011). The Driving Factors of Firm Investment: Latin American Evidence. *Emerging Markets Finance & Trade*, *47*(5), 4–26. doi:10.2753/REE1540-496X470501

Ferramosca, S., & Allegrini, M. (2018). The complex role of family involvement in earnings management. *Journal of Family Business Strategy*, *9*(2), 128–141. doi:10.1016/j.jfbs.2018.01.001

Ferraz, D. P., Lopes, I. T., & Kopliku, A. (2018). Can board diversity and choice of auditor enhance profitability? *International Journal of Business Performance Management*, *19*(3), 289–306. doi:10.1504/IJBPM.2018.092757

Fich, E. M., & Slezak, S. L. (2008). Can corporate governance save distressed firms from bankruptcy? An empirical analysis. *Review of Quantitative Finance and Accounting*, *30*(2), 225–251. doi:10.100711156-007-0048-5

Fidler, D. (2010). *The challenges of global health governance*. Council on Foreign Relations.

Filatotchev, I., Lien, Y. C., & Piesse, J. (2005). Corporate governance and performance in publicly listed, family-controlled firms: Evidence from Taiwan. *Asia Pacific Journal of Management*, *22*(3), 257–283. doi:10.100710490-005-3569-2

Findik, H. & Öztürk, E. (2016). Finansal Bilgi Manipülasyonunun Beneish Modeli Yardımıyla Ölçülmesi: BIST İmalat Sanayi Üzerine Bir Araştırma. *İşletme Araştırmaları Dergisi*, *8*(1), 483-499.

Firth, M., Lin, C., & Wong, S. M. L. (2008). Leverage and investment under a state-owned bank lending environment: Evidence from China. *Journal of Corporate Finance*, *14*(5), 642–653. doi:10.1016/j.jcorpfin.2008.08.002

Fischer, P. E., & Louis, H. (2008). Financial reporting and conflicting managerial incentives: The case of management buyouts. *Management Science*, *54*(10), 1700–1714. doi:10.1287/mnsc.1080.0895

Flayyih, H.H., Salih, J.I., Rahma, N.G.A., & Mohammed, Y.N. (2020). Earnings Management between the fact of manipulation and credibility of management procedures: a literature review. *SSHJ*, *4*(5), 1898-1908.

Fleet, R., Dupuis, G., Fortin, J., Gravel, J., Ouimet, M., Poitras, J., & Légaré, F. (2017). Rural emergency care 360°: Mobilising healthcare professionals, decision-makers, patients and citizens to improve rural emergency care in the province of quebec, canada: A qualitative study protocol. *BMJ Open*, *7*(8), e016039. doi:10.1136/bmjopen-2017-016039 PMID:28819068

Fooladi, M. Z. S. (2011). Corporate governance and disclosure of related party transactions. In 2nd International Conference on Business and Economic Research (pp. 1392-1405). ICBER.

Fortuny-Amat, J., & McCarl, B. (1981). A representation and economic interpretation of a two-level programming problem. *The Journal of the Operational Research Society*, *32*(9), 783–792. doi:10.1057/jors.1981.156

Francis, B. B., Hasan, I., & Wu, Q. (2012) *Do Corporate Boards Affect Firm Performance? New Evidence from the Financial Crisis*. Bank of Finland Research Discussion Paper.

Francis, B., Hasan, I., & Li, L. (2016). Evidence for the existence of downwards real-activity earnings management. *Journal of Accounting, Auditing & Finance*, *31*(2), 212–248. doi:10.1177/0148558X15582086

Francis, B., Hasan, I., & Wu, Q. (2015). Professors in the Boardroom and Their Impact on Corporate Governance and Firm Performance. *Financial Management*, *44*(3), 547–581. doi:10.1111/fima.12069

Francis, J. R., & Wang, D. (2008). The joint effect of investor protection and Big 4 audits on earnings quality around the world. *Contemporary Accounting Research*, *25*(1), 157–191. doi:10.1506/car.25.1.6

Francis, J., Schipper, K., & Vincent, L. (2005). Earnings and dividend informativeness when cash flow rights are separated from voting rights. *Journal of Accounting and Economics*, *39*(2), 329–360. doi:10.1016/j.jacceco.2005.01.001

Francis, J., & Wilson, E. (1988). Audit change: A test of theories relating to agency costs and auditor differentiation. *The Accounting Review*, *64*, 663–682.

Freeman, R. E., & McVea, J. (2001). *A Stakeholder Approach to Strategic Management*. Darden Business School Working Paper, 01-02. doi:10.2139srn.263511

Freeman, R. E. (1984). *Strategic Management: A Stakeholder Approach*. Cambridge University Press.

Friska, F., & Kashan, P. (2019). Company Characteristics, Corporate Governance, Audit Quality Impact on Earnings Management. *Accounting & Finance Review*, *4*(2), 43–49. doi:10.35609/afr.2019.4.2(2)

Fung, S., Jo, H., & Tsai, S. (2009). Agency problems in stock market driven acquisitions. *Review of Accounting and Finance*, *8*(4), 388–430. doi:10.1108/14757700911006958

Funken, K. (2003). *The best of both worlds: the trend towards convergence of the civil law and the common law system*. University of Munich School of Law.

Gandhi, A. V., & Sharma, D. (2018). Technical efficiency of private sector hospitals in India using data envelopment analysis. *Benchmarking*, *25*(9), 3570–3591. doi:10.1108/BIJ-06-2017-0135

Gao, L., & Zhang, J. (2015). Firms' earnings smoothing, corporate social responsibility. *Journal of Corporate Finance*, *32*, 108–127. doi:10.1016/j.jcorpfin.2015.03.004

Gao, Y., Zhang, G., Ma, J., & Lu, J. (2009). A ${\bm\lambda} $-Cut and Goal-Programming-Based Algorithm for Fuzzy-Linear Multiple-Objective Bilevel Optimization. *IEEE Transactions on Fuzzy Systems*, *18*(1), 1–13. doi:10.1109/TFUZZ.2009.2030329

García Lara, J. M., Osma, B. G., & Penalva, F. (2007). Board of directors' characteristics and conditional accounting conservatism: Spanish evidence. *European Accounting Review*, *16*(4), 727–755. doi:10.1080/09638180701706922

Garcia Osma, B., Scarlat, E., & Shields, K. (2020). Insider trading restrictions and earnings management. *Accounting and Business Research*, *50*(3), 205–237. doi:10.1080/00014788.2020.1712650

Garcia, A., Mendes-Da-Silva, W., & Orsato, R. (2017). Sensitive industries produce better ESG performance: Evidence from emerging markets. *Journal of Cleaner Production*, *150*, 135–147. doi:10.1016/j.jclepro.2017.02.180

García-Ramos, R., & García-Olalla, M. (2011). Board characteristics and firm performance in public founder-and nonfounder-led family businesses. *Journal of Family Business Strategy*, *2*(4), 220–231. doi:10.1016/j.jfbs.2011.09.001

Garcia-Teruel, P. J., Martinez-Sola, C., & Martinez-Solano, P. (2011). Corporate cash holdings and firm value. *Applied Economics*, *45*(2), 161–170.

GarmaiseM. J.LiuJ. (2005) Corruption, Firm Governance, and the Cost of Capital. https://ssrn.com/abstract=644017 doi:10.2139srn.644017

Gelb, D., & Strawser, J. (2001). Corporate social responsibility and financial disclosure: An alternative explanation for increased disclosure. *Journal of Business Ethics*, *33*(1), 1–13. doi:10.1023/A:1011941212444

Getz, R. V. (2001, March 1). Culture, perceived corruption, and economics: A model of predictors and outcomes. *Business & Society*, *40*(1), 1–24.

Ghazali, A. W., Nurullah, M., Ibrahim, S., Sanusi, Z. M., & Mohame, N. (2019). The effect of corporate board diversity: Real earnings management among malaysian listed firms. *International Journal of Business and Management Science*, *9*(2), 257–276. www.scopus.com

Gholami, R. A., Sandal, L. K., & Ubøe, J. (2020). A solution algorithm for multi-period bi-level channel optimization with dynamic price-dependent stochastic demand. *Omega*. doi:10.1016/j.omega.2020.102297

Ghorbani, A., & Salehi, N. (2020). Earnings management and the informational and disciplining role of debt: Evidence from Iran. *Journal of Asia Business Studies*. Advance online publication. doi:10.1108/JABS-11-2019-0336

Gibson, A. R. (2003). Management Is Responsible, Too. *Journal of Accountancy*.

Gilson, R. J. (2006). Controlling shareholders and corporate governance: Complicating the comparative taxonomy. *Harvard Law Review*, *119*(6), 1642–1679.

Gomez-Mejia, L. R., Haynes, K., Nunez-Nickel, M., Jacobson, K., & Moyano-Fuentes, F. (2007). Socioemotional wealth and business risks in family controlled firms. *Administrative Science Quarterly*, *52*(1), 106–137. doi:10.2189/asqu.52.1.106

Gomez-Mejia, L. R., Larraza-Kintana, M., & Makri, M. (2003). The determinants of executive compensation in family controlled public corporations. *Academy of Management Journal*, *46*(2), 226–237.

Gonçalves, T., Gaio, C., & Santos, T. (2019). Women on the board: Do they manage earnings? empirical evidence from european listed firms [Mulheres no Board: Elas gerem resultados? Evidência empírica das empresas europeias cotadas]. *Revista Brasileira de Gestão de Negócios*, *21*(3), 582–597. doi:10.7819/rbgn.v21i3.4010

González, J. S., & García-Meca, E. (2014). Does corporate governance influence earnings management in Latin American markets. *Journal of Business Ethics*, *121*(3), 419–440.

González, J. S., & García-Meca, E. (2014). Does corporate governance influence earnings management in Latin American markets? *Journal of Business Ethics*, *121*(3), 419–440. doi:10.100710551-013-1700-8

Gordon, E. A. E. H. (2006). Related party transactions: associations with corporate governance and firm value. *EFA 2004 Maastricht Meeting*, 1-59.

Gordon, E. H. (2004). Related party transactions and corporate governance. *Advances in Financial Economics*, 9.

Gordon, D., McKay, S., Marchildon, G., Sacha Bhatia, R., & Shaw, J. (2020). Collaborative governance for integrated care: Insights from a policy stakeholder dialogue. *International Journal of Integrated Care*, *20*(1), 3. doi:10.5334/ijic.4684 PMID:32089655

Gore, P., Pope, P. F., & Singh, A. K. (2007). Earnings management and the distribution of earnings relative to targets: UK evidence. *Accounting and Business Research*, *37*(2), 123–150. doi:10.1080/00014788.2007.9730065

Governance, F. C. (2000). *Malaysian Code on Corporate Governance, March 2000*. Malaysian Government.

Graham, J. R., Harvey, C. R., & Rajgopal, S. (2005). The economic implications of corporate financial reporting. *Journal of Accounting and Economics*, *40*(1), 3–73. doi:10.1016/j.jacceco.2005.01.002

Graves, S. B., & Waddock, S. A. (1990). Institutional ownership and control: Implications for long-term corporate strategy. *The Academy of Management Perspectives*, *4*(1), 75–83. doi:10.5465/ame.1990.4274714

Gregory, A., & Wang, Y.-H. (2013). Cash acquirers: Can free cash flow, debt and institutional ownership explain long-run performance? *Review of Behavioural Finance*, *5*(1), 35–57. doi:10.1108/RBF-02-2013-0010

Group, M. s. (2019, August). *MSWG*. Retrieved from Encouraging Minority Shareholder Activism: http://www.mswg.org.my/news/encouraging-minority-shareholder-activism

Gualtieri, G., Traverso, S., Pozza, A., Ferretti, F., Carabellese, F., Gusinu, R., & Coluccia, A. (2020). Clinical risk management in high-security forensic psychiatry residences. protecting patients and health professionals: Perspectives and critical issues of the law 81/2014. *La Clinica Terapeutica*, *171*(2), e97–e100. PMID:32141478

Guidry, F., Leone, A., & Rock, S. (1999). Earnings-based bonus plans and earnings management by business-unit managers. *Journal of Accounting and Economics*, *26*(1-3), 113–142. doi:10.1016/S0165-4101(98)00037-8

Gul, F. A. S. L. (2002, January 1). Audit quality, management ownership, and the informativeness of accounting earnings. *SAGE Journals, 17*(1), 25-49. Retrieved from https://journals.sagepub.com/doi/abs/10.1177/0148558X0201700102

Gul, F. A., Leung, S., & Srinidhi, B. (2003). *Informative and opportunistic earnings management and the value relevance of earnings: Some evidence on the role of IOS*. Available from https://papers.ssrn.com/sol3/papers.cfm?abstract_id=429800

Gulamhussen, M. A., & Guerreiro, L. (2009). The influence of foreign equity and board membership on corporate strategy and internal cost management in Portuguese banks. *Management Accounting Research*, *20*(1), 6–17. doi:10.1016/j.mar.2008.10.006

Gulamhussen, M. A., & Santa, S. F. (2015). Female directors in bank boardrooms and their influence on performance and risk-taking. *Global Finance Journal*, *28*, 10–23. doi:10.1016/j.gfj.2015.11.002

Gul, F. A., Srinidhi, B., & Tsui, J. (2011). Female directors and earnings quality. *Journal of Contemporary Accounting Research*, *28*(5), 1610–1643. doi:10.1111/j.1911-3846.2011.01071.x

Gündüz, M. (2016). Determination of earnings management: An application in BIST Kazanç yönetiminin tespiti: BIST'de bir uygulama. *Journal of Human Sciences*, *13*(3), 6080–6091. doi:10.14687/jhs.v13i3.4367

GuneyY.OzkanA.OzkanN. (2003) Additional International Evidence on Corporate Cash Holdings, Available at SSRN: https://ssrn.com/abstract=406721.2003 doi:10.2139srn.406721

Gutiérrez, M., & Sáez, M. (2013). Deconstructing Independent Directors. *Journal of Corporate Law Studies*, *13*(1), 63–94. doi:10.5235/14735970.13.1.63

Gu, Y., Zhou, Q., & Ho, K. (2020). Financial flexibility and managerial short-termism. *Annals of Economics and Finance*, *21*(1), 189–208. www.scopus.com

Habib, A. (2011). Growth opportunities, earnings permanence and the valuation of free cash flow. *Australasian Accounting, Finance, and Business Journal*, *5*(4), 101–122.

HabibA. 2005. Information Risk and the Cost of Capital: Review of the Empirical Literature. https://ssrn.com/abstract=722781 doi:10.2139srn.722781

Hai, V. D., Trung, L. H. P., Hung, P. M., Hung, D. V., Ngoc, P. P., Hung, P. D., Dan, C. Q., & Vi, T. Q. (2020). Design of noninvasive hemodynamic monitoring equipment using impedance cardiography. *IFMBE Proceedings*, *69*, 3-9. 10.1007/978-981-13-5859-3_1

Hambrick, D. C. (2007). Upper echelons theory: An update. *Academy of Management Review*, *32*(2), 334–343. doi:10.5465/amr.2007.24345254

Hambrick, D. C., & Mason, P. A. (1984). Upper echelons: The organization as a reflection of its top managers. *Academy of Management Review*, *9*(2), 193–206. doi:10.5465/amr.1984.4277628

Hamdani, A., & Yafeh, Y. (2013). Institutional investors as minority shareholders. *Review of Finance*, *17*(2), 691–725. doi:10.1093/rof/rfr039

Haniffa, R. M., & Cooke, T. E. (2002). Culture, corporate governance and disclosure in Malaysian corporations. *Abacus*, *38*(3), 317–349.

Haniffa, R., & Hudaib, M. (2006). Corporate governance structure and performance of Malaysian listed companies. *Journal of Business Finance & Accounting*, *33*(7-8), 1034–1062.

Han, S. H., Kim, M., Lee, D. H., & Lee, S. (2014). Information asymmetry, corporate governance, and shareholder wealth: Evidence from unfaithful disclosures of Korean listed firms. *Asia-Pacific Journal of Financial Studies*, *43*(5), 690–720. doi:10.1111/ajfs.12064

Happ, C., & Schiereck, D. (2017). Seasoned equity offerings and corporate governance in Europe. *Journal of European Real Estate Research*, *10*(2), 170–194. doi:10.1108/JERER-05-2016-0019

Harakeh, M., El-Gammal, W., & Matar, G. (2019). Female directors, earnings management, and CEO incentive compensation: UK evidence. *Research in International Business and Finance*, *50*, 153–170. doi:10.1016/j.ribaf.2019.05.001

Harford, J., Mansi, S. A., & Maxwell, W. F. (2012). Corporate Governance and Firm Cash Holdings in the US. In Corporate Governance (pp. 107-138). Springer.

Harris, L. (1994). Minimum Price Variations, Discrete Bid-Ask Spreads, and Quotation Sizes. *Review of Financial Studies*, *7*(1), 149–178. doi:10.1093/rfs/7.1.149

Hart, O. (1995). *Firms, Contracts, and Financial Structure*. Clarendon Press. doi:10.1093/0198288816.001.0001

Hartzell, J. C., & Starks, L. T. (2003). Institutional investors and executive compensation. *The Journal of Finance*, *58*(6), 2351–2374. doi:10.1046/j.1540-6261.2003.00608.x

Harvey, C. R., Lins, K. V., & Roper, A. H. (2004). The effect of capital structure when expected agency costs are extreme. *Journal of Financial Economics*, *74*(1), 3–30. doi:10.1016/j.jfineco.2003.07.003

Hashim, A. M. (2013). The Breadth and Depth of Related Party Transactions. *International Journal of Trade, Economics and Finance*, *4*, 388. Retrieved from https://www.researchgate.net/profile/Hafiza_Hashim/publication/272909338_The_Breadth_and_Depth_of_Related_Party_Transactions_Disclosures/links/558f5f6608ae1e1f9baceaba/The-Breadth-and-Depth-of-Related-Party-Transactions-Disclosures.pdf

Hashim, A. M. (2014, April 2). Accounting Irregularities in Related Party Transactions. International Journal of Trade. *Economics and Finance*, *5*, 181.

Hashim, H. A., & Devi, S. (2008). Board characteristics, ownership structure and earnings quality: Malaysian evidence. *Research in Accounting in Emerging Economies*, *8*(97), 97–123.

Haw, I. M., Ho, S. S., Hu, B., & Wu, D. (2010). Concentrated control, institutions, and banking sector: An international study. *Journal of Banking & Finance*, *34*(3), 485–497.

Health Services Circular (HSC). (1999). *Clinical Governance. Quality in the new NHS*. Available at http://www.dh.gov.uk/prod_consum_dh/groups/dh_digitalassets/@dh/@en/documents/digitalasset/dh_40120 43.pdf

Healy, H. B. (2004, August 18). Individualism and collectivism. *Industrial Relations*, *35*(5).

Healy, P. (1985). The impact of bonus schemes on the selection of accounting principles. *Journal of Accounting and Economics*, *7*(1-3), 85–107. doi:10.1016/0165-4101(85)90029-1

Healy, P. M., & Wahlen, J. M. (1999). A review of the earnings management literature and its implications for standard setting. *Accounting Horizons*, *13*(4), 365–383. doi:10.2308/acch.1999.13.4.365

Heenetigala, K., & Armstrong, A. (2011). The impact of corporate governance on firm performance in an unstable economic and political environment: Evidence from Sri Lanka. *Conference on financial markets and corporate governance, 13*, 1-17.

Heidrick & Struggles. (2003), Is Your Board Fit for the Global Challenge? Third annual survey conducted by Heidrick & Struggles. Chicago, IL: Academic Press.

Helmers, R. A., & Harper, C. M. (2019). The mayo clinic model of clinical integration. *Health Care*, *7*(3). PMID:29970294

Hepworth, S. R. (1953). Smoothing periodic income. *The Accounting Review*, *28*(1), 32–39.

HeremansD. (2007). Corporate governance issues for banks: a financial stability perspective. doi:10.2139srn.1024693

Herranz, C. Z., Iturriaga, F. J. L., & Reguera-Alvarado, N. (2018). The right person at the right time: Audit committee members and the quality of financial information 1. [La persona adecuada en el momento adecuado: Los miembros del comité de auditoría y la calidad de la información financiera] UCJC. *Business and Society Review*, *15*(2), 18–35. doi:10.3232/UBR.2018.V15.N2.01

Hilmola, O., & Henttu, V. (2016). Transportation costs do matter: Simulation study from hospital investment decision. *Journal of Modelling in Management*, *11*(2), 560–584. doi:10.1108/JM2-10-2013-0053

Hirsch, J. E. (2005). An index to quantify an individual's scientific research output. *Proceedings of the National Academy of Sciences of the United States of America*, *102*(46), 16569–16572. doi:10.1073/pnas.0507655102 PMID:16275915

Ho, F. N., Wang, H. M. D., Ho-Dac, N., & Vitell, S. J. (2019). Nature and relationship between corporate social performance and firm size: A cross-national study. *Social Responsibility Journal*, *15*(2), 258–274. doi:10.1108/SRJ-02-2017-0025

Hofstede, G. (1983, June 1). The Cultural Relativity of Organizational Practices and Theories. *Journal of International Business Studies*, *14*, 75–89.

Högfeldt, P. (2003). The history and politics of corporate ownership in Sweden. In R. A. Morck (Ed.), *History of corporate governance around the world* (pp. 517–579). The University of Chicago Press.

Holá, J., Moravcová, M., & Hlaváčková, E. (2020). Communication competency: The topic of lifelong learnifor nurse managers in hospitals [Komunikační kompetence: Téma celoživotního vzdělávání všeobecných sester manažerek v nemocnicích]. *Kontakt*, *22*(1), 33–39. doi:10.32725/kont.2019.053

Holmström, B. (1977). *On Incentives and Control in Organizations* (Unpublished PhD dissertation). Stanford University, Palo Alto, CA.

Hooghiemstra, R., Hermes, N., Oxelheim, L., & Randøy, T. (2019). Strangers on the board: The impact of board internationalization on earnings management of Nordic firms. *International Business Review*, *28*(1), 119–134. doi:10.1016/j.ibusrev.2018.08.007

House, M. J. (2001, October). Project GLOBE: An introduction. *Applied Psychology*, *50*(4), 489–505.

House, M. J. (2002). Understanding cultures and implicit leadership theories across the globe: An introduction to project GLOBE. *Journal of World Business*, *37*(1), 3–10.

Howorth, C., Westhead, P., & Wright, M. (2004). Buyouts, information asymmetry and family management dyad. *Journal of Business Venturing*, *19*(4), 509–534. doi:10.1016/j.jbusvent.2003.04.002

Hribar, P., & Collins, D. W. (2002). Errors in estimating accruals: Implications for empirical research. *Journal of Accounting Research*, *40*(1), 105–134. doi:10.1111/1475-679X.00041

Hsiao, C. (2014). *Analysis of Panel Data, 54*. Cambridge University Press. doi:10.1017/CBO9781139839327

Hsieh, H., & Shannon, S. E. (2005). Three approaches to qualitative content analysis. *Qual Health Res., 15*, 1277-1288.

Hsu, G. C. M., Clarkson, P., & Ouyang, A. X. (2019). Do biotechnology and health-care firms have poorer continuous disclosure practices as reflected in ASX queries? *Accounting Research Journal*, *32*(2), 88–112. doi:10.1108/ARJ-12-2015-0152

Hu, A., & Kumar, P. (2004). Managerial entrenchment and payout policy. *Journal of Financial and Quantitative Analysis*, *39*(4), 759–790. doi:10.1017/S0022109000003203

Huang, C. Y., & Ho, Y. S. (2011). Historical research on corporate governance: A bibliometric analysis. *African Journal of Business Management*, *5*(2), 276–284.

Huang, G., & Song, F. M. (2005). The financial and operating performance of China's newly listed H-firms. *Pacific-Basin Finance Journal*, *13*(1), 53–80.

Huang, K., Lao, B., & McPhee, G. (2017). Does stock liquidity affect accrual-based earnings management? *Journal of Business Finance & Accounting*, *44*(3-4), 417–447. doi:10.1111/jbfa.12236

Huang, W., Goodell, J. W., & Zhang, H. (2019). Pre-merger management in developing markets: The role of earnings glamor. *International Review of Financial Analysis*, *65*(C), 101375. Advance online publication. doi:10.1016/j.irfa.2019.101375

Huhs, E., Gliebe, W., & Sendlhofer, G. (2019). Qualitative analysis of lean management in healthcare: Perspectives of Austrian and swiss experts [Qualitative Analyse zu Lean Management im Gesundheitswesen: Sichtweisen österreichischer und Schweizer Experten]. *Zeitschrift für Evidenz, Fortbildung und Qualität im Gesundheitswesen*, *143*, 8–14. doi:10.1016/j.zefq.2019.05.003 PMID:31153810

Hunger, J. D., & Wheelen, L. T. (2002). *Strategic management: principles and practices*. Reichmann e Afffonso.

Hunjra, A. I., Perveen, U., Li, L., Chani, M. I., & Mehmood, R. (2020). Impact of ownership concentration, institutional ownership and earnings management on stock market liquidity. *Corporate Ownership & Control*, *17*(2), 77–87. doi:10.22495/cocv17i2art7

Hussain, H. I., Ali, A., Thaker, H. M. T., & Ali, M. (2019). Firm Performance and Family Related Directors: Empirical Evidence from an Emerging Market. *Contemporary Economics*, *13*(2), 187–204.

Hussain, N., Rigoni, U., & Orij, R. P. (2018). Corporate governance and sustainability performance: Analysis of triple bottom line performance. *Journal of Business Ethics*, *149*(2), 411–432. doi:10.100710551-016-3099-5

Hutton, A. P. (2007). A discussion of "Corporate disclosure by family firms". *Journal of Accounting and Economics*, *44*(1-2), 287–297. doi:10.1016/j.jacceco.2007.01.004

Huynh, Q. L. (2020). A triple of corporate governance, social responsibility and earnings management. *Journal of Asian Finance. Economics and Business*, *7*(3), 29–40. doi:10.13106/jafeb.2020.vol7.no3.29

Iatridis, G., & Kadorinis, G. (2009). Earnings management and firm financial motives: A financial investigation of UK listed firms. *International Review of Financial Analysis*, *18*(4), 164–173. doi:10.1016/j.irfa.2009.06.001

Ibáñez, N. (2001). Social health organizations: the model in the State of São Paulo. *ABRASCO, 6*(2).

Iglesias, A. (1999). Economic impact of pension reforms in Chile. In *International Conference "Universal Pension Funds Systems"* (pp. 19-20). Academic Press.

Ilaboya, J., & Ashafoke, T. (2017). Board Diversity and Firm Performance in Nigeria. *International Journal of Management, Accounting and Economics*, *4*(10).

International Family Enterprise Research Academy (IFERA). (2003). Family businesses dominate. *Family Business Review*, *16*(4), 235–240. doi:10.1177/08944865030160040201

International. A. s. (2018). ASI Final Assessment Report. Malaysia: ASI.

IPGC. (2018). *Código de Governo das Sociedades*. https://cgov.pt/images/ficheiros/2018/codigo_de_governo_das_sociedades_ipcg_vf.pdf

Isidro, H., & Gonçalves, L. (2011). Earnings management and CEO characteristics in Portuguese firms. *Corporate Ownership & Control*, *9*(1), 86–95. doi:10.22495/cocv9i1art5

Ismail, R. (2016). Impact of liquidity management on profitability of Pakistani firms: A case of KSE-100 index. *International Journal of Innovation and Applied Studies*, *14*(2), 304.

Ittner, C. D., Lambert, R. A., & Larcker, D. F. (2003). The structure and performance consequences of equity grants to employees of new economy firms. *Journal of Accounting and Economics*, *34*(1), 89–127. doi:10.1016/S0165-4101(02)00088-5

Iwu-Egwuonwu, D., & Chibuike, R. (2012). Does Corporate Governance Enhance Firm Performance? An Empirical Literature Evidence. *Romanian Statistical Review Supplement*, *60*(1), 53–56.

Jaafar, A., & El-Shawa, M. (2009). Ownership concentration, board characteristics and performance: Evidence from Jordan. *Research in Accounting in Emerging Economies*, *9*, 73–95. doi:10.1108/S1479-3563(2009)0000009005

Jaakko, H., & Tapani, J. (2005). Germanic and Nordic Fraud: A Comparative Look Under the Surface of Commonalities. *Global Jurist Advances*, *5*(2), 2–14.

Jacoby, G., & Zheng, S. X. (2010). Ownership dispersion and market liquidity. *International Review of Financial Analysis*, *19*(2), 81–88. doi:10.1016/j.irfa.2010.01.008

Jaggi, B., Leung, S., & Gul, F. A. (2007). *Board independence and earnings management in Hong Kong firms: Some evidence on the role of family ownership and family board control.* Working Paper. Department of Accounting and Information System, Rutgers University.

Jaggi, B., Leung, S., & Gul, F. (2009). Family control, board independence and earnings management: Evidence based on Hong Kong firms. *Journal of Accounting and Public Policy*, *28*(4), 281–300. doi:10.1016/j.jaccpubpol.2009.06.002

Jain, T., Aguilera, R. V., & Jamali, D. (2017). Corporate stakeholder orientation in an emerging country context: A longitudinal cross industry analysis. *Journal of Business Ethics*, *143*(4), 701–719.

Jebran, K., Chen, S., Tauni, M. Z., & Ahmad, H. (2019). Corporate governance, ultimate owner, and target cash holdings: Evidence from China. *SAGE Open*, *9*(4), 1–12. doi:10.1177/2158244019894293

Jensen, M. C. (1993). The modern industrial revolution, exit, and the failure of internal control systems. *The Journal of Finance*, *48*(3), 831-880.

Jensen, M. C., & Meckling, W. H. (1976). Theory of the Firm: Managerial Behaviour, Agency Costs and Ownership Structure. *Journal of Financial Economics*, *3*(4), 305–360.

Jensen, M. C. (1986). Agency costs of free cash flow, corporate finance, and takeovers. *The American Economic Review*, *76*(2), 323–329.

Jensen, M. C. (1993). The modern industrial revolution, exit, and the failure of internal control systems. *The Journal of Finance*, *48*(3), 831–880. doi:10.1111/j.1540-6261.1993.tb04022.x

Jensen, M. C. (1994). Self-interest, altruism, incentives, and agency theory. *Journal of Applied Corporate Finance*, *7*(2), 40–45. doi:10.1111/j.1745-6622.1994.tb00404.x

Jensen, M. C. (2001). Value Maximization, Stakeholder Theory, and the Corporate Objective Function. *Journal of Applied Corporate Finance*, *14*(3), 8–21. doi:10.1111/j.1745-6622.2001.tb00434.x

Jensen, M. C., & Meckling, W. H. (1976). Theory of the firm: Managerial behavior, agency costs and ownership structure. *Journal of Financial Economics*, *3*(4), 305–360. doi:10.1016/0304-405X(76)90026-X

Jensen, M. C., & Meckling, W. H. (1979). *Theory of the Firm: Managerial Behavior, Agency Costs, and Ownership Structure*. Springer.

Jensen, M. C., & Meckling, W. H. (1994). The Nature of Man. *Journal of Applied Corporate Finance*, *7*(2), 4–19. doi:10.1111/j.1745-6622.1994.tb00401.x

Jerbi Maatougui, A., & Halioui, K. (2019). The effect of outside blockholders on earnings management around seasoned equity offerings in french listed companies on the SBF120. *Journal of Financial Reporting and Accounting*, *17*(3), 449–467. doi:10.1108/JFRA-02-2018-0012

Jha, A. (2019). Financial Reports and Social Capital. *Journal of Business Ethics*, *155*(2), 567–596. doi:10.100710551-017-3495-5

Jiang, H. J., Lockee, C., & Fraser, I. (2012). Enhancing board oversight on quality of hospital care: An agency theory perspective. *Health Care Management Review*, *37*(2), 144–153. doi:10.1097/HMR.0b013e3182224237 PMID:21712722

Jiang, W., Lee, P., & Anandarajan, A. (2008). The association between corporate governance and earnings quality: Further evidence using the GOV-score. *Advances in Accounting incorporating. Advances in International Accounting*, *24*(2), 191–201. doi:10.1016/j.adiac.2008.08.011

Jiraporn, P., & DaDalt, P. (2009). Does founding family control affect earnings management? *Applied Economics Letters, 16*(2), 113–119. doi:10.1080/17446540701720592

Jiraporn, P., Miller, G. A., Yoon, S. S., & Kim, Y. S. (2008). Is earnings management opportunistic or beneficial? An agency theory perspective. *International Review of Financial Analysis, 17*(3), 622–634. doi:10.1016/j.irfa.2006.10.005

Jizi, M. I., & Nehme, R. (2017). Board gender diversity and firms' equity risk. *Equality, Diversity and Inclusion, 36*(7), 590–606. doi:10.1108/EDI-02-2017-0044

Joecks, J., Pull, K., & Vetter, K. (2013). Gender Diversity in the Boardroom and Firm Performance: What Exactly Constitutes a "Critical Mass?". *Journal of Business Ethics, 118*(1), 61–72. doi:10.100710551-012-1553-6

John, K., Litov, L., & Yeung, B. (2008). Corporate governance and risk-taking. *The Journal of Finance, 63*(4), 1679–1728. doi:10.1111/j.1540-6261.2008.01372.x

Johnstone, J. B. (2004, July 29). Audit firm portfolio management decisions. *Journal of Accounting Research, 42*(4), 659–690.

Jones. (1995). Instrumental Stakeholder Theory. *Academy of Management Review, 24*, 92–117.

Jones, J. J. (1991). Earnings management during relief investigations. *Journal of Accounting Research, 29*(2), 193–228. doi:10.2307/2491047

Jones, S., & Sharma, R. (2001). The impact of free cash flow, financial leverage and accounting regulation on earnings management in Australia's "old" and "new" economies. *Managerial Finance, 27*(12), 18–39. doi:10.1108/03074350110767420

Jones, T. M., & Wicks, A. C. (1999). Convergent Stakeholder Theory. *Academy of Management Review, 24*(2), 206–221. doi:10.5465/amr.1999.1893929

Kadri, M. I. (2009). Value relevance of book value and earnings: Evidence from two different financial reporting regimes. *The Journal of Finance, 7*(1), 1–16.

Kahle, K. M., & Stulz, R. M. (2013). Access to capital, investment, and the financial crisis. *Journal of Financial Economics, 110*(2), 280–299. doi:10.1016/j.jfineco.2013.02.014

Kahn, M., & Rock, E. (2007). Hedge funds in corporate governance and corporate control. *University of Pennsylvania Law Review, 155*(5), 1021–1093.

Kajola, S. O. (2008). Corporate governance and firm performance: The case of Nigerian listed firms. *European Journal of Economics, Finance and Administrative Sciences, 14*(14), 16-28.

Kajola, S. O. (2008). Corporate governance and firm performance: The case of Nigerian listed firms. European Journal of Economics. *Finance and Administrative Sciences, 14*(14), 16–28.

Kakemam, E., & Dargahi, H. (2019). Competencies gap in hospital management in Tehran, Iran: A cross-sectional survey. *Journal of Health Management, 21*(4), 451–464. doi:10.1177/0972063419884412

Kalcheva, I., & Lins, K. V. (2007). International evidence on cash holdings and expected managerial agency problems. *Review of Financial Studies, 20*(4), 1087–1112. doi:10.1093/rfs/hhm023

Kamal Hassan, M. (2008). The corporate governance inertia: the role of management accounting and costing systems in a transitional public health organization. In Corporate Governance in Less Developed and Emerging Economies (pp. 409-454). Academic Press.

Kamran, K., & Shah, A. (2014). The impact of corporate governance and ownership structure on earnings management practices: Evidence from listed companies in Pakistan. *The Lahore Journal of Economics*, *19*(2), 27–70.

Kao, L., Chen, A., & Lu, C. (2018). Ex ante and ex post overvalued equities: The roles of corporate governance and product market competition. *Asia Pacific Management Review*, *23*(3), 209–221. doi:10.1016/j.apmrv.2017.07.002

Kaper, M. S., Reijneveld, S. A., van Es, F. D., de Zeeuw, J., Almansa, J., Koot, J. A. R., & de Winter, A. F. (2020). Effectiveness of a comprehensive health literacy consultation skills training for undergraduate medical students: A randomized controlled trial. *International Journal of Environmental Research and Public Health*, *17*(1), 81. doi:10.3390/ijerph17010081 PMID:31861918

Kaplan, S. (1989). Management buyouts: Evidence on taxes as a source of value. *The Journal of Finance*, *44*(3), 611–632. doi:10.1111/j.1540-6261.1989.tb04381.x

Kaplan, S. N., & Minton, B. A. (1994). Appointments of outsiders to Japanese boards: Determinants and implications for managers. *Journal of Financial Economics*, *36*(2), 225–258. doi:10.1016/0304-405X(94)90025-6

Kapoor, N., & Goel, S. (2017). Board Characteristics, Firm Profitability and Earnings Management: Evidence from India. *Australian Accounting Review*, *81*(27), 180–194. doi:10.1111/auar.12144

Karaibrahimoğlu, Y. (2010). *The role of corporate governance on earnings management: Quarterly evidence from Turkey* (Unpublished Doctoral Dissertation). Izmir University of Economics, Turkey.

Karamanou, I., & Vafeas, N. (2005). The association between corporate boards, audit committees, and management earnings forecasts: An empirical analysis. *Journal of Accounting Research*, *43*(3), 453–486. doi:10.1111/j.1475-679X.2005.00177.x

Kasznick, R. (1999). On the Association between Voluntary Disclosure and Earnings Management. *Journal of Accounting Research*, *37*(1), 57–82. doi:10.2307/2491396

Kaya, U., & Yazan, Ö. (2017). Kurumsal Sosyal Sorumluluk-Kazanç Yönetimi ve Finansal Performans İlişkisi. *Muhasebe ve Denetime Bakis*, *17*(51), 15–40.

Kay, J. (2019). The Concept of the Corporation. *Business History*, *61*(7), 1129–1143. doi:10.1080/00076791.2018.1509956

Kennedy, M., Elcock, M., Ellis, D., & Tall, G. (2017). Pre-hospital and retrieval medicine: Clinical governance and workforce models. *EMA -. Emergency Medicine Australasia*, *29*(4), 467–469. doi:10.1111/1742-6723.12776 PMID:28378954

Khaddafi, M., Wahyuddin, Heikal, M., Falahuddin, & Maulida, R. (2018). Effect of corporate governance mechanism, independence and management of earnings integrity of financial statements (in manufacturing companies listed on the stock exchange). *Quality - Access to Success*, *19*(164), 94–97.

Khan, M., & Watts, R. L. (2009). Estimation and empirical properties of a firm-year measure of accounting conservatism. *Journal of Accounting and Economics*, *48*(2-3), 132–150. doi:10.1016/j.jacceco.2009.08.002

Khan, S. N., Yaseen, M. N., Mustafa, F., & Abbasi, S. (2019). The Interaction Effect of Financial Leverage on the Relationship Between Board Attributes and Firm Performance; Evidence of Non-financial Listed Companies of Pakistan. *Journal of Accounting and Finance in Emerging Economies*, *5*(1), 115–122. doi:10.26710/jafee.v5i1.681

Kholeif, A. (2008). CEO duality and accounting-based performance in Egyptian listed companies: A re-examination of agency theory predictions. In *Corporate governance in less developed and emerging economies* (pp. 65–96). Emerald Group Publishing Limited.

Kiel, G. C., & Nicholson, G. J. (2003). Board composition and corporate performance: How the Australian experience informs contrasting theories of corporate governance. *Corporate Governance*, *11*(3), 189–205. doi:10.1111/1467-8683.00318

Kim, I., & Venkatachalam, M. (2011). Are sin stocks paying the price for accounting sins? *Journal of Accounting, Auditing & Finance*, *26*(2), 415–442. doi:10.1177/0148558X11401222

Kim, Y., Park, M., & Wier, B. (2012). Is earnings quality associated with corporate social responsibility? *The Accounting Review*, *87*(3), 761–796. doi:10.2308/accr-10209

Kirzner, I. (1973). *Competition and Entrepreneurship*. University of Chicago Press.

Klapper, L., Laeven, L., & Rajan, R. (2006). Entry regulation as a barrier to entrepreneurship. *Journal of Financial Economics*, *82*(3), 591–629. doi:10.1016/j.jfineco.2005.09.006

Klein, A. (2002). Audit committee, board of director characteristics, and earnings management. *Journal of Accounting and Economics*, *33*(3), 375–400. doi:10.1016/S0165-4101(02)00059-9

Klemp, G. Jr. (2005). *Leadership skills. Nursing administration and leadership: theory and practice*. Artmed.

Knickman, J. R., & Snell, E. K. (2002). The 2030 problem: Caring for ageing baby boomers. *Health Services Research*, *37*(4), 849–884. doi:10.1034/j.1600-0560.2002.56.x PMID:12236388

Koh, P. S. (2003). On the association between institutional ownership and aggressive corporate earnings management in Australia. *The British Accounting Review*, *35*(2), 105–128. doi:10.1016/S0890-8389(03)00014-3

Kosuch, S., Le Bodic, P., Leung, J., & Lisser, A. (2012). On a stochastic bilevel programming problem. *Networks*, *59*(1), 107–116. doi:10.1002/net.20482

Kothari, S. P., Leone, A. J., & Wasley, C. E. (2005). Performance matched discretionary accrual measures. *Journal of Accounting and Economics*, *39*(1), 163–197. doi:10.1016/j.jacceco.2004.11.002

Kouloukoui, D., de Oliveira Marinho, M. M., da Silva Gomes, S. M., de Jong, P., Kiperstok, A., & Torres, E. A. (2020). The impact of the board of directors on business climate change management: Case of Brazilian companies. *Mitigation and Adaptation Strategies for Global Change*, *25*(1), 127–147. doi:10.100711027-019-09864-7

Kousenidis, D. V., Ladas, A. C., & Negakis, C. I. (2013). The effects of the European debt crisis on earnings quality. *International Review of Financial Analysis*, *30*, 351–362. doi:10.1016/j.irfa.2013.03.004

Krafft, J., Qu, Y., Quatraro, F., & Ravix, J.-L. (2014). Corporate governance, value and performance of firms: New empirical results on convergence from a large international database. *Industrial and Corporate Change*, *23*(2), 361–397. doi:10.1093/icc/dtt007

Krishnan, G. V. (2003). Audit Quality and the Pricing of Discretionary Accruals. *Auditing*, *22*(1), 109–126. doi:10.2308/aud.2003.22.1.109

Krishnan, G. V., & Visvanathan, G. (2008). Does the SOX definition of an accounting expert matter? The association between audit committee directors' accounting expertise and accounting conservatism. *Contemporary Accounting Research*, *25*(3), 827–858. doi:10.1506/car.25.3.7

Krishnan, J. (2005). Audit committee quality and internal control: An empirical analysis. *The Accounting Review*, *80*(2), 649–675. doi:10.2308/accr.2005.80.2.649

Krismiaji, P. M., & Prabhata, A. (2019). Corporate Governance, Earnings Management, and Economic Value Added Indonesian Evidence. *KnE Social Sciences*, 182-199.

Kuan, T. H., Li, C. S., & Chu, S. H. (2011). Cash holdings and corporate governance in family-controlled firms. *Journal of Business Research*, *64*(7), 757–764. doi:10.1016/j.jbusres.2010.07.004

Kuek, C. Y. (2015, June). *Shareholder activism through exit and voice mechanisms in Malaysia: A comparison with the Australian experience*. Research Gate.

Kuek, C. Y. (2015, June). Shareholder activism through exit and voice mechanisms in Malaysia: A comparison with the Australian experience. *Research Gate*, *26*(2), 1–179.

Kukah, M. A., Amidu, M., & Abor, J. Y. (2016). Corporate governance mechanisms and accounting information quality of listed firms in Ghana. *African Journal of Accounting. Auditing and Finance*, *5*(1), 38–58.

Kula, V. (2005). The impact of the roles, structure and process of boards on firm performance: Evidence from Turkey. *Corporate Governance*, *13*(2), 265–276. doi:10.1111/j.1467-8683.2005.00421.x

Kulkarni, S. S., Barnato, A. E., Rosengart, M. R., Fischhoff, B., Angus, D. C., Yealy, D. M., Wallace, D. J., & Mohan, D. (2019). Does preexisting practice modify how video games recalibrate physician heuristics in trauma triage? *The Journal of Surgical Research*, *242*, 55–61. doi:10.1016/j.jss.2019.04.013 PMID:31071605

Kumari, S. S. (2008). Multicollinearity: Estimation and elimination. *Journal of Contemporary Research in Management*, *3*(1), 87–95.

Kumar, P., & Zattoni, A. (2013). Corporate governance, board of directors, and firm performance'. *Corporate Governance*, *21*(4), 311–313. doi:10.1111/corg.12032

Kumar, S. (2016). Corporate governance and firm performance in Indian listed IT companies. *Corporate Governance*, *2*(10), 219–230.

Kuntz, L., Pulm, J., & Wittland, M. (2016). Hospital ownership, decisions on supervisory board characteristics, and financial performance. *Health Care Management Review*, *41*(2), 165–176. doi:10.1097/HMR.0000000000000066 PMID:25978002

Kusnadi, Y. (2011). Do corporate governance mechanisms matter for cash holdings and firm value? *Pacific-Basin Finance Journal*, *19*(5), 554–570. doi:10.1016/j.pacfin.2011.04.002

Kwakernaak, H. (1978). Fuzzy random variables—I. Definitions and theorems. *Information Sciences*, *15*(1), 1–29. doi:10.1016/0020-0255(78)90019-1

Kwakernaak, H. (1979). Fuzzy random variables—II. Algorithms and examples for the discrete case. *Information Sciences*, *17*(3), 253–278. doi:10.1016/0020-0255(79)90020-3

Kwan, J. H., & Lau, W. Y. (2019). The Effects of Country-Level Governance and Corporate Cash Holdings: Evidence from Hospitality Firms in ASEAN-5. *Humanities (Washington)*, *7*(3), 123–140. doi:10.18488/journal.73.2019.73.123.140

Kyaw, K., Olugbode, M., & Petracci, B. (2015). Does gender diverse board mean less earnings management? *Finance Research Letters*, *14*, 135–141. doi:10.1016/j.frl.2015.05.006

La Porta, R. F. L.-d.-S. (2002, June). Investor protection and corporate valuation. *The Journal of Finance*, *57*(3), 1147-1170. Retrieved from https://onlinelibrary.wiley.com/doi/full/10.1111/1540-6261.00457

La Porta, R., Lopez-de-Silanes, F., & Shleifer, A. (1999). Corporate ownership around the world. *The Journal of Finance*, *54*(2), 471–517. doi:10.1111/0022-1082.00115

La Porta, R., Lopez-de-Silanes, F., Shleifer, A., & Vishny, R. (2000). Investor protection and corporate governance. *Journal of Financial Economics*, *58*(1-2), 3–27. doi:10.1016/S0304-405X(00)00065-9

La Porta, R., Lopez-de-Silanes, F., Shleifer, A., & Vishny, R. W. (1998). Law and Finance. *Journal of Political Economy*, *106*(6), 1113–1155. doi:10.1086/250042

Labhane, N. B., & Mahakud, J. (2016). Determinants of dividend policy of Indian companies: A panel data analysis. *Paradigm, 20*(1), 36–55. doi:10.1177/0971890716637698

Lafond, R., & Watts, R. L. (2008). The information role of conservatism. *The Accounting Review, 83*(2), 447–478. doi:10.2308/accr.2008.83.2.447

Lai, T., Lei, A. C. H., & Song, F. M. (2019). The impact of corporate fraud on director-interlocked firms: Evidence from bank loans. *Journal of Business Finance & Accounting, 46*(1-2), 32–67. doi:10.1111/jbfa.12362

Lakhal, F., Aguir, A., Lakhal, N., & Malek, A. (2015). Do women on boards and in top management reduce earnings management? Evidence in France. *Journal of Applied Business Research, 31*(3), 1107–1118. doi:10.19030/jabr.v31i3.9236

Lal, P. (2019). Agency costs, corporate governance and the Fiji Sugar Corporation. *Pacific Economic Bulletin, 21*(2), 70–93.

Lang, H. P., René, M., Stulz, L., & Walkling, R. A. (1991). A test of the free cash flow hypothesis: The case of Bidder returns. *Journal of Financial Economics, 29*(2), 315–335. doi:10.1016/0304-405X(91)90005-5

Lang, M., Lins, K. V., & Maffett, M. (2012). Transparency, liquidity, and valuation: International evidence on when transparency matters most. *Journal of Accounting Research, 50*(3), 729–774. doi:10.1111/j.1475-679X.2012.00442.x

Larcker, D., Richardson, S., & Tuna, A. (2005). *How important is corporate governance?* SSRN Working Paper.

Lee, S., & Kim, W. G. (2009). EVA, refined EVA, MVA, or traditional performance measures for the hospitality industry? *International Journal of Hospitality Management, 28*(3), 439–445. doi:10.1016/j.ijhm.2009.01.004

Lefort, F., & Urzua, F. (2008). Board independence, firm performance and ownership concentration: Evidence from Chile. *Journal of Business Research, 61*(6), 615–622. doi:10.1016/j.jbusres.2007.06.036

Lehn, K., & Poulsen, A. (1989). Free Cash Flow and Stockholder Gains in Going Private Transactions. *The Journal of Finance, 44*(3), 771–787. doi:10.1111/j.1540-6261.1989.tb04390.x

Leitterstorf, M. P., & Rau, S. B. (2014). Socioemotional wealth and IPO underpricing of family firms. *Strategic Management Journal, 35*(5), 751–760. doi:10.1002mj.2236

Lel, U. (2019). The role of foreign institutional investors in restraining earnings management activities across countries. *Journal of International Business Studies, 50*(6), 895–922. doi:10.105741267-018-0195-z

Lemmon, M. L. K. L. (2001, April). Ownership structure, corporate governance, and firm value: Evidence from the East Asian financial crisis. *The Journal of Finance, 58*(4), 1445-1468. Retrieved from https://deepblue.lib.umich.edu/bitstream/handle/2027.42/39777/wp393.pdf?sequence=3

Lemmon, M. L., Roberts, M. R., & Zender, J. F. (2008). Back to the beginning: Persistence and the crosssection of corporate capital structure. *The Journal of Finance, 63*(4), 1575–1608. doi:10.1111/j.1540-6261.2008.01369.x

Lesmana, C. R. A., Gani, R. A., Hasan, I., Sulaiman, A. S., & Lesmana, L. A. (2017). Therapeutic interventional endoscopic ultrasound based on rare cases in indonesia: A single-center experience in unselected patients. *Case Reports in Gastroenterology, 11*(1), 72–77. doi:10.1159/000456606 PMID:28611556

Lethbridge, E. (1997). Corporate governance. *BNDES Journal, 4*, 209–231.

Leuz, C., Nanda, D., & Wysocki, D. (2003). Earnings management and investor protection: An international comparison. *Journal of Financial Economics, 69*(3), 505–527. doi:10.1016/S0304-405X(03)00121-1

Levitt, A. (1998). Speech by SEC Chairman: The numbers game. Remarks delivered at the NYU Center for Law and Business, New York, NY.

Liao, Q., & Ouyang, B. (2019). Shareholder litigation risk and real earnings management: A causal inference. *Review of Accounting and Finance*, *18*(4), 557–588. doi:10.1108/RAF-06-2018-0122

Li, B., Jiang, C., Zhang, G., & He, Y. (2018). Management and performance evaluation of DSR aggregator based on a bi-level optimization model. *IEEJ Transactions on Electrical and Electronic Engineering*, *13*(3), 432–441. doi:10.1002/tee.22584

Liew, P. K. (2008). The (Perceived) roles of corporate governance reforms in Malaysia: The views of corporate practitioners. *Corporate governance in less developed and emerging economies*, 455-482.

Liew, P. (2007, September). Corporate governance reforms in Malaysia: The key leading players' perspectives. *International Review (Steubenville, Ohio)*, *15*(5), 724–740. https://d1wqtxts1xzle7.cloudfront.net/52122942/Corporate_Governance_Reforms_in_Malaysia20170312-15935-kkvki3.pdf?1489326252=&response-content-disposition=inline%3B+filename%3DCorporate_Governance_Reforms_in_Malaysia.pdf&Expires=1605775918&Signature=WouDsU

Lim, R. (2011). Are corporate governance attributes associated with accounting conservatism? *Accounting and Finance*, *51*(4), 1007–1030. doi:10.1111/j.1467-629X.2010.00390.x

Linck, J. S., Netter, J., & Shu, T. (2013). Can managers use discretionary accruals to ease financial constraints? Evidence from discretionary accruals prior to investment. *The Accounting Review*, *88*(6), 2117–2143. doi:10.2308/accr-50537

Lin, J. W., & Hwang, M. I. (2010). Audit quality, corporate governance, and earnings management: A meta-analysis. *International Journal of Auditing*, *14*(1), 57–77. doi:10.1111/j.1099-1123.2009.00403.x

Lin, Q. L., Liu, L., Liu, H. C., & Wang, D. J. (2013). Integrating hierarchical balanced scorecard with fuzzy linguistic for evaluating operating room performance in hospitals. *Expert Systems with Applications*, *40*(6), 1917–1924. doi:10.1016/j.eswa.2012.10.007

Lin, Y. F. (2005). Corporate governance, leadership structure and CEO compensation: Evidence from Taiwan. *Corporate Governance*, *13*(6), 824–835.

Lin, Z., Liu, M., & Noronha, C. (2016). The impact of corporate governance on informative earnings management in the Chinese market. *Abacus*, *52*(3), 568–609.

Li, S., Fu, H., Wen, J., & Chang, C. P. (2020). Separation of ownership and control for Chinese listed firms: Effect on the cost of debt and the moderating role of bank competition. *Journal of Asian Economics*, *67*, 101179. doi:10.1016/j.asieco.2020.101179

Li, S., Selover, D., & Stein, M. (2011). "Keep silent and make money": Institutional patterns of earnings management in China. *Journal of Asian Economics*, *22*(5), 369–382. doi:10.1016/j.asieco.2011.06.003

Lisboa, I. (2016). Impact of financial crisis and family control on earning management of Portuguese listed firms. *European Journal of Family Business*, *6*(2), 118–131. doi:10.1016/j.ejfb.2017.06.002

Lisboa, I., & Esperança, J. P. (2010). Ownership structure and performance: Evidence from Portugal. *Corporate Ownership & Control*, *7*(3), 25–32. doi:10.22495/cocv7i3p2

Lisboa, I., Guilherme, M. C., & Teixeira, N. (2020). Corporate governance practices in Portugal. *Corporate Law & Governance Review*, *2*(1), 42–54. doi:10.22495/clgrv2i1p4

Listokin, Y. (2010). If you give shareholders power, do they use it? An empirical analysis. *Journal of Institutional and Theoretical Economics*, *166*(1), 38–53. doi:10.1628/093245610790711438

Li, T., Zhao, X., & Zhao, A. (2019). Voting with hands, earnings management and corporate governance. *Review of Accounting and Finance, 18*(2), 178–197. doi:10.1108/RAF-02-2016-0016

Liu, C., Chung, C. Y., Sul, H. K., & Wang, K. (2018). Does hometown advantage matter? the case of institutional blockholder monitoring on earnings management in korea. *Journal of International Business Studies, 49*(2), 196–221. doi:10.105741267-017-0093-9

Liu, L., Zhang, Y., Da, C., Huang, Z., & Wang, M. (2020). Optimal allocation of distributed generation and electric vehicle charging stations based on intelligent algorithm and bi-level programming. *International Transactions on Electrical Energy Systems, 30*(6), e12366. doi:10.1002/2050-7038.12366

Liu, Q., & Lu, Z. J. (2007). Corporate governance and earnings management in the Chinese listed companies: A tunneling perspective. *Journal of Corporate Finance, 13*(5), 881–906. doi:10.1016/j.jcorpfin.2007.07.003

Liu, Y., Miletkov, M. K., Wei, Z., & Yang, T. (2015). Board independence and firm performance in China. *Journal of Corporate Finance, 30*, 223–244. doi:10.1016/j.jcorpfin.2014.12.004

Liu, Y., Wei, Z., & Xie, F. (2014). Do women directors improve firm performance in China? *Journal of Corporate Finance, 28*, 169–184. doi:10.1016/j.jcorpfin.2013.11.016

Li, V. (2019). The effect of real earnings management on the persistence and informativeness of earnings. *The British Accounting Review, 51*(4), 402–423.

Li, W., & Zhang, R. (2010). Corporate Social Responsibility, Ownership Structure and Political Interference: Evidence from China. *Journal of Business Ethics, 96*(4), 631–645. doi:10.100710551-010-0488-z

LiZ. F.PatelS.RamaniS. (2019). The role of mutual funds in corporate social responsibility. doi:10.2139srn.3366100

Loasby, B. J. (2015). Ronald Coase's Theory of the Firm and the Scope of Economics. *Journal of Institutional Economics, 11*(2), 245–264. doi:10.1017/S1744137414000265

Lombardo, D., & Pagano, M. (2006). *Legal Determinants of the Return on Equity, Corporate and Institutional Transparency for Economic Growth in Europe*. SSRN Working Paper.

Lopes, P. T., & Rodrigues, L. L. (2007). Accounting for financial instruments: An analysis of the determinants of disclosure in the Portuguese stock exchange. *The International Journal of Accounting, 42*, 25-56.

Lopes, A. I., & Reis, L. (2019). Are provisions and contingent liabilities priced by the market? An exploratory study in Portugal and the UK. *Meditari Accountancy Research, 27*(2), 228–257. doi:10.1108/MEDAR-09-2017-0212

Lopes, I. T., Ferraz, D. P., & Martins, M. M. (2016). The influence of diversity on boards profitability: An overview across Iberian non-financial listed companies. *Corporate Ownership & Control, 13*(2), 454–460. doi:10.22495/cocv13i2c2p6

LRBM. (2014). Kuala Lumpur Stock Exchange (KLSE) Listing Requirements 2001. Kuala Lumpur, Malaysia: LRBM.

Lüleci, N. E., Gemlik, H. N., Bektas, G., & Manioglu, Y. (2015). The awareness of experience innovation and an application in private hospitals. *JPMA. The Journal of the Pakistan Medical Association, 65*(10), 1108–1111. PMID:26440843

Lumpkin, G. T., & Dess, G. G. (2001). Linking two dimensions of entrepreneurial orientation to firm performance: The moderating role of environment and industry life cycle. *Journal of Business Venturing, 16*(5), 429–451. doi:10.1016/S0883-9026(00)00048-3

Luo, L., Li, J., Liu, C., & Shen, W. (2019). Using machine-learning methods to support health-care professionals in making admission decisions. *The International Journal of Health Planning and Management, 34*(2), e1236–e1246. doi:10.1002/hpm.2769 PMID:30957270

Machlup, F., & Mansfield, U. (1983). *The study of information, interdisciplinary messages.* John Wiley & Sons.

MacVane Phipps, F. (2020). Challenges of 21st-century health governance. *International Journal of Health Governance, 25*(1), 12–18. doi:10.1108/IJHG-12-2019-0080

Madaleno, M., Vieira, E. S., & Teodósio, J. P. (2019). Corporate Female Leadership Effects Considering PSI20 and IBEX35 Companies' Performance. In Handbook of Research on Women in Management and the Global Labor Market (pp. 280-301). IGI Global. doi:10.4018/978-1-5225-9171-9.ch014

Madaleno, M., & Vieira, E. (2018). Volatility analysis of returns and risk: Family versus nonfamily firms. *Quantitative Finance and Economics, 2*(2), 348–372. doi:10.3934/QFE.2018.2.348

Mahadeo, J. D., Soobaroyen, T., & Hanuman, V. O. (2012). Board composition and financial performance: Uncovering the effects of diversity in an emerging economy. *Journal of Business Ethics, 105*(3), 375–388.

Mahenthiran, H. M., Rahman, R. A., & Hamid, N. A. (2006). Agency costs as a factor in the suspension of companies from the Kuala Lumpur stock exchange. *Journal of Contemporary Accounting & Economics, 2*(1), 99–121. doi:10.1016/S1815-5669(10)70018-7

Maijoor, S. J., & Vanstraelen, A. (2006). Earnings management within Europe: The effects of member state audit environment, audit firm quality and international capital markets. *Accounting and Business Research, 36*(1), 33–52. doi:10.1080/00014788.2006.9730005

Malaysia, B. (2015b, October). *Main market listing requirement.* Retrieved 2020, from Transactions: http://asklisting.bursamalaysia.com:8080/MainLR/Pages/MainChapter10.aspx

Malaysia, B. (2020). *Bursa Malaysia.* Retrieved from Listing on Bursa Malaysia: https://www.bursamalaysia.com/listing/why_bursa_malaysia/your_listing_destination

Malaysia, B. (n.d.a). *Bursa Malaysia.* Retrieved from Listing on Bursa Malaysia: https://www.bursamalaysia.com/listing/why_bursa_malaysia/your_listing_destination

Malaysia, B. (n.d.b). *Related party transaction requirements.* Retrieved from Main Market Listing Requirements: https://www.bursamalaysia.com/sites/5bb54be15f36ca0af339077a/content_entry5ce3b5005b711a1764454c1a/5ce3c84a5b711a13e3b4bbfa/files/MainApp2_RPT-final_22Jan2015_.pdf?1570701456

Malaysia, B. N. (2013). *Guidelines on related party.* Bank Negara Malaysia.

Malaysia. L. O. (Incorporating latest amendment - Act A1299 /2007). ACT 125, COMPANIES ACT 1965 (REVISED - 1973), Incorporating the latest amendment - Act A1299 /2007. Malaysian Government. Malaysia: Malaysian government.

Malaysia, B. (2015a). *Related party transaction requirements, main market listing requirements. Busra Malaysia.* Busra Malaysia. Retrieved from https://www.bursamalaysia.com/sites/5bb54be15f36ca0af339077a/content_entry5ce3b5005b711a1764454c1a/5ce3c84a5b711a13e3b4bbfa/files/MainApp2_RPT-final_22Jan2015_.pdf?1570701456

Malik, M. (2015). Value-enhancing capabilities of CSR: A brief review of contemporary literature. *Journal of Business Ethics, 127*(2), 419–438. doi:10.100710551-014-2051-9

Mang'Unyi, E. E. (2011). Ownership structure and Corporate Governance and its effects on performance: A case of selected Banks in Kenya. *International Journal of Business Administration, 2*(3), 2.

Mao, Y., & Renneboog, L. (2015). Do managers manipulate earnings prior to management buyouts? *Journal of Corporate Finance, 35*, 43–61. doi:10.1016/j.jcorpfin.2015.08.005

Marcelo, J. L. M., & Quirós, M. D. M. M. (2006). The role of an illiquidity risk factor in asset pricing: Empirical evidence from the Spanish stock market. *The Quarterly Review of Economics and Finance, 46*(2), 254–267.

Marchetti, P., Siciliano, G., & Ventoruzzo, M. (2017). Dissenting directors. *European Business Organization Law Review, 18*(4), 659–700. doi:10.100740804-017-0093-z

Marchini, P. L., Mazza, T., & Medioli, A. (2018). Related party transactions, corporate governance and earnings management. *Corporate Governance, 18*(6), 1124–1146. doi:10.1108/CG-11-2017-0271

Marianne Bertrand, P. M. (2002, February). Ferreting out tunneling: An application to Indian business groups. *The Quarterly Jounral of Economics, 117*(1), 121-148.

Markazi-Moghaddam, N., Arab, M., Ravaghi, H., Rashidian, A., Khatibi, T., & Zargar Balaye Jame, S. A. (2016). Knowledge Map for Hospital Performance Concept: Extraction and Analysis: A Narrative Review Article. *Iranian Journal of Public Health, 45*(7), 843–854. PMID:27516990

Market, T. E. (2013). *Patimas audit reveals irregularities*. Academic Press.

Market, T. E. (2014, March 19). *Patimas to be delisted from Bursa on Friday*. Retrieved from Patimas to be delisted from Bursa on Friday: https://www.theedgemarkets.com/article/patimas-be-delisted-bursa-friday

Marshall, A. (1920). *Principles of Economics*. Macmillan.

Martani, D., & Saputra, Y. E. (2009). The impact of corporate governance to the economic value added listed company in BEI 2003-2004. *China-USA Business Review, 8*(3), 26–40.

Martínez-Sola, C., García-Teruel, P. J., & Martínez-Solano, P. (2013). Corporate cash holding and firm value. *Applied Economics, 45*(2), 161–170. doi:10.1080/00036846.2011.595696

Martins, M. M., Morais, A. I., Isidro, H., & Laureano, R. (2018). Intellectual Capital Disclosure: The Portuguese Case. *Journal of the Knowledge Economy, 9*(4), 1224–1245. doi:10.100713132-016-0412-6

Martín-Ugedo, J. F., & Minguez-Vera, A. (2014). Firm Performance and Women on the Board: Evidence from Spanish Small and Medium-Sized Enterprises. *Feminist Economics, 20*(3), 136–162. doi:10.1080/13545701.2014.895404

Martín-Ugedo, J. F., Minguez-Vera, A., & Rossi, F. (2019). Female directors and firm performance in Italian and Spanish listed firms Does masculinity matter? *Academia (Caracas), 32*(3), 411–436. doi:10.1108/ARLA-06-2018-0124

Marzuki, M. M., Haji-Abdullah, N. M., Othman, R., Abdul Wahab, E. A., & Harymawan, I. (2019). Audit committee characteristics, board diversity, and fraudulent financial reporting in Malaysia. *Asian Academy of Management Journal, 24*(2), 143–167. doi:10.21315/aamj2019.24.2.7

MASB. (2012). *First-time Adoption of Malaysian Financial*. Retrieved from http://masb.org.my/article.php?id=270

Matteo, P., & Francesco, P. (2018). Earnings management in developing countries. the case of brazilian real estate industry. Academy of Accounting and Financial Studies Journal, 22(1).

Matteo, P., & Francesco, P. (2018). Earnings Management in Developing Countries. The Case of Brazilian Real Estate Industry. *Academy of Accounting and Financial Studies Journal, 22*(1), 1–12.

Maury, B. (2006, January). Family ownership and firm performance: Empirical evidence from Western European corporations. *Journal of Corporate Finance, 12*(2), 321–341. https://www.sciencedirect.com/science/article/pii/S0929119905000404

McNichols, M. F. (2000). Research design issues in earnings management studies. *Journal of Accounting and Public Policy*, *19*(4-5), 313–345. doi:10.1016/S0278-4254(00)00018-1

McNichols, M. F. (2002). Discussion of the Quality of Accruals and Earnings: The Role of Accrual Estimation Errors. *The Accounting Review*, *77*(1), 61–69. https://aaapubs.org/doi/10.2308/accr.2002.77.s-1.61

McNichols, M. F. (2002). Discussion of the quality of accruals and earnings: The role of accrual estimation errors. *The Accounting Review*, *77*(s-1), 61–69. doi:10.2308/accr.2002.77.s-1.61

Melis, A. (2000). Corporate governance in Italy. *Corporate Governance*, *8*(4), 347–355. doi:10.1111/1467-8683.00213

Melis, A., Carta, S., & Gaia, S. (2012). Executive remuneration in blockholder-dominated firms. How do Italian firms use stock options? *The Journal of Management and Governance*, *16*(3), 511–541. doi:10.100710997-010-9163-0

Mellado, C., & Saona, P. (2020). Real earnings management and corporate governance: A study of latin america. *Economic Research-Ekonomska Istrazivanja*, *33*(1), 2229–2268. doi:10.1080/1331677X.2019.1691930

Memiş, M. Ü. & Çetenak, E. H. (2012). Kurumsal Yönetimin Kazanç Yönetimi Uygulamaları Üzerine Etkisi: İmkb'de İşlem Gören Şirketler Üzerine Uygulama. *Çukurova Üniversitesi Sosyal Bilimler Enstitüsü Dergisi*, *21*(3), 205-224.

Meo, F. D., Lara, J. M. G., & Surroca, J. M. (2017). Managerial entrenchment and earnings management. *Journal of Accounting and Public Policy*, *36*(5), 399–414. doi:10.1016/j.jaccpubpol.2017.07.003

Merchant, K. A. (1990). The effects of financial controls on data manipulation and management myopia. *Accounting, Organizations and Society*, *15*(4), 297–313. doi:10.1016/0361-3682(90)90021-L

Merigó, J. M., & Yang, J. B. (2017). Accounting research: A bibliometric analysis. *Australian Accounting Review*, *80*(27), 71–100. doi:10.1111/auar.12109

Merika, A., Syriopoulos, T., & Negakis, C. (2007). Highly leveraged firms and corporate performance in distressed industries. European Journal of Economics. *Finance and Administrative Sciences*, *8*, 93–101.

Mertzanis, C., Basuony, M. A., & Mohamed, E. K. (2019). Social institutions, corporate governance and firm-performance in the MENA region. *Research in International Business and Finance*, *48*, 75–96. doi:10.1016/j.ribaf.2018.12.005

Mikkelson, W. H., & Partch, M. M. (2003). Do persistent large cash reserves hinder performance? *Journal of Financial and Quantitative Analysis*, *38*(2), 275–294. doi:10.2307/4126751

Miller, I. L.-M. (2006, March). *Family governance and firm performance: Agency, stewardship, and capabilities*. SAGE.

Miller, D., Breton-Miller, I. L., & Lester, R. H. (2013). Family firm governance, strategic conformity, and performance: Institutional vs. strategic perspectives. *Organization Science*, *24*(1), 189–209. doi:10.1287/orsc.1110.0728

Miller, D., Le Breton-Miller, I., Lester, R. H., & Cannella, A. A. Jr. (2007). Are family firms really superior performers? *Journal of Corporate Finance*, *13*(5), 829–858. doi:10.1016/j.jcorpfin.2007.03.004

Mindzak, J., & Zeng, T. (2018). The impact of pyramid ownership on earnings management. *Asian Review of Accounting*, *26*(2), 208–224. doi:10.1108/ARA-11-2016-0130

Mio, C., Soerger Zaro, E., & Fasan, M. (2020). Are loyalty shares an effective antidote against short-termism? empirical evidence from italy. *Business Strategy and the Environment*, *29*(4), 1785–1796. doi:10.1002/bse.2473

Miralles-Marcelo, J. L., Miralles-Quirós, M. M., & Lisboa, I. (2014). The impact of family control on firm performance: Evidence from Portugal and Spain. *Journal of Family Business Strategy*, *5*(2), 156–168. doi:10.1016/j.jfbs.2014.03.002

Miralles-Quirós, M., Miralles-Quirós, J., & Gonçalves, V. (2018). The value relevance of environmental, social, and governance performance: The Brazilian case. *Sustainability, 10*(3), 574. doi:10.3390u10030574

Mirsharafoddini, H. S., Farhani, M. G., Hajiha, Z., Yahaghi, E., Honarvar, M. S., Khodaverdi, E., Behnood, V., & Tousi, E. F. (2014). Characteristics of Board of directors and creating Economic Value Added: Evidence from Iran. *International Journal of Current Research and Academic Review, 2*(3), 149–162.

Mishra, M., & Malhotra, A. (2016). Earnings Management Practices in Indian Companies: A Cross-Sectional Analisis. *Journal of Modern Accounting and Auditing, 12*(6), 295–305. doi:10.17265/1548-6583/2016.06.001

Mishra, R. K., & Jhunjhunwala, S. (2013). *Diversity and the effective corporate board.* Academic Press.

Mishra, S., & Dasgupta, R. (2019). Cross-impact of leverage and firm performance: Developed vs frontier bank-based economies. *Managerial Finance, 45*(8), 982–1000. doi:10.1108/MF-09-2018-0435

Moardi, M., Salehi, M., Poursasan, S., & Molavi, H. (2019). Relationship between earnings management, CEO compensation, and stock return on tehran stock exchange. *International Journal of Organization Theory and Behavior, 23*(1), 1–22. doi:10.1108/IJOTB-12-2018-0133

Moche, S. W. (2014). *Corporate governance and firm performance of listed family- owned firms in Kenya* (Doctoral dissertation).

Mohammadkarim, B., Jamil, S., Pejman, H., Seyyed, M. H., & Mostafa, N. (2011). Combining multiple indicators to assess hospital performance in Iran using the Pabon Lasso Model. *The Australasian Medical Journal, 4*(4), 175–179. doi:10.4066/AMJ.2011.620 PMID:23393508

Mohammed, N. F., Ahmed, K., & Ji, X. D. (2017). Accounting conservatism, corporate governance and political connections. *Asian Review of Accounting, 25*(2), 288–318. doi:10.1108/ARA-04-2016-0041

Mohan, D., Wallace, D. J., Kerti, S. J., Angus, D. C., Rosengart, M. R., Barnato, A. E., Yealy, D. M., Fischhoff, B., Chang, C-C., & Kahn, J. M. (2019). Association of practitioner interfacility triage performance with outcomes for severely injured patients with fee-for-service medicare insurance. *JAMA Surgery, 154*(12).

MohanA.ChandramohanS. (2018) Impact of Corporate Governance On Firm Performance: Empirical Evidence from India, Available at SSRN: https://ssrn.com/abstract=3133491

Moll, M. C., Decavel, F., & Merlet, C. (2009). A quality evaluation tableau for health institutions: An educational tool [Tableau de bord d'évaluation du système qualité des pôles en établissement de santé: un outil pédagogique.]. *Recherche en Soins Infirmiers, 98*, 19–27. doi:10.3917/rsi.098.0019 PMID:19947122

Monks, R., & Minow, N. (1995). *Corporate governance.* Basil Blackwell.

Mora, A., & Walker, M. (2015). The implications of research on accounting conservatism for accounting standard setting. *Accounting and Business Research, 45*(5), 620–650. doi:10.1080/00014788.2015.1048770

Morck, R. B. Y. (2003, October). Agency problems in large family business groups. *SAGE, 27*(4), 367-382. Retrieved from https://journals.sagepub.com/doi/abs/10.1111/1540-8520.t01-1-00015

Morck, R., & Yeung, B. (2003). Agency problems in large family business groups. *Entrepreneurship Theory and Practice, 27*(4), 367–382. doi:10.1111/1540-8520.t01-1-00015

Morellec, E., Nikolov, B., & Zucchi, F. (2013). *Competition, cash holdings, and financing decisions.* Swiss Finance Institute Research Paper, 13-72.

Morlock, L. L., & Alexander, J. (1986). Models of Governance in Multi Hospital Systems Implications for Hospital and System-Level Decision. *Making. Medical Care, 24*(2). PMID:3796079

Morse. (2008). Entrepreneurs: Generating cash in a credit crunch. *Ivey Business Journal Online, 72*(6), 1.

Moscariello, N., Fera, P., & Cinque, E. (2020). The information content of discretionary accruals during systemic crises. *Journal of Applied Accounting Research, 21*(3), 455–476. doi:10.1108/JAAR-04-2018-0054

Moscariello, N., Pizzo, M., Govorun, D., & Kostyuk, A. (2019). Independent minority directors and firm value in a principal–principal agency setting: Evidence from Italy. *The Journal of Management and Governance, 23*(1), 165–194. doi:10.100710997-018-9421-0

Muda, I., Maulana, W., Siregar, H. S., & Indra, N. (2018). The analysis of effects of good corporate governance on earnings management in indonesia with panel data approach. *Indian Economic Review, 22*(2), 599–625.

Muda, I., Maulana, W., Siregar, H. S., & Indra, N. (2018). The analysis of effects of good corporate governance on earnings management in Indonesia with panel data approach. *Indian Economic Review, 22*(2), 599–625.

Mukhtaruddin, M., Zuryati, E., Robiani, B., & Saftiana, Y. (2018). Good corporate governance mechanism and earnings management: Study on manufacturing companies in indonesia stock exchange. *Journal of Applied Economic Sciences, 13*(8), 2298–2308. www.scopus.com

Mulford, C. W., & Comiskey, E. E. (2002). *The financial numbers game: detecting creative accounting practices*. John Wiley & Sons.

Munir, R. G. (2011). Related party transactions, family firms and firm performance: Some Malaysian evidence. *Corporate Governance Conference*.

Munisi, G., Hermes, N., & Randøy, T. (2014). Corporate boards and ownership structure: Evidence from Sub-Saharan Africa. *International Business Review, 23*(4), 785–796.

Musau, V. M., Waititu, A. G., & Wanjoya, A. K. (2015). Modeling panel data: Comparison of GLS estimation and robust covariance matrix estimation. *American Journal of Theoretical and Applied Statistics, 4*(3), 185–191. doi:10.11648/j.ajtas.20150403.25

Musteen, M., Datta, D. K., & Kemmerer, B. (2010). Corporate reputation: Do board characteristics matter? *British Journal of Management, 21*(2), 498–510.

Mutarindwa, S., Schäfer, D., & Stephan, A. (2020). Central banks' supervisory guidance on corporate governance and bank stability: Evidence from African countries. *Emerging Markets Review*.

Mutlu, C. C., Van Essen, M., Peng, M. W., Saleh, S. F., & Duran, P. (2018). Corporate governance in China: A meta-analysis. *Journal of Management Studies, 55*(6), 943–979. doi:10.1111/joms.12331

Myers, S. (1977). Determinants of corporate borrowing. *Journal of Financial Economics, 5*(2), 147–175. doi:10.1016/0304-405X(77)90015-0

Myers, S. C. (1984). The capital structure puzzle. *The Journal of Finance, 39*(3), 575–592. doi:10.2307/2327916

Myers, S. C., & Majluf, N. S. (1984). Corporate financing and investment decisions when firms have information that investors do not have. *Journal of Financial Economics, 13*(2), 187–221. doi:10.1016/0304-405X(84)90023-0

Naciti, V. (2019). Corporate governance and board of directors: The effect of a board composition on firm sustainability performance. *Journal of Cleaner Production, 237*, 117727. doi:10.1016/j.jclepro.2019.117727

Narang, S., & Kaur, M. (2014). Impact of firm-specific attributes on shareholder value creation of Indian companies: An empirical analysis. *Global Business Review*, *15*(4), 847–866. doi:10.1177/0972150914543422

Nasr, M. A., & Ntim, C. G. (2018). Corporate governance mechanisms and accounting conservatism: Evidence from Egypt. *Corporate Governance: The International Journal of Business in Society*, *18*(3), 386–407. doi:10.1108/CG-05-2017-0108

Navarro, T. M., Durán, F. M., & Santos, J. L. (2017). A regional competitiveness index for Spain [Un índice de competitividad regional para España]. *Revista De Estudios Regionales*, *109*, 67–94.

Nesbitt, S. L. (1994). Long-term rewards from shareholder activism: A study of the "CalPERS effect. *Journal of Applied Corporate Finance*, *6*(4), 75–80. doi:10.1111/j.1745-6622.1994.tb00251.x

Neves, J. B., Shepherd, S., Cullen, D., Powles, T., Aitchison, M., & Tran, M. G. B. (2019). Performance and cost of a renal cancer specialist multidisciplinary team meeting: Results from 1500 discussions. *Journal of Clinical Urology*, *12*(4), 314–319. doi:10.1177/2051415819829309

Ng, B. S. (2012). Corporate governance: Golden parachute for minority shareholders. *Business (Atlanta, Ga.)*.

Ng, C. Y. (2005). An empirical study on the relationship between ownership and performance in a family-based corporate environment. *Journal of Accounting, Auditing & Finance*, *20*(2), 121–146.

Ngo, A., Duong, H., & Chen, A. (2016). The Effects of Covenant Violations on the Underpricing of Seasoned Equity Offerings and the Implied Cost of Equity Capital. *The Quarterly Journal of Finance*, *06*(01), 1–33. doi:10.1142/S2010139216400036

Nishizaki, I., Sakawa, M., & Katagiri, H. (2003). Stackelberg solutions to multiobjective two-level linear programming problems with random variable coefficients. *Central European Journal of Operations Research*, *11*(3).

Noman, M., Din, B. H., & Mustafa, F. (2019). The influence of corporate governance on cash holdings; Empirical evidence from Jordan. *Asian Journal of Multidisciplinary Studies*, *7*(3), 1–5.

Nowell, L. S., Norris, J. M., White, D. E., & Moules, N. J. (2017). Thematic analysis: seeking to meet the reliability criteria. *Int J Qual Meth.*, *16*(1).

Nsamzinshuti, A., Van Elslande, C., & Alassane, N. B. (2014). Managing hospital efficiency and effectiveness: Designing a hospital performance measurement system. *Proceedings of 2nd IEEE International Conference on Logistics Operations Management, GOL 2014*, 188-200. 10.1109/GOL.2014.6887440

Ntim, C. G. (2009). *Internal corporate governance structures and firm financial performance: evidence from South African listed firms* (Doctoral dissertation). University of Glasgow.

Nuber, C., Velte, P., & Hörisch, J. (2020). The curvilinear and time-lagging impact of sustainability performance on financial performance: Evidence from Germany. *Corporate Social Responsibility and Environmental Management*, *27*(1), 232–243. doi:10.1002/csr.1795

Obiyo, O. C., & Lenee, L. T. (2011). Corporate governance and firm performance in Nigeria. *IJEMR*, *1*(4), 1–12.

OECD. (2015). *G20/OECD Principles of Corporate Governance*. OECD Publishing. doi:10.1787/9789264236882-

Office, U. S. (2003, June). *By the Comptroller General of the United States*. Retrieved from Government Auditing Standards, 2003 Revision: https://www.gao.gov/assets/80/76730.pdf

Oh, W. Y., Chang, Y. K., & Jung, R. (2019). Board characteristics and corporate social responsibility: Does family involvement in management matter? *Journal of Business Research*, *103*, 23–33. doi:10.1016/j.jbusres.2019.05.028

Oh, W. Y., Chang, Y. K., & Kim, T. Y. (2018). Complementary or substitutive effects? Corporate governance mechanisms and corporate social responsibility. *Journal of Management, 44*(7), 2716–2739. doi:10.1177/0149206316653804

Okaily, J. A., Dixon, R., & Salama, A. (2019). Corporate governance quality and premature revenue recognition: Evidence from the UK. *International Journal of Managerial Finance, 15*(1), 79–99. doi:10.1108/IJMF-02-2018-0047

Olheten, E., Theoharakis, V., & Travlos, N. G. (2005). Faculty perceptions and readership patterns of finance journals: A global view. *Journal of Financial and Quantitative Analysis, 40*(1), 223–239. doi:10.1017/S0022109000001800

Oliveira, J. S., Azevedo, G. M. C., & Silva, M. J. P. C. (2019). Institutional and economic determinants of corporate social responsibility disclosure by banks: Institutional perspectives. *Meditari Accountancy Research, 27*(2), 196–227. doi:10.1108/MEDAR-01-2018-0259

Oliveira, J., Rodrigues, L. L., & Craig, R. (2011). Risk-related disclosures by non-finance companies: Portuguese practices and disclosure characteristics. *Managerial Auditing Journal, 26*(9), 817–839. doi:10.1108/02686901111171466

Oliveira, J., Serrasqueiro, R., & Mota, S. N. (2018). Determinants of risk reporting by Portuguese and Spanish non-finance companies. *European Business Review, 30*(3), 311–339. doi:10.1108/EBR-04-2017-0076

Omware, I. M., Atheru, G., & Jagongo, A. (2020). Corporate governance and financial performance of selected commercial banks listed at Nairobi Securities Exchange in Kenya. *International Academic Journal of Economics and Finance, 3*(5), 75–91.

Önder, Ş. (2012). *İşletmelerin Kar Yönetimi Uygulamalarında Kurumsal Yönetim Yapılarının Etkisi İMKB üzerine Bir Uygulama.* Basılmamış Doktara Tezi, Kütahya Üniversitesi.

Ongsakul, V., Jiraporn, P., & Kim, Y. S. (2020). The effect of earnings management on shareholder value and the role of board gender diversity: Evidence from terrorism. *Pacific Accounting Review, 32*(3), 323–334. Advance online publication. doi:10.1108/PAR-09-2019-0110

Opler, T., Pinkowitz, L., Stulz, R., & Williamson, R. (1999). The determinants and implications of corporate cash holdings. *Journal of Financial Economics, 52*(1), 3–46. doi:10.1016/S0304-405X(99)00003-3

Orazalin, N., Orazalin, N., Mahmood, M., Mahmood, M., & Lee, K. J. (2016). Corporate governance, financial crises and bank performance: Lessons from top Russian banks. *Corporate Governance: The International Journal of Business in Society, 16*(5), 798-814.

Orazalin, N. (2019). Board gender diversity, corporate governance, and earnings management: Evidence from an emerging market. *Gender in Management, 35*(1), 37–60. doi:10.1108/GM-03-2018-0027

Osma, G., & Noguer, B. (2007). The Effect of the Board Composition and its Monitoring Committees on Earnings Management: Evidence from Spain. *Corporate Governance, 15*(6), 1413–1430. doi:10.1111/j.1467-8683.2007.00654.x

Ouyang, W., & Hilsenrath, P. E. (2017). Merger & Acquisition and Capital Expenditure in Health Care. INQUIRY. *The Journal of Health Care Organization, Provision, and Financing, 54*, 004695801769227. doi:10.1177/0046958017692275

Owusu, A., & Weir, C. (2018). Agency costs, ownership structure and corporate governance mechanisms in Ghana. *International Journal of Accounting. Auditing and Performance Evaluation, 14*(1), 63–84. doi:10.1504/IJAAPE.2018.089414

Özcan, A. (2019). Audit Quality and Earnings Management: Evidence From Turkey. *International Journal of Economic & Administrative Studies, 23*, 67–78.

Pacheco, L. (2019). Performance vs. Family Ownership and Management: The Case of Portuguese Wine Firms. *Entrepreneurial Business and Economics Review, 7*(3), 7–24. doi:10.15678/EBER.2019.070301

Paim, J., Travassos, C., Almeida, C., Bahia, L., & MacInko, J. (2011). The brazilian health system: History, advances, and challenges. *Lancet*, *377*(9779), 1778–1797. doi:10.1016/S0140-6736(11)60054-8 PMID:21561655

Paiva, I. S., Lourenco, I. C., & Branco, M. C. (2016). Earnings management in family firms: Current state of knowledge and opportunities for future research. *Review of Accounting and Finance*, *15*(1), 85–100. doi:10.1108/RAF-06-2014-0065

Pamburai, H., Chamisa, E., Abdulla, C., & Smith, C. (2015). An analysis of corporate governance and company performance: A South African perspective. *South African Journal of Accounting Research*, *29*(2), 115–131. doi:10.1080/10291954.2015.1006482

Paniagua, J., Rivelles, R., & Sapena, J. (2018). Corporate governance and financial performance: The role of ownership and board structure. *Journal of Business Research*, *89*, 229–234. doi:10.1016/j.jbusres.2018.01.060

Papadaki, A., & Tzovas, C. (2017). Financial crisis and accrual and real earnings management in Europe. *Corporate Ownership & Control*, *14*(3), 8–19. doi:10.22495/cocv14i3art1

Park, H. (2003, June 17). Determinants of corruption: A cross-national analysis. *Multinational Business Review*, *11*(2).

Park, K., & Jang, S. (2013). Capital structure, free cash flow, diversification and firm performance: A holistic analysis. *International Journal of Hospitality Management*, *33*, 51–63. doi:10.1016/j.ijhm.2013.01.007

Park, Y. W., & Shin, H. H. (2004). Board composition and earnings management in Canada. *Journal of Corporate Finance*, *10*(3), 431–457.

Peasnell, K. V., Pope, P. F., & Young, S. (2000). Accrual Management to meet earnings targets: UK evidence pre- and post-Cadbury. *The British Accounting Review*, *32*(4), 415–445. doi:10.1006/bare.2000.0134

Peasnell, K. V., Pope, P. F., & Young, S. (2005). Board Monitoring and Earnings Management: Do Outside Directors Influence Abnormal Accruals? *Journal of Business Finance & Accounting*, *32*(7-8), 1311–1346. doi:10.1111/j.0306-686X.2005.00630.x

Pedraza, A. (2018). Ownership concentration and market liquidity: Evidence from a natural experiment. *Economics Letters*, *167*, 56–59.

Peni, E., & Sami, V. (2012). Did good corporate governance improve bank performance during the financial crisis. *Journal of Financial Services Research*, *41*(1-2), 19–35. doi:10.100710693-011-0108-9

Pereira, I. N., & Esperança, J. P. (2015). Top executive compensation in less developed capital markets. *Corporate Governance*, *15*(1), 122–133. doi:10.1108/CG-11-2014-0128

Pereira, V. M. M., & Filipe, J. A. B. (2015). Measuring the Board's Members Effect on Banks' Performance: An Application to Portugal. *International Journal of Latest Trends in Finance and Economic Sciences*, *20*(10), 1–16.

Pereira, V. M. M., & Filipe, J. A. B. (2018). Quality of Board Members' Training and Bank Financial Performance: Evidence from Portugal. *International Journal of Economics and Business Administration*, *6*(3), 47–79.

Pericleous, L., Amin, M., & Goeree, R. (2019). The value and consequences of using public health technology assessments for private payer decision-making in Canada: One size does not fit all. *Journal of Medical Economics*, *22*(5), 478–487. doi:10.1080/13696998.2019.1582535 PMID:30757934

Perryman, A. A., Fernando, G. D., & Tripathy, A. (2016). Do gender differences persist? An examination of gender diversity on firm performance, risk, and executive compensation. *Journal of Business Research*, *69*(2), 579–586. doi:10.1016/j.jbusres.2015.05.013

Perry, S., & Williams, T. (1994). Earnings management preceding management buyout offers. *Journal of Accounting and Economics*, *18*(2), 157–179. doi:10.1016/0165-4101(94)00362-9

Persakis, A., & Iatridis, G. E. (2016). Audit quality, investor protection and earnings management during the financial crisis of 2008: An international perspective. *Journal of International Financial Markets, Institutions and Money*, *41*, 70–101. doi:10.1016/j.intfin.2015.12.006

Petera, P., Wagner, J., & Knorová, K. (2016). Perception and interpretation of sustainability among the largest corporations established in the Czech Republic. *Acta Universitatis Agriculturae et Silviculturae Mendelianae Brunensis*, *64*(3), 1053–1065. doi:10.11118/actaun201664031053

Pfeffer, J. (1972). Size and composition of corporate boards of directors: The organization and its environment. *Administrative Science Quarterly*, 218–228.

Pham, H. Y., Chung, R. Y., Roca, E., & Bao, B. (2019). Discretionary accruals: Signalling or earnings management in australia? *Accounting and Finance*, *59*(2), 1383–1413. doi:10.1111/acfi.12275

Pham, P. K., Suchard, J. A., & Zein, J. (2011). Corporate governance and alternative performance measures: Evidence from Australian firms. *Australian Journal of Management*, *36*(3), 371–386. doi:10.1177/0312896211413035

Phillips, R. (1997). Stakeholder Theory and a Principle of Fairness. *Business Ethics Quarterly*, *7*(1), 51–66. doi:10.2307/3857232

Pillai, R., & Al-Malkawi, H. A. N. (2018). On the relationship between corporate governance and firm performance: Evidence from GCC countries. *Research in International Business and Finance*, *44*, 394–410. doi:10.1016/j.ribaf.2017.07.110

Pillay, R. (2010). The skills gap in hospital management: A comparative analysis of hospital managers in the public and private sectors in South Africa. *Health Services Management Research*, *23*(1), 30–36. doi:10.1258/hsmr.2009.009015 PMID:20150608

Pinto, I., Gaio, C., & Gonçalves, T. (2019). Corporate governance, foreign direct investment, and bank income smoothing in african countries. *International Journal of Emerging Markets*, *15*(4), 670–690. doi:10.1108/IJOEM-04-2019-0297

Pizzo, M. (2009, July 31). *Related Party Transactions in Corporate Governance*. Retrieved from https://papers.ssrn.com/sol3/papers.cfm?abstract_id=1441173

Porter, M. E. (1992). Capital choices: Changing the way America invests in industry. *Journal of Applied Corporate Finance*, *5*(2), 4–16. doi:10.1111/j.1745-6622.1992.tb00485.x

Post, C., & Byron, C. (2015). Women on boards and firm financial performance: A meta-analysis. *Academy of Management Journal*, *58*(5), 1546–1571. doi:10.5465/amj.2013.0319

Pourmohammadi, K., Hatam, N., Shojaei, P., & Bastani, P. (2018). A comprehensive map of the evidence on the performance evaluation indicators of public hospitals: A scoping study and best fit framework synthesis. *Cost Effectiveness and Resource Allocation*, *16*(1), 64. doi:10.118612962-018-0166-z PMID:30534009

Prencipe, A., Bar-Yosef, S., & Dekker, H. (2014). Accounting research in family firms: Theoretical and empirical challenges. *European Accounting Review*, *23*(3), 361–385. doi:10.1080/09638180.2014.895621

Prencipe, A., Bar-Yosef, S., Mazzola, P., & Pozza, L. (2011). Income smoothing in family-controlled companies: Evidence from Italy. *Corporate Governance*, *19*(6), 529–546. doi:10.1111/j.1467-8683.2011.00856.x

Prencipe, A., Markarian, G., & Pozza, L. (2008). Earnings management in family firms: Evidence from R&D cost capitalization in Italy. *Family Business Review*, *21*(1), 71–88. doi:10.1111/j.1741-6248.2007.00112.x

Price, T., Tredinnick-Rowe, J., Walshe, K., Tazzyman, A., Ferguson, J., Boyd, A., Archer, J., & Bryce, M. (2020). Reviving clinical governance? A qualitative study of the impact of professional regulatory reform on clinical governance in healthcare organisations in england. *Health Policy (Amsterdam)*, *124*(4), 446–453. doi:10.1016/j.healthpol.2020.01.004 PMID:32044153

Prior, D., Surroca, J., & Tribo, J. (2008). Are socially responsible managers really ethical? Exploring the relationship between earnings management and corporate social responsibility. *Corporate Governance*, *16*(3), 160–177. doi:10.1111/j.1467-8683.2008.00678.x

Prommin, P., Jumreornvong, S., & Jiraporn, P. (2014). The effect of corporate governance on stock liquidity: The case of Thailand. *International Review of Economics & Finance*, *32*, 132–142.

Provan, K. G. (1980). Board power and organizational effectiveness among human service agencies. *Academy of Management Journal*, *23*, 221–236. PMID:10247028

Puri, M. L., Ralescu, D. A., & Zadeh, L. (1993). Fuzzy random variables. In *Readings in fuzzy sets for intelligent systems* (pp. 265–271). Morgan Kaufmann. doi:10.1016/B978-1-4832-1450-4.50029-8

Puryandani, S., Kusumawati, H. A., & Robiyanto, R. (2020). Corporate governance and earnings management practices in indonesian banking sector. *Quality - Access to Success*, *21*(176), 102–108.

Putra, A. A., & Mela, N. F. (2019). Effect of Ownership Types on Informative Earnings Management. *International Journal of Academic Research in Accounting. Finance and Management Sciences*, *9*(2), 74–82.

Radzi, M. N. (2017, June 30). The impact of internal factors on small business success: A case of small enterprises under the FELDA scheme. *Asian Academy of Management*, *22*(1), 27–55.

Raeisi, A., & Vaez, S. A. (2016). An evaluation of the relationships between the corporate governance mechanisms, the free cash flow, and earnings management in Tehran stock exchange listed companies. *International Journal of Humanities and Cultural Studies*, 122-140.

Raghunandan, K., & Rama, D. V. (2007). Determinants of audit committee diligence. *Accounting Horizons*, *21*(3), 265–279. doi:10.2308/acch.2007.21.3.265

Rahim, M. (2013). Legal Regulation of Corporate Social Responsibility: A Meta-Regulation Approach of Law for Raising CSR in a Weak Economy. Berlin: Springer.

Rahman, A. F., Hassan, M. S., Saleh, N. M., & Shukor, Z. A. (2013). The effect of underinvestment on the relationship between earnings management and information asymmetry. *Asian Academy of Management Journal of Accounting and Finance*, *9*(2), 1–28.

Rahman, A. H. A., & Muhamad, S. F. (2013). Corporate governance and firms cash holding in Malaysia. *Proceeding of the International Conference on Social Science Research*, 1236-1247.

Rahman, R. A., & Ali, F. H. M. (2006). Board, audit committee, culture and earnings management: Malaysian evidence. *Managerial Auditing Journal*, *21*(7), 783–804. doi:10.1108/02686900610680549

Rahmat, M. M., Iskandar, T. M., & Saleh, N. M. (2009). Audit committee characteristics in financially distressed and non-distressed companies. *Managerial Auditing Journal*, *24*(7), 624–638. doi:10.1108/02686900910975350

Rajgopal, S., & Venkatachalam, M. (1997). *The role of institutional investors in corporate governance: An empirical investigation*. Graduate School of Business, Stanford University.

Rasbash, J., Browne, W., Goldstein, H., Yang, M., Plewis, I., & Healy, M. (2000). *A User's Guide to MLwiN*. University of Bristol.

Rashidizadeh-Kermani, H., Vahedipour-Dahraie, M., Anvari-Moghaddam, A., & Guerrero, J. M. (2019). A stochastic bi-level decision-making framework for a load-serving entity in day-ahead and balancing markets. *International Transactions on Electrical Energy Systems*, *29*(11), e12109. doi:10.1002/2050-7038.12109

Rauch, M. F. (2000). *Psychological approaches to entrepreneurial success: A general model and an overview of findings*. Academic Press.

Razzaque, R., Ali, M., & Mather, P. (2016). Real earnings management in family firms: Evidence from an emerging economy. *Pacific-Basin Finance Journal*, *40*, 237–250. doi:10.1016/j.pacfin.2015.12.005

Reddy, K., Locke, S., & Scrimgeour, F. (2010). The efficacy of principle-based corporate governance practices and firm financial performance: An empirical investigation. *International Journal of Managerial Finance*, *6*(3), 190–219. doi:10.1108/17439131011056224

Reed, W. R., & Ye, H. (2011). Which panel data estimator should I use? *Applied Economics*, *43*(8), 985–1000. doi:10.1080/00036840802600087

Regulamento da CMVM nº 1/2007, Diário da República, 2ª série - Nº 224, 21 de novembro de 2007.

Regulamento da CMVM nº 1/2010, Diário da República, 2ª série - Nº 21, de 1 de fevereiro de 2010.

Regulamento da CMVM nº 10/2001, Diário da República, 2ª série Nº 222, 18 de novembro de 2005.

Regulamento da CMVM nº 4/2013, Diário da República, 2ª série - Nº 147, de 1 de agosto de 2013.

Regulamento da CMVM nº 7/2001, Diário da República, 2ª série - Nº 299, 28 de dezembro de 2001.

Reicher, R., & Ngo, T. N. (2020). The propensity for mandatory audit rotation and its impact on earnings management in Europe. *International Journal of Engineering and Management Sciences*, *5*(1), 1–10. doi:10.21791/IJEMS.2020.1.19

Ren, A., & Wang, Y. (2014). Optimistic Stackelberg solutions to bilevel linear programming with fuzzy random variable coefficients. *Knowledge-Based Systems*, *67*, 206–217. doi:10.1016/j.knosys.2014.05.010

Ren, A., & Wang, Y. (2015). An interval approach based on expectation optimization for fuzzy random bilevel linear programming problems. *The Journal of the Operational Research Society*, *66*(12), 2075–2085. doi:10.1057/jors.2015.13

Report, C. (1992). The *Financial aspects of Corporate Governance*. Retrieved from: https://ecgi.global/sites/default/files//codes/documents/cadbury.pdf

Report, O. E. C. D. (2010). *The OECD Principle of Corporate Governance*. The Organization for Economic Cooperation and Development.

Reverte, C. (2008). Institutional differences in EU countries and their relationship with earnings management differences. *Journal of Accounting & Organizational Change*, *4*(2), 182–200. doi:10.1108/18325910810878964

Riahi, Y., Lamiri, I., & Ben Arab, M. (2013). The Impact of Earnings Management on Liquidity: Case of the Tunisian Stock Market. *International Journal of Business and Commerce*, *2*(10), 38–57.

Richardson, S. (2006). Over-investment of free cash flow. *Review of Accounting Studies*, *11*(2-3), 159–189. doi:10.100711142-006-9012-1

Rodrigues, E. N. (2012). *Corporate Governance: A Relação entre As Características do Conselho de Administração e o Desempenho das Empresas na Euronext Lisbon* (Doctoral dissertation). Instituto Superior de Economia e Gestão.

Rodrigues, L. L., Tejedo-Romero, F., & Graig, R. (2016). Corporate governance and intellectual capital reporting in a period of financial crisis: Evidence from Portugal. *International Journal of Disclosure and Governance*, *14*(1), 1–29. doi:10.1057/jdg.2015.20

Roland, M., & Baker, R. (1999). *Clinical governance: a practical guide for primary care teams*. University of Manchester. Available at http://www. npcrdc.ac.uk/Publications/HANDBOOK%20CLINICAL%20 GOVERNANCE.pdf

Rommelfanger, H. (1996). Fuzzy linear programming and applications. *European Journal of Operational Research*, *92*(3), 512–527. doi:10.1016/0377-2217(95)00008-9

Ronen, J., & Yaari, V. (2008). *Earnings management* (Vol. 372). Springer US.

Rose, C. (2007). Does female board representation influence firm performance? The Danish evidence. *Corporate Governance*, *15*(2), 404–413. doi:10.1111/j.1467-8683.2007.00570.x

Roychowdhury, S. (2006). Management of earnings through the manipulation of real activities that affect cash flow from operations. *Journal of Accounting and Economics*, *42*, 335–370. doi:10.1016/j.jacceco.2006.01.002

Rubin, A. (2007). Ownership level, ownership concentration and liquidity. *Journal of Financial Markets*, *10*(3), 219–248.

Rusmin, R. W., Astami, E., & Hartadi, B. (2014). The impact of surplus free cash flow and audit quality on earnings management: The case of growth triangle countries. *Asian Review of Accounting*, *22*(3), 217–232. doi:10.1108/ARA-10-2013-0062

Sa'adiah Munir, N. M. (2013). Family ownership, related-party. *Asian Academy*, *9*(1), 129–153.

Saddour, K. (2006). *The determinants and the value of cash holdings: Evidence from French firms.* Cahier De Recherche n. 6.

Sadiq, M., Othman, Z., & Keong, O. C. (2019). A study of interaction effects of political influences and earnings management on organisational performance. *Asian Economic and Financial Review*, *9*(5), 642–653. doi:10.18488/journal.aefr.2019.95.642.653

Safiullah, M., & Shamsuddin, A. (2018). Risk in Islamic banking and corporate governance. *Pacific-Basin Finance Journal*, *47*, 129–149. doi:10.1016/j.pacfin.2017.12.008

Sakawa, M., & Katagiri, H. (2012). Stackelberg solutions for fuzzy random two-level linear programming through level sets and fractile criterion optimization. *Central European Journal of Operations Research*, *20*(1), 101–117. doi:10.100710100-010-0156-5

Sakawa, M., Katagiri, H., & Matsui, T. (2011). Interactive fuzzy random two-level linear programming through fractile criterion optimization. *Mathematical and Computer Modelling*, *54*(11-12), 3153–3163. doi:10.1016/j.mcm.2011.08.006

Sakawa, M., Katagiri, H., & Matsui, T. (2012). Stackelberg solutions for fuzzy random bilevel linear programming through level sets and probability maximization. *Operations Research*, *12*(3), 271–286. doi:10.100712351-010-0090-2

Sakawa, M., Katagiri, H., & Matsui, T. (2014). Interactive fuzzy stochastic two-level linear programming with simple recourse. *Information Sciences*, *278*, 67–75. doi:10.1016/j.ins.2014.03.020

Sakawa, M., & Matsui, T. (2013). Interactive fuzzy programming for fuzzy random two-level linear programming problems through probability maximization with possibility. *Expert Systems with Applications*, *40*(7), 2487–2492. doi:10.1016/j.eswa.2012.10.052

Sakawa, M., Nishizaki, I., & Uemura, Y. (2000). Interactive fuzzy programming for multi-level linear programming problems with fuzzy parameters. *Fuzzy Sets and Systems*, *109*(1), 3–19. doi:10.1016/S0165-0114(98)00130-4

Sakellarides, C. (2003). Health governance in a global post modern world - when Beauty meets the Beast. *Humanitas. Humanidades Médicas*, *1*(3), 91–100.

Salampessy, B. H., Bijlsma, W. R., Van Der Hijden, E., Koolman, X., & Portrait, F. R. M. (2019). On selecting quality indicators: Preferences of patients with breast and colon cancers regarding hospital quality indicators. *BMJ Quality & Safety*, *29*(7), 576–585. doi:10.1136/bmjqs-2019-009818 PMID:31831636

Saleh, N. M. T. I. (2005). Earnings management and board characteristics: Evidence from Malaysia. *Jurnal Pengurusan, 4*, 77-103. Retrieved from http://103.219.237.47/pengurusan/article/viewFile/1455/1265

Saleh, N. M. T. I. (2007, April 3). Audit committee characteristics and earnings management: Evidence from Malaysia. *Asian Review of Accounting, 15*(2), 147-163. Retrieved from https://www.emerald.com/insight/content/doi/10.1108/13217340710823369/full/html

Salehi, M., Mahmoudabadi, M., & Adibian, M. S. (2018). The relationship between managerial entrenchment, earnings management and firm innovation. *International Journal of Productivity and Performance Management*, *67*(9), 2089–2107. doi:10.1108/IJPPM-03-2018-0097

Salim, M. R. (2011). *Corporate governance in Malaysia: the macro and micro issues.* Handbook on International Corporate Governance.

Salvato, C., & Moores, K. (2010). Research on accounting in family firms: Past accomplishments and future challenges. *Family Business Review*, *23*(3), 193–215. doi:10.1177/0894486510375069

San Martin Reyna, J. M. (2018). The effect of ownership composition on earnings management: Evidence for the mexican stock exchange. *Journal of Economics, Finance and Administrative Science*, *23*(46), 289–305. doi:10.1108/JEFAS-01-2017-0011

Sani, A. A., Abdul Latif, R., & Al-Dhamari, R. A. (2020). CEO discretion, political connection and real earnings management in nigeria. *Management Research Review*, *43*(8), 909–929. doi:10.1108/MRR-12-2018-0460

Santos, J. C., & Melo, W. (2018). Comparative Health Study: Primary Health Care Models in Brazil, Canada and Cuba. *Interinstitutional Journal of Psychology*, *11*(1), 79–98.

Saona, P., & Muro, L. (2018). Firm- and country-level attributes as determinants of earnings management: An analysis for latin american firms. *Emerging Markets Finance & Trade*, *54*(12), 2736–2764. doi:10.1080/1540496X.2017.1410127

Saona, P., Muro, L., & Alvarado, M. (2020). How do the ownership structure and board of directors' features impact earnings management? the spanish case. *Journal of International Financial Management & Accounting*, *31*(1), 98–133. doi:10.1111/jifm.12114

Saona, P., Muro, L., San Martín, P., & Baier-Fuentes, H. (2019). Board of director's gender diversity and its impact on earnings management: An empirical analysis for select european firms. *Technological and Economic Development of Economy*, *25*(4), 634–663. doi:10.3846/tede.2019.9381

Sarig, O. H. (1998). The effect of leverage on bargaining with a corporation. *Financial Review*, *33*(1), 1–16. doi:10.1111/j.1540-6288.1998.tb01603.x

Sarkar, J., & Sarkar, S. (2008). Debt and corporate governance in emerging economies Evidence from India 1. *Economics of Transition*, *16*(2), 293–334. doi:10.1111/j.1468-0351.2008.00307.x

Sá, T. M., Neves, E. D., & Góis, C. G. (2017). The influence of corporate governance on changes in risk following the global financial crisis: Evidence from the Portuguese stock market. *The Journal of Management and Governance*, *21*(4), 841–878. doi:10.100710997-016-9361-5

Sauerwald, S., Heugens, P. P., Turturea, R., & Van Essen, M. (2019). Are all private benefits of control ineffective? Principal–Principal benefits, external governance quality, and firm performance. *Journal of Management Studies, 56*(4), 725–757. doi:10.1111/joms.12420

Schipper, K. (1989). Earnings management. *Accounting Horizons, 3*(4), 91–102.

Scholes, L., Westhead, P., & Burrows, A. (2008). Family firm succession: The management buy-out and buy-in routes. *Journal of Small Business and Enterprise Development, 15*(1), 8–30. doi:10.1108/14626000810850829

Schroeder, M. a. (1983). *Accounting Theory: Text and Readings* (Vol. 58). Pro Quest.

Schulze, W. S., Lubatkin, M., & Dino, R. N. (2003). Exploring the agency consequences of ownership dispersion among the directors of private family firms. *Academy of Management Journal, 45*(2), 179–194.

Schulze, W. S., Lubatkin, M., Dino, R. N., & Buchholtz, A. K. (2001). Agency relationships in family firms: Theory and evidence. *Organization Science, 12*(2), 99–116. doi:10.1287/orsc.12.2.99.10114

Schumpeter, J. (2008). The Theory of Economic Development: An Inquiry into Profits, Capital, Credit, Interest and the Business Cycle. *Journal of Comparative Research.*

Schwab, A., Werbel, J. D., Hofmann, H., & Henriques, P. L. (2016). Managerial Gender Diversity and Firm Performance: An Integration of Different Theoretical Perspectives. *Group & Organization Management, 41*(1), 5–31. doi:10.1177/1059601115588641

Securities and Exchange Commission (SEC). (2002). Available at http://www.cvm.gov.br

Securities Commission of Malaysia. (2017). *Malaysian Code on Corporate Governance.* Available at https://www.sc.com.my/api/documentms/download.ashx?id=70a5568b-1937-4d2b-8cbf-3aefed112c0a

Sehrawat, N. K., Kumar, A., Lohia, N., Bansal, S., & Agarwal, T. (2019). Impact of corporate governance on earnings management: Large sample evidence from india. *Asian Economic and Financial Review, 9*(12), 1335–1345. doi:10.18488/journal.aefr.2019.912.1335.1345

Sengupta, I. N. (1992). Bibliometrics, informetrics, scientometrics and librametrics: An overview. *Libri, 42*(2), 75–98. doi:10.1515/libr.1992.42.2.75

Shakina, E., Barajas, A., & Molodchik, M. (2017). Bridging the gap in competitiveness of Russian companies with intangible bricks. *Measuring Business Excellence, 21*(1), 86–100. doi:10.1108/MBE-03-2016-0017

Shamayleh, A., Awad, M., & Farhat, J. (2020). IoT based predictive maintenance management of medical equipment. *Journal of Medical Systems, 44*(4), 72. doi:10.100710916-020-1534-8 PMID:32078712

Shan, C. M., Razak, N. H. A., & Ali, A. B. I. (2018). The impact of board of directors' characteristics and remuneration on companies' performance in Malaysia. *Indian Journal of Public Health Research & Development, 9*(11), 1220–1221. doi:10.5958/0976-5506.2018.01625.X

Shao, L. (2019). Dynamic study of corporate governance structure and firm performance in China. *Chinese Management Studies, 13*(2), 299–317. doi:10.1108/CMS-08-2017-0217

Sharif, F. A., Bino, A., & Tayeh, M. (2015). The impact of ownership structure on stock liquidity: Evidence from Amman Stock Exchange. *Jordan Journal of Business Administration, 11*(1), 239–251.

Shen, C. H., & Chih, H. L. (2007). Earnings management and corporate governance in Asia's emerging markets. *Corporate Governance, 15*(5), 999–1021. doi:10.1111/j.1467-8683.2007.00624.x

Shepheard, J., Lapiz, E., Read, C., & Jackson, T. J. (2019). Reconciling hospital-acquired complications and CHADx+ in victorian coded hospital data. Health Information Management. *Journal of the Health Information Management Association of Australia*, *48*(2), 76–86. doi:10.1177/1833358318770282 PMID:29690788

Sherafat, A., Vaezi, A., Vafaeenasab, M., Ehrampoush, M., Fallahzadeh, H., & Tavangar, H. (2019). Responsibility-evading performance: The experiences of healthcare staff about triage in emergency departments: A qualitative study. *Iranian Journal of Nursing and Midwifery Research*, *24*(5), 379–386. doi:10.4103/ijnmr.IJNMR_217_18 PMID:31516525

Sherman, S. Y. (2001). Tread lightly through these accounting minefields. *Harvard Business*, 1-8.

Shleifer, A. (2004). *Does Competition Destroy Ethical Behavior?* Harvard University. doi:10.3386/w10269

Shleifer, A., & Vishny, R. W. (1997). A survey of corporate governance. *The Journal of Finance*, *52*(2), 737–783. doi:10.1111/j.1540-6261.1997.tb04820.x

Shleifer, A., & Wolfenzon, D. (2002). Investor protection and equity markets. *Journal of Financial Economics*, *66*(1), 3–27. doi:10.1016/S0304-405X(02)00149-6

Shoaib, A., & Siddiqui, M. A. (2020). Earning information content changes based on accrual measures and quality measures: Evidence from member countries of Asia Pacific trade agreement. *International Journal of Finance & Economics.*

Sial, M. S., Chunmei, Z., & Khuong, N. V. (2019). Do female and independent directors explain the two-way relationship between corporate social responsibility and earnings management of chinese listed firms? *International Journal of Accounting and Information Management*, *27*(3), 442–460. doi:10.1108/IJAIM-03-2018-0027

Simeonov, S., & Stefanova, M. (2015). Corporate Social Responsibility in Bulgaria: The Current State of the Field. In S. Idowu, R. Schmidpeter, & M. Fifka (Eds.), *Corporate Social Responsibility in Europe. United in Sustainable Diversity* (1st ed., pp. 313–332). Springer. doi:10.1007/978-3-319-13566-3_17

Singh, A. K., Singhania, S., & Sardana, V. (2019). Do Women on Boards affect Firm's Financial Performance? Evidence from Indian IPO Firms. *Australasian Accounting. Business and Finance Journal*, *13*(2), 53–68.

Singham, K. (2003). Corporate governance in Malaysia. *Bond L. Rev.*, *15*, i.

Singh, S., Tabassum, N., Darwish, T. K., & Batsakis, G. (2018). Corporate governance and Tobin's Q as a measure of organizational performance. *British Journal of Management*, *29*(1), 171–190. doi:10.1111/1467-8551.12237

Singh, V. P. (2020). An Approach to Solve Fuzzy Knapsack Problem in Investment and Business Model. In *Networked Business Models in the Circular Economy* (pp. 154–173). IGI Global. doi:10.4018/978-1-5225-7850-5.ch007

Singh, V. P., & Chakraborty, D. (2019). Solving Knapsack Problem with Fuzzy Random Variable Coefficients. In *International Conference on Innovation in Modern Science and Technology* (pp. 1037-1048). Springer.

Singh, V. P., & Sharma, K. (2020). Capacitated Vehicle Routing Problem with Interval Type-2 Fuzzy Demands. In *Advances in Mechanical Engineering* (pp. 83–89). Springer.

Singh, V. P., Sharma, K., & Chakraborty, D. (2020). Solving the shortest path problem in an imprecise and random environment. *Sadhana*, *45*(1), 1–10. doi:10.100712046-020-01403-4

Siskou, O., Kaitelidou, D., Papakonstantinou, V., & Liaropoulos, L. (2008). Private health expenditure in the greek health care system: Where truth and the myth begins. *Health Policy (Amsterdam)*, *88*(2-3), 282–293. doi:10.1016/j.healthpol.2008.03.016 PMID:18486985

Skinner, D. (1993). The investment opportunity set and accounting procedure choice. *Journal of Accounting and Economics*, *16*(4), 407–445. doi:10.1016/0165-4101(93)90034-D

Slater, S. F. (1997). Developing a Customer Value-Based Theory of the Firm. *Journal of the Academy of Marketing Science*, *25*(2), 162–167. doi:10.1007/BF02894352

Sloan, R. (2001). Financial accounting and corporate governance: A discussion. *Journal of Accounting and Economics*, *32*(1-3), 335–347.

Smith, A. (1759). *The Theory of Moral Sentiments*. Retrieved: http://metalibri.wikidot.com/title:theory-of-moral-sentiments:smith-a

Smith, A. (1776). *An Inquiry into the Nature and the Causes of the Wealth of Nations*. Retrieved: http://metalibri.wikidot.com/title:an-inquiry-into-the-nature-and-causes-of-the-wealth-of

Smith, A. (n.d.). *93-adam-smith-the-wealth-of-nations-on-joint-stock-companies*. Retrieved from http://media.bloomsbury.com/rep/files/primary-source-93-adam-smith-the-wealth-of-nations-on-joint-stock-companies.pdf

Smits, P., & Champagne, F. (2020). Governance of health research funding institutions: An integrated conceptual framework and actionable functions of governance. *Health Research Policy and Systems*, *18*(1), 22. doi:10.118612961-020-0525-z PMID:32070372

Soltani, B., & Maupetit, C. (2015). Importance of core values of ethics, integrity and accountability in the European corporate governance codes. *The Journal of Management and Governance*, *19*(2), 259–284. doi:10.100710997-013-9259-4

Soper, M. R., Stallmeyer, J. M., Bopp, K. D., & Wood, M. B. (1995). Balancing the Triad: Cost Containment, Quality of Service, and Quality of Care in Managed Care Systems. National Center for Managed Health Care Administration, University of Missouri.

Spigelman, A. D., & Rendalls, S. (2015). Clinical governance in Australia. *Clinical Governance*, *20*(2), 56–73. doi:10.1108/CGIJ-03-2015-0008

Staglianò, R., La Rocca, M., & Gerace, D. (2018). The impact of ownership concentration and analyst coverage on market liquidity: Comparative evidence from an auction and a specialist market. *Economic Modelling*, *70*, 203–214.

Stake, R. E. (1995). The art of case study research. *Sage (Atlanta, Ga.)*.

Standard, I. A. (2009, November 1). *IAS 24 — Related Party Disclosures*. Retrieved from Deloitte: https://www.iasplus.com/en/standards/ias/ias24

Stark, P. (2020). Advancing complex case management competencies in a health care system. *Professional Case Management*, *25*(1), 19–25. doi:10.1097/NCM.0000000000000361 PMID:31764712

Stathopoulos, K., & Voulgaris, G. (2016). The Impact of Investor Horizon on Say-on-Pay Voting. *British Journal of Management*, *27*(4), 796–818. doi:10.1111/1467-8551.12172

Steinberg, H. (2003). *The Human Dimension of Corporate Governance*. People.

Steurer, R., & Konrad, A. (2009). Business–society relations in Central-Eastern and Western Europe: How those who lead in sustainability reporting bridge the gap in corporate (social) responsibility. *Scandinavian Journal of Management*, *25*(1), 23–36. doi:10.1016/j.scaman.2008.11.001

Steurer, R., Martinuzzi, A., & Margula, S. (2012). Public policies on CSR in Europe: Themes, instruments, and regional differences. *Corporate Social Responsibility and Environmental Management*, *19*(4), 206–227. doi:10.1002/csr.264

Stockmans, A., Lybaert, N., & Voordeckers, W. (2010). Socioemotional wealth and earnings management in private family firms. *Family Business Review*, *23*(3), 280–294. doi:10.1177/0894486510374457

Strömberg, P. (2008). The new demography of private equity. *The Global Impact of Private Equity Report, 2008*, 3–26.

Strøm, R. Ø., D'Espallier, B., & Mersland, R. (2014). Female leadership, performance, and governance in microfinance institutions. *Journal of Banking & Finance*, *42*, 60–75. doi:10.1016/j.jbankfin.2014.01.014

Stulz, R. (1990). Managerial discretion and optimal financing policies. *Journal of Financial Economics*, *26*(1), 3–27. doi:10.1016/0304-405X(90)90011-N

Subramanyam, K. R. (1996). The pricing of discretionary accruals. *Journal of Accounting and Economics*, *22*(1-3), 249–281. doi:10.1016/S0165-4101(96)00434-X

Suleiman, S. (2014). Corporate governance mechanisms and accounting conservatism. *Journal of Management Policies and Practices*, *2*(2), 113–127.

Sundaramurthy, C., Rhoades, D. L., & Rechner, P. L. (2005). A meta-analysis of the effects of executive and institutional ownership on firm performance. *Journal of Managerial Issues*, *17*(4), 494–510.

Sun, L., & Al Farooque, O. (2018). An exploratory analysis of earnings management practices in australia and new zealand. *International Journal of Accounting and Information Management*, *26*(1), 81–114. doi:10.1108/IJAIM-09-2016-0087

Suntraruk, P. (2013). An empirical analysis on the association between corporate governance rating and firms' characteristics: Evidence from MAI Thailand. *International Journal of Academic Research in Business & Social Sciences*, *3*(12), 732–744. doi:10.6007/IJARBSS/v3-i12/488

Susanto, Y. K., Pradipta, A., & Cecilia, E. (2019). Earnings management: Esop and corporate governance. *Academy of Accounting and Financial Studies Journal*, *23*(1).

Suvankulov, F., & Ogucu, F. (2012). Have firms with better corporate governance fared better during the recent financial crisis in Russia. *Applied Economics Letters*, *19*(8), 769–773. doi:10.1080/13504851.2011.603685

Svejnar, J. (2002). Transition economies: Performance and challenges. *The Journal of Economic Perspectives*, *16*(1), 3–28. doi:10.1257/0895330027058

Tabachnick, B. G., & Fidell, L. S. (2001). *Using Multivariate Statistics*. Allyn and Bacon.

Tam, O. K., & Tan, M. G. S. (2007). Ownership, governance and firm performance in Malaysia'. *Corporate Governance*, *15*(2), 208–222. doi:10.1111/j.1467-8683.2007.00555.x

Tan, Q. M., Zhang, N., & Ma, M. Z. (2011, September). Empirical investigation on EVA and accounting performance measures: Evidence from China stock market. In *2011 IEEE 18th International Conference on Industrial Engineering and Engineering Management* (pp. 2054-2057). IEEE.

Tangjitprom, N. (2013). The role of corporate governance in reducing the negative effect of earnings management. *International Journal of Economics and Finance*, *5*(3), 213–220. doi:10.5539/ijef.v5n3p213

Tasi, M. C., Keswani, A., & Bozic, K. J. (2019). Does physician leadership affect hospital quality, operational efficiency, and financial performance? *Health Care Management Review*, *44*(3), 256–262. doi:10.1097/HMR.0000000000000173 PMID:28700509

Tauringana, V., Kyeyune, M. F., & Opio, P. J. (2008). Corporate governance, dual language reporting and the timeliness of annual reports on the Nairobi stock exchange. *Research in Accounting in Emerging Economies*, *8*(1), 13–37.

Teodósio, J., & Lisboa, I. (2020). Board gender diversity and Capital Structure: the case of Portuguese listed firms. *International Conference on Management, Technology and Tourism: Social Value Creation*.

Teoh, S. H., Welch, I., & Wong, T. J. (1998). Earnings management and the long run performance of initial public offerings. *The Journal of Finance*, *53*(6), 1935–1974. doi:10.1111/0022-1082.00079

Terjesen, S., Couto, E. B., & Francisco, P. M. (2016). Does the presence of independent and female directors impact firm performance? A multi-country study of board diversity. *The Journal of Management and Governance*, *20*(3), 447–483. doi:10.100710997-014-9307-8

Thaiyalnayaki, M., & Divakara Reddy, G. (2018). A brief analysis on dividend payout vs promoters share in corporate firms. *Indian Journal of Public Health Research & Development*, *9*(2), 19–24. doi:10.5958/0976-5506.2018.00084.0

Tham, Y. H., Sultana, N., Singh, H., & Taplin, R. (2019). Busy boards and earnings management – an australian perspective. *Asian Review of Accounting*, *27*(3), 464–486. doi:10.1108/ARA-08-2018-0149

The relationship between culture and corruption: A cross-national study. (2009, January 16). *Journal of Intellectual Capital, 10*(1), 165-184.

Thomas, W. (2002). The Rise and Fall of Enron. *Journal of Accountancy.*

Thomsen, S., & Conyon, M. (2012). Stakeholder governance in Scandinavia. In S. Thomsen & M. Conyon (Eds.), *Corporate Governance: Mechanisms and Systems*. McGraw Hill.

Thomson Reuters Corporate Responsibility Ratings (TRCRR). (2013). *Rating and Ranking Rules and Methodologies.* https://financial.thomsonreuters.com

Thomson Reuters. (2019). *Thomson Reuters ESG Scores*. https://www.refinitiv.com

Tierno, M. V. (2014). *Corporate governance and portuguese listed companies' performance* (Doctoral dissertation). Instituto Superior de Economia e Gestão.

Tirole, J. (2006). *The Theory of Corporate Finance*. Princeton University Press.

Tolulope, I., Uwuigbe, U., Uwuigbe, O. R., Emmanuel, O., Oriabie, S., & Asiriuwa, O. (2018). The effect of corporate governance attributes on earnings management: A study of listed companies in nigeria. Academy of Strategic Management Journal, 17(6).

Tomar, S., & Bino, A. (2012). Corporate governance and bank performance: Evidence from Jordanian banking industry. *Jordan Journal of Business Administration, 153*(655), 1–40.

Tong, Y. H. (2007). Financial reporting practices of family firms. *Advances in Accounting*, *23*, 231–261. doi:10.1016/S0882-6110(07)23009-3

Torres, J. A., Leal, M. D. C., Domingues, R. M. S. M., Esteves-Pereira, A. P., Nakano, A. R., Gomes, M. L., Figueiró, A. C., Nakamura-Pereira, M., De Oliveira, E. F. V., Ayres, B. V. D. S., Sandall, J., Belizán, J. M., & Hartz, Z. (2018). Evaluation of a quality improvement intervention for labour and birth care in brazilian private hospitals: A protocol. *Reproductive Health*, *15*(1), 194. doi:10.118612978-018-0636-y PMID:30477517

Toumeh, A. A., Yahya, S., & Amran, A. (2020). Surplus Free Cash Flow, Stock Market Segmentations and Earnings Management: The Moderating Role of Independent Audit Committee. *Global Business Review*, 1–30. doi:10.1177/0972150920934069

Toygar, S. A., & Akbulut, Y. (2013). An assessment of the decision making and problem-solving skills of hospital administrators. *International Journal of Healthcare Management*, *6*(3), 168–176. doi:10.1179/2047971913Y.0000000035

Trading Economics Database. (n.d.). www.tradingeconomics.com

Tran, D. V., Hassan, M. K., & Houston, R. (2019). Activity strategies, information asymmetry, and bank opacity. *Economic Modelling*, *83*, 160–172. doi:10.1016/j.econmod.2019.02.008

Triki Damak, S. (2018). Gender diverse board and earnings management: Evidence from french listed companies. Sustainability Accounting. *Management and Policy Journal*, *9*(3), 289–312. doi:10.1108/SAMPJ-08-2017-0088

Tsamenyi, M., & Uddin, S. (2008). Introduction to corporate governance in less developed and emerging economies. *Research in Accounting in Emerging Economies*, *8*(1), 1–11.

TulungJ. E.RamdaniD. (2018) Independence, Size and Performance of the Board: An Emerging Market Research. https://ssrn.com/abstract=3133857 doi:10.22495/cocv15i2c1p6

Tunger, D., & Eulerich, M. (2018). Bibliometric analysis of corporate governance research in German-speaking countries: Applying bibliometrics to business research using a custom-made database. *Scientometrics*, *117*(3), 2041–2059. doi:10.100711192-018-2919-z

Türegün, N. (2018). Effects of borrowing costs, firm size, and characteristics of board of directors on earnings management types: A study at borsa istanbul*. *Asia-Pacific Journal of Accounting & Economics*, *25*(1-2), 42–56. doi:10.1080/16081625.2016.1246192

Türegün, N. (2020). Does financial crisis impact earnings management? Evidence from Turkey. *Journal of Corporate Accounting & Finance*, *31*(1), 64–71.

Turner, J. (2014). Predicting long-term debt in the healthcare sector. Saarbrucken, Germany: Scholars' Press.

Turner, J. S., Broom, K., Elliot, M., & Lee, J. (2015). A comparison of capital structure: The use of debt in investor owned and not-for-profit hospitals. *Journal of Health Care Finance*, *41*(4).

Tutuncu, L. (2019). Earnings management and performance of management buyouts. *Managerial Finance*, *45*(10-11), 1363–1381. doi:10.1108/MF-01-2018-0007

Uadiale, O. M. (2010). The impact of board structure on corporate financial performance in Nigeria. *International Journal of Business and Management*, *5*(10), 155–166.

Uddin, S., Mori, Y., & Shahadat, K. (2020). Private management and governance styles in a japanese public hospital: A story of west meets east. *Social Science & Medicine*, *245*, 245. doi:10.1016/j.socscimed.2019.112719 PMID:31838335

Udomsirikul, P., Jumreornvong, S., & Jiraporn, P. (2011). Liquidity and capital structure: The case of Thailand. *Journal of Multinational Financial Management*, *21*(2), 106–117.

Upadhyay, A. D., Bhargava, R., & Faircloth, S. D. (2014). Board structure and role of monitoring committees. *Journal of Business Research*, *67*(7), 1486–1492. doi:10.1016/j.jbusres.2013.07.017

Utomo, S. D., Machmuddah, Z., & Oktafiyani, M. (2019). The associations between earnings management, corporate environmental disclosure, corporate financial performance and corporate governance mechanisms. *WSEAS Transactions on Business and Economics*, *16*, 345–354.

van de Riet, M. C. P., Berghout, M. A., Buljac-Samardžić, M., van Exel, J., & Hilders, C. G. J. M. (2019). What makes an ideal hospital-based medical leader? three views of healthcare professionals and managers: A case study. *PLoS One*, *14*(6), e0218095. doi:10.1371/journal.pone.0218095 PMID:31185051

Van den Berghe, L. A., & Levrau, A. (2004). Evaluating boards of directors: What constitutes a good corporate board? *Corporate Governance*, *12*(4), 461–478. doi:10.1111/j.1467-8683.2004.00387.x

Vaz, J. C. (2013). A OPA e o controlo societário: A Regra de não frustração [Lexical characteristics of Portuguese language]. Edições Almedina, S.A.

Velnampy, T. (2013). Corporate governance and firm performance: A study of Sri Lankan manufacturing companies. *Journal of Economics and Sustainable Development*, *4*(3), 228–235.

Velte, P. (2016). Women on management board and ESG performance. *Journal of Global Responsibility*, *7*(1), 98–109. doi:10.1108/JGR-01-2016-0001

Verrecchia, R. E. (1986). Managerial discretion in the choice among financial reporting alternatives. *Journal of Accounting and Economics*, *8*(3), 175–195.

Veselovsky, M. Y., Izmailova, M. A., Bogoviz, A. V., Lobova, S. V., & Alekseev, A. N. (2018b). Innovative solutions for improving the quality of corporate governance in Russian companies. *Quality - Access to Success*, *19*(162), 60–66.

Veselovsky, M. Y., Izmailova, M. A., Bogoviz, A. V., Lobova, S. V., & Ragulina, Y. V. (2018a). System approach to achieving new quality of corporate governance in the context of innovation development. *Quality - Access to Success*, *19*(163), 30–36.

Vieira, E., & Madaleno, M. (2019). Earnings Management and Corporate Governance in Family Firms: Evidence from a small market. In Handbook International Financial Reporting Standards and New Directions in Earnings Management. IGI Global. doi:10.4018/978-1-5225-7817-8

Vieira, E., & Neiva, J. (2019). Corporate governance board of directors and firm performance in Portugal. In Handbook of Board of Directors and Company Performance: An International Outlook (pp. 121-150). Virtus Interpress.

Vieira, E., & Neiva, J. (2019). Corporate Governance Board of Directors and Firm Performance in Portugal. In Handbook of Board of Directors and Company Performance: An International Outlook. Virtus Interpress.

Vieira, E. S. (2014). Corporate Risk in Family Businesses Under Economic Crisis. *Innovar (Universidad Nacional de Colombia)*, *24*(53), 61–73. doi:10.15446/innovar.v24n53.43909

Vieira, E. S. (2016). Earnings management in public family firms under economic adversity. *Australian Accounting Review*, *26*(2), 190–207. doi:10.1111/auar.12096

Vieira, E. S. (2016). Investor sentiment and share returns: Evidence on family firms. *Academia (Caracas)*, *29*(1), 65–83. doi:10.1108/ARLA-08-2015-0234

Vieira, E. S. (2017). Debt policy and firm performance of family firms: The impact of economic adversity. *International Journal of Managerial Finance*, *13*(3), 267–286. doi:10.1108/IJMF-03-2016-0062

Vieira, E. S. (2018). Board of directors characteristics and performance in family firms and under the crisis. Corporate Governance. *The International Journal of Business in Society*, *18*(1), 119–142.

Vieira, E. S. (2018). Board of directors characteristics and performance in family firms and under the crisis. *Corporate Governance: The International Journal of Business in Society*, *18*(1), 119–142. doi:10.1108/CG-01-2017-0010

Vieira, E. S., Neves, M. E., & Dias, A. G. (2019). Determinants of Portuguese firms' financial performance: Panel data evidence. *International Journal of Productivity and Performance Management*, *68*(7), 1323–1342. doi:10.1108/IJPPM-06-2018-0210

Vijayakumaran, S., & Vijayakumaran, R. (2019). Corporate governance and capital structure decisions: Evidence from Chinese listed companies. Journal of Asian Finance. *Economics and Business*, *6*(3), 67–79.

Villalonga, R. A. (2006, May 2). How do family ownership, control and management affect firm value? *Journal of Financial Economics*, *80*(2), 385–417.

Vo, D., & Phan, T. (2013). Corporate governance and firm performance: Empirical evidence from Vietnam. *Journal of Economic Development*, *7*(1), 62–78.

Volpin, P. (2002). Governance with poor investor protection: Evidence from top executive turnover in Italy. *Journal of Financial Economics*, *64*(1), 61–90. doi:10.1016/S0304-405X(02)00071-5

Wagstaff, A., & Culyer, A. J. (2012). Four decades of health economics through a bibliometric lens. *Journal of Health Economics*, *31*(2), 406–439. doi:10.1016/j.jhealeco.2012.03.002 PMID:22481096

Walker, D. (2009). *A review of corporate governance in UK banks and other financial industry entities*. Academic Press.

Walker, M. (2013). How far can we trust earnings numbers? What research tells us about earnings management? *Accounting and Business Research*, *43*(4), 445–481. doi:10.1080/00014788.2013.785823

Wan Hussin, W. N., & Ibrahim, M. A. (2003). Striving for quality financial reporting. *Akauntan Nasional*, *16*(3), 18–24.

Wan Mohammad, W. M., & Wasiuzzaman, S. (2019). Effect of audit committee independence, board ethnicity and family ownership on earnings management in malaysia. *Journal of Accounting in Emerging Economies*, *10*(1), 74–99. doi:10.1108/JAEE-01-2019-0001

Wang, D. (2006). Founding family ownership and earnings quality. *Journal of Accounting Research*, *44*(3), 619–656. doi:10.1111/j.1475-679X.2006.00213.x

Wang, G. Y. (2010). The impacts of free cash flows and agency costs on firm performance. *Journal of Service Science and Management*, *3*(04), 408–418. doi:10.4236/jssm.2010.34047

Wang, T., Lin, Y., Werner, E. M., & Chang, H. (2018). The relationship between external financing activities and earnings management: Evidence from enterprise risk management. *International Review of Economics & Finance*, *58*, 312–329. doi:10.1016/j.iref.2018.04.003

Warfield, T., Wild, J., & Wild, K. (1995). Managerial Ownership, Accounting Choices and Informativeness of Earnings. *Journal of Accounting and Economics*, *20*(1), 61–91. doi:10.1016/0165-4101(94)00393-J

Waryanto, E. (2010). *Pengaruh Karakteristik Good Corporate Governance terhadap Luas Pengungkapan Corporate Social Responsibility di Indonesia. Skripsi*. Universitas Diponegoro.

Wasan, P., & Mulchandani, K. (2020). Corporate governance factors as predictors of earnings management. *Journal of General Management*, *45*(2), 71–92. doi:10.1177/0306307019872304

Watkins, K., Spronk, J., & Dick, V. D. (2009). Corporate governance and performance during normal and crisis periods: Evidence from an emerging market perspective. *International Journal of Corporate Governance*, *1*(4), 382–399. doi:10.1504/IJCG.2009.032726

Watts, R. L. (2003). Conservatism in accounting part I: Explanations and implications. *Accounting Horizons*, *17*(3), 207–221. doi:10.2308/acch.2003.17.3.207

Watts, R. L., & Zimmerman, J. L. (1978). Towards a positive theory of the determination of accounting standards. *The Accounting Review*, *53*(1), 112–134. https://www.jstor.org/stable/245729

Watts, R. L., & Zimmerman, J. L. (1986). *Positive Accounting Theory*. Prentice Hall.

Watts, R. L., & Zimmerman, J. L. (1990). Positive accounting theory: A ten year perspective. *The Accounting Review*, *65*(1), 131–156.

Waweru, N. M., & Prot, N. P. (2018). Corporate governance compliance and accrual earnings management in eastern africa: Evidence from kenya and tanzania. *Managerial Auditing Journal*, *33*(2), 171–191. doi:10.1108/MAJ-09-2016-1438

Wei, T. S. (2014, June 30). *SKRINE*. Retrieved 2020, from Proposed Amendments to Related Party Transactions: https://www.skrine.com/insights/newsletter/june-2014/proposed-amendments-to-related-party-transactions

Weir, C., Laing, D., & Wright, M. (2005). Undervaluation, private information, agency costs and the decision to go private. *Applied Financial Economics*, *15*(13), 947–961. doi:10.1080/09603100500278221

Weisbach, M. (1998). Outside directors and CEO turnover. *Journal of Financial Economics*, *20*, 431–460. doi:10.1016/0304-405X(88)90053-0

Wen, U. P., & Hsu, S. T. (1991). Linear bi-level programming problems—A review. *The Journal of the Operational Research Society*, *42*(2), 125–133.

Wen, U. P., & Hsu, S. T. (1992). Efficient solutions for the linear bilevel programming problem. *European Journal of Operational Research*, *62*(3), 354–362. doi:10.1016/0377-2217(92)90124-R

Wernz, C., Zhang, H., & Phusavat, K. (2014). International study of technology investment decisions at hospitals. *Industrial Management & Data Systems*, *114*(4), 568–582. doi:10.1108/IMDS-10-2013-0422

Westhead, P. (1997). Ambitions, external environment and strategic factor differences between family and non-family companies. *Entrepreneurship and Regional Development*, *9*(2), 127–157. doi:10.1080/08985629700000007

Westhead, P., & Howorth, C. (2006). Ownership and management issues associated with family firm performance and company objectives. *Family Business Review*, *19*(4), 301–316. doi:10.1111/j.1741-6248.2006.00077.x

White, H. (1980). A heteroskedasticity-consistent covariance matrix estimator and a direct test for heteroskedasticity. *Econometrica*, *48*(4), 817–838.

Williamson, O. (1973). Markets and Hierarchies: Some Elementary Considerations. *The American Economic Review*, *63*(2), 316–325.

Wilson, N., Wright, M., & Scholes, L. (2013). Family business survival and the role of boards. *Entrepreneurship Theory and Practice*, *37*(6), 1369–1389. doi:10.1111/etap.12071

Winberge, D., & Randolph, P. (2004). *Corporate Social Responsibility: What every In-House Council Should Know.* ACC Docket, 72. World Bank Database. www.worldbank.org/

Wiseman, L. G.-M. (1998, January 1). A behavioral agency model of managerial risk taking. *Academy of Management Journal*, *23*(1), 133–153.

Wong, M. J. (2008, September 20). *Propping through related party transactions*. Springer. Retrieved from https://link.springer.com/article/10.1007/s11142-008-9081-4

Wong, T. J. M. J. (2003). Earnings management and tunneling through related party transactions: Evidence from Chinese corporate groups. In *EFA 2003 Annual Conference Paper* (pp. 1-44). Academic Press.

Woolsey, D. R. (2003, March). The use of tv in teaching physiology and anatomy: 1956. *Academic Medicine*, *78*(3), 264.

World Economic Forum Database. (n.d.). www.weforum.org

World Health Organization (WHO). (1998a). *Health for All in the 21st Century.* World Health Organization. Available in: https://apps.who.int/iris/bitstream/handle/10665/55721/WHSQ_1998_51__p3-6_eng.pdf?sequence=1&isAllowed=y

World Health Organization (WHO). (2009). *Who are health managers: Case studies from three African countries.* Human Resources for Health Observer - Issue No. 1. Geneva, Switzerland: World Health Organization. Available in: https://www.who.int/hrh/resources/hrh_observer/en/

World Health Organization (WHO). (2020). *Regional Office for Europe. Hospital Readiness Checklist for COVID 19.* Available in: http://www.euro.who.int/_data/assets/pdf_file/0010/430210/Hospital-Readiness-Checklist.pdf?ua=1

World Investment Report. (n.d.). https://unctad.org/en/

Wright, M., Thompson, S., & Robbie, K. (1992). Venture capital and management-led, leveraged buy-outs: A European perspective. *Journal of Business Venturing, 7*(1), 47–71. doi:10.1016/0883-9026(92)90034-O

Wulferth, H. (2013). *Managerial Discretion and Performance in China.* Springer-Verlag Berlin and Heidelbe. doi:10.1007/978-3-642-35837-1

Wu, W. Y. (1997). Management buyouts and earnings management. *Journal of Accounting, Auditing & Finance, 12*(4), 373–389. doi:10.1177/0148558X9701200402

Xie, B., Davidson, W. N. III, & DaDalt, P. J. (2003). Earnings management and corporate governance: The roles of the board and the audit committee. *Journal of Corporate Finance, 9*(3), 295–316. doi:10.1016/S0929-1199(02)00006-8

Xie, E., Reddy, K. S., & Liang, J. (2017). Country-specific determinants of cross-border mergers and acquisitions: A comprehensive review and future research directions. *Journal of World Business, 5*(2), 127–183. doi:10.1016/j.jwb.2016.12.005

Xue, S., & Hong, Y. (2016). Earnings management, corporate governance and expense stickiness. *China Journal of Accounting Research, 9*(1), 41–58. doi:10.1016/j.cjar.2015.02.001

Xue, Y., Liang, H., & Boulton, W. (2008). Information technology governance information technology investment decision process: The impact of investment characteristics, external environment, and internal context. *Management Information Systems Quarterly, 32*(1), 67–96. doi:10.2307/25148829

Yaghoobnezhad, A., Roodposhti, R. F., & Zabihi, A. (2011). The study of relationship between institutional ownership and stock liquidity in Tehran stock exchange. *Journal of Basic and Applied Scientific Research, 12*(1), 2736–2742.

Yang, Y., & Abeysekera, I. (2019). Duration of equity overvaluation and managers' choice to use aggressive underlying earnings disclosure and accrual-based earnings management: Australian evidence. *Journal of Contemporary Accounting and Economics, 15*(2), 167–185. doi:10.1016/j.jcae.2019.04.004

Yaşar, A. (2013). Big Four Auditors' Audit Quality and Earnings Management: Evidence from Turkish Stock Market. *International Journal of Business and Social Science, 4*(17), 153–163.

Yasser, Q. R., Al Mamun, A., & Rodrigs, M. (2017). Impact of board structure on firm performance: Evidence from an emerging economy. *Journal of Asia Business Studies, 11*(2), 210–228. doi:10.1108/JABS-06-2015-0067

Yasser, Q. R., Al Mamun, A., & Seamer, M. (2017). Do corporate boards affect firm performance? New evidence from an emerging economy. *International Journal of Productivity and Performance Management, 66*(6), 724–741. doi:10.1108/IJPPM-06-2015-0085

Yavuzaslan, S. & Kalmis, H. (2016). İşletmelerin Kurumsal Yönetim Uygulamalarinin Kâr Yönetimi Üzerindeki Etkisi ve Borsa Istanbul AS Sirketleri Üzerinde Bir Uygulama. *Çanakkale Onsekiz Mart Üniversitesi Yönetim Bilimleri Dergisi, 14*(27), 353-384.

Yendrawati, R., & Asy'ari, E. F. (2017). The Role of Corporate Governance as a Leverage Moderating and Free Cash Flow on Earnings Management. *Jurnal Keuangan dan Perbankan, 21*(3), 412-424. doi:10.26905/jkdp.v21i3.704

Yeoh, P. (2010). Causes of the global financial crisis: Learning from the competing insights. *International Journal of Disclosure and Governance*, *7*(1), 42–69. doi:10.1057/jdg.2009.18

Yin, R. K. (1994). Case study research: Design and methods. Academic Press.

Yin, R. K. (2003). *Case study research: Design and methods* (3rd ed.). Sage.

Yoo, S. W., Lee, G., Shin, J. E., & Kim, J. (2020). Firm performance and the adoption of a co-CEO structure: Evidence from Korea. *Asia Pacific Journal of Management*, 1–18. doi:10.100710490-020-09713-1

Yosra, G., & Sioud, O. B. O. (2011). Ultimate ownership structure and stock liquidity: Empirical evidence from Tunisia. *Studies in Economics and Finance*, *28*(4), 282–300.

Yusoff, W. F. W., & Alhaji, I. A. (2012). Corporate governance and firm performance of listed companies in Malaysia. *Trends and Development in Management Studies*, *1*(1), 43–65.

Zabri, S. M., Ahmad, K., & Wah, K. K. (2016). Corporate governance practices and firm performance: Evidence from top 100 public listed companies in Malaysia. *Procedia Economics and Finance*, *35*, 287–296. doi:10.1016/S2212-5671(16)00036-8

Zahra, S. A., & Stanton, W. W. (1988). The implications of board of directors' composition for corporate strategy and value. *International Journal of Management*, *5*, 229–236.

Zahra, S., & Pearce, J. II. (1989). Boards of Directors and Corporate Financial Performance: A Review and Integrative Model. *Journal of Management*, *15*(2), 291–344. doi:10.1177/014920638901500208

Zaid, M. A., Abuhijleh, S. T., & Pucheta-Martínez, M. C. (2020). Ownership structure, stakeholder engagement, and corporate social responsibility policies: The moderating effect of board independence. *Corporate Social Responsibility and Environmental Management*, *27*(3), 1344–1360. doi:10.1002/csr.1888

Zalata, A. M., Tauringana, V., & Tingbani, I. (2018). Audit committee financial expertise, gender, and earnings management: Does gender of the financial expert matter? *International Review of Financial Analysis*, *55*, 170–183. doi:10.1016/j.irfa.2017.11.002

Zhai, W., Zhao, Y., Lian, X., Yang, M., & Lu, F. (2014). Management planning of fast-growing plantations based on a bi-level programming model. *Forest Policy and Economics*, *38*, 173–177. doi:10.1016/j.forpol.2013.08.009

Zhang, G., & Lu, J. (2005). The Definition of Optimal Solution and Extended Kuhn-Tucker Approach for Fuzzy Linear Bilevel Programming. *The IEEE Intelligent Informatics Bulletin.*

Zhang, G., & Lu, J. (2010). Fuzzy bilevel programming with multiple objectives and cooperative multiple followers. *Journal of Global Optimization*, *47*(3), 403–419. doi:10.100710898-008-9365-z

Zhang, J., & Aboud, A. (2019). Determinants of economic value added (EVA) in Chinese listed banks. *Asian Review of Accounting*, *27*(4), 595–613. doi:10.1108/ARA-11-2018-0216

Zhong, L., Chourou, L., & Ni, Y. (2017). On the association between strategic institutional ownership and earnings quality: Does investor protection strength matter? *Journal of Accounting and Public Policy*, *36*(6), 429–450. doi:10.1016/j.jaccpubpol.2017.09.002

Zhu, L., Peng, Z., Liu, L., & Ling, S. (2019). Combining resource, structure and institutional environment: A configurational approach to the mode selection of the integrated healthcare in county. *International Journal of Environmental Research and Public Health, 16*(16), 2975. doi:10.3390/ijerph16162975 PMID:31430889

Zimmermann, H. J. (2011). *Fuzzy set theory—and its applications*. Springer Science & Business Media.

About the Contributors

Elisabete S. Vieira is Coordinator Professor, ISCA-UA, University of Aveiro. She is researcher at the Research Unit on Governance, Competitiveness and Public Policies (GOVCOPP), being Vice Co-ordinator of the Competitiveness, Innovation and Sustainability (CIS) Research Group. She has a Ph.D. in Finance from the ISCTE, Lisbon. Her research topics include corporate finance, corporate behavior finance, and corporate governance.

Graça Azevedo has a PhD in Management (scientific field: Accounting) at the Institute of Higher Labor and Enterprise – ISCTE. She has published and presented several articles in national and international journals and conferences as well. She is a member of the Editorial Board of international journal "Accounting and Finance Research". She currently teaches courses in scientific field of Financial Accounting at the Institute of Higher Learning in Accounting and Administration of the University of Aveiro. Her research interests are related to financial reporting, impression management strategies and international accounting standards.

* * *

Siti Zaleha Abdul Rasid has received her B.Sc., M.B.A., and Ph.D. degrees. She is currently an Associate Professor in accounting with the Azman Hashim International Business School, Universiti Teknologi Malaysia (UTM), Kuala Lumpur. She has also served as a Research Panelist with the Centre of Excellence, Chartered Institute of Management Accountants (CIMA), Southeast Asia. She is actively involved in research activities and has authored or co-authored more than 100 articles and research articles in journals, conference proceedings, and technical reports. Her research interests are in management accounting, risk management, corporate governance, and performance management. She is also an Associate Member of the Malaysian Institute of Accountants and a member of the British Accounting and Finance Association. She is also the Associate Chair of the School of Postgraduate Studies, UTM.

Rohaida Basiruddin holds a PhD in Accounting and Finance from Durham University Business School, UK and currently teaches accounting subject for MBA and DBA programs. She has been involved in academic research for the last ten years and supervised PhD students for the last seven years. Her research interests are corporate governance, audit, earnings management and Islamic banking.

Susana Callao has a Degree and Doctorate in Economics and Business Studies and Professor of Financial Economics and Accounting at the University of Zaragoza (Spain). The main lines of research:

international financial information; analysis of financial statements; earnings management; corporate social responsibility; and circular economy. Some of the scientific journals where I have published are The Spanish Journal of Finance and Accounting, The International Journal of Accounting, The European Accounting Review, Journal of International Accounting, Auditing and Taxation, Accounting in Europe, Advances in Accounting or Journal of Business Economics and Management, among others. Some of the studies carried out have been distinguished with awards such as "José María Fernández-Pirla" and "Carlos Cubillo Valverde" granted by the Spanish Association of University Professors of Accounting (ASEPUC) and the Institute of Accounting and Auditing (ICAC).

Kiarash Ehtiat Karrahemi is a market researcher and technology advisor and responsible for the business and marketing department of Ustartup company in Vancouver, Canada. He is holding a PhD in finance from Universiti Teknologi Malaysia in Kuala Lumpur, Malaysia. He has extensive experience in academic research in corporate governance, finance, economics, business, and management. He currently lives in Vancouver, Canada, where he recently acquired his Master of admin science in computer security and forensics.

Pietro Fera (born 1985) is an Assistant Professor of Accounting and Financial Analysis at the University of Campania, Luigi Vanvitelli. He was a Ph.D. Fellow at the University of Naples "Federico II" and a visiting Ph.D. Fellow at the Kristianstad University in Sweden. He is the author of various contributions published in scientific journals and books in the field of financial reporting and disclosure, earnings quality and earnings management, corporate governance, and auditing.

José Ignacio Jarne holds a Bachelor's and PhD in Economic and Business Sciences and Professor of Financial Economics and Accounting at the University of Zaragoza since 1998. He has been a member of several committees of the University of Zaragoza and the Management Team of its Department of Accounting and Finance, and Director of the Master in International Business Management and Foreign Trade of the University of Zaragoza. He has been a visiting researcher at the University of Surrey in England. He has taught at several foreign universities such as the Universidad del Litoral in Argentina or the Portuguese University of Minho.He is an author and has participated in several books on Accounting and Finance, and has published a large number of articles in national and international scientific journals such as the Spanish Journal of Financing and Accounting, The International Journal of Accounting, The European Accounting Review, Journal of International Accounting, Auditing and Taxation, Accounting in Europe, Advances in Accounting,Journal of Business Economics and Management, Journal of Cleaner Production or Journal of East European Management Studies, among others. He has been awarded the National Accounting Research Award "José María Fernández-Pirla" and the "Carlos Cubillo Valverde" Award for Accounting Research awarded by the Spanish Association of Accounting Teachers (ASEPUC) and the Institute of Accounting and Auditing (ICAC). He has participated in numerous research projects in the field of accounting and finance with public and private funding. His area of work focuses on financial accounting, financial analysis, international accounting, the quality of financial information and earnings management.

Ines Lisboa is Professor at the School of Technology and Management of the Polytechnic Institute of Leiria (ESTG/IPLeiria). Effective researcher at Centre of Applied Research in Management and Economics (CARME). PhD in Financial Economics and Accounting, with specialization in Family Business, from the University of Extremadura, Spain (Thesis title: "Differences between Family and Non-Family Companies, Evidence for the Portuguese and Spanish Stock Markets"). Master in Finance, ISCTE, Portugal (Title of dissertation: "Does Ownership Influence Performance? Evidence From Europe."). Degree in Organization and Management of Companies, by the Faculty of Economics of the University of Coimbra, Portugal. She is author of diverse papers published internationally and evaluator of some conferences. She has participated in several national and international conferences.

Isabel C. P. Marques is a Ph.D. student in Management at the University of Beira Interior (UBI), Covilhã, Portugal. Grant-holder in the UBI_SantanderTotta Study Grant Programme. Master's in administration of Potiguar University (UnP), Natal – Rio Grande do Norte, Brazil and Degree in Nursing from the State University of Campinas (UNICAMP), São Paulo, Brazil. She has published in various journals: Scientometrics, Health and Technology, Journal of Governance and Regulation, Journal of Orthopaedics and Sports Medicine and other journals.

Maizaitulaidawati Md Husin, PhD, is an experienced academician with strong enthusiasm and passion for Islamic banking and finance. She is currently a Senior Lecturer at the Azman Hashim International Business School, Universiti Teknologi Malaysia and an adjunct research fellow at University of Business and Technology, Jeddah, Saudi Arabia. She has over 12 years of experience in teaching and supervision. Maizaitulaidawati holds a PhD in Islamic Economics from the University of Malaya, MSc in Banking and BBA in Finance. She is also a certified Islamic financial planner in Malaysia.

Jacinta Raquel Moreira is Assistant Teacher at the School of Technology and Management, Politécnico de Leiria - Portugal. The academic degree includes a Ph.D. in Management, with specialization in Marketing and Master in Management. She is coordinator of the degree in Marketing at ESTG - IPL and is a member of CARME - Center of Applied Research in Management and Economics. Areas of Interest: Marketing, Innovation, Advertising, Brands and Consumer Behavior.

Nicola Moscariello (born 1977) is a Full Professor of Business Groups and Consolidated Financial Statements at the University of Campania, Luigi Vanvitelli. He is co-editor-in-chief of the journal "Corporate Board: role, duties, and composition". He was a lecturer of Financial Accounting and Reporting at the Brunel University in London. He has published about 3 books and several articles on Accounting and Business Research, Journal of Management & Governance, Meditari Accountancy Research, and Journal of Applied Accounting Research. His research interests embrace financial reporting and corporate governance.

Samuel Mutarindwa holds a PhD in Business Administration from Jönköping University and is a Lecturer in the Department of Accounting, School of Business, College of business and Economics at the University of Rwanda where he teaches accounting and finance related courses in both undergraduate and graduate levels. Samuel's main research interests lie in law, finance, and growth. Specifically, he is interested in regulations and governance for firms' financing. Samuel's research has recently been published in the Journal of International Financial Markets, Institutions and Money, Emerging Markets Review, and South African Journal of Higher Education. Other papers are to be published in the Journal of Institutional Economics, Journal of Financial Stability, and the African Finance Journal. He has also published several book chapters in Springer and Edgar Publishers.

Alvaro Nascimento is Professor of Economics and Finance at Católica Porto Business School –having been dean from 2008 to 2013 – and member of the board of Católica Luanda Business School. Non-executive director on several boards: president of the Board of the Auditing and Finance Committee of SonaeMC, non-executive director at NORS, president of the Auditing Boards of Novabase and Vallis SCR, member of the Auditing Committee of Unicer, president of the Advisory Board of the Portuguese Regulatory Authority for Water and Waste (ERSAR), and board member of FAE (Portuguese Association of Corporate Managers). In the past he served as Chairman of Caixa Geral de Depósitos, president of the Auditing Committee at Banco Carregosa, independent director of Euronext Lisbon, and the Portuguese Institute for Corporate Governance (IPCG). He holds a PhD in Banking and Finance – Cass Business School (London) –and a MSc in Internal Trade and Finance –University of Lancaster (UK). He was a research fellow at London Business School on regulation and competition. He has research and publications in finance, telecommunications, and competition and regulation. Professional consultant on competition to private organisations and government agencies, such as the Portuguese Competition Authority, Health and Telecom Regulators. He is regularly invited to presentations, seminars and conferences to professional audiences in subjects related to asset valuation, risk management, corporate governance, and regulation of the financial and telecommunications sectors.

Fernanda Maria Duarte Nogueira is an Associate Professor with Aggregation in the area of Administration and Public Policies, has a PhD in Management from the University of Trás-os-Montes and Alto Douro (UTAD) and a Masters in Instruments and Techniques for Development. Is Professor at the University of Lisbon, School of Social and Political Sciences (ISCSP), where he teaches in the Administration with emphasis in Health Administration and the Public Policy. Collaborating Professor at the Military Academy as a teacher in the Leadership Masters Course - People and Organizations, researcher at the Center for Administration and Public Policies (CAPP) at the University of Lisbon and Coordinator of the Health Gov: Management and Policies in Health research line. Main Interests Research areas are: Public Policy Management and Implementation; Management of Organizations in the Health Sector and Organizational Behavior.

Ahmet Özcan is a faculty member of Faculty of Business at Adana Alparslan Türkeş Science and Technology University. He received his Ph.D. in accounting and finance from Marmara University in 2014. His research interests include auditing, IFRS and cost accounting.

Hakan Özkaya received his BSc degree from Dokuz Eylül University, İzmir, Turkey. He received one of his MSc degrees from Dumlupınar University, Kütahya, Turkey and the other one from Erasmus University, Rotterdam, the Netherlands. Having completed his PhD at Dokuz Eylül University, Dr. Hakan Özkaya started to work at Pamukkale University, Denizli, Turkey and is currently working as an assistant professor at Dokuz Eylül University at the Department of International Trade. He has been teaching financial accounting, cost and managerial accounting and financial analysis courses. His main research interests include IFRS, cost behavior, healthcare costing and auditing.

Michele Pizzo (born 1962) is a Full Professor of Business Administration and Financial Accounting at the University of Campania, Luigi Vanvitelli. He is a member of the "OIC" (Organismo Italiano di Contabilità), i.e. Italian accounting standard setter, and of the editorial board of the journal "Financial

Reporting". He was visiting Professor at many universities. He has published several books and research articles in the field of financial reporting and corporate governance.

Neuza Ribeiro is professor of human resources management and organizational behavior at the School of Technology and Management, Polytechnic Institute of Leiria, and coordinator of the Centre of Applied Research in Management and Economics (CARME). She received a Post-doc in Management and a Doctorate in Industrial Management with a specialization in organizational behavior from Aveiro University, in 2010. Her research focuses broadly on human resources management and organizational behavior.

Giorgio Ricciardi (born in 1992) is a Ph.D. Fellow at the University of Campania "Luigi Vanvitelli". He is author of some contributions focused on earnings management and corporate governance.

Eleonora Santos is a researcher at the Centre of Applied Research in Management and Economics (CARME) of the Polythecnic Institute of Leiria. She holds a PhD in Economics, from the Faculty of Economics, University of Coimbra. She is a collaborating researcher at the Center for Business and Economics Research (CeBER) at the Faculty of Economics, University of Coimbra; and a consultant at the Interdisciplinary Center for Marine and Environmental Research (CIIMAR) of the University of Porto. From 2005 to 2014, she was Adjunct Professor at the D. Dinis Higher Education Institute (ISDOM) where she coordinated and taught 14 Courses in Accounting and Business Administration, Solicitor, Human Resources Management and Management and Informatics. She was awarded with 4 scholarships and 3 scientific merit awards from the University of Coimbra, Calouste Gulbenkian Foundation (Portugal), Oxford University (UK) / General Electric Healthcare Budapest (Hungary), Tokyo Foundation (Japan) and Polytechnic of Bragança. Her scientific areas of interest and research are: Foreign Direct Investment, Economic Growth, Productivity, Industrial Organization, Tourism; Corporate Governance; Marine Economics and Health Economics. In addition, she has published several articles in the field of Medical Physics; and has been nominated as a participant in the Fourth Technical Meeting on Modelling and Data for Radiological Impact Assessments (MODARIA) at the Headquarters of the International Atomic Energy Agency (IAEA) in Vienna.

Zélia Serrasqueiro is full professor at University of Beira Interior and Researcher in CEFAGE-UE. She has published in various journals: Entrepreneurship Theory & Practice, Research Policy, Journal of Evolutionary Economics, Small Business Economics, Industrial and Corporate Change, Journal of Business Research, Journal of Service Management, the Services Industries Journal and other journals.

Pierre Sindambiwe currently works as Lecturer at School of Business, University of Rwanda (UR). He holds a Ph.D. in Business Administration at the Center for Family Enterprise and Ownership (CeFEO), Jönköping International Business School (JIBS), Sweden. His research interests are in the longevity of family businesses, leadership, strategy, entrepreneurship, and corporate governance. Dr Pierre has a decade of experience in teaching and curriculum development. He worked with different banks, and occupied different administrative as well as academic positions at the University of Rwanda.

João Teodósio has a PhD, MSc and MBA in Management from ISCTE – Lisbon University Institute. He is graduated in Management and Public Administration from Technical University of Lisbon.

Currently, he is doing a second PhD in Finance at University of Aveiro. He is Professor of the Accounting and Finance Department at School of Management and Technology from Polytechnic Institute of Santarém, Portugal. He lectures accounting and finance subjects at graduate and post graduate levels. His research interests are related with Corporate Governance, Finance, Management Control and Cross-cultural Management.

Lokman Tutuncu currently works as Assistant Professor at Bulent Ecevit University, and holds a Ph.D. in finance from University of Birmingham. He has works published in established business and finance journals such as Journal of Business Economics and Management, Eurasian Business Review, Managerial Finance and Eurasian Economic Review. His research interests include corporate finance subjects such as initial and secondary public offerings, earnings management, disclosure and management buyouts.

Index

F

G

H

I

L

M

N

O

P

Q

R

S

T

U

www.ingramcontent.com/pod-product-compliance
Lightning Source LLC
LaVergne TN
LVHW062109300926
849161LV00010B/2415